C0-DLS-600

POVERTY, U. S. A.

THE HISTORICAL RECORD

ADVISORY EDITOR: David J. Rothman
Professor of History, Columbia University

ANNUAL REPORTS
OF THE NEW YORK ASSOCIATION
FOR IMPROVING
THE CONDITION OF THE POOR

Nos. 1–10

1845–1853

Arno Press & The New York Times
NEW YORK   1971

Reprint Edition 1971 by Arno Press Inc.

Reprinted from a copy in
The University of Illinois Library

LC# 77—137179
ISBN 0—405—03117—3

POVERTY, U.S.A.: THE HISTORICAL RECORD
ISBN for complete set: 0-405-03090-8

Manufactured in the United States of America

Publisher's Note: Research indicates
Second Annual Report never published.

THE FIRST ANNUAL REPORT

OF THE

NEW-YORK ASSOCIATION

FOR THE

IMPROVEMENT OF THE CONDITION OF THE POOR,

FOR THE YEAR 1845,

WITH

THE CONSTITUTION, VISITOR'S MANUAL,

AND

A LIST OF MEMBERS.

"The quality of Mercy is not strain'd;
It droppeth as the gentle rain from heaven
Upon the place beneath: it is twice bless'd;
It blesseth him that gives and him that takes."

NEW-YORK:
PRINTED BY JOHN F. TROW & COMPANY,
33 ANN-STREET.
1845.

PROCEEDINGS
OF THE
ANNUAL MEETING
OF THE
NEW-YORK ASSOCIATION FOR THE IMPROVEMENT OF THE CONDITION OF THE POOR,

Held in the Hall of the Public School Society, December 15, 1845.

The President of the Institution, JAMES BROWN, in the chair.

The Treasurer, ROBERT B. MINTURN, read an abstract of his report; and on motion of A. R. WETMORE, seconded by PHILO DOANE, it was approved, adopted, and ordered on file.

The Corresponding Secretary read abstracts from the minutes of the Executive Committee, as the report of their proceedings to the meeting; and on motion of LUTHER JACKSON, seconded by THOMAS COCK, M. D., it was approved.

He also read the Annual Report of the Board of Managers, which, on motion of JOHN R. LUDLOW, seconded by THOMAS B. STILLMAN, was approved, adopted, and referred to the Executive Committee for publication.

It was moved by THOMAS DENNY, seconded by A. R. WETMORE, and after an animated discussion,

Resolved, That in the event of a new application being made by our fellow-citizens to the state legislature for the extension of the new license law to this city, the Executive Committee be instructed to memorialize the legislature to the same effect, provided, in their judgment, such a measure shall not be deemed prejudicial to the interests of the association.

On motion of JOS. B. COLLINS, seconded by JAMES O. POND, M. D., it was

Resolved, That the By-Laws be so altered, as that the monthly meetings of the Advisory Committees and Visitors be held on some day during the first week in every month, instead of the last Wednesday, as now provided; also, so as to refer the call of the monthly meetings, during July and August, to the discretion of the Advisory Committees.

The meeting next proceeded to the election of Officers and Managers for the ensuing year, when the following were chosen, viz. :

President.
JAMES BROWN.

Vice Presidents.
GEORGE GRISWOLD,   JAMES BOORMAN,
J. SMYTH ROGERS, M. D.   WILLIAM B. CROSBY,
JAMES LENOX.

Treasurer.
ROBERT B. MINTURN.

Corresponding Secretary and Agent.
ROBERT M. HARTLEY.

Recording Secretary.
JOSEPH B. COLLINS.

Board of Managers.

First District.*
John R. Ludlow,
Lora Nash,
Ira Bliss,
James Cruikshank,
John A. Crum.

Second District.
William Gale,
George W. Abbe,
Joseph A. Riley,
William Sharp,
William E. Barnes.

Third District.
F. S. Winston,
B. L. Woolley,
Jonathan Sturges,
William Walker,
James Van Nostrand.

Fourth District.
Philo Doane,
Archibald Hall,
Hugh Aikman,
Abraham Fardon, Jr.
Henry Whittlesey.

Fifth District.
A. R. Wetmore,
William Forrest,
William H. Richards,
G. T. Cobb,
Lyman Clapp.

Sixth District.
E. P. Woodruff,
Stephen Conover,
O. E. Wood,
N. C. Everett,
Jared L. Moore.

Seventh District.
John H. Griscom, M. D.
Josiah Rich,
Stephen Cutter,
G. S. Conover,
G. S. Price.

Eighth District.
Joseph B. Collins,
William Johnson,
O D. McLain,
John Endicott,
Charles C.-Dyer.

Ninth District.
James O. Pond, M. D.
James S. Miller, M D.
Thomas B. Richards,
Jeremiah Terbell,
J. Van Doren.

Tenth District.
John Falconer,
William Truslow.
David Schenck,
Joseph M. Bell,
Samuel W. Scofield.

Eleventh District.
Thomas B. Stillman,
Abner Mills,
L. L. Johnson,
Dudley Sheffield,
Nehemiah Miller.

Thirteenth District.
E. D. Comstock.
John Conger,
Lewis Chichester,
Peter Balen,
Thomas Kennedy.

*Note.—Districts correspond to the wards. These Managers constitute the Advisory Committees of their respective districts.

1845.) VISITORS. 5

FOURTEENTH DISTRICT.
William Bloodgood,
M. P. Prout,
Benj. F. Howe,
Thomas B. Rich,
William Willmarth.

FIFTEENTH DISTRICT,
Erastus C. Benedict,
Stewart Brown,
William G. Bull,
Thomas Denny,
Stephen M. Chester.

SIXTEENTH DISTRICT,
Tayler Lewis,
S. A Lawrance,
E. Holbrook,
S. P. Smith,
Luther Jackson.

SEVENTEENTH DISTRICT,
S. C Lynes,
John R. Gibson,
G. Manning Tracy,
Herman Griffin,
Timothy Ensign.

Elected Members of the Board.

John C. Green,
William S. Wetmore,
Jonathan Sturges,
William H. Macy,
E. J. Woolsey.
Peter Cooper,
Jno. C. Baldwin,
George Douglass,
Josiah Mann, Jr.
Willia G. Bull.

Benjamin Ellis,
George P Pollen,
Walter Edwards,
John P. Crosby,
J. T. Adams,
Lora Nash,
James Van Nostrand,
Daniel Stanton,
Thomas Denny,
Daniel Trimble.

Executive Committee.

John R. Ludlow,
William Gale,
F. S. Winston,
Philo Doane,
A. R. Wetmore,
E. P. Woodruff,
John H Griscom, M. D.
Jos. B. Collins,

James O. Pond, M. D.
John Falconer,
Thomas B. Stillman,
E. D. Comstock,
William Bloodgood,
Erastus C. Benedict,
Tayler Lewis, LL. D.
S. C. Lynes.

Elected Members of the Executive Committee.

Horatio Allen,
James Brown,
George Griswold,

Stewart Brown,
R. B. Minturn,
J. Smyth Rogers, M. D.

Thomas Cock, M. D.

Visitors
Appointed by the Advisory Committees for the Ensuing year.

First District.
Quincy C. Degrove,
Ira Bliss,
A. Q. Thompson,
James M. Raymond,
James Cruikshank,
John R. Ludlow,
Peter Naylor,
John A Crum,
Lora Nash,
William M. Lathrop,
John C. Cass,
Daniel N. Tucker,
Lewis B. Loder.

Second District.
William E. Barnes,
Isaac Philips.
Charles Wilber,
John A. Riley,
William Sharp,
George W. Abbe.

Third District.
Marcus Mitchell.
Paul Babcock,
P. G. Arcularius,
Frederick S. Winston,
E. L Fancher,
W. D Harris,
J. Van Nostrand,
James Beatty.

Fourth District.
Adam Pierson,
Samuel Sparks,
J. Chapman,
Roland Gelston,
John V. Tilyou.
E. Wade, Jr.
G W. Rose,
Frederick Reimer.
Harman King,
T. R. Ryers,
Wm. C. Sparks,

D. Moffat,
John Hagadorn,
R. R. Johnson,
H. Whittlesey.

Fifth District.
J. J. Greenough,
A. R. Wetmore,
R. Warnock,
P. R. Bonnett,
David Terry, Jr.
D. S. Clark,
S. Williams,
William Forrest,
Lyman Clapp,
Robert Carter,
B. Skidmore,
J. Minor,
W. H Scrymser,
Robert Pattison,
John Scrymser,
Moses Allen,

6 VISITORS. (1845.

J. H. Bockover,
S. S. Ward,
W. C. Redfield,
George T. Cobb,
R. J. Brown,
William H. Richards,

Sixth District.
William Ballagh,
Henry Worrell,
Leonard Crocker,
Charles D. Brown,
S. C. Hills,
T. Lippencott,
Moses B. Taylor,
Sylvester Tuttle,
John P. Ware,
Joseph Whittemore,
Simon Clannon,
George B. Alvord,
E. P. Woodruff,
Benjamin W. Benson,
Abraham Florentine,
John G. Sperling,

Seventh District.
A. Decker,
A. Morehouse,
A. G. Hanford,
Josiah Rich,
Jona B. Horton,
E. W. Chester,
A. G. Crane,
C. S. Atwood,
J. A. Williamson.
J. Skidmore,
J. B. Dickinson,
B. F. Camp,
A. B. Ludlam,
G. Gordon,
Gilbert Woodhull,
S. Cutter,
Hewlet Smith,
John H. Griscom, M. D.
G. J. Price,

Eighth District.
Joseph B. Collins,
William B. Bradbury,
Anthony Civill,
N. T. Eldridge,
M. R. Berry,
Ira Burdge,
William H Van Dalsem,
James R. Westervelt,
Luke Kelly,
Robert Murlis,
Charles C. Dyer,
J. W. Kellogg,
C. P. Dakin,
W. W. Dwight, M. D.
John Douglass,
William M. Wilson,
John Endicott,
James G. Barbour,
William Johnson,
H. Cogswell,

Ninth District.
Reuben Ayres,
John Parr,
Nathan Peck,
Edward Bleecker,
Henry P. Lee,
Roderick Sedgewick,
H. W. Deems,
Richard R. Palmer,
O. S. Bartles, M. D.
Daniel French,
William Dunning,
W. R. Halsey,
Simon Shindler,
Edward Earle,
F. S. Cortelyou,
Thomas Fessenden,
J. W. G. Clements, M. D.
Hunting Sherrill, M. D.
Richard Horton,
Daniel Crane,
Horatio Mott,
Jacob Bogert,

Tenth District.
Hiram Raynor,
Joseph M. Bell,
Isaac B. Condit,
James Dunbar,
David Schenck,
Isaac Seaman,
Edward A. Fraser,
John Falconer,
Laban Jacobs,
E. Wheeler.
Thomas Lewis,
William Truslow,
A. P. Wood,
William Way,
William Miller,
Samuel W. Scofield,
William C. Bradley,
Cornelius Clarkson.

Eleventh Distriet.
Isaac Taylor,
Joseph Leggett,
James Barkley,
Jeremiah Green,
L. Delong,
S. L. Newman,
J. G. Lugar,
David L. Young,
E. Stebbins,
L. L. Johnson,
Jacob Stillman,
Samuel P. Patterson,
E. C. Cook,
Benjamin Wooster,
J. Townsend, Jr.
Abner Mills,
F. W. Stillman,
Nehemiah Miller,
James Little,

Thirteenth District.
Isaac Stelle,

John Hutchings,
Josiah King,
James H. Fletcher,
John R. Marsh,
Joseph Seeley,
Woodhull Smith,
James Forrester,
L. M. Sammis,
Charles Meril,
Samuel Valentine,
William A. Walker,
Abraham Trafford,
William G. Boggs,
Samuel McCorkle.
John J. Gantz,
James Remsen,
Joab Young,
Hiram Russell,
B. T. Dean,

Fourteenth District.
Charles Redman,
Abraham Bell,
Addison A. Jayne,
Adam Blackledge,
Bezaleel Howe,
Thomas B. Rich,
J. M. Howe,
Josiah Hopper, M. D.
Nelson Sammis,
Ransom Beach,
Joseph B. Weeden,
J. Allen,
William Willmarth,
B. F. Howe.

Fifteenth District.
Richard Hale,
Edward Newlin,
Henry A. Field,
Frederick Pattillow,
James Goodliff,
A. O. Willcox,
Rev. Isaac Orchard,
R. H. Winslow,
Israel Russell,
Benjamin Lord,
John Mollard,
Samuel B. Barlow,
O. W. Morris,

Sixteenth District.
J. Cowl,
Joseph Merrill.
Charles C. Darling,
Charles Roome,
Samuel Smith,
A. Young,
S. Wiswall,
D. Tompkins,
Holbrook Chamberlin,
Thomas Cummings, Jr.
J. B. Peabody,
James Millward,
John Seaman,
William Rudd,
J. L. Stephens,

1845.) VISITORS. 7

James Van Valkenburgh,
William C. Dusenberry,
A. A. Denman,
William Haydon,
Lorenzo Moses,
James F. Chamberlain,
C. Dewitt Tappan,
J. F. Joy,
Anson Willis,
S. B. Stanton,
William Thompson,
James S. King,

George Lees,
James Vanderwater,
J. Cary,
J. C. Huntington,
J. M. Woolley,

Seventeenth District

N. B. Lane,
R. Albro,
John T. Duff,
John Valentine,
Herman Griffin,

William B. Humbert,
Timothy Ensign,
George M. Tracy,
Adam Leach,
H. G. Smith,
William Stebbins,
Daniel Y. Townsend,
G. W. Edwards,
S. C. Lynes,
Joshua Butts,
John Wiley,

CONSTITUTION AND BY-LAWS.

CONSTITUTION.

ARTICLE I.

This Institution shall be called the NEW-YORK ASSOCIATION FOR THE IMPROVEMENT OF THE CONDITION OF THE POOR.

ARTICLE II.

Its design is the elevation of the moral and physical condition of the indigent ; and so far as compatible with these objects, the relief of their necessities.

ARTICLE III.

Every person who becomes an annual subscriber, or a Visitor, shall be a member of this Association.

ARTICLE IV.

The affairs of the Association shall be managed by a President, five Vice Presidents, a Treasurer, a Secretary and General Agent, and one hundred members, including the Advisory Committees, who shall constitute a Board of Managers. Nine members shall form a quorum for the transaction of business.

ARTICLE V.

The President and Secretary shall perform such duties as usually pertain to their office.

ARTICLE VI.

The Treasurer shall give such security for the faithful performance of the trust reposed in him, as the Association may demand and approve.

He shall take in charge all funds ; keep an account of all receipts and expenditures; and pay all duly authorized drafts. At the annual meeting, he shall render a particular and correct statement of all his receipts and disbursements to the Association. He shall also exhibit a summary report to the Board of Managers at their stated meetings, and to the Executive Committee whenever called upon for that purpose.

ARTICLE VII.

The Board of Managers shall have exclusive control of the funds of the Association, and authority to make by-laws ; to fill vacancies ; appoint all committees ; and generally to adopt such measures as the objects of the Institution may require. Its stated meetings shall be held on the second Monday of January, March, and November, and the Annual Meeting of the Association shall be convened on the third Monday of November, when the Board shall submit a Report of its proceedings, and the Officers and Managers be chosen by ballot.

ARTICLE VIII.

An office shall be opened in an eligible situation, for the purpose of concentrating and diffusing all information pertaining to the Society's operations and objects, and for the transaction of its general business.

ARTICLE IX.

It shall be the duty of the General Agent to devote himself with diligence and fidelity to the affairs of the Association.

ARTICLE X.

The city shall be divided into seventeen Districts, each Ward forming a District ; and the Districts be subdivided into Sections. Each District shall have an Advisory Committee, to consist of five members ; and each Section a Visitor.

ARTICLE XI.

It shall be the duty of the Members of the Association to endeavor, in all suitable ways, to give practical effect to its principles ; especially to discountenance indiscriminate alms-giving and street-begging ; to provide themselves with tickets of reference ; and instead of giving aid to unknown applicants, whose case they cannot themselves investigate, to refer such applications to the Visitor of the Section in which the applicants reside, in order that they may be properly inquired into, and, if deserving, relieved.

ARTICLE XII.

The form of Tickets shall be determined by the Board of Managers, and no other form shall be used.

ARTICLE XIII.

Special meetings of the Association may be called by the Secretary, at the request of the President, or on receiving a requisition signed by five members. Two days' notice must be given of the time of meeting.

ARTICLE XIV.

This Constitution shall not be altered except at a General Meeting of the Association, and by a vote of two-thirds of the Members present.

BY-LAWS.

ARTICLE I.

There shall be an Executive Committee, to consist of seven elected members and the Chairmen of the Advisory Committees, on whom shall devolve all the business of the Association during the recess of the Board. It shall meet on the second Mcnday of every month; and report its proceedings at each Stated Meeting of the Managers. Five members shall constitute a quorum for business.

ARTICLE II.

It shall be the duty of the Advisory Committees to divide their Districts into such Sections as to apportion to each about twenty-five families requiring attention; endeavor to obtain suitable Visitors for each section; supply vacancies which may occur; make the necessary arrangements for placing at the disposal of the Visitors, food, fuel, and clothing, for distribution; and on some day in the first week of every month (excepting the meetings in July and August, which are referred to the discretion of the Committees), to convene all the Visitors of the

Sections, for the purpose of receiving their returns, and conferring with them on the objects of their mutual labours. The Committees, moreover, shall duly draw upon the Treasurer for such proportion of the funds as may be appropriated to their District; they shall keep a strict account of all their disbursements, and only in extreme cases make donations of money; they shall monthly render an account of their expenditures to the Executive Committee; and in default of this duty, shall not be entitled to draw upon the funds of the Association. Each Committee shall appoint its own Chairman, Secretary, and Treasurer, and shall transmit the Reports of the Visitors, immediately after each Monthly Meeting, with any other information they may think desirable, to the General Secretary.

ARTICLE III.

It shall be the duty of the Sectional Visitors to confine their labors exclusively to the particular Section assigned them, so that no individual shall receive relief, excepting in the Section where he is known, and to which he belongs. They shall carefully investigate all cases referred to them before granting relief; ascertain their condition, their habits of life, and means of subsistence; and extend to all such kind services, counsel, and assistance, as a discriminating and judicious regard for their present and permanent welfare requires. And in cases of sickness and want, it will be their duty to inquire whether there is any medical or other attendance; whether relief is afforded by any religious or charitable society, and what assistance is needed. To provide themselves with information respecting the nearest Dispensary, and in all cases, when practicable, to obtain aid from existing charitable societies. And when no other assistance is provided or available, then to draw from the resources of this Association—not money, which is never allowed to be given, except with the consent of the Advisory Committee or a member thereof—but such articles of food, fuel, clothing, and similar supplies, as the necessities of the case require. And in all cases of want coming to the knowledge of the Visitors, they will be expected to perform the same duties although no application has been made. It shall be their duty, moreover, to render a report of their labors, and also an account of all their disbursements, to their respective Committees, on the last Wednesday of every month. No Visitor neglecting these duties will be entitled to draw on the funds of the Association.

ARTICLE IV.

Special Meetings of the Board of Managers may be called by the

Secretary, at the request of the President, or on receiving a requisition signed by five members. Two days' notice must be given of the time of meeting.

ARTICLE V.

These By-laws can only be altered at a Meeting of the Board of Managers, and by a vote of two-thirds of the Members present.

ANNUAL REPORT

OF THE

NEW-YORK ASSOCIATION FOR THE IMPROVEMENT OF THE CONDITION OF THE POOR.

THE Association, at the previous Annual Meeting, having been recently organized, and being then in a formative state, the Board of Managers deemed it premature to publish a Report. Having now entered upon the third year of their labors, they feel that it is due to the community and to the Association to refer, in this Report, to the causes of its origin, and to the incipient measures which have given to this Institution its present responsible position among the organized charities of the city.

In referring to the origin of the Association, it is not inappropriate to remark, that the inspired declaration, " The poor shall never cease out of the land," has ever been as applicable to other nations, as it was to the peculiar people to whom it was originally addressed. Man, in his present state, is encompassed with numerous physical and moral evils, with which the necessities of his condition require him constantly to conflict. His subsistence is made to depend upon labor, and toil or penury is the common lot. But as various unavoidable causes often unfit him for toil and deprive him of the rewards of his industry, without the interpositions of benevolence, suffering and death would inevitably ensue. Hence the duty of providing for the destitute, has been acknowledged in all civilized communities; and the more enlightened and humane, the more systematic and ample has been the provision for this object.

But while revelation and experience forbid the hope that poverty will ever entirely cease, they furnish the assurance that by appropriate means its prevalence may be diminished and its pressure mitigated. To effect these beneficent results, such measures should be pursued as have been dictated by observation and sanctioned by experience. The want of due caution, in this respect, has been productive of incalculable injury to the poor, and to the welfare and security of communities. Ignorant benevolence can never be beneficial, for it gives without discrimination, and instead of attaining its objects, augments and perpetuates the evils it aims to remove.

In this community, there appears to the Managers not to have been due care in adapting the systems of relief to the progressive exigencies of the city. It is true, that when the population was small and the solicitations for aid infrequent, the character and condition of applicants were so generally known, that the same degree of circumspection in extending relief was not then required which afterwards became indispensable. Hence a few associations that were chiefly guided by their own limited experience in their methods of charity, answered all the demands which the welfare of society and the condition of the needy required.

But the rapid growth of the city rendered a more ample charitable fund, and a different system of distribution, necessary. For as the population multiplied and became mixed with large accessions of pauper immigrants, the difficulty of judicious alms-giving was greatly increased, and the number of the dependent poor permanently augmented, in a ratio far exceeding that of the population.

To meet this state of things, numerous associations were instituted on the principle of providing for particular classes of the indigent, which united moral objects with the relief of physical want. And so successfully were these views prosecuted, that in 1843 between thirty and forty alms-giving societies of this description were in operation amongst us. But it was evident, from the results, that their modes of relief were defective. For even with this enlarged provision, in addition to the supplies of legal charity, and while every class of the indigent appeared to be provided for, the streets were still filled with mendicants, the benevolent harassed with applications, and importunate impostors constantly obtaining the aid which was designed only for the needy and deserving. Such being the general effect of our city charities, a few friends of the poor became deeply impressed with the importance of ascertaining the cause of their failure, and of devising, if practicable, a better system of dispensing relief.

For this purpose, a number of gentlemen, in the winter of 1842-3, appointed a select committee and an agent, to whom the whole subject was referred for careful examination; the results of which, in the form of conclusions, may here be summarily stated. It appeared,

First. That the want of *discrimination in giving relief* was a fundamental and very prevalent defect in most of these schemes of charity. They had no adequate arrangement by which it was possible to learn the character and condition of applicants. Of course, no sound judgment could be exercised in distributing aid; and the societies being subjected to constant imposition, large sums were so misapplied as to create more want than they relieved.

Second. The societies were found to act *independently of each other*, which was another very fruitful source of evil. For as there was no concert of action or reciprocation of intelligence between them, they were ignorant of each other's operations: and artful mendicants so turned this ignorance to their own advantage, as often to obtain assistance from many of the societies at the same time, without detection. The most undeserving, consequently, received the largest amount of assistance, and were thus encouraged in dissolute and improvident habits; while the better class of the needy not only obtained less aid, but often far less than their necessities required and the benevolent would have bestowed, provided such a knowledge of their character and circumstances had been possessed, which a better system would have conferred.

Third. They made no adequate provision for *personal intercourse* with the *recipients* of *alms* at their dwellings, nor for such sympathy and counsel as would tend to encourage industrious and virtuous habits, and foster among them a spirit of self-dependence. In short, the final and prospective end of all true charity was generally unattained by them, inasmuch as, in addition to other defects, they failed to provide for the *permanent* physical and moral improvement of those their alms relieved.

Fourth. The inquiries of the Committee also embraced the *legal provision for the poor*, which resulted in the conviction, that no form of public charity which has not especial reference to the removal of the causes of pauperism, can fail to increase its amount; and it appeared equally certain, that no such provision could embrace all the objects of private benevolence or supersede its efforts; and after the laws had done their utmost, an immense work would remain unaccomplished, which could not be effected by isolated individual exertions.

Such, without referring to matters of minor character, being a brief and general outline of their conclusions, their next object was to devise a better system, and adapt it to the practical exigences of the city. But to do this was a complex and difficult work; for, in social evils of long standing, a change from wrong to right is not easily effected. Continuing, however, to prosecute their investigations, they discovered that in addition to the local knowledge already possessed, it was important to obtain the results of experience in other places. For this purpose the agent visited Boston. Philadelphia, and Baltimore; and by correspondence in this country and abroad, gathered up whatever practical information could be obtained on the subject from every available source. This cautious and deliberative course, was deemed essential to avoid the adoption of any principles or modes of action, that were opposed by facts and experience.

The result, in short, of their various inquiries and labors, was the establishment of this Institution; and although it has now been some time before the public, it is here deemed in place to exhibit a brief exposition of its principles, objects, and modes of operation.

Its primary object is to discountenance indiscriminate alms-giving, and to put an end to street-begging and vagrancy. Secondly, it proposes to visit the poor at their dwellings, carefully to examine their circumstances, and to extend to them, appropriate relief; and through the friendly intercourse of Visitors, to inculcate among them habits of frugality, temperance, industry, and self-dependence.

To effect these desirable objects, the city, from the Battery to Fortieth-street, is divided into *sixteen districts*, which are sub-divided into *two hundred and seventy-eight sections*. Each district has a responsible Committee, and each section an efficient Visitor. Connected with the arrangement, are a General Agent and a Central Office, where is kept a register of persons who receive aid from this and other benevolent associations, and from the city authorities. A Pocket Directory is furnished to every member of the Association, (that is, every contributor to its funds), which shows the name and residence of each Visitor and the section committed to his care; also, printed tickets for referring mendicants to Visitors. By this arrangement, the prompt visitation and relief of the poor are secured, and the public no longer constrained by appeals to their humanity to bestow alms on unknown applicants, who may be deserving or otherwise.

With a view to uniformity of action, and to aid Visitors in the discharge of their duties, a "Manual"* has been printed for their use, containing a series of rules and instructions supplementary to those prescribed in the By-Laws. Each Visitor is also furnished with printed tabular forms of a Report,† with appropriate

*See Appendix A. †See Appendix B & C.

columns for the name, residence, character, &c., of every person relieved, which being filled up monthly, and transferred to the General Agent, he prepares therefrom a condensed report, and submits it to the Executive Committee, at their stated meetings, who are thereby made acquainted with the labors of the Visitors, and all statistical and other necessary information effectually secured.

Such, without enlarging, is a general outline of the causes that induced, and the labors which preceded the establishment of this Institution; also of the objects it contemplates, and of the means employed for their attainment. It now remains for them to show to what extent the favorable anticipations of its success have been justified by the results.

The Association having now commenced the third year of its operations, it is with devout gratitude to Providence, the Managers are enabled to say, that nothing has yet transpired to diminish their confidence in its principles or modes of action. Experience has shown it to be a comprehensive, uniform, and systematic plan of charity, so arranged as effectually to guard against the evils usually attendant on other systems of dispensing relief. Its machinery, though extensive, is easily managed, and works with admirable precision, economy, and effect. It has proved its adaptation to the wants of the city, by doing for the benevolent what they cannot accomplish for themselves, inasmuch as, by its personal intercourse with the poor, it offers a permanent channel through which their charities will reach their object with beneficial results; and, with the general co-operation of the public, they see not how it can fail to expel idleness and beggary from the city.

As several incidental means of aiding the poor have been adopted during the past year, they may here receive a passing notice.

First. Arrangements for *loaning stoves* to needy persons, who were otherwise unable to procure them. It was found that many persons gratuitously supplied with fuel, had no means of using it to the best advantage. Stoves of a suitable description were therefore provided, and loaned to such poor families as the Visitors, after careful inquiry, designated for that purpose. The results, in many instances, were highly gratifying; and in general sufficiently satisfactory to warrant the repetition of the same course another year.

Second. Clothing. Notwithstanding the existence of many associations of benevolent ladies for providing clothing for the needy, it was deemed advisable to establish depots in the several districts, for the collection and distribution of cast-off clothing, etc., to which persons having such articles to give were requested to send them. In several districts, although the season was far advanced before the arrangement was made, the call was generously and promptly responded to.— The third and fifth districts reported the distribution of about four hundred articles, consisting chiefly of garments, hose, hats, quilts, etc., and the excellent lady who had charge of the depository declined any remuneration for her services.

Third. Cold Victuals. From a variety of circumstances, it was ascertained, that a considerable proportion of the cold victuals given away by families, fell into the hands of the undeserving, and was appropriated to improper uses. The Board conceiving that good would result, instituted a plan by which, through the action of the Visitors, a communication might be arranged between those who gave them out, and deserving recipients. This system, so far as it was adopted, answered every reasonable anticipation. The advantages that would result from its extension over the city, it is not important here to attempt to compute. It may, however, be remarked, that the families who favor it, will soon be relieved from the annoyance with which they are now beset, by the almost incessant application for broken victuals, the deserving poor will be relieved, impostors detected, and that which is now a standing temptation to vagrancy and vice, become a valuable charity.*

* See Appendix, D

As the vast field for benevolent effort which this city affords has been deliberatively surveyed, several other subjects of great practical moment to the poor have been urged upon the attention of the Board, and such measures have been adopted in regard to them, as their relative importance appeared to demand. These measures being now in a course of development, it may be premature, before the results are known, to refer to them more particularly.

The Board takes great pleasure in publicly acknowledging, that the success of the Institution thus far has, with the favor of Providence, mainly depended on the very efficient manner in which the Advisory Committees and Visitors have performed their self-denying and arduous labors. The Association has just cause of gratitude that it has been enabled to entrust the details of the undertaking to gentlemen so well qualified to discharge its duties. But however faithfully these duties are performed, it is scarcely to be expected, that the class of persons mainly affected by them will, in every case, be satisfied. Some few complaints have been made by the poor of inattention to their wants, and of receiving articles insufficient in quantity, or inferior in quality. In respect to these and to similar cases, the Board regard it as due to the public and to the Institution, to remark, that it considers all applicants for aid as entitled to relief, until a careful examination proves the contrary; and it provides that all cases failing of attention from the Visitors, shall, upon reference to the General Agent, receive his personal investigation.

But it does not thence follow, that all applicants will be relieved by the Association: for some have claims on charities founded for specific objects; many are only fit subjects for the Alms-House; others are paupers by profession, and impostors; while not a few are recent immigrants, legally entitled to a support from shippers or consignees, who have given bonds of indemnity to the city authorities for this purpose. Let it, however, be distinctly understood, that in the cases named, and in all of similar character, if there is risk of actual suffering, assistance is given by the Association, until relief from the appropriate source is made available for their benefit.

But if all are not relieved, let the fact be borne in mind, that visitation is not neglected. Through the complete supervision which this system of charity extends over its almoners, all cases of alleged neglect receive immediate investigation, and such action as they severally require.

Some few have also objected to the *dietary* system, which has been observed in giving relief. In this they have overlooked some of the fundamental rules of the Institution, which require the Visitor—

To give what is least susceptible of abuse.

To give even necessary articles in small quantities, in proportion to immediate need.

To give assistance, both in quantity and quality, inferior, except in case of sickness or old age, to what might be procured by labor.

To give assistance at the right moment ; and not to prolong it beyond the duration of the necessity which calls for it ; but to extend, restrict, and modify it with that necessity.

While the observance of these rules enables the Association to accomplish much more with the means entrusted to it, than if a more liberal system had been adopted, their tendency and design is to induce persons to prefer a life of labor to dependence upon alms. If these principles are correct, as the Board maintain, then the complaints against them are inconsiderate and injudicious.

Of practical results a volume might be written, which would probably interest the benevolent, and still leave much unsaid. The Institution has been instrumental in feeding the hungry, clothing the naked, reclaiming the vicious, and ministering to the sick. And while it has sympathized with man as a responsible and intelligent being,—traversed the narrow lanes and crowded alleys of this metropolis on its errands of kindness,— while it has sat by the side of the wretched in their comfortless hovels, to listen to the tales of their sufferings, to soothe their sorrows, and to extend relief,—yet it has not blindly dispensed its favors, so as to discourage struggling virtue, or to encourage in vicious courses the idle and depraved. On the contrary, it has detected the impostor, and arrested the vagrant, while it has stimulated the inert and desponding, and relieved the distresses of the deserving. Possessing superior facilities for collecting and diffusing information, its action, free from prejudices and preferences, has been liberal and comprehensive. In inculcating temperance, frugality, and industry, it has stood as the hand-maid of Christianity, in its endeavors to meliorate the condition of the indigent. And though it may not have accomplished all that was needful to be done, nor as perfectly as could be desired, yet with the means at their disposal, the Board believes, with better effects, and with approximations to a better system, than had hitherto been acted upon in this city.

Of direct results they will attempt no estimate, beyond the following summary statements, which they respectfully submit, viz:

Amount of receipts to Nov. 10th, 1844,	$10,514 15
Expenditures do. do. do.	8,696 20
Balance in Treasury at the above date,	1,817 95
Receipts from Nov. 1844, to Nov. 1845,	16,692 72
Amount for disbursement,	18,510 67
Expenditure from November 1844, to November 1845,	17,938 09
Balance in Treasury, Nov. 10, 1845,	572 58
Expenditures in two years,	27,206 87
Total Receipts in two years,	27,779 45

Up to November 10th, 1845, the Register shows the relief of 8013 applicants, *nearly all of whom represent families;* while the extent of personal exertion in behalf of its objects, may be inferred from the number of visits of inquiry and sympathy made to them, which according to the Visitors' reports, amount to 28,086.

The Board acknowledges, with peculiar emotions, a bequest of *one thousand dollars*, by Charles D. Betts, Esq., deceased, (son of the Hon. Judge Betts,) whose many virtues, in public and private life, endeared him to an extensive circle of friends, and whose early death is deplored as an irreparable loss.

In conclusion, they tender their thanks to the numerous contributors who have so generously and promptly furnished the means of sustaining this extensive charity; and in behalf of the needy, they earnestly solicit the continuance of their sympathy and support. The position of this Institution will be seen to involve great pecuniary responsibilities, which cannot be met without adequate resources. For these, its sole dependence is upon the contributions of the benevolent, which, from the past experience of their kindness, they believe will not be withheld. And let none imagine, that *liberal* contributions will favor idleness and improvidence, or tend to profuse or indiscreet charity. For as the Association aims, to the extent of its means, to promote the greatest good of all its beneficiaries with the fewest possible evil results, so its principles and action unite to afford the strongest guaranty that this philanthropic object will be attained. The more ample, therefore, its means, the greater will be its usefulness; for all will be so used, as shall tend to shed blessings on donors and recipients, and dry up the causes of poverty and wretchedness at their source.

TREASURER'S ACCOUNT. (1845.

R. B. MINTURN, Treasurer, in account with Association for Improving the Condition of the Poor.

Dr.					Cr.
1844	Disbursements to Nov. 10th,	$9,268 78	1844	Receipts to Nov. 10th,	$11,086 73
1845	Ditto to Nov. 10th,	17,938 09	1845	Ditto to Nov. 10th,	16,692 72
	Balance in hand to date,	572 58			
	Total disbursements and balance,	$27,779 45		Total receipts to date,	$27,779 45

The undersigned, having examined the Treasurer's accounts, found vouchers for all the sums charged, and a balance in his hands to the credit of the Association, of Five Hundred and Seventy-Two Dollars, Fifty-Eight Cents.

JOS. B. COLLINS, } *Auditing Committee.*
F. S. WINSTON,

NEW-YORK, Nov. 10th, 1845.

APPENDIX.

A.

VISITOR'S MANUAL.

WITH a view to promote uniformity of action, and to aid Visitors in the discharge of their responsible duties, the following series of Rules and Instructions, supplementary to those prescribed in the By-Laws, have been adopted by the Association, and are hereby earnestly recommended to the careful attention of all who may engage in carrying out its principles.

ARTICLE I.

The first principle of this Association is founded in the admission, that the Alms of Benevolent Societies, and of private liberality, are often misapplied, and as often abused by those who receive them. As a visitor of this Association, therefore, be especially careful to do all that a cautious and discriminating judgment may suggest, to prevent every abuse of the charity you may dispense. But if, after suitable precaution on your part, to guard against the misapplication of charity, it should appear, that it has been bestowed on objects of pretended distress, or upon those who may be receiving adequate relief from other sources, it will be your immediate duty to report all such cases to your

Committee, that the names of the undeserving applicants may be placed upon record at the General Office, and become known to every Visitor and member of the Association.

ARTICLE II.

The persons who will address themselves to your sympathies, though differing in many particulars, may here be divided into three classes. *First*, those who have been reduced to indigence by infirmity, sickness, old age, and unavoidable misfortune; *Second*, those who have brought themselves to want and suffering by their improvidence and vices; and, *Third*, persons who are able but unwilling to labour, and are beggars and vagrants by profession. The well-being of these different classes evidently requires a mode of treatment adapted to each. And as this cannot be applied without a knowledge of their character and circumstances, your first duty is, *to withhold all relief from unknown persons.* Let this rule be imperative and unalterable.

ARTICLE III.

In all cases referred to you for aid, if the applicants reside in your section, remember they have claims upon your sympathies and kind offices which belong to no other Visitor of this Association, and if neglected by you, they may suffer unrelieved. Without delay, therefore, visit them at their homes; personally examine every case; ascertain their character and condition; and carefully inquire into the causes which have brought them into a state of destitution. You will become an important instrument of good to your suffering fellow-creatures, when you aid them to obtain this good from resources within themselves. To effect this, show them the true origin of their sufferings, when these sufferings are the result of imprudence, extravagance, idleness, intemperance, or other moral causes which are within their own control; and endeavour, by all appropriate means, to awaken their self-respect, to direct their exertions, and to strengthen their capacities for self-support. In your intercourse with them, avoid all appearance of harshness, and every manifestation of an obtrusive and a censorious spirit. Study to carry into your work a mind as discriminating and judicious as it is kindly disposed, and a heart ready to sympathize with the sick and the infirm, the widow and the orphan, the tempted and the vicious.— In short, if you would confer great and permanent good upon the needy, you first must distinctly understand in what that good consists; and as this knowledge can only be acquired by personal intercourse with them at their dwellings, the second rule becomes as absolute as the first, viz.—*Always to visit those for whom your benevolent services are required, before granting relief.* Having given these general instructions in relation to visitorial duties, it may be useful to present a few practical directions concerning each of the classes of the poor before named.

First. Those who have been reduced to indigence by unavoidable causes.

In your intercourse with this class, if you meet with industry, frugality, and self-respect, and a preference for self-denial to dependence upon alms, let not your charities become the means of undermining one right principle, or of enfeebling one well-directed impulse. Alms in such cases must often be given, and the temptation is to bestow freely; but let them be administered with great delicacy and caution. The most effectual encouragement for such persons is not *alms chiefly*, or any other form of charity as a substitute for alms, but that sympathizing counsel which re-enkindles hope, and that expression of respect for character, which such individuals never fail to appreciate. A wise distribution of charity, connected with a deportment of this kind towards the deserving poor, will often save them from pauperism, when the absence of these may degrade them to habitual dependence on alms for subsistence.

Second. Individuals who have become mendicants through their own improvidence and vices.

The evils of improvidence can never be diminished, except by removing the cause; and this can only be done by elevating the moral character of the poor, and by teaching them to depend upon themselves. Many able-bodied persons apply for alms who earn enough for their own maintenance, but expend their earnings in improper indulgences, with the calculation of subsisting on charity when their own resources fail them, who might have obviated this necessity by proper self-denial and economy. In respect to these cases, if relief must be given,—and it sometimes must be,—it should never be of a kind, or to a degree, that will *make this dependence preferable to a life of labour.* And it should not be forgotten, that many would be economical and saving *if they knew how to be.* Let it be your endeavour, therefore, to instruct them; to encourage deposits in savings banks for rent, fuel, and winter supplies; and by all the motives which you can present, stimulate them to habits of thriftiness, industry, and foresight. The rule is, *that the willingly dependent upon alms should not live so comfortably with them as the humblest independent labourer without them.*

In this class is also included those who have been reduced to want by their vices. Among these, the vice of *Intemperance* is the most prolific source of pauperism and abject poverty. How to act wisely in reference to this class of applicants, is a most perplexing question, yet, as it will frequently occur, it must be met. As a general rule, *alms should, as far as possible, be withheld from the drunkard.* But here, perhaps, is the inebriate's family in actual want of the absolute necessaries of life. Still the rule is, that *relief should never be given to the families of the intemperate, beyond the demands of urgent necessity.* You should, if possible, become the instruments of their rescue; but any alms you can bestow may only perpetuate their misery. They may minister to the drunkard's recklessness, and induce him to feel that he is relieved from the necessity, perhaps from the moral obligation of providing for his wife and children. Much must here be left to your discretion. Seek, however, by all the means of which you can avail yourself, to save the intemperate from ruin. Depraved though he be, shut not your heart against him. Though apparently lost, he is not beyond hope. Act on this principle, and you may be the instrument of his recovery. But whatever may be your success with the guilty, and perhaps incorrigible parent, never abandon your interest in the welfare of his children.

Third. To the third general class specified, viz., those who are able but unwilling to labour, and professional paupers, the Scriptural rule applies without qualification: "This we command you, that if any will not work, neither should he eat." If the entire community were to act on this principle, some of this class might be exposed to the risk of starvation. But as such unanimity is not likely to occur, this Association cannot, by bestowing alms on objects so undeserving, become a willing accessory in perpetuating the evils of vagrancy and pauperism.

ARTICLE IV.

Another rule is, *where there are relatives of the indigent who are able to provide for them, alms should never be so given as to interfere with the duties of such relatives.* If those alms are evil which become substitutes for industry and economy, in a still higher sense are they evil because they offend against a higher law, when their tendency or result is to cancel just claims on kindred or consanguinity. Let it therefore be your endeavour so to awaken and strengthen the natural sympathy of relatives, that those who have the means of aiding their dependent connexions, may never suffer them to be cast upon the charity of the world.

ARTICLE V.

Endeavour by a systematic attention to the education and religious instruction of the children of the poor, through the aid of the Public and Sunday Schools, to fit them for the proper pursuits of life; and as they arrive at suitable age, to assist those parents who of themselves are unable, to provide eligible situations for their children, in such useful occupations or trades as will qualify them in after life to obtain their own support, and to be introduced into society as industrious and useful citizens.

ARTICLE VI.

In all your intercourse with the poor, endeavour to gain their respect and confidence. Be careful to encourage habits of cleanliness, both of houses and persons. Show them the absolute necessity of employment, and, as far as in your power, aid them in obtaining it. Be particularly attentive to the infirm, the sick, and the aged. Sympathize with the widow, have compassion on the fatherless, and endeavour to promote the good of all, by pointing out the advantages of education, the duty of religiously observing the Sabbath, the importance of attending a place of worship, and the value of the Sacred Scriptures.

ARTICLE VII.

You will observe, that it is not the design of this Association to extend relief to the poor indiscriminately. Those who are accustomed to avail themselves of the public provision made them at the Alms House, and who leave it in summer to pass a few months in idleness, and return to it again when other means fail, are considered as undeserving our aid; but even persons of this class should not be wholly disregarded. You must advise and encourage them to change their habits of life; but until they manifest by their exertions to assist themselves a disposition to reform their course of conduct, they have no claims for relief on this Association. To the needy, however, who have no other resource, it will be your duty to extend a friendly hand in providing food, fuel, clothing, and shelter; and in your visits to the abodes of suffering and sorrow to provide, for the sick, medical aid, by means of the public dispensaries or otherwise, and such necessary comforts as their condition may require. And ever endeavour to evince a deep and permanent interest in the social and moral welfare of the persons whom your charities relieve.

ARTICLE VIII.

As there are certain fundamental rules to be observed in the distribution of charity which cannot be too familiar to your minds, they will here be summarily stated. It is best, as far as possible,

First. To give the necessary articles, and what is immediately necessary.

Second. To give what is least susceptible of abuse.

Third. To give even necessary articles only in small quantities, in proportion to immediate need.

Fourth. To give assistance, both in quantity and in quality, inferior, except in cases of sickness, to what might be procured by labor.

Fifth. To give assistance at the right moment; and not to prolong it beyond the duration of the necessity which calls for it; but to extend, restrict and modify it with that necessity.

ARTICLE IX.

In case of the removal of a family into your section who may solicit aid, it is recommended that you call upon the Visitor in whose section they had previously resided, for information respecting them; but in no case communicate to them the names of the individuals who informed you concerning their condition and character. When persons are referred to you for aid, who do not reside in your section, direct them to the Visitor of the section in which they belong. And in all cases of difficulty, consult your Advisory Committee, and be guided by their judgment; thus you will avoid the censure of the public and the reproaches of the undeserving poor.

ARTICLE X.

Bear in mind that two prominent and serious evils exist in this city, in relation to pauperism. The one is, that the worst class among the poor stands the best chance of obtaining, and do in fact obtain, the greatest amount of charity. The other is, that of the best class of poor, including all who are more or less in want, and who are not vicious, some obtain much less, and others far more than they deserve. These evils are chiefly attributable to the injudicious mode of bestowing alms, which has too generally prevailed in this city. The benevolent, by acting independently of each other, have necessarily been ignorant of each other's doings, and the artful and designing have turned this ignorance to their own advantage, and to the injury of the deserving. Now, it is one object of this Association, by establishing a comprehensive, uniform, and systematic mode of distributing charity, and by an intelligent co-operation on the part of all who engage in the work, greatly to facilitate the detection of imposture. To this important reform, therefore, let your attention be vigilantly directed.

ARTICLE XI.

Use every exertion in your power to advance the cause of temperance, by imparting judicious advice, and the circulation of tracts and other useful publications on the subject.

ARTICLE XII.

The objects of the Association require, that you furnish your Committee, at each monthly meeting, with a *written report*, containing an accurate statement of the number of persons you have assisted during the preceding month; the names of the persons thus assisted; the residence, occupation, and character of each; and of the kind and amount of relief afforded; according to a form provided by the Association. This will explain to the benevolent, who, through this organization, have made you their almoner, the manner in which their charities have been applied; and the information, moreover, will be generally available, for the prevention of fraud, and the detection of imposture. Do not fail to have your report prepared in time, and be punctual in attending the monthly meetings.

ARTICLE XIII.

Record in a book the names of the persons you visit, and the relief afforded them, with such facts and observations on the state of your section, as may be useful in preparing your report; also such notice of any particular circumstance as will tend to illustrate character, evince improvement, or call for special advice. Upon your removal or resignation, give immediate notice thereof to the Secretary of the Advisory Committee, and transfer to him your books and papers, with such information concerning your section, as you think may be useful to your successor.

B.

PRINTED FORMS USED BY THE ASSOCIATION.

Ticket of Reference for the Use of Members.

Mr.   Visitor,

  No.   St.

is requested to visit

at No.

                                              Member

                    N. Y. Association for the
             Improvement of the Condition of the Poor.

Visitor's Order.

Mr.

No.   *St.*

Please let

have the value of

in

                    184

                                        Vis.

                    N. Y. Association for the
             Improvement of the Condition of the Poor.

C.

Monthly Report.

Subjoined is a condensed plan of a Sectional Monthly Return. The original occupies a large page of foolscap, with appropriate columns, 38 in number, which enable Visitors to give the following particulars of every family relieved. 1st. Name, residence, place of birth, sex, color, occupation, time in the city, number in family, and number of visits. 2d. Statements of character,—as being temperate or intemperate, virtuous or vicious, industrious or idle. 3d. Unavoidable causes of indigence, such as sickness, infirmity, or old age. 4th. Whether they can read or write; whether the children attend Public School, or Sabbath School; and also particularly concerning the kind and amount of relief given, either in food, fuel, clothing, or medicine, with space for marginal remarks.

New-York Association for the Improvement of the Condition of the Poor.

VISITOR'S MONTHLY REPORT, OF SECTION No. ____ DISTRICT No. ____ Dated ____

☞ *A mark with a pen thus ,, in the columns, will point out the class to which the person named belongs.* ☜

Nos. of Persons.	Names of Persons Visited.	Residence of Persons.	Foreigners.	Natives.	Colored Persons.	Males.	Females.	Kind of occupation.	Time in City.	No. in Family.	No. of Visits.	Character: Temperate.	Intemperate.	Provident.	Improvident.	Virtuous.	Vicious.	Industrious.	Idle.	Unavoidable causes: Sickness.	Infirmity.	Misfortune.	Old Age.	Education: Can rd & write.	Cannot do.	Child'n to a S.	do. Public.	Kind of Relief: Food.	Fuel.	Clothing.	Shelter.	Money.	Medicine.	Physician.	Amount Expended. Dols | cts.	Remarks.

Total. ____

Remarks.

Signed, _____ Visitor.

184

D.

CIRCULAR ON COLD VICTUALS.

To the Citizens of New-York:

There are *several thousand families* in the city, the refuse of whose tables, if carefully gathered up, and as carefully dispensed, would go far towards relieving an *equal number of families,* among the needy and deserving. But, with few exceptions, cold victuals are given by servants at the door, without any knowledge of the recipients, or of the use to which the charity is applied. It is notorious, that such alms are often abused. Sometimes they are fed to swine, or sold to keepers of low boarding-houses, to obtain the means of improper indulgence ; and in all cases, the giving of refuse victuals in this way encourages street begging and vagrancy, with the various evils inseparable from indiscriminate charity.

Now, with the concurrence of our citizens, these evils may be corrected ; and the way of doing it is extremely simple. If you are willing to *give your refuse victuals on the order of our Visitors, to the exclusion for the time being of all other applicants you do not know to be deserving, and will insert your name and residence in the subjoined card, and send it without delay as addressed,* all that is desired from you for the cure of these evils, will be accomplished. Please do this, and the arrangement will be completed by our Visitors, who will be careful to send for your charity deserving persons, with whom you can so adjust the *time for calls,* as will subject your family to the least inconvenience.

} *Advisory Committee th District.*

To the
No.   Street,
M.. Residence,
No. .... Street,
Will give Cold Victuals on the Orders of your Visitors.

LIST OF MEMBERS.

Owing to inadvertence in the returns from some of the Districts, it is feared that the list of Members may not be perfectly accurate. The *amounts* received were duly credited, as may be seen by an inspection of the Treasurer's account, at the General Office. But as the names of some who contributed small sums, did not accompany their donation, with all the efforts subsequently made to obtain them, the list may still be incomplete. Measures are taken to avoid this omission in future.

Adams, J. T.
Adams, O.
Adams Tiffany & Co.
Arms,
Adams, F. M.
Adams, J. K.
Allen Horatio
Allen, John B.
Allen, H.
Allen, G. H.
Allen, H. P.
Allen, Joseph,
Allen, Rev. J. M.
Addison, Thomas,
Aikman, Hugh
Aspinwall, W. H.
Andrews, George
Ayres, Reuben
Ackerley, Richard
Abeel, John H.
Abeel, George
Allen, Stephen
Anderson, Albert
Anderson. Mrs.
Avery, John S.
Asten, B. C.
Ackerman, Mrs.
Attenbury, Lewis
Anderson, W. C.
Avery, F.
Anderson, G. V.
Anderson, William
Ackerman, Hiram
Anderson, N. P.
Anderson, Walter,
Angel, J.
Alfred & Co.
Allen, Gilbert,
Atwell, J.
Amerman, P.
Austen, David,
Anderson, John
Averill, Augustus
Addis, C. J.
Ashfield, A.
Atiles, Mr.
Aguire, P.
Aspinwall, J. S.
Alwick, Miss
Austin,
Aspinwall, J. M.
Archibald, J. M.
Aimes, J.

Andriance, Charles,
Arsnigg, B.
Alsop, Joseph W. Jun.
Anthony, Jacob
Alvord, G. B.
Arnold, B. G.
Armstrong, John
Astor, William B.
Astor, John Jacob.
Barry, S. S.
Blatchford, S. M.
Balen, Peter
Baldwin, John C.
Barnes, William E.
Barbour, James G.
Barmore, Garret
Blake, Eli C.
Bradley, William C.
Baldwin, Jotham
Barker, Stephen
Blackledge Adam
Blakeman William M. M. D.
Bayard, R.
Bradish, Mrs. L.
Bartlett & Miller,
Battelle, Thomas
Bennet, J. L.
Beers, C.
Bell, Joseph M.
Bevier Rev. John H.
Bell, Abraham
Brewster, J. B.
Bridgham, G. W.
Bowne, Mr.
Baldwin, Mrs.
Baldwin, D. A.
Blaine, Mr.
Bayle, W. F.
Barker, J. S.
Barker, C., M. D.
Bacot, M. E.
Brady, J. T.
Bragg,
Baylis, Henry
Banyer. Mrs.
Blatchford, R. M.
Barstow & Co. J.
Barlow, W. J.
Barker, Mrs.
Baldwin, Joshua
Babcock, Paul
Baldwin, Jotham M.
Bradbury, William B.

Bacon, George
Barlow, Samuel B., M. D.
Barker, Joseph D.
Barron, Wm.
Blackwell, J.
Brainerd, Mrs. G. W.
Badleston, E.
Banger, Wm.
Bradhurst, J. M.
Blake, M. B.
Bartlett C.
Baker, A,
Bradford, W. H.
Barker, N.
Barker, Thomas D.
Barker, Thomas
Baldwin, Luther
Ballard, William
Beech, Mr.
Bedell Knapp
Beul, Thomas
Benedict, C. S.
Breath, Mrs.
Beekman, J. N.
Beckwith, W. M.
Belcher, George E., M. D.
Bremner James P.
Bell, James
Benton, Lewis
Berry, M. R.
Beach Street, 10
Bethune, Mrs.
Bren, Mrs. William
Brevoort, Henry,
Beals, C.
Bleecker Mrs. A. N.
Betts, Mr.
Betts, Charles D.
Beck, John B.
Belcher, E. P., M. D.
Beckman, S. B.
Bisby, L. S.
Brigham, Mrs.
Birdsall, Rowland & Co.
Bridge, J.
Bridge, Edward
Bridges, J. F.
Brinckerhoff, James L.
Bishop, John
Bliss, James C.
Bonus, Mr.
Booth, Mrs.
Brooks, Mr.

LIST OF MEMBERS.

Brooks, James,
Brown, S.
Browne, George W.
Brown, E. M.
Brooks, D. H.
Bogart, Mrs. C. M.
Brower, J. D.
Boswell, S.
Bromham, G. W.
Brown & Dimock,
Boggs, William G.
Bloodgood, William
Brooks, A.
Bloodgood, N.
Bolton, C.
Bonnet, R. R.
Bronson, F.
Borrowe, J. H.
Brown, E. J.
Bogert, Cornelius
Brown, B.
Brooks, J.
Boorman, R.
Bogart, H. R.
Brown, Lewis
Browning, William
Booth, Jonas
Brown, Alexander
Brower, Thomas M.
Burr, A. C.
Brush, J. E.
Buntun, R.
Bunker, Mr.
Butler, Charles
Burnes, James
Bulkley, Thomas,
Bryan, J. S
B. R.
Burritt & Johnson,
Burritt,
Bunce, L.
Blunt, George W.
Buck, G.
Burrell, Samuel
B. D.
Burling, L. S.
B. W. & S.
Brown, James
Boorman, James
Brown, Stewart
Benedict, E. C.
Bliss, Ira
Briant, Daniel S.
Bockover, J. H.
Brown, Charles D., M. D.
Brown, Silas
Bronson. Arthur,
Bronson, Mrs. Isaac
Bowne, William & John
Bull, William G.
Butler, George B.
Burdge, Ira
Bussing, E. K.
Bushnell O.
Blunt & Syms,
Bryson, David,
Boyd, Mr.
Boyle, E. J.

Briggs, Mrs.
Bennett, N. L.
Bremner, J. B.
Bunker, Paul
Brown Edward
Bennett, P.
Cass, J. C.
Caulkins, William H.
Carter, R.
Carpenter, N. B.
Carey, Josiah,
Chapman. William S.
Chauncey, Henry
Chauncey, William
Caswell, J.
Cary, W. F.
Clark. John
Caffee, John
Clark, Nathaniel,
Cassody, Samuel
Canfield, D. N.
Callender, Mrs. Thomas
Cassavere, H. A.
Cape, Mrs. C.
Clark Gerardus
Clarkson, Mrs.
Clarkson Thomas S.
Cartledge,
Carle, J.
Cape & Trowbridge
Clarke, D. S.
Clapp. Lyman
Camp B. F.
Crane, A. G.
Clarke, J. Henry, M. D.
Crane, Daniel
Crane, Morris,
Clark, G.
Cash,
Clark, A. H
Candee, E. W.
Chapman, Mrs.
Chaffle, Mrs.
Cambreling, Mrs.
Cammann, O.
Cammann, P. G.
Craig, Mrs. L.
Carrall, N. T.
Carman, S. A.
Carne, D.
Carter, H.
Carter, H. C.
Carney, N. B.
Chandler. J.
Cary, S. T.
Cape, John J.
Cartwright, A. F.
Cartwright. William
Clarkson, C. V , M. D.
Clayton, Charles H.
Clark, J.
Clark, Mr.
Chester, Stephen M.
Center. E. C.
Clements, J. W. G., M. D.
Chester, W. W.
Chesterman, James
Cheseborough, Mr.

Clendennen, P.
Chichester, L.
Clinch, C. P.
Cripps & Co.
Christie, Albert
Crosby, William B.
Collins, Joseph B.
Cock, Thomas, M. D.
Comstock, E. D.
Colgate. Wiliam
Cornell, Samuel M.
Crocker, Leonard
Conover, G. S.
Conger, John
Cooper, Peter
Crosby, John P.
Cortelyou. F. S.
Cook, Edward
Cooper, John
Colden, David C.
Colden, Frances
Colt. Harris
Cook, Levi
Cobb, James N.
Coit, H. A.
Crolius, William J.
Connolly, Edward
Corbet, Mr.
Codman, M.
Cook, Mrs.
Cornell, H.
Cameron, J.
Conkling, Jonas
Cottenet, F.
Cockroft. W.
Cornell, T. F.
Coster, C. M.
Cook. Zebedee
Crolius, W A.
Cobb, George T.
Cook, E. C.
Cook, James
Copcutt, Mrs.
Cook, Mrs. Edward
Colden, Mrs.
Crooks. R.
Coffin, Edmund
Cormin, O.
Corning, W. B.
Coddington, J. J.
Cogswell, Mrs.
Couch, William
Collins, S. B.
Cox, A. B.
Coit, M. A.
Cockroft, James
Cromwell, Daniel
Coe, Rev. David B.
Crosby, A. S.
Conover, Peter
Cottrier, John
Cruikshank, James
Cutter, Stephen
Cutter, William T.
Crum, John A.
Culver, John
Cutler, Miss
Crum, J. A.

LIST OF MEMBERS.

Cummings, John
Curtiss, M. O.
Cushman, D. A. & Co.
Cumming, T. B.
Chute, Richard
Chub, Mrs.
Cummings, T. S.
C. & E. W.
C. S.
C. N. D.
Colon John R
Crampton, Henry
Cromwell, Wm. A.
Catron, David W.
Dakin, C. P.
Darling, C. C.
Dawson, W.
Dawson, G. H.
Daken, George
Davis Mr.
Day, Mahlon,
Davison, Erastus
Davis, E. R.
Davis, H. E.
Davies, T. E.
Dawson, B. F.
Draper, W. B.
Drake, I.
Drake, Mrs. S.
Dayton, G.
Dashwood, Mrs.
Davis, E. P.
Denny, Thomas
Deming, Barzillai
Depeyster, Frederick
Degrove, Quincy C.
De Rham, H. C.
Demarest J. D.
Dettmer, Frederick
Delprat, J. B.
Dennistown, W.
Dery, S. P.
Devenport, Mrs.
Decoppit, Mr.
Dewey, Orville
Delafield, Mr.
Decker, A.
Deems, H. W.
Dean, Benj. T.
Denison, G.
Demarest, Mrs.
Dekham & Moore,
Delafield, E.
De Forest, W. W.
Delano, E.
Dewitt, Thomas
Denison, Mrs. A.
Delafield, Joseph
Dean, Thomas
Delaney, John F.
Decan, I.
Dwight, W. W., M. D.
Dirker, Mr.
Dibblee & Pray,
Dickinson, J. B.
Dickson, E.
Doane, Philo
Douglass, George

Douglass, John
Donaldson, Thomas
Donaldson, J.
Downer, S.
Dorr, G. B.
Doolittle. A., M. D.
Dodd, John M.
Dominick, J. W., Jr.
Dominick, James W.
Dodge, Samuel M.
Douglass, J. H.
Dominick-street 42,
Drondon, Mr.
Dyer, Charles C.
Dusenberry, William C.
Dubois, Cornelius, Jr.
Duyckinck, E. & G.
Dunn, Mrs.
Duryea, Jacob
Dyckman, Jacob
Dyson, A.
Dupuy, Mr. E.
Dubois, Cornelius,
Dunning, William
Dunbar, James
Duff, James
Draper, Simeon
D. J. S.
D. H. V.
Dormin, Oscar
Dormin, Wm. P.
Dewey, Nathaniel
Dewey, James
Drake, Wm. J.
Easton, George S.
Eastmond J.
Eastman, S. J.
Easknas, Mrs. C.
Eaton. D. C.
Earl. Edward
Eaton. A. B.
Earl, Robert
Eagle, Mrs. H.
Everett, N. C.
Edwards, Walter
Eggleston, Thomas
Emmet, W. C.
Eversley, Charles
Edwards, A. B.
Everdell, William
Ellsworth. W.
Ebaugh, Rev. J. S.
Ensign, Timothy
Ellis, Benjamin
Endicott, John
Ely & Wilcox,
Ely, Charles
Ellison, J.
Eustice, W.
E. J. E.
Edwards, Ogden E.
Eno, Amos R.
Falconer, J.
Fancher, E. L.
Fanshaw, Daniel
Fraser, E. A.
Flaylor, T.
Fraser, Henry F.

Francis, Charles
Franklin, William H.
Franklin, S.
Francis, Dr.
Fanning, James
Ferdon, Abraham, Jr.,
Fessenden, Thomas
Ferguson, James
Fendall. J L.
Fenn, Jason
Fenn, Gairus
Ferris, Isaac
Fredericks,
French, Daniel
Fletcher, James H.
Fellows, W. M.
Fleming, Thomas
Ferr, Mrs. C
Ferris, J. H.
Feeks, Abijah S.
Forrest, William
Foy, John
Ford, Ebenezer
Forrester, James
Frost, Samuel
Fisher, Richard
Fisher, George C.
Fitch, William
Fisher, John G.
Field, Henry A., M. D.,
Fitch, Hanlin & Co.
Friend, A
Field, Edward
F. L R
Field, Thomas W.
Field, Benjamin H.
F. W. F.
Fink, Mrs. Elizabeth
Fowler, J. W.
Frost, William
Fox, Livingston & Co.,
Fowler, B M.
Ford, Isaac,
Fortentack, W.
Foster, James, Jr.,
Fox, S. M.
Furst, J. P.
Fry, Jacob
Fulton, George
Fuller, Mrs.
Frink, F.
Gale, William
Gray, J. A. C.
Gantz, John I.
Gates, William
Graves. Edward B.
Gray, Thomas R.
Grayden, John
Gray, John
Garner, Mrs.
Garner, T.
Guns, M.
Galletin, Albert R.
Graham, John A.
Gray, W. C.
Graham,
Graham, Mrs.
Gardner, Mrs.

40 LIST OF MEMBERS. (1845.

Graigley, Mrs.
Gray, E.
Gallatin, Albert
Gray, Niel,
Gardner, William
Green, John C.
Gelston, Roland,
Green, David. M. D.
Greenough, J. J.
Geery, J. & W.
Green, Garret
Green, E.
Green, Walter C.
Green, Miss
Griswold George,
Griscom J. H., M. D.
Griffin, Herman
Grinnell, Moses H.
Gibbs, John
Griswold, John
Gilliland, C. H.
Gills, Mrs.
Griffin, Lewis B.
Griffing, Samuel
Gifford, M. Y.
Gibbs, G.
Gilchrist,
Gillman, Mr.
Gilpin, S. S.
Griffith, Mr.
Grice, C. C.
Goodhue, Jonathan
Gould, Edward L.
Gollier, Mr.
Gross, John L.
Glover, Daniel T.
Gross & March,
Gould, Wm. R., Jr
Gorden, G.
Godine, Francis
Goodliffe, James
Goodwin, E.
Grosvenor, S.
Grosvenor, J.
Goddard, G. C.
Gould, Mr.
G. D.
G. G. W. & B.
Grum, J. N., M. D.
Gunn, George O.
Hartley, R. M.
Hance, Revo C.
Hall, Archibald
Harris. J.
Hagedorn, John
Halsey, A. P.
Harris, Wm. D
Hanford, Albert G.
Hamilton John
Halsey James
Havens, Renselaer, Jr.,
Haggerty, Ogden,
Haggerty, C. M.
Halstead, Wm. M.
Hadley, Robert,
Hammersly, J. W.
Hart, Eli

Harrison, Misses
Harris, J.
Hawxhurst, J. W.
Hawley, J.
Hall, James
Harriet, James
Harmony, Peter, & Co.
Halley, Irad
Harmer, Charles G.
Harrison. Miss
Haines, R. T.
Hammersly, Gordon
Hallet, William R.
Havens, H.
Havens, Augusta S.
Hatch. George W.
Hadden, D., & Son
Haviland. John
Haynes, Thomas
Hatch, C. B.
Halstead, Mr.
Havemeyer, F. C.
Hammersly, Mr.
Hart, James
Hallock, Dr. L.
Hale, James W.
Hall, P.
Halstead, A. L.
Harris. D.
Hamilton, J. C.
Haggerty, J.
Halsted, S.
Halsted, Schureman
Havens. C.
Hewlet, O. T.
Heard, James
Heiser, Henry
Hedenburgh, Mrs.
Hertell, Thomas
Hewlett, Joseph
Hedges, Timothy
Hechschier,
Heath, Mrs. F.
Hearry, Elizabeth
Heyer, Edward
Heyer, Isaac
Herring, Silas C.
Hendricks, Mrs.
Hewit, Charles
Hendrick, Miss
Herbert, Mr.
Hepburn, Mrs.
Hicks, John H.
Hinchelwood, Robert
Hillman, W.
Hale, Richard
Hurd, Mrs.
Hills, Mrs H. W.
Hickok, Wm. C., M. D.
Hitchcock, Mrs.
Houghton, E.
Howe, Benj. F.
Howland Samuel S.
Horton, Richard
Howe, John M.
Hoyt, Calvin
Howe, J. W.

Hoffman, L. M.
Howland, G. G.
Hoffman, Philip
Howe, Mr.
Howe, Benjamin
Holman, John
Hopping. A.
Holensworth, S.
Holden, Horace
Holmes, Madison
Holmes, James E.
Hoe, R. M.
Hoe, Robert
Hone, James
Howe, John
Hoit, Dr.
Houghtwout,
Hoyt, J. J.
Hocth, George W.
Hosmer & Sherman
Hosack, N. P.
Howe, Bezaleel
Hogg & Delematre,
Hoyt, Mrs. J. M.
Howe, Calvin W.
Holmes, H. L.
Holmes, O.
Howse, Mrs. D.
Howell, Charles J.
Hosack, Alexander
Howard,
Holmes, Samuel P.
Horn, James
Houghton, T. L.
Hoyt, A.
Hoag, G. B.
Hobey, T.
Hurlbut, H. A.
Hurry, Edmund
Hunter, Charles
Hutchings, John
Hunt, Thomas
Hubbell, H. W.
Hurry, William
Hunter, Jacob
Hyatt, E.
Hubbs & Buxby,
Huntington, J. C.
Humbert, W. B.
Hutchinson, Mr.
Hunter, Dr.
Hyatt, T.
Hutton M. S.
Hunt, Edwin
Humphrey, Mrs. S.
Hull, J. S.
Hunn, S.
Hussey, G.
Hutchinson, S.
Hendricks, H.
Hefan, D.
Hart, Mrs.
Irvin, Richard
Irvin, John
Inpler, John H.
Ireland, George
Irvin, Mrs.

1845.) LIST OF MEMBERS. **41**

Inkley, George
Jackson, Wm. H.
Jay, Miss
Jackson, John
Jacobs, Laban
Jackson, L. E.
Jauncey, J.
Jackson, Luther
Jessup, Samuel
Jemmenson, J. F.
Jeremiah, J.
Jennings, Ezra
Johnson, William
Jordan, Andrew
Joline, D.
Johnson, W. M.
Jones, James J.
Johnson, Wm.
Jones, George
Jones,
Jones, Isaac
Jones, A. T.
Johnson, Dr.
Joy, J. F.
Jones, A. P., & Co.
Jones, John Q.
Johnson, J. K.
Jones, A.
Jones, Rev. E. S.
Just, Mrs.
Knapp, Shepherd
Knapp, Rev. M.
Knapp, James S.
Kennedy, Thomas
Kennedy, James
Kellogg, J. W.
Kennedy, D. S.
Keeht, George
Kendall, Thomas
Krebs, John M.
Keeler, L. M.
Kemble, William
Kemeys, William
Kellogg, E.
Keeler, R. N.
Kernechan, W. S.
Kermit, Robert
Ketchum, John W.
Kingsley, E. M.
Kilbourne, J. S., M. D.
Knight, Daniel
King, R. S.
King, Josiah
Kingsley, H., M. D.
King, J. G.
Kip, L. W.
Kip, B. L.
Kidder, Mrs.
Kitletas, E.
King, Harman
Kingsland & Co.
King, W. L.
Kip, Mr.
Kingsland, D.
Kingsland, Mrs.
Kilree, W. H.

King, P. V.
Kip, F. A.
Knipe, William
Kozzell, C.
Kobbe, W.
Kummell, H.
Kuested A.
Klotts, John J.
Kelly, F. W. & W. F.
Laight, Edward W.
Lawrence, Joseph
Lawrence, S. A.
Lander, Wm. P.
Lane, N. B.
Lain, Mrs. M.
Lawrence, G.
Laton, Mr.
Lawrence, Isaac
Lawrence, A. M.
Langdon, E.
Lathrop, W. M.
Lathrop, D.
Lawrence, Alexander
Lawrence, J.
Laing, E.
Lawrence, Mrs.
Lane, Josiah
Lamb, A.
Laye, Mrs. D.
Law, James
Lawrence, H.
Leavitt, John W.
Leavitt, Rufus
Lewis, Professor T.
Leavenworth, Mrs.
Leupp, C. M.
Levy, Kurmann
Levenworth, M.
Lewis, Mr.
Lefferts, James
Leversay, Jane
Lewis, Thomas
Lent, J. W.
Lewis, Mrs.
Lewis, A.
Leroy, Jacob R.
Leeds, Samuel, Jr.
Leroy, Wm. H.
Leland, Francis
Lee & Brewster,
Le Barbier, A.
Leslie, Edmund S.
Ledyard, D. J.
Leon, P. W.
Lippincott, Thomas
Little, James
Livingston, Lewis
Lillie, William
Lillie, Rev. M.
Lindsley, C. F.
Livingston, Schuyler
Livingston, Mrs.
Lockwood, Benj.
Lord, Benjamin
Longstreet, Samuel
Lowrie, Jno. C.

Lorillard, P.
Lowery, John
Loomis, Judson
Lossing, B. J.
Lord, R. L.
Lowther & Son,
Lorton, W. H.
Ludlow, John R.
Lynes, S. C.
Lugar J. G.
Lydig, P. M.
Ludlam, W.
Lyons, E. T.
L. J.
Loder & Co.
Lee, Robert R.
M'Laine, O.
Macy, Wm. H.
Mann, Josiah, Jr.
Marselis, Robert,
Marsh, John R.
May, Charles W.
McCracken, John H.
Mackie, John
May, Mrs. E. H.
Martin, C. L.
M'Carty, John J.
Mayor, A.
M'Clawry, Dr.
Maas, Philip
Marston, Lemuel
Mason, Miss
Mason, Ebenezer
Martin, Robert
Mace, John
Marsh, Mr.
Mather, George
M'Call, James
Manning,
Markoe, Francis
Marvin, A. S.
March, Charles
Manice, D. F.
Mason, Mrs. L.
Mague, D.
Magill, James
Mayer, W.
McArthur, Mr.
Maxwell, J. B.
McElrath, Thomas
McLean, D.
McElroy, J., M. D.
Merritt, Miss
McGeah, John
Messerau, T. W.
McLeod, Alexander
McPhearson, R.
Mease,
Melvin, S.
Mead,
McCrea, J.
Messerole, B. J.
Meril, Charles,
Messenger, Brothers
Merrill, H.
Medicott, Wm. G.

LIST OF MEMBERS. (1845.

Melly, A.
Meyer, Mrs.
McEvers, Mrs. B.
Meyer, G.
Metcalf, James W.
Minturn. Robt. B.
Miller, Jas., M. D.
Miller. Nathaniel
Miller, Wm. P.
Mills, Thomas
Minturn, C.
Miller, Jonathan
Miller, H.
Miller, Horatio
Middleton. Thos. D.
Mills, A. B.
Mitchell, Marcus
Mills. Abner
Miller, J. A.
McBride, James
McVicar, Mrs. Jane
McKie, Thomas
Minturn, Mrs.
Miles, A.
Miles. W. B.
Morris, Oran W.
Moore, President
Moore, William
Morgan, John J.
McDonald, M. D.
Moore, T. D.
McCord, Mr.
Mott, Samuel F.
Mott, W. F.
McCooon, M.
Morton, H. G.
Morse, Mr.
Montgomery James
Moore, H.
Morrison William
Moore, S W.
Moore, J. W.
Moore, Matilda
Mowatt, E.
McCorkle, Samuel
Mollard, John
Moses Lorenzo
McDonald, A., Jr.
Moore, W. T.
Morris, G. W.
Morris, Mrs. R. V.
Morgan, J. J.
Morgan. Mrs. E. D.
Moore, Dr. F. G.
Mott, W. T
Morrison. David
McLure, Alexander
Munson, John
Murdock, A. A.
McCurdy, R. H.
Murray. Lindley
Munn, S. B.
Mulligan. H. S.
Murlis, Robert
Myers, John R.
Mulligan John
Miller, Mrs.
Moger, Simeon

Marchwald, M. B.
Matford, Joseph
Mackrel, James,
McGlyn, J. A.
Nash, Lora
Nap, W. Curtis
Naylor, Peter
Nevins, P. S.
Nelson, Thomas
Nealy, John
Newell, Mr.
Newbold, George
Newell, Robert
Newman, S. L.
Nelson, W. B.
Neule, C.
Noyes, J. R.
Norris. R. T.
Norn, T.
Noe, Charles L.
Nostrand, Mrs. C.
N. T B.
Ostrander, Mr. Gideon
Owens. J. J.
Oneil, E.
Olssen, Richard
Ogden, H. L.
Orchard, Rev. Isaac
Oliver, John W.
Olyphant, David
Olitler, Wm.
Pattison, Robert
Patillow, Frederick
Palmer, Miss C.
Parsons, Matilda
Paine, Mr.
Page, Thomas
Palmer, John J.
Page, P P.
Platt, E.
Patton, Mrs.
Parr, John
Patterson, Samuel P.
Palmer, Mrs
Phelps, Anson G.
Paige. Robert George
Pattison, Godfrey
Paret, John
Prall, W. L.
Palmer, W. C.
Place. R. S.
Prankhard, John B.
Patterson, Mr.
Price, G. J.
Pinckney, Peter
Pierson, Daniel B.
Price, James B.
Prime, Edward
Pinquent, M. L.
Price, J. B.
Pickersgill, W. C.
Phillips,
Phillips,
Pierson, J Green
Pitcairn, Joseph
Pierson, Mrs. C. E.
Pillow, W. H.
Price, P.

Prime. P.
Pond, J. O., M. D.
Pollen, P.
Prout, M. P.
Polhamus, Cornelius
Powers, T. W.
Potts, George
Post, A. R.
Post, G.
Post, J. J.
Post, W. B.
Post, Alfred C.
Post, Henry
Pope, Henry
Purdy, J.
Phyfe. John
Pearson, Adam
Peabody, J. B.
Persse, Dudley
Pearson, A.
Passenger Jacob
Peeker, A.
Phelps, John J.
Pearse, Mrs.
Peck, N.
Perry, S.
Pearson, Mrs.
Peck, Lewis
Peshine. John
Prescott, Mr.
Peck, H. N.
Phelps, George
Phelps, J. N.
Pearsall, Mrs.
Peters, Dr. J. C.
Pell, Mrs. J. B.
Perrit, P P.
Pryer. Grace
Puysley, T.
Purdy, Dr.
Purdy, Richard E.
Purdy, J. B.
Pyne. Smith
Purdy, Jonathan
Puthers. J. H.
Pray. David
Peleg David
Philips, John J.
Quackenbush, Wm.
Quackenbush, B.
Quack, Mrs.
Quanhal!, David T.
Raymond, James M.
Radan, Gilbert
Ray, Wm. Richard
Ramppen, G. H.
Raynor,
Ransom, J. H.
Randolph, Wm. B. F.
Ramsay, J. C.
Raynor, John
R. A. R.
Ray, Robert
Rait, Mrs.
Randolph. P. F.
Raynor, Mrs.
Reimer, Frederick
Reed, John M.

LIST OF MEMBERS.

Requa. Austin
Remsen, James
Reeve, Henry
Redman, Charles
Reed, William
Remsen, J. Henry
Remsen, Mrs.
Remsen, H. R.
Renwick, Wm. P.
Renwick, Mrs. M. H.
Remsey, J. H.
Rich, Josiah
Richards, T. B.
Riley, John A.
Riggs, E.
Rhinelander, W. E.
Rhinelander, Bernard
Richards N G.
Richards, James
Richards, E. C.
Raynor, Nathan
Riker, James
Richards, W. H.
Rich, Thomas B.
Rich Crandall
Rigny, William
Rogers, J. Smyth, M. D.
Rockwell. Samuel D.
Roome, Samuel
Robinson George
Robinson, Jacob
Roe. F.
Rollins, G. B.
Rosevelt, C. V. S.
Rogers, A. R.
Robinson, Nelson
Robinson, E.
Robert & Williams
Roome. Charles
Rogers, C.
Robertson Frederick
Rondon, Freeman,
Rosevelt, James
Robertson, J. A.
Root. R. C.
Rhoades, Daniel
Robertson, H. P.
Rhoades, E. H.
Robert G.
Russell, Israel
Rudd, Wm. H.
Ryan, Maurice
Ryden, Edgar T.
Ryers, T. R.
Russell Hiram
Russell. A.
Russell Theop
Rusline Charles
Sayre. John N.
Sparks, Samuel
Sparks, Walter
Sands, Daniel H.
Sammis, Leander
Sampson, Joseph
Saltus, Francis
Shaw, William
Spaulding, James
Sands, Dr.

Sabine, Mrs. G. A.
Sanford, M.
Sparks Mrs
Swain James
Sanger, R., & Co.
Saunders, W. S.
Shannon, R. H.
Sharp, William
Sammis, Nelson
Sprague, Mr.
Swain, J. P.
Sampson, George G.
Swan, C.
Safford. John L.
Savage, N.
Sanderson, John
Stark, Rev. A.
Swansnick, Thomas
Sampson, Mrs.
Shannon. William
Staples, Joseph
Schafer, P.
Sawyer, Rev. T. S.
Sarget, Mrs.
Small, Wilson
Stanton, J. A.
Smack, Elijah
Seaman W. S.
Sedgwick, Theodore
See, H. P.
Schenck, David
Seymour. Charles
Sheffield, Dudley
Stebbins, Elias
Stelle, Isaac
Seeley, Joseph
Sherrill, Franklin
Sheafe, J Fisher
Sheldon, Henry
Schermerhorn, P. A.
Stebbins, D. G.
Spencer, A.
Stewart, Daniel
Spencer, Capt., for a Lady
Scheper, Alrick
Stephens R.
Srenchard, S.
Seymour, W. N.
Sterling, R.
Seguine. C.
Seymour, J.
Stevens, C.
Stewart, David
Stevens. H. H.
Schieffelin,
Schieffelin. H. H.
Stevens, Horatio G.
Spencer, G G.
Sedgwick, Roderick
Stewart, Lispenard
Street. Mr.
Selby. John
Stevens, J A.
Sedgwick, C. M.
Sedgwick, Mrs. Robert
Smedes, Mrs.
Sheldon, F
Sherwood, Mrs. S.

Seon, Mrs. A. F.
Stevens. Mrs B. K.
Secor, Mrs. H.
Secor, Mrs. Charles
Stewart, A T.
Sheldon, Henry
Stewart, James
Seney, Rev. Robt.
Seaman, G.
Stillman, T. B.
Smith, S P.
Skidmore, B.
Smith, Jacob
Slipper J. F.
Smith, Hiram G.
Shipman. George P.
Smith, Ruel
Schmidt. T. W.
Smith & Co C. W.
Smith, S T.
Simpson, Andrew
Smith, Samuel
Steinly. Mr.
Smith, Jane M.
Schieffelin, R. L.
Smith. S.
Simons, W. W.
Smith J A.
Smith, W. H.
Skinner T. H.
Smith. George
Shindler Simon
Smith, William
Stillman, Francis W.
Smith, Woodhull
Smith, Mr.
Smith, G. G.
Skiddy, F.
Simmons, H.
Smith, Mrs. E.
Spier, G. M.
Skilman, Joseph
Stillwell, Rev. Wm.
Simpson Wm D.
Simmerson, W.
Stoddart, Thos. P.
St. John, Milton
Scofield, Samuel W.
Stone, Asaph
Somer, L.
Stone, E.
Snowden, John
Stone, Henry A.
Story, Benjamin
Story, T. W.
Southmayd, S. D.
Stone. L. B.
Shotwell, Joseph
Strong, James
Spofford, James
Stokes & Anthony,
Stone & Starr,
Southart. Jacob
Strong T. W.
Stout, A. G.
Spofford, C. N.
Strong, Mr.
Strong, B.

LIST OF MEMBERS.   (1845.

Stohlman, Charles H.
Story, Rufus
Scofield, P.
Shoemaker, Isaac L.
Scofield, Legrand,
Sturges, Jonathan
Shultz, John M.
Scrymser, Wm. H.
Suffern, T.
Scrymser, John
Sturges, Miss
Suydam, Sage & Co.
Stuart, Mrs.
Stuart, J. H.
Suydam, Lambert
Systare,
Sturgis, William
Schuyler, Mrs. G. L.
Schunhardt, F.
Sully, William
Schureman, N.
Storr, Wm.
Smith, Philetas
Smith, Mrs.
Tracy, John R.
Taylor, Isaac
Trafford, Abraham
Talbot, C. N.
T. C. N.
Taylor, Moses
Taylor, John S.
Tracy, George M.
Taggard, William
Tracy, Emily
Taylor, Isaac
Taylor, D. G.
Taylor, T. H.
Thanksgiving
Taggard, W. H.
Taylor, J. R.
T. A.
Terbell, J.
Terret, G. R.
Tweedy, O. B.
Tebor, Peter
Temigreu, Bartholomew
Tweed, Richard
Terry, David, Jr.
Trenchard, S.
Teney, Mrs. R.
Teets, Philip
Trimble, Daniel
Tieman, George
Timpson, Mr.
Tiebout, N.
Titus, S. L.
Tilford, I. L.
Titus, M.
Tillotson, I. C.
Tileston, T.
Tiers, Edward W.
Thibout, Lewis
Tillon, F. R.
Tilden, William
Tompkins, Daniel
Tompkins, Mrs. James
Thorn, Jonathan
Thorp, Gould

Townsley, I. H.
Thorn, Cornelia
Townsend, Effingham
Trowbridge, Henry
Townsend, P.
Town Charles
Tompson, Thomas
Trowbridge,
Thorn,
Townsend, Caleb A.
Trowbridge, Dwight & Co.
Townsend, J. Jr.,
Thompson, W. J.
Townsend, Daniel Y.
Tobias, T. J.
Thompson, David
Thompson, W. B.
Tone, Wolfe, Miss
Townsend, Wm. H.
Trowbridge, G. A.
Thorp, Isaac
Thompson, B. M.
Tuckerman, J.
Truslow, W.
Twyle, Mr.
Turner, Mr.
Tucker, Daniel N.
Tuttle, Sylvester
Turner, D. S.
Tucker, F. C.
Trusdale, E. D.
Turbell, Mrs. H. S.
Turbell, Isabel
Trumbull, Mrs. C.
Turner, D. H.
Utter, Mrs. Samuel
Underhill, W.
Underhill, Abraham
Underhill, J. S.
Underhill, G.
Van Nostrand, James
Vanderhoof, C.
Van Dalsen, William
Vanderhoof, Matthew
Valentine, Samuel
Van Wagenen, W. H.
Van Valkenburgh, Jas.
Vanderwater, J. H.
Van Rennselar, Mrs.
Van Rennselar, Miss C. P.
Van Rennselar, Alexander
Van Wagenen, W. S.
Vanhook, William
Vantine, Thomas
Van Winkle, J.
Van Winkle, Jane
Van Wyck, Stephen
Van Vort, John V.
Vantice, J.
Van Zant, P.
Van Horne, A.
Van Voorhis, E. W.
Vail, Stephen
Vanderwater, James
Vann, G.
Van Wart, Irving
Van Winkle, Mr. & Mrs.
Van Aulin, J. C.

Van Wagenen, Mrs. Ann
Vandervoort, Henry
Valentine, H.
Verian, J. M.
Verian, A.
Verrato, J. F.
Vanderbilt, Jeremiah
Vancott, J.
Valentine, B. W.
Vanarsdale, Peter
Ward, Isaac
Warnock, R.
Ware, John P.
Walker, Wm. A.
Walsh, A. Robinson
Wagstaff, Miss S. A.
Wagstaff, D.
Wagstaff, Mrs.
Warnick, Miss E.
Ward, Samuel
Ward, Augustus H.
Wallace, Joseph C.
Wagner, Anthony G.
Warren, Samuel B.
Watan, J.
Walldorf, H.
Washburn, J.
Waterbury, S.
Warring, Amos
Walter, S. B.
Wagener, A. C.
Washington, James
Walker, William
Waldo, Charles B.
Ward & Heath,
Walbridge, Mr.
Watts, Mrs. Ann
Wainwright, Rev. J. M.
Water, J
Warner, Miss
Walker, William
Warner, George
Warren, Richard
Washington, George
Walter, W. H.
Ward, Mrs.
Watts, G.
Waydell, J.
Walter, W.
Warren, N.
Wetmore, A. R.
Wetmore, W. S.
Weeden, Joseph B.
Westervelt, James
Weed, Nathaniel
Wells, Lloyd W.
Weeks, R. D.
Wheden, Wm.
Wheeler, Mr.
West, Joseph
Weisman, Aug.
Weller, James
Wells, Thomas L.
West, Joseph
Wells, Mary Ann
Wells, G., Jr.
Wetmore, L.
Wheeler, R. C.

1845.)   LIST OF MEMBERS.   **45**

Wells, John D.	Williams, John H.	Woolsey, E. J.
Wheaton, Abel	Willis, John R.	Woolley, J. M.
Weeks, N. T.	White, J. T.	Woodward, W. A.
Westtin, John	Wright, A.	Woodruff, T. T.
West, J. P.	White, S. P.	Wood, W. A.
Weeks, Edward A.	Wight, Edward	Woodhouse, Mrs. C.
Wessels, Francis	Wilbur, J.	Wood, A. P.
Weteran, J. B.	Willets, Samuel	Woram, William
Winston, F. S.	Whitlock, B. M.	Wood, Mrs. E.
Whittlesey, Henry	Williams, D. S.	Wolfe, Chrys.
Wilson, Thomas	Wilbur, Charles W.	Wooster, Benjamin
White, Edward	Willis, Anson	Wood, S. B.
Witter, J. B.	Williams, E.	Wood, D. A.
Wiley, John	Williams, Rankin & Co.	Woodhull, William
Whitlock, William, Jr.	Williams, Mr.	Wood, R. W.
Wilkes, Ann	White, Eli	Woodhead,
Wilson, John	Wilson, James C.	Woolcocks, Thos. J.
Wright, Edward	White, Mr.	Wyeth, L. J.
White, Mrs. Amelia	Wilkes, H.	Wycoff, Mrs.
Winter, Mrs. Elizabeth	White, G. B.	Wyley, Thomas
Wilson, R. B.	White, A.	Wurts, John
Wigham, Mr.	Winthrop, Mr.	Winship, Thomas,
Wickham, Mrs. Daniel	White, H. D. D.	Willet, Margaret
Wright, Joseph W.	Wright, N.	Wines, Charles
White, Captain	Williams, S. C.	Yates, F. L.
Willis, Samuel	Williams, A. G.	Yelverton, H. R.
Wilson, Harris	Wright, E.	Young, D. L.
Witherspoon, James	Whitewright, Wm.	Young, Joab
Williams, William R.	Woodruff, E. P.	Youle, George
Wilmerding, W. E.	Woolley, Brittain L.	Young, E.
Willis, Samuel J.	Wolcott, F. H.	Young, Alexander
Willet, Samuel	Wood, O. C.	Zabriskie, Andrew C.

The following Names were obtained after the foregoing were in type, viz:

Adams, F. M.	Eagle, Captain	Meikleham, David S.
Adams, I. K.	Fox, S. M.	McCormick, Richard E.
Anderson, John	Feeks, Abijah S.	Magie, D.
Allen, Rev. J. M.	Fink, Mrs. Elizabeth	Mandevell, H.
Anderson, S. N.	Friend, A.	Neule, C.
Boyd, Daniel	Goodrich, Elisha B.	Neely, R. N.
Baxter, E. S.	Green, Miss	O'Conner, C. L.
Burr, J.	Geraghty, H.	Odell, Mr.
Bear, Wm. H.	Grant, Mrs.	Quanhall, David T.
Brady, John	Gibson, Mr.	Rigny, Mr.
Brush, L.	Hitchcock, Cyrus	Ridley, Mr.
Betts, M.	Halsted, A. L.	Robinson, C.
Berenbroisky, Lewis	Jauncey, J.	Stokes, James
Burne, E.	Jennings, Ezra	Smith, Rev. Hugh
Bird, Fisher	Kneeland, Mr.	Stott, Alexander
Burges, Mr.	Kursheedt, A.	Smith, Sheldon
Carter, Mrs.	Kimball, Mrs.	Sackett, Wm. H.
Cometh, H. P.	Kemple, A.	Sherman, Mr.
Codwise, Mrs.	Luquer, F. J.	Thompson, B. M.
Cheesebrough, Mr.	Loryman, I.	Trenchard, Samuel
Centre, E. L.	Lorton, W. V.	Trow, John F.
Chandler, Job	Lowden, R.	Whitmore, Wm., Jr.
Collin, Mrs.	Lamb, A.	Wagner, Erastus
Curtis, J. L.	Mott, W. T.	Wilkins, Mr.
Demike, A. C.	Magill, James	White, H.
Deforest, L.	Miles, W. B.	Wright, A.
Deluze, Mrs.	Mayer, W.	Weeks, E. C.
Derbro, Mr.	McArthur, Mr.	Withers, R.
Divine, Mrs.	Morrison, David	
Erven, Charles	Maxwell, J. B.	

THE THIRD ANNUAL REPORT

OF THE

NEW-YORK ASSOCIATION

FOR THE

IMPROVEMENT OF THE CONDITION OF THE POOR,

FOR THE YEAR 1846,

WITH

THE CONSTITUTION,

AND

A LIST OF MEMBERS.

> "The quality of mercy is not strain'd;
> It droppeth as the gentle rain from heaven
> Upon the place beneath : it is twice bless'd;
> It blesseth him that gives and him that takes."

NEW-YORK:
PRINTED BY LEAVITT, TROW & COMPANY,
33 Ann Street.
1846.

PROCEEDINGS

AT THE

ANNUAL MEETING

OF THE

NEW-YORK ASSOCIATION FOR THE IMPROVEMENT OF THE CONDITION OF THE POOR,

Held in the Hall of the Public School Society, Nov. 16, 1846.

In the absence of the President, the Chair was taken by George Griswold, Esq., one of the Vice-Presidents.

The minutes of the last Annual Meeting were read by the Recording Secretary, and on motion approved.

The Treasurer presented his Annual Report, which was accepted and ordered on file.

The minutes of the Executive Committee, exhibiting their operations during the recess of the Board, were read by the Corresponding Secretary and approved.

The Annual Report was read, accepted, and ordered to be printed under the direction of the Executive Committee.

On motion, the Constitution was amended, by inserting in the Seventh Article, after the word November, "provided they deem it expedient."

The first Article of the By-Laws was also so amended, as that the Officers of the Association be hereafter Members, *ex officio*, of the Executive Committee.

A Resolution offered by a Member, restricting the Visitors to the use of printed orders on groceries, was referred to the Executive Committee, with power.

Voting by ballot, having by resolution been dispensed with, the Association proceeded to the election of the following Officers and Managers, for the ensuing year, after which the meeting adjourned.

President.
JAMES BROWN.

Vice-Presidents.
GEORGE GRISWOLD,   JAMES BOORMAN,
J. SMYTH ROGERS, M. D.,   WILLIAM B. CROSBY,
JAMES LENOX.

Treasurer.
ROBERT B. MINTURN.

Corresponding Secretary and Agent.
ROBERT M. HARTLEY.

Recording Secretary.
JOSEPH B. COLLINS.

Board of Managers.

FIRST DISTRICT.
John R. Ludlow,
James Cruikshank,
John A. Crum,
Q. C. Degrove,
A. Q. Thompson.

SECOND DISTRICT.
William Gale,
George W. Abbe,
Joseph A. Riley,
John N. Sayre,
William Sharp.

THIRD DISTRICT.
F. S. Winston,
B. L. Woolley,
Jonathan Sturges,
William Walker,
P. G. Arcularius.

FOURTH DISTRICT.
Abraham Fardon, Jr.
Archibald Hall,
Hugh Aikman,
Walter C. Sparks,
Charles Chamberlain.

FIFTH DISTRICT.
A. R. Wetmore,
William Forrest,
G. T. Cobb,
Leonard Kirby,
William H. Richards.

SIXTH DISTRICT.
E. P. Woodruff,
Stephen Conover,
Leonard Crocker,
N. C. Everett,
N. D. Herder.

SEVENTH DISTRICT.
Josiah Rich,
Stephen Cutter,
J. S. Skidmore,
G. S. Price,
A. G. Crane.

EIGHTH DISTRICT.
Joseph B. Collins,
William Johnson,
O. D. McClain,
John Endicott,
Charles C. Dyer.

NINTH DISTRICT.
James O. Pond, M. D.,
James S. Miller, M. D.,
Thomas P. Richards,
Jeremiah Terbell,
J. Van Doran.

TENTH DISTRICT.
John Falconer,
William Truslow,
Joseph M. Bell,
Samuel W. Scofield,
E. Wheeler.

ELEVENTH DISTRICT.
Thomas B. Stillman,
Abner Mills,
Samuel P. Patterson,
Dudley Sheffield,
Nehemiah Miller.

THIRTEENTH DISTRICT.
Peter Balen,
Lewis Chichester,
Thomas Kennedy,
Gabriel P. B. Hoyt,
Charles Merrill.

FOURTEENTH DISTRICT.
William Bloodgood,
M. P. Prout,
Benjamin F. Howe,
Thomas B. Rich,
Ransom Beach.

FIFTEENTH DISTRICT.
Erastus C. Benedict,
Stewart Brown,
William G. Bull,
Thomas Denny,
Joseph Lawrence.

SIXTEENTH DISTRICT.
Luther Jackson,
Tayler Lewis, LL. D.

S. A. Lawrence
Charles Roome.
W. Vermilyea.

SEVENTEENTH DISTRICT.
S. C. Lynes,
James R. Gibson,
Geo. Manning Tracy,
Herman Griffin,
Timothy Ensign.

EIGHTEENTH DISTRICT.
J. F. Joy,
E. Holbrook,
E. F. Mather,
S. P. Smith,
John Campbell.

Elected Members of the Board.

John C. Green,
William S. Wetmore,
Jonathan Sturges,
William H. Macy,
E. J. Woolsey.

Peter Cooper,
John C. Baldwin,
William G. Bull,
Lora Nash,
J. T. Adams.

Executive Committee.

John R. Ludlow,
William Gale,
F. S. Winston,
Abraham Fardon, Jr.,
A. R. Wetmore,
E. P. Woodruff,
Josiah Rich,
Joseph B. Collins,

James O. Pond, M. D.,
John Falconer.
Thomas B. Stillman,
William Bloodgood,
Erastus C. Benedict,
Luther Jackson,
S. C. Lynes,
J. F. Joy.

Elected Members of the Executive Committee.

Horatio Allen,
James Brown,
George Griswold,
Stewart Brown,
Robert B. Minturn,
Thomas Cock, M. D.,
John H. Griscom, M. D.

Visitors.

Appointed by the Advisory Committees for the ensuing year.

First District.
Quincy C. Degrove,
Charles H. Starin,
A. Q. Thompson,
D. S. Briant,
James Cruikshank,
John R. Ludlow,
Peter Naylor,
John A. Crum,
William M. Lathrop,
John C. Cass,
Lewis B. Loder.

Second District.
Charles Wilber,
William Gale,
William Sharp,
Daniel N. Tucker,
George W. Abbe,
Joseph A. Riley,

Third District.
Marcus Mitchell.
Paul Babcock,
John Campbell,
William Walker,
E. L. Fancher
W. D. Harris.
Edward Field,
A. Williams,
Stephen Burkhalter.

Fourth District.
Adam Pierson,
Samuel Sparks,
J. Chapman,
Roland Gelston,
Ralph Hall,
E. Wade, Jr.,
Thomas Ritter, M.D.,
Charles G. Christman,

Hiram Hurd,
T. R. Ryers,
John V. Tilyou,
D. Moffat,
John Hagadorn,
John Gates,
Thomas H. Burras.

Fifth District.
J. J. Greenough,
A. R. Wetmore,
Samuel G. Evans,
R. Warnock,
J. C. Hines,
David Terry, Jr.,
D. S. Clark,
Samuel Heuston,
William Forrest,
Lyman Clapp,
Robert Carter,

VISITORS. (1846

Wm. Van Allen,
Israel Minor,
W. H. Scrymser,
Robert Pattison,
John Scrymser,
J. F. Bridges,
Leonard Kirby,
J. H. Bockover,
S. S. Ward,
J. H. Redfield,
George T. Cobb,
R. J. Brown,
J. O. Door,
William Steele.

Sixth District.
William Ballagh,
J. I. Perry,
Leonard Crocker,
Charles D. Brown,
D. B. Hunt,
A. D. Herder,
T. Lippincott,
Moses B. Taylor,
Sylvester Tuttle,
Daniel Oakley,
Joseph Whittemore,
Simon Clannon,
W. P. Cook,
E. P. Woodruff,
John V. B. Roome,
Abraham Florentine,
John G. Sperling.

Seventh District.
Linus Pratt,
A. Morehouse,
A. G. Hanford,
Josiah Rich,
Jonathan B. Horton,
C. Tracy,
A. G. Crane,
C. S. Atwood,
J. A. Williamson,
J. Skidmore,
William Pease,
Peter Doig,
H. C. Martin,
Ed. L. Chichester, M. D.,
G. J. Price,
J. B. Dickinson,
Matthew Bird,
A. B. Ludlum,
John Hecker,
Shelden Martin,
S. Cutter.

Eighth District.
Joseph B. Collins,
O. D. McClain,
Peter Roome,
N. T. Eldredge,
M. R. Berry,
Ira Burdge,
William H. Van Dalsem,
Robert Murlis,

Francis Patterson,
R. H. Nodine,
Charles C. Dyer,
J. W. Kellogg,
C. P. Dakin,
W. W. Dwight, M. D.,
John Douglass,
William M. Wilson,
John Endicott,
James G. Barbour,
William Johnston,
Josiah S. Ferris.

Ninth District.
Reuben Ayres,
W. J. Demarest,
Nathan Peck,
W. R. Demarest,
Henry P. See,
Roderick Sedgwick,
Henry W. Deems,
Cornelius Lefferts,
Edward Bleecker,
Daniel French,
John Cameron,
James Kearney,
Joseph Carter,
Edward Earle, M. D.,
Isaac See,
Thomas Fessenden,
Gustavus Reid,
Hunting Sherrill, M. D.,
John Murry,
Daniel Crane,
Oliver Loveland,
Jacob Bogert.

Tenth District.
Peter Aims,
Smith Downs,
Joseph M. Bell,
Isaac B. Condit,
James Dunbar,
William Wheaton,
Isaac Seaman,
Edward A. Fraser,
John Falconer,
Laban Jacobs,
E. Wheeler,
Thomas Lewis,
William Truslow,
A. L. White, M. D.,
Stephen P. Fowler,
Walter Anderson,
Samuel W. Scofield,
William C. Bradley,
Cornelius V. Clarkson.

Eleventh District.
Samuel Brotherston,
Joseph Leggett,
J. V. D. B. Fowler,
Joel Kelly,
Jeremiah Green,
Benjamin Perine, Jr.,
Caleb Miller,

Charles Perley,
Jonathan Remer,
James Barkley,
William Bennet,
Jacob Stillman,
Samuel P. Patterson,
Alexander Black,
Grant Dubois,
Benjamin Wooster,
J. Townsend, Jr.,
S. L. Newman,
Ambrose Paris,
Augustus Williams,
D. G. Wells,
Nehemiah Miller,
James Little.

Thirteenth District.
Isaac Stelle,
John Hutchings,
John J. Gantz,
James H. Fletcher,
John R. Marsh,
Joseph Seely,
Woodhull Smith,
James Forrester,
Henry Guernsey,
Charles Merrill,
Henry Esler,
William A. Walker,
Abraham Trafford,
William G. Boggs,
Harman Tremper,
Francis A. Roe,
James Remsen,
Joab Young,
Thomas Brown,
Joab Young.

Fourteenth District.
Anderson Bogart,
Nelson Stelle, M. D.
Adam Blackledge,
Adam W. Spies,
Bezaleel Howe,
Thomas B. Rich,
J. M. Howe,
Josiah Hopper, M. D.,
William Bloodgood,
Ransom Beach,
John Fowler,
A. D. Jayne,
J. Allen, M. D.,
A. D. Clement, M. D.,
B. F. Howe.

Fifteenth District.
Richard Hale,
Edward Newlin,
James Goodliff,
Frederick Pattilow,
Samuel B. Barlow, M. D.,
James L. Dayton,
Isaac Orchard,
William Archer,
Sidney Wetmore,

1846.) VISITORS. 7

Benjamin Lord,
John Mollard.

Sixteenth District.
Charles J. Day,
D. Tompkins,
Joseph Merrill,
Charles C. Darling,
D. Coleman,
Samuel Smith,
Charles Roome,
J. Cowl,
S. Wiswall,
William Tate,
Charles Roff,
Joseph T. Williams,
P. H. Williams,
Thomas Cummings, Jr.,
J. B. Peabody,
John Cummings,
James Millward,
J. F. Chamberlin,

H. S. Benedict, M. D.,
William Haydon,
William Rudd,
J. L. Stevens,
M. L. Weston,
William C. Dusenberry,
John Cable,
Lorenzo Moses.

Seventeenth District.
N. B. Lane,
R. Albro,
John T. Duff,
Jonathan Taft,
Herman Griffin,
William B. Humbert,
Timothy Ensign,
George M. Tracy,
Sylvanus Warren,
John Valentine,
William Stebbins,
Richard Horton,

James R. Gibson,
S. C. Lynes,
James Scrymser,
J. Curtis,
William P. Woodcock,
I. Caughey.

Eighteenth District.
O. P. Woodford,
Lewis Atterbury,
J. F. Joy,
Ira M. Allen,
George W. Savage,
William J. Thompson,
J. M. Woolley,
George Lees,
John Campbell,
Royal West,
S. P. Smith,
Samuel Thompson,
James Stokes.

CONSTITUTION AND BY-LAWS.

CONSTITUTION.

ARTICLE I.

This Institution shall be called the NEW-YORK ASSOCIATION FOR THE IMPROVEMENT OF THE CONDITION OF THE POOR.

ARTICLE II.

Its design is the elevation of the moral and physical condition of the indigent ; and so far as compatible with these objects, the relief of their necessities.

ARTICLE III.

Every person who becomes an annual subscriber, or a Visitor, shall be a member of this Association.

ARTICLE IV.

The affairs of the Association shall be managed by a President, five Vice-Presidents, a Treasurer, a Secretary and General Agent, and one hundred members, including the Advisory Committees, who shall constitute a Board of Managers. Nine members shall form a quorum for the transaction of business.

ARTICLE V.

The President and Secretary shall perform such duties as usually pertain to their office.

ARTICLE VI.

The Treasurer shall give such security for the faithful performance of the trust reposed in him, as the Association may demand and approve.

He shall take in charge all funds; keep an account of all receipts and expenditures; and pay all duly authorized drafts. At the annual meeting, he shall render a particular and correct statement of all his receipts and disbursements to the Association. He shall also exhibit a summary report to the Board of Managers at their stated meetings, and to the Executive Committee whenever called upon for that purpose.

ARTICLE VII.

The Board of Managers shall have exclusive control of the funds of the Association, and authority to make by-laws; to fill vacancies; appoint all committees; and generally to adopt such measures as the objects of the Institution may require. Its stated meetings shall be held on the second Monday of January, March, and November, provided the Board deem it expedient, and the Annual Meeting of the Association shall be convened on the third Monday of November, when the Board shall submit a Report of its proceedings, and the Officers and Managers be chosen by ballot.

ARTICLE VIII.

An office shall be opened in an eligible situation, for the purpose of concentrating and diffusing all information pertaining to the Society's operations and objects, and for the transaction of its general business.

ARTICLE IX.

It shall be the duty of the General Agent to devote himself with diligence and fidelity to the affairs of the Association.

ARTICLE X.

The City shall be divided into eighteen Districts, each Ward forming a District; and the Districts be subdivided into Sections. Each District shall have an Advisory Committee, to consist of five members; and each Section a Visitor.

ARTICLE XI.

It shall be the duty of the Members of the Association to endeavor, in all suitable ways, to give practical effect to its principles; especially to discountenance indiscriminate alms-giving and street-begging; to provide themselves with tickets of reference; and instead of giving aid to unknown applicants, whose case they cannot themselves investigate, to refer such applications to the Visitor of the Section in which the applicants reside, in order that they may be properly inquired into, and, if deserving, relieved.

ARTICLE XII.

The form of Tickets shall be determined by the Board of Managers, and no other form shall be used.

ARTICLE XIII.

Special meetings of the Association may be called by the Secretary, at the request of the President, or on receiving a requisition signed by five members. Two days' notice must be given of the time of meeting.

ARTICLE XIV.

This Constitution shall not be altered except at a General Meeting of the Association, and by a vote of two-thirds of the members present.

BY-LAWS.

ARTICLE I.

There shall be an Executive Committee, to consist of seven elected members and the Chairmen of the Advisory Committees, on whom shall devolve all the business of the Association during the recess of the Board. It shall meet on the second Monday of every month; and report its proceedings at each Stated Meeting of the Managers. Five members shall constitute a quorum for business. The officers of the Institution shall be members, *ex officio*, of the Executive Committee.

ARTICLE II.

It shall be the duty of the Advisory Committees to divide their Districts into such Sections as to apportion to each about twenty-five families requiring attention; endeavor to obtain suitable Visitors for each Section; supply vacancies which may occur; make the necessary arrangements for placing at the disposal of the Visitors, food, fuel, and clothing, for distribution; and on some day in the first week of every month (ex_ cepting the meetings in July and August, which are referred to the discretion of the Committees), to convene all the Visitors of the Sections, for the purpose of receiving their returns, and conferring with them on the objects of their mutual labors. The Committees, moreover, shall duly draw upon the Treasurer for such proportion of the funds as may be appropriated to their District; they shall keep a strict account of all their disbursements, and only in extreme cases make donations of money; they shall monthly render an account of their expenditures to the Executive Committee; and in default of this duty, shall not be entitled to draw upon the funds of the Association. Each Committee shall appoint its own Chairman, Secretary, and Treasurer, and shall transmit the Reports of the Visitors, immediately after each Monthly Meeting, with any other information they may think desirable, to the General Secretary.

ARTICLE III.

It shall be the duty of the Sectional Visitors to confine their labors exclusively to the particular Section assigned them, so that no individual shall receive relief, excepting in the Section where he is known, and to which he belongs. They shall carefully investigate all cases referred to them before granting relief; ascertain their condition, their habits of life, and means of subsistence; and extend to all such kind services, counsel, and assistance, as a discriminating and judicious regard for their present and permanent welfare requires. And in cases of sickness and want, it will be their duty to inquire whether there is any medical or other attendance, whether relief is afforded by any religious or charitable society, and what assistance is needed; to provide themselves with information respecting the nearest Dispensary, and in all cases, when practicable, to obtain aid from existing charitable societies. And when no other assistance is provided or available, then to draw from the resources of this Association—not money, which is never allowed to be given, except with the consent of the Advisory Committee or a member thereof—but such articles of food, fuel, clothing, and similar supplies, as the necessities of the case require. And in all cases of want coming to the knowledge of the Visitors, they will be expected to perform the same duties although no application has been made. It shall be their duty, moreover, to render a report of their labors, and also an account of all their disbursements, to their respective Committees, on the last Wednesday of every month. No Visitor neglecting these duties will be entitled to draw on the funds of the Association.

ARTICLE IV.

Special Meetings of the Board of Managers may be called by the Secretary, at the request of the President, or on receiving a requisition signed by five members. Two days' notice must be given of the time of meeting.

ARTICLE V.

These By-laws can only be altered at a Meeting of the Board of Managers, and by a vote of two-thirds of the members present.

Note. The Visitors' Manual may be obtained at the office of the Association, corner of Grand and Elm streets.

THIRD ANNUAL REPORT

OF THE

NEW-YORK ASSOCIATION FOR THE IMPROVEMENT OF THE CONDITION OF THE POOR.

NEXT to a grateful recognition of the continued favors bestowed upon the Association by an ever beneficent Providence, the Board of Managers feel bound to express their sincere thanks to the numerous contributors who have generously supplied the means necessary to sustain this extensive charity, during the operations of another year.

They would also acknowledge their appreciation of the lively interest evinced by the public in this undertaking; and of the confiding manner in which many, by making this the channel of their charities, have been instrumental in correcting numerous evils inseparable from indiscriminate alms-giving, and of introducing a better system of relief into the city.

Nor would the Board omit publicly to acknowledge a bequest of *one thousand dollars* by Samuel Demilt, Esq., deceased, who while living was numbered among the friends of the Institution, and who in prospect of that world where beneficent actions never lose their reward, admitted its abiding claims upon his sympathies.

And it is with peculiar satisfaction that they refer to the very efficient manner in which the District Committees and Visitors have performed their labors. To their indefatigable exertions the Association, in an important sense, owes its usefulness, and the poor commiseration and relief. The annals of benevolence in this city afford, perhaps, no instances of greater devotion to the good of others, than is evinced by the almoners of this Institution. They have to do with the virtuous and the vicious, the thankful and the unthankful; and to witness and endure much that is painful to their sensibilities. But charity suffereth long and is kind; it thinketh no evil; it seeketh not its own; but hopeth all things, and endureth all things, if thereby human suffering may be alleviated. And such, pre-eminently, is the spirit by which the Visitors have been animated. By night and by day, in storm and sunshine, regardless of their own ease or convenience, and with none to witness or reward their toils, they have been found by the beds of the sick, and in the hovels of the indigent, the unfortunate and depraved, administering consolation, or proffering their counsel and aid. The economy, moreover, and discrimination with which their multiform labors have been performed, are most satisfactorily attested by statistical reports and results.

Nor would the Board withhold the expression of their thanks from the Rev. Clergy who have called the attention of their congregations to the objects of the Association, and who have thereby diffused, more widely than would otherwise have been done, the practical benefits of an organization, through which the charities of the benevolent may flow to the needy, without risk of perversion.

Their acknowledgments, moreover, are justly due to the Editors of the religious and secular press, to whose co-operation they feel that the Association is greatly indebted. For many of them have not only opened their columns to give publicity to its principles, but have themselves become the exponents and advocates of those principles, whereby light has been scattered, sympathy excited, and the public mind led to a juster appreciation of its objects.

The Board having thus been encouraged and sustained in their labors, and having, as they progressed, the advantages of a more enlarged experience, they trust they have been better enabled to give effect to the principles on which gratuitous relief should be administered, than in any previous year. And the results, though surpassing their own expectations, they regard but as an earnest of greater good yet to be realized, when the strict principles on which alone relief should be given are introduced, so far as practicable, into every family, and are generally adopted by our citizens.

But they deem it unadvisable, though possessing ample materials, to dwell upon results, for it would require an extremely voluminous report to detail the benefits conferred upon the numerous families assisted by the Association during the operations of a single month. Nor yet is it their design, as the plan of this charity has already been spread before the public, here to enlarge upon it. As this document, however, may fall into the hands of persons unacquainted with the Institution, they deem it important to refer, though briefly, to its principles and mode of action, inasmuch as such reference may impart information to those who desire it, and who thereby will be enabled to judge of the adaptation of the means to the end, and of the degree of success that might reasonably be expected from such an organization.

It may be preliminarily remarked, that if we except the pauperism occasioned by immigration, to which this city is peculiarly exposed, the chief cause of its increase among us is the *injudicious dispensation of relief*. The evils incident to misapplied charity are universally admitted; but only those who have studied the subject are aware how much harm is thereby inflicted upon communities and individuals. By the indiscriminate supply of all who ask, the most clamorous and worthless usually supersede the most modest and deserving; while to make want the sole measure of supply, without regard to character, conduct or consequences, is to subvert temperance, economy and industry, and to encourage pauperism with its attendant evils. If these views are correct, aid cannot be safely given without certain knowledge of the character and condition of the recipient; and as this knowledge is unattainable except by personal intercourse with the poor at their homes; and this intercourse impracticable, in a large community like this, by separate individual effort, there remains but one way by which it can be effected, to wit, *united systematic action.*

Now, such is the action this Association supplies. And for this purpose its organization is at once so comprehensive and minute as that while it covers the entire city, it reaches, by the personal investigations of *two hundred and ninety-seven* Visitors, the dwelling of every applicant. And vast as is the work, it is readily accomplished by a division of labor and responsibility which assigns to each Visitor a definite field of labor, and the care of all the poor resident therein. As the Visitor is not allowed to give relief out of his own Section, nor the poor to receive it out of the Section where they belong, vagrancy is prevented, imposture detected, and the whole system of giving and receiving reduced to the utmost precision and certainty. For in whatever part of the City the needy apply to the Members of the Association for aid, by means of a Directory and printed tickets, they are sent back to their appropriate Section and Visitor, whose proximity to the residence of the applicant enables him, by personal visitation and inquiry, to extend, withhold, or modify relief, on well-defined principles, according to the deserts and necessities of every case.

But relief merely of *physical* want, is not all the poor need, nor all the Association contemplates. There are numerous *economic derangements* among them which require correction. Idleness and improvidence are the sure harbingers of poverty and suffering, while industry and forethought seldom fail to confer upon their possessor comfort and respectability. Many would be prudent and saving, if they knew how to be; but through ignorance or inattention, they fail to make the labor of one portion of the year compensate for the loss of it during another. In every thing indeed, pertaining to their economic condition, many need to be instructed. The Visitor is therefore required to inculcate prudential habits and self-reliance; and not by indiscreet alms either to encourage dependence upon charity, or by relief to render their condition as comfortable as that of the humblest independent laborer. But, on the contrary, he endeavors to show them the origin of their sufferings, when attributable to causes within their own control, to encourage deposits in Savings Banks for rent, fuel, and winter supplies, and by all appropriate means so to direct their exertions and stimulate them to habits of thriftiness and industry, as to strengthen their capacity for self-support.

There is, however, still another higher and more important department of charity than either alms-giving or economic reform, to which the Board would briefly advert. Want, sickness and suffering, are often the direct consequences of intemperance, profligacy, and other vices, which can only be removed by elevating the character. The Visitor is therefore expected to minister to the *moral* necessities of the destitute, which are often the cause of every other, wherever his alms gain him access; and, as opportunity offers, to others beyond the cases relieved. This principle pervading the whole system, each Visitor's circle of effort is compressed to a limit that will admit of his attention to those duties; and he consequently regards his work as incomplete, while the moral object is unattained. This beautiful feature of the system has already been productive of very salutary results. Where such improvement is effected, it is uniformly followed by a corresponding change in the habits of families and individuals, which restores them to permanent self-maintenance. There is a moral grandeur and interest in the enterprise, as thus contemplated, which should secure it a place in every bosom that expands with sympathetic benevolence. It indeed promises much, and great results might reasonably be expected. More than *twenty-six thousand visits* of sympathy and aid have been made the past year, to the dwellings of the poor, by nearly *three hundred visitors ;* and it would be an anomaly in morals, if these instrumentalities had been employed in vain. Good results, though difficult to compute, have been produced; and the fruit will eventually appear in the brightened prospects and improved condition of the classes the Institution is designed to benefit. Any other conclusion would be at variance with the established succession of cause and effect.

But while of results, as before intimated, the Board would speak cautiously, there are some of so obvious a character, they should receive a passing notice. It is evident that better methods of dispensing charity, than had previously existed, are now gradually pervading the city. Former modes of assisting the poor were extremely defective. There are certain economical laws of universal adaptation, which if disregarded by the benevolent will disappoint their expectations and injure the recipient. These laws have not been understood, or if understood there have been no adequate arrangements to give them effect; and hence, it has been the tendency of our city charities, individual, associated and legal, to aggravate the evils they were intended to remove. But the introduction of a better system, tending to give discrimination and a right direction to the hitherto misapplied or perverted charities of this great community, is of itself an important result.

It is also certain that *street-begging*, to a great extent, has been repressed. This also is an extremely valuable result, not merely because it has rid the city of a nuisance, and our citizens of annoying applications; but for an incomparably better reason—it has inculcated principles and habits that are incompatible with beggary, and saved the poor from its demoralizing influences. These effects were very strikingly exemplified the past winter, which was unusually severe, and a very trying one. Employment failed, fuel and provisions were dear, and owing to the extraordinary influx of pauper immigrants, the number of the dependent poor was unprecedentedly great. Such a concurrence of unfavorable circumstances in former years would have filled our streets with importunate mendicants, and required the establishment of soup-houses and other local exertions, to prevent suffering and starvation. But nothing of the kind was in requisition the past winter; yet it is admitted that never before was there so little mendicity or distress, which, in the absence of other causes, can only be attributed to the preventive action of this Association.

Again: The *friendly intercourse maintained with the poor*, through the indefatigable labors of the Visitors, has made those hitherto neglected to feel that they sustain relations and duties and responsibilities to the community around them they never felt before, and produced in them some corresponding desires and interests. Thousands of our fellow-beings at the end of the year are less debased, less wretched, and more disposed to good objects, than they would otherwise have been. Inebriate and dissolute fathers have been reclaimed; mothers, whose hearts have been wrung with anguish, because of the wickedness, disobedience, and prospective ruin of their children, have found sympathy, encouragement, and aid. Vagrant children have been supplied with places and employment, and great numbers, recovered from the streets, have been brought into the Public and Sabbath Schools. The Association, moreover, has served as a chain of communication between the poorest and the richest, the highest and the lowest in the city; generating kinder and juster feelings between them, while the moral interests of the rich themselves have been promoted by the blessings they have been induced to confer upon the poor, through this instrumentality.

But probably in no other way has the usefulness of the Institution been more clearly evinced, than by *preventing the increase of pauperism.* In the vast and growing population of this city, there is always a numerous class of persons, who have been accustomed to provide their own support, and prefer self-dependence to reliance upon alms; but who, being reduced to want by unavoidable causes, require temporary assistance. And experience has abundantly shown, that the danger to be apprehended for this class, is, that after buffeting awhile with the difficulties of their condition, they will accept of alms-house relief, rely upon it, lose their self-respect, and descend from the respectable and independent position they had previously maintained, to that of the vagrant pauper class. Thus, without the preventive action of this Association, pauperism and mendicity would, as hitherto, continually increase by large accessions from this class, and no subsequent exertions, likely to be made, would ever effect their rescue from it. Though previously unreached by all other instrumentalities, multitudes are now reached by this Institution; and by cutting off this prolific source of pauperism, the aggregate of the evil will be constantly diminishing, until, eventually, few will be found dependent upon public charity, except imported paupers or those who from bodily infirmity are incapable of providing their own support.

The Board in passing are gratified to remark, that the movements of this Institution are exerting an influence which is felt far and near. Similar Associations, adopting this for a model, have been formed in Brooklyn and Albany; and they learn that others are in progress in other cities. They feel that the object they are seeking is a great public good; and would desire, by kindly intercourse with kindred Institutions, to impart or receive whatever observation or experience suggests, that may be useful in future labors.

Several means of aiding the poor, noticed in previous Reports, have been employed during the year, with results which justify their continuance, to wit: the *loaning of stoves*, and the systematic distribution of *cast-off clothes*, and *cold victuals*. With respect to the two latter, they believe much greater good may be done than has yet been effected. Several merchants the past year contributed blankets, hosiery, and materials for clothing, and many families, garments, hats, quilts, etc., which were gratefully accepted and usefully applied. But how inadequate the supply to the demand, and to the ample means and well known liberality of our citizens! It is evident that this mode of doing good has not been appreciated. There are, doubtless, very many families, and also persons in business, having articles of a kind or in a condition to be of little value to themselves, that would be wealth and comfort to the needy, if prepared for their use, and judiciously distributed. The plan for this object is to provide depots in each Ward, from which the articles are given out on the order of the Visitors, who knowing the applicants, imposition is prevented, and the deserving supplied. They here refer to the subject, to excite a deeper interest and wider co-operation therein than has hitherto been evinced. The location of the Depositories, and further information will be given, when a public appeal is made for the object.

So also with respect to the subject of *cold victuals*. There are thousands of families in the city, the refuse of whose tables, if carefully gathered up, would go far towards relieving an equal number of deserving and needy families. But generally, broken victuals are given away by servants, without any knowledge of the recipients; and it is notorious, that such alms are often abused, while street-begging and all the evils incident to indiscriminate relief, are thereby encouraged. The Board have therefore instituted a plan, by which the benefits of this important charity may be made available, and the mischiefs of the present mode of dispensing it avoided. For this plan they would bespeak the concurrence of the benevolent, when arrangements are made in their respective Wards for the purpose.

The Eighteenth Ward having been formed, by dividing the Sixteenth, it has been organized by the appointment of an Advisory Committee and Visitors. As the new District was unsupplied with gratuitous medical attendance and medicines for the indigent, the Board has effected an arrangement at the expense of the Association, by which the wants of the poor in this respect, it is believed, will be adequately provided for. The chief advantages of the system adopted are, that it brings the physician and the dispensary near the patients, whereby medical attendance and medicines are readily obtained, while it provides so thorough a supervision, that every alleged neglect will be inquired into and corrected. As this arrangement, however, has been in operation but a few months, it would be premature to speak very confidently respecting it.

The Association, in the fulfilment of its objects, has devoted much inquiry during the year to the dwellings of the poor, with a view to the adoption of the best means for their improvement. And though nothing very definite has been done beyond a full examination of the subject, the way is now prepared for the intelligent presentation of plans, the advantages of which, it is hoped, will at no distant period be realized. Several other reformatory measures have also been considered, some of which are in successful progress, and in due season will be made public.

Desirous of introducing into the organization whatever would augment its completeness and effect, the Board addressed a circular letter to each Visitor, requesting their opinion of its action, and any suggestions by which its efficiency might be increased. These gentlemen, being most intimately conversant with all the practical working of the plan and results, and consequently best qualified to speak intelligently respecting them, concurred in expressing their confidence in the system, without intimating any desire of change, except in the area of some Sections and the addition of a few Visitors.

There is, in the view of the Board, just cause of self-gratulation, that an experiment of four years has detected no radical defects either in the principles of the Association, or in the means of their attainment; and that the only modification required has been in the division of labor, by which the Sections have been increased from 276 to 297. Extensive as is the organization, it has been managed with increasing ease and effect, as those connected with it have acquired that knowledge and familiarity with their duties, which experience alone can give. The system, in short, appears suited to its objects, and it needs no higher praise.

To sustain the Association, however, in vigorous and progressive action, has required a vast amount of labor, which has been performed by those to whom it has been intrusted with singular devotedness and fidelity. The Executive Committee, on whom devolves the business of the Association during the recess of the Board, has held its meetings monthly throughout the year, exclusive of incessant sub-committee labors, also performed by members of that body. During the same period, the District Committees and Visitors held more than 200 meetings for conference on the objects of their mutual labors. The Visitors, meanwhile, transmitted to the Secretary, an average of about 250 written Reports each month, or more than 3,000 during the year, furnishing all necessary information relative to their labors; and these returns having been condensed into a general Report, and submitted to the Executive Committee at their stated monthly meetings, a thorough knowledge of the operations of the Institution, as indicated by the separate action of each individual and by statistical returns, has been obtained, possessing all the certainty of arithmetical computation.

The following is a summary statement of the receipts and expenditures, which they respectfully submit :—

Amount of Receipts from November 10th, 1845, to November 1st, 1846, - - - - - $24,144 13
Expenditures do. do. do. 24,327 90

The above receipts include two Bequests of $1000 each, yet the expenditures show an outlay beyond the total receipts of $183 77.

Subjoined is a tabular statement of the monthly district returns for the past year, to wit, from November 1st, 1845, to November 1st, 1846.

1845.	Number of Families Relieved.	Number of Persons.	Number of Visits.
November, . . .	577	1,639	1,215
December, . . .	1,978	6,154	3,879
January, 1846, .	3,296	10,084	6,136
February, . . .	2,918	8,207	5,642
March, ...	2,410	8,815	3,089
April, ...	880	3,213	1,549
May, ...	378	1,402	1,225
June, ...	232	825	741
July, ...	89	327	289
August, ...	152	571	468
September, . . .	276	993	807
October, ...	368	1,344	922

In conclusion, the Board again recur with gratitude to the Unseen Hand that has guided, and to the benevolence that has sustained the Association through another year, and to the same kind Providence and liberality they commit it for time to come. The favor with which the public has regarded this organization by making it supersede other Societies, and consequently multiplying references to it for aid, has in the same ratio increased its pecuniary responsibilities. These responsibilities, it is evident, can only be met by corresponding advances by the public. The Association guarantees the economical and judicious disbursement of the means placed at its disposal. If these are adequate to the demands upon it, all apprehension of suffering from want may be dismissed, for in that case it engages to care for all the uncared-for indigent in the city. If, however, support should be withheld, it will be unable to fulfil its humane objects.

But all their experience of public liberality rebukes distrust, and inspires them with confidence for the future. For they address not a community unaccustomed to feel for the needy, but those who are distinguished for deeds of benevolence. And pleading, as in this instance, for the most imperative of all objects, they feel that it will not be in vain. They ask not means for a profuse or incautious expenditure, but that, with the advantages of a system securing far greater economy and discrimination than individual charity can exercise, the resources of the Association may be equal to the increased demands upon it.

Another inclement season is at hand, when the expenses of living will increase, employment fail, and sickness and want invade numerous households. On many of you, fellow-citizens, Providence has bestowed affluence, and upon others security from want, and the comforts of a well furnished home. As all is bleak and dreary without, how much more cheering will be your own bright fire, and home enjoyments, as you recollect that you have done what you could—all that God and humanity requires of you for the children of want and misfortune. And as you look within your own breast, and up to Him whose omniscient eye is upon your heart and thoughts, and hear a voice within distinctly saying, "You have done your duty," you will desire no other approbation or reward.

Statement of the Receipts and Expenditures of the Association for the Improvement of the Condition of the Poor, for the year ending Nov. 1st, 1846.

Dr.

1845–6. Receipts per Contributions, &c., from Nov. 10, 1845, to Nov. 1, 1846,	$22,144	13
Do. two Bequests, $1,000 each	2,000	00
Excess of Expenditures over Receipts,	183	77
	$24,327	90

Cr.

1845–6. Disbursements from Nov. 10, 1845, to Nov. 1, 1846,	$24,327	90
	$24,327	90

The undersigned, having examined the accounts of the Treasurer, R. B. Minturn, and found vouchers for all the sums charged, hereby certify the same to be correct.

F. S. WINSTON, } *Auditing Committee.*
R. M. HARTLEY,

NEW-YORK, December 1, 1846.

PRINTED FORMS USED BY THE ASSOCIATION.

Ticket of Reference for the Use of Members.

Mr.	Visitor,
No.	St.
is requested to visit	
at No.	
	Member

N. Y. Association for the
Improvement of the Condition of the Poor.

Visitor's Order.

Mr.	
No.	St.
Please let	
have the value of	
in	
184	
	Vis.

N. Y. Association for the
Improvement of the Condition of the Poor.

Monthly Report.

Subjoined is a condensed plan of a Sectional Monthly Return. The original occupies a large page of foolscap, with appropriate columns, 38 in number, which enable Visitors to give the following particulars of every family relieved. 1st. Name, residence, place of birth, sex, color, occupation, time in the city, number in family, and number of visits. 2d. Statements of character,—as being temperate or intemperate, virtuous or vicious, industrious or idle. 3d. Unavoidable causes of indigence, such as sickness, infirmity, or old age. 4th. Whether they can read or write; whether the children attend Public School, or Sabbath School; and also particularly concerning the kind and amount of relief given, either in food, fuel, clothing, or medicine, with space for marginal remarks.

New-York Association for the Improvement of the Condition of the Poor.

VISITOR'S MONTHLY REPORT OF SECTION No.   DISTRICT No.   Dated   184

☞ *A mark with a pen thus ╲, in the columns, will point out the class to which the person named belongs.* ☜

Nos. of Persons.	Names of Persons Visited.	Residence of Persons.	Foreigners.	Natives.	Coloured Persons.	Males.	Females.	Kind of occupation.	Time in City.	No. in Family.	No. of Visits.	Character.								Unavoidable causes.				Education.			Kind of Relief.							Amount Expended.	Remarks.
												Temperate.	Intemperate.	Provident.	Improvident.	Virtuous.	Vicious.	Industrious.	Idle.	Sickness.	Infirmity.	Misfortune.	Old Age.	Can read & write	Cannot do.	Children to S. S.	do. Public.	Food	Fuel.	Clothing.	Shelter.	Money.	Medicine	Physician.	Dol's. cts.	

Total.

Remarks.   Signed,
                                                                    Visitor.

LIST OF MEMBERS.

Owing to inadvertence in the returns from some of the Districts, it is feared that the list of Members may not be perfectly accurate. The *amounts* received were duly credited, as may be seen by an inspection of the Treasurer's account, at the General Office. But as the names of some who contributed small sums, did not accompany their donation, with all the efforts subsequently made to obtain them, the list may still be incomplete.

A.

Ackerman, D. D.
Anliss, Mrs.
Anderson, L.
Ambler, John
Anthon, E. H.
Andrews, Mr.
Anderson, James B.
Angle, J.
Anthony, N. H.
Allen, G.
Angevine, D.
Armstrong, George
Armstrong, James
Allen, Ira M.
Abbott, Mrs.
Aickman, Hugh
Anderson, John
Anderson, William
Avery
Andrews, R. C.
Applegate, Joseph
Alley, Saul
Avin
Anderson, E.
Anon
Adams
Abbott, William M.
Anthony, I.
Adams, S. H.
Anderson, J.
Ackerman, I. C.
Ayers, A.
Andereise, J. W.
Astor, William B.
Austen, David
Alosp, J. W.
Allen, Stephen
Anthon, John
Allen, Horatio
Anthon, Rev. H.
Astor, John Jacob
Abeel, John H.
Aymar, William
Aspinwall, J. S.
Adams, J.
Andrews, H. O.
Ackerman, S.
Anthon, H.
Averill, A.
Anthony, E.
Aymar, B.
Atkin, J. H.
Aspinwall, W. H.
Allen, Gibert
Allison, M.
Andrews, L.
Ambler, J. G.
Ackerman, S. H.
Allen
Ashford, Mrs.
Allen, William
Allen, J.
Ackley, J. A.
Andrews, Benjamin
Avery, I. S.
Alison, Mr.
Abbe, George W.
Ayers, Reuben
Archer, William
Albro, R.
Angevine. L.
Allison, T. H.
Andrews, James E.
Anderson, W. T.
Armour, Jacob
Ammon, Frederick
Atkinson. Samuel
Aherns, G.
Ammerman, J. W.
Alicotes, John M.
Alford, E. M.
Arcularius, P. G.
Atterbury, Lewis
Anderson, S. W.
Arcularius, M. A.
Ames, Jacob
Achmuty, Mrs.
Adriance, Thomas M.
Arden, John B.
Ammerman, Mr.
Appleton, D.
Andrews, J. D.
Aikman, Robert
Allen, George F.
Akerly, Hiram
Attridge, John
Atwood, C. S.
Andrews. Josiah B., M. D.
Aupoix, Charles
Aycrigg, B.
Allen, Alexander
Ash, Joseph H.
Aitken, John
Atwill, J. F.

B.

Bushnell, J.
Bolton, Henry
Burke, Jonah
Bromley, R.
Bosworth, J. S.
Banister, George
Bremner, Andrew A.
Barker, Mr.
Berry, Miss
Bowman, G.

LIST OF MEMBERS. (1846.

Bloom, Mrs.
Benjamin, Mr.
Bowen, Mr.
Blanco, B.
Banker, Edward
Brooks, George
Bruen, W. D.
Borden, William
Barker, James W.
Bowie, J. H.
Boggs, Mrs.
Brown, Stewart
Butler, B. F.
Bedell, Rev. S. T.
Bell, Joseph M.
Bradley, Wm. C.
Booth, Jonas
Bird, Matthew
Branch, Wm. L.
Blackwell, Josiah
Barker, N.
Blake, C. F.
Barker, Stephen
Brown, Alexander
Brewster, Joseph
Babbot, W. H.
Belcher, M. D., Elisha R.
Burdsall, E.
Belcher, Geo. E.
Bond, Thomas E.
Barrett,
Buckhalter, C.
Born, Jacob
Burritt, W.
Brower, I. S.
Bergen, L. T.
Bliss, T. E.
Barnes, J. N.
Burdge, J. W.
Bussell, George
Browne, Geo. B.
Burr, M.
Bailey, T.
Berry, S. J.
Bayles, James
Boswell,
Bartram, Geo. M.
Butler,
Bull, Miss
Bissell, Mrs. J.
Blondell, W.
Burrell, G.
Boyce, W. V.
Blauvelt, J. A.
Buckmaster, T. O.
Burnton. J. T.
Baird, T.
Blanck, T. J.
Bailey, S.
Brower, Mrs.
Brower, James H.
Bremner, G. H.
Bloomfield. William
Blauvelt, D. T.
Brown, James G.
Brownson, William M.

Bridge, L. K.
Butler, C. E.
Baldwin. D. T.
Belden. G.
Bellows. Mr.
Brown, G. H.
Branch, Wm. L.
Butler, Charles
Burnham, Mrs. Elizabeth
Brush, Joshua
Bussing, John S.
Bigelow, Richard
Barton, William
Benson, C. B.
Bussing, E. K.
Barton, John G.
Barton, Wm. B.
Bervear, John H.
Bogardus, Wm. H.
Breath. Mrs.
Bell, John
Bostwick, C. J. Mrs.
Bussing, T.
Butler, Mr.
Bushnell, O.
Bartlett, Frances
Baker, David
Bowen, George
Benedict, S. H.
Beardsley, M.
Bumney, T. W.
Barlow, E.
Banta, Soloman
Bleecker, W. V.
Brownell, I Sherman
Boggs, Wm. G.
Briggs, I.
Bond, David
Behell, David
Bebee, A. P.
Bond, W. S.
Burdett, N.
Belden, H.
Burdett, H. C.
Brigham, J. C.
Brunt, B.
Barrow, James
Basset, A.
Bourn & Co.,
Brown & Co., E. J.
Barstow, C.
Burr, Edwin
Burrows, P.
Beck & Co., Edward
Brush, J E.
Boyle. E. J.
Baldwin, Luther
Burlen. Mr.
Baker, C.
Barnes, A.
Beers, N.
Barker, E. C.
Babcock, Mr.
Bacline, Mr.
Bayard, John
Brown, James

Boorman, J.
Banyer, M. Mrs.
Bartlett, Edwin
Briggs. E.
Baldwin, John C.
Barrow, Mrs.
Birdsall & Rowland,
Bedient, L., Mrs.
Baker, David
Bingley, G. W.
Burdett N. Y.
Bronson, F.
Bronson, Mrs.
Bartlett, A.
Boyenten, E.
Bethune, Mrs.
Bradish, Mrs. L.
Bull, W. G.
Bush, W..J.
Ballding, M. G.
Buckley, C. A.
Board of Brokers
Benedict. E. C.
Brush, Mr.
Barclay, George
Benjamin, F. A.
Bronson. Arthur
Bailey, James Mrs.
Brown, Francis
Brown, William
Bolton, Dr.
Bard, Wm.
Bonnet, P.
Bradford, W.
Bird, George
Butler, Mrs.
Bowne, Walter
Brandreth, B., M. D.
Bliss, Mrs. Dr.
Betts, S. R.
Bowne, Richard H.
Berrian, W. J.
Bangs, D.
Boorman, R.
Brown, William
Baird, R , Rev.
Butterworth, J. T.
Barnes & Pharo
Brown, E. M.
Booing & Witte
Burgs, James
Barry, Sam'l F.
Brenchley, John
Basseur, Mr.
Bishop, Joseph
Boardman, William, Jun'r.
Birdsell, H.
Boyce, James
Brasted, J.
Bartholomew, Susannah
Brooks, P.
Beekman. Abram
Belnap, D. D.
Baker, Treble
Barret. S. H.
Bation, David W.

1846.) LIST OF MEMBERS. **33**

Bennet, William
Butler, Mrs.
Bellanac, M.
Buckhalter, Stephen
Brotson. A., Mrs.
Brooks, William
Bunker, B. F.
Bonnet, P. R.
Belnap, J.
Brown
Butler, T. C.
Bannen. Peter
B———, Mr.
Bronson. Isaac, Mrs.
Ballow, J.
Bruce, George
Belnap. E. S.
Barker, J. S.
Beardsley, Lucas
Brown, George W.
Brower, Abraham
Bleecker, G. N.
Bulkley, E.
Bouce, J. M.
Baker, Dabel
Buchannan, Mary
Briggs, N.
Brooks, D. H.
Bran, William
Brooks, A.
Buck, John
Bowne, John L.
B. F. A.
Burnes, William
Briant, D. S.
Berry, M. R.
Burdge, Ira
Barbour, James G.
Bleecker, Edward
Bogart, Jacob
Barlow, Samuel B., M. D.
Buckley, T.
Benedict, S. C.
Bird, E. W.
Bulkley, G.
Barstow, S.
Bonnell, Mrs.
Boyd, Daniel
Burke, William
Berrian, James
Bayan, W. J.
Burnette. William
Bunker. P.
Brown, Ellen
Badger, Mrs.
Burrows, Sarah
Bell, Mrs.
Baldwin, Charles A.
Beekman, Mr.
Brommer, Mr.
Bennett, Mr.
Bostwick, Wm. M.
Bennett, N. L.
Boyle, Thomas
Bussing. Geo. H.
Braisted, John

Burd, G.
Boyd, Nath'l J.
Briggs, George S.
Bryant, Mrs.
Baker, J. R.
Baldwin, Nehemiah
Babcock, Paul
Brown, Thomas
Bridges, J. F.
Brockover, J. H.
Brown, R. J.
Bartles, O. S.
Bell, Joseph M.
Bleecker, Edward
Ballagh, William
Brown, Charles D., M. D.
Benedict, H. S., M. D.
Brother-ton, Samuel
Barkley, James
Bennet, William
Black, Alexander
Bird, Matthew
Barron, Thomas
Bailey, Mr.
Buloid, R. W.
Binsse, L.
Bostwick, Charles B.
Bonatic, M. H., M. D.
Bonnett, Mrs.
Brooks, Joshua
Burrall, Samuel
Brinkeroff, Mrs.
Benkerd, James
Beers, O.
Belmont, Augustus
Bailey, A. P.
Beck, Mr.
Boyd, Wm., Mrs.
Brown, A. H.
Baker
Bradburge
Billings, E.
Baxter, Miss
Bolmer, M. T.
Babcock, Nathan
Benedict, A. C.
Bradish, Mr.
Bellamy, Mr.
Bartlett
Ballow, William
Bontadeau, Peter
Bartow, Edgar J.
Burgess & Stringer
Buck, W. J.
Bowne, Samuel
Bell, George
Barnes, A. S.
Baack, E.
Barenbroik, F.
Boker, H.
Bache, G.
Blake, O. V.
Blackman, Thomas
Baur, T. N.
Bumstead & Co., J. N.
Bonderet, C.

Bon, L.
Bridges, Mr.
Bedwell, Mr.
Bostwick, John
Baber, Alfred
Boyer, A., Jr. & Co.

C.

Cottenett & Co., F.
Cook, Edward
Comstock, D. A.
Cummings, Thomas
Campbell, M. S.
Curtis, S.
Chandler, Mr.
Crane, C. C.
Cox, C. B.
Cooper, William
Crane, H. A.
Crolins, John
Cole, George
Comstock, N.
Chamberlin, C.
Cannon, A. V.
Cox, Mrs.
Cornell, B. F.
Christie, P.
Coutant, E. H.
Cotton, E. L.
Clearman, H. V.
Cox, C.
Clinch, C. P.
Carter, Mrs.
Cooper, P.
Clinch, G.
Contoit, Mrs.
Collins, John
Cairns, B. F.
Clinch, Mr.
Cram, J.
Chamberlain, William
Coster, J. G., Mrs.
Coster, H. T., Miss
Cheesman, Dr.
Coster, G. H.
Clark, Mathias
Collins, G. C.
Carroll, Nicholas
Carpenter, G.
Church, William
Campbell, J.
Craig, J. J.
Chalmers, James
Cornell, John H.
Clark, P.
Carle,
Campbell, James
Collin, E.
Crum, A. J.
Christy, Thomas
Cannon, Charles
Carroll, J. B.
Cornell & Amerman
Cunningham, Walter

2*

Cape, H. M., Mrs.
Cockroft, James
Cape, John
Clendening, P.
Cole, Rhoades
Coe, David B.
Crosby, N. S.
Cox, Jemison
Cromwell, Daniel
Cahart, William
Colton, C.
Chanfrau, P. J.
Clark, J.
Clark, S.
Camp, J. D.
Conant, Wm. A.
Conner, E.
Clapp, B.
Colby, A. J.
Chichester, Aaron
Christopher, R.
Church, E. M.
Cowpethwait, J. K.
Cauldwell, E.
Cromwell, Edward
Clapp, S. H.
Chardivine, W. B.
Carle, John
Child, W. L.
Castles, M.
Clarke, H.
Crane, John J.
Connor, Mrs.
Comstock, Dr.
Crawford, Mr.
Carey, Mrs.
Cooper, John
Cragen, B.
Cashman, D. A.
Curtis, John B.
Carrill, Mrs.
Cooper, Peter
Cairns, B. F.
Corse, C.
Campbell, Matthew
Clark, Thomas
Carray, Mrs.
Cooper, John
Cushing,
Chauncy, Henry
Cripps & Co.
Caswell, J.
Cook, Levi
Coles, W. H.
Callihan, Mr.
Campbell, M. S.
Coggill, Henry
Church, S.
Carey, W. F.
Carey, S. T.
Colden, Mrs.
Cammon, G. P.
Corwin, E. C.
Canning, T. P.
Camman, Oswold
Crosby, John B.

Craig, Mrs.
Cuming, James
Carlisle, Thomas
Chagany, Mrs.
Chalmers, A.
Chifneau, Mrs.
Carrow, J.
Cobb, James N.
Crane, D. P.
Carpenter, J. S.
Cock, Dr.
Chilton, J. R.
Corwin, J. B.
Clark, Edwin
Cox, J. & J.
Cheesbrough, Mrs.
Christer, Albert
Collins, S. B.
Carter, E. C.
Cotheal & Co., H. & D.
Codwin, D.
Coggshall, George
Cheever, George B.
Campbell, John
Campbell
Clark, George
Clapp, John
Civil, Action
Collins, P. D.
Colton, F.
C.
Conger, John, M. D.
Churchman, O.
Colgate, R.
Collins, Mr.
Clearman, G. M.
Chichester, Mr.
Chase, H., Rev.
Clark, R. W.
Cleveland, John
Cogswell, Mrs.
Cheffman, Miss
Cruger, Douglass, Mrs.
Cruikshank, James
Crum, John A.
Cass, John C.
Cortilyou, F. S.
Crane, Daniel
Corkle, Samuel M.
Crosby, W. B.
Currick, Mrs.
Carragher, John
Cromwell, Mr.
Conway, Richard
Cumings, Mr.
Corwith, Luther
Cooper, John
Chambers, James L.
Curtis, S.
Congrest, Thomas
Cunningham, Patrick
Chichester, Lewis
Cornwall, Mrs.
Corwin, Silas
Cunningham, P.
Cunningham, James

Comstock, E. D.
Chichester, H., Mrs.
Covert, Geo. H.
Clotts, John J.
Cook, Alfred
Cain, Peter
Covert, Mr.
Crane, Philander
Clussman, Mr.
Clark, Mr.
Conger, John
Cook James H.
Conant, F. J.
Clark, D. S.
Clapp, Lyman
Carter, Robert
Condit, Isaac B.
Clarkson, Cornelius V.
Cameron, John
Carter, Joseph
Crocker, Leonard
Clannon, Simon
Cook, W. P.
Coleman, D.
Covil, J.
Cummings, Thomas, Jun.
Cummings, John
Chamberlin, James F.
Cbale, John
Crane, I. G.
Chichester, Edward L., M.D.
Cutter, S.
Campbell, John
Cochran, Samuel
Cowl, J. J.
Cannye, A. J.
Chapman, J. G.
Carmer, C. W.
Charraud, J. J.
Contoit
Cassebur
Chambers, M.
Caffey & Blood
Cahill
Cox, J. and I.
Collamore, E.
Crocker, E. B.
Chauncy, Wm.
Cornell
Corwin, O.
Cooper, Miss
Covell, L.
Cranch, C. P.
Chesterman, J.
Center, A. H. & Son
Colgate, Charles C.
Colgate, William, & Co.
Cowdry, P. A.
Cargill, Abraham
Colton, George H.
Cahoone, W.
Clinch, Joseph W.
Cleveland, Augustus
Curtis, Charles
Clark, I. B.
Corney, I. C.

1846.) LIST OF MEMBERS. 35

Communion Fund, St. Mark's Church.
Chapman, I.
Collins, Joseph B.
Civill, Anthony
Curtis, J.
Caughey, J.
C. I. N.

D.

Dunshee, Samuel
Dunshee, Mrs.
Downey, Mrs.
Dunn, Hugh
Duchard, Jacob
Dawson, B. F.
Day, Mahlon
Doan, P.
Davis, E. P.
Dunn, Mr.
Deveau, S.
Durbrow. J.
Deff, Michael
Duncombe, A. H.
Daud, Mr.
Davis, J. W.
Dodworth, A.
Dyckman, W. N.
Dargavel, Thomas
Dewill, G.
Dayton, G. C.
Duneson, James
Donington, O.
Door, W. S.
Davie, E. G.
Delluc & Depuy
Delluc, M.
Dashwood, Mrs.
Dean, N.
Dawson B. V.
Dillon, R. J.
Dickenson, J. S.
Dixon, H. W.
Dewey, S. P.
Declyne, W.
Dana, R. P.
Denny, I.
De Graw, I.
Dunbar, C.
Denlin, John
Dowling, John
Day, Thomas
Davidson, James
Dill, James
Day, A. M.
Dodge, E. L.
Demarest, Abraham
Dewili & Son
Demarest, W.
De Graw, J. L.
Dudley, G.
Dyckman, J. G.
Dickinson, Charles
Dunham, Charles

Demarest, James B.
Demarest, David
De Forest, Benjamin
Dow, A. F.
Dutilth & Courtney
Dow
Door & Beastry
Dewey, O.
De Peyster, J F.& daughter.
Delafield, Dr.
Donaldson, James
Drake, Susannah
Douglass, H. B.
Douglass, William
Douglass, George
De Forest, L.
Dean, Thomas
Daniels, George
Donnelly, S.
Drisle, Henry
Dibble, W. W.
Donaldson, Mrs.
Dodge, D. L., Mrs.
Davenport, Quincey & Co.
Draper, C. E.
Delaehause & Maire
Dubois, Francis & Co.
Davis, J. M. & Jones
Devau, John A.
De Long, Lemuel
Delamater, W.
Denison, C.
Duryee, Jacob
Duff, James C,
Duchardt, H.
Decker, A.
Devoo, Mr.
Dodge, S N.
Dobbin, C., Mrs.
Degrove, Quincy C.
Dyer, Charles C.
Dakin, C. P.
Dwight, W. W.
Douglass, John
Deems, H. W.
Dunning, William
Dean, Benjamin T.
Dayton, James L.
Duff, John T.
Dominick, J. W.
Dominick, J. W. Jun.
Denike, A.
Dennis, O.
Dougherty, I. H.
Dunlap, A. B.
Dornin, Oscar
Dornin. Wm. H.
Duke, W. S.
Duff, William
Davis, R. E.
Davis, Stephen A.
Dimon, James
Dewey, Mrs.
Downing, Silas
Dunnell, Doctor

Duncan, Francis
Durye, Mrs.
Dowie, John J.
Dickson, Robert
Deleplain, J.
Downs, Smith
Door, J. O.
Dunbar, James
Demarest, W. I.
Demarest, W. R.
Day, Charles J.
Dusenberry, W. C.
Dubois, Grant
Doig, Peter
Dickinson, J. B.
Delafield, R. K.
Dunscomb, G. A.
Defeganier, L. E.
Delluc, F.
Delafield, William
Drake, Misses
Duncan, John
Dalryple
Delafield, Joseph

E.

Easton, Geo. S.
Earle, Abm. L.
Easton, N. W.
Erven, Charles
Engle, Samuel S.
Earl, Wm. H.
Everett, W. L.
English, C. B.
Eaton, A. B.
Elwo.th, H.
Earle, Miss
Earle, Mr.
Eaton, J. A.
Ellison. Richard
Ely & Harrison
E. A. R., Lady from the South
Ewen, Charles
Edwards, A.
Edgar, W.
Eastman, Charles
Ensign, E. H.
Eagle, Henry, Jun.
Eilts, R. S.
Ely, N. C.
Edwards, G. W.
Everdell, Wm.
Eusheyreve, A.
Elsworth, E.
Eden, H.
E. D.
Eastman, Mr.
Elder, George
Earle, Phillip
Eldridge, N. T.
Edicott, John
Earl, Edward M. D.
Ensign, Timothy

LIST OF MEMBERS. (1846.

Ewen, Daniel
Edwards, Sylvanus
Evelith, Mrs.
Esler, Henry
Evans, Sam'l G.
Edgar, H. Mrs.
Edgar, James

F.

Fry, I.
Fairbanks, D.
Fellows, Mrs.
Freeman, L.
Fowler, Charles
Furgurson, James
Frazee, Abraham
Ford, E.
Frazer, Alexander
Forsters & Livingston
Fearing & Hall
Furgurson, J.
Farquharson, James
Frasee, John
Fraser, Thomas
Foster, George
Fisher, George H.
Fuller, William
Falconer, John
Field, Josiah
Favor & Briggs
Foulke, Thomas
Fraser, Edward A.
Fanning, Mr.
Fitzgerald, Elisha
Ferry, Darius
Fink, Mrs.
Fowler, John
Ford, Isaac
Fabie, L.
Farnam, J. B.
Foster, J. W.
Fitch, G. P.
Fox & Livingston
Fuller, M. E.
Fryer, Mrs.
Foster, James, Jun.
Finn, A. J.
Forest, Edwin
Ferris, L. C., M. D.
Few, Mrs.
Fitch, A.
Farrand, I. F.
Furgurson, William
Field, E.
Faxen, H., Mrs.
Field, H. W.
Fowler, T. O.
Frelinghuysen, Theodore
Fash, Mrs.
Freeland, R. P.
Field, Jude
Folger, B. H.
Frazee, Henry F.
French, W.

Fowler, L. N.
Futcher, E. W.
Fisher, John F.
Fanshaw, D.
Francis, Joseph
Fowler, J H.
Follet, Jacob
Fowler, H.
Ferris, John H.
Freebold, P. E.
Fish, J. R.
F.
Fowler, J. W.
Franklin, W. M.
Ferris, L.
French, J.
Ferris, Josiah S.
French, Daniel
Fessenden, Thomas
Fletcher, James H.
Forrester, James
Fitzgend, John H.
Field, David
Fity, H, Jun.
Fisk, Mrs.
Ford, Mr.
Feeks, Stephen
Finch, Ferris
Fowler, Duncan S.
Fowler, Stephen P.
Fancher, E. L.
Field, Edward
Forrest, William
Florentine, Abraham
Fabriquetts, E.
Fried——, J. H.
Falconer, Mrs.
Fisher
Frost, Mrs.

G.

Gillelan
Green, Mrs.
Gillelan, Edward H.
Gilpin, S. S.
Gerard, J. P.
Gilman, Nathan
Gray, Niel
Godine, Francis
Gardnier, William
Guhneur
Green, Anson
Gilchrest, J. P.
Gibson, Isaac
Graham, John A.
Gethe, R. P.
Gallier, John
Gilman. C. R.
Gregory, W D.
Groesbeck, W W.
Giesenhaimer, F. W.
Gardner, Thomas
Gatty, George
Geerelly, J. G.
Gourlie, Mrs.

Gilroy. George
Galbraith, John
Griffin, Francis
Godfrey, Pattison & Co.
Grant & Barton
Green, James
Gray, Morrison
Goff, R. H.
Goff, R. S.
Green, Edward
Greenleaf, Joseph
Gamble, Linus K.
Gubandon, A. W.
Greig, William
Groshon. John
Griswold, George
Green, John C.
Grinnell, Henry
Griswold, John
Green, Miss
Goldsmith. Hannah
Goodhue, Jonathan
Graves, E. Boonen & Co.
Gallatin, Albert
Gallatin, Albert, Jun.
Green, M.
Green, D
Griffin, George
Garner, Thomas
Glover, Samuel
Gelston & Treadwell.
Grant, S. N.
Gunning, Mr.
G. C.
Gillet, Mrs.
Gantz, John I.
Griffin, Herman
Gibson, James R.
Gilley W. & S. F.
Grey, William
Ganter, John
Goodrich, E. R.
Groan, John C.
Grimbs, John
Goodwin, James
Gumbs, Mrs.
Germond, Wellington
Gravis, Zelotus
Graham, John S.
Graydon, J.
Ganis, Simon M.
Gurnsey, Henry
Greenhough, J. J.
Green, Jeremiah
Grosvenor, Seth
Geraud, Mr.
Glover, John B.
Green, T. T., M. D.
Gale, D.
Grange, H. D.
Gamaleel
Gasguet
Gemmel, Mr.
Gouraud, Felix
Grosvenor, Jasper
Grant, O De Forrest

LIST OF MEMBERS.

Gihon, John
Green, Misses
Gibson, J. R.
Germind, George C.
Graydon, Samuel
Graspdon, Joseph
Gale, William
Godfrey, E.
Gilbert, Joshua
Groseland, Mr.
Gurney
Gascoigne
Goubelman, R.
Goll, John J.
Gorsuch, Robert B.
Groff, F.
Godfrey, Edward J.
Gage. William
Gelston, Rowland
Gray, Nathaniel
Goodliff, James
Gerry, T. A.
Galvan, Daniel

H.

Hays, H. M.
Hessenbergh, G.
Hosmer, O. E.
Havemeyer, F. C.
Hall, H.
Hinshelwood, R.
Hertell, Thomas
Holt, P. H.
Haxton, A. B.
Hillingsworth, S.
Herring, Silas
Hendzell, H. S.
Hawxhurst, Charles
Harriot, James
Hand, J. R.
Huse, John B.
Hall, Charles
Howe, Mr.
Haynes, S.
Hoffman, Mrs.
Hovey, Thomas
Humphries, John
Houghtaling, Albert
Howel. Mrs.
Holt, E
Hall, A B.
Hoose, P.
Hull, D. K.
Herman, George
Hull & Sons, W.
Hubbard, A.
Holberton, W.
Holmes, E.
Harper, James
Hall, Archibald
Hom, James
Holmes, Samuel P.
Hussey, George F.
Hoyt, John W

Halstead, Schureman,
Hinsdale, S. G.
Hilman, William
Halsey, J. B.
Harmer, Charles G.
Hitchcock, W.
Hunt & Hunter.
Hunt, James
Hicks, E.
Houghton, T. L.
Hunn, John
Hibbard, R. F.
Hucker, Edward
Hisser, John
Herriman, M. A.
Hughs, Thomas
Haws
Huntley, John S.
Hubbart, Mr.
Holmes, George
Hill, John A.
Hagard, Mr.
Head, Mr.
Halstead, Mr.
Haviland, Mr.
Hoyt, W. S.
Hechscher, Charles A.
Haughwout, E. W.
Harsen, J.
Hartley, R. M.
Harson, M. E.
Halsey, E. C.
Hall, Thomas
Hyde, Joseph
Henry, Robert
Hearne, Brothers
Harrison, I.
Havemeyer, William
Haff, Mrs.
Hart, G. A.
Hallock, W. A.
Hawkins, Willet
Hampson, R.
Herbert, J.
Housman, I. R.
Hedges, William
Hays, John
Hutchinson, Ira
Hardgert, Matthias
Harris, C. F.
Heywood, Mr.
Havemeyer, George
Havemeyer, C.
Hunt, W. S.
Hoyt & Hodges
Hoffman, W.
Halpin, James C.
Hornby, John
Howland, G. G.
Harris, Townsend
Haskins, Elizabeth, Mrs.
Hoffman, L. M.
Haggerty, Ogden
Henderson, S. P.
Hoyt, Emily, Miss
Hoyt, Goold

Hitchcock, C.
Hoyt, Jared
Hall & Fuller
Hoyt, S. M., Mrs.
Haddon & Son, D.
Haggerty, J.
Hubbard, L. P.
Hustace, John
Hitchcock, W. R.
Haberson, Mr.
Heard, James
Hone, Mr.
Houghton, John
Horton, Mrs.
Holmes, S. S.
Haynes, W. A.
Hamersly, J. W.
Hoadley, Phelps & Co.
Haughtwait
Hale & Hallock
Hyatt, E.
Hoffman, D.
Hoffman, M.
Hadden, D.
Hale, J. L.
Halsted, Wm. M.
Hoppoc, Ely
Howland, John H.
Hull, James S.
Heath L C.
Hill, Mrs.
Howland, S. L.
Halsted, P. S.
Heeler, Mr.
Harvey, T. W.
Hasluck & Co.
Howe, C. W.
Hayden, N.
Hoyt, S.
Hewlett, Joshua
Hunter, W. G., M. D.
Holden, Horace
Hoppoc & Son
Hurlburt, Henry A.
Hemphel, F.
Hovey, J.
Horton, Mr.
Happ, Mr.
H. Mr.
Hunt, Thomas
Hoxie, J.
Hanford, P.
Hopkins, G.
Haydock
H. L. W.
Hillsburgh, C.
Halleck, Doctor
Hoe, R. M.
Holt, Henry
Haydock, R.
Hancock, John
Hoe, Robert
Hoogland, A. C.
Holmes, Madison
Hauxhurst
Hoyt, Charles

LIST OF MEMBERS. (1846.

Hollingsworth, Thomas
H. M. S.
Hagadorn, John
Halsey, Wm. B.
Horton, Richard
Hutchings, John
Hale, Richard
Hall, William
Humbert, William B.
Hawley, J.
Hewlett, O. T.
Holmes, J.
Harper, J.
Haight, Rev. B.
Heidenhem, A.
Howe, Mr.
Hart, Mrs.
Henly, Joseph
Hobby, E. B.
Hallet, George
Hawkins, Elkanah
Hoey, John
Hesse, Henry
Hesler, Mrs.
Haight, Samuel
Hoyt, G. P. B.
Huinason, L. H.
Hargen, James
Hunt, Mr.
Hartshorne, W. R.
Harris, W. D.
Hines, J. C.
Heuston, Samuel
Hunt, D. B.
Herder, N. D.
Haydon, William
Hicks, Charles A., Jr.
Hanford, A. G.
Horton, J. B.
Hecker, John
Howell, Charles J.
Hyall, Jacob
Hunter, A. T., M. D.
Hunt, Mrs.
Hyatt, Mrs.
Hyett
Hastee
Huntington & Savage
Heyer, Jane M., Mrs.
Hardenburgh, J. B., Rev.
Hill, John
Halsey, Stephen
Hunt, John
Henricks, C. & A.
Hosland, J.
Hewitt, M. P.
Hammon, J. B.
Hague, John
Halsted, Benjamin
Hawkins
Henry, John & Co.
H. H. William
Harbeck, John H.
Hall, A. D.
Horton, William

Harris, J. C.
Hedden, John
Hamill, John
Harrison, Hiss H.
Hopper, Henry
Hopkins, E. A.
Harper, John
Hull, Wakeman
Holland, Richard
Hatfield & Bertine
Hoyt, N.
Hacket, John
Hope & Co., Thomas
Higby, Dr.
Hays, H.
Haws, G. E.

I. & J.

Joly Charles
Jaffray, E. S.
Jaffray, A. W.
Jones & Snow
Irvin, O.
Johnson, E. A.
Jessey, William
Irvin, O. M.
Ireland, W. B.
Irving, P. P., Rev.
Jay, Elizabeth C., Miss
Jay, Matilda, Miss
Jones, John Q.
Jenkins, Mr.
Jones, John
Jones, Thomas
Jacobus, David
Jones, Wm. T.
James, S.
Jones, Andrew A.
Jaques, J.
Jones, J.
Johnson, Samuel
James, Thomas
Johnston, John
Jones, Rebecca, Mrs.
Jones, Isaac
Irvin, Richard
Jones, George
Jay, Ann, Miss
Irving, Judge
Jones, J. J.
Judd, Samuel
Johnson, J.
Judson, W. D.
Johnson, Mr.
Johnson, H.
Ingraham
Jacot & Curvoiseir
Innis, Adrian
Jeremiah, Thomas
Ingolsby, Felix
Johnson, W.
Journay, Albert, Jr.
Jackson, Mrs.

Jenkins, T. L.
J. S.
Jones, W. P.
Judson, D.
Jenkins, T. W.
Jackson, L. E.
Johnson, R. R.
Johnston, Wm.
Irwin, Mr.
Janbun, Y.
Johnson, Albinus
Jewel, Leander
Ingersol, Chandler
Jackson, Thomas
Isman, Michael
Jacobs, Bernardo
Jacobs, Laban
Joy, J. F.
Jane, Edmund S., Rt. Rev.
Jordon, A. L.
Jenkins, J. S.
Jones, Henry
Jones, A. T.
Jones, William
Jeffries, Wm.
Jones, Mrs.

K.

Kipp & Brown
King, James G.
King, John A.
Kent, Chancellor
Knapp, R.
Kipp, L. W.
Kissam, J. B.
Keyser, W. H.
Kiersted, H. J.
Kellogg
Ketcham, T.
Knapp, L. B.
Knapp, P. B.
Kane, Miss
Kipp, F. A.
Ketcham, J. R.
Knapp, J. H.
Knipe, William
Knapp, J. P.
Kaezer, John
Kerkman, John
Kipp, P. L.
Knapp, W. H.
Knapp, H. G.
Kiny, R. S.
Kirby, William
Kissam
Kimball
Ketcham, Rogers & Bement
Ketcham, M.
Knapp, Shepherd
Kemble, William
Kirby, V.

LIST OF MEMBERS.

Kellogg, E.
Kelly, Mr.
Kummell, H.
Kemsted, Mr.
Kent, James
Kenedy, D. S.
Kelly, Robert
Kernochan, Joseph
King, P. V.
Kelly, Hugh
Kimball, Richard B.
Kenny, George
Kingland, D. D.
Kissam, A. B.
Kingsbury, O. R.
Kissam & Keeler
Knox, Edward
Kelsey, John
Knouse, C.
Keeler, D. B.
King, Harman
King, Josiah
Kellogg, J. W.
K. J.
Kelly, James
Kelly, John
Koe, Gilbert
Ketchum, E. W.
King, John
King, Sarah
Kennedy, Thomas
Kidder, Samuel
Kirby, Leonard
Kearny, Iames
Kelly, Joel
Kinnan, Mrs.
Kihlbrick, Wm.
Kingsland

L.

Lowndes, Thomas
Lamb, John
Loder & Co.,
Loder, Benjamin
Leary
Little, A.
Lockwood, S.
Low, A.
Lee, Jno. A.
Luckey, Mr.
Lawrence, Mr.
La Forge, C.
Leonard, M.
Lee, D. F.
Lester, I.
Lawrence, S.
Leggett, A.
Leller & Pearson,
Lord, Samuel
Lightbody, John G.
Lewis, Thomas
Lewis, W.
Luther, F. A
Le Ross, Daniel

Livingston, S. M.
Latou, Samuel
Livingston, Martin
Lawson, R.
Loweree, Seaman
Loder, Lewis B.
Lambert, J.
Lewis, Elizabeth
Lewis, I. W.
Lodwick, J. M.
Lane, Adolphus
Lent, E., Mrs.
Lzaarus, M.
Lowerie, M.
Ludlum, N.
Livingston, F. A.
Leake, C. T.
Leonard, Mr.
Lindsley, J.
Livingston, Mr.
Lippit, C. H.
Levenworth, Mrs.
Lillie, John
Lewis, Tayler, LL. D.
Lane, A.
Lenox, James
Lorillard, P.
Leupp, Charles M.
Le Barbiere, A.
Lownsbury, N.
Leller
Long, Davenport & Co.,
Leon, A. F.
Lawrence, Richard
Livingston, Maturin
Lot, John G.
Lee, James
Leveridge, J. C. W.
Lynch, Elias
L———
Lawrence, S. A.
Lambert, B.
Lawrence, Isaac, Mrs.
Ludlow, John R.
Lathrop, Wm. M.
Lord, Benjamin
Lane, N. B.
Lynes, S. C.
Linsey, Jane
Lyles, H.
Langsheath, F. & B.
Levy, B.
Lee, Thomas
Lichstenstan, Solomon
Lucy, Abraham G.
Lyon, W. E.
Latton, Robert
Losee, Henry
Legget, Stephen
Losee, G. R.
Lefferts, Cornelius
Loveland, Oliver
Lippincott, T.
Leggett, Joseph
Little, James
Ludlow, A. B.

Lees, George
Lawrence, Mr.
Ladd, Wm. F.
Lines, F.
Lawrence, C. W.
Lockwood, R.
Little, J.
Lord, R. L.
Lydig. P. M.
Lowther & Son
Lyon, P. P.
Lugar, I. C.
Lang, E.
Lorillard, J., Mrs.
Lawrence, J.
Lee, James, & Co.
Lane, D.
Livingston, M.
Laight, Edward
Lewin, R.
Le Roy, Jacob
Lord, D., Jr.
Leroy, Herman
Lee, David
Lawrence, Joseph
Laight, H.
Lovett, James
Lamb, A.
Livingston, Schuyler
Landrine, W. B.
Leggett, William
Leggett, A. A.
Lane, R.
Lasack, F. W.
Leise, F.
Locke, J. D.
Leonard & Wendt,
Ludwig, H.
Latham, E.
Lockwood, George

M.

McGough
McGrath
McLaren, William
Mackie, John
Mercantile Library
McGrath, of Pennsylvania
Manning & Richards
Maguin, John, & Co.
Murbury, Mrs.
Moses, Mr.
Morse, R. C.
Mace, John
Mildeberger
Minton, C.
McMartin, D
Miller, Jno. R.
Meigs, C. A.
McLeod, A.
Messereau, J. W.
Many, V. W.
Meigs, H.
Miller, Jonathan

LIST OF MEMBERS. (1846.

Marsh, P. S.
McLoughlin, Alexander
McAlister, D.
Martin, William
McCarren, Michael, Rev.
Marsh, Mr.
Marsh, N.
Maltby, E.
McColter, A.
Mitchell, J. F.
Moore, S. V. K.
Morton, Thomas
McDonald. Mr.
Marshall, Mr.
Munn, Stephen B.
Morgan, M.
Martin, C. J.
Moore, Clement C.
Maitland, R.
Mott, W. F., Jr.
McClain, O. D.
Mygatt, E., Jr.
Martin, R. W.
Mould, Charles
Murry, Martin
Miller, Geo. C.
Macy, C. B.
Montgomery, S. I.
Metz, Julius
Morse, Mrs.
Manning, Mrs.
Mooney, E. C.
Moir, J & W.
Miller, C.
Martin, W.
McIntire, C. H.
McKenzie, Wm.
Mercerau & Anderson,
McCuller, David
Mook, Thomas
Meikleham, David S.
Magill, James
Miles, A.
Mitchell, James
Mumford, T. V.
Morrison, Daniel
McKee, Joseph
Meserole, B. I.
Morris, L. B.
Mooney, R.
Mannwaring, D. W.
Merserau, John
Ming, Alexander, Jr.
Merserole, Jacob
Mott, D. S.
Marsh, Mr.
Merritt, L.
Mayo, Mrs.
Merle, G.
Mills, Charles
Mulerhell, Patrick
Matthews, William
Moore, J.
Minturn, Robert B.
Merritt, Ely & Co.,
McCleland, William

McSorley,
McCaffray, Mr.
McCormick, John
Morris & Williams,
Murry, J. B.
Murry, Mr.
Murry, Charles H.
Minturn, Miss
Morewood, G. B.
Manten, Mr.
McCurdy & Aldrich,
Marshall, C. H.
Meyers, J. K.
Miller, Daniel S.
Maitland, Mrs.
Metcalf, J. W.
Mann, Moses
Milbank, Mr.
McBride, J.
Mason, Sidney
Man, E. J.
McVicar, D.
McComb, John
Murphy, James
Meed, F.
Mitchell, Jno. W.
McCullum, Mrs.
Morrison, I. M.
Mass & Kattenhorn,
Mahony, I. H.
Mandeville, Stephen
Marsh, Samuel
Mills, T. H., & Sons
Mathiesons, J.
Martin & Lawrence,
Morgan, Walker & Smith,
Megary, A.
Moore & Co., John I.
McCullough, Mr.
Medlicott. Wm. G.
McLeod. Daniel
Meeks, J. C.
McVelner, J.
Mortimer John, Jr.
Metcalf. J.
Miller, N.
Miller, Jacob
Mills, Abner
Mills, Andrew
Munson, Samuel T.
Moffatt, D.
Murlis, Robert
Mott, Horatio
Marsh, John R.
Mallard, John
Murry, L.
Mott, S. F.
Mott, W. F.
Macy, Josiah
Milbank, Samuel, Sen.
Mather, G.
Macy, William
McCoon, Mrs.
Millbank, C. W.
Moore
M. A.

Mitchels S.
Moulton, T.
Mott, I.
Mount, Timothy
McCartine, Bernard
Miins, Alexander
Marks, Moses
Marsh, John R.
Moore, Mr.
Musliner, Josiah
Misplei, S.
McCreary. I. D.
Merrill, Charles
Miller, Mrs.
Moss, Doctor
Morris, John
McKenzie, Mr.
Morton, Murry & Co.,
Mitchell, Marcus
Micheals, J. A.
McClain, O. D.
Murry, John
Merrill, Joseph
Millward, James
Moses, L.
Morehouse, A.
Martin, H. C.
Martin, Shelden
Miller, Caleb
Miller, Nehemiah
Mullegan, John, Rev.
McMullen, Lewis
McCauley, Mrs.
Murray, Miss
Murray, John R.
Morton, W. G.
Manly, John
Marlen, J. B.
Moffat, John
Morrison & Allen
Mather, W. L.
Masterton, J. B.
Meyer, G.
McLelland, Thomas
McElrath, T.
McCoun, W. T.
Montgomery, Maria, Mrs.
Minor, Israel
Minor, Henry
Miller, W. S.
McGuire
Moore, I.
Mott, S. F., Jr.
Mitchell, Miss
Millbank, Samuel
Millbank, C. W.
Merritt, N. S.
Marriott, Mrs.
McGrath, M.
Mills, Zophar
Murphy, John
McCullough, James
Mulholland, Miss
Miller, Mrs.
Montgomery, E.
Minturn, Wm. H. & Edward

1846.) LIST OF MEMBERS. 41

Mann, Josiah
Minturn, M., Mrs.

N.

Noyes, I. R.
Nostrand, C., Mrs.
Noe, Charles L.
Nelstein, Mr.
Newman, H., Mrs.
Nicoll, Mrs.
Noble, John
Nants, Mrs.
Norton, H. C.
Nelson, R.
Nivin, G. I.
Nelson, J. B.
Noah, M. M.
Nesmith, John P.
Norris, N. F.
Noble, James
Newbold, H. Leroy
Nunns & Clark
Nicholl, J. W.
Norice, A.
Naylor, Mr.
Norris, H. & Brother
Nicholls, Elias S.
Nott, Hiram
Nichol, R.
Norris, R. T.
Newton, I.
Nevins & Co.
Norton, C.
Naylor, Peter
Newlin, Edward
Nostrand, E.
Norman, Thomas
Nodine, R. H.
Newman, S. L.
Newbold, G.

O.

Oelrichs & Kruger
Olcott, John
Onderdonk, J. R.
Ogden, J. G.
Ogden, John
Ogden, E. D.
Ogden, Mary Mrs.
Obrien, Mrs.
Olmsted, F.
Olyphant, D. W. C.
Ogsbury, F. W.
Olmsted, Charles
Ostrander, Gideon
Orven, D.
Oakley, Daniel
Oakes, Josiah
Oakley & Platt
Otheal, H. L.
Osborn & Sons
Oliver, Thomas

Ogden, T. W.
O'Connor, C.
Owen, J hn J.
O'Neil, Rev. E.
Osborn, William
Osborn & Little
Onderdonk, W. H.
O'Brien, Lewis
Ostrander, Mary
Orchard, Isaac Rev.
Owen, St. John
Osborn, J. P.

P.

Page, P. P.
Prime, Frederick
Parsons, A. B., Mrs.
Parsons, W. B.
Penfold, J.
Page, S. P.
Priel, J. L. B.
Place, R. S.
Peircy, Henry
Purch, Mrs.
Palmer, Walter C.
Purdy, J.
Pillow, W. H.
Pape, Henry
Pryer, Grice
Page, Thomas
Polhamus, Cornelius
Pershall, D. T.
Pessenger, Jacob
Polhamus, R. J.
Perry, J.
Pecher, Antonia
Pinner, S. B.
Pine, J.
Pine, Mr.
Phelps, Anson G.
Platt, Mr.
Putnam, Mrs.
Philips, W. W.
Palmer, Mrs.
Piggott, Samuel
Porter, John
Pringle, C. M.
Paulin, William
Pullin, S.
Purdy, Dr.
Parsall, A.
Philpont, M. J.
Platt, George W.
Pollock, James
Parse, Miss
Platt, Z.
Phelps, John Jay
Porter, William V.
Price, C. W.
Parmley, Mrs.
Pringle, T.
Packard, A. R.
Pengnet, H.
Pell, Charles S.

Parsons, Joseph
Parsons, W. E.
Pray, Henry
Payne, Theodore
Pugsley, T.
Prime, Edward
Pickersgill, W. C.
Parish, Henry
Parker. H.
Prall, Miss
Post, A.
Post, Mrs.
Pitrie, Joseph
Pitrie, John
Pullman, John
Perkins, J. W.
Paulding, N.
Pell & Co., D. C. W.
Platt, George
Post, J.
Perego, J.
Paton & Stewart
Peudleton, E. H.
Peck, E.
Polhamus, Abraham
Pell, Mr
Packwood, Mr.
Powell, Wm. H.
Powell, George B.
Price, Joseph H.
Paine, John
Pon. P. & Co.
Parker, Charles
Parkhurst, Mr.
Park, J. B.
Persee & Brooks
Poilon, P.
Pierson, Adam
Patterson, Francis
Pair, John
Peck, Nathan
Palmer, Richard R.
Pearce, N.
Parsons, J. B.
Pool, W. W.
Phillips, Samuel
Pease, John C.
Phelps, Mrs.
Pape, C.
Pitman, John
Pye, Peter
Powell, Allen
Peters, V.
Polhamus, John
Prime, John D.
Passmore, Doctor
Pratt, J. R.
Pattison, Robert
Perry, J. J.
Peabody, J. B.
Pratt, Linus
Perine, Benjamin, Jun.
Purley, Charles
Patterson, Samuel
Paris, Ambrose
Price, G. J.

LIST OF MEMBERS. (1846.

Prescott, Mr.
Purdy, J. B.
Pell, T. B.
Parret, John
Pike, Benjamin
Poilen, G. P.
Pearsall, E. L.
Parsons, Joseph
Perine, Benjamin Jun.
Phillips, John P.
Phyfe, H.
Palleseu, R.
P. B.
Platt, E.
Penfold, Wm.
Prior, Mr.
Platt, Medad
Prior, Ann, Miss
Purdy & Co.
Perry, S.
Pease, William
Patrick, Richard
Purdy, R. E.
Prindle, E.
Prior, Mr.
Penniman, I. F.
Price, Thompson
Pinkney, W. T.
Prout, M. P., Mrs.
Prout, M. P., Mr.
Prentis, John
Pattillon, Frederick

Q

Quackenbosh, B.
Quin, Dr.
Quarrier, Mrs.

R

Riker, Mrs.
Rogers, Charles H.
Raynor, Hiram
Ryder, Edgar T.
Ryder, Mrs.
Raynor, Samuel
Ritter, C.
Roach, C. H.
Riblet, Mr.
Robins, William
Robestoon, John
Roll, Wm. F.
Ryna, Mr.
Robinson, Morris
Rudd, Joseph
Roome, Peter
Rohr, John G.
Rolfe
Ridner, Mrs.
Richards, I. H.
Rolpans, D.
Rutan, E. A., Mrs.
Rust, L.

Richards, Thomas B.
Roid, Geo. M.
Robinson, Beverly
Roach, P. R.
Rowland. C. N. S.
Ritter. Mr.
Rice, I. N.
Roche, Edward C.
Rodman, John
Remson Mr.
Ruston, John
Reynolds, P. M.
Ritter, Misses
Richardson, Oliver
Rully, I.
Roberts, E.
Rawdon, F.
Roberts & Freeman
Riley, A.
Rising, Mrs.
Redman, Charles H.
Riley, Thomas
Ray, Robert
Rosevelt, H.
Rosevelt, C. S. V.
Rogers. J. Smyth, M. D.
Rogers. I. Mrs.
Rosevelt, James
Rasselby, Mr.
Reid, John
Ray, Richard
Rogers, Catherine
Randolph, S. F.
Romer, T.
Riggs, A.
Richardson, Capt. E.
Richardson, T. S.
Reed, Mr.
Riley, James
Randolph, Mr.
Rapelye, G.
Riker, A.
Riley, John A.
Rose, C. W.
Reiner, Frederick
Ryers, T. R.
Remsen, James
Russell, Hiram
Robert, C.
Roberts, E. S.
Riker, Stephen
Robjohn, T.
Richter, Daniel A.
Robinson, William
Roberts, Nathan
Rosenburgh, S.
Riker & Hutchings
Roe, Francis A.
Redfield, W. C.
Reed, Gustavus
Roome. John V. B.
Roff, Charles
Rudd, William
Rich, Josiah
Rollins, John T.
Riley, F. & Co.

Raddie, W.
Rodh, D.
Riddle, G. T., Rev.
Roberts & Spencer
Ruggles, Mr.
Rogers, J.
Redmond, Mrs.
Ronalds, Mrs. T. A.
Rogers, Archibald
Rhinelander, Wm. C.
Remsen, Wm.
Robertson, James
Robinson, A.
Ransom, J. H.
Russell, J. G.
Rumsey, J. W.
Reading, Mrs.
Richards, S. P.
Riker, J. L.
Russell, J.
Rockwell, J. S.
Richardson, Michael
Reed, Cornelius
Roff, Almond
Roshore, John
Rabold, Daniel
Riley, Philip
Rick, Thomas
Reed, James
Rutgers, N. G.

S.

Skidmore, T. S.
Sheffilin, H.
Snowdon, John
Stock Exchange
Stokes, James
Smith, Hugh, Rev.
Sherwood, B.
Scofield, A. R.
Stiveson, Mrs.
Sedgwick, T.
Snodgrass, Dr.
Smith, G. B.
Scudder, E.
Sherman, B. H.
Scribner, E.
Shuchardt, F.
Spies, Christ & Co.
Staples, S. P.
Sandford, Edward
Sherman, Doctor
Sloe, Fredrick
Suydam, A.
Seixas, J. B.
Schaals, F. P.
Southmayd, S. G.
Smith, Thomas C.
Shaler, M. & Son,
Seymore, McNeil
Sage, Mr.
Sarvan, D.
Sterling, R.

LIST OF MEMBERS.

Styles, A. W.
Stanley. W. W.
Scott, C. J.
Sedwick, R.
Sutton, George
Stokes, B. J.
Stilt, George S.
Smith, A. P.
Stephens, C.
Smith, H. H.
Suydam, Lambert
Smith, James B.
Selmes, James
Strang, John
Seguine, C.
Simpson, Mrs.
Stagg, P.
Schofield, W. H.
Salisbury, H.
Sherman, A.
Schoonmaker, H. E.
Sharp, J. R.
Stillheimer, J.
Seixas, I. R. T.
Swaine, E.
Smith, D., M. D.
Scott, William
Stewart, William
Stevens, John
Stagg, C.
Shults, Charles
Secor, O.
Sanford, M.
Sweet, W. H.
Steele
Schureman, N.
Simpson, George
Smith, Richard
Story, Rufus
Sarget, Mrs.
Smith, C. W. & Co.
Sherman, W.
Stohlman, Charles G. E.
Shipman, Asa L.
Staples, Joseph
Small, Wilson
Straede, Charles
Scofield, Philo
Stamler, J. A.
Sonney, William
Statehinron, S.
Scofield, S. W.
Scharpe, Philip
Seaman. Wm. I.
Scott, Mrs.
Stone & Starr
Shaw, James M.
Shirman, G. & I.
Sturges, Jonathan
Stewart, L.
Stewart, R. L. & A.
Storms, Garrit
Schermerhorn, A.
Sampson, Joseph
Suydam, Sage & Co.
Strong, George D.

Skidmore, S. T.
Spohes, B. G.
Swaren, L. S.
Sturges, Bennet & Co.
Saltus, F.
Swain, L. S.
Seller, Thomas
Smith, I. E.
Sampson, G. G,
Skidmore, L. F.
Stagg, J. P. & Co.
Stevens, John A.
Schermerhorn, Mrs.
Strang, J. D.
Stuyvesant, P. G.
Scott, Mr.
Sheldon, H.
Swan, B. F.
Sheriff, Mr.
Spencer, W. A.
Sheffelin, H. M. & Fowler
Sandson, C. W.
Stebbens, W.
Smith, I. I.
Smith, W. I.
Smith, H. M.
Shelden, F.
Stevens, R. L.
Suydam, Jane, Miss
Suydam, John
Sydam, S. I.
Stebbins, R.
Smith, Sheldon
Scrymser. J., Jun.
Smith, Edwin
Scrymser, John
Seaman, S. M.
Stratton, J. L.
Smith, Asa D.
Spaulding, John
Somers, F.
Spier, G. M.
Schenck, C., Jun.
Smith, Lemuel
Sheppard & Morgan
Smith, James
Storms, J.
Scole
Sterling & Walter
Smith
Smith, H.
Stokes, Mrs.
Shields, Mrs.
S. I.
Sniffin, John
Skaden, Mr.
Sheeff, Mrs.
Smith, Jesse
Smith, James
Shotwell, William
Sweesy, N. T.
Small, Thomas
Sands, A. B.
Seymour, C. N.
Scott, Mr.
Smith, Mr.

Smith, C.
Schefflin, Alderman
Stone
S. B.
Sanford, C. W.
Stebbins, W.
Starin, Charles H.
Sharpe, William
Sparkes, Samuel
Sparkes, W. C.
See, Henry P.
Sedgwick, Roderick
Shindler, Simon
Shirrill, Hunting, M. D.
Stille, Isaac
Seely, Joseph
Smith, Woodhull
Sammis, Leander M.
Stebbins, William
Schrymser, James
Seymour, N. & Father
Sturges, L. L.
Smith, U. S.
Strang, G. D.
Starr, William, Rev.
Stout, A. V.
Sammis, Mr.
Sharpe, R.
Stickney, Charles L.
Smith, Wm.
Struthers, James
Stebbins, B. W.
Shonard, Peter
Searles, Mr.
Sheridan, John
Stapenhaven, E. C.
Skidmore, Thomas
Scott, Alexander
Smith, Elias L.
Shippy, Wm.
Skidmore, B.
Scrymser, W. H.
Steele, Wm., Jun.
Seaman, Isaac
Scofield, Samuel W.
See, Isaac
Sperling, John G.
Smith, Samuel
Stevens, J. L.
Stillman, Jacob
Skidmore, J.
Savage, George W.
Smith, S. P.
Stokes, James
Spicer, C. B.
Schlisinger, F. S.
Schlisinger, Alfred
Schufelin, J. H.
Skiddy, F.
Schalzel, Mrs.
Schuylers
Stewart, James
Steele, Miss
Smith, T. U.
S—, James
Scudder, Mrs.

LIST OF MEMBERS. (1846.)

Scharfenburgh, Wm.
Smith & Cornwell
Strong, B.
Shumway, James
Scott, John
Sill, H.
Sarles, H.
Smith, R. C.
Stokes, Henry
Shepherd
Scott, Henry
Sniffin, J. Jun
Shiefflen, S. A.
Shiefflen, S. B.
Stedman, W. S.
Sill & Thompson
Swanwick, Thomas
Sheafe, J. F.
Stillman, F. B.
Stratton, R. M.
Schureman, Isaac
Stillman, Alfred
Smith, M. G.
Secor, T. F.
Steams, John G.
Sheffield, D.
Selleck, Gould
Spelman, Wm. B.
Schulce, G.
Schenck, H.
Sammis, E. R.
Sheldon, James
Smith, William
St. John, B. G.
Strange, E. B.
Smith, J. & N.
Stelle, Nelson, M. D.
Simonson, Miss

T.

Tuttle, Sylvester
Terry, David
Trowbridge, George A.
Truslow, William
Thorn, T. W.
Tilden, William
Thorp, Isaac O.
Thorp, S. S.
Titus, Samuel L.
Taylor, Mr.
Tucker, William
Tillotson, Mrs.
Tallman, S S.
Todd, W. W.
Trowbridge, T. H.
Thompson, Thomas
Tate, Mrs.
Teele, George
Truesdell, T. P.
Towers, James
Taylor, Lyman
Turner, Charles D.
Thompson, S. M.
Taylor, Richard

Tooker, D. E.
Tenbrook, Mr.
Trudean, James
Torry, William
Tilford, Mr.
Townsend. J. H.
Tinkham, Joseph
Taylor, Moses B.
Tremper, Harmen
Torry, Joseph
Tunis, C. C.
Totten, Mr.
Thompson, M.
Torry, E. P.
Towsley, Charles
Tallman, A.
Tobit, J. H.
Taylor, D. C.
Titus, George W.
Tunison, Mrs.
Townsend, Elihu
Tucker, Joseph
Tonnelly, John
Taylor, W. R.
Talbot, Charles A.
Taylor, Mr.
Taylor, Moses
Tracy, F. A., Mrs.
Thorne, Jonathan
Thompson, David
Tappen, George, Jun.
Taft, J. H.
Trimble, D.
Thompson, T. F.
Tiers, E. W.
Tweedy, O. B.
Tweedy, E. S.
Thatcher, Mr.
Thompson, Mr.
Tighe, Mr.
Turrell, W.
Templeton's Concert, proceeds
Thompson, W. D.
Townsend, P.
Tuckerman, Joseph
Tatham, B.
Tatham, W.
Tisdale, S. T. & Co.
Treadwell, Adam
Thompson, Wm. B.
Tompkins, W. W.
Tier, J. W.
Tonnele & Hall
Trowbridge, Henry
Townsend, J. P.
Tomes, Francis & Son
Trenkamp, F.
Trow, William
Taff, Henry
Taylor, H.
Turpenny, Nathaniel
Trumpy, C.
Thomas, Augustus
Tattersell, W. R.
Trooley, Charles

Tay, Casper
Turner, Mrs.
Thompson, J.
T——, Mrs.
Truman, G. R.
Townsend, J. Jun.
Tompkins. D.
Tate, William
Tracy, C.
Thompson, W. S.
Thompson, Samuel
Tredwell, George
Tait, Isaac E.
Talman, John H.
Terbell, Henry S.
Turnbull, W. C.
Terbell, J.
Thorn, H.
Thorn & Jarvis
Tappan, David
Terrett, G. R.
Tweed, R.
Thorp, A.
Turnure, A.
Thorp, Mr.
Tucker, E.
Thompson, A. Q.
Tucker, Daniel N.
Tilyou, Jno. V.
Trafford, Ahraham
Taft, Jonathan
Tracy, George Manning
Townsend, D. Y.
Trimble
Tracy, C.
Thomas, John
Thurston, Henry
Troutman, S.
Tucker, Stephen V.
Tappan, C. B.
Trite, James, Jun.
Topping, Thomas
Turrell, Richard
Talbot, Bethuel
Titus, Charles F.
Tyler, Isaac
Taylor, Wm.
Tappan, Prof.

U.

Underwood, B.
Underhill, Abraham
Underhill, T. N.
Underhill, G.
Ustick, Richard
Underhill, A. S.
Underhill, W.
Underhill, J. S.

V.

Vyse & Sons
Van Winkle, Tunis

1846.) LIST OF MEMBERS. 45

Vose, R.
Van Norden, Wm.
Van Buskirk, W. I.
Van Antwerp, Mrs.
Van Saun, Abraham
Vanderwoort, Henry
Vincent, Leon M., Rev.
Van Voorhies, E. W.
Valentine, Henry
Van Arsdale
Vantine, R.
Vanarsdale, Dr.
Vermilye, W. M.
Van Wagner, W. I.
Van Vleck, Jasper T.
Van Doran, John
Van Nest, John
Vanderburgh, P.
Vanderbilt, John
Van Ostrand, Jacob
Van Dusen, A.
Van Zant
Valentine, D.
Van Riper, J. A.
Van Winkle, J.
Van Black, D. S.
Vandervoort, P.
Victor, F. & Archelis
Van Winkle, Edgar S.
Van Renssalear, Mrs.
Van Renssalear, Cornelia, Miss
Van Renssalear, Alexander
Van Nostrand, S.
Verplanck, G. C.
Van Ransalear, H. R.
Van Wagner & Tucker
Van Schaick, M.
Verplank, S.
Vermilie, Thomas, Rev.
Valentine, John
Vernon, Thomas
Vogley, T.
Van Vleeck, Abraham K.
Vandervoort, B. B.
Valentine, A. G.
Van Hosen, M.
Van Dalsem, Wm. H.
Valentine, Samuel
Valentine. John
Vreeland, Jacob M.
Vermule, W., M. D.
Vroome, Michael
Van Valkenburgh, James
Vanderwerken, A W.
Van Benschoten, J.
Van Allen, W.
Van Duser, S.

W.

Williams, Richard S.
White, John
Wood, James
Wickham, James
Whitfield, G. & J.
Wiflan, M.
Ward
Wilson, B. M.
Woodruff, Amos
Weed, Wm. H
Wilson, Dawson
Wight, Richard
Walton, J. B.
Whitewright, William
Walter, Israel D.
Wiseman, Augustus
Wheeler, Epenetus
Warren, H. M.
Wood, Wm. H.
Waydel, Mr.
White, A. L.
Wardell, T.
White, James H.
Wilsey, John G.
Willizan, J. B.
Welch, Mr.
Williams, F.
Wolf, M.
Wright, Mr.
Wheaton, Abel
White, Thomas
Whittemore, Timothy
Wallace, J.
Walton, W.
Winant, S.
Wykoff, Mrs.
Webb, W. P.
Withey, Ezra
Westervelt. P.
Wenman, Mr.
Wallace, Mr.
Wood, J. B.
Williams W. R.
Williams, John
Williams, Stephen H.
Warriner, P. R.
Westervelt, James
Wright, James
Walbuck, R. M.
White, John
Westervelt, Samuel D.
Westervelt, John, Jr.
Woodruff. H.
Walcot, F. H.
West, Professor
Worcester, I. C.
Way, E. R.
Wheeler, H. H.
White, Norman
Woodford, O. P.
Wainwright E.
Wood, W.
Ward, Mr. and Mrs. M.
Wheelwright, B. F.
Waits, John
Wessels, F.
Whittlesey, Henry
Warnock, R.
Woodruff, Thomas P.
White William,

Wetmore, A. R.
Wilmerding, W. E.
Wells, Lloyd W.
Wolf, John David
Weeks, Edward A.
Weeks, Robert D.
Ward, Samuel
Whittemore, Mr.
Winston, F. S.
Whitlock, William
Wyeth, L. I.
Woran, Wm.
Walker
Wilkes, Miss
Wetmore, L.
Walker, G.
Wilkes, Mrs.
Warren, R.
Winslow R. H.
Webb, J. W.
Wiseman, F.
Wight & Sturges.
Wetmore, A.
White, F. & E.
Woolsey, E. I.
Waldo, S. L.
Walker, S.
Walker, Wm.
Ward, R.
Westlake, C. J.
White, Miss
Woodward, R. P.
White, Charles
Worth, J. F.
Wright, N.
Wiley, John
Warner, E. I.
Wallin, Samuel
Waite, Edward P.
Weeks, E. C.
White, Henry
Wood, David
Willets, Samuel
Winchester, H.
Woodhull, C. S.
Williams, I H.
West, Joseph
Walsh, Richard
Wilcox, S. L.
Webb, Wm. H.
Wright, Horace
Watts, L. H.
Williams, Jabes
Wilkinson, James
White, James
Wright, D. D.
Wells, D. Gordon
Williams, Daniel
Westlake, Samuel
Whittemore, R. I.
Wilson, Harris
Wray, J.
Wood, Mr.
Wiegand, F. W.
Williamson, William
Walker

Williams, Richard
Willet, Samuel
Whitlock, Andrew
Westervelt, J. A.
Wood, Isaac, M. D.
Webbs, Misses
Willets, D. T.
Wheeler, E.
West, John
Williams, Thomas
Woodward. Mr.
Wheeler, Ezra
Willets, E.
Waterbury, A. G.
Walker, Samuel
Wilbur, Charles
Wade, E , Jr.
Whittlesey, H.
Wilson, William A.
Warren, Sylvanus
Woodcock, Wm. P.
Whiting, J. R.
Whittemore, J. C.
Williamson, D. D.
Willet, Margaret, Mrs.
Winship, Thomas
Weeks, Philip
Woolly, Mr.
Williamson, Josiah R.
White, E.
Wiley, William

Woods, John
Ward, Adam
Watterbury, John W.
Warner, Henry R.
Wheeler, Timothy
Warren, A. K.
Walters, Doctor
Wilson, Mrs.
Weeks, A.
Whittaker, Mrs.
Webb, Willet
Wheaton, William
Woolman, John
Williams, A.
Ward, S. S.
Wood, E. A.
Wetmore, Sidney
Whittemore, Joseph
Woodruff, E. P.
Wiswall, S.
Williams, Joseph T.
Williams, P. H.
Wooster, Benjamin
Williams, Augustus
Wells, D. G.
Williamson, J. A.
Woodford, O. P.
Woolley, J. M.
West, Royal
Waggin, Wm. H.
Wainwright, Rev. Dr.

Watts, A., Mrs.
White, Eli
Woodbury, D.
Walter
Woodsworth
Wooley
Whitlock, Mr.
Walker, D. N.
Woodruff, T. T.

Y.

Young, E. M.
Young, S. S.
Young, John
Young, Joab
Young, A.
Young, S. B.
Yates, F. L.
Yelberton, H. R.
Young, D. L.
Young, E.

Z.

Zabriskie & Van Riper
Zabriskie, George
Zabriskie, C.
Zabriskie, A. C.

THE FOURTH ANNUAL REPORT

OF THE

NEW-YORK ASSOCIATION

FOR

IMPROVING THE CONDITION OF THE POOR,

FOR THE YEAR 1847.

WITH

THE CONSTITUTION,

AND

A LIST OF MEMBERS.

> "The quality of mercy is not strained;
> It droppeth as the gentle rain from heaven
> Upon the place beneath: it is twice bless'd;
> It blesseth him that gives and him that takes."

NEW-YORK:
PRINTED BY LEAVITT, TROW & COMPANY,
33 ANN-STREET.
1847.

PROCEEDINGS

AT THE

ANNUAL MEETING

OF THE

NEW-YORK ASSOCIATION FOR IMPROVING THE CONDITION OF THE POOR,

Held in the Hall of the Public School Society, Nov. 24, 1847.

The President, JAMES BRWON, Esq., in the chair.

THE minutes of the last Annual Meeting were read by the Recording Secretary, and on motion approved.

The Treasurer presented his Annual Report, which was accepted and ordered on file.

The minutes of the Executive Committee, exhibiting their operations during the recess of the Board, were read by the Corresponding Secretary, as their report to that body, and approved.

The Annual Report was read, accepted, and ordered to be printed under the direction of the Executive Committee.

On motion, the Constitution was amended by inserting in the Fourth Article, after the words " General Agent," and " not less than."

It appearing that some embarrassments had occurred with respect to a proper provision for newly arrived indigent emigrants, the subject on motion was referred, with power, to the consideration and action of the Executive Committee.

Several subjects of a desultory character, for a little season, occupied the attention of the meeting.

Voting by ballot having by resolution been dispensed with, the Association proceeded to the election of the following Officers and Managers for the ensuing year, after which the meeting adjourned.

OFFICERS AND MANAGERS. (1847.

President.
JAMES BROWN.

Vice-Presidents.
GEORGE GRISWOLD, JAMES BOORMAN,
J. SMYTH ROGERS, M. D. WILLIAM B. CROSBY,
JAMES LENOX.

Treasurer.
ROBERT B. MINTURN.

Corresponding Secretary and Agent.
ROBERT M. HARTLEY.

Recording Secretary.
JOSEPH B. COLLINS.

Board of Managers.
The first in order is the Chairman of each District Committee.

FIRST DISTRICT.
Quincy C. Degrove,
D. S. Briant,
John Clitz Morrison,
John Cruikshank,
Joseph W. Moulton.

SECOND DISTRICT.
William Gale,
George W. Abbe,
Joseph A. Riley,
John N. Sayre,
William Sharp.

THIRD DISTRICT.
P. G. Arcularius,
B. L. Woolley,
Jonathan Sturges,
William Walker,
Edward Field.

FOURTH DISTRICT.
Abraham Fardon, Jr.,
Archibald Hall,
Hugh Aikman,
Charles Chamberlain,
John Hagadorn.

FIFTH DISTRICT.
A. R. Wetmore,
William Forrest,
G. T. Cobb,
Leonard Kirby,
William H. Richards.

SIXTH DISTRICT.
N. C. Everett,
Stephen Conover,
N. D. Herder,
Thomas Lippincott,
John G. Sperling.

SEVENTH DISTRICT.
Josiah Rich,
Stephen Cutter,
J. S. Skidmore,
G. S. Price,
Calvin Tracy.

EIGHTH DISTRICT.
Joseph B. Collins,
William Johnson,
O. D. McClain,
John Endicott,
Charles C. Dyer.

NINTH DISTRICT.
James O. Pond, M. D.,
James S. Miller, M. D.,
Thomas P. Richards,
Jeremiah Terbell,
J. Van Doran.

TENTH DISTRICT.
John Falconer,
William Truslow,
Joseph M. Bell,
Samuel W. Scofield,
E. Wheeler.

ELEVENTH DISTRICT.
S. P. Patterson,
Abner Mills,
Peter McPherson,
Dudley Sheffield,
Nehemiah Miller.

THIRTEENTH DISTRICT.
Peter Balen,
Lewis Chichester,
Thomas Kennedy,
Gabriel P. B. Hoyt,
Charles Merrill.

FOURTEENTH DISTRICT.
William Bloodgood,
M. P. Prout,
Benjamin F. Howe,
Thomas B. Rich,
Adam W. Spies.

FIFTEENTH DISTRICT
Erastus C. Benedict,
Stewart Brown,
William G. Bull,
Thomas Denny,
Joseph Lawrence.

SIXTEENTH DISTRICT.
Luther Jackson,
Tayler Lewis, LL. D.,
L. B. Woodruff,
Charles Roome,
W. Vermillyea.

SEVENTEENTH DISTRICT.
S. C. Lynes,
James R. Gibson,
George Manning Tracy,
Herman Griffin,
Timothy Ensign.

EIGHTEENTH DISTRICT.
J. F. Joy,
E. Holbrook,
E. F. Mather,
S. P. Smith,
John Campbell.

VISITORS.

Elected Members of the Board.

John C. Green,
William S. Wetmore,
Jonathan Sturges,
William H. Macy,

E. J. Woolsey,
Peter Cooper,
John C. Baldwin,

William G. Bull,
Lora Nash,
J. T. Adams.

Executive Committee.

Quincy C. Degrove,
William Gale,
P. G. Arcularius,
Abraham Fardon, Jr.,
A. R. Wetmore,
N. C Everett,

Josiah Rich,
Joseph B. Collins,
James O. Pond, M. D.,
John Falconer,
S. P. Patterson,

William Bloodgood,
Erastus C. Benedict,
Luther Jackson,
S. C. Lynes,
J. F. Joy.

Elected Members of the Executive Committee.

Horatio Allen,
James Brown,
George Griswold,

John R. Ludlow,
John H. Griscom, M. D.,
Stewart Brown,

Robert B. Minturn,
Thomas Cock, M. D.

Visitors,

Appointed by the Advisory Committees for the ensuing year.

FIRST DISTRICT.
Quincy C. Degrove,
Joseph W. Moulton,
Edmund Griffin,
D. S. Briant,
Geo. Hatt,
John Clitz Morsison,
Peter Naylor,
James Giffin,
Ira Brown,
John C. Cass,
L. B. Loder.
Geo. Hatt, Sec'y.

SECOND DISTRICT.
Charles Wilbur,
William Gale,
G. W. Abbe,
D. N. Tucker,
Wm. Sharp,
Joseph A. Riley.
Geo. Hatt, Sec'y.

THIRD DISTRICT.
H. Armfelt,
Paul Babcock,
N. T. Jennings,
L. Wetmore,
E. L. Fancher,
W. D. Harris,
Edward Field,
A. Williams,
Stephen Burkhalter.
David Terry, Sec'y.

FOURTH DISTRICT.
Adam Pearson,
Samuel Sparks,
Alexander J. Henderson,
Ralph Hall,
George Newcomb, M. D.,
E. Wade,
Thomas Ritter, M.D.,
Samuel Shurdlow,
Hiram Hurd,
T. R. Ryers,

Thomas F. Peers,
David Moffat,
John Buxton,
John Gates,
T. H. Burras.
Henry Whittelsey, Sec'y.

FIFTH DISTRICT.
J. J. Greenhough,
A. R. Wetmore,
Lemuel G. Evans,
J. M. Holley,
C. Adams,
James Smith,
D. S. Clark,
John Thomson,
William Forrest,
R. Lawrence,
Robert Carter,
Wm. Van Allen,
Israel Minor,
Cyrus Curtis,
Robert Pattison,
John Scrymser,
J. F. Bridges,
David Terry,
C. C. Savage,
S. S. Ward,
J. H. Redfield,
George T. Cobb,
Mason Thomson,
J. O. Dorr,
W. Steele.
David Terry, Sec'y.

SIXTH DISTRICT.
Wm. Ballagh,
J. Perry,
Harvey Hunt,
Dr. Benjamin Marshall,
D. B. Hunt,
Nicholas D. Herder,
Thomas Lippincott,
Moses B. Taylor,
Sylvester Tuttle,
Daniel Oakley,

Joseph Whittemore,
Simon Clannon,
W. B. Cook,
Michael R. Walsh,
William Phelps,
Abraham Florentine,
John G. Sperling.
Amzi Camp, Sec'y.

SEVENTH DISTRICT.
Linus Pratt,
George Gordon,
Hiram Warner,
Josiah Rich,
Jonathan B. Horton,
C. Tracy,
C. S. Atwood,
J. P. Bremner,
S. S. Broad,
R. T. Thorn,
Wm. Pease,
Peter Doig,
H. C. Martin,
Ed. L. Chichester, M. D.,
G. L. Price,
J. B. Dickinson,
Matthew bird,
A. B. Ludlum,
Warren Rowell,
Z. C. Inslee,
S. Cutter.
Jonathan B. Horton, Sec'y.

EIGHTH DISTRICT.
Joseph B. Collins,
O. D. McClain,
Warren Jenkins,
N. T. Eldridge,
John Cameron,
Ira Burdge,
Wm. H. Van Dalsem,
Edward Field, M. D.,
Francis Patterson,
Richard H. Nodyne,
Charles C. Dyer,
J. W. Kellogg.

VISITORS. (1847.

C. P. Dakin,
W. W. Dwight, M. D.,
William Johnson,
William M. Wilson,
John Endicott,
John Jones,
James G. Barbour.
J. S. Ferris.
 Samuel Russell, Sec'y.

NINTH DISTRICT.
J. W. Rumney,
W. J. Demorest,
Nathan Peck,
W. R. Demarest,
Edward Earle, M. D.,
Roderick Sedgwick,
Henry W. Deems,
Cornelius Lefforts,
Edward Bleecker,
Daniel French,
Wm. Marten,
Wm. A. Foster,
J. Carter,
Robert Pugsley.
Isaac See,
Thomas Fessenden,
Daniel F. Lee,
John Murray,
George W. Pearcy,
Daniel Crane,
Geo. D. Cragin,
John B. Hering.
 Nathaniel Gray, Sec'y.

TENTH DISTRICT.
Peter Aims,
Smith Downs,
Joseph M. Bell,
James Horn,
James Weir,
William Wheaton,
Isaac Seaman,
Edward A. Fraser,
John Falconer,
Laban Jacobs,
E Wheeler,
Henry Vanarsdale, M. D.,
William Truslow,
Isaac Ford,
James T. Perry,
Joseph D. Barker,
Samuel W. Scofield,
Wm. C. Bradley,
Cornelius V. Clarkson, M. D.
 E. A. Fraser, Sec'y.

ELEVENTH DISTRICT.
Wm. R. Siney,
Charles Logan,
J. V. D. B. Fowler,
Joel Kelly,
Thomas Hogan,
Wm. Murphy, M. D.,
Wm. R. Tattersall,
Peter McPherson,
Simon Howout,
John Philips

Wm. Bennet,
John Young,
S. P. Patterson,
Caleb Miller,
B. Wooster,
J. Townsend, Jr.,
Allerton Cushman,
Richard Slocum,
Concklin Seamen,
J. W. D. Stillman, M. D.,
John Camron,
James Little.
 Grant Dubois, Sec'y.

THIRTEENTH DISTRICT.
Isaac Stelle,
John Hutchings,
John J. Gantz,
Myron Finch,
John R. Marsh,
Joseph Seely,
Woodhull Smith.
James Forrester,
Henry Wood,
Charles Merrill,
Jeremiah Cornwell,
Wm. A. Walker,
Abraham Trafford,
Andrew V. Stout,
Ferris Finch,
Joseph H. Vandewater,
Samuel Fisk,
Joab Young,
Thomas Brown,
Thomas Dean.
 John H. Bulen, Sec'y.

FOURTEENTH DISTRICT.
Benjamin Ogden, M. D.,
Nelson Stelle, M. D.,
Adam Blackledge,
Adam W. Spies,
Bezaleel Howe,
Thomas B. Rich,
J. M. Howe,
Josiah Hopper, M. D.,
William Bloodgood,
James L. Phelps, M. D.,
C. L. Straight, M. D.,
Robert Rae,
James Allen, M. D.,
A. D. Clement, M. D.,
B. F. Howe.
 Amzi Camp, Sec'y.

FIFTEENTH DISTRICT.
Richard M. Bolles, M. D.,
G. S. Chapin,
James Goodliff,
Frederick Pattilow,
Samuel B. Barlow, M. D.,
James L. Dayton,
Isaac Orchard,
William Archer,
Alfred Riggs, M. D.,
Benjamin Lord,
John Mollard.
 Isaac Orchard, Sec'y.

SIXTEENTH DISTRICT.
Charles J. Day,
D. Tompkins,
Jos. Merrill,
Charles C. Darling,
D. Coleman,
William Rudd,
Wm. Comb,
James Cowl,
Alexander S. Holt,
Asa Smith,
Joseph Williams,
James Millward,
Thomas Cummings, Jr.,
John Cummings,
H. Cyphers,
H. S. Benedict, M. D.,
James Muir,
Wm. Heydon,
William Rudd,
J. L. Stevens,
Thomas G. Row,
Wm. Dusenberry,
David House,
Wm. J. Peck,
J. F. Chamberlain.
 Chas. C. Darling, Sec'y.

SEVENTEENTH DISTRICT.
N. B. Lane,
R. Albro,
J. T. Duff,
Charles Eversley,
H. Griffin,
Wm. B. Humbert,
C. B. White,
Geo. Manning Tracy,
S. Warren,
J. Valentine,
Wm. Stebbins,
Richard Horton,
Jas. R. Gibson,
Wm. P. Woodcock,
James Scrymser,
Jonathan Dibble,
B. W. Merriam,
Geo. J. Hill,
John Caughey,
 Richard Horton, Sec'y.

EIGHTEENTH DISTRICT.
O. P. Woodford,
Wm. J. Lewis,
J. F. Joy,
Jas. Armstrong,
S. B. Stanton,
L. B. Hardcastle,
Nicholas Sebur,
John Trigler,
George Lees,
R. West,
Simeon P. Smith,
Stephen Bonnell,
J. F. Gilchrist,
 Royal West, Sec'y

CONSTITUTION AND BY-LAWS.

CONSTITUTION.

ARTICLE I.

This Institution shall be called the NEW-YORK ASSOCIATION FOR IMPROVING THE CONDITION OF THE POOR.

ARTICLE II.

Its design is the elevation of the moral and physical condition of the indigent; and so far as compatible with these objects, the relief of their necessities.

ARTICLE III.

Every person who becomes an annual subscriber or a Visitor, shall be a member of this Association.

ARTICLE IV.

The affairs of the Association shall be managed by a President, five Vice-Presidents, a Treasurer, a Secretary and General Agent, and not less than one hundred members, including the Advisory Committees, who shall constitute a Board of Managers. Nine members shall form a quorum for the transaction of business.

ARTICLE V.

The President and Secretary shall perform such duties as usually pertain to their office.

ARTICLE VI.

The Treasurer shall give such security for the faithful performance of the trust reposed in him, as the Association may demand and approve. He shall take in charge all funds; keep an account of all receipts and expenditures; and pay all duly authorized drafts. At the annual meeting, he shall render a particular and correct statement of all his receipts and disbursements to the Association. He shall also exhibit a summary report to the Board of Managers at their stated meetings, and to the Executive Committee whenever called upon for that purpose.

ARTICLE VII.

The Board of Managers shall have exclusive control of the funds of the Association, and authority to make by-laws; to fill vacancies; appoint all committees; and generally to adopt such measures as the objects of the Institution may require. Its stated meetings shall be held on the second Monday of January, March, and November, provided the Board deem it expedient, and the Annual Meeting of the Association shall be convened on the third Monday of November, when the Board shall submit a Report of its proceedings, and the Officers and Managers be chosen by ballot.

ARTICLE VIII.

An office shall be opened in an eligible situation, for the purpose of concentrating and diffusing all information pertaining to the Society's operations and objects, and for the transaction of its general business.

ARTICLE IX.

It shall be the duty of the General Agent to devote himself with diligence and fidelity to the affairs of the Association.

ARTICLE X.

The City shall be divided into eighteen Districts, each Ward forming a District; and the Districts be subdivided into Sections. Each District shall have an Advisory Committee, to consist of five members; and each Section a Visitor.

ARTICLE XI.

It shall be the duty of the Members of the Association to endeavor, in all suitable ways, to give practical effect to its principles; especially to discountenance indiscriminate alms-giving and street-begging; to provide themselves with tickets of reference; and instead of giving aid to unknown applicants, whose case they cannot themselves investigate, to refer such applications to the Visitor of the Section in which the applicants reside, in order that they may be properly inquired into, and, if deserving, relieved.

ARTICLE XII.

The form of Tickets shall be determined by the Board of Managers, and no other form shall be used.

ARTICLE XIII.

Special meetings of the Association may be called by the Secretary, at the request of the President, or on receiving a requisition signed by five members. Two days' notice must be given of the time of meeting.

ARTICLE XIV.

This Constitution shall not be altered except at a General Meeting of the Association, and by a vote of two-thirds of the members present.

BY-LAWS.

ARTICLE I.

There shall be an Executive Committee, to consist of seven elected members and the Chairmen of the Advisory Committees, on whom shall devolve all the business of the Association during the recess of the Board. It shall meet on the second Monday of every month; and report its proceedings at each Stated Meeting of the Managers. Five members shall constitute a quorum for business. The officers of the Institution shall be members, *ex officio*, of the Executive Committee.

ARTICLE II.

It shall be the duty of the Advisory Committees to divide their Districts into such Sections as to apportion to each about twenty-five families requiring attention; endeavor to obtain suitable Visitors for each Section; supply vacancies which may occur; make the necessary arrangements for placing at the disposal of the Visitors, food, fuel, and clothing, for distribution; and on some day in the first week of every month (excepting the meetings in July and August, which are referred to the discretion of the Committees), to convene all the Visitors of the Sections, for the purpose of receiving their returns, and conferring with them on the objects of their mutual labors. The Committees, moreover, shall duly draw upon the Treasurer for such proportion of the funds as may be appropriated to their District; they shall keep a strict account of all their disbursements, and only in extreme cases make donations of money; they shall monthly render an account of their expenditures to the Executive Committee; and in default of this duty, shall not be entitled to draw upon the funds of the Association. Each Committee shall appoint its own Chairman, Secretary, and Treasurer, and shall transmit the Reports of the Visitors, immediately after each Monthly Meeting, with any other information they may think desirable, to the General Secretary.

ARTICLE III.

It shall be the duty of the Sectional Visitors to confine their labors exclusively to the particular Section assigned them, so that no individual shall receive relief, excepting in the Section where he is known, and to which he belongs. They shall carefully investigate all cases referred to them before granting relief; ascertain their condition, their habits of life, and means of subsistence; and extend to all such kind services, counsel, and assistance, as a discriminating and judicious regard for their present and permanent welfare requires. And in cases of sickness and want, it will be their duty to inquire whether there is any medical or other attendance, whether relief is afforded by any religious or charitable society, and what assistance is needed; to provide themselves with information respecting the nearest Dispensary, and in all cases, when practicable, to obtain aid from existing charitable societies. And when no other assistance is provided or available, then to draw from the resources of this Association—not money, which is never allowed to be given, except with the consent of the Advisory Committee or a member thereof—but such articles of food, fuel, clothing, and similar supplies, as the necessities of the case require. And in all cases of want coming to the knowledge of the Visitors, they will be expected to perform the same duties although no application has been made. It shall be their duty, moreover, to render a report of their labors, and also an account of all their disbursements, to their respective Committees, on the last Wednesday of every month. No Visitor neglecting these duties will be entitled to draw on the funds of the Association.

ARTICLE IV.

Special Meetings of the Board of Managers may be called by the Secretary, at the request of the President, or on receiving a requisition signed by five members. Two days' notice must be given of the time of meeting.

ARTICLE V.

These By-laws can only be altered at a Meeting of the Board of Managers, and by a vote of two-thirds of the members present.

Note: The Visitors' Manual may be obtained at the office of the Association, corner of Grand and Elm streets.

FOURTH ANNUAL REPORT

OF THE

NEW-YORK ASSOCIATION FOR IMPROVING THE CONDITION OF THE POOR.

THE Board of Managers, to whose care the affairs of the Association have been intrusted, in compliance with the provisions of the Constitution, respectfully submit their Fourth Annual Report.

A retrospective glance at the operations of the year just closed, awakens emotions of devout gratitude to Divine Providence, for the various means, both pecuniary and moral, by which the Association has been sustained, and for the signal success that has hitherto crowned its exertions. Committing again the cause of the poor to the beneficent Being who ever careth for them, in humble reliance upon His guidance, with animated hopes, we enter anew upon our labors.

But at the very threshold of the year, we are again most forcibly reminded of the mutability of all earthly relations, by the recent decease of ELIJAH P. WOODRUFF, Esq., an esteemed member of this Board, and Chairman of the Advisory Committee in the Sixth District. By this mournful event, the poor have lost a sincere friend, and the Association an efficient helper.

Experience has shown, that there exists in a community like this, all the elements essential to its own conservation. If there is much of indigence, vice, and wretchedness, there is more of wealth, virtue, and Christian compassion, which needs only to be drawn out and applied, to ameliorate the condition of the poor, and do all that human sympathy can effect, for their elevation and happiness. And if alms-giving were all that is required, our city might be said to fulfill its obligations, in this respect; for the voluntary private beneficence amongst us is immense. But giving alms is not all of charity or of duty. It is only one of the instruments of social benevolence; and one too, which, if not rightly managed, will defeat its own objects. It is a good thing to have relieved the wants of the famishing to-day, but if nothing more is done, their necessities may not be the less urgent to-morrow; and the more frequent and freely they are aided, the more entire will be their feeling of dependence upon others, and the more importunate and craving their demands. Nor does the evil here find its limit. Self-respect and self-reliance may thus be undermined, and the most effectual of all inducements to idleness and imposture be presented. And by rendering a higher standard of comfort necessary, without riveting upon their minds the obligation to provide what they feel to be needful, for themselves, every failure of supply is attended with clamorous discontent and aggravated wretchedness: consequently, the great objects of true charity —the promotion of temperance, industry, economy, and general elevation of character—are subverted. We need not cite facts in evidence of these tendencies and results, for they are familiar to all who are conversant with the subject.

Such being the deplorable effects of a faulty administration of alms, it follows, not that the poor should suffer unrelieved, but that aid be dispensed in accordance with principles which will subserve the best interests of the recipient and of the community. We do not here propose to enter upon an exposition of these principles, farther than to remark that they require nothing less than a *volunteer individual guardianship over the poor*, with faithful efforts for their moral and physical elevation. And very much is implied in such a guardianship. In most cases, their destitution and misery are owing to moral causes, and will admit only of moral remedies. Condition must consequently be improved, by improving character. If able-bodied and idle, they should be compelled to work, or left to suffer the consequences of their misconduct; if uneconomical, be taught to make, mend, and save; if intemperate and profligate, the sources of their wretchedness ought, if practicable, to be dried up, by recovering them from these vices. And if their children are growing up in vice and ignorance, they should be brought under moral and mental culture, that they may not become a burthen and curse to the community. Or it may be, that the needy are the virtuous poor—for such a class there is—who are struggling with unavoidable calamities, and require not only substantial aid, but the encouragement, counsel, and solace of human sympathy. There are, in short, almost endless diversities in the character and circumstances of the poor, which demand a corresponding adaptation of means; and this it is that renders judicious relief so exceedingly difficult. Yet, whatever is peculiar to each, should be known, before they can be aided with proper discrimination; and as this knowledge can only be obtained by visiting them at their homes, and by habits of personal intercourse with the humblest and lowest, it is evident that the exercise of a careful guardianship, and the immense work of distributing the charities of this great city with due care, cannot be effected by isolated or impulsive individual efforts.

But what is impracticable to unassociated action, this Institution, by a systematic and minute division of labor, has undertaken to perform. Its mode of operation having been fully spread out in previous publications, to many it is well known; but for the information of those who desire it, into whose hands this Report may fall, we will briefly state some of its leading features.

The organization is designed to be of the simplest form that is compatible with efficiency. Its first general division of labor is into *Districts*, corresponding to the Wards, (*eighteen* in number,) over each of which is appointed an Advisory Committee, consisting of five persons, (ninety in all,) to whose careful supervision and control the diversified labors pertaining to their respective divisions are intrusted.

The next partition is made by subdividing the Districts into *two hundred and ninety-eight Sections*, and the appointment of a Visitor to each. Thus each has a definite field of labor, compressed to a limit which will admit of his attention to all the needy resident therein; and no Visitor being allowed to give, nor the poor to receive relief out of the Section to which they belong, vagrancy is prevented, imposture detected, the physical and moral necessities of the indigent provided for, and the whole system of giving and receiving reduced to the utmost precision and certainty. For, in whatever part of the city the needy apply to the members of the Association for aid, by means of a Directory and printed tickets, they are sent back to their appropriate Section and Visitor, whose proximity to the residence of the applicant enables him, by personal visitation and inquiry, to extend, withhold, or modify relief, on well-defined principles, according to the deserts and necessities of every case.

These particulars have been introduced, to show how readily the difficulties usually inseparable from other modes of judiciously dispensing relief, are overcome by the provisions of this system. And it would be gratifying to show the operations of the system by copious extracts from the

Visitors' returns; but as details would be incompatible with the necessary brevity of such a Report, we subjoin only a few condensed statements, illustrative of particular features.

The following facts show how effectually *vagrancy* and *imposture* would be broken up, if our citizens generally made this organization the channel of their charities.

Says a Visitor:—" One evening, a colored woman, wretchedly clad, but seemingly in health, brought me a ticket, signed J—— M——, Union Square. Perceiving she had other tickets, on examining them I found that they were all from persons in the upper part of the city, and addressed to myself. Inquiring how she came by so many tickets, she replied, that having had nothing to eat all day, she had asked for food at many places, but got nothing but tickets. I said that I would go with her to her home, and if she was as destitute as she represented, I would aid her. At this she hesitated, and urged me most earnestly to help her on the spot, which awoke in me the suspicion that all was not right. Finding me resolute to go, she led the way, and I followed. We had not gone far, when I observed that she had not taken the most direct road to her house, which strengthened the suspicion that there was deception in the case. In short, though I was on my guard, favored by the darkness of the night she managed to run away from me, and I returned, satisfied that she was an impostor."

"Some time afterwards, happening in that neighborhood, I saw the same woman in the street, and, unobserved myself, followed her, and noted the house she entered. On inquiry I was informed that she lived there, that her husband drove a cart, owned some property, and was unusually well off, for a person of his class; that the wife pursued begging about as regularly as the husband his work, and had continued this course for years. This information coming from different respectable persons, I could not doubt its truth. I therefore called on the woman, and charged her with these habits, who, when she saw denial would be vain, attempted to justify herself on the ground that there could be no harm in a poor woman like herself begging a little from the rich. I tried to impress on her mind the wickedness of such a life of deceit and imposture, with the warning that I would watch her, and if she was again seen begging it would be my duty to report her as a vagrant, and the police would probably send her to the penitentiary. She became alarmed, and promised to do better in future, and, I have no doubt, is entirely cured of her begging and vagrant propensities."

Another.—Says a gentleman living up town :—" My door was so frequented by vagrants and beggars, chiefly foreigners, as to prove a most serious annoyance; and yet so importunate were they, and so pitiful often were their tales of distress, that we knew not how to send them empty away. At the same time, I observed that my neighbor, who lived in a more splendid and attractive house than my own, appeared to have very few calls from persons of this class. Wondering at this, I asked him how it happened that his door was so much less beset by beggars than mine. 'Oh, ho,' said he, we give them nothing but tickets, and they never come back.' 'Tickets!' I rejoined; 'what do you mean?' He then explained the nature of the Association, and among other things said, 'that tickets were given to direct beggars to the Visitor, who, if they were deserving and needy, gave them relief; and if undeserving, or impostors, led to their detection; so that in either case it would do them no good to come to his house again; and by these means they were properly cared for, and he got rid of them altogether.' Learning this, I made the trial myself; and in the course of a week, the evil at my door was pretty much cured; and now, six months after, we only have an occasional call." He adds :—" Of all the cures for vagrancy, this is the most complete. But if families will still persist in giving to, they know not who, at their doors, they will, of course, be run down with beggars; and since this organization has been formed, they can blame no one but themselves. I feel bound to pay this tribute of commendation to this noble and widely extended effort for the relief of the poor and the suppression of street-begging."

As indolence and vice almost necessarily imply deception, *duplicity* enters largely into the condition of poverty, and is the expedient to which the debased generally resort. But the facilities of detecting such persons when they least expect it, may be inferred from the following fact.

A woman being refused assistance, because of her intemperate habits, she made her complaint at the general office. Being asked by the Secretary whether she had ever been aided by the Association, she replied that she had not. Examining the Register, he ascertained that for a long time she had been occasionally relieved; and wishing her to correct her misstatement, he called her attention to what she had said. "And sure," she replied, "no one knows better than myself, that I never had any thing from your Society." "But, good woman," said he, "two years since, you lived in Houston-street, and were helped one month by the Visitor; next you removed to Ludlow-street, where you were helped until your character was found out; then you went to Forsyth-street, and being sick, a physician was sent you, and you were aided until you recovered; now you live in Mott-street, and because of your intemperance, the Visitor believes it to be his duty to refuse you relief." "Och," said she, rising in a passion, "if your honor has nothing better to do than to follow honest women about the streets, I'll have nothing to do with your Society."

It being one of the prominent objects of the Association to *prevent pauperism*, by extending timely aid, and judicious counsel to those who have never been debased by vagrancy or alms-house relief, the following facts may illustrate the methods of obtaining this important result.

"My attention," says a Visitor, "was called to a family of newly arrived immigrants, consisting of a man aged 56 years, his wife, two sons, and three daughters. Though not literally falling within the scope of our objects, with the consent of the Advisory Committee, I extended to them the sympathies and aid of the Association. When they landed, all they had was five dollars, which being soon expended, they were moneyless, friendless in a strange land, without work, and destitute. To add to their trials, the wife and mother was lying on the floor of their wretched apartment, so reduced by sickness, that she despaired of her own recovery. Her first anxiety was to have the counsel and sympathies of a Christian friend, and her next a physician. In both these capacities, I was enabled to serve her, by imparting religious instruction and consolation, and such medicine and assiduous attendance, that in the course of three weeks her health was restored. Meanwhile, from the funds of the Association, I supplied them with many necessaries, and also from other sources provided them relief.

"But it being my great object to put them in a way of self-support, in a few weeks I succeeded in obtaining permanent employment for the father and one of the sons, who were blacksmiths, at Mr. W.'s factory, in Elm-street, where both are spoken of as worthy men. The elder, indeed, is a constant attendant at a Protestant church, where he esteems it his privilege to pay something weekly for the minister's support. For the other son, who is a saddler, I procured work in Broadway; and soon also good situations were found for the three girls. Thus by the expenditure of very few dollars, a worthy family were rescued from the darkest penury, and placed in comfortable circumstances, bidding fair to be valuable members of society. Many more such immigrants would not be undesirable."

Another case narrated by the same Visitor, illustrating the generally beneficent character of these labors, is not without interest.

"Mrs. R. was left a widow with six children, the eldest a cripple. The next two earned about three dollars a week, and on this scanty sum the family subsisted. But unfortunately, the children's employer dismissed them, having no longer need of their services; and thus, in the depth of winter, the family was deprived of all means of support. In this condition I was called to visit them. I found the apartment clean, and the children comfortably clad; still it was the abode of gaunt want and suffering. The widow related her tale of sorrow; and pleasant was it to sympathize in her afflictions, and to comfort her with the consolations of that religion, which for years had been her hope. I should here remark, that through my solicitations, the gentleman who had previously employed the children, again gave them work; so that, with a little assistance from the Association, they were enabled to get comfortably through the winter. I regard it as a great privilege to be a Visitor. When I most feel like yielding to discouragement, cases like these occur, which afford an ample reward for all my anxieties and toils."

Of a similar kind, are the following characteristic statements, and facts.

"Having been a Visitor of the Association ever since its formation, many facts have come under my observation, which I think are calculated to increase the confidence of the public in the 'heavenly benevolence' of an organization, that spreads its broad sheltering wings over the whole city, from the Battery to Fortieth-street, and from river to river.

"And here I am at a loss, not for the want of materials, but from their abundance. For in the course of about two years I have, as Visitor, assisted more than a hundred different families, embracing all the varied grades of morals and destitution, which, probably, can be found in this great city. I will, however, begin with a poor Irish family, in ——— street. The father of the family, a common laborer, lay dangerously ill; his wife, from recent confinement, was scarcely able to crawl about; they had two helpless children; and were destitute of all that could sustain life. The husband, I supposed, was rapidly sinking with consumption, and incurable. I however supplied the family with provisions for a season, by an order on our grocer, and procured for the sick man the services of Doctors G. and H., who generously attended without fee or reward of an earthly kind. For many months I visited this family, and nearly sustained them by gratuitous aid; and with the blessing of Heaven upon the Association's gifts, and the physicians' skill, I at length had the pleasure, the great pleasure, of seeing this once emaciated, dispirited, unhappy man, look sleek, fat, and plump, and again able and ready to follow his usual hard labor.

"Another case. A few months since, I found a very interesting Scotch woman, a widow with four children, in a small attic room, in a miserable house, in a more miserable street! She had seen good days, but was now more than doubly wretched, for she was not only a widow, but was sick and destitute, and her eldest child, a girl of seventeen years, a cripple for life! This widow, reduced by coughing and raising blood almost to a skeleton, lay in one corner of her desolate chamber, on the floor, without any thing in the hape of a bed under her! (O ye sons and daughters of wealth, who recline on your couches of velvet and down, remember the sorrows of the poor sick widow and her famishing orphans, and in some way hasten to their relief!) Her condition was truly heart-rending! She was intelligent and virtuous, and while her health lasted, had been laborious;

but when sickness came, she was forced to pawn one thing after another for the means of subsistence, until the bed she so much needed was in the pawnbroker's shop.

"The Association, through me, supplied the family with necessary food, whilst private benevolence raised the sick sufferer from the hard floor, to a comfortable bed. Meanwhile, having procured an excellent cough remedy, I soon had the satisfaction of seeing her health so far restored, that she again was able to return to her daily toil. Speaking with her of her forlorn condition when I first visited her, she said, with grateful emotion, that had she not thus been timely discovered and rescued, she would now have been dead. And I have little doubt that these instrumentalities saved her life. Many, many more facts could I relate, but I only add that a society, which thus blesses the sick poor, the suffering widow and the fatherless, deserves the patronage of all, and receives the smile of approving Heaven."

The limits of the Report will not permit, or a volume of similar facts might be compiled. But probably enough have been introduced for the object in view, which is, to show by the testimony of those most conversant with the system, the nature of its operations and results.

Of the incidental operations of the year, a few may be concisely noticed.

First.—*The Nursery Children.* Among the objects which have claimed the notice of the Association, the numerous body of children, under the care of the city authorities, and now temporarily on Blackwell's Island, is one of the most interesting. Emphatically the offspring of misfortune, and exposed from their birth or tenderest infancy to deprivation on the one hand, and the corrupting influence of dissolute parents on the other, their condition called forth the sympathy of the Board. In the hope of being useful in promoting their welfare by assisting the Commissioner of the Alms

House in his supervision over them, the Association memorialized the Common Council for the passage of a Resolution authorizing the Commissioner to accept the gratuitous aid of a Committee in that department. The application has been successful; but the Committee having been but recently organized, can as yet speak only of their hopes and wishes. Meanwhile the Board rest in the belief that our present worthy Commissioner is doing every thing in his power, to accomplish the same desirable object.

SECOND.—*Stoves, Clothing, &c.* It being the design of the Institution to economize its means, and to adapt relief so far as is practicable to the diversified wants of the poor, it has during the past, as in previous years, *loaned stoves, distributed clothing* and *broken victuals,* with results which justify their continuance. In regard to the two latter descriptions of aid, though much more has been done than in former years, it is believed they might still be greatly extended with advantage. Great good has thus been done by comparatively few families; and as these methods of benefiting the poor are equally practicable to thousands of others, who doubtless would as cheerfully co-operate therein, if as well acquainted with the beneficial effects, the Board here refer to the subject to bespeak the general concurrence of the benevolent therein, when arrangements shall be announced in their respective Wards for the purpose.

THIRD.—*Dwellings for the Laboring Classes.* The subject of improving the tenements of the laboring classes noticed in the last Report, has also continued to receive the attention of the Board, the result of whose investigations may be thus summarily stated.

I. That the tenements of the poor in this city, are generally defective in size, arrangement, supplies of water, warmth, and ventilation; also that the yards, sinks, and sewerage are in bad condition. The occupants, consequently, often suffer from sickness and premature mortality; their ability for self-maintenance is thereby impaired or destroyed; social habits and morals are debased, and a vast amount of wretchedness, pauperism, and crime is produced.

II. Defective as are these tenements, they frequently pay rents which, increased by a system of sub-tenantcy, become very oppressive, and as this system in other respects is adverse to the interests of the tenants, it should be superseded by a more equitable and less oppressive system.

III. Buildings may be erected for the laboring classes, with all the requisites for health, comfort, and economy, and let at rents sufficient to give a fair remuneration to the capitalist, and at the same time be within the reach of the less wealthy.

IV. Great value should be attached to this much desired reform, seeing it lies at the basis of other reforms; and as the health and morals of thousands are injured or destroyed by the influence of circumstances around them, an improvement of the circumstances in connection with other appropriate means, afford the only rational hope of effectually elevating their character and condition, and of relieving the city from numerous evils which now exist.

V. The subject has peculiarly urgent claims upon the wealthy, because it is one which they alone are competent to effect; and they may enter upon it either from philanthropic or pecuniary considerations, with the assurance of advantage to themselves, to the community at large, but especially with benefit to great numbers of their suffering fellow men.

The Board lithographed their plans for building, and were, by a mature consideration of the subject, otherwise prepared for an immediate prosecution of the undertaking. But it being evident to the gentlemen who propose to furnish the capital, that it would be impracticable for them to attend personally to the details of the business, measures have been taken to create a distinct organization, for the purpose of carrying out these plans.

FOURTH.—*Dispensary Arrangements.* It having appeared from the report of our Visitors, that the present dispensary arrangements for supplying the sick poor with medical aid were insufficient, measures were adopted by the Association to provide additional resources of a temporary character. After some months' trial, the expenses exceeding the sum which the Association could readily spare for this object, it was discontinued, and the less unwillingly, as one of the dispensaries extended its facilities, so as in a measure to supply the deficiency in that section of our city most needing it.

To the Northern Dispensary great praise is due for its exertions to keep pace with the increase of population, by extending its action to Forty-second street, and establishing two new central dispensary offices, with a corresponding increase of physicians. Recognizing the principle, that those systems of charity are essentially defective which cannot be promptly made available in time of need, it has endeavored to place its provisions within the reach of all it is designed to benefit. The Eastern Dispensary is also, with commendable zeal, endeavoring to effect a like extension of its labors over the Eighteenth Ward, which, when accomplished, will meet the urgent demands that have arisen from the rapid increase of population, in that quarter of the city.

FIFTH.—*Commissioners of Emigration.* The vast influx of sick and destitute emigrants to this country from Europe the past year, filled our city with persons of this class to an extent which rendered some new legal provision necessary. The Legislature consequently appointed a Board of Commissioners, with power to enforce such regulations as the dictates of humanity and the public interest required, which have now been in operation more than six months. This Association, acknowledging a deep interest in whatever relates to the well-being of the poor, refer with gratification to this new action in their behalf, anticipating therefrom, under the able management of the intelligent and efficient Board of Commissioners, results far exceeding any that could be attained by the operations of the old system.

SIXTH. *Tracts.* Poverty being often produced and perpetuated by ignorance of thrift, want of forecast, and mismanagement of household affairs, the Board, believing that plain, popular tracts, treating of those matters, would be beneficial to the poor, have commenced the publication of a series, on economical subjects. Of the first, entitled the "Economist," 10,000 copies have been distributed by the Visitors, who have found it a valuable auxiliary in their labors, inasmuch as it prepared the way for imparting useful counsel, and deepened upon the minds of the poor, the salutary impression produced by faithful conversation. This tract is designed to be followed in due time by others on kindred subjects; and as improvement of condition necessarily succeeds the correction of economic derangements, useful results from this effort may reasonably be expected.

Among the labors of the year, the moral objects of the Association have held a very prominent place. Its best energies have been employed to elevate the character of the poor, while it has ministered to their physical necessities. This being the most difficult as it is the most important object of this scheme of benevolence, its indefatigable and self-denying almoners have addressed themselves to this philanthropic work, with an earnestness and zeal becoming its claims. Whilst they have given food to the famishing, clothing to the naked, and necessaries to the sick, they have endeavored to enlighten the ignorant, stimulate the inert, reclaim the vicious, and to impress upon all, men, women, and children, such a sense of their respective duties to themselves, to others, and to their Maker, as might lead them to self-support, to useful lives, and to the possession and practice of those religious principles which, above all other influences, tend to the elevation of character here, and to the felicities of an endless hereafter.

A Tabular Exhibit of the Monthly District Returns, from November 1st, 1846, to November 1st, 1847.

1846–7.	Number of Families Relieved.	Number of Persons.	Number of Visits.
November, . . .	857	2,890	1,052
December, . . .	2,031	6,970	3,172
January, ...	3,472	12,455	5,888
February, . . .	3,592	13,090	5,805
March, ...	2,919	10,859	4,716
April, ...	1,131	4,246	1,656
May, ...	732	2,668	964
June, ...	227	879	376
July, ...	73	288	102
August, ...	238	877	469
September, . . .	287	1,045	596
October, ...	354	1,251	634

In the above table, there are unavoidable repetitions, occasioned by the same families being sometimes relieved through different months. We therefore annex the following statements, which contain the actual aggregate relief, to wit:—

Number of different Families relieved from November 1st, 1846, to November 1st, 1847, . . 5,580
Number of Persons, ... 25,110
Number of Visits, ... 26,435
Amount of Receipts for the same period, . . $24,659 35
Amount of Expenditures, . . . 24,040 00

Excess of Receipts over Expenditures, . . 619 35

The most striking fact brought to view by the above statements, is the economy of this system, by which so large a number of the destitute have been materially aided, through the agency of the Visitors.

As the success of the Association is mainly attributable to the efficiency of the Advisory Committees and Visitors, to them the Board, in passing, would say: Yours is truly a great and noble employment. It is one in which, could angels covet, they might desire to share. The more humble, obscure, and inglorious your toils, the closer their resemblance to that highest pattern of excellence, who, identifying himself with the poor, came not to be ministered unto, but to minister. And is it not enough for the *disciple* to be as his *Master*, and the *servant* as his LORD? It is a small matter to be commended of man's judgment; but appreciating your patient and assiduous efforts to raise the fallen children of want and suffering to happiness and virtue, we bid you God-speed, and point you to the highest recompense and encouragement which await all who with right motives persevere in this self-denying service, "Inasmuch as ye have done it unto the least of these my brethren, ye have done it unto me."

In conclusion, they only add,—To the favor of a beneficent Providence, and to the friends of the poor, they again, with unwavering confidence, commit the interests of the Association, and the sacred cause it represents. It cannot be, at a time when our own cup is filled with blessings to overflowing, that the widow and the fatherless will be left to commune with want and wretchedness, unrelieved. If thou draw out thy soul to the hungry, and satisfy the afflicted soul, then shall thy light arise in obscurity, and thy sympathies and alms come up as a memorial before God. But he that hardeneth his heart, and shutteth his hand against his brother who is waxen poor, shall himself come to a morsel of bread.

Statement of the Receipts and Expenditures of the Association for Improving the Condition of the Poor, for the Year ending Nov. 1, 1847.

Dr.			Cr.		
1846–7. Receipts per Contributions, &c., from Nov. 1, 1846, to Nov. 3, 1847,	$24,659 35		1846–7. Disbursements from Nov. 1, 1846, to No. 3, 1847,	$24,040 00	
			Receipts over Expenditures,	619 35	
	$24,659 35			$24,659 35	

The undersigned, having examined the accounts of the Treasurer, Robert B. Minturn, Esq, and found vouchers for all the sums charged, hereby certify the same to be correct.

JOS. B. COLLINS, } *Auditing Committee.*
F. S. WINSTON,

NEW-YORK, November 3, 1847.

PRINTED FORMS USED BY THE ASSOCIATION.

Ticket of Reference for the Use of Members.

Mr.   Visitor,
  No.   St.
is requested to visit
at No.

                                    Member

N. Y. Association for
Improving the Condition of the Poor.

Visitor's Order.

Mr.
No.   St.
Please let
have the value of
in
               184
                                      Vis.

N. Y. Association for
Improving the Condition of the Poor.

Monthly Report.

Subjoined is a condensed plan of a Sectional Monthly Return. The original occupies a large page of foolscap, with appropriate columns, 15 in number, which enable Visitors to give the following particulars of every family relieved. 1st. Name, residence, place of birth, sex, color, occupation, time in the city, number in family, and number of visits. 2d. Statements of character,—as being temperate or intemperate. 3d. Unavoidable causes of indigence, such as sickness, infirmity, or old age, with space for marginal remarks.

PRINTED FORM USED BY THE ASSOCIATION.

New-York Association for Improving the Condition of the Poor.

VISITOR'S MONTHLY REPORT OF SECTION No.   DISTRICT NO.   DATED   184

☞ *A mark with a pen thus ,, in the columns, will point out the class to which the person named belongs.*

FAMILIES RELIEVED. Always give full Name, and *male* Head of Family, if living.	RESIDENCE OF FAMILIES. Which must be reported every month.	Foreigners.	Natives.	Colored Persons.	Males.	Females.	No. in Family.	No. of Visits.	KIND OF OCCUPATION.	Temperate.	Intemperate.	Sickness.	Misfortune.	Old Age.	AMOUNT EXPENDED. $	cts.	REMARKS.

Signed,   Visitor.

LIST OF MEMBERS.

Owing to inadvertence in the returns from some of the Districts, it is feared that the list of Members may not be perfectly accurate. The *amounts* received were duly credited, as may be seen by an inspection of the Treasurer's account, at the General Office. But as the names of some who contributed small sums did not accompany their donation, with all the efforts subsequently made to obtain them, the list may still be incomplete.

A.

Astor, John Jacob
Astor, Wm. B.
Anderson, Capt.
Arnold, W. V.
Amerman, J. W.
Angevine, L.
Archer, Moses
Alicotus, John M.
Alford, Edwin M.
Arnold, James
Alexander, Isaac
Aller, Joseph B.
Andrew, J. E.
Allison, H.
Achbold, Henry
Allen, Andrew
Allen, G. F.
Attrige, John
Avery, Stephen
Allen, William
Anderson, Wm.
Allison, J.
Andrews, J. B.
Aymar, William
Atwill, J. F.
A. N.
Averill, H. & W. J.
Avery, F.
Allen, Horatio
Adams, J.
Alley, Saul
Austen, John H.
Arnold, A.
Anthony, J. H.
A Friend, H. J.
A.
Abbott, Mr.
Ackerly & Briggs
Appleton, Daniel
Allen, Wm. C., Mrs.
Allen, Wm. M.
Auchmuty, Mrs.
A Lady
A. F.
Alsop, J. W.
Austin David
Aspinwall, J.
Ackerman, S. H.
Aspinwall, John

Allen, Stephen
Abbatt, J.
A Friend
Angel, J.
Aspinwall J. S.
A Friend, by Mrs. Scott through Jas. Boorman.
Aspinwall, J. L.
Aldis, Charles J.
A Lady
Aycrigg, B.
Auten, Mr.
A. B.
A Subscriber
Allen, W. C., Mrs.
Abbatt, Wm.
Ackerman, James
Anderson & Demarest
Aitkin, John
Alvane, U.
Adriance, James B.
Ayres
American Museum
Appleton, John A.
Aford, S. M.
Aikman, Robert
Ahrenfeldt, Charles
A. S. B.
A.
Atkinson, A. S.
Atwater, Wm.
Adriance, Thos. M.
Anderson, S. W.
Allen, Gilbert
Aimes, J. C.
Ackerly, R. C.
Arcularius, A. M.
Ackles
Andrews
Albertson, Mr.
Albro, Wm.
Andrews, Josiah B., M.D.
Abeel, John H.
Avery, John W.
A. T. H.
Allen, John
Anderson, C. V.
Ash James
Alexander, James, M. D.
Allen, Henry
Allen, Samuel

Alling, H. M.
Ackerman, John
Anderson, David
Archer, Mr.
Abbe, George W.
Arcularius, P. G.
Aikman, Hugh
Adams, J. T.
Allen, Mr.
Aldrich, H. D.
Abbe, G. W.
Atwood, C. S.
Arnfeldt, H.
Adams, C.
Aims, Peter
Allen, James, M. D.
Archer, William
Albro, R.
Armstrong, James

B.

Baush, Ann
Brown, James
Brown, Stewart
Bronson, F.
Bronson, F., as Executor
Burr, Wm. I.
Butler, C. E.
Bellows, C. N.
Brown, W. S.
Brown, S. J.
Bailey, W. A.
Belden, C. & G.
Baldwin, H.
Bradley, Wm. C.
Booth, Jonas
Bergen, James
Bell, Joseph M.
Baldwin, Luther
Belcher, Dr.
Brush, J. E.
Bedell Knapp
Backus, C.
Becker, Mr.
Bunker, J. D.
Brewster, J.
Barker Stephen
Barker, Joseph D.
Bruce, Robt. M.

LIST OF MEMBERS. (1847.

Bruce, John T.
Babbitt, Wm. H.
Belcher, Geo. E.
Barlow, Richard
Barker, N.
Brown, Wm. H.
Boardman, Wm.
Bennet, Wm.
Bishop, J.
Birdsall, H.
Brasted, John
Boice, James
Broad, John H.
Bartholomew, Susan
Bevan, Edward
Brooks, Rufus
Belkman, Abram
Burger, William
Brommer, Mr.
Bunker, P.
Briggs, J. H.
Bausher, Henry
Badger, Mrs.
Baker, E. S.
Balen, Peter
Burrall, H. & Co.
Betts, John
Bennet, Phineas
Bell, Mrs.
Baldwin, Charles A.
Barnett, S.
Boyle & Colman
Bishop, William
Bennett, N. L.
Bennett, John A.
Burke, Wm.
Boyd, Daniel
Bacon, F. S.
Boggs, Wm. G.
Brown, E. D.
Briggs, T. Alanson
Burr, G. W.
Briggs, John
Briggs, G. S.
Bettman, A. M.
Bates, J. Y.
Bremmer, Andrew
Baker, J. R.
Boyd, N. J.
Brush, Moses
Boyle, James
Barritt, John
Bassett, George
Bapp, John
Boyd & Paul
Byrd, Geo. J.
Benjamin, W. Jr. & Co.
Bowne & Co.
Blanco, B.
Booth & Edgar
Bechtel & Drayer
" B. & H."
Barrows J. R.
Brochelman, T. & T.
Baldwin & Starr
Brown & Dimoch
Brigham, D. & Co.

Bird, George
Brown, L. W.
Bourdine, Mr.
Beck, James & Co.
Butler, Frances
Brown, Thomas
Burchard, J.
Bonnett, Mrs.
Blukard, James
Brinckerhoff, J. S., Mrs.
Bethune, J., Mrs.
Bowden, A.
Brush, P.
Brown, P. H.
Banta, Wm.
Bell, Benjamin
Brown, Nathan
Barron, Thomas
Browning, Wm.
Brower, J. L.
Brooks, J.
Burrell, Samuel
Betment, A.
Burrett, J.
Biglen, D.
Bancroft, Mr.
Bosch, B.
Burke, M.
Burr, A. C.
Brewster, J.
Bouyee, Mr.
Bradbury, Mr.
Belden, Rev. Mr.
Balte, H. S.
Beach, M. S.
Bunting, C. T.
Boyd, A. P.
Barry, J. T.
Brower, A.
Baltzer, F. A.
Banks, R.
Bailey, Mrs.
Brown, E. J. & Co.
Butler, B. F.
Bonnett, Peter A.
Beals, H. C.
Brown, Paul S.
Breath, J.
Barrow, Wm. J.
Beebe, A. P.
Bagley, Wm.
Boils, E. S.
Brownell, J. S.
Baldwin, D. T.
Bell, Thomas
Barnes, Daniel
Bervier, John H.
Burdett, Mr.
Briggs, George
Broadhead, E.
Bennett, M. A.
Bingham, J. C., Rev.
B.
Bebell, David
Brush, R. P.
Beebe, Philo
Babb, Mr.

Barton, J. G.
Barton, Wm. B.
Buloid, R. W.
Baddy, G.
Broon
Barker, J. W.
Brooks, S. & T.
Bennet
Brennen, M. D.
Banks, Mr.
Buckley, J. L.
Bruce, John M.
Brooks, George
Bowie, John H.
Boyle, H. P.
Bitter, Henry
Bryson, David, Jr.
Bennett, Mr.
Bruce, George
Ballagh, W. & R.
Browning, W.
Beams, J.
Buloid, R.
Barker, Luke
Bleeker, Jane, Mrs.
Baker
Banks, Wm.
Bunn, Mrs.
B & Mellvin
Bosworth, J. S.
Branch. Wm. L.
Billings, D. & E.
Bache, Geo. P.
Burdick, Perrin
Bride, D. K.
Barmer, W. H.
Bennen, Owen
Blythe, Robert
Bacon, D. R.
Bell, Joseph M.
Bloodgood, Wm.
Benedict, E. C.
Benedict, C. S.
Bleecker, G. N.
Bartow, Samuel
Bulkley, George
Bulkley, E.
Bruce, J. M.
Baker, Dobell
Bacon, J. E.
Brown, Charles P.
Bonsall, R. W. S.
Bayles
Buckmaster, T. O.
Burnton, J. T.
Brown, W. H.
Baxter, J. C.
Blauvelt, D. S.
Bronsan, Mrs.
Bull, Susan, Mrs.
Bogert, R.
Brady, N. C.
Brackett, Mr.
Banks, Mrs.
Blondel, Wm.
Berry, S. J.
Benson, A. N.

1847.)   LIST OF MEMBERS.   33

Blackall, Mr.
Brinkerhoff
Brown, Geo. B.
Burdge, John W.
Biggs, J. A.
Burr, H. Mrs.
Bansen
Brower, John
Brittan, Mr.
Burdsall, Mr.
Brackett, Mr.
Bloodgood, M.
Baley, Mrs.
Bloomfield, Wm.
Brown, L. W., Jr.
Belden, Wm., Jr.
Batta, Mr.
Baird, F.
Brinkerhoff, Walter
Bartow, Edgar J.
Bishop, T.
Burgess & Stringer.
Blunt & Syms
Brooklyn White-Lead Co.
Beers, Mr.
Bennet. Mr.
Bowman, S. S.
Boyd, J. S., M. D.
Brewer, Wm.
Bartholomew
Boker, H.
Briggs, George.
Baur, T. N.
Brack, E.
Banderett
Bache, G.
Bon, Las.
Bostwick, F.
Bidwell
Berrian, W. D.
Browne, Richard H.
Betts, T. R.
Barnes George
Baird, Rev. Robert
Barry, Mrs.
Badeau, P.
Boorman, R.
Burnham, E., Mrs.
Bigelow, Richard
Brush, Joshua
Butler, Charles
Bradley, J. N.
Budd, Joseph
Burck, Wm. J.
Barrell, George
Blatchford, E. H.
Booth, D. A.
Burrows, P.
Blackett, J.
Blackett, Wm.
Blois, Samuel, M. D.
Bolles, R. M., M. D.
Bache, Ann E., Mrs.
Brown, Robert W.
Bunn, C.
Brown, J. F.
Buchanan, R. S.

Buckland, Alex.
Bond, W. S.
Buchanan, H. P.
Bridge, John
Bell, A.
Baldwin, John C.
Bartlett, Edwin
Benson, Arthur
Barber, James
Banger, Miss
Bagley Wm. A.
Brown, Silas
Ball, Tompkins, & Co.
Brush, Mr.
Bartlett, A.
Bradford, W. H.
Brown, J. A.
Beers, Mr.
Butler, B. F.·
Boorman. James
Brown, E. M.
Boden
Benjamin, F. A.
Bond, Mr.
Blunt, George W.
Bell. H. K.
Beebe, Miss
Bostwick, Mrs.
Brown, T. S.
Bedell, G. T., Rev.
Brush, Mr.
Bailey, J.
Babcock, F. M.
Banger, Mrs.
Burr, Isaac, Mrs.
Bull, J. H.
Brown, W. S.
Brown, W. S., Mrs.
Bruen, A. M.
Brower
B. D.
Brumley, R.
Bromass, Mr.
Bartlett, Edwin.
Buckhalter, C.
Brewster, J. B.
Born, J.
Bussell, Mr.
Beekman, J. W.
Boyce, Gerardus
Berrian, J. H.
Beales, J C.
Burritt, W.
Blackstone, W.
Barker, J. S.
Belknap, E. S.
Bradley, J.
Bucknam, Ezra
Brooks, D. H.
Briant, D. S.
Brown, Ira
Brenner, J. P.
Broad, S. S.
Bird, Matthew
Babcock, Paul
Burkhalter, Stephen
Buxton, John

Burras, T. H.
Bridges, J. F.
Ballagh, Wm.
Burdge, Ira
Barbour, James G.
Blucker, Edward
Bell, Joseph M.
Barker, Joseph D.
Bradley, Wm. C.
Bennet, William
Bulen, John H.
Brown, Thomas
Blackledge, Adam
Barlow, Samuel B., M. D.
Benedict, H. S., M. D.
Bonnell, Stephen

C.

Caughey, John
Charlton, John
Chataway, Samuel
Crosby, Wm. B.
Chauncy, Henry
Cox, J. & P.
Cahill, Mr.
Crary, E. C.
Chamberlain, Wm.
Cotheal & Co., H. D.
Cummings, T. P.
Conant, F. J.
Candee & Scribner
Carpenter, W.
Campbell, D. P.
Carfrac & Blood
Collamore, Mr.
Colby, Lewis, Rev.
Clark, J. L.
Clark, John
C. F. L.
Congdon, George
Clark, Alexander
Covert, G. H.
Colton, Mrs.
Callis, T.
Chichester, Asa
Crawford & Cutter
Cooper, J.
Cooper, T.
Cheesbrough, Mrs
Castree, Mr.
C B. S.
Covel, L.
Cooper, Benj. F.
Craft, W. S.
Cammann, O. S.
Couch, Wm.
Cambreling, Stephen
Catlin, D. W.
Clark, E. S.
Cox, A. B.
Cowling, Henry G.
Coursen, Mrs.
Collins, D. C.
Clark, James A.
Crump, F. R.
Clinch, James
Corwin, Thomas J.

2*

LIST OF MEMBERS. (1847.

Cantrell, S.
Cronklute, J. P.
Cox, Dr.
Cary, W. F.
Coles, J.
Cooper, Peter
Cushman, D. A.
Crosby, J. B.
Carr, A. S.
Caswel & Co., John
Clark, Edwin
Collins, Joseph B.
Christmas offering, from young lady
Cumming, T. B.
Carey & Co.
Crane, D. B.
Concklin Jonas
Communion fund St. Mark's Church, by the Rev. H. Anthon
C. A. L., Mrs.
C. & T.
Chester, W. W.
Cook, Z.
Carrow, Isaac
Conover, G. S.
Cockroft, D. W., M. D.,
Cook, James B.
Cash
Cape, Mrs.
Clendenen, P.
Cockburn, Elizabeth
Cockroft, James
Clarkson, C. V.
Colton, C.
Camp, Mrs.
Cox, Mrs.
Coe, D. B., Rev.
Cook, E.
Cole, Rhodus
Church, F.
Crosby, A. S.
Cromwell, Daniel
Cromwell, Edward
Cromwell, J. D., Mrs.
Chegary, H. D., Madam
Carter, L.
Curtis, Charles
Cornell, J F., M. D.
Chambers, William
Clark, J. B.
Corlis, Edward
Cummings, Wm.
Crane, Mr.
Caruck, Robert
Currahger, John
Craft, Andrew
Coster, Mrs.
Crooker, John
Colt, A. H.
Cain, Peter
Crooker, Wm.
Craig, Mrs.
Cook, James H.
Clark, S.
Chambers, J. L.

Cornell, Joseph
Cook, M. L.
Cation, W. D.
Conger, John
Clark, James
Chichester, L.
Clark, Ira A.
Cornings
Cronin, John R.
Cottenett & Co., F.
Clark, W.
Carey, Samuel F.
Cogswell, Crane & Co.
Curtis, D. Jr.,
Comstock, D. A.
Cochran, Samuel
Cropsey, James
Cook, John
Coffin, Mr.
Colden, Mrs.
Charraud, J. J.
Camman, G. P.
Carmer, C. W.
Coit, Henry
Copcutt, J.
Cook, Edward,
Castre, John
Contoit, Mr.
Carter, Robert
C.
C. H.
Cooper, P.
Callender, Miss
Carter, Joseph, Rev.
Coster, John G. Mrs.
Coster, W. T.
Curtis, P. A.
Chalmers, James
Cook
Connah, John
Campbell, James
Clark, M.
Cornell, F. F.
Carpenter, George
Collamore, D.
Collins, G. C.
Curtis, L.
Curtis, Joseph
Clark, Miss
Cooper, F. N.
Connor, Noah
Couenhoven, M., Mrs.
Canfield, D. W.
Cornell & Ammerman
Cornell, J. H.
Capan, E. A.
Church, Wm.
Crane, A. S.
Conger, John, M. D.
Chesterman, J.
Center, A. H.
Cludius, Charles
Craighead, R.
Cummings, Dodge, & Co.
C. F. W.
Comstock, U
Crips, B. & Co.

C. S.
C. W. V.
Crump
Clark
Coggswell, George
Chandler, Mrs.
Chauncy, Wm.
Cornell, Elijah
Cheavis, Geo. B.
Collord, Mrs.
Carter, J. M.
Codwise, D.
Conoly, Charles M.
Cotheal, Henry L.
Cahoon, B. J.
Conover, G. A.
Carron, Michael M., Rev.
Cummings, Thomas P.
Clinch, C. P.
Chamberlain, E.
Curtis, S.
Carlin, Mrs.
Cox, C. B.
Crocker, Wm. H.
Cook, Mr.
Clover
Caggill
Christie, P.
Cooper, W.
Cummings, A.
Chapman, E.
Carlin, J.
Coutant, E. H.
Cromwell, Edward
Craft, John
Cowperthwait, J. K.
Church, Charles M.
Christopher, Richard
Carl, John
Clark, H.
Caldwell, E.
Crane, Mr.
Chadavoyne, W. & T. C.
Cooledge, Geo. F. & Co.
Curier, N.
Canton Tea Company.
Childs, C. C.
Childs, W. L.
Chamberlin, C.
Columbian Foundry
Cortelyea, Peter C.
Carland
Cassebeer, J.
Conover, Stephen
Coutant, J. A.
Chalmers, Wm.
Curtis, Geo. B.
Chrysty, Thomas
Cole, R.
Conway, Mrs.
Cooper, John
Carns, D.
Clark, George
Cowl, James
Curry, D. F.
Connor, James E.
Constant, Samuel S.

1847.) LIST OF MEMBERS. **35**

Caldwell, Mr.
Cochran, Mr.
Connell, John
Crawford, George
Cruikshank, James
Crum, John A.
Cobb, G. T.
Crocker, Leonard
Cutter, Stephen
Crane, A. G.
Campbell, John
Cock, Thomas, M. D.
Chichester, Lewis
Chamberlain, Charles
Clapp, John
Camp, B. F.
Colton, F.
Churchman, O.
Corwin, E. R.
Cass, John C.
Cook, Wm. B.
Chichester, Ed. L.
Cutter, S.
Clark. D. S.
Carter, Robert
Curtis, Cyrus
Cobb, George T.
Clannon, Simon
Camp, Amzi
Cameron, John
Carter, J.
Crane, David
Cragin, Geo. D.
Clarkson, Cornelius V., M. D.
Cushman, Allerton
Camron, John
Cornwell, Jeremiah
Clement, A. D., M. D.
Chapin, G. S.
Coleman, D.
Comb, William
Cowl, James
Cummings, Thomas
Cummings, John
Cyphors, H.
Chamberlain, J. F.

D.

Dibble, Jonathan
Doolittle. L. F.
Day, John
Duncan, John
Dalrymple, Mr.
D.
Dows & Cary
Douglas, A.
Deveau, John A.
Dunham, Francis
Delong, L.
Day, Mary
Donnelly, N. S.
Durbrow, J.
Dittenhœffer, Isaac
Dunn, Mrs.
Davis, S. A.
Duryea, G. W.
Dickson, James

Duffy, E.
Duffy, Patrick
Dornin, William
Dornin, Oscar
Duke, W. S.
Dewey, James
Duryea, Mrs.
Duncan, Georgiana, Mrs.
Duncan, Francis
Dimm, H.
Downs, William
Dunlap, E. B.
Dowe, John J.
Doty, Charles
Dunham, H. R.
Dryden, George
Donington, Ogden
Delafield, R. K.
Dibble & Richardson
Dennistown & Disbrow
Dixon, C. P.
Donaldson, James
Dodge, W. E.
Deveau, John
Delafield, Joseph
Dale, Thomas N.
Devoe, John
Doneghen, M.
Delprat, Mr.
Dunn, Mr.
Doolittle, Dr.
Du Bois, Wm.
Dolan, Thomas
Diefenthaler, V.
Dunson, Mr.
Deming, B.
Driggs, Chester
Durand, A. B.
Douglass, J. H.
Downer, Eliza, Mrs.
Dashwood, Emma, Mrs.
Dean, Henry
Dustan, Mr.
Drysdale, Mrs.
Douglass, H.
Darby, Geo. F.
Davy, James S.
Dowley, John
De Forrest, B. & Co.
Depeyster, Susan M. C.
De Forrest, Lockwood
Demerest, Mrs.
Devin, Richard
Delefield, Rufus
Delafield, E.
Dean, Thomas
Douglass, George
Denniston, Wood, & Co.
Davis, D. H.
Douglass, W.
Denney, T.
Delano, F. H.
Delano, Warren, Jr.
De Peyster, F.
Dutilth, E.
Dutilth & Cousinary
De Forrest, A. W. & Co.

Dando, Stephen
Day, Mr.
De Ruyter, John
Davis, John F.
Duncan, James
Deberuan, L.
Davison, James
Desseir, J.
Dickie, P.
Dillinger, C.
Daniels, C. F.
Dugan, Thomas,
Drinker, W. W.
Demerest, Mr.
Door, S., Mrs.
Dyer, Thomas
Delluc & Co.
Dyckman, W. N.
Drucker, Mrs.
Dickie, Edward P.
Dodworth, T.
De Veaux, Frederick
Duryea, Jacob
Dunshee, Samuel
Dawson, Mrs.
Driggs, Dr.
Davis, J. M. & James
De Rosset & Brown
Drummond, J. P.
Dunn & Co., S. H.
Dubois, Francis, & Co.
Delenhaus, A.
Del Vechio
Dubois, E.
Dejonze, L.
Deitz, Brothers, & Co.
Dummer & Lyman
Draper & Richards
Donnelly, T.
Dickinson, R. W., Rev.
Dodge, Mrs.
De Forrest, L.
Dickerson, J. S.
Dewey, S. P.
Darrogh, John
Dixon, H. U.
Dill, James
Dana, Mrs.
Denta, E.
Day, Thomas
Dellyon, W. F.
Demarest, W. J.
De Klyne, Wm.
Day, Mahlon
Derby, Richard, of Boston
Durell, J. G.
Deguire, Joseph
De Forest, L.
Depyster & Friend
De Worken, E. V.
Doughty, E.
Douglass, Earl
Dunnel, Patrick
Davis, Evan
Denham, J.
Devoe, H. F.
Diacon, A.

LIST OF MEMBERS. (1847.

Dunn, Hugh S.
Davis, R. E.
Door, Henry
Demarest
Degraw, Mrs.
Dubois, J. B,
Denman, A. A.
Davidson, John H.
Dainty, J.
Dexter, A.
Dyer, Charles C.
Deveau, Mr.
Decker, A.
Dominick, J. W.
Dominick, J. W., Jr.
Dodge, S. N.
Degrove, Quincy, C.
Doig, Peter
Dickinson, J. B.
Door, J. O.
Davis, Thomas
Dyer, Charles C.
Dakin. C. P.
Dwight, W. W., M. D.
Demorest, W. J.
Demarest, W. R.
Deems, Henry W.
Downs, Smith
Dean, Thomas
Dayton, James L.
Darling, Charles C.
Day, Charles J.
Dusenberry, Wm.
Duff, J. T.

E.
Earle, Edward, M. D.
Eversley, Charles
Earle, S. W.
Ely & Harrison
Eno, Amos R.
Edgar, W. A.
Everets, Wm. M.
Earle, Morris
Edmonds, F. W.
Eveleth, Mrs.
Egbert, James
Ewen, Daniel
E. B.
Eastwood, James
E. L.
Ely, George
Evans, Mr.
Edgar, James E.
Earl, M.
Elderd, H.
Everson, Henry
Edgar, D. M.
Eigenbrodt
E. A. R., by L. P. Stone
Egliston, Thomas
Engles, S. S.
Elliott, H. H.
Elsworth, H.
Earle, Thomas
Eastman, O.
Earle, R. W.

Earle, Mrs.
Effray, Felix
Eaton, John A.
Eagle, Henry, Jr.
Eggert, D., & Son
Everdell, Wm.
E. W. M. S..
Elliot
Easton, Charles
Ensign, E. H.
E. W. H.
Earle, Abraham L.
Evans, Thomas
Eating House
Everdell, James
Everett, N. C.
Engle, Samuel S.
Erskine, John
Endicott, John
Ensign, Timothy
Eastman, S. J.
Elder, George
Evans, Lemuel G.
Eldridge, N. T.
Endicott, John

F.
Ford, Mr.
Fredricks, Mrs.
Faile, Thomas H.
Fellows, Louis S., & Schell
Fellows, James
Frost, Samuel
Frost, James
Fellows, Richard S.
Folger, B. H.
Fraser & Everitt
Fischell, T. S. & Vonstrade
F. & L.
Fellows, W. W.
F. E. B.
F. B.
Frankamp
Frosse, Henry K.
Forward, Oliver
Farrand, Joseph
Frye, J.
Fitch, G. S.
Freeman, C.
Fowler, Charles
Frazee, Abraham
Forbes, J. M.
Fox, Charles
Falkner, J. C., Jr.
Fenn, G.
Foster, A. S.
Foster, J. W.
Falkner, J. C., Senior
Fardon, A.
Francis, C.
Frost, Mrs.
Fallon, Mr.
Forbes, Mrs.
Foot, C.
Farquhar, James
Farrell, John
Finley, Daniel F.

Flanagan, W B.
Fardon, Abraham, Jr.
Forrest, William
Fowler, J. W.
Friends
Freeman, E. R.
Franklin, M.
Florentine, Abraham
Fancher. E. L.
Field, Edward
Forrest, William
Field, Edward, M. D.
Ferris, J. S.
French, Daniel
Foster, Wm. A.
Fessenden, Thomas
Fraser, E. A.
Ford, Isaac
Fowler, J. V. D. B.
Finch, Myron
Forrester, James
Finch, Ferris
Fisk, Samuel
Ferris, L. C.
Foster, T. V.
Foster, William
Forbs, H. M., Mrs.
Flint, S. S.
Fisher, Richard
Farmer, Edgar
Fearing & Hall
F. & Co.
Franklin, Richard L.
Freeman, Alfred, M. D.
Fisher, J. J.
Fancher, D.
Follet, Jacob
Field, Jude
Frech, Jacob
Ferris, John H.
Falconer, John
Fraser, E. A.
Field, J.
Fabre, L.
Fowler, S. T.
Ford, J.
Fanning T.
Furnold, F. P.
Fink, Mrs.
Freeman, Wm.
Folger, Robert B.
Fletcher, James
Finch, Ferris
Field, D.
Fisk, Samuel
Fisk, Mrs.
Fowler, D. S.
Flood, Patrick
Franklin, Henry
Farrel, John
Field, H. W.
Fox, George S.
Fasten, James
Frey, Jacob
Flandrau, Mr.
Fisher, T. J.
Ferguson, J.

1847.) LIST OF MEMBERS. 37

Fray, J. M.
Fendall, John L.
Finn, A. T.
Frazer, William
Folke, J., Jr.
Francis, Dr.
Fellows, J. P.
Fuller, Wilson
Foster, James
Fox & Livingston
Field, Edward
Foster, J., Jun.
Felton, D. B.
Furguson, M.
Ferguson, John
Few, Mrs.
Ford, James
Fisher, George H.
Fonda, A. P.
Foster, George
Farnsworth, Joseph
Fuller, C. A.
Fraser, G. W.

G.

Griswold, George
Green, John C.
Given, M. A.
Gilchrist, J. T.
Gums, J. D.
Goodrich, E. B.
Goodsman, Mrs.
Goodwin, Mr.
Germond, Wellington
Galvan, Daniel
Grimes, John
Gruver, J. C.
Grumbes, Mrs.
Gould, Thomas C.
Glover, A. B.
Gilley, Messrs.
Gardner, H.
Gooderson, Frederick
Gray, Niel
Gardiner, H. M.
Glover, James M.
Goldsmith, Mrs.
Gage, Wm. C.
Goll, John J.
Goff, D.
Godfrey, Edward J.
Griscom, John H., M. D.
Goodhue, Jonathan
Grant & Barton
Guerber, A.
Graubner, Ferdinand
Gibhard, Frederick C.
Goddard, J. W.
Gross & March
Guest, Wm. A.
Gerardin, Mr.
Green, Dr.
Gilmore, J. & J.
Grosvenor, Seth
Gibson, Joseph H.
Ginochio, Jno. B.
Gurnee, Benjamin

Gubrauer, Wm.
Giles, J. H.
Goadby, Thomas
Groesbeck, Nicholas
Gilmore, John
Gibson, George
Gates, T.
Gabaudan, A. W.
Gallatin, Albert
Gelston, M.
G. A.
Gardiner, Mrs.
Green, Horace.
Gray, F.
Gilsuite, R. V.
Gilston, Mr.
Glover, R. Ogden
Graves, E. Boonen
Glover, S.
Green, the Misses
Grosvenor, Jasper
Gilpen, T. S.
Goddard, G. C.
Griswold, John
Green, W. C.
Getty, R. P.
Griffin, George
Green
Grand Jury, Court of Sessions
Gray, J. A. C.
Gillen, Isaac
Graham, John A.
Gregory & Co., W. G.
Geissenheimer, F. W.
Gilroy, George
Greenman, J. B.
Gardner, Thomas
Geer, Darius
Girard, H. A.
Galley, Mrs.
Gatty, G.
Graves, E. Boonen, Mrs.
Goodwin, Eli
Grinnell, Moses H.
Gans, M.
G. F. J.
Gordon & Talbot
Gilbert, C.
Griffin, Thomas
G. H. K. & Co.
Goublemon, R.
Gumand, Emily
Gale, Wm.
Germond, G. C.
Graydon, Samuel
Gibson, James R.
Getty, Robert P.
Gunn, A. N., Dr.
Groshon, John
Green, James
Gunther, Christopher G.
Gillett, Ann, Mrs.
Gillman, Nathaniel, Jun.
Gratacap, G. R.
Gratacap

Geiry
Gemmel, James, Jun.
Gurley, R.
Groning, Thomas
George, C. L.
Gottesberger, George
Gray, John
Gregory, John
Griffin, Herman
Gerry, T. A.
Griffin, Solomon
Gillett, Mrs.
Giffin, Edmund
Griffin, James
Gordon, George
Gates, John
Greenhough, J. J.
Gray, Nathaniel
Gantz, John J.
Goodliff, James
Griffin, H.
Gibson, James R.
Gilchrist, J. F.

H.

Howland, S. S.
Howland, G. G.
Hamilton, J. C.
Hummel, H. E.
Hardenburgh, James B
Hunter, A. T.
Hamilton, A., Miss
Hodges, Dr., Mrs.
Hall, A. D.
Haight, G.
Hyatt, Mr.
Hill, John
Huxthall, B.
Holdridge, Wm.
Hays, H. M.
Herring, S. C.
Hutton, B. H.
Halsted & Dash
Hansher & Unkart
Horne & Buchard
Hoadly & Phelps
Hecksher, Mr.
Hatfield & Bertinie
Harbeck, J. H.
Harper, John
Harrison, A., Miss
Harris, J. C.
Hatfield, Amos F.
Hutchinson, Dr.
Hull, Wakeman
Hedden, John
Hicks, John
Hoyt, A.
Hackler, John
Horton, Wm.
Harris, R.
Hoyt, J. M., & Son
Hall, Wm., and J. T.
Holmes, Samuel P.
Halsted, Schureman
Hillman, W.
Horn, James

LIST OF MEMBERS. (1847.

Hutchinson, S.
Hoag, G. B.
Hurton, John H.
Healey, E.
Hepburn, Mrs.
Hadley, John S.
Haley, Thomas
Hickock, & Co.
Hunn, John
Hunt, A. Mrs.
Houghton, T. L.
Huff, Mrs.
Hoey, John
Huested, T. S.
Hoffman, Mr.
Holston, John
Hawkins, Elkanah
Hutchins, J.
Hutchinson, B.
Hughs, Wm.
Haight, Samuel
Holmes, A. B.
Hugh, Mr.
Harger, J.
Hartshorne, Mr.
Hoyt, G. P. B.
Howes, T. A.
Hitchcock, Edward
Huddard, Rev. Dr.
Huntington, F. A.
Hine, James
Heusted, M.
Hoyt, J. B. & W.
Havemeyer, Geo. L.
Howe, John W.
Hunt, W. S.
Holly, Alexander
Husband, Dr.
Heisser, Jacob
Hays, Samuel
Halley, Robert
Horsfield, Dr.
Hindman, Mr.
Hoey, John
Hartley, Robert M.
Herder, N. D.
Hoyt, G. P. B.
Howe, Benjamin F.
Hawley, Irad
Hoe, R. & R.
Haydock, H. W.
Hewlett, O. T.
Hilleburgh, Charles
Hanford, P.
Holt, H.
Hancock, J.
Holmes, Madison
Hunt, T.
Hawkhurst
Hoyt, E. A.
Hidden, E.
Hallock, Lewis, M. D.
Hurlbutt, H. A.
Henderson, Alexander J.
Hall, Ralph
Hatt, George Rev.
Horton, Jonathan B.

Harris, W. D.
Hurd, Hiram
Holly, J. M.
Hunt, Harvey
Herder, Nicholas D.
Hunt, D. B.
Herring, John B.
Horn, James
Hogan, Thomas
Howout, Simon
Hutchings, John
Howe, Bezaleel
Howe, J. M.
Howe, B. F.
Hopper, Josiah, M. D.
Holt, Alexander S.
Heydon, William
House, David
Horton, Richard
Humbert, W. B.
Hill, George J.
Hardcastle, L. B.
Hows, A. B.
Hitchcock, W. R.
Holbrook, E.
Harsen, Jacob
H. B.
Hobby, E. B.
Hayes, H. M.
Hobert, Mrs.
Heiser, Mr.
Hadley, R.
Harman, P.
Hand, George
Hinds, Mr.
Howell, G. R.
Hiler, Selah
Hicks, J. J.
Hauptman, A. B.
Hook, C. G.
Haws, J. C., Jun.
Hoffman, L. M.
Hoppock, Ely
Hendricks & Brothers
Howe, C. W.
Haight, D. L.
Haight, D. H.
Hutton, M S.
Hawkins, J. S.
Hunt, Edwin
Hogan, R.
Holmes, S.
Holmes, L. R.
Houghton, R.
Harison, C. J.
Hargous, L. C.
Hargous, P. A.
Hyer, E. P.
Hadden, David
Hale & Hallock
Harsen, M. E., Miss
Harsen, J.
Hammersly, J. W.
Hitchcock, Mrs.
Hall
Harrison, the Misses
Herring, J. B.

Henery, E.
Haggerty, John
Haggerty, W. C.
Hone, John, Jun.
Herran, Lees, & Co.
Halsted, Wm. M.
Hoffman, Martin
Harris, J. W.
Hamilton, Wm.
Havemeyer, W. F.
Hyde, Joseph
Harris, Dennis
Hall, James F.
Houston, J. C.
Havemeyer, C. H.
Hearn, Brothers
Hutchins, G. H.
Haughurst, C. V.
Hutchings, E. N.
Henry, Robert
Hallock, James C.
Hutchinson, Ira
Hall, Thomas
Hevemeyer, Wm.
Halstede, J. W.
Halsey, E. C.
Hazelton, F.
Harrison, J.
Hays, John
Hagadorn, Wm.
Harris, D., Mrs.
Heskner, Henry
Henry, Wm. G.
Hart, G. H.
Herbert, J.
Huntington, R. G.
Huddarts, R. T., Rev.
Hall, Valentine G.
Hayden, N.
Hunter, James
Hastman, Sons, & Dracke.
H. S. L.
Henry, John, & Co.
Hewlett, James
Hayden, P. & T.
Halstead, Benjamin
Hague, John
H. & Co. Wm.
Hoyt, S.
H. H. S.
Hewlett, Wm. S.
Hibbard, Rufus F.
Holt, C., Jun.
Hampton, A.
Heitkemp, Carle
Henricks, M.
Hunt, Wilson G.
Howland, John H.
Hopkins, R. H.
Heath, L. C.
Howe, F. W.
Halsted, A. L.
Hubbs & Clark
Hertell, Thomas
Henshelwood, R.
Hall, Herbert
Howes, M.

LIST OF MEMBERS.

Hubble, G. R.
Hart, James
Haxton, A. B.
Hegenon, P. A.
Hustice, Mrs.
Howell, Mrs.
Henry, John
Hill, Mrs.
Holleysmith, S.
Heyer, Jane M., Mrs.
Hosack, N. B.
Hosack, A. E.
Howell, Charles J.
Hogg & Delamater
Hubbard, Archibald
Holmes, Eldad
Hall, A.
Hall, H.
Hall, Wm.
Hall, D. K.
Harper, James
Harper, John
Hull, John C.
Hull, Wager
Hart, H. A. N.
Holt
Harding, Richard
Harding, Catherine
Hall, Archibald
Hicks, C. C.
Hamersly, the Misses

J.

Johnston, John
Jones, Miss
Ingolsby, Felix
Jones, D. S.
Johnson, L. L.
J. F.
Judson, D.
Jaffray, J. R., & Sons
Jones, Walter, Jun.
Johnson, Henry W.
Johz, C.
Jesup, Frederic S.
Jones
Johnes, Otis, & Co.
J.·H. H. H.
Jennings, G. W.
Jones, J.
Jewel, Leander
Jones, D.
Jenkins, R.
Jarvis, Dr.
Jessup, Samuel
Jacobs, John
Johnson, Joseph
Ireland, George
Jones, William
Josephi, H.
Jones, Henry
Ingersol, Chandler
J. N. K.
J. H. S.
J. V. N.
Jackson, Mrs.
Johnson, W.

Jarvis, Z.
Jones, Morris
Jayne, Mr.
Inwright, Mr.
Jenkins, Hannah
Jones, George
Jones, Colford, Mrs.
Jones, E. S.
Jervis, John B.
Irving, John T.
Jephson, Wm. H.
Jones, L.
Irvin, Richard
Judd, Samuel
Jay, Ann, Miss
Jarvis, Mrs.
Jay, Elizabeth Clarkson
Jay, Susan Matilda
Irving, P. M.
Irving, Richard
Jones, J. J.
Jones, S. S.
Ireland, W. B.
Irving, P. P., Rev.
Irvin, Judge, Mrs.
Jacobus, David
Jones, A. S.
Immen, John H.
Jacobus, C.
Jenkins, Warren
Johnson, H. F.
Jones, W. B.
Johnson, A.
Jones, John
Jones, W. T., Mrs.
Ingraham, S. R.
Jordo), Mrs.
J. S.
J. D. W.
J. Sd.
Johnson, H.
J. D. P.
J. R. & Co.
Jordon, David C.
Jubin, Charles
J. J. B.
Ivison, H.
Jaffrevs, Wm.
Jillet, A. J.
Ironsides
Josslin
Janes, Edmund S., Rt. Rev.
Jones, Bindfall, & Rowland
Johnson, John
Jackson, George A.
Janeway, J. J.
Janeway, George
James, Mr.
J. K.
Johnston, R. R.
Johnson, Wm.
Jacques, Eden
Ivins, J.
Johnson, Wm. M.
Jackson, Wm., Mrs.
Johnson, Stephen
Jones, Alfred

Irwin, Mr.
Judah, Charles D.
Joy, J. F.
Jackson, Luther
Johnston, A.
Jones, W. P.
Jenkins, T. W
Jennings, J. E.
·Inslee, Z. C.
Jennings, N. T.
Jenkins, Warren
Johnston, William
Jones, John
Jacobs, Laban

K.

Kennedy, D. S.
Kirby, Leonard
Keese, John M.
Kenney & Sampson
King, Mrs.
Kelly, Wm.
Keyser, Mr.
Ketchum, Edward
Ketchum, Philip
Kreps, Henry
Kelly, James
Kahn, Isaac
Kelly, Malachi
Kennedy, Thomas
Ketchum, J. R.
Kipp, F. A.
Knipe, Wm.
King, Wm. R.
Kirk, Robert
Knapp, James S.
Keese, Theodore
Ketcham, Rogers, & Bement
Ketcham, Morris
Ketcham and Perry
Knouse, Charles
Kelsey, John
King, Charles
Keys, John
Kenan, Mrs.
Kennedy, Duncan
Kinsley, H., Dr.
King, James G.
Knapp, Shepherd
Kelly, Robert
Kane, M.
Kane, J. J.
Kipp, Leonard W.
Kiersted, H. T.
Knapp, P. B.
Kennedy, Wm.
Keyser, W. H.
Kidder
Kipp, B. Livingston
Keer, John
Kissam, T. T.
Kipling
Kimball
Keese, John D.
King, Mr.
K. L. R.
King, C. W., Mrs.

Kelly, Hugh,
Kingsland
Kingsland, Mrs.
King, R.
Kirby, V.
Kerrigan, James
Kerkman, John
Kensett, Thomas
Kenedy, T.
Kurtze, T.
Kobbe, Wm.
King, Wm.
Kirnie, Asa
Krowl, James
Kay & Barden
Keeler, D. B.
Kellogg, J. W
Kelly, Joel

L.

Lenox, James
Leroy, J.
Livingston, Mortimer
Long & Davenport
L. H. S.
L. T. D.
Latham, E.
Lowrey, J. & A.
Leeds, Samuel
Loewig & Sheneider
Lowndes, Thomas
Leonard, Hone, & Nicoll
Langley, W. C., & Co.
Loss, Daniel L.
Lewis, Thomas
Linsley, Mrs.
Lewis, H. H.
Lewis, Wm.
Ludlum, John
Latham, J. S.
Losee, Jeffree
Lickstenstan, S.
Laton, Robert
Lamb, B. S.
Lewis, James
Lavoe, J. G.
Lane, N.
Ludlum, T. B.
Laurence, Wm.
Lockwood, Mr.
Lawrence, Rodrick
Laight Street, 28
Lawrence, A.
Lagrave, J. J.
Lagrave, A. F.
Lord, R. L.
Lydig, P. M.
Lekack, A.
Laey, B.
Lynch, Mr.
Lathrop, Edward
Lyons, J. S. Rev.
Leger, Dr.
Littell, John
Littell, Andrew
Lockwood, Roe
Lawrence, Joseph

Low, Cornelius
La Farge, John
Laight, Wm. E.
Lawrence, Thomas
Lowndes, Rawlins
Lee, John H.
Ludlow, Mrs.
Lynch, Mrs.
Lewis, C.
Lewis & Brown
Laight, E. W.
Livingston, C. C., Miss
La Barbier, A.
Le Roy, J.
Lord, Daniel, Jun.
Lee, James, & Co.
Le Roy, H.
Lee, David
Livingston, M. & W.
Leake, S. T.
Lane, W. J.
Lee, J. A.
Livingston, Wm.
Livingston, C. R.
Lewis, Gale
Leon, A. F
Lawrence, M.
Laight, W. E.
Levenworth, Mrs.
Luep, C. M.
Lawrence, Isaac
Linsey, J. H.
Lillie, Wm.
Laverty, H.
Lorillard, Peter
Lawrence, R. M.
Labagh, J.
Lomas, W. H.
Lewis, J. S.
Lambert, J.
Lewis, W.
Lowerre, Seaman
Lent, Mr.
Loutrel, Wm. M.
Laurie, W. E.
Lane, Adulphus
Lowrie, Wm.
Lord, J. C.
Lasak
Lueisseu, G.
Lane, M.
Lang, L.
Lewis
Lawrence, George N.
Leise, F.
Leonard & Wendt
Lewis, John
Love, Robert
Lee & Brewster
Lane, Anthony
Livingston, Schuyler
Leggett, Wm. F.
Le Roy, David
Lane
Leggett, W. H.
Loder, Benjamin
Leggett, Samuel M.

Low, A.
Lee, John, Jun.
L. S.
Ladd, Wm. F.
Lawton & Slocum
Law, G. M.
Luther & Chuch
Leggett, A.
Leggett, W. E
Lord & Taylor
Lester, James W.
Lightbody
Lamphier, J. C.
Ludlaw, Mr.
Ludlam, Mr.
Lynch, Joseph
Lothian, Mr.
Lawrence, C. W.
Lewis, S. W.
Longstreet, Samuel
Lamb
Leonard, E.
Linsay, Jean
Lippitt, C. H.
Longking, Mrs.
Ludlow, John R.
Lewis, Tayler, LL. D.
Lawrence, S. A.
Lynes, S. C.
Lyles, Henry
Lake, E. E.
Linsey, Dr.
Loder, L. B.
Ludlow, A. B.
Lawrence, R.
Lippincott, Thomas
Lefforts, Cornelius
Lee, Daniel F.
Logan, Charles
Little, James
Lord, Benjamin
Lane, N. B.
Lewis, W. J.
Lees, George

M.

Minturn, Robert B.
Moore, Elnathan
Mann, Josiah, Jun.
Maberry, F. F.
Minor, W. W., M. D.
Michaels, Mrs.
Maby, Mr.
Mayhew, P. S.
McAllister, J. R.
Milne, A.
Miller, Mrs.
Martin, Mr.
Moody, Mr.
Moore, Charles
Moulton, Mr.
Marsh, J. R.
Miller, Isabella
Mensher, H.
McDonald, J. H.
M'Keage, Wm.
Moores, C. W.

1847.) LIST OF MEMBERS. **40**

Mitchell, Peter
Mather, E. W.
Miller, Hester
Moss, Dr.
Merrill, Manning
Merrill, Charles
Marmadell, F.
McFarlan, Mr.
M'Kinney, Wm.
Moran, Patrick
Molloy, Frances
Myers, George W.
Montgomery, Maria, Mrs.
Martin, David R.
McElrath, T.
Merry, C. H.
Magill, James
Moore, H.
Morris, L. B.
Mattison, M.
Ming, H.
Ming, Alexander, Jun.
Morrison, David
Miles, Charles
Marvin, A. S.
McNulty, M.
Moran & Mellen
Moore, Thomas D.
March, P. S.
Moore, L. H.
Messinger, Brothers
Meyer & Stucker
McCurdy, R. H.
Meir, Taylor, &Co.
Miller, Nehemiah
Mills, Abner
Miller, Jacob
Milliken, John M.
Mills, Andrew
Masterson, John H,
Mather, W. L.
Martin, Dr.
Mlller, Dr.
Minor, J.
Murray, Mary
Murray, John R.
Morton, W. Q.
Mortimer, John, Jun.
Munn, Stephen B.
McAuley, C.
Marriner, James
Morton, John
Miller, J. B.
Morrisou & Allen
Moffat, Dr.
Morton, Mrs.
Miller, Mr.
McAuley, Mrs.
Moore, James
M'Guire, James
McCready
McGrau, N.
Miller, L.
Morrison, Mr.
Merritt, Mrs.
Martin, Mr.
McClauny, Dr.

Marsh, M.
Martin, Charles
Morton, Thomas
McEmmons, Mr.
Moore, O. J.
Maggs, J.
McIntire, Wm. N.
Miller, G. & H.
Myers, Myer S.
Man, Albon P.
Morgan, J. J.
Morris & Williams
Marsh, James
Munsell, H. H.
Mead, Wm., Mrs.
Maltby, O. E.
Meakim, J. & A.
Morris, Gerard W.
Mott, Wm. F., Jr.
Maxwell & Co.
Mann, F.
Mason, J. L.
Mitchell, Wm.
McDonald, S.
Merritt, A.
McEvers, Bache, Mrs.
Morgan, Nathan
Milbank, J. M.
M.
Maury, M.
Moore, N. F.
Maitland, Mrs.
Mann, E. J.
Mcore, A.
Moore, W.
Mason, Sidney
Mackay, Mr.
Morgan, M.
Mills, Drake
Moore, James L.
Murray, J. B.
Maury, Matthew
Martin, Charles J.
McIlvain, R. B.
Megrath, George
Minturn, Wm. H.
M. H.
Marshnll, Charles H.
Mackie,
Mackie, John F.
Moses, D. B.
Martin
Moody, E.
Morrts, Wm. L.
Mildeberger, Mr.
Many, V. W.
McMillen, James
Marshall, Mr.
Morgan, A. W.
Magereal, D. A.
Myers, Mr.
Monroe, Daniel
Mann & McKim
McVean, Charles
Messerau, John W.
Mount, Elizabeth
Millbank, C. & S.

Merritt, J. G.
Morrell, Thomas
Moffatt, D.
Mitchell, Mr.
Matthews, Wm.
Mayo, Mrs.
Me-riam, Mr.
Morrison, Mr.
Mearl, Mr.
Mills, Charles
Miller, E.
Moore, Joseph
Marshman, B.
Mullens, Alderman
Miller, Geo.
Moulton, John
McNeish, G.
McAlpin, D. H.
Martine, T.
Myers, M.
McIntosh
March, T. E.
Marsh, Alex.
Montgomery, Elizabeth
Meyers, Henry
Merritt, Stephen
Martin, Alfred
Mead, Daniel
McAdam, Thomas
Mapes, W. H.
Mayhew
Mitchell, Mr.
McNee, James
Merritt, Geo.
May, E. H., Rev.
McBride, Ab'm
Maguire, John
Moffatt, Patrick
Meyer, John
Miller, James S., M. D.
Mather, E. F.
Macy, Wm. H.
McClain, O. D.
Mather, G.
Macy, Josiah
Mott, Wm. F.
Macy, Wm. H.
Murphy, Wm. J.
McCoon, Mrs.
Millbank, S., Jr.
Moore, Joseph
Mills, Z.
Martin, R. W.
McCrea, Mrs.
Mead, Wm. H.
McCotter, A.
Miller, Geo. C.
Martin, Wm. C.
Morrison, James
Mygatt, E., Jr.
Morrison, Wm., Jr.
Murray,
Melvin, Mr.
Moro, W.
McIntire, C. H.
Marius, Zopher
Myers, Erastus

LIST OF MEMBERS. (1847.

Miller, G. B.
Merle, Charles
Mooney, E. C.
McMann, James D.
Marooney, W. J.
Montgomery, Samuel J.
Mitchell, Catharine
Marsh, M. L.
Martin, William
Marshall, Mrs.
Martin, Samuel
McWilliam, J. H.
Mauld, C.
McKinsley, B. M.
Montgomery, J. P.
Middleton, J. D.
Murray, Robert J.
Murray, Mary
Moore, Baltis
Marsh, S.
Merrill, N. W.
McKesson, J.
McCullough, James
McCullough
Martin & Lawrence
Mills
Mathieson, J.
McKewan, John
Megary, J.
Martelle & Co.
M. M. B.
Mitchell, R. H.
Morgan, Walker & Smith
McGowan, J. R.
McCleod, Daniel
Major, H. B.
McKenna, J.
McBean, L.
Marr, C.
Mason
Mortimer, John, Jr.
McComb, John
Mangam, W. D.
Mead, F.
Mackerell & Richards
Martin, Samuel
Morrison, Mrs.
Mahony, J. H.
Morse, Richard C.
McLeod, Alexander
Minturn, Charles
McMartin, D.
Mumford, B. A.
Mace, John
McEllight, J. N.
Moulton, John W.
Morrison, John Citz
Marten, H. C.
Moffatt, David
Minor, Israel
Marshall, Benj., M. D.
McClain, O. D.
Marten, William
Murray, John
Murphy, William, M. D.
McPherson, Peter,
Miller, Caleb

Marsh, John R.
Merrill, Charles
Mollard, John
Merrill, Joseph
Milward, James
Muir, James
Merriam, B. W.

N.

Newbold, Geo.
Nichols, Elias S.
Nurans & Suber
Newbold, C.
Noyes. J. R.
Noe, Mr.
Nostrand, Mrs.
Norrie, Adam
Nesmith & Co.
Noble, J.
Nostrand, E.
Norman, Thomas
Nicoll, George
Nesmith, Thomas
Newton, James W.
Nason, H.
Nash, M.
Neeves, James
Nathan, B.
Nevins, Townsend & Co.
Newbold, H. L.
Naylor & Co.
Newman, Mrs.
Nichols, Samuel
Nickoll, J., Mrs.
Nelson, Wm.
Norris, H.
Norton, H. G., Mrs.
Nichols, F. L.
Newhouse
Nelson, Mr.
Nesbitt, G. F.
Nanry, C. H.
Newell, D. C.
Nash, Lora
Norris, R. S.
Newton, J,
Naylor, Peter
Newcomb, George
Nodyne, Richard H.

O.

Ogsbury, F. W.
Oliver, Thomas
Oliff, Mr.
Oldring, Mr.
Oliver, Isaac
Owen, St. John
Ormsby, Royal
Osborn, J.
Ostrander, G.
Owen, D.
Owen, James
Otis & Woodward
Oakey, W. F.
Otten, H.
Oakley, Morris

Ockerhausen, H. J.
Oliver, James D.
Owens, P. S.
Ogden, T. W.
Ogden, M.
Outhout, John
Ogden, T. G.
Olsen, Andrew J.
Olmsted, J.
Oakley, Mrs.
O'Connor, C.
Olcott, John N.
Onderdonk, J. R.
Olwell, Matthew
Obear, Mr.
Oliff, Dr.
Oakley, Daniel
Ogden, Benjamin, M. D.
Orchard, Isaac, Rev.

P.

Prime, Edward
Prime, Frederick
Pratt, Dr.
Potter, Joseph
Parish, James
Prescott, J. M.
Purdy, J. B.
Paillet, H.
Parsons, Joseph
Perine, Benjamin
Petrie, Mr.
Phillips, J. W.
Peck, G. M.
Pearce, George & Co.
P. V. H.
Pinned, W. W. & Co.
Parker, T.
Paul, Schmid & Andrea
Patridge, Mr.
Polhamus, C.
Polhamus, R. J.
Perrine, Mr.
Palmer, M. C., M.D.
Pillow, W. H.
Pearson, Adam
Price, P.
Pope, Henry
Peck, Curtis, Capt.
Place, R. S.
Price, Harrison
Purdy, Jonathan
Painter, W. R.
Platt, George
Pease, Erastus
Pooton, Wm.
Phelps, A. G.
Palmer, Mr.
Pray, David
Phillips, John J.
Phillips, Samuel
Pease, John
Pomroy, J. B.
Peters, Mrs.
Preston, David
Polhamus, J.
Peck, J. B.

1847.) LIST OF MEMBERS. 43

Peppers, M. C.
Powell, Joseph
Pachman, F. W.
Peterson, Mr.
Pitman, C.
Pierson, C.
Pringle, A. Y.
Power, Mr.
Pendleton, E. H.
Paton & Stewart
Palmer, J. J.
Platt, N. C.
Post, Alfred C.
Post, Edward
Parmley. J.
Peet, Mrs.
Parsons, W. B.
Poillon, J.
Phalen, James
Parker, Wm.
Purser, Charles E.
Pickersgill, W. C. & Co.
Perego, Ira, Jr.
Palmer, Capt.
Perkins, J. A.
Patridge, C.
Pearson, J. G.
Phillips, Lewis
Patterson, Godfrey, Mrs.
Patterson, Godfrey, Miss
Pell, John B.
Porter, Mortimer
Prout, M. P.
Prout, M. P., Mrs.
Palmer, Mrs.
Phillips, James B.
Pinner, H.
Powell, A. G.
Parcell, Abraham
Piggott. S.
Porter, John
Perry, Mr.
Pierson, S. H
Peck, Edwin
Putnam, Nathaniel
Putnam, Elizabeth, Mrs.
Pearson, J.
Pinkney, W. T.
Page, R. P.
Pearson, J. Green
Penfold, Edmond
Pon & Palanca
Peyser, D. M.
Prasser, T.
Platt, J. S.
Priestley, J.
Parkhurst
Parks, J. B.
Peck, Elisha
Polhemus, Abraham
Pollock, Alderman
Pollock, John
Powell, Wm. H.
Powell, Geo. B.
Pollen, Geo. P.
Post, R.

Pharo, Jos. W.
Pinkney, J. G.
Pryer, G. Mrs.
Porter, H. C.
Phelps, John Jay
Powers, Lorenzo
Porter, William
Price, C. W.
Payne, Theodore
Phillips, Dr.
Pringle, Thomas
Pott, F.
Peck, N.
Palmer, Mrs,
Potter, Mrs.
Provost, S. H.
Page, P. P.
Price, Mr.
Penfold, John
Purdy
Pinchback, Mr.
Purnie, P., Jr.
Pike, B., Jr.
Prall, W. H. H.
Parr, Mr.
Peck, C. A.
Prime, Mrs.
Pearse, A. F.
Pickering, Thomas
Parker, Moses
Patton, Andrew
Price, S. S.
Pond, James O., M. D.
Patterson, Samuel P.
Price, T.
Pearce, J. N.
Platt, Isaac
Purdy & Packer
Prier, J.
Parsons, J. B.
Patrick, R.
Purdy, R. E.
Pease, W. J.
Platt, Medad
Pegg, R.
Paxson, S. C.
Penfold, Wm.
Platt, E.
Prior
Philps, William
Pratt, Linus
Pease, Wm.
Price, G. L.
Pearson, Adam
Peers, Thomas F.
Pattison, Robert
Perry, J. I.
Patterson, Francis
Peck, Nathan
Pugsley, Robert
Pearcy, Grorge W.
Perry, James T.
Phillips, John
Phelps, James L., M. D.
Pattilow, Frederick
Peck, Wm. J.

Q.

Quidort, Mr.
Quinn

R.

Richards, M. H.
Roosevelt, S. Weir
Root, Geo. F.
Rumsey, J. W.
Reid, William
Roosevelt, James
Ray, Robert
Renaud, Mr.
Ryan, Mr.
Robjohn, Mr.
Romeo, Mr.
Richter, D. A.
Randall, W. R.
Riker, James
Roberts, George
Roberts, Alderman
Rose, Mr.
Rosenbury, Mr.
Rodgers, B.
Raynor, Mr.
Ryerson, Peter
Remor, Oliver
Robinson, Mr.
Remsen, D.
Read, C.
Roff, Almona
Roshore, J.
Robold, Daniel
Raiby, Philip
Richardson, E. & Co.
R. U. M.
Roberts, E. G.
Rogers, Charles H.
Ryder, Edgar T.
Roger, P. L.
Ryder, Mrs.
Raynor, Hiram
Reed, Almet
Rodh, David
Richmond, Otis T.
Riley, Mr.
Rupeh, A.
Raynor, S.
Roe, F. A.
Reed, N.
Rockwell, Dr.
Ryers, H. S.
Rankin, A.
Ryan, Mr.
Rose, Mr.
Rogers, W. S.
Robinson, John A.
Redfield, Charles B.
Ronalds, T. A., Mrs.
Russell, W. H.
Robertson, James A.
Richards, G.
Routh, H. L. & Son.
Rachan, J. A. F.
Robbins, G. S.
Richardson, T.

LIST OF MEMBERS. (1847.

Romaine, S. B.
Remsen, Wm.
Remsen, C. B., Mrs.
Roosevelt, C. S. V.
Ray, Richard, Mrs.
Rogers, J. Smyth, M. D.
R. G. P.
Rogers, Catharine
Reed, Taylor & Co.
Ruggles, H.
Rigney, Mrs.
Russell, Mrs.
Robinson, M.
Rutgers, G., Jr.
Rogers, Mrs.
Redmond, W.
Rodewald & Brothers
Riggs, E.
Rogers, Mrs.
Rockland, G. O. V.
Russ, Brothers
Robinson, Dr., Rev.
Reeve, Henry
Redman, Charles H.
Requa, A.
Roome, Peter
Raymond, Samuel G.
Russell, John
Rolfe, C.
Randle, J. & S.
Roux, A.
Reynolds, C.
Ruton, Mrs.
Rohr, John G.
Reeve, Henry
Ramsey, P. P.
Rankin, Duryee & Co.
Riker, J. L.
R. & W.
Rosselot, P. A.
Reckard, L. B.
R. C. B.
R. H.
Robertson, James
Reyburn, James
Robinson, M.
Richardson, Watson & Co.
Ruderford, Mrs.
Ransom, J. H.
Rodman, John
Roach, P. R.
Raymond, H. J.
Reid, George M.
Roach, Edward
Robinson
Richards, John W.
Roberts, Mr.
Rice, S. N.
Roy, Jennet
Ramsay, H.
Rhodes, Josiah
R: C. B.
Ritters, Misses
Richell, T. B.
Richards, James
Rader, Mr.
Ricker, Abraham

Rockwell, Mr.
Rose, J.
Rowell, Charles S.
Reed, C, H., Rev.
Rabadan, C.
Reial, H. E.
Riley, A.
Robinson, Mrs.
Rockhill, Jane
Riley, John
Rainer, A.
Richmond, Robert
Rogers, Joseph
Ritter, Mr.
Ross, George
Riley, Joseph A.
Richards, Wm. H.
Rich, Josiah
Richards, Thomas P.
Rich, Thomas B.
Roome, Charles
Rappelye, George
Riker, Abraham
Randolph,
Richards, Mrs.
Robert, C. R.
Ritche, H. L.
Riley, Joseph A.
Rich, Josiah
Rowell, Warren
Ritter, Thomas, M. D.
Ryers, T. R.
Redfield, J. H.
Russell, Samuel
Rumney, J. W.
Rae, Robert
Riggs, Alfred
Rudd, Wm.
Row, Thomas G.

S.

Southart, Jacob
Stewart, Lispenard
Schuyler, Mrs.
Smedberg, Mrs.
Sampson, G. G.
Strong, Mr.
Sill, Horace
Silcock, P. M.
Schlesinger, A.
Shabzell, Mrs.
Smith, C. A.
Scharfenburgh, Wm.
Smith & Cornwall
Sheffield, Mrs
Stewart. R. L. & A.
Station House of 13th Ward
Simmons, Mrs.
Smith, J. S.
Squire & Brother
Sneckner, J.
Snowden, Thomas
Selpho, Wm.
Silver, Mr.
Smeads, Mrs.
Street, C., Mrs.
Spencer, E. S.

Suffern, Thomas
Schuchardt, F.
Suydam, J.
Stout, A. G. M.
Sanderson, C. F.
Schenck, W. L.
Stilwell, John
Stephens, B S.
Starr, Nathan
Sampson, A. W.
Stanton, John
Skiddy, W.
Schenck, D. S., Mrs.
Sevre, J. P.
Starr, Elias
Sherman, Dr.
Swan, Benj. L.
Shaddle, H. V.
Swarez, S. W.
Swords, R. B. S.
Stagg, John P. & Co.
Steward, J. Jr.
Skiddy, F. Mrs.
Sturges, Jonathan
Sheldon, Henry
S. & S.
Stewart, John
Smith, D. Gilbert
Seaman, Isaac
Saltus & Co.
Stuyvesant, P. G.
Swords, R. S.
Schieffelin, H. H.
Stone & Swan
Skiddy, F.
Shepherd, Mrs.
Smith, H. M.
Schieffelin, P.
Spence, W. A.
Stewart, L. J.
Schermerhorn, Abraham
Spofford & Tileston
Sturges, Bennet & Co.
S. R.
Stevens, John A.
Spenser, A.
Stuckley, Rutun
Strong, Angelina & Amelia
Sabine, Dr.
Simons, Lewis
Simonson, Miss
Seguine, C.
Seymour, J. Mrs.
Stoneburdge, J.
Scott, A. M L.
Scott, Wm. & Co.
Salisbury, H.
Schoonmaker, H. E.
Sessel
Steavens, John
Suydam, Henry
Swain, E.
Starr, Charles, Jr.
Smith, S. A.
Southmayd, H.
Smith, A.
Slaughter, S.

1847.) LIST OF MEMBERS. 45

Stansbury, J. F.
Sherman, A.
Smith, Dr.
Strauss, S.
Sloan, George
Skidmore, S. H.
Seon, A. F., Mrs.
Stevens, T. I.
Smith & Co., Wm. H.
S. S.
Sandford, H. J.
Sprague, Robinson & Co.
Spaulding, Thomas & Vail
Scoville, A. M. S. & W. H.
Smith, Torrey & Co.
Staples, G. W.
Schiefflen, A. B.
Smith, L.
Shepherd & Morgan
Smith, Catharine P.
Schuster
Schiefflen
Sawyer & Hobby
Smith, M. M.
Smith, Wright & Co.
S A.
Smith, R. C.
Struller, L.
Smith, S.
Stedman, W. S.
Starr, Wm. H.
Scott
Scrymser, James
Smith, Sheldon
Stebbins, Russel
Smith, J. E.
Seaman, J. M.
Sutherland, Wm.
Salisbury, W. D.
Smith, A. D.
Stone, G. C.
Schoals, F. P.
Smith, Thomas C.
Sage, G. E.
Shelton, S. B.
Smilie, J.
Sampson, Joseph
Storm, Garret
Skidmore, S. T.
Sedgwick, Theodore
Southard, S. L.
Smith, F.
Stone, E.
Sanford, C, W.
Strange, E. B.
Stevens, John C.
Seaman, G.
Stohlman, Charles F. E.
Shafer, P.
St. John, Lewis
Smith, C. W.
Smith, John J.
Shannon, Wm.
Schureman, N.
Staples, Joseph
Stillwell, Wm. M., Rev.
Smith, Jesse

Souter, Brothers & Co.
Smith, R.
Schieffelin, H. M.
St. John, Burr & Co.
Scribner, U. K.
Sterling, Robert Richard
Sprague, E. D.
Spies, Christ & Co.
Sacket, Belcher & Co.
Stevens, L. M.
Syz, Irminger & Co.
Smith, Richard
Smythe, H. A.
Schmidt, J. W.
Swan, Caleb
Stillman, T. B.
Shurman, Isaac
Smith, Wm.
Smith, M. G.
Steanes, John G.
Sheldon, James
Sellick, Gonld
Spelman, W. B.
St. John, B. G.
Summers, Alex. B.
Sheffield, D.
Sanford, N.
Sneeden, Mr.
Sarles, Mr.
Sniffin, John
Stout, A. O.
Smith, W. N.
Smith, Peter
Sneeden, Mr.
Stickney, C. L.
Sprague, George
Spencer, Warner
Stephenhagen, E. C.
Smith, C. E.
Smith, James L.
Snyder, A.
Smith, H.
Scurman, Sopwal
Stott, Alexandsr
Sewell, Thomas
Smith, E. L.
Steers, Thomas
Saffin, David
Steele, Wm.
Smith, T. U.
Seon, A. F., Mrs.
Smith, A.
Smilie, Wm.
Schenck, W. E.
Starr
Sutton, George
Still, G. S.
Sarvan, David
Seabury, Dr., Rev.
Scott, John D.
Standley, Wm. W.
Sherwood, B.
Smith, Andrew
Sanford, Mrs.
Salter, Benjamin, Jr.
Somerindyck, G. W.
Smith, H. H.

Small, Thomas
Sherman, G. & I.
Stopnhazen, M.
Sweeny, D.
Shaw, James M.
Sears, R.
Schultz, J. S.
Scott, J. G.
Starr, Mr.
Simpson
Shead
Sollomon, Dr.
Smith, Miss
Sorier, J.
Smith, A. M. C.[1]
Saroni & Archer
Sweeny, Hugh, M. D.
Stoppani, Charles G.
Smith, Washington
Scudder, E.
Smith, Mr.
Scott, Ann
Sapher, George
Schafer, F. & M.
Sherwood, B.
Smith, John
See, Wm.
Sloam, Thomas G.
Smith, James R.
Smith, Isaac B.
Smith, E. Dunlap
Smith, Floyd
Smith, Fletcher
Stirling & Walton
Smith, Daniel Drake
Sayer, John N.
Sharp, William
Sparks, Walter C.
Skikmore, J. S.
Scofield, Samuel W.
Sheffield, Dudley
Smith, S. P.
Smith, James
S. M.
Sanford, M.
Smith, Jesse
Swazy, N, T.
Sands, A. B,
Scott, Wm. B.
Seymour, Charles
Saxton, J.
Seymour & Low
Sharp, William
Sperling, John G.
Sparks, Samuel
Shurdlow, Samuel
Smith, James
Scrymser, John
Savage, C. C.
Steele, W.
Sedgwick, Roderick
See, Isaac
Scofield, Samuel W.
Siney, Wm. R.
Slocum, Richard
Seaman, Concklin
Stillman, J. W. D.

46 LIST OF MEMBERS. (1847.

Stelle, Isaac
Seely, Joseph
Smith, Woodhull
Stout, Andrew V.
Stelle, Nelson, M. D.
Spies, Adam W.
Straight, C. L., M. D.
Smith, Asa
Stevens, J. L.
Stebbins, William
Schrymser, James
Stanton, S. B.
Sebur, Nicholas
Smith, Simeon P.

T.

Thorne & Jarvis
Tredwell, George
Terbell, J.
Tracey, F. A., Mrs.
Thorne, Herman
Thompson, Daniel
Terenly, E.
T. D. L.
Talbot, Charles N.
Thornton, A.
Thurston, Henry
Tier, Margaret
Tromley, Owen
Tyson, Mrs.
Terrill, Caleb
Tienza, Mr.
Timpson, T. B.
Tucker, S. D.
Titus, Charles F,
Tappen, B., Col.
Tyler, Isaac
Thatford, J.
Till, Peter
Tice, Peter
Tappen, David
Taylor, Wm.
Thomas, Augustus
Tottersall, W. K.
Trippe, J, & J. F.
Thompson, J.
Taylor, A.
Thompson, J., Jr.
Townsend, G. E.
Toole, Wm. S.
Trowbridge, G. A.
Truslow, Wm.
Trenchard, S.
Taylor, G. G.
Taylor, R.
Tappen, Geo., Jr.
Thorp, Samuel
Thorp, Isaac O.
Tredwell, Adam
Taff, H.
Taylor, Henry
Towle, John H.
Trumpy, C.
Thompson, B. M.
Taylor, W, B.
Thomas, J. C.
Thorne, J.

Thompson, D.
Townsend, Caroline, Mrs.
Thurston, R. H., Mrs.
Thurston, C. M.
Tillinghast, P.
Tobias, J. J.
Taylor, Moses
Tooker, Mead & Co.
Thompson, T. F.
Tuckerman, Jos.
Thomas, Mr.
Taft, J. H.
Tiffany, Young & Ells
Thompson, W. D.
Taylor, F. H.
Turrell, Wm.
Tracy, J. W.
Tillotson, J. C.
Tappen, Prof.
Teale, John P.
Tallman, S. S.
Todd, Wm. W.
Thompson, Joseph P.
Thorn, Wm.
Tuthill, Geo. M.
Thomas, Elias
Tate, Mrs.
Thwing, C.
Teel, Miss
Topham, Wm.
Townsend, C. P.
Trowbridge, F. H.
Thompson, Thomas
Tucker, William
Tomes, Francis
Taylor, R. H.
Tomes, F. Jr.
Towsey, Sinclair
Talmadge, Wm. F.
Tracy, J. & Co.
Taham & Brothers
Tarbox & Kingsley
Tisdale, Samuel J.
Trowbridge, Henry T. B.
Tones & Friedel
Trow, Wm.
Tubell, H. S.
Thompson, W. B.
Tinkham, J.
Todel, D. P.
Townley, Mrs.
Thompson, G.
Ten Brook, R.
Tunis
Taylor, Joseph D.
Tweedy, O. B.
Tweedy, Edward
Trotter
Tierman, George
Taylor, Mr.
Tenatt, H. E.
Towl, Charles
Tompson, Thomas
Towl
Topping, H.
Thorn, Charles E.

Thurston
Townsend, Mr.
Thomas, T.
Taylor, J.
Thompson, J. B.
Thompson, Wm.
Tunnier, Elizabeth
Tucker, Joseph
Tom, James
Towers, J.
Thompson, John
Teague, Edward
Thorn, N. T.
Tracy, Geo. M.
Thompson, A. Q.
Tweed, R.
Turneur, Abraham
Thorp, A.
Thorp, Henry,
Terrett, G. R.
Tucker' N. D.
Tracy, Calvin
Thorn, R S.
Thomson, John
Terry, David
Thomson, Mason
Taylor, Moses B.
Tuttle, Sylvester
Tattersall, W. R.
Townsend, J.
Trafford, Abraham
Tompkins, D.
Trigler, John

U

Underhill, Doct.
Underhill, T. N.
Unknown
Ulshoeffer, M.
Underhill, J. W.
Underwood, J.
Underhill, J. S.
Underhill, Wm.
Underhill, A. S.
Underhill
Ustick, Richard

V

Venables, Richard
Vaughan, G.
Van Voorhees, Mr.
Vreeland, Mr.
Vroom, Mr.
Vermule, F., M.D.
Vermule, W., M.D.
Van Tassel, Albert
Van Vleek, Abr'm.
Vogely, Frederick
Van Kleeck, Wm. H. & Co.
Van Ransellaer, H. R.
Vandervoort, Henry
Van Arsdale, H.
Van Tuyl, B. S.
Vincent, L. M., Rev.
Van Voorhis, E. W.
Van Nest, John
Vyse & Sons

LIST OF MEMBERS.

Versfelt, Mr.
Van Buren, G. A. C.
Van Rensselaer, Miss
Van Wyck, Henry L.
Vermilye, W. M.
Van Blarcom, A.
Vose, C. L.
Van Duran, D.
Van Renselaer, Mr., Rev.
Verplank, G. C.
Van Vleek, W.
Van Wagner & Frazier
Van Hook, W.
Van Antwerp, Mrs.
Vose, Reuben
Van Norden, Wm.
Van Antwerp, M. Mrs.
Van Buskirk, S.
Van Saun, Mr.
Van Winkle, Tunis
Van D——, A. W.
Vandenburgh, Mrs.
Van Nests
Valentine, R. C.
Vernon, Thomas
Van Deventer, J. G.
Vernon, E.
Vermilye, Dr., Rev.
Van Wagner, Wm.
Vreedenburgh, P.
Van Arsdale, John
Van Doren, J.
Vandervoort, P.
Van Houghton, John
Vorhiss, Richard
Vermulle, William
Van Nest, Abm.
Vosburgh, J.
Vernal, Mr.
Vultee, F.
Vail, H.
Vail, G.
Vultee, F. L.
Verplank, Saml
Vosburgh, John S.
Van Winkle, N. H.
Vandenburgh, James
Vosburgh, A. P.
Van Dolsen, J.
Vermilye, W.
Valentine, A. G.
Van Allen, Wm.
Van Dalsom, Wm. H.
Van Arsdale, Henry, M.D.
Vandewater, Joseph H.
Valentine, J.

W.

Ward, Edward F.
Wetmore, W. S.
Wolfe, Jno. D.
Wainwright, Dr., Rev.
Waddell, Wm. C. H.
Whitaker, Dr.
Wood, Messrs.
Westchester House
Wood, Mr.
Woodward, J. S.
Wilson, B.
Wetmore, N.
W B.
Ward, J.
Wynkoop, F. S.
Wilds, J.
Wolfe, N. H.
Wilson, J. B.
Waller, R.
Waddington, W. D.
Weller, John
Wetmore, W. C.
Wells, E. H.; Mrs.
Watts, R. Jun.; Mrs.
Wetmore, S.
Wilson, N.
Wilson, Rob't. M.
W. B.
Wilmerding, W. E.
Woolsey, E. J.
Whitlock, Wm., Jun.
Wells, Brothers
Wright, Largo & Lattimer
Waldo, Chas. B.
Weeks, R. D.
Weeks, E. A.
Walker, Wm.
White, R. H.
Ward, Samuel
White, Miss
Whiting, A.
Warren, Mr.
Ward, H. Miss
Walker, A.
W.
White, F. & Co.
Wyeth, L. J.
Wiley, J.
Wells, Ralph
Weed, A.
Wright, James
Walsh,
Walsh, A. R.
Walsh, Hugh
Woodruff, T. T.
Woodford, O. P.
Webb, J. Watson
Winslow, R. H.
Warrol, Henry
Woodruff, Amos
Whitman, L.
Walker, J., Mrs.
Woram, Wm.
Wilson, B. M.
Wright, Richard
Woodbridge, W. E.
Walton, J. B.
Wright, John G.
Williston, J. T.
White, John
Ward, Mrs.
Wood, Mr.
Wilkes, S.
Williams, P. H.
Wheelock, A.
Wead, Edward N.
Watt Wm.
Warback, G. C.
Wilson, Dorson
Wise, M.
Wooding, James
W. H. M.
Wheelright, B. F.
Wright, Sturges & Shaw
Ward, A. H.
Williamson & Co., S. P.
Wilber, Wm. B.
Windle, W. B.
Williams Brothers
Wilson, James C.
W. M. B.
Wyck, J.
W. & T. A.
Weitick.
Watkins, Henry M.
West
Wendle, J. D.
Winant, Mr.
Wright, N.
Williams, Charles
Willis, W. H.
Woodward, R. T.
Williams, E. H.
Wiley, J.
White, Charles B.
W. S.
Whittemore, Timothy
Wallace, J.
Williams, Wm. R., M. D.
Wood, Wm. R.
Whittemore, Mr.
Wells, Mr.
Winthrop, T. C.
Williams, H. D.
Walton, W.
W. E. L.
Wright, Mr.
Waite, Mrs.
Williams, Mrs.
Wilson, Mr.
Westervelt, S. D., Rev.
Wood, D. A.
Williams, Rich'd S.
Williams & Hinman
Williams, Peter
Wood, James L.
Whitfield, G. & J.
Wheeler, L. F.
White, John
West, Mr.
Wedemeyer, George
Worrell & Co.
Warner, Thomas
Wallin, Sam'l
Walker & Linden
Wark, W. A.
Williams, Mrs.
Woodruff, E. P.
Woodruff, L. B.
Waters, Geo. G.
Wheeler, H H.
Warner, George
Wilson, J. D.

Wheeler, A.
Wortendyke, D. A.
Wheeler, Lucius
Woolley, B. L.
Winston, F. S.
Weld, Henry
Wicksted, John
Wyckoff, W. H.
Wetmore, A. R.
White, Eli
Wetmore, L.
Wood, B.
Wilson, D. M.
Wiggins, W. H.
West, Wm.
Woodworth, Mr.
White, N.
White, Mr.
Wellman, J. R.
Wilmot, Mr.
Waterhouse, Mr.
Welling, J. T.
Waterbury, J.
Warner, H. R.
White, Doct.
Wardell, N.
Winant, Jacob
Woods, John
Ward, Adam
Wagner, J.
Willett, Mrs.
West, John
White, Mrs.
Weeks, Absalom
Walker, Mrs.
Welford, Mr.
Wall, Andrew
Wood, James
Webb, W. H.
Williams, Jabez
Wooster, Benjamin
Wright, D. D.
Wilkinson, James
Whitmore, R. J.
Wranglir, James

Wood, H. L.
Wenman, Andrew J.
Wooley, Charles
Williams, D. S.
West, Wm. G.
Wilson, Harris
Wotherspoon, Geo.
Wheeler, E.
Weismann, Aug's
Whitewright, Wm., sen'r
Whitewright, Wm., jr.
White, A. L.
White, J. H.
Wiggins, Mr.
Wetteran, John B.
Weir, J.
Wood, W. H.
Waydell, J.
Wardle, Thomas
Wolfe & Gillespie
West, E. G.
W. P. & K.
Whitlock, Aug's
W. K. C.
Williams, F B.
Woolcott & Slade
Waldo, Francis
Wiches, Wm. W.
Woolsey & Woolsey
Whitmore, J. C.
Williamson, D.
Willets, Daniel T.
Westervelt, J. A.
Wheeler, Ezra
Willets, S.
Willets, R. R.
Woodhull, Wm.
Woodward, Tho's
Wright, Horace
Williams, J. H.
Williams, Thomas
Wright, J. D.
Wood, B. M. D.
Webbs, Misses
Williams, R.

Whitlock, Andrew
Watkiss, Mr.
Wood, James R., M. D.
Wilbur, Charles
Walsh, Michael R.
Wetmore, L.
Williams, A.
Wade, E.
Ward, S. S.
Whittemore, Joseph,
Warner, Hiram
Wilson, Wm. M.
Weir, James
Wheaton, William
Wheeler, E.
Wooster, B.
Wood, Henry
Walker, Wm. A
Williams, Joseph
White, C. B.
Warren, S.
Woodcock, W. P.
West, Royal, Rev.
Woodford, O. P.

Y.
Youle, G. W.
Young, Thomas
Young, John
Yelvertons & Fellows
Young, Mr.
Yates, A. E., Mrs.
Young, George
Young, L.
Yenton
Young, Miss
Young, Joab

Z.
Zabriskle, C. A.
Zodeivick, P.
Zabriskie & Van Riper
Zabriskie, George

THE FIFTH ANNUAL REPORT

OF THE

NEW-YORK ASSOCIATION

FOR

IMPROVING THE CONDITION OF THE POOR,

FOR THE YEAR 1848.

WITH

THE BY-LAWS AND A LIST OF MEMBERS.

"The quality of mercy is not strained;
It droppeth as the gentle rain from heaven
Upon the place beneath: it is twice blessed;
It blesseth him that gives and him that takes."

NEW-YORK:
PRINTED BY LEAVITT, TROW & CO.,
49 ANN-STREET.
1848.

PROCEEDINGS

AT THE

ANNUAL MEETING

OF THE

NEW-YORK ASSOCIATION FOR IMPROVING THE CONDITION OF THE POOR,

Held in the Hall of the Public School Society, Nov. 21, 1848.

The President, JAMES BROWN, Esq., in the chair.

The minutes of the last Annual Meeting were read by the Recording Secretary, and on motion, approved.

The Treasurer presented his Annual Report, which was accepted, and ordered on file.

The minutes of the Executive Committee, exhibiting their operations during the recess of the Board, were read by the Corresponding Secretary, as their report to that body, and approved.

The Annual Report was read, accepted, and ordered to be printed as read, under the direction of the Executive Committee.

After remarks explaining the advantages of incorporate privileges, by one of the Vice-Presidents, on motion, it was unanimously

Resolved, That it is expedient to incorporate the Association.

The "Certificate of Intention," as required by law, was then read and approved; and on motion, it was

Resolved, That the necessary measures be taken to consummate the incorporation of the Institution, under the General Law for such purposes, passed April 12th, 1848.

At this stage of the proceedings the Corresponding Secretary being called upon, addressed the meeting;—after which a communication from a member was read, recommending a freer distribution of Directories and Tickets, than had hitherto been practised. This gave rise to a discussion, which was arrested by referring the whole subject, with power, to the consideration and action of the Board of Managers.

Several subjects of a desultory nature, having for a little time occupied the attention of the members, on motion, the meeting adjourned.

OFFICERS, MANAGERS,

AND

SUPERVISORY COUNCIL.

President.
JAMES BROWN.

Vice Presidents.
GEORGE GRISWOLD,   JAMES BOORMAN,
J. SMYTH ROGERS, M. D.,   HORATIO ALLEN.
JAMES LENOX.

Treasurer.
ROBERT B. MINTURN.

Corresponding Secretary and Agent.
ROBERT M. HARTLEY.

Recording Secretary.
JOSEPH B. COLLINS.

Supervisory Council.
The first in order is the Chairman of each District Committee.

FIRST DISTRICT.
D. S. Briant,
James Cruikshank,
James Giffin,
Peter Naylor,
James C. Ramsey.

SECOND DISTRICT.
William Gale,
George W. Abbe,
John N. Sayre,
Wm. Sharp,
Charles Wilbur.

THIRD DISTRICT.
P. G. Arcularius,
William Walker,
Jonathan Sturges,
E. Cauldwell,
J. L. Baldwin.

FOURTH DISTRICT.
Abraham Fardon, Jr.,
Archibald Hall,
Hugh Aikman,
Charles Chamberlain,
John Hagadorn.

FIFTH DISTRICT.
A. R. Wetmore,
Wm. Forrest,
G. T. Cobb,
Wm. H. Richards,
Leonard Kirby.

SIXTH DISTRICT.
N. C. Everett,
Stephen Conover,
James B. Thompson,
Thomas Lippencott,
John G. Sperling.

SEVENTH DISTRICT.
C. Tracy,
A. B. Ludlum,
G. J. Price,
Stephen Cutter,
J. Skidmore.

EIGHTH DISTRICT.
Joseph B. Collins,
Wm. Johnston,
John Endicott,
Charles C. Dyer,
O. D. McClain.

NINTH DISTRICT.
James O. Pond, M. D.,
James S. Miller, M. D.,
Thomas P. Richards,
Jeremiah Terbell,
Daniel French.

VISITORS. (1848.

TENTH DISTRICT.
James Horn,
Joseph M. Bell,
Samuel W. Scofield,
Peter Aims,
Henry Van Arsdale., M. D.

ELEVENTH DISTRICT.
S. P. Patterson,
Abner Mills,
Peter McPherson,
Dudley Sheffield,
Nehemiah Miller.

THIRTEENTH DISTRICT.
Lewis Chichester,
Thomas Kennedy,
G. P. B. Hoyt,
Charles Merrill,
Wm. A. Walker.

FOURTEENTH DISTRICT.
Adam W. Spies,
William Bloodgood,
J. M. Howe,
S. M. Blatchford,
William Post.

FIFTEENTH DISTRICT.
Thomas Denny,
Stewart Brown,
Wm. G. Bull,
Joseph Lawrence,
Henry E. Davies.

SIXTEENTH DISTRICT.
Luther Jackson,
Tayler Lewis,
L. B. Woodruff,
W. Vermilye,
Charles Roome.

SEVENTEENTH DISTRICT.
S. C. Lynes,
James R. Gibson,
Timothy Ensign,
George Manning Tracy,
Herman Griffin.

EIGHTEENTH DISTRICT.
F. E. Mather,
J. F. Joy,
E. Holbrook,
J. W. Benedict,
John Campbell.

Elected members of the Supervisory Council.

John C. Green,
William S. Wetmore,
Jonathan Sturges,
William H. Macy,
Thomas Cock, M. D.,

E. J. Woolsey,
Peter Cooper,
John C. Baldwin,
Wm. B. Crosby,

William G. Bull,
Lorin Nash,
J. T. Adams,
Josiah Rich.

Elected members of the Board of Managers.

Stewart Brown,
John R. Ludlow,

Frederick S. Winston,
Erastus C. Benedict.

VISITORS.

Appointed by the Advisory Committees for the ensuing year.

FIRST DISTRICT.
William P. Sell,
James C. Rumsey,
D. S. Briant,
Palmer Sumner,
William Stoddart,
Peter Naylor,
James Giffin,
David Meeker,
John C. Cass,
Lewis B. Loder,
George Hatt, Sec'y.

SECOND DISTRICT.
Charles Wilbur,
William Gale,
G. W. Abbe,
D. N. Tucker,
William Sharp,
Joseph F. Sanxay,
George Hatt, Sec'y.

THIRD DISTRICT.
Henry Ahrenfeldt,
John Ramsay,

N. T. Jennings,
L. Wetmore,
E. L. Fancher,
W. D. Harris,
Samuel Hopkins,
C. C. Colgate,
Stephen Burkhalter,
David Terry, Sec'y.

FOURTH DISTRICT.
Adam Pearson,
Samuel Sparks,
Alexander J. Henderson,
Ralph Hall,
George Newcomb, M. D.,
E. Wade, jr.,
Arch'd Hall,
John Barry,
Hiram Hurd,
T. R. Ryers.
Henry G. Leask,
David Moffatt,
John Buxton, jr.,
John Gates,
T. H. Burras,
Henry Whittelsey, Sec'y.

FIFTH DISTRICT.
J. J. Greenough,
A. R. Wetmore,
Lemuel G. Evans,
T. V. Forster,
C. Adams,
James Smith,
E. D. Truesdale,
John Thomson,
S. Cochrane,
R. Lawrence,
H. Cole,
William Van Allen,
J. Prescott,
William Forrester,
J. H. Redfield,
L. P. Hubbard,
J. F. Bridges,
Robert Pattison,
C. C. Savage,
S. S. Ward,
Robert Carter,
George T. Cobb,
Mason Thomson,
J. O. Dorr,
W. Steele,
David Terry, Sec'y.

1848.)   VISITORS.   7

Sixth District.
William Ballagh,
George Pollock,
Andrew Hume,
Benjamin Marshall, M. D.,
James Rogers,
James B. Thompson,
Thomas Lippencott,
Moses B. Taylor,
Silvester Tuttle,
George W. Lowerre,
Joseph Whittemore,
Simon Clannon,
Daniel A. Webster,
Samuel Baxter,
Benjamin B. Forbes.
Reuben S. Carpentier,
John G. Sperling,
Amzi Camp, Sec'y.

Seventh District.
Linus Pratt,
George Gordon,
Charles L Nichols,
William Faulkner,
Jonathan B. Horton,
C. Tracy,
A. P. McNaughton,
J. P. Bremner.
S. S. Broad,
B. R Smith,
William Pease,
Peter Doig,
H. C. Martin,
Edward L. Chichester, M.D.,
G. J. Price,
J. B. Dickinson,
Phineas Burgess,
A. B. Ludlum,
Warren Rowell,
Z. C. Inslee,
S. Cutter,
Jona. B. Horton, Sec'y.

Eighth District.
Joseph B. Collins,
O. D. McClain,
Isaac Gibson,
Daniel Conover,
J. H. McWilliams,
Ira Burdge,
William H. Van Dalsom,
William Johnston,
J. S. Holt,
Charles C. Dyer,
William Scott,
W. W. Dwight, M. D.,
C. P. Dakin,
William M. Wilson,
John Endicott,
Edward Fields,
Henry W. Ryerson,
L. B. Wright, M. D.,
Darius Geer,
J. S. Ferris,
Samuel Russell, Sec'y.

Ninth District.
John C. Myers,
S. B. Philips, M. D.,
Nathan Peck,
W. R. Demarest,
William Cargill,
A. D. F. Randolph,
H. W. Deems,
Cornelius Lefferts,
N. S. Davis, M. D.,
Daniel French,
William Marten,
William A. Foster,
William Harned,
Robert Pugsley,
J. Danforth,
Thomas Fessenden,
Daniel F. Lee,
John Murray,
E. H. Payton,
H. S. Whittemore,
George D. Cragin,
M. H. Howell,
Nathaniel Gray, Sec'y.

Tenth District.
Peter Aims,
Smith Downs,
Joseph M. Bell,
James Horn,
James Weir,
William Wheaton,
Isaac Seaman,
Ed. A. Fraser,
Conelius V. Clarkson, M.D.,
Laban Jacobs,
Josiah W. Wentworth,
Henry Van Arsdale, M. D.,
Richard Hayter,
Isaac Ford,
James T. Perry,
Joseph D. Barker,
Samuel W. Scofield,
W. C. Bradley,
John D. McCreary,
E. A. Frazer, Sec'y.

Eleventh District.
Adam C. Leach,
Charles Logan,
Joel Kelly,
Thomas Hogan,
William Murphy,
Philip Killy,
J. W. Rickard,
Simon Houghwout,
John Philips,
William Bennett,
John Young,
S. P. Patterson,
Caleb Miller,
Benjamin Wooster,
John Townsend, jr.,
John A. Deveau,
Cornelius Waldron.
Joseph Hall.

M. A. Southworth, M. D.,
John Camron,
James Price,
Grant Dubois, Sec'y.

Thirteenth District.
Isaac Stelle,
John Hutchings,
John J. Gantz,
Myron Finch,
John R. Marsh,
Joseph Seely,
Woodhull Smith,
James Forrester,
Henry Wood,
Charles Merrill,
Jeremiah Cornwell,
John W. Conover,
Abraham Trafford,
Francis Duncan,
Ferris Finch,
Silvanus Edwards,
Samuel Fisk,
Joab Young,
Thomas Brown,
Charles S. Loper,
Noah Coe, Sec'y.

Fourteenth District.
Benjamin Ogden, M. D.,
Nelson Stelle, M. D.,
William Post.
Adam W. Spies,
Bezaleel Howe,
J. M. Howe,
Charles Speaights,
Eli Goodwin,
William Bloodgood,
J. J. Jenkins,
Thomas W. Strong,
Robert Rae,
John W. Weed, M. D.,
Samuel M. Blatchford,
Daniel W. Teller,
William Gray, Sec'y.

Fifteenth District.
Richard M. Bolles, M. D.,
Louis Pignolet, jr.,
Frederick Patillow,
James Goodliff,
James L. Dayton,
Rev. Isaac Orchard,
Elisha Corwin,
Rufus R. Skeel,
Benjamin Lord,
John Mollard,
Isaac Orchard, Sec'y.

Sixteenth District.
Charles J. Day,
D. Thompson,
Joseph Merrill,
B. M. Fowler,
D. Coleman,

8 VISITORS. (1848.

William Rudd,
William Comb,
James Cowl,
John P. Hamilton,
Asa Smith,
Joseph Williams,
Joseph Longking,
James Millward,
John Parr,
H. Cyphers,
H. S. Benedict, M. D.,
John Ives, M. D.,
William Hayden,
Thomas Darling,
T. L. Stevens,
Charles C. Darling,
H. K. Bull,
William Heyden,
Darius Newell,
J. F. Chamberlain,
Charles C. Darling, Sec'y.

SEVENTEENTH DISTRICT.
N. B. Lane,
B. Albro,
James Duff,
C. H. Redman,
H. Griffin,
William B. Humbert,
Jonathan Wilt,
George M. Tracy,
S. Warren,
J. Valentine,
William Stebbins,
James Robertson,
James R. Gibson,
Eliphalet Wheeler,
Isaac Labagh,
James M. Cockcroft,
D. C. Weeks,
George J. Hill,
Jonathan Dibble,
Richard Horton, Sec'y.

EIGHTEENTH DISTRICT.
O. P. Woodruff,
Leonard Hazeltine,
C. H. Baldwin,
James Armstrong,
C. R. Harvey,
Richard Kelly,
Edward Roberts,
John Hurley,
John Evans,
Royal West,
R. T. Gill, M. D.,
J. W. Benedict,
J. T. Gilchrist,
George Lees,
Royal West, Sec'y.

BY-LAWS.

ARTICLE I.

Every person who becomes an annual Subscriber, a member of an Advisory Committee, or a Visitor, shall be a member of the Association.

ARTICLE II.

The President and Secretaries shall perform such duties as usually pertain to their office.

ARTICLE III.

The Treasurer shall give such security for the faithful performance of the trust reposed in him, as the Association may demand and approve. He shall take in charge all funds; keep an account of all receipts and disbursements; and pay all duly authorized demands. At the annual meeting, he shall render a particular and correct statement of all his receipts and disbursements to the Association. He shall also exhibit a summary report to the Board of Managers at their stated meetings, and whenever called upon by them for that purpose.

ARTICLE IV.

The Board of Managers shall have exclusive control of the funds of the Association, and authority to make by-laws; to fill vacancies; appoint all committees; and generally to adopt such measures as the objects of the Institution may require. It shall meet for the transaction of business, on the second Monday of every month; and the annual meeting of the Association shall be convened on the third Monday of

November, when the Board shall submit a report of its proceedings, and the officers and managers be chosen. In case of a failure to hold the specified meeting in November, a special meeting for the same purpose shall be convened in the course of the ensuing month.

ARTICLE V.

Special meetings of the Board of Managers and of the Supervisory Council, may be called by the Secretary, at the request of the President, or on receiving a requisition, signed by five members. Two days' notice must be given of the time of meeting.

ARTICLE VI.

The Managers may at any time make such alterations in these By-Laws, as may be deemed necessary; provided they be not contrary to the Act of Incorporation, and that such alteration shall be submitted to the Board of Managers at least one meeting before the same is acted upon; and that it shall not be passed upon unless specified in the call of the meeting, and when a majority of the whole number of the Board of Managers is present.

ARTICLE VII.

An office shall be opened in an eligible situation, for the purpose of concentrating and diffusing all information pertaining to the Society's operations and objects, and for the transaction of its general business.

ARTICLE VIII.

It shall be the duty of the General Agent to devote himself with diligence and fidelity to the affairs of the Association.

ARTICLE IX.

The City shall be divided into eighteen Districts, each Ward forming a District; and the Districts be subdivided into Sections. Each District shall have an Advisory Committee, to consist of five members; and each Section a Visitor.

ARTICLE X.

It shall be the duty of the Advisory Committees to divide their Districts into such Sections as to apportion to each about twenty-five families requiring attention; endeavor to obtain suitable Visitors for each Section; supply vacancies which may occur; make the necessary arrangements for placing at the disposal of the Visitors, food, fuel, and clothing, for distribution; and on some day in the first week of every month (exceping the meetings of July and August, which may be omitted in the discretion of the Committees), to convene all the Visitors of the Sections, for the purpose of receiving their returns, and conferring with them on the objects of their mutual labors. The Committees, moreover, shall duly draw upon the Treasurer for such proportion of the funds as may be appropriated to their District; they shall keep a strict account of all their disbursements, and only in extreme cases make donations of money; they shall monthly render an account of their expenditures to the Board of Managers; and in default of this duty, shall not be entitled to draw upon the funds of the Association. Each Committee shall appoint its own Chairman, Secretary, and Treasurer, and shall transmit the Reports of the Visitors, immediately after each Monthly Meeting, with any other information they may think desirable, to the General Secretary.

ARTICLE XI.

It shall be the duty of each Visitor to confine his labors exclusively to the particular Section assigned him, so that no individual shall receive relief, excepting in the Section where he is known, and to which he belongs. The Visitors shall carefully investigate all cases referred to them before granting relief; ascertain the condition, habits of life, and means of subsistence of the applicants; and extend to all such kind services, counsel, and assistance, as a discriminating and judicious regard for their present and permanent welfare requires. And in cases of sickness, it will be their duty to inquire whether there is any medical or other attendance needed; whether relief is afforded by any religious or charitable society; to provide themselves with information respecting the nearest Dispensary, and in all cases, when practicable, to refer applicants for aid to appropriate existing societies. When no other assistance is provided or available, they shall draw from the resources of this Association—not money, which is never allowed to be given, except with the consent of the Advisory Committee or a member thereof—but such articles of food, fuel, clothing, and similar supplies, as the necessities of the case require. In all cases of want coming to the knowledge of the Visitors, they will be expected to perform the same duties, although no application has been made. It shall be their duty, moreover, to render a report of their labors, and also an account of all their disbursements, to their respective Committees, at the stated monthly meeting. No Visitor neglecting these duties will be entitled to draw on the funds of the Association.

ARTICLE XII.

The Board of Managers, the members of the Advisory Committees, and certain Elected Members, shall together constitute a Supervisory Council, whose duties shall be deliberative and advisory; and its annual meetings be held on the third Monday of November, in each year. Special meetings of this body shall be held, when called by the Board of Managers.

ARTICLE XIII.

It shall be the duty of the members of the Association to endeavor, in all suitable ways, to give practical effect to its principles; especially to discountenance indiscriminate alms-giving and street-begging; to provide themselves with tickets of reference; and instead of giving aid to unknown applicants, whose case they cannot themselves investigate, to refer such applications to the Visitor of the Section in which the applicants reside, in order that such cases may be properly inquired into, and, if deserving, relieved.

ARTICLE XIV.

The printed forms of Tickets and orders for relief, shall be designated by the Board of Managers, and no other shall be used.

FIFTH ANNUAL REPORT

OF THE

NEW-YORK ASSOCIATION FOR IMPROVING THE CONDITION OF THE POOR.

THE Board of Managers respectfully present their congratulations to the numerous friends of the Association, on again being permitted to assemble, under the auspices of a benign Providence, to observe the return of another Anniversary.

As each succeeding year demonstrates the necessity of an organization like this, to meet the wants, and to regulate the alms-giving of the City, it is a source of gratification that its operations are constantly developing new proofs of its usefulness, and of its adaptation to its designs.

The various objects of the Institution are now resolved into an intelligible system, and the means for the attainment of these objects are believed to be guided by principles which are accordant to reason and Revelation. By observing these principles, success, with Divine favor, appears as certain as are the laws of antecedent and result. That, consequently, which we should most fear, is not the system we have satisfactorily tried, but ourselves, lest being intrusted with the power of benefiting our fellow-men, we fail through a misapprehension or a misapplication of our own principles. But let these principles be understood and applied, and the condition of the indigent amongst us, it is hoped, will not only be improved, but some progress be made in solving for the advantage of our own City, at least, that great and difficult problem which now so extensively agitates the world— the best remedy for social evils, in populous communities.

It is, therefore, with peculiar satisfaction the Board are enabled to report, that the operations of the past year have been distinguished beyond all others, by a careful adherence to principles and to system in the dispensation of relief. This is not attributable to any change in the organization or in the mode of its administration, but chiefly to the maturer experience of the Visitors, who, as they become practically acquainted with the rules by which aid should be given, find greater ease in their application, and greater encouragement in the results.

The Board regard it as worthy of distinct and grateful notice, that in an organization consisting of nearly four hundred individuals, but one, SIMEON P. SMITH, Esq., a member of the Advisory Committee, and a Visitor in the Eighteenth District, has been removed by death. And he died, not in this City, but abroad. He was taken away in the meridian of life from a position of usefulness, to his reward. Loved by the poor and respected by his associates, we pay this passing tribute of regard to the memory of a Christian brother, and a devoted philanthropist.

The vast amount of labor performed by the Visitors, would appear incredible, if not well attested by facts. Their services are volunteer, gratuitous, without intermission, and chiefly for natives of foreign countries, and of a different faith. During the six most inclement months of the year, they made more than twenty-seven thousand visits of sympathy and aid, besides rendering numerous other services, which admit of no statistical enumeration. Some of them, at certain seasons, devote, perhaps, one-third of their time, to the objects of this Charity. And though self-gratification with them, is neither the rule nor the end of their exertions, their labors are not wholly uncompensated. "Among my happiest hours," says a Visitor, "were those when at night, with lantern in hand, I threaded my way, through dark alleys to dreary cellars and garrets, bearing relief to the needy, and consolation to the wretched. As I witnessed the sorrows of others, and sympathized with the afflicted, my own cares and disquietudes were banished, and my peace flowed as a river. Though now obliged by ill health to relinquish these labors, their recollection is refreshing to my spirits, and will be remembered among the most pleasant of my life." Another remarks, "It was not much I gave; but it sent a new impulse of joy to a smitten heart, which spoke in her eye, and vented itself in tears. I would rather be the occasion of such tears, than possess the wealth of Crœsus or Alexander's glory." Such, leaving out of view the future, are the immediate rewards of beneficence. Toil and sacrifice are sweet in such a service. It has ennobling joys, with which no stranger intermeddles, "blessing him that gives, and him that takes."

Impulsive benevolence is selfish, indolent, indiscriminating, and generally produces evil. Not so true Charity. It is governed by principle. It is intelligent and judicious. It ascertains the character and condition of the needy, and graduates relief in amount and extent, according to their necessities. It seeks, in a word, the highest good of its object, and is satisfied with nothing else. And such, both in a physical and moral view, being the kind of Charity this Institution is pledged to bestow, if it is not all that philanthropy desires, it at least aims to become such, and regards improvement and progress, among its fundamental elements.

So frequently have the nature, necessity, and objects of

the Association been presented in previous Reports, it is unnecessary here to dwell upon them farther than to state, for the information of those who have not had access to those documents,

1. " That the Institution is founded upon those clear and repeated injunctions of Scripture, which inculcate care and sympathy for the poor, and a persevering endeavor to alleviate their sufferings and improve their condition."

2. That its arrangements for the attainment of its objects, are by making, *first*, a general division of the City into *Eighteen Districts*, corresponding in number and area to the Wards, and the appointment of an Advisory Committee of *five* persons, in each; and next, by a farther division of the Districts into *two hundred and ninety-eight Sections*, and the appointment of a Visitor to each Section.

Thus it will be seen, that the diversified labors of each District are confided to the careful supervision and control of a separate committee; and that each Section has its Visitor, whose field of labor is compressed to a limit, which will admit of his personal attention to all the needy therein; and no Visitor being allowed to give, nor the poor to receive relief out of the Section to which they belong, vagrancy is prevented, imposture detected, the physical and moral necessities of the indigent provided for, and the whole system of giving and receiving reduced to the utmost precision and certainty. For in whatever part of the City, the needy apply to the members of the Association for aid, by means of a Directory and printed tickets, they are sent back to their appropriate Section, and Visitor, whose proximity to the residence of the applicant, enables him, by personal visitation and inquiry, to extend, withhold, or modify relief, on well-defined principles, according to the deserts and necessities of every case.

Incorporation. For the purpose of securing to the Association the privileges peculiar to a Corporate Body, it has, by complying with the law, become a body politic, and corporate under the general Incorporation Act, passed April 12th, 1848. The Act requiring the business of the organizations formed under it, to be transacted by a majority of the Managers, as that body in this Institution originally consisted of one hundred members, a considerable reduction of the number became unavoidable, in order to obtain a legal quorum for the transaction of business. Besides that change, no other has been found necessary, excepting the appointment of a Supervisory Council, of one hundred members, consisting of all the Advisory Committees in the different Districts, the officers of the Association, and four elected members. In all other respects, the organization continues as it was, previous to its incorporation.

The *Nursery Committee* state that, "Since the last Report of the Board, the Nurseries on Randall's Island, under the charge of the Alms House Commissioner, have been conducted in a satisfactory manner. The spacious and convenient buildings erected by the City Authorities, on an admirable site, have contributed greatly to the welfare of their numerous inmates, in every respect. Admitting of separate classification as to health, age, and sex, together with an excellent suite of school-rooms, opportunities for promoting their physical, moral, and intellectual improvement, have abounded; and in the main, the character of the immediate caretakers of the children has been of an unobjectionable kind. It would be a source of profound regret, should the example and influences of any portion of the domestic establishment be such, as in any degree to counteract the sound moral influences, so much needed by the youthful inmates of the establishment. And it can hardly be, that an Institution embracing so very large a number of children, the offspring of indigent and depraved parents, should not exercise a large influence on the lowest class of our population. That it may be conducted with wisdom from on high, and a single eye to the immortal interests of the infant objects of its care, is devoutly to be hoped."

Dwellings for the Laboring Classes. The subject of "Improving the dwellings of the laboring classes," noticed in previous Reports, has continued to receive the attention of the Board. During the year, the Committee to whom the business was referred, gathered up, through the agency of the City Missionaries, much valuable information relative to the tenements of the poor, in different parts of the city; and of so startling a character were some of the facts, as to strengthen the conviction, that more should be done to arouse public attention to the subject, than had yet been attempted. The original view of the Board involved the idea of a separate and distinct organization, which should employ its own funds to erect one or more *Model Dwellings* on the most approved designs, to be let to suitable tenants, at a rent not exceeding that ordinarily paid for the worst description of tenements. But owing to causes beyond their control, such an organization has not been yet formed; they have, however, the gratification to state, that the attention of capitalists and builders having been drawn to the subject, some improvement in this class of tenements has already been made, and the hope is indulged that they will be progressive. Extensive observation and experience, both in America and Europe, having shown the connection which exists between the physical elevation of the poor, and the advancement of their social, civil, and religious condition, the Board regard the subject not only interesting in itself, but as legitimately falling within the objects of the Association. They design, therefore, so far as in their power, to give it the attention its importance demands; and the Committee having the business in charge, still intend to erect Model Buildings, when the temporary hinderances to their action shall be removed.

Tracts for the Laboring Classes, on economical and moral subjects, have also continued to receive attention. During the year, a second edition of the "Economist," consisting of 10,000 copies, has been distributed with very gratifying results. Numerous cases have been related of idle, filthy, improvident families, who through its influence have been so reformed, as to exercise a wise forecast, improve their domestic habits, and become industrious and respectable. One Visitor reports forty-five families which were thus benefited, and another, twenty-nine. Many of these had long been indolent and dependent upon charity, and were perfectly amazed to find their own exertions adequate to their support. Tracts, in short, for the correction of economic and social derangements, have been found so valuable an auxiliary, that another, the *second* in the series, entitled the "Way to Wealth," has been published, and an edition of 10,000 is now in the course of distribution. And for a *third*, on promoting habits of economy and good management among the poor, with special reference to the fluctuations of demand for labor, the Board have felt justified in offering a premium of *Fifty Dollars*.

The loaning of Stoves, and the distribution of *Broken Victuals*, by arrangement between the givers and receivers, have been continued with satisfactory results. And through the liberality of numerous ladies, merchants, and other benevolent individuals, a considerable amount of *new* and *second-hand* clothing, materials for clothing, blankets, shoes, hose, &c., has also been distributed to the destitute, as the most acceptable gifts that could have been bestowed. To several persons special acknowledgments are due, for their repeated, timely, and generous supplies. If affluent families and persons in business generally knew how articles of little value to them, may become wealth and comfort to the needy, donations of this kind would freely flow in, and the donors feel themselves a thousand-fold compensated.

The Board being desirous of comparing efforts with results, requested the Visitors to report for this purpose some of the most remarkable cases of improvement, which had been effected in the character and condition of families and neighborhoods within their respective sections. Numerous communications were consequently received from them, many of which were of the most encouraging kind; but the statements were generally found so nearly to resemble each other, and were, moreover, so voluminous as to preclude their publication in this Report. The Board have, therefore, deferred any present action upon these returns, farther than to deposit them among their records, as documents of great interest and value for future use.

In endeavoring, however, to form something like a just estimate of what has been done, we should look to moral rather than to satistical evidences; to facts rather than to figures. Within the year *twenty-eight thousand visits* have been made, and in five years, more than *one hundred and thirty-five thousand* visits, by two hundred and ninety-eight philanthropic laborers, solely intent on alleviating the sufferings, and on elevating the social and economic condition of the indigent. What an immense expenditure of means and of efforts is here exhibited! Yet who will undertake to compute the good effected, or give a tabular form to the results? Though such a computation may be declined as impracticable, it is not the less certain that substantial advantages have accrued to the community, beyond the eleemosynary benefits conferred upon the poor, which may be thus summarily stated.

I. It has provided for the city a system of relief, which being alike available to donors and recipients, all may now withhold alms at their doors, with the certainty that the needy unrelieved by them and referred to it, will be humanely and discreetly cared for; while the indigent, having no other resource, may with like facility, without resorting to vagrancy, find near their own homes, the aid their condition requires. And thus, it has already materially relieved our citizens who have strictly complied with its requisitions, from the annoying applications of street beggars; and by diminishing the aggregate of the evil, has practically demonstrated its ability, so far as relied upon, to remove them entirely from the city.

II. There being no public provision as formerly, for the *out-door* relief of newly arrived indigent immigrants, it was reasonable to expect, that mendicity would have increased in some ratable proportion to the recent extraordinary influx of that class of persons into the city; merely, therefore, to have prevented such increase, would of itself have been an important work, and a conclusive proof, that powerful counteracting influences against pauperism had been successfully exerted. Now there is statistical proof which shows that mendicity has not only been kept in check, but that such an aggression has been made upon it, as to diminish its numbers. According to official records, *two hundred and sixty persons* less required aid during the last, than in the previous year. This, under the existing circumstances, the Board regard as a very remarkable result, especially as it has occurred when the increased thoroughness and expansion of the Association's labors, were least likely to overlook any needing relief; at a period too, when the tide of foreign immigration has been pouring like a constant flood upon our city—300,000 having arrived at this port, within the past eighteen months!

III. It appears not more certain that mendicity and vagrancy have been repressed, than that the correction of these evils, with respect to many, will be *permanent*. For it has been a specific object to eradicate the spirit of beggary and vagrancy, by the inculcation of principles which are incompatible with such habits. This effects a radical cure. Important and humane as it is to help the needy, it is much more important and charitable, to teach them to help themselves. Hence, many long addicted to vagrancy and imposture have been induced to change their course of life; and a vastly greater number, who by injudicious relief would probably have been made paupers for life, by timely aid and proper management are now depending upon their own industry for support.

IV. The moral influence of the Visitors, incident to their frequent and familiar fireside intercourse with the poor, is too important to be overlooked. Moral results being usually of slow growth under the most favorable circumstances, their development has been watched with solicitude, and statements in regard to them have been received with caution. But the Visitors uniformly affirm, that many persons have been recovered from vicious courses, some from intemperance, and a still greater number saved from falling into this vice; and that others have been brought within the reach of religious influences, which have effected radical reformations of character. And by imparting instruction in domestic affairs, and aiding parents in the management of their children, a degree of order and comfort has been brought into numerous households, to which the inmates had long been strangers. By the introduction also of children—often wicked and disobedient—to Sabbath and day schools, or by putting them to some useful calling, many have become a present help and comfort to their parents, and qualified to obtain an honorable support for themselves in after life.

V. It may be received as an axiom in social economy, that there must be a balance somewhere in society to preserve its equilibrium—an influence somewhere to overcome the repellencies between classes, and the unnatural repression of benevolent sympathies so generally consequent upon inequality of condition, in populous communities. These influences, this Association, in an humble degree, may be said to supply. Serving as a chain of union between the highest and the lowest, the richest and the poorest, it connects the extremes of society—not by fear or dependence, but by affection and gratitude, and binds all harmoniously together. The rich thus recognizing by their kind acts their relation and duty to the poor, meet the claims of religion, and fulfill the designs of that overruling Providence, which has made them to differ; and by manifesting a feeling of brotherhood, in their endeavor to advance the virtue and happiness of others, most effectually promote their own. The poor, on the other hand, by the sympathy expressed in their behalf, and the liberal expenditure of money, means, efforts, and personal attentions for their benefit, have new and juster feelings awakened towards their benefactors, and new interests and desires in relation to society around them, making them better citizens, and tending to prevent some of the most dangerous evils, to which a populous community is exposed.

But, without enlarging on particulars of this kind, there is on a general survey, in the opinion of the Board, ample evidence that the Association during another year, has faithfully met its assumed responsibilities, fulfilled the reasonable expectation of its friends, and given encouraging promise of increasing usefulness in future. It has, with a degree of energy and success far exceeding the ability of the most devoted unassociated efforts, promptly ministered to the necessities of the sick, the destitute, the helpless and deserving of every class, without respect to persons—encouraged the industrious, reproved the indolent, detected imposture, suppressed beggary, diminished pauperism—and developed, fostered, and diffused such views and feelings in respect to the reciprocal relations and duties of the different classes to each other, as are calculated to promote the welfare of the entire community. And these results have been secured, as the expenditures will show, with an economy of means, which demonstrates, that the cheapest exercise of philanthropy and benevolence is that which is most comprehensive, systematic, and complete.

A Tabular Exhibit of the Monthly District Returns, from November 1st, 1847, to November 1st, 1848.

1847–8.	Number of Families Relieved.	Number of Persons.	Number of Visits.
November,	720	2477	1400
December,	1703	6144	3945
January,	3558	12,663	5995
February,	3653	13,295	6767
March,	3058	11,361	4934
April,	1049	3881	1485
May,	396	1453	596
June,	203	716	301
July,	62	239	76
August,	269	1010	395
September,	231	821	461
October,	451	1690	686

As unavoidable repetitions occur in the above table, occasioned by the same families being sometimes relieved through different months, the following statements are annexed, which exhibit the actual aggregate relief, to wit:—

FIFTH ANNUAL REPORT.

Number of different Families relieved from November 1st, 1847, to November 1st, 1848, . . 5,340
Number of Persons, ... 24,030
Number of Visits, ... 28,040
Disbursements for the same period, . . $25,413 59
Receipts do. . . 25,78 29

Excess of Disbursements over Receipts, . . $335 30

The Board, in concluding their Report, would not omit to acknowledge their deep obligations to the numerous friends and patrons of the Institution, by whose liberality and co-operation, under Divine Providence, it has hitherto been sustained. They scarcely need add, that though willing themselves again to enter upon this arduous and gratuitous service, and bear their full proportion of the expense and responsibility, the Association must continue to depend for its existence and means of usefulness, upon the intelligent benevolence of the city. It is to the intelligent and humane, who can appreciate the advantages to the community of an extensive, well-devised, and judiciously administered system of relief, that this charity especially appeals. From such, its aims, operations and results invite the closest scrutiny; and to such, who feel their accountability to God and their duty to the poor, it is believed the appeal will not come in vain.

Statement of the Disbursements and Receipts of the Association for Improving the Condition of the Poor, for the year ending November 16, 1848.

Dr.		
1847–8. Receipts per Contributions, &c., from Nov. 1, 1847, to Nov. 16, 1848,	$25,078	29
Balance in Treasury last year,	1,936	92
	$27,015	21

Cr.		
1847–8. Disbursements from Nov. 1, 1847, to Nov. 16, 1848,	$25,413	59
Balance in Treasury Nov. 16, 1848,	1,601	62
	$27,015	21

The undersigned, having examined the accounts of Stewart Brown, Esq., Treasurer pro tem., and found vouchers for all the sums therein charged, hereby certify the same to be correct.

FREDERICK S. WINSTON,
JOSEPH B. COLLINS,
} *Auditing Committee.*

NEW-YORK, November 16, 1848.

PRINTED FORMS USED BY THE ASSOCIATION.

Ticket of Reference for the use of Members.

Mr.   Visitor,

   No.   St.

is requested to visit

at No.

                                                             Member

                         N. Y. Association for
               Improving the Condition of the Poor.

Visitor's Order.

   Mr.

No.   *St.*

Please let

have the value of

in

                             184

                                                          Vis.

                       N. Y. Association for
            Improving the Condition of the Poor.

Monthly Report.

Subjoined is a condensed plan of a Sectional Monthly Return. The original occupies a large page of foolscap, with appropriate columns, fifteen in number, which enable Visitors to give the following particulars of every family relieved. 1st. Name, residence, place of birth, sex, color, occupation, time in the city, number in family, and number of visits. 2d. Statements of character,—as being temperate or intemperate. 3d. Unavoidable causes of indigence, such as sickness, infirmity, or old age, with space for marginal remarks.

PRINTED FORM USED BY THE ASSOCIATION. (1848.)

New-York Association for Improving the Condition of the Poor.

VISITOR'S MONTHLY REPORT OF SECTION No.   DISTRICT No.   DATED   184

☞ *A mark with a pen thus ,, in the columns, will point out the class to which the person named belongs.* ☜

FAMILIES RELIEVED. Always give full Name, and *male* Head of Family, if living.	RESIDENCE OF FAMILIES. Which must be reported every month.	Foreigners.	Natives.	Colored Persons.	Males.	Females.	No. in Family.	No. of Visits.	KIND OF OCCUPATION.	Temperate.	Intemperate.	Sickness.	Misfortune.	Old Age.	AMOUNT EXPENDED. $	cts.	REMARKS.

Signed,   Visitor.

LIST OF MEMBERS.

Owing to inadvertence in the returns from some of the Districts, it is feared that the list of Members may not be perfectly accurate. The *amounts* received were duly credited, as may be seen by an inspection of the Treasurer's account, at the General office. But as the names of some who contributed small sums did not accompany their donation, with all the efforts subsequently made to obtain them, the list may still be incomplete.

A

Alsop, J. W.
Allen, Horatio
Aldrich, H. D.
Allen, Geo. F.
Aguirre, Peter A.
Allen, J. G.
Andrews, Mrs.
Adams, John
Averill, A
Allen, Stephen
Alley, Saul
Astor, Wm. B.
Astor, J. J. Jun.
Adams, William
Allen, Wm. M.
Ashton, George
Abbott, Gorham D.
Allen, Wm. C.
Aspinwall, W. H.
Appleton, A. Mrs.
Acton, John W.
Appleton, W.
Appleton, D.
Auchmuty, Mrs.
Alston, J.
A Friend,
A Friend.
Anonymous,
  Do.
Allen, William
Anonymous,
  Do.
Arcularius, M.
Anonymous,
A Friend,
Austin, Henry
A. & S.
Anthon, John
Alexander, J. W.
Allison, M.
Armstrong, M.
Arnold, Wm.

Anderson,
Archer,
Andrews,
Anderson, E. J.
Adams, J. T.
Abbott
Anderson, Capt.
Allen, Geo. W.
Arnold, Mr.
Andrews, Mr.
Anthon, Henry, Rev.
Allen, G.
Adriance, Thos. M
Aims, Jacob
Anderson, S. W.
Anstice, Henry
Adrance, Abm.
Anderson, P.
A. L. H.
Anderson, James
Aymar, William
Adolphus & Moser,
Andrew, J. B. M.D.
Adikes, M. H.
Alcock, H.
Ayres, Mrs.
Atwill, J. F.
Alexander, Wm.
Aikman,
Allen, Henry
Anderson, Jas. B.
Asten, Joseph
Ackerman, John
Angevine, O.
Adams, H. C.
Albro, Richard
Anderson, C, V.
Abbe, G. W.
Ahremfeldt, Henry
Adams, C.
Aims, Peter
Albro, B.
Armstrong, James
Alexander, J.

Adelsdorfer, Mr.
Adburgher, H.
Abeel, Mrs.
Arnold, James
Aler, J. B.
A Friend, by B. McCartin.
Alford, Edwin M.
Amerman, J. W.
Ambler. J. G.
Ahrens,
Akerly, R. C.
Abbott, Mr.
Anderson, John
Aims, Peter
Anderson, Wm.
A Friend,
Allen, Wm.
A Friend.
Abeel, John H. A.
Avery, John W.
Aikman, Hugh
Allen, Wm. A.
A Friend, by H.
Ahles, Mrs.
Aken, J.
Ayers, Reuben
Andrews, H. M.
Amertage, E. R.
Amerman, Rev. Mr.
Anonymous, by J. Lenox,
Austin, David
Abbott, S.
Allen, S.
Aspinwall, J. L.
Ayerigg, B.
A Friend, by W. E. Laight,
Arcularius, A. M.
A sincere Friend,
Arnold, A.
American Museum,
A. & S.
Appleton,
Atwater, W.
A. & H. S. T. & Co.

LIST OF MEMBERS. (1848.

Aikman, Robert
Auchincloss, H. & Sons,
A. H.
Angell, Mr.
Aldrich, H. D.
Anthony, J.
Allen, George F.
Avery, Stephen
Attridge, John
Arcularius, Andrew M.

B.

Bailey, Theo. W.
Brooks, John
Bennett, A. H.
Burnham, M.
Bigelow, Richard
Butler, Charles
Bushnell, O.
Brush, Joshua
Brown, Charles P.
Breath, James
Brown, P., Mrs.
Bradley, John N.
Burton, Wm.
Benson, C.
Bell, Thomas
Beebe, Philo
Burr, S. P.
Briggs, George
Bussing, E. K.
Banta, S.
Brownell, J. Sherman
Burrows, J.
Broadhead, E.
Bignell
Butler, Henry
Beadleston, E.
Bogardus, Wm. H.
Bervier, J H.
Bowen, George
Brigham
Blondel, Charles
Barton, J. G.
Bond
Bostwick, Charles J.
Bulby
Burdett
Bluxon
Benedick, S.
Burnston
Brown J.
Baldwin, J. C.
Baggs, Mrs.
Bronson, Arthur, Mrs.
Bartlett, A.
Brinckerhoff, N. G.
B., Mrs., by Rev. G.T.Bedell.
Ball, Tompkins & Black.
Blunt, George W.
Beers, A.
Brush, Mrs.
Briesse, L. B.
Bridge, John
Burley, James E.

Brain, J. H.
Bunker, B. F.
Beveridge
Baldwin, N. G. & Co.
Butts, O. T.
Bonnet, P.
Blain, D.
Bell, J. T.
Baker, Mr.
Blachman, Dr.
Bogardus
Blakely
Brown
Brinckerhoof
Boyd, J.
Bogardus
Briggs
Benson
Brown
Bulkley
Browning, Wm.
Buckingham, Chs.
Burritt, Francis
Boudouine, C. A.
Burdett, S. C.
Bellows, Henry W.
Burgess
Brumley, R.
Belknap, E.
Butler, H. V.
Belden, George
Baker, A. S.
Brown, Lewis B.
Baldwin, C. P.
Bausher, Mr.
Bennet, Mr.
Berrian, Mr.
Bunker, Paul
Brommer, John
Badger, Mrs.
Brown, G. W.
Blakely, Mr.
Bacon
Butts, P
Brown, E D.
Bremner, E.
Bachman, A.
Burd, G. W.
Baker, J. R.
Boyd, N. J.
Briggs, John
Bell, Mrs.
Beangers
Babcock, Nathan
Burnham, G. W.
Blatchford, E. H.
Bage, Robert
Buckland, Alexander
Bogart, Cornelius
Brown, John J.
Brown, Edwin J.
Beale, Samuel J.
Bull, Wm. G.
Baldwin, Simeon
Brady, Wm. V.
Buchanan, R. S.
Bulkley, D. V. J. D.

Bleecker, T.
Bawden, W. T.
Blumsted, J.
Brown, J. F.
Bogert, Cornelius
Baltzer, F. A.
Blakeman. W. A., M. D.
Barbour, P. G.
Benson, C. S.
Barker, U. P.
Bulkley, C. A.
Barrell, George
Buck, Wm. J.
Boorman, James
Brown, Silas
Barclay, George
Bradford, William
Butler, Benjamin F.
Brooks, Horace
Blashfield, W. H.
Bedell, Rev. Dr.
Ball, H.
Bullard, Mrs.
Bedford, Dr.
Burr, Edwin
Benninger, A. G.
Bartlett, Edwin
Brown, J. M.
Brown, Stewart
Beach, Henry
Benedict, E. C.
Booth, D. A.
Bell, Wm. H.
Blunt, Geo. W.
Bidwell, W. H.
Bussing, John S.
Bonnett, P. R.
Bolton, Doctor
Bolton, Curtis
Biddle, Edw'd R.
Barkley, James
Bartholomew, S.
Broad, John H.
Beekman, Ab'm
Bartlett, A. M.
Burn, Mr.
Brigham & Miller
Boorman, Robert
Brown, E. M.
Berrian, W. D.
Baird, R., Rev.
Bogart. Henry K.
Barclay, Mrs.
Braduer, A.
Barnes, George
Bruce, Mrs.
Babcock, Mr.
Brouwer, J.
Bearns, W. F.
Badeau, Peter
Banks, Theo.
Burgers, C. A.
Brinchley, John
Brinckerhoff, Mrs.
Bethune, Mrs.
Bleecker, J. W., Mrs.
Bowden, Andrew

1848.) LIST OF MEMBERS. 31

Botine, Peter
Bornholt, Mrs.
Brower, Ogden & Co.
Brower, J. L.
Beesley, J.
Brooks, George
Brooks, Joshua
Burrell, Sam'l
Bronson, E C., Mrs.
Boyd, Wm.
Bouchaud, J.
Brewer, R.
Boudoine, C. A.
Breweck, Jacob
Brown, F.
Barclay, Mr.
Byrnes, E.
Beukard, J.
Bachmann, Mr.
Button, John
Bostwick, Mrs.
Bailey, Mr.
B. F. A
Butler, Francis
Brissel, John
Bennett, Dan'l
Baley, S.
Blondel, Chs.
Burke, Mich'l
Burdett, Mrs.
Barden, Wm.
Beavers, Jesse
Bannister, George
Babcock, F. H.
Beam, M. R.
Belcher, P.
Bishop, Peter V. W.
Brooks, Benj. Y.
Branch, Wm. L.
Barker, John
Bell, Richard
Banks, Mark
Butt, John
Brown, J. H.
Bosworth, J. S.
Barkley, Mr.
Bannan, Owen
Beenan, J. & C.
Ballagh, W. & R.
Barber, Mr.
Briant, D. S.
Burkhalter, Stephen
Barry, John
Buxton, John, Jr.
Burras, T. H.
Bridges, J. F.
Ballagh, Wm.
Baxter, Samuel
Broad, S. S.
Bremner, J. P.
Burgess, Phineas
Burdge, Ira
Bell, James M.
Barker, Joseph D.
Bradley, W. C.
Brown, Thomas
Bloodgood, William

Blatchford, Samuel M.
Bolles, Richard M.
Benedict, H. S., M. D.
Bull, H. K.
Baldwin, C. H.
Benedict, J. W.
Beers, J. D.
Bridge, Mrs.
Bronson, F., Ex'r.
Blunt, N. B.
Brown, James
Burr, Isaac, Mrs.
Bininger, Abraham
Brush, Stephen
Brown, R. J.
Bolles, Dr.
Boyd, Thomas
Blois, Dr.
Buel, Dr.
Beebe, S. J.
Brown, R. W.
Birdsall, James
Burkhardt, C. B.
Banyer, M., Mrs.
Brooks, Sidney.
Bronson, A. E., Mrs.
Barnes, D. H., Mrs.
Brevoort, Henry
Banks, Wm.
Beekman, J C.
Brown, Richard
Blackett, John
Bedell, Henry
Bruce, George
Bishop, Japhet
Bayard, Robert
Bartlett, J. R.
Barrows & Pitcher
Barnet, Mr.
Brown, John P.
Bache, G. P.
Brown, Mr.
Binsse, Louis B.
Bird, George
Belding, Wm., Rev., Jr
Beals, Sam'l J.
Babcock, Mrs.
Brandreth, Benj., M. D.
Banyer, Mrs.
Brunson, Silas
Barclay, Anthony
Brodie, Mr.
Bellnap, A.
Burger, Wm.
Brown, J. F.
Brown, A. & J.
Burkhalter, Stephen
Bininger, A. G.
Bard, Wm.
Burns, H.
Boyle & Coleman
Bennett, N. L.
Bruister, T. H.
Bell, Mr.
Bennett, P.
Baldwin, N.
Butcher, J. H.

Brush, Moses
Barker, Capt.
Boyd, Daniel
Burr, J.
Burke, Wm.
Baldwin, C. A.
Booth, Mr.
Brons
Bigler, D.
Bunting, C.
Bowyee, A.
Banks, Wm.
Brinckerhoof
Butt, C.
Benedict, M.
Baker, Mr.
Batte, H. S.
Bruce, J. & R.
Bell, Joseph M.
Babbitt, W. H.
Booth, Jonas
Berger, James
Bradly, Wm C.
Burling, S. S.
Brush, J. E.
Baldwin, Luther,
Brewster, Joseph
Brown, G. P. G.
Bogardus, J. P.
Berlew, R.
Bleecker, G. N.
Bradley, J.
Buckman, Ezra
Blackmer, J.
Burks, C. C.
Board of Brokers
Bruen, A. M.
Bunce, N.
Blanco, B.
Burtus, James A.
Banker, Ewdard
Bristol, W. B. & Co.
Boddy, G.
Brombacher, Jacob
Barlow, B. R.
Bunce, Geo. F.
Buchanan, Mr.
Bryson, Mr.
Bell, F. W.
Brown, W. S.
Brown, W. C. Mrs.
Beebe
Barrows & Pitcher
Breese & Elliot
Brown, De Rossett & Co.
Burgess, Stringer & Co.
Backus & Osborn
Bangs, L.
Bowman, Samuel S.
Bell, A. & Son.
Benjamin, W. M.
Barker, G.
Burns, W. D.
Bon, Ls.
Banderet, C.
Barker, James
B. H. Mr.

LIST OF MEMBERS. (1848.

Burt, W.
B. E. T.
Burk, F.
Boarders at Mrs. Crooker's
Bowne & Co.
Blanco, B.
Baldwins, Dibble & Work
Brown, Bartholomew
Badger, Jacob
Byrd, George J.
Bowen & McNamee
Blake, B. Marshall
Burkhalter, C.
Blackstone, W.
Burritt, Mrs.
Blondell, Wm.
Bloodgood, M.
Bloomfield, E. S.
Bond, Thos. E. Rev.
Beales, J. C.
Beekman, J. W.
Banks, Martha
Born, J.
Bussle, George
Boyce, Geradus
Buckhalter, R.
Binsse, L. B.
Bayles, J.
Benson, Mrs.
Benson, J. G.
Brown, W. H.
Bishop, J.
Boardman, Wm.
Birdsall, Hosea
Bennet, Wm.
Boyce, James
Brooks & Cummings,
Burkley, Wm.
Breasted, Mr.

C

Collins, Joseph B.
Cash, R. K.
Cash, E. P.
Cash, J. P.
Clark & West
Crane, Wm. W.
Canfield, D. W.
Center, A. H.
Cash, D. A.
Cash, (Ely)
Clossen, Aaron
C. W. F. & Co.
Craighead, R.
Cash, B.
Constant, Samuel S.
Cash, J. L. R.
C. & D.
Cottenet, F. & Co.
Cotheal, H. & D.
Carey, S. T.
Collins, E. K.
Comstock, D. A.
Cook & Co. Levi
Corlies, Haydock & Co.
Coster, H. A.

Course, Israel
Curtis, P. A.
Campbell, James
Collins, G. C.
Curtis, Joseph
Cornell & Ammermann
Clark, Matthias
Capen, H. T.
Collamore & Davis
Clarke, P. Mrs.
Cash
Connah, J.
Cornell, T. F.
Cornell, J. H.
Curtis, Charles
Chambers, W.
Craft, Joseph
Clark, J. B.
Collins, Mr.
Carpenter, G.
Cornell, S. M.
Chauncey, Wm.
Curtis, C. E.
Creighton, Frederick
C. H. M.
Cahoune, W.
Colton, Thomas
Crane
Coe, Mrs.
Campbell, J. D.
Coit, Levi
Clark, E. S.
Coit, Henry A.
Clark, J. L.
Cook, Z. jun'r.
Colwill, A.
Clark, F. H.
Cruft, Wm. S.
Cohen, L. I.
Cuming, T. B.
Cooper, F. Dr.
Cutler
Cox, A. L. Dr.
Clark, P. F. Dr.
Couch, William
Clark, J. A.
Crump, F. R.
Coe, B. H.
Cutting, R. L.
Collins, S. B.
Clements, J. W. G., M. D.
Cooper, H. T.
Chauncey, Henry
Concklin, Jonas
Champlin, Dr.
Cariyl, N. T.
Carpender, J. S.
Cruger, J. C.
Crane, D. B.
Coddington, T. B.
Cronkite, J. P.
Currie, William
Canfield, M.
Cammann, O. J.
Center, E. C.
Colles, James
Cash

Cobb, James N.
Clinton, George
Coursen, Mrs. A.
Currier, N.
Clinch, James
Cuyler, V.
Covell, L., M. D.
Campbell, D.
Crosby, John P.
Catterfield, Wm. F.
Cooper, W. S.
Chapin, G. S.
Coddington, J. J.
Cisco, John J.
Clark, Geradus
Clarkson, J. C.
Clark, R. S.
Crosby, Wm. B.
Connor, Mr.
Cash
Conway, Mr.
Clark, James
Cook, Alderman
Copeman, J.
Cash
Cash
Conger, John
Cook, Miss
Carpenter, E.
Cash
Cash
Clark, Samuel
Corey, Mr.
Cockle, Samuel M.
Cash
Chambers, J. L.
Craig, Mr.
Chichester, Lewis
Caverly, J. R.
Clickman
Clinch
Cordell, S. C. M.
Contort, J. H.
Cheesbrough, Mrs.
Coates, J. H.
C.
Cooper, John
Cash for Tea
Cash
Chatain, H.
Colman, Mrs.
Coey, Wm. John
Chain, Mr.
Clendenen, P.
Cape, J. J.
Cape, Hannah M. Mrs.
Cockcroft, James
Cook, Ebenezer
Cornwell, J. D.
Clark, Miss
Campbell, Thomas P.
Cooke, S. G.
Colten, C.
Crasley, Mr.
Churchman, O.
Cary, W. F.
Cholwell, Jacob

1848.) LIST OF MEMBERS. **33**

Cromwell & Birdsel
Coggeshall, George
Craft, John
Cooledge & Brother, J. F.
Canton Tea Company
Cargill, Wm.
Cragin, George D.
Clarkson, Cornelius D.
Corwin, Elisha
Comb, William
Coleman, D.
Cowl, James
Cyphers, H.
Chamberlain, J. F.
Cockcroft, James M.
Chardavoyne, W. & T.
Cowperthwaite, J. R.
Cludius, Charles
Carroll, A. B.
Clarke & Co.
Church, Charles M.
Cauldwell, Elizabeth
Currier, N.
Childs, Caspar C.
Carl, J.
Crawford, E.
Childs, W. L.
Chamberlain, Charles
Clark, H.
Christopher, Richard
Crowe, Mrs.
Conroy, Mrs.
Christial & Draper
Crawford, M. A.
Campbell, Geo. W.
Campbell, W. S.
Cahoon, B. J.
Conover, D. D.
Connoly, Charles M.
Curtis, L.
Catheal, H. S.
Cummings, Thomas
Coggill, Henry
Clinch, Charles P.
Chamberlain, E.
Conover, Gustavus A.
Curtis, S.
Carlin, John
Cox, Charles B.
Cunningham, W. S.
Cary, George D.
Cotton, C.
Cooper, William
Courtland, E. H.
Conner, D. T.
Collins, J. B
Clark, E.
C. S.
Collection from Church of
 Ascension
Carey, S.
Chesterman, James
Condit & Noble
Carnes, D. C.
C . . . The Misses
Cartmen in employ of Kennys, Breese & Sampson

Collins, D. C.
C. R. S. 5th Ward
Cooper, Peter
Colgate, Charles C.
Curry, D. F.
Camp, B. F.
Constant, S. S.
Campbell, D. P.
Caswell, John
Cutting, F. B.
Cock, Thomas, M. D.
Coles, H
Colgate, Mrs.
Cannon
Carman
Cash
Cattenhorn
Cox, Joseph
Cash
Chilton, James R.
Cash
Cordey
Cash
Cook & Adell
Cain & Company
Cash
Cromwell
Currin
Cash
Childs
Cahoone, Mr.
Cash
Corlies, H.
Camman, Oswald
Colgate, Robert
Cheever, George B.
Chegary, H. D.
Cash
Cash
Coffin, E.
Cummings, T. P.
Cash, 32, East 20th stret
Cash, 48, West 21st "
Cash, East 15th
Crocker, John
Cash, 361, Grand
Cash, 77, Suffolk
Clarkson, William
Cash, 7 Suffolk
Campbell, Mr.
Crane, Mr.
Carrick, Mr.
Curragher, Capt.
Cash
Clussman, Mrs.
Cain, Peter
Cash
Cash
Coe, D. J. Rev.
Church, Mrs.
Colden, Mrs.
Cochran, S.
Carter, R.
Copcutt, J. & F.
Carmer, C. W.
Cannon, C.
Charraud, J.

Copcutt, J.
Cook, E.
Collamore, E.
Conklin, W.
Cammann, Dr.
Cornell, G. J.
Chapman, J. G.
Caffrey & Blood
Campbell, Mrs.
Cunningham, Wm.
Conover, J. S.
Cairns, David
Cole, R.
Case, George
Cole, Mrs.
Combs, John.
Conant, F. J.
Cummings, Silas
Cornell, Mark
Cook, James
Coles, G. Rev.
Clark, George
Crawley, P.
Campbell, Matthew
Curtis, George B.
Cammann, F. W.
Christy, Thomas
Cooper, John
Cowl, James
Crouch, John
Connor, James E.
Conacher, Mr.
Cranna, George
Churchward, Mr.
Columbian Foundry,
Cass, John C.
Colgate, C. C.
Cochrane, S.
Cole, H.
Carter, Robert
Cobb, George T.
Camp, Amzi, Rev.
Clannon, Simon
Carpentier, Reuben S.
Chichester, Edward L.
Cutter, S.
Conover, Daniel
Ca

D.

Denny, Thomas
Douglass, J. H.
Davis, Thomas E.
Davies, H. E.
Downer, Samuel, Jr.
De Witt, Thomas, Rev.
Deming, B.
Depeau, Madame
Depeau, L.
Davis, Prof. Charles
Delafield, Dr.
De Wolf, J., Mrs.
Dawson, B. F.
Dwight, Mrs.
Dibble, Henry E.

34 LIST OF MEMBERS. (1848.

Dibble, Ezra
Durrand, A. B.
Dustan, S., Mrs.
Denison, L.
Delano, Warren, Jr.
Delano, Franklin H.
De Forest, George B.
Dykers, J. H.
Dickson, Sam'l Henry
Davison, Mrs.
Dashwood, Emma, Mrs.
Dowling, C. E., Rev.
Durbrow, John B.
Dale, T. N.
De Peyster, Fred'k
Dawson, William
D....., Doctor and Mrs.
Draper, Dr.
Dennis
Detmold, Dr.
Draper, G.
De Lanney, A. & V.
De Peyster, James E.
De Forest, Benjamin
Davis, Gilbert
Donaldson, James
Downes, Mrs.
Dunlap, T.
Davies, Thos. A.
Driggs, Chester
Dean, Henry
Dodd, John B.
Day, Mahlon
Dean, Thomas
Dunshee, Samuel
Dickinson, Charles, M. D.
Douglas, Mr.
Dickerson, J. S.
Dale, N. T.
Delapierre Chs. B.
Dana, R. P., Mrs.
Deaney, John
Darling, Danl. S.
Demming, C. W.
De Klyne, Barent
Dolbear, Thos. W.
De Klyne, Wm.
De Forest
Dickerson, Charles
Dill, M.
Demarest, David
Degraw, John
Dunlap, Mrs.
Daw, J.
Dudley, A. T.
Dutilh, E.
Dutilh & Cousinary
Dennistown, Wood & Co.
De Rahm & Moore
De Peyster, Mrs.
Delafield, E.
Douglass,Mr.,byJ.B.Fleming.
De Forest, L.
Dord, C.
Davis, J. M., Jones & Co.
Drummond, J. P.
D. M.

D. B. & Co.
Delluc & Co.
D. U.
D. & D.
Doubleday, U. F. & E.
D. & B.
Dibblee, Richardson & Co.
Dannistown & Disbrow.
De Ruter, John
Day & Newell
Dickie, Patrick
Drillinger, C.
Dickie, Edward J.
Dyckman, Wm. N.
Ducker
Deveau, John A.
D., Mr.
Douglass, A.
Duncan, Francis
De Forest, L.
Duke, W. S.
Dayton, James L.
Darling, Charles C., Rev.
Day, Charles J.
Darling, Thomas
Duff, James
Dibble, Jonathan
Dodge, Mr.
Dodge, David L., Mrs.
Donnelly, T.
Dibble, W. W.
Donnelly, N. T.
Daniels, George
De Wint, J. C.
Donelsen, James, Mrs.
De Leon, Mrs.
Delafield, Joseph
Dryden, George
Dean, W. E.
Dolsen, G. L.
Dubois, Wm.
Dixon, J.
Drake, Mrs.
Disbrow, Mrs.
Dalrymple
Davis, Evan
Draher, Mrs.
Denham, Mrs.
Denham, Mr.
Davidson, F.
Dwyer, John
Dunn, James
Dougherty, M.
Downing, Agustus C.
Down, Thomas
Downer, S. P.
Dean, Nicholas
Dansforth, M. J.
Dixon, C. P.
Denniston, Chs. C.
Dunn, Hugh S.
Davis, Robt. E.
Dunn, Mr.
Denman, A. A.
Darling, George
Doolittle, L. F.
Doremus, Henry

Duckstador, B.
Drinker, W. W.
Duberceau, L.
Dunn, E. F. C.
Donover, Wm.
Dorr, J. O.
Doig, Peter
Dickinson, J. B.
Dyer, Charles C.
Dwight, W. W., M. D.
Dakin, C. P.
Demarest, W. R.
Deems, H. W.
Davis, N. S., M. D.
Danforth, J.
Downs, Smith
Dennis, S. A.
Dowley, J.
Denistown
Dows & Cary
Denison, C., Jr.
Douglass, Wm.
Day, H. H.
Dayton, S.
Duchworth
Dwyer
Deen & Thornton
Dole, N. J.
Deane
Dodge, Wm. E.
Duffy, Patrick
Davidson, Jos.
Davis, S. A.
Dickson
Duncan, F.
Dearborn, J.
Degrove, Mrs.
Doman, A.
Downing, T. K.
Decker, J. H.
Dowe, John J.
Dennis, Oliver
Dennis, J. B., M. D.
Dusenbury, J. H.
Duncan, G., Miss
Dimm, Henry
Dearborn, J.
Deal, Martin
Demarest, T. M.
Dortick
Depster, H. N.
Dowling, Robert
Dunshee, Samuel
Delprat, John C.
Daniel, W.
Dieffenbach, Henry
Dailey, Timothy
Drake, Benjamin, M. D.
Dodd, John M.
Dunn, Mr.
Dissenhoefer, Isaac
Dunn, or Danie, W. A.
Dennistown
Dannat, W. H.
Daniels, W. A.
Downer & Son
Dare & Webb

Doblin, A.
Dando, S.
Decker, Charles
Dobson, A. W.

E.

Ellison, Richard
Edwards
Eaton, D. C.
Emmett, Robert
Elliman, J. B.
Endicott, George
Edgar, M. B.
Everitt, S. K.
Evesson, Henry
Evans, Mrs.
Ely, J. M.
Eustapieve, Alexis
Edgar, William
Edwards, S. J.
Elliman, C. B.
Engle, Samuel S.
Elsworth, E.
Ensworth
Edmonds, F. W.
Earle, Morris
Everts, W. M.
Eveleth, John H.
Ely, H. G.
Elstroth, J. G.
Eveleth, E., Miss
Evans, Jos. T.
Ewen, Ogilvie
Ewen, Daniel
Elliott, Mrs.
Earl & Bartholomew
Emmons, Geo. F.
Ellerson, John
Eversley, Charles
Eastman, S. J.
Eastman
Egleston & Battell
Evans, Thomas
Ewry
Erk, C.
Emmet, T. A.
Elder, George
Earle, Abm. L.
Enge, P. W.
Endicott, M.
Eaton, A.
E. A. R., by Stone & Starr.
E. W., Jr.
"Earnings for the Society for the Relief of the Poor," through Stewart Brown.
Engle, J.
Everdell
Eagle, H.
E. H. W.
Eggert, D. & Son
Elliot, Mr.
Eno, A. R.
Elsworth, H.

Earle, Miss
Earle, Thomas
Eastwood, James
Easton, Charles
Elder, Robt.
Ensign, Edward
Ebbetts, Daniel
Edwards
Eaton, Horace
Everts, W. W., Rev.
Esler, Edward
Edelmayer, John
Evans, Lemuel G.
Endicott, John
Evans, John

F.

Freeman, N. A.
Ferguson, D.
Frink, J. B.
Freeman, G. Mrs.
Forster, T. V.
Freelinghuysen, T.
Fortenbach, Mr.
Foster, Mrs.
Fowler, Mrs.
Forrest, Edwin
Fisher, John F.
Flood, Mrs.
Farquhar, Jas.
Fredov, George
Fancher, E. L.
Forster, T. V.
Forrester, William
Forbes, Benjamin B.
Faulkner, William
Fields, Edward M.D.
Ferris, J. S.
French, Daniel
Foster, Wm. A.
Fessenden, Thomas
Fraser, E. A.
Ford, Isaac
Foulke, Joseph
Fowler, T. O.
Fox, S. M.
Foster, Dr.
Fomachon, Mrs.
Foulke, M. P.
Fowler, Joseph
Frelinghuysen, Theo.
Fuller, D. B.
Finley, J. B.
Finn
Fleming, John B.
Fitzgerald, W. G.
Friend, A.
Field, B. H.
Foster, S. H.
Fraser, William
Fraser
Fisher, G. H. Rev.
Foster, C. W.
Franklin, J.
Francis, J. W. Dr.

Folger, R. W.
Forniss, Wm. P.
Fiedler, Ernest
Foster, James Jr.
Franklin, R. L.
Few, Mrs. Catharine
Flower, A.
Fowler & Odell
Fish
Fowler
Ford
Ferris
Furman
Fillman, W.
Fox, G. S.
Foster, James
Forester, Charles
Fowler, Duncan S.
Flandour, E.
Fagan, Mrs.
Fincher, J. F.
Francis, W. H.
Fowler, J. O.
Frink, Mrs.
Forster, James
Ferrero, S.
Forrester, G.
Fanning, Edward
Falconer, John
Fraser, Edward A.
Field, J.
Furnald, F. P.
Fanning, F.
Fiell, H. E.
Fent, E.
Friends
Faile, Thos. H.
Francis Norman
French, R.
Faulkner, J. C.
Fardon, A. Jr.
Fenn, Gaius
Franke, C.
Fryer, Francis
Frazee, Abm.
Fry, J.
Ford, E.
Fitch, George S.
Fairbanks, Peter
Freeman, M. N.
Fellows, Mrs.
Fowler, Chas.
Fox & Livingston
Falen, James
Ferguson, E.
Fellows & Schell
Frost, Samuel
Fellows, James
F. & L.
F. L.
Fellows, M.
Fabrequetts, E.
Fraser & Everett
F. D.
Fisher, I. J.
F. B.

LIST OF MEMBERS. (1848.

F. D. & Co.
Frasse, Henry F.
Ferguson, John
Fearing & Hall
Fulton, George
Fomer, Thomas
Fletcher, Edward H.
Fowler, John H.
Fanshaw, D.
Frances, Mr.
Field, Jude
Follet, Jacob
Frech, Jacob
Freelan, R. J. Mrs.
Fitch, Miss
Ferris, L. C.
Ferris, John H.
Fish, S., M. D.
Francis, James
Fisher, R. Jr.

G

Grosvenor, S.
Gray, John A. C.
Gibson, Isaac
Guillaume, J.
Getty, R. P.
Gallier, John,
Geissenhainer, F. W.
Geer, D.
Gradner, Thomas,
Goll, John J.
Grandy, Wm.
Godfrey, E. J.
G. E. C.
Groff, C. F.
Grocer
Gans, S. M.
Gregory, Mr.
Green, Miss.
Gruyden, Samuel,
Griffing, Samuel
Garr, A. S.
Guion
Greenwood, Mrs.
Glover, Miss
Gurnie, B.
Graham, J. L.
Grice, C. C.
Guire, A. Mrs.
Green, T. T.
Gasquet, Jos.
Gilbert, Mrs.
Gash, Peter
Gregory, J.
Gilligan, Peter
Gunning, E.
Gurley, Royal
Gantz, Geo. W.
Gallagher, Mr.
Geer, Samuel W.
Geiry
Giffin, James
Gates, John
Greenhough, J. J.
Gordon, George

Gibson, Isaac
Geer, Darius
Gray, Nathaniel
Gantz, John J.
Gray, William Rev.
Griffin, H.
Gill, R. T.
Gilchrist, J. T.
Goodwin, Eli
Goodliff, James
Green, Horace M. D.
Gray, Farley
Gould, Edward S.
Givan, M. A. Mrs.
Green, Wm. C.
Grosvenor, Jasper
Gelston, Maltby
Gallatin, Albert, Jr.
Gaw, Arch'd.
Georger, L.
Griswold, George
Green, J. C.
Gardner, J. Mrs.
Gabauden, A. W.
Gilbert, Clinton
Greenway, Wm. W. T.
Guion, F. A.
Goddard, G. C.
Giraud, D. & J.
Gould, Charles
Graham, Mrs.
Graham, Mrs. (boarders)
Gourlie, A. T.
Griffin, Francis
Grinnell, Henry
Gunning, T. B.
Green, the Misses
Goodwin
Gillilan, E. H.
Gans Meyer
Greenway, J. Henry
Greeley H. (from the country)
Grant & Barton
Gens, Meyer
Graham, Mrs. (Boarders)
Graves, E. Boonen Mrs.
Griscom, John H. M. D.
Gelston & Treadwell
Gibson, Wood
Gilsey, Peter
Gillespie, G.
Gilmore, J.
Gordon, Peter
Gavott, A. T.
Gardiner
Gardner
Gardner
Greenwood
Gleason
Griswold, John
Goodyear, H. B.
Gibbs, R. W.
Griffith, W. H.
Gibson, James R.
Goodwin, James
Goodrich, E. B.
Green, H.

Goodman, Mr.
Gillie, W. & W. F.
Glover, A. B.
Grumbes, Mrs.
Grimbs, John
Groover, J. C.
Goldsmith, D.
Galvan, Daniel
Gerow, Hiram C.
Gibert, N.
Gillespie, Mr.
Gillies, Mr.
Grey, Samuel S.
Griffin, Thomas B., M. D.
Gray, Niel
Gardner, Wm.
Gevand, H. A.
Gillman
Gelston, Mrs.
Gillett, Mrs.
Gilmour, John A.
Godwin, H. M.
Guinam, Mr.
Gaffrey, E S.
Gunn, A. N., Dr.
Groshon, John
Gabaudan, A. W.
Gregory, L.
Glosford, R. W.
Green, E.
Galloby
G., Miss
Goldane, W. C.
Gidhens, Robert
Griffith, George
Grinnell, Moses H.
Goodman, Ely
Graves, Boonen & Co.
Gallatin, Albert
G..ball, Valentine
Gordon & Talbot
Griffin & Palmer
Gale, William
Gunther, C. G.
G. N. S.
Gennin, J. N.
Gelmartin, D.
Gumand, D.
Goubleman, R.
Gardener
Goodhue, Jonathan
James R. Gibson

H

Harrison C. J., Miss
Heyer, J. Mrs.
Harrison, Jane Miss
Hoffman, P. V.
Heyer, E. P.
Hopkins, E. N.
Habicht, Edward C.
Hutton, M. S. Rev.
Hatch, Charles B.
Hopkins, Edward M.
Hendricks, Henry
Hicks, Wm. T.

1848.) LIST OF MEMBERS. 37

Holmes, Luke H.
How, Calvin W.
Hoffman, Martin
Hart, Joseph C.
Hill, A. Mrs.
Herring, J. J.
Hendricks, U.
Hendricks, W. M.
Hesser, Professor
Holton, Dr.
Holden, H. N.
Hassenberg, G.
Howland, G. G.
Hubbard, N. T.
Hadden, David & Sons
Hone, Philip
Hyatt, Edmund
Herrick, J. B.
Hills, Henry W.
Hoppock, Eli
Howes, M.
Hunt, Edwin
Holden, Horace
Havens, Henry
Hoyt, John W.
Hart, John
Holmes, John
Hoover, C.
Hoppock, Howel, Mrs.
Hendricks, Mrs.
Hall, Wm.
Howland, John
Hook, C. G.
Halstead, J. M.
Henriques, M.
Hargous, P. A.
Hall, J. Prescott
Holmes, Silas
Herrick,
Hamersly
Holmes & Co.
Hitchcock, W. R.
Hagaman, D.
Hutchinson, Mr.
Hamilton, Mr.
Hatch, E. Mrs.
Hull, W.
Hope & Co.
Hoadley, David
Hughs, Rev. Dr.
Hoyt
Howell, G. R.
Higgins, Mr.
Harman, Philip
Hadley, R.
Haws, G.
Holt, Mr.
Holmes, Samuel P.
Hunn, John
Halsted, S.
Hillman, Wm.
Horn, James
Hennesey, D.
Houghton, T. L.
Huchings, S.
Hepburn, Mrs.
Hill, J. J,

Haviland, Mrs.
Hoag, G. D.
H. W. B.
Hadley, J.
Halleck, Lucius E.
Heard, Charles
Hurton, J. H.
Hall, Harison
Hull, J. C.
Hull, Wager
Hennell, F.ederick
Harper, James
Hubbard, Archibald
Hall, Wm.
Hagadorn, John
Howard, Mrs.
Hoyt, J. B. & W.
Hoyt, C.
Holmes, Eldad
Hall, Archibald
Hart, H. &'M.
Havermeyer, F. C.
Herd, John R.
Hunt, J.
Henderson, J. C.
Hertell, Thomas
Henshelwood, Robert
Hall, Willis
Hertzell, Jacob Z.
Hall, J. F.
Hatfield, Abraham
Haughwout, Simon
Hull, Wakeman
Harrison A. Miss
Heddon, John
Hutchinson, Dr.
Hodgkinson, W.
Horton, Wm.
Hackett, John
Hammell, John
Halsted, C. O.
Howes, R. W.
Harper, Fletcher
Harper, John
Howland, Wm. H.
Hinth, S.
Hoffman. Mr.
Harper, S. B.
Haynes, Mrs.
Halsted, Mr.
H. M. F.
Howland, E.
Hunter, A. T. M. D.
Holmes, Mrs.
Hobart, Dr.
Hines, James
Henderson, R.
Hyatt, G. E. L.
Heckert, C.
Humbert, Mr.
Hoffman, Mrs.
Hardenburgh, J. B. Rev.
Hazard, S
Hoagland, J. S.
Hill, J.
Hall, E. Mrs.
Hyslop, Mrs.

Havemeyer, Geo. L.
Hays, Wm.
Harrison, Benj.
Harrison, S.
Hays, Samuel
Halley, Robert
Hahn, Christopher
Hurd, Chauncey D.
Holmes, A. B.
Halsey, Chas. H. Rev.
Hallock, James C.
Haven, John P.
House, Mrs.
Hunt, Wm. S.
Horsfield, R. T. M. D
Hinton, J. H.
Hemming, Mr.
Hanshe, J.
Harkins, B.
Hudgin, Sylvanus
Hornby, John
Hay, Peter
Hay, Allen
Hatt, George, Rev.
Harris, W. D.
Hopkins, Samuel
Hall, Ralph
Hall, Archibold
Hurd, Hiram
Henderson, Alexander J.
Hubbard, L. P.
Hume, Andrew
Horton, Jonathan B.
Holt, J. S.
Harned, William
Howell, M. H.
Horn, James
Hayter, Richard
Hogan, Thomas
Howe, Bazeleel
Howe, J. M.
Heyden, William
Horton, Richard, Rev.
Hamilton, John P.
Humbert, Wm. B.
Hill, George J.
Hazeltine, Leonard
Harvey, W. R.
Hurley, John
Hutchinson, D. R.
Hegeman, E. P.
Harriet, James
Hutchinson, Ira
Hopkins, N. F.
Hayes, J. P.
Harris, S.
Hurry, Edmund
Hay, Charles M.
Harned, Wm.
Hogland, J. E.
Hale
Howey, Thomas
Haxon
Hunt, H. W.
Hamersley, J. W.
Hoffman, L. M.
Hagerty, Draper & Jones

LIST OF MEMBERS. (1848.

Hitchcock, C.
Hone, John
Hagden, Capt.
Holmes, S.
Hopkins & Weston
Hubbard, L. P.
Holt & Pease
Hall, Valentine G.
Hicks, John H.
Hunt, Wilson G.
Horstman, Sons & Drucker.
Hayden, N.
Hunter, James
Hague, John
Hickman, Robt.
Hine, C. D.
Hutchings, S.
Hills, S. C.
Hewett, M. S.
Hoyt, S.
Heitcamp, Chs.
H..., Captain
H. A.
H. D. P.
Herring, Silas C.
Hayes, H. M.
Hechsher, Chs. A.
Harnden & Co.
Hendricks, H. M.
Havemyer, Wm. F.
Hearn, Brothers
Haveymer, Wm.
Haveymer, C. H.
Henry, Robt.
Halsey, E. C.
Hubbert, J.
Houghwout, E. V.
Halsted, J. W.
Halsted, W. M.
Hilger
Hallock, Lewis, M. D.
Hunt, Thomas
Haight, David L.
Hobbe, Mr.
Hoyt, Gould
Hoyt, James
Hoppock, H.
Hoppock, George
Hunter, W. A.
H. & V.
Hopkins
Hustice
Hasbrogh
Howell, C.
Halsey & Gastin
Hopping
Holt, C.
Hays
Hopkins & Co.
Hone
Hoes, Miss
Hawks
Higby, J. S.
Husted
Hagerty & Bench
Hyde
Houghton

Hull's Truss Office
Holbrook, E.
Halsted, W. M.
H. L. & Co.
High, Edwin
Haines, Wm. A.
Hubbs, F.
Howell, D.
Hutchings, John
Hurley, Peter
Holand, Mr.
Hatfield, Mr.
Harvey, C. A.
Higgins, S.
Houston, W.
Holston, John
Halsey, S. R. & Co.
Hoey, John
Howe, Mr.
Husted, Thos. S.
Hoyt, G. P. B.
Hobby, Mr.
Haight, E. M.
Hall, Andrew
Harger, James
Holmes, A. B.
Hartley, R. M.

I. & J.

Innes, Edward S.
Irving, John T.
Jessup, F. S.
Jessup, A. S., Mrs.
Ireland, William B.
Johnson, Wm. M.
Johnston, John
Jones, George
Iselin, A.
Jones, James J.
Jervis, J. B.
Iselin, John A.
Irving, A. S., Mrs.
Johnston, Bradish
Jones, R., Mrs.
Jones, Isaac
Jones, Wm. P.
Jones, E., Miss
Jay, Ann, Miss
Jones, Lott, Rev.
Jay, Elizabeth Clarkson, Miss
Jay, Matilda, Miss
Irving, Richard, Mrs.
J. M. H.
Jay, John
J. & S.
Jones, Walter R.
J. H.
Janes, E. S.
Jennings, N. T.
Jefferson
Johnson
Ibbotson, Henry
Janes, A.
J. W. B.
Ives, R. A.

Jenkins. Wm.
Jayne, Hamilton
Jones, D.
Ingersol, Chandler
Jaquith
Johnson, N S.
Jenkins, J. J.
Jenkins, Hannah, Mrs.
Jones, Morris
Jacobson, Joseph
Jefferies, George C.
Johnson, Saml. S.
Jackson, Thomas
I. I. D.
I. H. S.
J. P. B.
J. D.
Jackson, Geo. A.
Jennings, N. T.
Inslee, Z. C.
Johnston, Wm.
Jacobs, Laban
Jenkins, J. J.
Ives, John, M. D.
Jimmerson, R. J.
Jones, Burdsall & Rowland
Jessup & Co.
Johnson, J. E.
Johnston, R. R.
Jackson, John
Johnson, John
Ivison, H.
Johnson, F.
Jacot, E. H.
Jaffreys. Wm.
Jarvis, W. H.
Jarvis
J. C.—A Subscriber
Irving, Richard
J. C. S.
Ingolsby, M.
Jordan, C.
J. C. & F.
Johnson, H.
John, P., Son
Jones & Needel
J. L.
Johnson, Henry W.
Jones, Walter R.
Jennings, Chester
Jones, S. T.
Isaacs, Samuel, Rev.
Inman, John H.
Jacobus, David
Jacobus, C. C.
Joyce, Samuel
Jones, J. M.
Jones, W. F.
Johnson, L. L.
Jackson, James L.
J. W. R.
J. A.
J. J. H.
Johnson, Mr.
Judd, E., Mrs.
Ireland, G.
Jones, M. S., Miss

1848.) LIST OF MEMBERS. 39

J. H.
Jacobus, James G.
Jost, Frederick
Johnson, Wm. M.
Johnston, Mr.
Johnson, Wm.
Jaques, Eden F
Irving, Wm.
Johnson, Stephen
Irwin, David
Jones, Charles
Jeremiah, J.
Luther Jackson

K.

Kurshedt, J. B.
Kelly, Ely
King, J., Mrs.
Kratrenburgh & Co.
Knapp, Shepherd
Knox, John M.
Kendall, J. C.
Ketcham, Morris
Kermit, Robert
Kimball, E. W.
Knox, John, Rev.
Kinsley, Dr.
Kennedy, David S.
Kane, Delancy
Kelly, Robert
King, Mr.
King, Peter V.
Knox, Edward
Knapp, B.
Kieran
Kinnedy
Knapp
King, C. E.
Kellogg, S. O.
Kayser, Henry
Keeps, Henry
Kissam, George
Kellogg, J. D.
Keage, Wm M.
Kennedy, Thos.
Ketchum, E. W.
Kuner, Frederick
Knapp, James H.
Kipp, F. A.
Ketchum, J. R.
Knapp, S. P.
Kirk
Knipe, Wm.
Knapp, F. A.
Ketchum, John W.
Kensett & Wheeler
Kingman, H. W.
Kirks, C. C.
King, C., Mrs.
Ketchell, Mr.
Knapp, G. Lee & Palen
Kirby, Valentine
Knolton, D.
King, R. S.
Knapp, Wm. H.
Kissam

King, J. G.
Kane, J. J.
Kingsley, E.
K. & Son
Kreymborg, G. H.
Ketcham, Morris
Kemble, Wm.
Knapp, P. B.
Karr, D.
Knapp, R.
Keese, Wm. M.
Kennedy, Wm.
Knapp, Wm. R.
Knouse, Charles
Kidder, Mr.
Kelsey, John
Kelly, R. W.
Kinny, George
Kingsland, D.
Kissam, A. B.
Keen, R.
Kingsford, T. J.
Kingsbury, O. R.
Kirby, L.
Kentgen, Mrs.
Kettell, G. F., Rev.
Kummell, H. E.
King, William
Kirnaen, John
King, George
Kydd, Wm.
Kaus, J. P.
Kelly, Richard

L.

Leonard & Wentd
Lester, Andrew
Leeds, Samuel
Laverty, Henry
Livingston, B.
Lawrence, R. M.
Lowerre, Seaman
Loines, Wm. H.
Lent, Mortimer
Lane, Anthony
Lowerie, W.
Lambert, J.
Lewis, J. W.
Lewis, J. S.
Lane, M. A.
Lodewick, J M.
Ludlow, John
Lugar, Mr.
Lathan, E.
Lewis, E.
Lloyd & Wells
Lee & Brewster
Land, A.
Lohman, Isaac
Lewis, J., Rev.
Le Roy, Danl.
Lawrence, Mrs.
Lawrence, R.
Lee, Wm.
Lydig, P. M.

Lane, Mrs.
Lawrence, R.
London, Mrs.
Ladd, W. S.
Lee, J. A.
Lord, R. L.
Lane, Mis.
Litton, J.
Leonard, John
Love, Joseph
Lamb, Thomas
Lit, Domingos
Lightowler, John
Lewis, S. W.
Longking, John
Lawrence, Richard
Lister, Joseph
Lawrence, S. A.
Link, Cutlep
Lupton, Chs.
Longking, Joseph
Loder, Lewis B.
Leask, Henry G.
Lawrence, R.
Laight, E. W.
Lawry, John
Livingston, John R.
Lawrence, Joseph
Le Roy, Jacob
Leeds, Samuel, Jr.
Ludlum, H.
Leland, Francis
Livingston, M.
Livingston, V.
Lockwood, Roe
Lee, John H.
Litgur, F.
Livermore, W. W.
Lentillon, Eugene
Lathrop, Dwight
Lane, D.
Livingston, F. H.
Le Barbier, A.
Lownds, R., Mrs.
Lownds, J., Miss
Lowrie, Walter
Lawson, James
Lyn h, Jane, Mrs.
Loeschigk, W.
Luquer, R. S.
Lawrence, Thomas
Lord, B.
Luyster, P. J.
Ludlow, J. R.
Low, Cornelius
Leverich, H. S.
Lenox, James
Ludlow, G., Mrs.
Lovett, G.
Locke, John D.
Lorillard, P.
Leupp, Charles M.
Lawrence, Isaac
Lyons, Mr.
Lord, D.
Lee, David
Lawson, Miss

LIST OF MEMBERS. (1848.

Lillienthal, L.
Lee, D. L.
Le Comte, N.
Lindsey
Lewis & Jenkins
Lam, or Lane, Mrs.
Ludwig
Laquin
Lockwood, W.
Lane
Le Comte
Lindsley
La Fever
Langdon
Leverich, Mrs.
Livingston, J. W.
Lane, Mr.
Ludlum, Mr.
Laroe, J. C.
Lamb, B. F.
Levy, Mr.
Lane, N.
Lay, Mrs.
Lynch, Mrs.
Lawrence, Wm.
Lane, Mrs.
Ludlum, N. S.
Lynch, Mrs.
Lewis, W.
Lewis, W. H.
Lounsbery, N.
Lilienthal, D., Rev.
Lynes, B.
Lord & Taylor
Lane, J. A.
Leggett, Abm.
Lester, J. B.
Lander, T. D.
Ludlam, Wm.
Lyon, Wm.
Low, M. P.
Leroy, Thomas Otis, & Co.
Loder, Benjamin
Leavenworth, R., Mrs.
Lathrop, Wm. K.
Leary, J.
Lucas, Archd.
Lawrence, W. E.
Little, A.
Lee, John, Jr.
Lee, D. F.
Laight, W. E.
Leavitt, Trow & Co.
Livingston, M., Mrs.
Lenox, Miss
Laing, E. H.
Le Roy, J. H.
Le Roy, J. C.
Lewis, James T.
Lang, L.
Lord, J. C.
Long & Davenport
L. C.
Luersen, G.
Little, Chs. L.
Luckey, James C.
Longstreet, S.

Lippencott, Thomas
Lowerre, George W.
Ludlum, A. B.
Lefferts, Cornelius
Lee, Danl. F.
Loper, Charles S.
Lord, Benjamin
Longking, Joseph
Lane, N. B.
Labagh, Isaac
Lees, George
Lay, J. C.

M.

Mather, Eliza G.
Mather, Ellen L.
Meakim, J. & A.
Morris, Anne, Mrs.
Messerole, Abraham
Majie, David, Jun.
Merwin, T. T.
Manigault, Mrs.
Morris, Anna E. Miss
M'Jimsey, J. M.
Montant, A. P.
Marie, C.
Mitchell, Wm.
Muller, Charles C.
Man, A. P.
Moore, Samuel
Miller, William
Mead, William
Maitland, W. C.
McCracken, Francis
Myers, M. S.
Malcom, W. H.
Mott, Wm. F. Jr.
Munro, Hugh
McArthur, Wm.
Morgnn, E. D.
Maltby, O. E.
Morgan, Matthew
Morrell, Mrs.
Mitchell, Mrs.
Manson, D.
Munsell, H. H.
Meyer, Henry
Marwin, E. E.
McNamee, Theodore
Meletta, Charles
Mills, T. H.
Mead, Mrs.
Meeks
Marshall, C. H.
Mortimer, John H.
Mann, Francis
McCall, J. H. Mrs.
McCurdy, R. H.
Maggs, Joseph
Mason, E. Rev.
Mann, William
Morgan, John J.
Minturn, S. Mrs.
Morris, Gerard W.
Marsh, James
Minturn, Robert B.

Maitland, E. S. Mrs.
McCall, James
Minturn, Edward
McVicker, Dr.
Moore, Dr.
Meich, R.
Moses, D. B. & W.
Martin, H.
Micoll
Morrison, Samuel
Meiggs
Moore, J. C.
Maverick
Miller, C.
McLauren
Merritt, Miss
Martin, Charles
Metcalf, A. W.
McChain
Marwedell, F.
Magill, James
McCreary, John D.
Morrison, David
Miles, A.
Morris, B. L.
Murphy, W. J.
Millbank, S. Jun.
Miner, W. W. M. D.
Moore, J. L.
Merritt, W. H.
McGarvy, William
Merritt, Joseph G.
Many, Francis
Merle, G.
Modert, Z.
Moseman, Mr.
Moore, S. W.
Miller, E.
Morrell, Thomas
Mount, Elijah
Matthews, William
Maguire, B.
Mullins, D.
Mathey, A.
Mayo, Ann, Mrs.
Mattison
Moffat, David
McKay, Mr.
Moreau, Mr.
Miller, Charles
Morse, Richard C.
McCarron, Michael, Rev.
Mann & McKimm
Milnor, E. Mrs. Rev.
Minturn, C.
McMartin, Duncan
McLeod, A.
Manning, M. D. Mrs.
McKewan, John
Marshman, B.
Marshall, D. D. T.
Miller, N.
Mills, A.
Miller, Jacob
McPherson, P.
Morgan, C. W.
Metzgar, C.

1848.)   LIST OF MEMBERS.   41

Millikin, Charles
Masterson, John H.
Mason, T.
Mills, Andrew
Maybe, Mr.
Mortimer, John, Jun.
Miles, C.
Murphey, James
McComb, John
Murray, Robert J.
Murray, Mary
M'Cready, D. A., Mrs
McLord, Helen
McLord, Eliza
Mead, Frederick
Mackrell & Richardson
Martin, S.
Morrison
Maas, H.
Mooney, B.
Martin, L.
Matthews, J. H.
McGuire. P.
Morton, W. Q.
McAuley, Mrs.
McDonald, S.
Mettler, S.
Millet, M. E.
Myers, F.
Myers, Mrs.
McKah, Mr.
McCoy, S.
Moley, E. Miss
Merry, C. H.
Menzies, Mr.
Mott, Mrs.
Morton, J.
Morris & Allen
Maxwell, W. H. Mrs.
Miller, John
Masterson Michael
McFarland, Ann
Myers, Christian
McQuoid, William
McFord, Thomas
Myers, Henry
Moriarty, A. P.
Musgrif, William
McKona, Thomas
Martin, Alfred
McBride, Abram
May, E. H. Rev.
Morrison, Mrs.
Myers, M.
Meikleham, Dr.
Miller, James
Mayhew, George A.
March, Thomas E.
McAdams, Thomas
Merritt, S.
Moore, Richard
Myol, Frederic
Menzies, William
McCutchen, Hugh
Maidment, John
Mapes, W. H.
Mitchell, Robert

Martin, W. S.
Mitchell, George
Matt, E.
McKiernan, Thos.
Moses, Lorenzo
Muhlenburg, W. A., Rev. Dr.
Mangam, W. D.
McCoon, Mr.
Meeker, David
Moffatt, David
Marshall, Benjamin, M. D.
McNaughton, A. P.
McClain, O. D.
McWilliams, J. H.
Myers, John C.
Martin, William
Martin, H. C.
Murray, John
McCreary, John D.
Murphy, William
Miller, Caleb
Marsh, John R.
Merrill, Charles.
Mollard, John
Merrill, Joseph
Millward, James
Mather, F. Ellsworth
Mumford, A. B.
Miller, Jonathan
Messereau, W.
Marsh, P. S.
Martin, D. Randolph
Miller, J. R.
Messett, B. W. Cary
Meigs, H., Jr.
Many, Vincent W.
McVean, C.
McCotter
Moses, D. B.
Maltby, E.
Mitchell
Moor
McAdams, Mrs.
Meigs, C. A.
Mildeburger, John A.
Moore, N. F.
Metcalf, J. W.
McWhorter, Miss
Moore, J. L.
Munn, Stephen B.
Mills, Drake
Mackay, Wm.
McKee, Jos., Rev.
Merritt, Ely & Co.
Montgomery, Mrs.
M. C. P.
Moore, Baltis
Marsh, Samuel
Meyer, E.
Morrison, Wm.
McKesson, J.
M. & L.
Marr, C.
Megary, A.
M. L.
McLeod, D.
McKenna, J.

Morgan, A. W.
Mott, Lawrence P.
Morewood, Geo. B. & Co.
Moran & Iselin
McCurdy, R. H.
Martin, W. C.
Miller, Geo. C.
May, John A.
McIntire, C. H.
Moffett, James G.
McCrea, J., Mrs.
Mygatt, E., Jr.
Monroe, Ebenr.
Moir, J. & W.
Montgomery, J. J.
McEvers, Bache
Mortimer, R.
Mason, J. W.
McBride, James
Morley, J., Jr.
McLaren, Wm., Rev.
Moore, N. F.
Miller, Mr.
Moulton
Meritt, W. H.
McGrath, T.
Miller
McWhorten, A.
Muller, John
Maitland, R. L.
Mason, Sidney
Myers, John K.
Miller, W. P.
McCready, Ann
Marbury
Metz, J.
Martin, C. J.
Moore, John M.
McIlvaine, B. R.
McNamee, R.
Marston, Isaac
Montfort, Henry
Michaels, Mrs.
Miller, Mrs.
Mott, Mr.
Myers, Daniel
Milne, A.
Mount, Timothy
Myers, James
Mills, Elias
McDonough, Wm.
McAlarny, B.
McKenzie, John
Marks, Moses J.
Marsh, J. R.
Moore, James
Marten, B.
Mead, Mrs.
Mather, E.
Moubry, J.
Moss, Dr.
Merkle, Dr.
Moore, T.
Marr, A.
Mushner, J.
McCue, Mrs.
Merritt, C.

4

42 LIST OF MEMBERS. (1848.

Marten, M.
Martin & Witchief
Meeks, J. W.

N.

Noyes, Wm. Curtis
Newbold, F. H.
Newbold, C.
Nevins, P. I.
Noble, J.
Nichols, E. C.
Newman, W.
Nelson, J. G.
Nye, Gideon Jun.
Norsworthy, Mrs.
Naylor, Peter
Newhouse,
Nefus,
Nash, Mrs.
Nostrand, E.
Northrop, C. B.
North, Mr.
Noe, C. L.
Nostrand, Mrs.
Noyes, Isaac R.
Nelson, H. A.
Nanny, C. M.
Norton, C. L.
Nelson, R.
Norton, H. G.
Nichols, J. L.
Newell, G. S.
Naylor & Co.
Nevins, R. H.
Nielson, John, Jun.
Nevins, Townsend & Co.
Nottebohm, A.
Nelson, Wm.
N. W. M.
Nesmith, John P.
Nash, Lora
Newman, W. H.
Newcomb, John
Newman, Mr.
Newbold, George
Nodine, Mrs.
Norris, J. D.
Neilly, Mrs.
Neville, Francis
Naylor, Peter
Newcomb, George
Nichols, Charles C.
Newell, Darius

O.

Ogden, Benjamin, M. D.
Oliver, James D.
Oliver, Wm. H.
Ogden, Henry
Owen, Edward
Oelricht & Kruger
Okay, Wm. F.
Outhout, John
Otis, A. W.

O'Hara, Chas. H.
Oliff, W. J., M. D.
Ogsbury, Francis W.
Olwell
O'Brien
O'Rourke
Oldring, Mr.
Olliff, Wm.
Osborne, J. D.
Osborn, H. B. & Brother
Owen, St. John
Ogilvie, William
Onthout, Gatharine
O'Meara
O'Meara
Otto, Mr.
Osborn, C. F.
Owen, D.
Ostrander, G.
Osborn, W. W.
Oakley, Jacob F.
Onderdonk, Levi
Olcott, John N.
Ogden, E. D.
Ogden, T. W.
Oakey, W. F.
Oakes, Josiah
Ogden, .T G.
O'Connor, Charles
Ockershasen, A. F.
Ogden, John, jr.
Onderdonk, J. R.
Orchard, Isaac, Rev.

P.

Putnam, Tarrant
Phelps, Isaac N.
Perkins, Newton
Phelps, George D.
Post, Alfred C. M. D.
Parsons, W. B. (R. N.)
Pendleton, E. H.
Ponvert, Elias
Poillon, George W.
Pierce, James
Pittsfield, C. R.
Post, James M.
Platt, George W.
Pickersgill, Wm. C.
Platt, Nathan C.
Post, John H.
Peet, E.
Pell, Alfred
Purdy, Samuel A.
Paul, Stephen
Pell, F.
Pierce, George
Paine, John
Post, Edward
Post, W. B.
Popham, W. H.
Petrie
Petrie, J. S.
Partridge, Charles
Phillips, L.
Pierson, Dr.

Penniman, James F.
Phalen, James
Palmer, John J.
Parmly, E.
Penfold
Prall, Mrs.
Phyfe, Isaac M.
Peters, J. C., M. D.
Punnett, John. M. D.
Post, Jehial J., by A. W. Spies
Page, P.
Perkins, Mr.
Pistor, Mr.
Phillips, James W.
Pell, J. R.
Phelps, Royal
Parker, Charles
Phyfe, Duncan
Pell, James
Payne, Mrs.
Parshall, James L.
Phillips, Mr.
Provost, S. H.
Page, S. P.
Planten, Mr.
Piernie, John
Pearson, A.
Policemen of the Fourth Ward Station House
Platt, C.
Phelps, John Jay
Powell, M. M.
Poultney, B.
Price, C. W.
Pengnet, H.
Pound, J., Rev.
Powell, A. G.
Phillips, Rev. Dr.
Packard, A. R.
Porter, Wm.
Pringle, Thos.
Povey, C.
Parker, A. H.
Pratt
Platt, F.
Patridge
Perego, Ira, Jr.
Prime, T.
Phayse, P.
Pearsall, T. W.
Post, George D.
Pell, D. C. & W. & Co.
Paid
Pon & Palanca
Platt, J. S.
Phelps, G. D. & Dodge
Priestly, J.
Purdy, J.
Prosser, Thomas
Parkhurst
Parks, J. B.
P. & T. H.
Phillips, J. W.
Petrie, J. & A.
Phelps, George D.
Palmer, N. T.
Putman, E., Mrs.

LIST OF MEMBERS.

Putman, N.
Pearson, S H.
Pierson, Edwin
Prine, Mr.
Perley, Charles
Patterson, S. P.
Plumb, Wm.
Pesinger, J.
Parsons, Joseph
Peck, E.
Perry, Samuel
Polhamus, Abm.
Pell, Mrs.
Panter, H. A.
Pinkney, J. G.
Post, Ralph
Pryer, Mrs.
Porter, H. C.
Porter, Mr.
Phelps, Royal
Purdy, J. B.
Paret, John
Pierce, J. D.
Paillet, H.
Pierson, Dr.
Page, E.
Parks, S. A.
Paton & Stewart
Pattee, Mrs.
Phelps, Simon
Pollock, J.
Parker, Moses
Pickering, Thos.
Pearse, A. F.
Porter, J. S.
Pearson, Adam
Prescott, J.
Pattison, Robert
Pollock, George
Pratt, Linus
Pease, William
Price, G. J.
Phillips, S. B.
Peck, Nathan
Pugsley, Robert
Payton, E. H.
Perry, James T.
Post, William
Pignolet, Louis, Jr.
Patillon, Frederick
Parr, John
Price
Pike, L. B.
Pendleton
Potter
Parmly, Dr.
Phelps, Anson G., Jr.
Peck, Elisha
Paton, W.
Phelps, T., Mrs.
Pell, Walden
Parker, A. C.
Prime, E
Palmer, Stephen
Pray, D.
Philips, Col.
Pooton, Mr.

Pease, Jno. C.
Phillips, Samuel
Pinkerton, Mr.
Pease, John
Platt, John A.
Prime, J. D.
Polhamus, John
Preston, D.
Pomroy, J. B.
Porter, Wm.
Peck, J. B.
Patterson, A. K.
Painter, W. K.
Pheland, M.
Peet, M.
Pollock
Pretlove
Prout, M. P.
Peck, George
Price, A.
Peirce, H.
Purdy
Pitman, C.
Polhamus, Richard
Parker, Asa
Purdy, Elijah
Purdy, Jonathan
Place, Robt. S.
Patterson, W. T.
P. S.
Peck, A. L.
Purdy, E. P.
Parchall, Mr.
Parkhurst, Mr.
Perse
Platt, Isaac
Patrick, R.
Purdy, R. E.
Pease, W. J.
Paxson, S. C.

Q.

Quincey, John W.
Quintard, Mrs.
Quackenbush
Quidort, E. T.
Quiggin, George
Quin, James M.
Quackenbosh, R.

R.

Renwick, W. R.
Richards, M. H., Mrs.
Reese, Jacob, Jr.
Richards, Guy
Robins, George S.
Randolph
Romaine, S. B.
Roosevelt, James, Mrs.
Rhinelander, F. W., Mrs.
Rogers, J Kearny, M. D.
Roberts, Mrs.
Ross, J. H.

Rachan, John A. F.
Rhinelander, Wm. C.
Robertson, J. A.
Robert, C. R.
Russell, Charles H.
Rogers, Archibald
Reed, Almet
Richardson, Thomas
Remsen, R., Mrs.
Remsen, William
Rodgers, Robert
Renwick, R.
Robbins, C.
Robison, Morris
Robinson, Nelson
Rankin, A.
Riggs, Dr.
Rutgers
Robinson, E.
Roach, P. R.
Richards, Josiah
Rudderow, John
Rogers. J. Smyth, M. D.
Rogers, J., Mrs.
Russell, W. H.
Roosevelt, James J.
Richards, E. B.
Reeve, Henry
Rutgers, N. G., Mrs.
Robinson, Rev. Dr.
Roxford, A.
Robinson, Robt. F.
Renwick, A., Mrs.
Romer & Riggs
Rowe
Reeve
Renwick, Mrs.
Randall
Rumsey
Reed
Kichards, E. C.
Rumsey, J. W.
Rogers, C., Miss
Reade, R. S.
Rutherford, L. M., Mrs.
Rutgers, N. T.
Redmond, W.
Riggs, Dr.
Rogers, A., Mrs.
Rexford, A.
Rutgers, N. G., Mrs.
Rogers, John, Mrs., by Dr. B. Ogden
Rosevelt, C. V. S.
Roberts
Rikman, Robert
Read, Taylor & Co.
Rankin, D. & Co.
Reckhard, S. B.
Roselot, P. A.
Riggs, E.
Reis, Bro's & Co.
Robinson, Mr.
Rider, John P.
Raymond, Saml. C.
Requa, Austin
Russell, John

LIST OF MEMBERS. (1848·

Reasanis
Roff, A.
Read, C.
Reily, Philip
Reed, P. A.
Rossman, N.
Rubold, Danl.
Russell, J.
Rawdon, Freeman
R. L.
Russell, J. G., Mrs.
Roshore, John
Redfield, W. C.
Redfield, J. H.
Rankin, Wm.
Riley, F. & Co.
Riker, J.
Rogers, A.
Randolph, S. F.
Roger, H. L.
Russell, R., Mrs.
Read, C. H., Rev.
Roller, Mrs.
Ronalds, Eleanora, Miss
Robinson, Mrs.
Riley, Michael
Rae, Mr.
Ray, Robert
Rainer, A.
Roof, Milton
Ruton, Benj. B.
Ritter, W.
Roberts, Frazier
Richmond, Robt.
Russell, T.
Richardson, Mrs.
Riley, Asahel
Rumsey, James C.
Ramsay, John
Ryers, T. R.
Redfield, J. H.
Rogers, James
Rowell, Warren
Ryerson, Henry W.
Randolph, A. D. F.
Rickard, J. W.
Rae, Robert
Rudd, William
Robertson, James
Roberts, Edward
Redman, C. H.
Root, Geo. F.
Russel, Wm. C.
Ryan, M. C.
Roberts, Mr.
Richter, D. A.
Rapelyea, George
Reed, N.
Ryerson, Peter
Rose, Peter
Ross, James
Roberts, N.
Roberts, George
Rosenburgh, J.
Rosenkun, Mr.
Rogers, B.
Remsen, Daniel

Renoud, H.
Robinson, Wm.
Raynor, N.
Rennie, James
Rice, Mrs.
Rowell, Dr.
Rankin, A.
Raynor, Samuel
Rogers, C. H.
Ryder, Edgar T.
Ranney, A. & H. M.
Rushton, B. G.
Riker, A., Jr.
Raynor
Rappelye, George
Retche, H. L.
Robert, E. C.
Rockwell, B.
Rafferty & Leask
Rader, M.
Rose, Joseph
Rogers, R. P.
Rees, Hans
Reed, John
Richards, Henry J.
Reid, Geo. W.
Rudd, Joseph
Roe, Charles S.
Raymond, H. J.
Roberts, M. O.
Roach, Edward
Rodman, John
Rowland, C. N. S.
Reynolds, P.
Rumney, T. W.
Ropes, John P.
Remsen, John
Robinson, Mrs.
Russell
Ritter, R.

S.

Smith, Dan'l H.
Scott, H.
Smith, Charles
Stevens, Mr.
Scofield, Nathaniel
Sebastian L.
Secord, John
Smith, Fletcher
Sherman, Benj. F.
Smith, Hugh, D.D.
Smith, E. Dunlap, Rev.
Simpson, William
Smith, James B.
Swaney, Thomas
Sloan, Thomas G.
Simpson, Mrs.
Scudder, Egbert
Smith, Charles W.
Schaeffer, Frederick
Simpson Richard
Simpson, Mr.
Snedecor, John D.
Smith, Dan'l Drake

Stewart, John M.
Stoppani, Chas. G.
Sell, Wm. P.
Sumner, Palmer
Stoddart, William
Sharp, William
Sanxay, Joseph F.
Sparks, Samuel
Smith, James
Savage, C. C.
Steele, W.
Sperling, John G.
Smith, B. R.
Scott, William
Seaman, Isaac
Scofield, Sam'l W.
Southworth, A. M. M. D.
Stelle, Isaac
Seely, Joseph
Stelle, Nelson, M. D.
Spies, Adam W.
Speaights, Charles
Strong, Thomas W.
Skeel, Rufus R.
Stevens, T. L.
Smith, Asa
Stebbins, William
Sutphen, John
Sylvester, S. J.
Smith, James
Sealey, B. T.
Scofield, J. L.
Scardefield, Mr.
Sneeden, Mr.
Searls, H. R.
Sammis, Daniel P.
Simpson, Mr.
Skillman, John
Smith, Henry F.
Smith, Peter
Spencer, Wm.
Smith, E. L.
Stott, J.
Sommers, Mrs.
Schwab, M.
Silverman, J.
Strauss, J.
Stapenhagen, Mr.
Smith, Shadrach
Serrimer, L
Smith, Mr. Rev.
Stickney, C. L.
Smith, Wm. N.
Stout, Andrew V.
Smith, C. E.
Sneeden, James
Skillman, Judge
Sherridan, Mrs. & Sister
Sanford, C. W.
Schott, George
Southart & Kissam
Smith, W. D.
Smith, J. N.
Seignett, Mrs.
Schieffelin, James L.
Snowden, Thomas
Sneckner, John

LIST OF MEMBERS.

Sands, Benjamin
Surget, James
Smith, C. W.
Simpson, Wm.
Shoemaker
Seaman, G. S.
Stohlmann, C. H. E.
Staples, J.
Stillwell, J. N.
Short, John
Sackett, J. L.
S. S.
Skinner, Otis A.
Skeel, Rufus R.
Schmidt, John W.
Shaw, William
Sherwood, Wm.
Seton, Alfred
Swan, Caleb
Sherwood, Samuel
Stout, Aquilla G.
Schermerhorn, John
Skiddy, Francis
Stanton, Thomas P.
Skiddy, Wm. Capt.
Stewart, A. T.
Smith, Gilbert, M. D.
Stevens, J. A.
Shaddle, H. V.
Shearman, J. H., M. D.
Scribner, A. S.
Smedes, Mrs.
Southmayd, A.
Southmayd, S. C.
Seymour, P. W., Mrs.
Stephens, Benjamin
Suffern, Thomas
Swan, B. L.
Stevens, Byam K.
Starr, Nathan
Schermerhorn, Peter
Sanderson, E. F.
Schuchardt, F.
Sprague, Roswell
Shaw, J. B.
Sanford, L H.
Spear, Alva
Sturgis, Wm. Jr.
Saltus, Francis
Sheffield, J. B.
Stebbins, Mrs.
Speir, G. M.
Sherman. R. B.
Strang, T.
Sanders, Geo. N.
Samson, Abijah
Seaman, D.
Sturges, Thos. T.
Schenck, D. S.
Staples, G. W.
Storer, G. L.
Secor, C. A.
Stanton, John
Smith, Uriah J.
Salter. W. D.
Sheldon, Frederick
Sage, F. P.

Smith, A.
Stewart, J.
Schoot
Strang,
Sanford, Mrs.
Shuart, Wm.
Smith, J. C.
Stuyvesant, P. G., Mrs.
Skeel, R. B.
Stewart, Paton
Stagg, J. P. & Co.
Shaherie, Dr.
Sheldon, H.
Stevens, J. A.
S. & Sister
Smith, Mrs.
Swarez, L. J.
Sheriff's Jury, 2d Panel, by C. N. S. Rowland, Treasurer
Smith, W. H. & Co.
S. T. & V.
S. P. W.
Sanford, H. J.
S. K.
Smith, L.
Sheffelin, S. B.
Sheffelin, S. A.
S. V.
Simpson, J. T.
Sayer, J. N.
Smith, W. A.
Scott, H.
S. & C.
Sillicks,
Sill, H. L.
S. C.
Stryling, Henry
Sackett, Belcher, & Co.
Stone & Starr
Shugardt, F.
Shmidt, J. W.
Stewart, John Jr. & Co.
Strong, Geo. W.
Stuart, James
Strong, Geo. W., for Wife and Daughter
St. John, Burr & Co.
Scheffelin, H. M. & Fowler
Spies, Christ & Co.
Scribner, U. K.
Seguine, C.
Scharfenberg & Lewis
Sherman, A.
Salisbury, Henry
Southmayd, H.
Scott, A. M. L.
Scott, Mr.
Schoonmaker, H. E.
Stillwill, H.
Stillman, T. B.
Shawman, Isaac
Secor, T. F.
Sterns, John G.
Summers, Alex. B.
Smith, Wm.
Sageman, John W.

Spellman, W. B.
Sheffield, J. M.
Stark, Mr.
Scott, James N.
Sudlow, John
Selleck, Gould
Seely, Mr. Rev.
Schutz, L.
Sparks, Jared
Suckley, Rutsen
Smith, Sheldon
Stebbins, Russel
Scrymser, James
Sherrerd, Mrs.
Sutherland, Wm.
Smith, N. D. Rev.
Seaman, J. M.
Shipman, Wm. B.
Sanford, G.
Sawtell, Mrs.
Schuyler, Mrs.
St. John, Square
Swords, Miss
Strong. Benjamin
Sheffield, Mrs.
Sampson, Geo. G.
Stanley, P. Mrs.
Scrymgeour, James
Smith, E. J.
Stebbins, Miss
Smith, W. D.
Seaman & Muir
Scott, Wm.
Symes, Wm.
Sieger, Mr.
Smith, James
Smedberg, Mrs.
Shelley, Mr.
Steel, Wm.
Sears, E. P.
Skillman, J.
Stewart, D.
Spicer, C. B.
Smets, Wm.
Sabine, P. A., M. D.
Stevens, A. W.
Skidmore, S. T.
Soffie, H.
Skinner, Dr. Rev.
Stimson, C. Mrs.
Starling, Lyne Jr.
Schermerhorn, A.
Stagg, John P.
Searles, H.
Stewart, F. C., M. D.
Shepherd, T.
Sherwood, B., M. D.
Spofford, G.
Sus, A. W.
Spencer, W. A.
Scribner, U. R.
Stevens, H. G.
Schiefflin, H. H.
Swords, George H.
Snow, Dr.
Schieffllin,
Sturges, Jonathan

LIST OF MEMBERS.   (1848.

Sweeny, N. T.
Strange, E. B.
Slone,
Sears H. B.
St. John, George
Sanford, H. J.
Stewart, Ann, Miss
Sampson, J. C.
Suydam, S. A.
Stewart,
Sears, H.
Sherwood, H.
Stewart, S. D.
Sumner,
Swartz, G.
Saunders, G.
Seely, Mrs.
Shepherd,
Shepherd,
Sheafe, J. F.
Scheiffelin, Philip
Staples, S.
Smith, C.
Sanford, E.
Stewart, Alvan
Stone, R. C.
Somerville, Mrs.
Smith, Wm. E.
Smith, Lemuel
Stamler, J. A.
Screvener, Abm. S.
Seymour & Son
S. M.
Sanford, Memnon
Smith, Jesse
Sweezy, N. T.
Shultz, J. S.
Southack, John W.
Scribner, A.
Skidmore & Littell
Sherman, G. & J.
Shed, E. R.
Stopenhagen, John
Somerville, A & M.
Sparks, S.
Serviera, J. B.
Sather & Church
Simpson, J. B. & S.
Smith, E.
Sears, R.
Smull, Thomas
Stewart & Coffin
Seaich, Mr.
Solomon, Dr.
Slack, R.
Schlessenger, F. S.
Smith, Andrew
Schenck, M. E., Rev.
Smith, A. P.
Schroeder, C. G.
Smith, Thomas C.
Sage, G. E.
Stokes, Henry
Schoals, Francis P.
Shelton, Dr.
Smith, J. Lee
Smilie, James

Staren, J. K.
Skiddy, Mr.
Stitt, George S.
Stevens, O.
Stokes B. G.
Spring, Mr.
Springsteen, Abraham
Skinner, T. H., Rev.
Stott, C. G.
Sarvan, David
Savoy, E.
Stimle, P.
Segwick, R.
Stowle, C.
Sykes, L. A.
Sutton, George
Stanley, Wm. W.
Storms, W. P.

T.

Tallman, S. S.
Todd, W. W.
Trowbridge, F. H.
Trussell, Richard
Taylor, Isaac C.
Taff, H.
Taylor, H.
Trumpy, Casper
Tuckey, J.
Tinkham, O.
Thompson, W. B.
Tallmadge, R. F.
Tilerson, W. H.
Tinkham, Joseph
T. E. T.
Townsen, D. Y.
Tredwell, George
Taylor, J. D.
Terbell, H.
Terbell, Jubal
Tenny, Mrs.
Tompkins, Mrs.
Tidal, J. C. B.
Tait, Isaac E.
Truesdell, E. D.
Thomas, John
Thomas, Mrs.
Taylor, John
Tucker, Joseph
Thacker, Mrs.
Talcott, A.
Turfler, G. C.
Towers, James
Thompson, John
Townsend, Wm.
Taberle, Philip
Tucker, D. N.
Te ry, David, Rev.
Truesdale, E. D.
Thomson, John
Thomson, Mason
Thompson, James B.
Taylor, Moses B.
Tuttle, Silvester
Tracy, C.

Townsend, John, Jr.
Trafford, Abraham
Teller, Daniel W.
Thompson, D.
Tracy, George Manning
Taylor, Moses
Tillottson, J. C.
Titus, Geo. N.
Tappan, Henry P.
Talbot, Charles N.
Thorne, Jonathan
Tallmadge, J.
Thompson, David
Townsend, J. R., Mrs.
Thompson, A. R.
Tooker, John S.
Taylor, J. J.
Townsend, F. L.
Tracy, Samuel F.
Toblas, Albert
Taylor, John S.
Treadwell, S. L.
Talman, S. S.
Tome
Towley, Sinclair
Tracy, Frederick
Taylor, W. B.
Tuttle, A. C.
Trenor, Dr.
Thurston, C. M., Mrs.
Thurston, R. H.
Thomas, J. A.
Trimble, D.
Tileston, T.
Thayer, N.
Taylor, L. E., M.D.
Todd, James L.
Trustee
Taylor, James O.
Townsend, Peter, Mrs.
Tredwell, Adam
Tarrant, James
Treadwell, Son
Treadwell
Taylor, R.
Tryon
Tillcomb, Dr.
Trenor
Titus
Thompson, Wm. D.
Turell, W.
Thomson, David
Tyhe, R.
Tyng, Stephen H., Rev. Dr.
Thompson, J. and H.
Tyson, Wm.
Thurston, H.
Terrill, Caleb O.
Timpson, C. B.
Thompson, Mrs.
Turner, Henry
Tucker, S. D.
Titus, Charles F.
Taylor, S. G.
Tyler, J. W.
Thatford, J.
Tappen, David

LIST OF MEMBERS.

Thomas, James
Taylor, John
Tyler, Isaac
Thompson, H.
Tappen, Charles
Tremper, Harman
Trafford, A.
Tupper
Tyack, Mr.
Thompson & Weller
Tucker, J. C.
Talbot, W. R.
Tucker, Thos. W.
Taylor, B. S.
Tyler, W. A.
Todd, John
Tryon
Truslow, Wm.
Trowbridge, G. A.
Towle, S.
Tilden, Wm.
Tappan, George, Jr.
Thompson, S. W.
Taylor, G.
Tatham
Thorn, Charles E.
Tompson, Thomas
Tieman, George
Taylor, A. B.
Topping, H.
Thompson, Samuel M.
Timpson, George
Torry, Joseph
Tallman, A. S.
Tenbrook
Towsley, Charles
Tunis, C. C.
Tomes, Francis and Son
Tracy, Irwin & Co.
Tapscott, W. & J. T.
Tisdale, Samuel T.
T. M.
Trowbridge, Henry
Tweedy, O. B.
Toole, Wm. S.
Thompson, J.
Thomas & Co.
Tucker, Wm.

U.

Ulshooffer, Michael
Ulhorn, Caspar F.
Underhill, J. S.
Underhill, Wm.
Underhill, A.
Underwood, H.
Underhill, P. R.
Underhill, Mrs.
Underwood, Joshua
Ustick, Richard

V.

Van Renselear, J. C.
Vermilye, W. M.
Vyse, Charles

Van Buren, Dr.
Van Blarcom, A.
Van Beuren, G. A. C.
Varnum, J. B.
Van Dyck, H., Mrs.
Verplank, Mrs.
Van Santvoord, C.
Van Nortwick, W. B.
Vanduzer, Daniel
Van Nest, A. R.
Van Hook, Wm.
Van Rensselear, Dr.
Varick, Richard
Vose, A. Troy, Mich.
Van Kleeck & Co.
Van Ankin and Son
Van Wagner
Van Antwerp, J.
Vail Aaron
Van Renselaer, W. C.
Van Horn, D.
Van Duser, S.
Van Duser, Miss
Van Ant werp, John
Van Alst, David
Vreeland, J. M.
Vermule, F., M. D.
Vermule, W., M. D.
Vantassel, J., Mrs.
Van Dien, Mrs.
Van Voorhis, E. W.
Vanderwoort, Henry
Van Tuyl, B. S.
Van Wort, J.
Vandewater, E. D.
Vanderpool, Mrs., Senr.
Vernon, L. & T.
Van Nest, Abm.
Vermilye, Wm. R.
Van Doren, John
Van Pelt, P. J.
Vreedenburgh, Peter
Vanvleck, Jasper T.
Van Nest, John
Van Arsdale, J.
Vanwagener, Wm.
Vandervoort, Mrs.
Varick, T. R.
Van Winkle, A. J.
Vandervoort, P.
Van Zant
Vorhiss, Richard
Van Howden, John
Vernon, Thomas
Van B. and H.
Vanderbilt, J.
Vernon, D. D.
Vose, Reuben
Van Winkle, Tunis
Van Saun, Abm.
Vogley, Frederick
Vanpelt, J. J.
Van Vliet, Sarah
Vincent, L. M., Rev.
Vau Winkle, Mrs.
Vandrail, Mrs.
Van Winkle, Wm.

Vaniderstine, Peter
Viets, Wm. A.
Vermilye, Isaac D.
Vosburgh, John S.
Valentine, Wm.
Van Winkle, David J.
Vandolsen, J.
Van Allen, William
Van Dalsom, Wm. H.
Van Arsdale, Henry, M. D.
Valentine, J.

W.

Wetmore, A. R.
Warren, Richard
Wright, Edward
Walsh, A. R.
Whitehead, John
Wayne, Henry C., Capt.
Wilkes, Henry
Watts, R. Jr., M. D.
Wyles, John
Weston, Edward
Wilson
Waddington, Mrs.
Waddington, W. D.
Weeks, R. D.
Ward, Wm. G.
Worster, J., M. D.
Wurts, John
Wainright, Eli
West, E. T.
Warthouse
Wurner, E. B., M. D.
Whitttemore, Wm. T.
Wilks, M.
Weed, Nathaniel
Whittemore, Timothy
Waller, Robert
Wilson, N.
Walker, Geo. S.
White, Mrs.
Ward, Henry
Wetmore, W. S.
Wagstaff, Alfred
Wolcott
Whittemore, C. R.
Wilson, John
Woram, Wm.
Wisner
Way, William
Wilson, S. D., Mrs., Dr.
Ward, J.
Whiting, Augustus
Weeks, E. A.
Ward (a friend), Dr.
Wheelwright, B. F.
Weyman, E. H.
Woodhead, J.
Wetmore, S.
Wynkoop, F. S.
Wetmore, Wm. C.
Wheeler, Wm. A.
Wood, Fernando
Windle, J. B.

Ward, E. H., Mrs.
Winthrop, Henry R.
Warren, J.
Wood, John
Ward, Adam
Woods, James
Withington, Lewis
Wiggins
Wilson, Harris
Waller
Wilk and Shaw
Weeks, S.
White, Wm. W.
Willson
Whitewright, W., Jr.
Wheeler, E.
Weisman, A.
Wandell, S. S.
Whitewright, W.
Waydell, John
Whitney, M. R.
Walsh, Wm.
Weir, J.
Willets, Daniel S.
Willetes, S.
Williams, R.
Whitlock, Andrew
Watkiss, Mr.
Williamson, G. A.
Walton, E. L.
Wetmore, Mary, Mrs.
Wheeler, L. F.
Williams & Hinman
Wentringham, J.
Westfall, J and D.
Weeks, A. F.
Witherold, Mrs.
Williams, Peter
Williams, R. S.
Wood, F. W.
Whitney, G. C.
Waller, J.
White, James
Witte, D.
Williams, Thos. H.
Wing, G. T.
Wood, James L.
Walker, S. G.
Wyckoff, A., Mrs.
Winship, Thomas
Williams, Wm. R., Rev.
Walton, W.
Wallace, J.
Wells, N. M.
Wight, Richard
Wood, Benjamin
Worrall, Henry
Wood, Fernando
Woram, Wm.
Weed, Wm. H.
White, John
Wilson & Bailey
Walton J. B.
Williston, J. T.
Webb, W. H.
Williams, Jabez
Wright, H.

Wright, James W.
Wood, A. L.
Witty, Catherine
Walters, W. A., Dr.
Wright, D. D.
Whittemore, R. J.
Williams, Daniel
Wheelwright, Charles
Westlake, Mr.
Withers, R.
Williams, Charles
Wheaton, M. A.
Walter, Mrs.
Ward, Issac
W. A. B.
Wright, Neziah
Willet, E. W.
Washburn, H. B.
White, H. Rev.
White, F.
Wilkes, Miss
Watts, Mrs.
White, L.
Waller, Mrs.
Worley, Mrs.
Walker, G. Mrs.
Walker, G.
Woodworth, F. A.
Weyman, Rebecca
Wetstien, Mr,
Wood, David
Wright, W. W.
White, E.
Warsawer, S.
Widow's Mite,
Wiggins, W. H.
Wilson, Geo. Mrs.
White, Chs.
Weaver, John
Williams, John
Weed, H. A.
Walker, James
Whitney, B. S.
Westervelt, J. J. V.
Waters, John G.
Weston, Mrs.
Wheeler, H. H.
Weed, H. O.
Wells, F. C.
Wellstood, John G.
Withey, Ezra
Whittemore, John
Wilks, Thomas
Williams, T. D.
Wheeler, L.
Woodruff, L. B.
Ward, S.
Wooding
Winslow, Wm.
Wiese, C.
Waters, John
Wixon, S.
Worrell & Co.
Warner, Thomas
Wallace, George
Wilbur, Charles
Wetmore, L.

Wade, E., Jr.
Whittelsey, Henry
Ward, S. S.
Whittemore, Joseph
Webster, Daniel A.
Wilson, Wm. M., M. D.
Wright, L. B., M. D.
Whittemore, H. S.
Weir, James
Wheaton, William
Wentworth, Josiah W.
Wooster, Benjamin
Waldron, Corns.
Wood, Henry
Weed, John W., M. D.
Williams, Joseph
Wilt, Jonathan
Warren, S.
Wheeler, Eliphalet
Weeks, D. C.
West, Royal, Rev.
Woodruff, O. P.
Warren, P. R.
Williams, J.
Woodhouse
Ward, W. C.
Westervelt, S. P.
Westervelt, Abm. D.
Walduck, R. M.
Westerfield, C.
Waterberry, Wm. R.
Wirton, A.
Wilson, Mrs.
Wood, J.
Westervelt
Weeks, R. D.
Weeks, E. N.
Walker, Samuel
Wetmore, S.
Wiley, John
W. L. A.
Wood, Silas
Whittemore, J. C.
Whitlock, W., Jr.
Wolfe, Charles
Wells, J. N.
Ward, A. H.
W. W. De F. & Co.
Woodward & Connor
Williams, Bros.
Windle, W. B.
Wilder, A.
Williams, C. F.
Wendle, J. D.
W. H. F.
Winchester, H.
Whittemore, J. M.
W. & B.
W. H.
W. K.
W. C.
Woods, David
West, John N.
White, W. Asa M.
W. M. S.
Woolsey, J.
Woolcott & Slade

LIST OF MEMBERS.

Wyth, L. J.
Waldo, C. & F.
Whitlock, Augustus
Williams, F. B.
Wolfe & Gillespie
Winslow, R. H.
Wilson, B. M.
Wolfe, N. H.
Wetmore, P. H.
Watson, J., M. D.
Wendle, J. D.
Weller, John
Wolfe, Chris'r
Wolfe, J. Æ.
Wagner, D. B.
Wyeth, L. J.
Winters, Mrs.
Wright, Sturgis & Shaw
West, J. J.
Webb, James Watson
Warren, James
Williams, Mr.
Winston, F. S.
Wells, Lloyd W.
Wood, William
Willets, Samuel
Watkiss, Charles
Weeks, John A.
Waldo, S. L.

Wyman & Dinby
Willoughby, Mr.
Wentworth
Wildry, A.
Wells, W.
Whitney
Wheeler, A.
Whittlesey, Mrs.
Wetmore, L.
Wells, Thomas
Willey
Whittemore, J. B.
Warner, C. L.
White, N.
Watson, R. S.
Wells, Charles
Woodford, O. P.
West, Joseph
Wilmott, Thomas
Weeks, Charles
Waterbury, Wm. M.
White, Mr.
Williamson, J. R.
Welling, John T.
Walsh, George
Walker, Mrs.
Weeks, Absalom
Welford, Mr.
West, J. S.

Withers, R.
Waterbury, John
Wardell, N.
Wagner, G.
Wallace, Wm.

Y.

Yates, Charles
Yates, Benjamin S.
Yates, F. L.
Young, Ab'm
Youle, G. W.
Young, S. & Co.
Young, Miss
Youle, Mr.
Yereyence, C.
Young, E. M.
Youngs, D. L.
Young, John
Young, Joab

Z.

Zimmerman, J. C.
Zabriskie, A. C.
Zabriskie, A. C. & Co.
Zabriskie, George

CERTIFICATE OF INTENTION

TO INCORPORATE THE NEW-YORK ASSOCIATION FOR IMPROVING THE CONDITION OF THE POOR.

THE undersigned, being each and every of them, of full age, and citizens of the State of New-York, desiring to associate themselves for the benevolent and charitable objects hereinafter expressed, that they may become a body politic and corporate, and be enabled to conduct the business of the Association in the City and County of New-York, according to the provisions of an "Act for the Incorporation of Benevolent, Charitable, Scientific, and Missionary purposes," passed April 12th, 1848, do for these purposes hereby certify,

I. That the name and title by which such Institution shall be known in law, is the "New-York Association for Improving the Condition of the Poor."

II. That the particular business and objects of such Association shall be the elevation of the physical and moral condition of the indigent; and so far as is compatible with these objects, the relief of their necessities.

III. That the Board of Managers to manage the same shall consist of one President, five Vice-Presidents, one Treasurer, one Corresponding Secretary and General Agent, one Recording Secretary, the Chairman of each Advisory Committee, or as his proxy, some other member of said Committee, and four members to be chosen by said Board of Managers.

IV. That the following named persons shall constitute the Board of Managers for the first year, to wit: James Brown, President; George

Griswold, J. Smyth Rogers, James Boorman, James Lenox, and Horatio Allen, Vice-Presidents; Robert B. Minturn, Treasurer; Robert M. Hartley, Corresponding Secretary and General Agent; Joseph B. Collins, Recording Secretary; together with the following Elected Members and Chairmen of the Advisory Committees, namely: Stewart Brown, Frederick S. Winston, Erastus C. Benedict, John R. Ludlow, Daniel S. Briant, William Gale, Peter G. Arcularius, Abraham Fardon, Jr., Apollos R. Wetmore, Nicholas C. Everett, Calvin Tracy, James O. Pond, James Horn, Samuel P. Patterson, Lewis Chichester, Adam W. Spies, Thomas Denny, Luther Jackson, Stephen C. Lynes, and F. Ellsworth Mather.

In witness whereof, we hereunto have subscribed our names, in the City of New-York, this the Eleventh day of December, in the year of our Lord One Thousand Eight Hundred and Forty-eight.

JAMES BROWN,	APOLLOS R. WETMORE,
GEORGE GRISWOLD,	NICHOLAS C. EVERETT,
J. SMYTH ROGERS,	CALVIN TRACY,
JAMES BOORMAN,	JAMES O. POND,
HORATIO ALLEN,	JAMES HORN,
ROBERT M. HARTLEY,	LEWIS CHICHESTER,
JOSEPH B. COLLINS,	ADAM W. SPIES,
STEWART BROWN,	THOMAS DENNY,
FREDERICK S. WINSTON,	LUTHER JACKSON,
DANIEL S. BRIANT,	STEPHEN C. LYNES,
PETER G. ARCULARIUS,	F. ELLSWORTH MATHER.
ABRAHAM FARDON, JR.	

Witness as to all the signatures   D. F. CURRY.

City and County of New-York, [ss]: On the Eleventh day of December, A. D. 1848, before me came George Griswold, J. Smyth Rogers, Horatio Allen, Joseph B. Collins, Luther Jackson, Abraham Fardon, Jr., Lewis Chichester, Daniel S. Briant, Nicholas C. Everett, James O. Pond, Adam W. Spies, F. Ellsworth Mather, James Horn, Frederick S. Winston, Peter G. Arcularius, Stephen C. Lynes, Calvin Tracy, and Robert M. Hartley; and on the 12th day of December, A. D. 1848, before me came James Brown, Stewart Brown, and James Boorman; and on the 13th day of December, A. D. 1848, before me came Apollos R. Wetmore, and Thomas Denny, to me known to be the same persons described in and who executed the foregoing instrument, who severally acknowledged that they executed the foregoing instrument, for the purposes therein mentioned.

D. F. CURRY, Commissioner.

I approve of the within Certificate, and allow the same to be filed.
H. P. EDWARDS, Justice Supreme Court.
New-York, December 14, 1848.

STATE OF NEW-YORK, }
SECRETARY'S OFFICE,   } Albany, Dec. 16, 1848.

I certify that the Certificate of Incorporation of the "New-York Association for Improving the Condition of the Poor," was received and filed this day in this office.

ARCH'D CAMPBELL,
Dep. Sec. of State.

THE SIXTH ANNUAL REPORT

OF THE

NEW-YORK ASSOCIATION

FOR

IMPROVING THE CONDITION OF THE POOR,

FOR THE YEAR 1849.

WITH THE BY-LAWS AND A LIST OF MEMBERS.

ORGANIZED, 1843—INCORPORATED, 1848.

"The quality of mercy is not strained;
It droppeth as the gentle rain from heaven
Upon the place beneath: it is twice blessed;
It blesseth him that gives and him that takes."

NEW-YORK:
JOHN F. TROW, PRINTER, 49 & 51 ANN-STREET.
1849.

PROCEEDINGS

AT THE

ANNUAL MEETING

OF THE

NEW-YORK ASSOCIATION FOR IMPROVING THE CONDITION OF THE POOR.

Held in the Hall of the Public School Society, Nov. 26, 1849.

The President, JAMES BROWN, Esq , in the Chair.

The Minutes of the last Annual Meeting were read by the Recording Secretary, and on motion, approved.

The Treasurer's Annual Report was presented by a member of the Auditing Committee, which was accepted, and ordered on file.

The minutes of the Board of Managers, exhibiting their operations during the recess of the Supervisory Council, were read by the Corresponding Secretary, as their annual report to that body, and approved.

The Annual Report being read, Dr. J. SMYTH ROGERS moved its acceptance and publication under the direction of the Board of Managers, accompanying his motion with the relation of several incidents, illustrating the interest with which the Association was regarded by distinguished strangers, and recommending the adoption of measures to give to the leading views of the Report, a wider circulation than they were likely to obtain in pamphlet form.

Voting by ballot having by previous resolution been dispensed with, on motion of A. R. WETMORE, Esq., seconded by HORATIO ALLEN, Esq., the meeting proceeded to the election of the officers of the Association and the Supervisory Council for the ensuing year.

At this stage of the proceedings, the Corresponding Secretary being called upon, addressed the meeting on the " Moral evils of indigence and dependence." He was followed by PETER COOPER, Esq., on the subject of " Providing employment for the unemployed poor ;" after which, on motion, the meeting adjourned.

OFFICERS, MANAGERS,

AND

SUPERVISORY COUNCIL.

President.
JAMES BROWN.

Vice Presidents.
GEORGE GRISWOLD,   JAMES BOORMAN,
J. SMYTH ROGERS, M. D.,   HORATIO ALLEN,
JAMES LENOX.

Treasurer.
ROBERT B. MINTURN.

Corresponding Secretary and Agent.
ROBERT M. HARTLEY.

Recording Secretary.
JOSEPH B. COLLINS.

Supervisory Council.
The first in order is the Chairman of each District Committee.

FIRST DISTRICT.
D. S. Briant,
James Cruikshank,
James Giffin,
Avery Brumley,
James C. Ramsey.

SECOND DISTRICT.
George W. Abbe,
Joseph F. Sanxay,
John N. Sayer,
Wm. Sharp,
Charles Wilbur.

THIRD DISTRICT.
E. Cauldwell,
Jonathan Sturges,
J. L. Baldwin,
C. W. Carmer,
C. C. Colgate.

FOURTH DISTRICT.
Abraham Fardon, Jr.,
Archibald Hall,
Hugh Aikman,
Charles Chamberlain,
John Hagadorn.

FIFTH DISTRICT.
A. R. Wetmore,
Wm. Forrest,
G. T. Cobb,
Wm. H. Richards,
Leonard Kirby.

SIXTH DISTRICT.
N. C. Everett,
Stephen Conover,
Daniel Fisher,
Thomas Lippencott,
John G. Sperling.

SEVENTH DISTRICT.
C. Tracy,
A. B. Ludlum,
G. J. Price,
Stephen Cutter,
J. Skidmore.

EIGHTH DISTRICT.
Joseph B. Collins,
Wm. Johnston,
John Endicott,
Charles C. Dyer,
O. D. McClain.

NINTH DISTRICT.
James O. Pond, M. D.,
James S. Miller, M. D.,
Thomas P. Richards,
Jeremiah Terbell,
Daniel French.

Tenth District.
James Horn,
Joseph M. Bell,
Isaac Ford,
Peter Aims,
H. Van Arsdale, M. D.

Eleventh District.
S. P. Patterson,
Abner Mills,
Peter McPherson,
Dudley Sheffield,
Nehemiah Miller.

Twelfth District.
Oran W. Morris,
Josiah Cary,
L. B. Ward,
John C. Miller,
Marvin W. Fox.

Thirteenth District.
Lewis Chichester,
Thomas Kennedy,
John Pearsall,
Charles Merrill,
Wm. A. Walker.

Fourteenth District.
Adam W. Spies,
Robert Rae,
Alexander W. Murray,
William Post,
J. J. Jenkins.

Fifteenth District.
Thomas Denny,
Stewart Brown,
Wm. G. Bull,
Joseph Lawrence,
Henry E. Davies,

Sixteenth District.
Luther Jackson,
Charles Roome,
L. B. Woodruff,
W. Vermilye,
H. K. Bull.

Seventeenth District.
S. C. Lynes,
James R. Gibson,
John Falconer,
Geo. Manning Tracy,
Herman Griffin.

Eighteenth District.
F. E. Mather,
William Walker,
E. Holbrook,
J. W. Benedict,
John Campbell.

Elected members of the Supervisory Council.
J. C. Green,
Wm. S. Wetmore,
Jonathan Sturges,
Wm. H. Macy,
Thos. Cock, M. D.,

E. J. Woolsey,
Peter Cooper,
John C. Baldwin,
Wm. B. Crosby,

George T. Trimble,
Lorin Nash,
John L. Mason,
Josiah Rich.

Elected members of the Board of Managers.
Stewart Brown,
John T. Adams,

Frederick S. Winston,
Erastus C. Benedict.

VISITORS.

Appointed by the Advisory Committees for the ensuing year.

FIRST DISTRICT.
John Harris,
Wm. P. Sell,
James C. Ramsey,
D. S. Briant,
Palmer Sumner,
Wm. Bogardus,
John A. Hatt,
James Giffin,
John Davidson,
George Hatt,
Avery Brumley,
David Meeker,
H. M. Baldwin,
George Hatt, Sec'y.

SECOND DISTRICT.
Charles Wilbur,
Joseph F. Sanxay,
G. W. Abbe,
D. N. Tucker,
William Sharp,
John N. Sayer,
George Hatt, Sec'y.

THIRD DISTRICT.
Henry Ahrensfeldt,
John Ramsay,
C. W. Carmer,
L. Wetmore,
Jas. Beatty,
W. D. Harris,
V. Lecount,
C. C. Colgate,
R. Lewis,
David Terry, Sec'y.

FOURTH DISTRICT.
Adam Pearson,
Samuel Sparks,
Alexander J. Henderson,
H. Whittlesey,
S. Fanning,
Wm. D. Abbott,
George W. Rose,
John Barry,
Hiram Hurd,
T. R. Ryers,
George W. Alston,
David Moffat,
John Buxton, jr.
John Gates,
T. H. Burras,
Henry Whittlesey, Sec'y.

FIFTH DISTRICT.
J. J. Greenough,
A. R. Wetmore,
Lemuel G. Evans,
T. V. Forster,
C. Adams,
D. Terry,
A. Wakeman,
John Thomson,
H. S. Terbell,
R. Lawrence,
H. Cole,
Wm. Van Allen,
J. Prescott,
Wm. Forrest,
J. H. Redfield,
L. P. Hubbard,
J. F. Bridges,
Robert Pattison,
W. D. Smith.
S. S. Ward,
Robert Carter,
George T. Cobb,
Mason Thomson,
J. E. Goddard,
W. Steele.
David Terry, Sec'y.

SIXTH DISTRICT.
William Ballagh,
Daniel Fisher,
Andrew Hume,
Benjamin Marshall, M. D.,
James Rogers,
J. McClaury, M. D.,
Thomas Lippencott,
Moses B. Taylor,
A. Florentine,
Geo. W. Lowerre,
Joseph Whittemore,
Abraham Forbes,
Daniel A. Webster,
Samuel Baxter,
Benjamin B. Forbes,
Reub. S. Carpentier, M. D.,
John G. Sperling,
Amzi Camp, Sec'y.

SEVENTH DISTRICT.
J. Sammis,
C. L Nichols,
T. Warren,
J. B. Horton,
C. Tracy,
A. P. McNaughton,
N. P. Beers,
B. R. Smith,
J. P. Bremner,
H. C. Martin,
G. J. Price,
A. B. Ludlum,
B. G. Bruce,
Wm. A. Van Nostrand,
J. W. Pease,
Stephen Cutler,
Jona. B. Horton, Sec'y.

EIGHTH DISTRICT.
Joseph B. Collins,
O. D. McClain,
Isaac Gibson,
Daniel Conover,
James F. Stansbery,
Albert S. Smith,
W. H. Van Dalsem,
William Johnston,
J. S. Holt,
Charles C. Dyer,
Wm. Scott,
Henry W. Ryerson,
C. P. Dakin,
W. R. Janes,
John Endicott,
Edward Fields, M. D.,
John Gillelan,
Stewart E. Clark,
Darius Geer,
J S. Ferris,
William Kirby, Sec'y.

NINTH DISTRICT.
John Ruston,
S. B. Phillips, M. D.,
Nathan Peck,
Reuben Ayres,
Benjamin Salter,
A. D. F. Randolph,
H. W. Deems,
Cornelius Lefferts,
C. P. Tucker, M. D.,
Daniel French,
William Martin,
William A. Foster,
Preston Sheldon,
Preston Hickok,
Leander See,
Thomas Fessenden,
Daniel F. Lee,
John Murray,
E. H. Payton,
John Carson,
George D. Cragin,
M. H. Howell,
John Ruston, Sec'y.

TENTH DISTRICT.
Peter Aims,
Smith Downs,
Joseph M. Bell,
James Horn,
James Weir,
William Wheaton,
Andrew V. Stout,
Edward A. Fraser,
Corn. V. Clarkson, M. D
Laban Jacobs,
Joseph W. Wentworth,

VISITORS. (1849.

Hen. Van Ardsdale, M. D.,
Fitz Edwin Jones,
Isaac Ford,
Thomas Jackson,
Charles Place,
Edmund Anderson,
William C. Bradley,
John D. McCreary,
E. A. Fraser, Sec'y.

ELEVENTH DISTRICT.

A. C. Leach,
Edward Bevan,
Joel Kelly,
Thomas Hogan,
William Murphy,
G. E. Cowperthwait,
John Lewis,
S. Houghwout,
E. Montross,
William Bennett,
John Young,
Henry Taff,
John Camron,
J. F. Jones,
Benjamin Wooster,
C. Waldron,
Richard H. Teller,
W. C. Barbour,
Joseph Hall,
C. B. Daton, M. D.,
John Myers,
Wesley Smith,
Grant Dubois, Sec'y.

TWELFTH DISTRICT.

D. C. Bartlett,
J. C. Miller,
J. A. Cary,
C. B. Ryer,
J. Cary,
O. W. Morris,
J. C. Hepburn, M. D.,
Theodore Hyatt,
J. Wilson,

THIRTEENTH DISTRICT.

Amos Bailey,
John Hutchings,
C. F. L. Hibbard,
Viner L. Cornell,
John R. Marsh,
Stephen Haff,
Charles A. Merrick,
Charles I. Harris,
Henry Wood,
Charles Merrill,

Isaac Abrams,
John W. Conover,
Abraham Trafford,
Francis Duncan,
Ferris Finch,
George W. Bowne,
Erastus Williams,
Joab Young,
Thomas Brown,
Woodhull Smith,
Noah Coe, Sec'y.

FOURTEENTH DISTRICT.

Robert Morton,
Nelson Stelle, M. D.,
William Post,
Adam W. Spies,
Bezaleel Howe,
M. Benedict,
Charles Speights,
Eli Goodwin,
Peter Carter,
J. J. Jenkins,
Thomas W. Strong,
Robert Rae,
Gideon Peck,
Alexander W. Murray,
Daniel W. Teller,
William Gray, Sec'y.

FIFTEENTH DISTRICT.

Richard M. Bolles, M. D.,
James Cole,
Frederick Pattillow,
John L. Fendall,
Rev. Isaac Orchard,
Elisha Corwin,
Cornelius R. Disosway,
Benjamin Lord,
John Mollard,
Isaac Orchard, Sec'y.

SIXTEENTH DISTRICT.

H. K. Bull,
Joseph Merrill,
H. Silleck,
B. M. Fowler,
L. W. Halsey,
Wm. Rudd,
D. Coleman,
James Cowl,
William Vanwinkle,
Asa Smith,
John Taylor,
D. Chichester,
Joseph Longking,

D. S. Young,
John Parr,
James Millward,
B. Pettit,
E. T. Winter, M. D.,
John Brady,
John Ives, M. D.,
Wm. Heydon,
Myron Finch,
James F. Duff,
J. D. Adams,
James Kerney,
Richard Davies,
D. Newell,
J. F. Chamberlain,
Charles C. Darling, Sec'y.

SEVENTEENTH DISTRICT.

John P. Thatcher,
R. Albro,
James Duff,
C. H. Redman,
H. Griffin,
Wm. B. Humbert,
Wm. A. Lockwood,
J. S. Bowron, M. D.,
George Manning Tracy,
L. K. Osborn,
Thomas Jeremiah,
William Stebbins,
Chauncey Shaffer,
James R. Gibson,
Levi Duryea,
James M. Cockcroft,
Isaac Labagh,
D. C. Weeks,
William Wagstaff,
A. Messerole,
Jonathan Dibble,
Richard Horton, Sec'y.

EIGHTEENTH DISTRICT.

J. W. Benedict,
Leonard Hazeltine,
Royal West,
James Armstrong,
C. R. Harvey,
Edward Campbell,
Edward Roberts,
J. W. Warner,
John Hurley,
C. C. Savage,
W. I. Thompson,
N. R. Long,
George Lees,
Royal West, Sec'y.

BY-LAWS.

ARTICLE I.

Every person who becomes an annual Subscriber, a member of an Advisory Committee, or a Visitor, shall be a member of the Association.

ARTICLE II.

The President and Secretaries shall perform such duties as usually pertain to their office.

ARTICLE III.

The Treasurer shall give such security for the faithful performance of the trust reposed in him, as the Association may demand and approve. He shall take in charge all funds; keep an account of all receipts and disbursements; and pay all duly authorized demands. At the annual meeting, he shall render a particular and correct statement of all his receipts and disbursements to the Association. He shall also exhibit a summary report to the Board of Managers at their stated meetings, and whenever called upon by them for that purpose.

ARTICLE IV.

The Board of Managers shall have exclusive control of the funds of the Association, and authority to make By-laws; to fill vacancies; appoint all committees; and generally to adopt such measures as the objects of the Institution may require. It shall meet for the transaction of business, on the second Monday of every month; and the annual meeting of the Association shall be convened on the third Monday of

November, when the Board shall submit a report of its proceedings, and the officers and managers be chosen. In case of a failure to hold the specified meeting in November, a special meeting for the same purpose shall be convened in the course of the ensuing month.

ARTICLE V.

Special meetings of the Board of Managers and of the Supervisory Council, may be called by the Secretary, at the request of the President, or on receiving a requisition signed by five members. Two days' notice must be given of the time of meeting.

ARTICLE VI.

The Managers may at any time make such alterations in these By-Laws, as may be deemed necessary; provided they be not contrary to the Act of Incorporation, and that such alteration shall be submitted to the Board of Managers at least one meeting before the same is acted upon; and that it shall not be passed upon unless specified in the call of the meeting, and when a majority of the whole number of the Board of Managers is present.

ARTICLE VII.

An office shall be opened in an eligible situation, for the purpose of concentrating and diffusing all information pertaining to the Society's operations and objects, and for the transaction of its general business.

ARTICLE VIII.

It shall be the duty of the General Agent to devote himself with diligence and fidelity to the affairs of the Association.

ARTICLE IX.

The city shall be divided into eighteen Districts, each Ward forming a District; and the Districts be subdivided into Sections. Each District shall have an Advisory Committee, to consist of five members; and each Section a Visitor.

ARTICLE X.

It shall be the duty of the Advisory Committee to divide their Districts into such Sections, as to apportion to each about twenty-five families requiring attention; endeavor to obtain suitable Visitors for each Section; supply vacancies which may occur; make the necessary arrangements for placing at the disposal of the Visitors, food, fuel, and clothing, for distribution; and on some day in the first week of every month (excepting the meetings of July and August, which may be omitted in the discretion of the Committees), to convene all the Visitors of the Sections, for the purpose of receiving their returns, and conferring with them on the objects of their mutual labors. The Committees, moreover, shall duly draw upon the Treasurer for such proportion of the funds as may be appropriated to their District; they shall keep a strict account of all their disbursements, and only in extreme cases make donations of money; they shall monthly render an account of their expenditures to the Board of Managers; and in default of this duty, shall not be entitled to draw upon the funds of the Association. Each Committee shall appoint its own Chairman, Secretary, and Treasurer, and shall transmit the Reports of the Visitors immediately after each monthly meeting, with any other information they may think desirable, to the General Secretary.

ARTICLE XI.

It shall be the duty of each Visitor to confine his labors exclusively to the particular Section assigned him, so that no individual shall receive relief, excepting in the Section where he is known, and to which he belongs. The Visitors shall carefully investigate all cases referred to them before granting relief; ascertain the condition, habits of life, and means of subsistence of the applicants; and extend to all such kind services, counsel, and assistance, as a discriminating and judicious regard for their present and permanent welfare requires. And in cases of sickness, it will be their duty to inquire whether there is any medical or other attendance needed; whether relief is afforded by any religious or charitable society; to provide themselves with information respecting the nearest Dispensary, and in all cases, when practicable, to refer applicants for aid to appropriate existing societies. When no other assistance is provided or available, they shall draw from the resources of this Association—not money, which is never allowed to be given, except with the consent of the Advisory Committee or a member thereof—but such articles of food, fuel, clothing, and similar supplies as the necessities of the case require. In all cases of want coming to the knowledge of the Visitors, they will be expected to perform the same duties, although no application has been made. It shall be their duty, moreover, to render a report of their labors, and also an account of all their disbursements, to their respective Committees, at the stated monthly meeting. No Visitor neglecting these duties will be entitled to draw on the funds of the Association.

ARTICLE XII.

The Board of Managers, the members of the Advisory Committees, and certain elected members, shall together constitute a Supervisory Council, whose duties shall be deliberative and advisory; and its annual meetings be held on the third Monday of November, in each year. Special meetings of this body shall be held, when called by the Board of Managers.

ARTICLE XIII.

It shall be the duty of the members of the Association to endeavor, in all suitable ways, to give practical effect to its principles; especially to discountenance indiscriminate alms-giving and street-begging; to provide themselves with tickets of reference; and instead of giving aid to unknown applicants, whose case they cannot themselves investigate, to refer such applications to the Visitor of the Section in which the applicants reside, in order that such cases may properly be inquired into, and, if deserving, relieved.

ARTICLE XIV.

The printed forms of tickets and orders for relief, shall be designated by the Board of Managers, and no other shall be used.

SIXTH ANNUAL REPORT

OF THE

NEW-YORK ASSOCIATION FOR IMPROVING THE CONDITION OF THE POOR.

The Board of Managers, in presenting their Sixth Annual Report, congratulate the members of the Institution and of the organization, on the auspicious circumstances under which they are again permitted to convene.

Ever appropriate as it is to the return of this season to acknowledge our dependence upon Divine Providence, such an expression of gratitude appears peculiarly suitable to the present occasion, when called to review the recent trials and dangers through which we have been safely brought.

The past year has been marked by disaster and vicissitude. Owing to the visitation of the pestilence, the labors of the Association have been unusually severe, and not without peril to human life, especially to the Visitors who have been subjected to the toils and exposures of ministering to the indigent sick. Yet, in this organization of four hundred individuals, but one, Mr. IRA BURDGE, Visitor of Section 210, has been removed by death. He fell a victim to the epidemic early in June, having been an efficient Visitor from the establishment of the Association until his decease. Whilst we deplore the loss of an esteemed associate, suddenly cut down in the strength of his age, we would derive from our own preservation new motives to fidelity in the work intrusted to our hands.

The past season has been one of trial and suffering to the poor. In this City, as elsewhere, the squalid abodes of poverty and their miserable inmates, have been the chief seats and subjects of the epidemic. Numerous families have been bereaved of those on whom they had leaned for support, the sick increased beyond example, widows and orphans multiplied, and many before self-dependent were reduced to want. And these distresses were aggravated by the failure of the employment and aid, which numbers were accustomed to receive from the affluent, many of whom early left the City. It is worthy of remark, that during the recent calamity, the humanity of the arrangement by which this Institution extends relief throughout the year, was strikingly exemplified. Other alms-giving societies retire from their labors with the return of spring; even the Corporation at that time discontinues its winter system of out-door visitation and relief. But this organization being ever in the field, when the City was smitten with cholera, aid was not only promptly given, but with a liberality which the exigencies of the poor required. Greatly aggravated, doubtless, would have been their sufferings, if this unfailing charity had not interposed for their relief.

The Board are gratified to state, that notwithstanding the severity of the past winter, the scarcity of employment, the expensiveness of living, and the many who by reason of sickness, were unable to labor, they have no ground for the inference that the number having legitimate claims on this charity, was greater than the average of the previous year. The statistics accompanying this Report show that *six thousand six hundred and seventy-two families*, containing *twenty-nine thousand eight hundred and forty-four persons*, were relieved by the Association during the year; but of this number at least *twenty-five* per cent. should have been provided for by the Alms-House and Emigration departments, without charge to this Institution, which would have reduced the aggregate below that of 1848. By referring to the previous Annual Report it will be seen, that the applicants for relief had decreased that year, as compared with 1847; and but for the very defective action of our public charities, notwithstanding the rapid increase of the population, a like decrease would have marked the operations of the present year. The Board would call attention to these facts, because they show that the tendencies of the Institution are not, as some have mistakenly alleged, to increase pauperism, but to diminish it, and that such hitherto have been the results. By these remarks, no reflection on the very respectable individuals having control of the public establishments is designed. The Board well know, that the immense influx of indigent foreigners at this port, suddenly thrown upon the Commissioners of Emigration, and the multitudes arriving by the way of Quebec and Montreal, chargeable to the City Authorities, required an extent of arrangements for their relief which could neither be anticipated nor immediately supplied. Many of the destitute were consequently thrown upon the community; and this Association sanctioning the temporary aid of suffering persons having claims on existing charities, until such claims could be made available for their benefit, the needy eagerly turned this provision to their own advantage, and from this source obtained relief. Nor could such relief, once granted, be suddenly withdrawn, without exposing many to suffering, and in some instances to starvation. Hence, though the number relieved during the year has been considerably augmented, the increase is neither attributable to the Institution, nor an indication of its tendencies. Such increase, in fact, may be regarded as temporary, and as likely to be reduced, when the Authorities to whom the matter exclusively belongs, bring the reformatory action they now promise, to bear upon the subject.

Special exertions have been made during the year to disencumber the Association, and so far as practicable the City, of all persons able to labor, who from time to time have evinced a disposition to subsist on the toil of others, rather than by their own. In prosecuting this work, a large amount of *voluntary destitution* has been discovered, chiefly among persons of foreign birth, who appear to regard labor as the greatest of evils, and exemption therefrom as their peculiar privilege. They live in indolence, intemperance, and filth, are abjectly obsequious for favors, and resort to any pretexts, however degrading or fraudulent, rather than to honest industry, for support. They are importunate for alms, which some claim as their prescriptive right. If once aided, they will certainly apply again; and if helped through a winter, will not only look for it as long as they live, but probably so train their children as to expect it after them. To this class, the discrimination and decision of the Visitors have caused great discomfort. The resentment of not a few has been shown, on finding their long-practised impositions detected, and themselves reduced to the comparatively hard condition of earning their bread by the sweat of their brow. But the results to many, by coercing them to industry and self-reliance, have been beneficial; whilst the general effects are to shield the community from one of the worst of evils—the prevalence of able-bodied pauperism.

The Board have learned during the year, with regret, that the Visitors in the discharge of their duties are sometimes severely tried by the well-meant but injudicious interference of donors. A person, for example, asking alms, is sent to the Visitor, who on careful investigation finds, perhaps, that the applicant is a recent emigrant, for whom the law provides relief, which he refuses to accept; or that he is otherwise aided, so that his own industry would readily supply what is deficient for his support; or he is idle, improvident, and intemperate, so that alms in his case would encourage vice, and be worse than wasted. Whatever the facts, the Visitor being fully acquainted with them, is best qualified to decide wisely and discreetly in the case. What then is his course? He interests himself in the applicant, and gives him appropriate counsel; but he cannot, perhaps, with the approval of his own judgment, grant any, or if any, only very limited relief. If the grounds of his decision were known to others, they would doubtless be satisfactory. But there being, unfortunately, no reciprocation of intelligence between the Visitor and donor, the disappointed applicant returns to the latter, we may suppose, with such a report as he trusts will turn most to his advantage. This report passing uncontradicted, his piteous tale and seeming wretchedness enlist the sympathies of the over-credulous donor, who sends the Visitor a hasty, probably an anonymous note, charging him, more or less directly, with inhumanity, unfaithfulness, or niggardly economy, accompanied with the intimation that if such treatment of the poor is sanctioned by the Association, he will choose some other channel for his charity.

Incredible as it may appear, the Visitor is sometimes subjected to trials like these. Is it then surprising that he is grieved, discouraged, nay, even impelled to leave a service which is so imperfectly understood and appreciated, especially by those from whom he has a right to expect sympathy and co-operation? Is it not obvious, that the complaining class referred to, do not enter into the spirit of the far-reaching principles by which the Visitor is governed, when they expect him to violate these principles merely to gratify their benevolent impulses? Comparatively easy would it be for him to yield to impulse, and give to importunity. But this would be to repeat what is reprehensible in indiscriminate relief, and to perpetuate the very evils which the systematic action of this Institution, is designed to prevent. Very different from this are the Visitor's duties. The comprehensive physical and moral reforms which his labors contemplate, require him first, personally to investigate the character and condition of the applicant, and afterwards to grant, withhold, or modify relief, according to the exigencies of each individual case. He is pre-eminently the poor man's friend, whose alms respect not merely his present necessities, but his permanent benefit.

Many appear to forget that this is a *voluntary* Association, all of whose Visitors are of the highest respectability, and their labors entirely gratuitous. None but the truly philanthropic will engage in so disinterested a service, or are qualified for it. It is not, however, for the defence of the Visitor merely that the subject is presented, but for an important practical object. Whatever embarrasses the Visitor, or induces him to relinquish his labors, wrongs the poor, and injures the community. So arduous are the duties of the organization, few comparatively will engage in them. Those, therefore, who are willing to endure the toils and sacrifices, should not only be highly esteemed for their own and their work's sake, but aided and encouraged by every citizen—for all have a common interest in their efforts and success.

There is unfortunately amongst us, though not peculiar to our city, a false philanthropy—a sickly sentimentality, whose tendencies are to relax the restraints which this Association has found necessary to apply. The Board would, therefore, earnestly, yet respectfully, urge upon all, as they dread the growth of pauperism, and value the best interests of the poor, to cease from weakening these restraints, and also from dictation and interference in the Visitor's duties. Let them either examine the case of unknown applicants themselves, or refer them to the Institution; and by their steady co-operation therewith, endeavor to subject to its strict principles and systematic control the mendicity of the city. And as mutual interchange of information between Visitors and members would greatly facilitate so desirable a result, the *Reference Tickets* have been enlarged, so that those who subscribe them may, by giving their *residence* with their name, be called upon, or corresponded with, by the Visitors, when necessary. The Board would call the special attention of members to this improved form of the tickets, with the earnest request that they be filled up, as the blanks therein indicate.

The Board, in this review, regard it also as a duty to advert to some causes which have steadily resisted the efforts of the Association to repress street-begging and vagrancy, *for which it is not responsible.*

Whilst the law confides the care and control of the city poor to the Alms House and Emigration Departments, and provides for the arrest of vagrants at the instance of any person making complaint, it obligates no person to proceed against them. Hence what may be done by any may be so neglected by all, that the community may be overrun with vagrants, as has been the case to a shameful extent in this city. Blame for this result may, with some reason, attach to the statute itself, because it has failed to lodge any where the obligation to arrest the vagrant. Be that, however, as it may, the Alms House Department, until the recent change in its government, assumed the charge of enforcing the vagrant law; and the right of doing this being universally conceded to it, as the legally constituted guardian of the poor, it is obvious that no voluntary institution like this, without legal power, could with any propriety interfere in the matter. The new government possessing the same rights, and incurring the same obligations which belonged to the old, was justly responsible for their exercise in suppressing vagrancy. Failing, however, to do this, the vagrant law became a dead letter, and street-begging being without this restraint, rapidly increased. But the Alms House Governors, having recently taken up the subject, the evil, so far as their department is concerned, will probably be corrected. If, as is earnestly hoped, the Emigration Board adopt similar measures with respect to the indigent which have claims upon them, then this Institution will be relieved of a burden which it has no funds to sustain, and the city be delivered from the annoyance of a class for which the Legislature, by a compulsory tax on the emigrants themselves, has amply provided.

Another, and no less fruitful cause of street-begging and vagrancy, for which this Association *is not responsible*, is the habit of many of our respectable citizens, especially ladies, of giving alms to unknown mendicants. The Board having frequently before called public attention to this great evil, the continuance of the habit is their apology for referring to it again. And here let them not be understood as disapproving private charity, or a quick sensibility to suffering, and a readiness to relieve, which are worthy of all praise; much less as wishing to take from any the opportunity or the duty of personally caring for the poor. It is one of the beautiful characteristics of our city, that so many families have each their select circles of charity, in which they endeavor to exert beneficent influences. They would rejoice to witness the increase of this spirit and action an hundred-fold, if regulated by the principle recognized by the patriarch who " sought out the cause he knew not." But the spirit which they would rebuke is that which gives merely or mainly to be relieved from importunity, or to avoid the pain, denial would inflict upon themselves. Such inconsiderate impulsiveness is not charity, but selfishness; and those who yield to it, may prove themselves the foes rather than the friends of humanity. Alms, without a knowledge of the applicant, or investigation of character, will fill the city with beggars, and produce incalculably more evil than good. As vain the hope of repressing vagrancy, whilst thus encouraged, as would be the attempt to extinguish fire by adding fuel, or of curing drunkenness by using stimulants. If we would exhaust the streams, we must seal up the fountain. But if we encourage, and, in effect, bribe the needy to vagrant habits by indiscriminate relief, the wisest measures human sagacity can devise will fail to correct the evil. There is high authority for the belief, that "the poor shall never cease out of the land." They have been left as a perpetual legacy to the benevolent by Him whose Providence extends over the universe. But street-begging and vagrancy are self-inflicted evils, for which there is neither necessity nor apology. No proposition is more certain, than whilst our citizens continue to give indiscreetly, they will continue to suffer this annoyance; but let them deny all aid to strange applicants, and refer them to the Association, and the ills of poverty in this form, will be speedily and effectually removed. The only alternative, therefore, is either to abandon this mistaken mode of relief, or the expectation of ridding the city of this intolerable evil.

But regarding indiscriminate alms merely as annoyances, does not express half their mischievous consequences. It is their deteriorating *moral effects* for which they are chiefly to be deprecated. There are facts enough to establish the assertion, that in nine cases out of ten, indolence, intemperance, deception, and profligacy, are thus encouraged; and these evils, be it remembered, are additional to the pecuniary burdens and annoyances which the curse of pauperism entails upon the community. There may be some few seeking aid in this way that deserve it, and would be benefited by it. For such, we repeat, and, indeed, for applicants of every grade and character, whether known or unknown, deserving or undeserving, this Institution is provided; and it invites the reference of all persons to its care who are beyond the range of individual knowledge and inquiry. For it can easily accomplish by its comprehensive system of visitation and investigation what is impracticable to unassociated effort. No individual can visit every one, but this reaches all. And not only so, but, like a vast sieve, it separates the precious from the vile; and whilst it disposes of all, so that none are left to suffer, except by their own choice, it goes beyond any scheme of mere temporary physical aid, and endeavors to exert over all appropriate moral influences. And that the system may have a city-wide universality, no one is precluded from sharing in its advantages by pecuniary considerations. Every donor, whether he gives little or much, becomes a member, and is entitled to tickets, and a Directory, by which he can refer applicants to the proper Visitor for aid. Should those, however, who decline membership, adopt the Association's principle of *never giving relief to strangers without personal inquiry*, the objects here contemplated would be attained. More than this is not asked of any; less than this, no well-disposed citizen can consistently do. It is alike demanded by public honor and public safety; by religion and philanthropy.

The heterogeneous character of the needy in this city greatly augments the difficulty of judicious relief. Here the indigent are chiefly of foreign birth—many speak a foreign language, and the greater proportion profess the Roman Catholic faith. They have not only their national peculiarities, but are so pauperized in spirit, and practised in deception, that the Visitor is frequently perplexed to discriminate between pretext and necessity. There is danger, moreover, of the deserving degenerating into impostors. If aided because of sickness or infirmity, they are tempted by the desire of an easier mode of life than labor, to feign illness, that relief may be continued. So numerous and embarrassing, in short, are the difficulties of the work, that if long-suffering charity was not an element of Christianity, it would fail amidst such trials and discouragements. That it is such, is both the guaranty of its perpetuity and of its unwearied endeavors so to dispense relief, as permanently to benefit its objects. As it is as much a duty to give with prudence as to give at all, by what other means could such prudence be more effectually exercised than by carrying out, on a scale commensurate with the city, that very system of relief which discreet private charity, in its narrower sphere, would adopt for itself? Hence the machinery, the arrangements, and regulations of this Institution; its minute divisions of labor, its numerous Visitors, its personal visitation and rigid scrutiny of character,—all are not only designed, but are essential to promote the best interests of the poor, and to prevent the enormous evils and abuses which would result, in a population so peculiar, from any mode of relief less thorough, exact, and comprehensive.

The *General Results*, the Board believe, have met every reasonable expectation. By a more thorough co-operation of the community, more doubtless would have been effected. But is it a small achievement to have corrected in any considerable degree the prevalent evils of indiscriminate relief, and to have instituted a system of charity in which six years' experience has discovered no radical defects;—a system at once so comprehensive and minute, that, while it embraces the entire city, overlooks not a single needy individual;—a system which does for, and in the name of the benevolent donor, what he cannot himself do, with a degree of promptness, intelligence, and economy, that isolated efforts in such a field could never attain;—a system which, while it neither supersedes private nor public charity, supplies, so far as is practicable, the acknowledged deficiencies of both, by caring for a numerous class of the most deserving not otherwise provided for, so as to save them from suffering, and from the degradation of Alms House relief? A system, in a word, whose principles they believe must remain unchanged; but whose efficiency and usefulness will progress, as, year by year, their application is better understood by the Visitors, and more generally appreciated and acted upon by the community. And what more than this can philanthropy desire, or humanity hope for?

In respect to *General Results,* it may be further said, that much of the good done, consists of the evil prevented. With the unprecedented flood of European pauperism, which for the past three years has been pouring upon our shores, this City would have been deluged with vagrants of the worst class, unless very energetic measures had been used to prevent it. And have not those relied upon been effectual? The emigration to this port alone, exceeds that of all the other ports of the Union combined; and yet the City of New-York, considering the number of its population and peculiarly exposed position, will, with respect to paupers and vagrants, favorably compare with any of our Atlantic cities. This Institution would not claim for itself an undue share of influence in saving the community from such degradation, to the disparagement of other agencies. "It is but one wheel in the vast machinery of moral forces." Yet, spread as it is over the entire City, and having an organization more numerous, more minutely diffused, more systematic and unintermitted in its labors and activity than any, or indeed, than all other institutions for the same object, either legal or voluntarily united, it may, without arrogance, claim a humble share of the praise for whatever has been done to guard the City from an appalling increase of pauperism.

On *Specific Results,* the Board might indefinitely enlarge, but for the difficulty of making selections, and of compressing them into the limits assigned this Report. It would be impracticable to refer even succinctly to the individuals and families that have been rescued from abject want, and placed in circumstances of comparative comfort; or to those provided with employment, which they had failed to obtain for themselves, so as to render gratuitous aid unnecessary; much less to those who have been morally as well as physically elevated to the rank of virtuous and useful citizens. And it is worthy of passing remark, that whilst alms to the needy are indispensable, and often open hearts to moral influences that would otherwise be closed against them, yet the most useful Visitors are not the most lavish of relief. Experience, on the contrary, shows that without great caution, the poor may be debased in proportion to the amount they receive. In some parts of the City, almost the entire population of certain Sections, have been clamorous for aid. They appeared, indeed, to subsist chiefly by street-begging, and what their well practised arts could get from organized charities. So numerous were the applicants, and so idle and degraded generally their character, as almost to discourage effort in their behalf. Many of them really supposing that they could not earn their own support, did not attempt it, and were content to live as paupers. But sagacious Visitors, in many instances, have dispelled such notions, and corrected such habits. Kind words, good counsel, and heart-felt sympathy—timely rebuke and occasional aid, have almost wrought miracles for the abject and the helpless, arousing them to efforts for themselves and families, when a more liberal but less considerate policy would, doubtless, have confirmed them in indolent and vicious courses, from which there would have been no after rescue. The appearance of some neighborhoods has entirely changed, with the improved character of the people. The number of applicants, in certain Sections, at the beginning of winter, has been so great, as to oppress and nearly overwhelm the Visitors. But aid being given only to those who by unavoidable causes were needy, the dependent list was soon reduced to *one third* or *one fourth;* whilst the able-bodied were so managed, as to enable them to subsist chiefly on their own resources. The beneficial results, in short, of such labors, to which more than *three hundred Visitors* are devoted, though not admitting of a Statistical Exhibit, are not less real and important, than if attested by an elaborate enumeration of facts.

The loaning of Stoves, and the distribution of *new and second-hand Clothing*, have received attention as in former years. For the latter, the Association has been indebted to many benevolent ladies, merchants and others, to whom the Board would thus publicly present their thanks. No donations are more gratefully received or usefully applied than clothing, or materials for clothing, hose, shoes, blankets, quilts, &c., which, though of little value to those who can spare them, are health and comfort to many a deserving but destitute fellow-creature, who would otherwise be subjected to exposure and suffering. All such articles being distributed by the Visitors to those whom they personally know, there is little risk that they will be perverted or abused. Will not the rich send of their abundance, and persons of less ample means spare something from their supplies, to cover the sick and clothe the destitute widow and orphan? All such donations may be sent either to the office of the General Agent, or to any of the members of the organization, by whom they will be placed in the hands of the Visitors.

The Circulation of Tracts on moral and economical subjects, has been continued, as in previous years, with encouraging results. The *fifth five thousand* of the "Economist," and the *third five thousand* of the "Way to Wealth," have been distributed since the previous Report. The *third* in the series, a premium Tract, is now in the course of publication, and will soon be put into the hands of the laboring classes, for whom it is especially designed. So manifestly useful are tracts of this kind, as, in the judgment of the Board, fully to justify the expense of their publication.

The Board take pleasure in acknowledging a donation from the Sanitary Committee of the Board of Health, by their Treasurer, ROBERT T. HAWS, Esq., of $465 73, being the balance remaining in their hands of moneys collected in different churches in the City, during the late epidemic; also of a lot of clothing from the same Committee, to be distributed by the Visitors of the Association, among the poor.

Nor would they omit to mention, the announcement of a bequest of *three thousand dollars,* by Miss ELIZABETH DE-MILT of this City, recently deceased. The Board gratefully appreciating these, and similar expressions of confidence in the Institution, by benevolent and philanthropic individuals, have referred to the consideration of a Committee, the expediency of appropriating legacies and special donations to the establishment of some permanent Institution, for the benefit of the indigent in this City.

Among other gratifying and encouraging incidents, may be noticed the steadily augmenting number of the friends and patrons of the Institution. The year just closed exhibits an increase of more than *one thousand members,* which is an unequivocal proof of the growing confidence of the community. They desire to express their sincere gratitude for past encouragement and pecuniary aid, which they regard, under the auspices of a benign Providence, as a pledge for the future.

Any concern they may at present feel, does not arise from a fear that the Association will fail of support; but from the conviction that they have themselves hitherto failed so to impress on the public mind the necessity of this great charity, as to secure for it more extensive co-operation. But they would not be impatient for such a result. As from the known laws of the human mind, reforms to be thorough must be the work of time, they indulge no visionary expectations of an immediate prevalent change. Large masses of mind are not *suddenly* reached and united into an effective public sentiment. It is prolonged effort, having truth for its basis, that must be successful. They therefore look to the future with confidence, for a widening appreciation of the Association's principles. These principles, it is believed, will ultimately be adopted, if not for philanthropic considerations, in self-defence. As a community, we are peculiarly exposed to pauperism; these principles are adequate to guard us against its incursions. As a City, multitudes will be thrown upon it who need sympathy and aid; in these principles there is sufficient power to meet the demands of duty and humanity. Having, in short, such claims to the patronage of an intelligent Christian people, it is not deemed too much to expect, that the principles of this system will make their way to public favor; and gradually gaining strength and extension, accomplish the objects for which they have been diffused.

A Tabular Exhibit of the Monthly District Returns, from November 1st, 1848, to November 1st, 1849.

1848–9.	Number of Families Relieved.	Number of Persons.	Number of Visits.
November . .	934	3336	1546
December . .	2250	8129	3817
January . . .	4733	17,380	8338
February . .	4756	18,328	7724
March	3072	11,959	4573
April	1111	4310	1773
May	330	1275	487
June	132	525	163
July	201	700	401
August . . .	160	645	320
September . .	403	1516	713
October . . .	417	1592	735

The following exhibits the aggregate relief, without repetition, which is unavoidable in the foregoing table, to wit:—

Number of different families relieved from November 1st, 1848, to November 1st, 1849, - - - - - 6,672
Number of persons, - - - - - - - 29,844
Number of visits, - - - - - - - - 30,590
Receipts for the same period, - - - - - $28,753 15
Disbursements do. - - - - - 26,550 65

Excess of Receipts over Disbursements, - - - $2,202 50

The Board, in conclusion, commend the Institution, its interests and objects, to the care of a beneficent Providence during another year, trusting that a deep sense of gratitude for the numerous manifestations of Divine goodness to ourselves as individuals, and as a people, will not fail to impress on all the duty and the privilege of exercising enlarged sympathy for the suffering and liberality to the destitute. "If thou draw out thy soul to the afflicted, and satisfy the afflicted soul, then shall thy light rise in obscurity, and the Lord guide thee continually." Thus shall a sacred and imperative obligation be fulfilled, and thy prayers and thine ALMS come up as a memorial before God.

Statement of the Disbursements and Receipts of the Association for Improving the Condition of the Poor, for the year ending November 5th, 1849.

Cr.			Dr.		
1848-9. Receipts per Contributions, &c., from Nov. 16, 1848, to Nov. 5, 1849,	$28,753	15	1848-9. Disbursements from Nov. 16, 1848, to Nov. 5, 1849,	$26,550	65
Balance in hand Nov. 16, 1848,	1,601	62	Balance in Treasury Nov. 5, 1849,	3,804	12
	$30,354	77		$30,354	77

The undersigned, having examined the accounts of Stewart Brown, Esq., Treasurer pro tem., and found vouchers for all the sums therein charged, hereby certify the same to be correct.

FREDERICK S. WINSTON, } *Auditing Committee.*
JOSEPH B. COLLINS,

NEW-YORK, November 5, 1849.

PRINTED FORMS USED BY THE ASSOCIATION.

Ticket of Reference for the use of Members.

Mr.   Visitor,
   No.   St.
is requested to visit
at No.

                                               Member

                              N. Y. Association for
                      Improving the Condition of the Poor.

Visitor's Order.

Mr.
No.   *St.*
Please let
have the value of
in
                               184
                                                   Vis.
                              N. Y. Association for
                      Improving the Condition of the Poor.

Monthly Report.

Subjoined is a condensed plan of a Sectional Monthly Return. The original occupies a large page of foolscap, with appropriate columns, fifteen in number, which enable Visitors to give the following particulars of every family relieved. 1st. Name, residence, place of birth, sex, color, occupation, time in the city, number in family, and number of visits. 2d. Statements of character,—as being temperate or intemperate. 3d. Unavoidable causes of indigence, such as sickness, infirmity, or old age, with space for marginal remarks.

PRINTED FORM USED BY THE ASSOCIATION.

New-York Association for Improving the Condition of the Poor.

VISITOR'S MONTHLY REPORT OF SECTION No.　　DISTRICT No.　　DATED　　184

☞ *A mark with a pen thus ,, in the columns, will point out the class to which the person named belongs.*

FAMILIES RELIEVED. — Always give full Name, and *male* Head of Family, if living.	RESIDENCE OF FAMILIES. — Which must be reported every month.	Foreigners.	Natives.	Colored Persons.	Males.	Females.	No. in Family.	No. of Visits.	KIND OF OCCUPATION.	Temperate.	Intemperate.	Sickness.	Misfortune.	Old Age.	AMOUNT EXPENDED. $	cts.	REMARKS.

Signed,　　　　　　　　　　　　　　　　　　　　　　　Visitor.

LIST OF MEMBERS.

Owing to inadvertence in the returns from some of the Districts, it is feared that the list of Members may not be perfectly accurate. The *amounts* received were duly credited, as may be seen by an inspection of the Treasurer's account, at the General Office. But as the names of some who contributed small sums did not accompany their donations, with all the efforts subsequently made to obtain them, the list may still be incomplete.

A.

Astor, Wm. B.
Alsop, J. W.
Anonymous, by James Millward
Anonymous, by A. W. Spies
Anonymous
Austin, David
Astor, J. J., Jr.
Aspinwall, Jas. S.
Anonymous
Anonymous
Anonymous
Aspinwall, Wm. H.
A Lady, by W. E. Laight
A Merchant
Aspinwall, John L.
A. L.
A Friend
Allen, G. F.
Allen, Stephen
A Friend, by H. S. Whitteman
Adams, John
A Lady
A Lady, by Naylor & Co.
Astor, J. J., Mrs.
Allen, Horatio
Anten, J. W.
Abbe, Geo. W.
Ahrensfeldt, Henry
Abbott, Wm. D.
Alston, Geo. W.
Adams, C.
Ayres, Reuben
Aims, Peter
Anderson, Edmund
Abrams, Isaac
Adams, J. D.
Albro, R.
Armstrong, James
Aikman, Hugh
Adams, J. T.
A. W. & Co.
Aymar & Co.
Aymar, Wm. & Co.
Alexander, G. C.
Avery, C. A.
A. G.
Alexander, Revd. Dr.
Allen, Dr.
Anthon, John
Allison, M.
Armstrong, M.
Ambler, Mr.
Adams & Co. C.
Andrus, Mr.
Apgar, Mahlon
Ambler, J.
Allen & Rose
Anderson, E.
Anderson, C. E.
Arcularius, Geo.
Arnold, A.
Andrews, Dr.
Alnwick, Mr.
Atwell, Mr.
Ackerman, Mr.
Ahles & Sattler
A Friend
Aymar, Wm.
Anderson, James
A Lady, by Mr. Forest
Allen, John
Allen, William
Aikman, Robert
Abbott, J. S. C.
Andrews, S. Mrs.
Aymar, Charles
Aldrich, H. D.
Anderson, Mr.
Abernethy, C.
Ashton, George
Aguirre, P. A.
Allen, Wm. M.
Aimes, Peter
Anderson, John
Anderson, Wm.
Armitage, Thos. Revd.
Allen, Isaac
Amerman, J. W.
Andrews, J. E.
Alexander, Isaac
Abeel, Miss
Anderson, Capt.
Alford, Edwin M.
Adeldorfer & Neustacer
Adriance, Isaac
Aldis, W. H.
Adriance, J.
A Friend
Ash, Joseph H.
Adolphus, A.
A Friend
Aikman, Hugh
A. G. S.
Allen, W. A.
Allen, E. P.
Adolphus, P.
Austin, John A.
Adams, J. T.
Anderson, E. J.
Alexander, F.
Allen, D. B.
Atterbury, L. Jr.
Alvord, A. A.
Abbott, Gorham D.
Austin, David
A., Mrs.
Ammerman, Richard
Aldrich, Mr.
Alcock, R. E.
Armstrong, George
Acklandone, J.
Anderson, Hiram
Allen, John
Anthon, Henry, Revd.
Abeel, John H.
Arcularius, A. M.
Auchmuty, Mrs.
Anstice, Henry
Aims, Jacob
Adriance, Thos. M.
Averill, Horatio
Abbott, W. M.
Albro, R.
Arden, J. B., M.D.

LIST OF MEMBERS. (1849.

A. C. B.
Anderson, P.
Allee, Mrs.
Appleton, Daniel
Appleton, John A.
Appleton, Wm. H.
A. J. L. & Co.
Ahrenfeldt
Ashley & Fenn
Atwater, Wm.
Aguir; B. C.
Atkinson, A. S.
Aycrigg, B.
Aliles, Mrs.
Andrews, H. M.
Amerman, J.
Atwater, W. L.
Ayres, Albert
Ackerman, Jas.
Allen, Thos. E.
Atwater, Mr.
Allen, George
Arcularius, Geo.
Anthony, J.
Aitkin, Walter
Anderson & Demarest
Atkins & Miller
Althouse, Mr.
Adams, H. C.
Ayres, Mrs.
Allen, Mr.
Ammen, C.
Allen, G. C.
Ackland, John
Ayres, Ann, Miss
A Heaven Send
A ———
A Friend, by Dr. Griscom
Abraham, J. D.
A Gentleman
A Lady
Abbott, Isaac
A Poor Woman
A Clerk
Anonymous
Aspinwall, Jno. Mrs.

B.

Brown, James
Brown, Stewart
Bartlett, Edwin
Bennett, Mr.
Banyer, Mrs.
Ball, Tompkins & Black, and Friend
Brown, John
Bull, Wm. G.
Baldwin, Jno. C.
Brooks, Miss, by the Revd. Mr Martin
Beales, Saml. J.
Bradford, Wm.
Belden, Wm. Revd.
Bird, George
Bruen, A. M.

Bruen, A. M. Mrs.
B. Robert
Butler, Benj. F.
Benedict, E. C.
Benjamin, F. A.
Banks, Mrs.
B. ———
Blunt, G. W.
Bronson, Arthur
Bruce, George
Brown, Richard
Brown, W. & S.
Bulkley, E.
Briant, D. S.
Bogardus, Wm.
Brumley, Avery
Baldwin, H. M.
Beatty, James
Barry, John
Buxton, John
Burras, T. H.
Bridges, J. F.
Ballagh, Wm.
Baxter, Samuel
Beers, N. P.
Bremner, J. P.
Bruce, B. G.
Bell, Joseph M.
Bradley, Wm. C.
Bevan, Edward
Bennett, Wm.
Barbour, W. C.
Bartlett, D. C.
Bailey, Amos
Bowne, Geo. W.
Brown, Thomas
Benedict, M.
Bolles, Richard M., M.D.
Bull, H K.
Brady, John
Bowron, J. S.
Benedict, J. W.
Baldwin, J. L.
Benedict, J. W.
Boorman, James
Blackwell, Josiah, per Mr. Hall
Bolton, Curtis
Bonnet, P. R.
Bussing, Jno. S.
Burr, E. Mrs.
Blatchford, E. H.
Bogert, Corn's
Brown, E. J.
Borrowe, J. H., M.D.
Bernard, A.
Buckland, Alex.
Bartow, Theodosius
Browne, Mr.
Berrian, J. M.
Bell, Wm. H.
Buck, Gurdon, M.D.
Barnes, D. H., Mrs.
Blunt & Syms
Bradley, Wm. C.
Bell, Joseph M.
Bruce, Jno. T.

Bruce, Robt. M.
Babbitt, Wm. H.
Bergen, James
Barker, Stephen
Bradford, N. G.
Burlew, R.
Brush, J. E.
Burling, L. S.
Belcher, E. R., M.D.
Baldwin, Luther
Brewster, Joseph
Belcher, H. W.
Brady
Browne
Burton
Bogue, Thos.
Baldwin, Chs.
Brown, E. D.
Brommer, J.
Bausher, Mr.
Badger, Mrs.
Bonvay, Mr.
Brown, G. F.
Blatchley, John
Burr, John
Boyd, Daniel
Burke, Edmund
Bacon, F. S.
Boyle & Coleman
Bachman, Mr.
Burns, Wm. S.
Bennett, N. L.
Boyd, N. J.
Bell, Mrs.
Baker, Jno. R.
Briggs, J. V.
Boyce, J. W.
Bolt, D.
Ballagh, W. & R.
Barbour, Wm. B.
Barker, Luke
Bulvid, Robert
B. B.
Baldwin, Dibblee & Work
Bowne & Co.
Badger, J.
Benedict, H. M.
Blake & Brown
Burritt, Francis
Benjamin, Jr. & Co. Wm.
Burnhiemer, Newhouse & Co.
Boicean & Bush
Boyd & Paul
Bigelow, R.
Babe & Brothers
Brown
Burritt, H. & Co.
Boker, E.
Buckman
Beach, W N.
Baker & Wanger
Bent
Brink, J.
Bartlett & Wilford
Bronson, Silas
Baldwin, J. L.
Brody, Mr.

1849.) LIST OF MEMBERS. 35

Baker, Dr.
Bevridge & Co.
Bonnet, Mr.
Butts, Mr.
Bulkey, Dr.
Bininger, A. M.
Butler, S. M.
Bininger & Cozzens
Boyd, John
Burkhalter, Stephen
Blair, H. B.
Brown, A. N.
Burdet, Mr.
Belnap, A.
Bradner, Bell & Co.
Booth, G. C.
Butterworth, Mr.
Barclay, Anthony
Bronson, Fredk.
Bronson, Miss
Beach, Mr.
Burt, Mr.
Boyce, John
Battin, Jos. Mr.
Brower, A. & J.
Basset, N.
Baldwin & Saxton
Baker & Scudder
Brez, Paul
Bard, Wm.
Blane, Mr.
Barnes & Mackey
Bell, J.
Britton, Mr.
Banta, Mr.
Bailey, W.
Barron, Mr.
Bloodgood, N.
Bulois, Mr.
Baily, Mr.
Brouwer, Jacob
Burke, M.
Banks, Theodore
Barry, A., Mrs.
Badeau, P.
Banell, Mrs.
Brinckley, John
Barnum, P. T.
Bartow, Edgar J. & Co.
Backus, Osborn & Co.
Burling Slip
Bishop
Bartholomew, W. H.
Bangs, Platt & Co.
Bostwick, Z.
Bushnell, L.
Bate, T. & T. H.
Benjamin, Wm. M.
Baldwin, A. D.
Brewer
Bourleir, P.
Bache, G.
Bond, Mr.
Bauduet, C.
Brown, Wm.
Benedict, S. W.
Bell, A.

Burnham, E. Mrs.
Barton, Wm.
Butler, C.
Buchanan, R.
Brown, Chs. P.
Blackwell, J. M.
Bell, Thomas
Bushnell, O.
Buxame, J.
Beales, H.
Breath, James
Beadleston, Ebnr.
Baker, J. W.
Briggs, Geo.
Bush, Richard J.
Benson, C. S.
Barrow, James
Beebe, W. H.
Brown, S. L. Mrs.
Bantie, S.
Bagley, A. G.
Bell, John
Bevier, John H. Revd.
Bates, Mrs.
Burdett, Henry C.
Brown, H.
Bradly
Bogardus, W. H.
Burdett, J.
Bower, Reuben,
Brinck, J. C.
Bond, W. S.
Bunn, Martin
Benedict, S. H.
Balch, W. S.
Brown, J.
Butterworth, J.
Blandell, Charles
Burkhalton, Chas.
Blondell, Wm.
Barritt, Mrs.
Bruce, Jno. M.
Blackstone, W.
Bloomfield, E. S.
Birdsall and Co., S.
Born, Jacob
Bleakley, Andrew
Brinkerhoff, Walter
Bussell, Geo.
Binse, L. B.
Bliss, Mr.
Badeau, E. C.
Barnes, J. N.
Bayles, J.
Blauvelt, D. T.
Berry, S. J.
Bogert, Wm. M.
Bailey, W.
Bull, Mr.
Bailey, S.
Bogert, C.
Burnton, J. F.
Blanck, T. J.
Blakeney, D.
Baker, Jno. D.
Brownson, Wm. M.
Bogert, Peter A.

Bloomfield, Wm.
Brown, Geo. B.
Bootman, E.
Brown, P.
Bruce, Chas.
Bull, Mrs.
Banks, Mrs.
Broadhead, L.
Biggs, Robert
Burns, Wm.
Benson, Mrs.
Berrenbrock, Mr.
Bloodgood, Mathias
Bellman, L. J.
Booth, Mr.
Barkley, James
Brown & De Rosset
Betts, Jno. S.
Banks
Barkley, Jno
Berdick, Mr.
Burr, Mr.
Barker, Mr.
Brunel, Christian
Bird, Mr.
Babcock, Mr.
Bride, A. W.
Barkly, Robt.
Broadhead, E.
Betts, Mr.
Brown, Mr.
Bellow, Hervey W.
Ballard, F. W.
Belknap, A. B.
Burs, Abm.
Battelle & Renwick
Brown, Silas
Boyd, Wm.
Bent, Mr.
Burkhalter, Mr.
Bennet, Mr.
Bissel, John
Benkard, James
Burger, Wm.
Browning & Durham
Betkam, Mrs.
Beers, C.
Bowden, Andrew
Burhans, Saml.
Brinkerhoff, Mrs.
Brinkerhoff, P. R
Bachelder, Mary, Mrs.
Butler, Samuel
Brooks, J.
Brown, Samuel
Black, Mr.
Brower & Ogden
Brown, J. H.
Brainard, G. W.
Briggs, Mr.
Bartholomew, S.
Bochaud, J.
Brelling
Beck & Co.
Baudoine, Mr.
Baker, Mr.
Brown, Thomas

LIST OF MEMBERS. (1849.

Bleecker, G. N.
Barker, J. S.
Blackmer
Bulkley, G.
Buckman, Ezra
Brooks, C. C.
Barstow, Samuel
Baker, Dobel
Belknap, E. S.
Barker, J. W.
Bulkley, E.
Beadle, Dr.
Bulkley, Dr.
Brown, J. V.
Brundige, Dr.
Bleecker
Bailley
Bairden
Bossuet, Mr.
Baker, L. Mrs.
Banyer, Mrs.
Buckley, Mrs.
Bolles, Dr.
Burnham, G. W.
Bacon, B. P.
Bronson, F.
Bininger, A.
Bedell, Henry
Burrows, Philip
Beckwith, N. M.
Bishop, Japhet
Bolton, J., M.D.
Beers, Joseph D.
Bleeker, A. J.
Brush, Stephen
Bridgham, S. W.
Blackett, J.
Blanco, B.
Banker, Edward
Bunce, Nath.
Banks, Theo.
Brombacher, J.
Bristol, W. B. & Co.
Boddy, George
Bowie, John H.
Burtus, Jas. A.
Bennett, Andrew H.
Bitte, H.
Buhler, D.
Billings, N.
Bradley, J. N.
Belknap, Edward
Breese & Elliot
Brown, Thos. P.
Brooks, D. H. Mrs.
Buckley, John L.
Belden, George, Mrs.
Brumley, R.
Bayard
Baudine, Chas. A.
Bryce, J.
Butler, Henry V.
Baker, Susan, Mrs.
Beekman, Wm. F.
Brown, A. A.
Benjamin, J. A.
Burdett, S. C.

Busteed, G. W.
Bell, James C.
Beach, H. C., Mrs.
Bloodgood, Mrs.
Beckwith, H. W.
Berrian, H. P.
Ballow, Wm. B. Mrs.
Birch, Thomas
Brady, Mrs.
Bard, J. S.
Blackwell, R.
Bouyee, A.
Belcher, G. E., M. D.
Bell, Abm.
Bosh, B.
Baily, J. H.
Baldwin, J. M.
Boardman, Mr.
Booth, Samuel
Burritt, Mr.
Black, Mr.
Bennet
Boorman, Robt.
Berrian, W. D.
Bowne, Richard H.
Brown, Edgar
Baird, R. Revd.
Brush, W. F.
Bleecker, G. N., Mrs.

C.

Collins, Joseph B.
Cary, W. F.
Cheesborough, Mrs.
Cottinet, F. & Co.
Cleveland, A.
Crosby, Wm. B.
Chauncey, Henry
C. S.
Committee of Taylor Festival, per J. F. Butterworth,
Cumming, T. B.
Conkling, F. A. Mrs.
Collins, Stacy B.
Cummins, Collins & Seaman.
Coe, Anderson, & Co.
Clark, Southworth & Tilden
Cruger, Harriet Douglas Mrs.
Cragin, Geo. D.
Carmer, C. W.
Colgate, C. C.
Cole, H.
Carter, Robert
Cobb, Geo. T.
Camp, Amzi, Revd.
Carpentier, Reuben S.
Cutter, Stephen
Conover, Daniel
Clark, Stewart E.
Carson, John
Clarkson, Cornelius C., M.D.
Cowperthwait, G. E.
Camron, John

Cary, J. A.
Cary, Josiah
Coe, Noah Revd.
Cornell, Viner L.
Conover, John W.
Carter, Peter
Corwin, Elisha
Coleman, D.
Cowl, James
Chichester, D.
Chamberlain, J. F.
Cockcroft, James M.
Campbell, Edward
Cole, James
Cruikshank, James
Cauldwell, A.
Chamberlain, Chas.
Cobb, G. T.
Conover, Stephen
Chichester, Lewis
Campbell, John
Cock, Thomas, M. D.
Cooper, Peter
Collins, E. K.
Cotheal & Co. H. & D.
Chouteau, P. Jr. & Co.
Cook, Levi & Co.
Camfield, M.
Cash
Camman, O. J.
Cornwell, Wm. K.
Conklin & Smith
Cartwright, Harrison & Co.
C. F. H.
Chamberlain & Phelps
Colton, G.
Coit, J.
Condit, J. S.
Caldwell, C. B.
J. S. Clark
Cushman & Co.
Crumb, W. S.
Cromwell, Wm.
Campbell, Duncan P.
Cutting, F. B.
Colgate, C. C.
Clark, Thos. L.
Colgate, Mrs.
Cozzens, Wm. B.
Clossin, Mr.
Cock, Thomas, M. D.
Cock, Thomas F., M. D.
Cary, Mr.
Caswell, John
Crommell, Henry
Cox, Joseph
lark, B. G.
Cox, John V.
Coe, F. A. Mrs.
Carroll, Mrs.
Croney, Mrs.
Carter, Lamson, Revd.
Colgate, M. & L. Misses
Cheesborough, Mrs.
Contoit, J. H.
Cobb, Mr.
Calhoun, Robt.

1849.) LIST OF MEMBERS. **37**

C. J.
Carpenter, G.
Codwise, D.
Chandler, Mrs.
Creighton, Mrs.
Cornell, S. M.
Cahoone, W.
Curtis, Mrs.
Church, L. H.
Clayton, Chas. H.
Coe, D. B. Revd.
Curtis, Adelaide
Campbell, A. P.
Cooper, Peter
Cock, E. W. & Co.
Chapman, L.
Canfield, D. W.
Chandler, Job & Foster
Center, A. H. & Son
Cliff St., 30
C. D. W. L.
Calkins & Darrow
Cash, J. D. W.
Cash, Carneben
Collis, A. H.
Cash, C. S.
Crowley, Wm. Jr.
Corry, J.
Cash, Elliot
Clark & West
Cash, Front Street
Cash, 196 Front
Connolly, Chas. M.
Curtis, L.
Connor, D. D.
Cotheal, Henry L.
Child, Asa
Cook, R. S.
Campbell, W. S.
Cummings, Thos.
Carlin, Jno.
Clark, S. M.
Camp, Henry
Chamberlen, E.
Clink, C. P.
Clayton, E. B.
Clarke, Saml.
Conklin, P. F.
Coggill, H.
Cox, Chas. B.
Cunningham, W. S.
Cooper, W.
Cornell, J. H., Jr.
Curtis, P. A.
Colt, S. Mrs.
Curre, J. H.
Collins, G. C.
Campbell, A. E. Revd.
Clark, Mathias
Chichester, C.
Curtis, G. H.
Cornell & Amerman
Cook, Wm. E.
Cooper, Thos. S.
Connah, John
Candee, E. W.
Camerdon, H.

Clayton, Alex. T.
Cooks, Westley
Cheesbro, A.
Carpenter, W. C.
Creighton, T.
Cook, G. H.
Clark, Mr.
Cameron, Mr.
Clark, M.
Coles, C.
Cogswill & Le Amoureux
Cooke, Mr.
Campbell, G.
Carroll, J. B.
Clark, A. G.
Collamer, David
Cheeseman, W.
Curtis, Charles
Clikner, David
Cole, Henry
Cogswell, Mr.
Clothing
Clothing
Cairns, David
Church, Dr.
Constant, S. S.
Christy, Thomas
Cash, from Conant
Cammon, Mr.
C. C. M.
Cash, from Concert
Coil, Mrs.
Cook, Edward G.
Cammon, Mr.
Cowls
Coursen, Mrs.
Coursen, Miss
Clark, C. W.
Cobb, Jas. W.
Clark, R. S.
Colles, J.
Clark, F. H.
Camman, O. J.
Catlin, D. W.
Clarkson, J. C.
Coit, Henry A.
Clark, E. S.
Colvill, A.
Cohen, L. J.
Curtis, C.
Carryl, N. T.
Carpenter, J. S.
Cronkhite, J. P.
Clark, George
Colt, James E.
Coddington, T. B.
Cash, Mr. Paine
Clapp, O. W.
Cockroft, J., M. D.
Cape, H. M.
Cape, John J.
Clendenen, P.
Cook, Ebenezer
Crane, Stephen M.
Clarkson, C. P.
Cromwell, D.
Cooley, Mary Mrs.

Cook, S. G.
Cornell, Stephen
Cahill, M. Thos.
Campbell, Thos.
Clussman, C. L.
Carrick, M. Mrs.
Craig, Mrs.
Craft, Andrew
Crane, Philander
Clark, James
Cook, James H.
Colt, Mr.
Carrahger, Capt.
Chambers, Jas. L.
Clark, Ira A.
Coapman, John
Cook, Miss
Clarkson, William
Craig, Miss
Cain, Peter
Chichester, Lewis
Conger, John
Campbell, Mr.
Conover, Stephen
Cortelyou, Peter
Chardavoyne, W. & T. C.
Coolidge, Geo. T. & Botrhers
Coggershall, Geo. D.
Cauldwell, E. Miss
Cludius, C.
Clark, H.
Carle, J. Jr.
Christopher, Richard
Clark, John
Cromwell & Birdsall
Currier, N.
Chamberlain, Charles
Church, C. M.
Carter, A.
Christian, C. G.
Costin, H.
Cottier, Mrs.
Cross, John
Cornish, David H.
Carson, A. B. Mrs.
Cholwell, J.
Chassagne
Church, J.
Coster, G. W.
Coffin, G. P.
Cheever, George B.
Colgate, Robert
Chegary, W. D.
Carpenter, N. F.
Cooper & Brothers
Clinch, James
Coles, Mrs.
Cromwell, Mr.
Crary, E. C. Mrs.
Camman, Mrs.
Comstock, S. S.
Churchill, T. G.
Crane, A. G.
Conway, E. H.
Corry, U.
Clark, J. H.
Colgate, Edward

LIST OF MEMBERS. (1849.

Clark, Mr.
Cragen, Mr.
Clark, J. A.
Chamberlain, E.
Corwin & Morgan Call
Craig & Teal
Carmer, Charles
Corbyn, Mrs.
Cook, J.
Coswell, Solomon
Cochran, J. Mrs.
Cropsey, James
Childs, Evan
Conover, James S.
Cully or Curry, Mr.
Chalmers, Dr.
Cochrane
Campbell, Mr.
Charters, Mr.
Camman, Dr.
Coleman, Mrs.
Corning. Wm. B.
Campbell, Mr.
Cornell, R. C.
Cunningham, Mr.
Corby, C. G.
Cook, J.
Copcutt, Mr.
Cook, E.
Collamore, Mr.
Cassebur, Henry
Coit, Henry
Crosby, Wm. B.
Clapp, John
Corlies, Miss
Churchman, O.
Couch, Wm.
Copeland, Mr.
Cutting, R. L.
Clark, James A.
Cummings, J. B.
Caffray, C. W.
Clark, H.
Caffray, Mr.
Cook, Mr.
Covanow, Mr.
C. Cottage, 29
Chamberlain, J.
Cowl, Mr.
Cogswell, Mr.
Callen, G.
Cobb, Mr.
Crane, D. B.
Caldwell, W. M.
Clapp, Caleb. Revd., by Dr. B. Ogden.
Carter, L. C., by Rev. Royal West.
Camman, Maria. Miss, by the Revd. Mr. Martin
Clark, Alexander
Crosby, J. P.
Christie, A.
Collins, David C.
Cushman, D. A.
Callender, Stanhope Mrs.

C. H. S.
Coe, B. H.

D.

Dutilth & Cousinary
Dawson, B. F.
Delafield, E., M. D.
De Forrest & Co., B.
Davenport, Henry
Donaldson, James
Depeyster, Susan M. C.
Depeyster, James F.
Dater, Miller & Co.
Deneson, Lyman
Douglas, George
Dutilth, Eugene
Dennistown, Wood & Co.
Douglas, William
Duryee, Jacob
Davidson, John
Dyer, Charles C.
Dakin, C. P.
Deems, H. W.
Downs, Smith
Daton, C. B., M. D.
Duncan, Francis
Disosway. Corns. R.
Darling, Chas. C. Revd.
Duff, James F.
Davies, Richard
Duff, James
Duryea, Levi
Dibble, Jonathan
Dubois, Grant
Denny, Thomas
Davies, Henry E.
Dibble, Richardson & Co.
Dunbar, F.
Dennistown & Desbrow
Dibblee, Albert
Dambmann, Charles F.
Duryee, M. A. Mrs.
Drew, S M.
Delafield, Wm.
Donaldson, J.
Demarest, Mr.
Duckworth, M. H.
Day, Horace
Dusenbury, W. C.
DeRahm & Moore
Douglass, George
Duryee, P.
Doscher, C.
Duckforth, Mr.
Dows & Cary
Denison, C. L.
Dunn, Mr.
Dryden, Geo.
Delhoys, Mr.
Delafield, Dr.
Dash, Daniel
Depuga, M. J.
Donnington, Mr.
Drake, Mrs.
Darin, Mrs.

Dayton, Mr.
Door, Mr.
Decaismet, M.
Duncan, J.
Dalrymple, A.
Dubois, Wm.
DeForest, Mr.
Dominick, J W.
Dominick, J. W., Jr.
Duryea, Jacob
Denike, Abm.
Dodge, S. N.
Devoe, Wm. L.
Decker, A.
Dominick, Elizabeth
Denistown, Mr.
Dannat, Wm. H.
Davis, Charles
Delafield, Dr.
Dawson, B. F.
Davis, Gilbert
Drew, Daniel
Davis, Dr.
Dustin, Mrs.
DePeyster, Fredk.
Dashwood, Mrs.
DuBois, Corns.
DeRuyter, John
Dickson, S. H., M.D.
Dale, Thos. W.
Downer, Samuel, Jr.
DeForest, Mrs.
Deming, Barzillai
Dodd, Jno B.!
Davis, D. H.
Dickson, Jas.
Dillinger, C.
Dyckman, W. N.
Duncan, James
Demarest, John
Dubois, Dr.
Devoe, D. M.
Drucker, G. Mrs.
Door, Wm. S.
Dufour, Thos.
Decker, Thos.
Demarest, D.
Daniels, J. L. B.
Demott, H.
Dodworth, A.
Delvechio, Mr.
Dupuy, E.
Dessoir, J.
Dav & Newell
Dodworth, Mrs.
Dusenbery & Miller
Dupond, T. H.
DeWaahia
Denny, Wm. H.
Downs, Mrs.
Danforth, M. J.
Douglass, Mr.
Downing, Mr.
Demarest, P. P.
Dwight
Dawson, Mrs.
Driscoll, Mr.

1849.) LIST OF MEMBERS. 39

Denham, Mr.
Downer, Mr.
Daguer
Daily, Miss
Davis, R. E.
Douglass, David
Dunn, Hugh S.
Davey, Thos.
Day, C. J.
Dunscomb, Mr., by the Revd. Mr. Martin
Dubois
Douglass, J. H.
Dean, Thos.
Day, Mahlon
Davis, Chs. Mrs.
Disosway, C. B., by Revd. Isaac Orchard
Dittenhoefer, Isaac
Dodd, John M.
Drake, Benjamin, M.D.
Dunn, A. Mrs.
DeCamp, Mrs.
Dunning, Chs E.
Dollens, H.
Dame, W. H.
Davidson, Joseph
Davis, Stephen A.
Dickson, James
Deverman, Mr.
Duncan, Mr.
Duff, James
Dennis, Mrs.
Decker, Joseph H.
Duncan, Mrs.
Demarest, S. D.
Dudley, M. Miss
David, Stephen
Dittenhoffen, E.
D. H.
Dare & Webb
Dawson, Geo. W.
Dodge, W. E.
Duer, John
Delafield, H.
Dean, Mrs.
Devlin, C. Mrs.
Doty, F. V. Mrs.
Dwight, Mrs.
Duffy, Corns. R.
Duvell
Dunshee, Samuel
Delpratt, Mr.
Donnelly, T. W.
Duke, Wm. S.
Deleplaine, Miss
Donelson, Mrs.
Dibblee. W. W.
Dodge, D. L. Mrs.
DeForrest, W. W. & Co.
Davis, J. M., Jones & Co.
Draper, C. E.
Deitz, Brothers & Co.
Davids & Black
Doubleday, U. F.
Delapierre, C. B.
Dana, Mrs.

Davis, C. N.
DeForest, H. G.
Dickenson, J. S.
Doubleday, T. D.
Dudley, Gilman
Dickinson, Chs., M.D.
Degraw, J.
Dolbear, Thomas P.
Dunshee, H. W.
Day, Thomas
Demarest, David
Dumont, R.

E.

Edgar, William
Enty, J. F.
Evans, Lemuel G.
Endicott, John
Everett, N. C.
Eighth Ward
Ely & Kent
Emmerson, C.
Eno, Amos R.
Ely, Richard S.
Earle, Daniel
Elliot, B.
Ellsworth, E.
Ely, M.
Egan
Ellsworth, W.
Everdell, Mr.
Embury, Peter
Embury, Peter, Jr.
Eastman, J. S.
Eaton, Mr.
Emmet, R.
Eversly, Charles
Earl, Mrs.
Everett, W. L.
Eagan, M.
Eveleth, Mr.
Elsbech, Isaac
Englebrecht, John C.
Ewen, Daniel
Eveleth, Emma
Egleston & Battelle
Evans, Thomas
Evans, John
Ely, E. C.
Elliot, G. T.
Evarts, William M.
E. ———
Eagle, H.
Eastman, Charles
Ellis, K. S.
Eggert, D., & Son
Engle, James
Everdell, William
Eldridge, C. B.
Ellis, George
Emmet, Thomas
Elder, George
English, W. C. R.
Engs, P. W.
Ellison, Richard

Earle, A. S.
Endicott, William
Eaton, Augustus
Elsworth, H.
Engles, S. S.
Earle, Miss
Eaton, J. A.
Erben, Henry Mrs.
Egbert, S. D.
Eveleys, Francis
Effray, F.
Evland & Brewer
Erving, G. W.

F.

Field, Cyrus W. & Co.
Faile, T. H.
Foster, J., Jr.
Folger, R. W.
Field, C. W. & Co.
Ferguson, Edward
Foster, F. G.
Fleming, Jno. B.
Folwell, S. P.
Fanning, S.
Forster, T. V.
Forrest, William
Fisher, Daniel
Florentine, A.
Forbes, Abraham
Forbes, Benjamin B.
Fields, Edward, M.D.
Ferris, J. S.
French, Daniel
Foster, William A.
Fessenden, Thomas
Fraser, E. A.
Ford, Isaac
Fendall, John L.
Fowler, B. M.
Finch, Myron
Finch, Ferris
Fardon, Abraham, Jr.
Fisher, Daniel
Fox, Marvin W.
Falconer, John
Feidler, Ernest
Fearing & Hall
Ferguson, John
Farrand, Joseph S.
Fuller, B., M.D.
Frothingham & Beckwith
Fenniman, M.
Frink, F.
Fowler & Odell
Fair, J. & G.
Foster, James
Fish, Mr.
Finch, A.
Fowler, J. O.
Fuller, Mr.
Francis, C. S.
Furman, P. H.
Friends
Felton, Silas
Flint, S. S.

Fabrequette, E.
Fisher, Mr.
Furguson, Mr.
Farwell, E.
Ferris, Dr.
Freeman, Mr.
Foster, W.
Ferris, J. H.
Fuller, Mr.
Fisher, Richard
Frost, Mrs.
Foster, T. V.
Falkner, Mr.
Friends, Rutgers Place
Friend, 230 Madison
Freeman, Alfred, M.D.
Francis, J. W.
Furniss, Wm. P.
Finn, A. T.
Finlay, J. Beekman
Field, E.
Foulke, Joseph, Jr.
Ferris, A. M.
Fraser, Edward A.
Furnald, F. P.
Ford, Isaac
Field, Josiah
Farrell, Edward
Fanning, T.
Fink, F. Miss
Forgey, William
Forester, Charles
Fisher, J. F.
Folger, Doctor
Fowler, D. S.
Finch, Myron
Fox, M. W.
Francis, Norman Mrs.
Fenno, J.
Fanning & Brother
Fanning, S.
French, R.
Frost, Mrs.
Favereau, F.
Fish, D.
Fox, C.
Fenn, G.
Faulkner, J. C.
Furman, G. C.
Fox, G. S.
Flagg, A. C.
Fearing, D. B.
Foulke, W.
Field, D. Dudley
Franklin, Thomas M.
Fletcher, Edward H.
Faulkner, Mrs.
Ferrego, S.
Fink, Arnest
Fraser, Mr.
Falconer, John
Freelan, R. J.
Forty-three, Fifth S.
Fellows, L. S. & Schell
Fellows, Wadsworth & Co.
Frost, S.
Fulton Street, 79

Fellows, William W.
Fraser & Everett
Frey, W. H. & Brothers
Frasse, H. F. & Son
Frazee, Abraham
Forrest, A. P.
Fitch, George
Fowler, Charles
Fellows, Mrs.
Forbes, Mr. Revd.
Frye, Jed.
Freeman, C.
Fairbanks, D.
Fullargh, William
French, William
Fonda, A. P.
Fatman, Joseph
Forbes, William
Freeman's Boarding House
Faht, F. H.
Farrell, J. & J.
Fowler, John H.
Fansher, David
Field, Jude
Foggin & Utter
Forest, Mrs.
Frasure, Mr.
Forbs, Mr.
Frith, Mr.
Farquer
Fergus, Mr.
Freeman, J. V.
Fowler, John W.
Two Young Ladies

G.

Griswold, George
Green, J. C.
Griswold, John
Gibbes, R. M.
Green, Horace, M.D.
Gillelan, E. H.
Graves, E. Boonen
Giraud, Jacob P.
Graves, Mrs.
G. A. H.
Gans, Meyer
Grosvenor, Jasper
Grinnell, Henry
Grant & Burton
Griffin, George
Giffin, James
Gates, John
Greenough, J. J.
Goddard, J. E.
Gibson, Isaac
Gillelan, John
Geer, Darius
Goodwin, Eli
Griffin, H.
Gibson, James R.
Gray, William, Revd.
Griffin, Herman
Galloway, Thomas
Gifford, Mr.

Gelson, Mr.
Gardner, H.
Griggs, S.
Gilpin, S. S.
Goddard, George C.
Gilbert, Cobb & Johnson
Goodhue & Co.
Greenway, J. Henry
Guillaume, S.
Gurgens, Henry
Gilbert, John S.
Gilsey, J.
Greenly, George
Gilbert, Mr.
Greenwood, Mr.
George, C. L.
Gavit, Mr.
Gillis, W. G.
Gray, J. S.
Gibson, G.
Goldsmith, D.
Gardner, Mr.
Gerdon, L.
Gutlin & Co.
Ginnochio, Mr.
Graham, James L.
Grosvenor, Seth
Green, Mr.
Gordoni, Mr.
Green, Mr.
Gilmour, Mr.
Gasquet, Mr.
Gemmel, Mr.
Griffin, Solomon
Gray, John
Gaunt, F. S.
Goodwin, Jacob
Gelston
Giraud, P. T.
Georger, L.
Glover, Mrs.
Goelet, Mr.
Gilbert, Clinton
Gould, Charles
Gordon, A. R.
Green, Misses
Graham, Mrs., and other Ladies
Green, William C.
Griswold, Mrs.
Gardiner, William
Gray, Niel
Gregory, S.
Golden, J. C.
Golden, F. W.
Griffiths, J. M.
Gantz, J. J.
Goodrich, E. B.
Gilman, George H.
Goodsman, Thomas
Goldsmith, David
Gumbs, Mrs.
Gardner, Mr.
Glover, Mr.
Grimbs, Lawrence
Garrish, Joseph
Galland. A., & Co.

1849.) LIST OF MEMBERS. 41

Gray, John
Garvey, William M.
Green, Mr.
G. & J.
Gilman, John A.
G. L. K. & P.
Gerard, J. W.
Green, George
Goelet, Robert
Gibbs, T. S. Mrs.
Gaul, Laura M.
Gay, J. A.
Gillen, Mrs.
Garabrant, D. Mrs.
Geery, Mr.
Goodly, Thomas
Griffith, Mr.
Geah, J.
Gilley, J. W.
Gillies, Mrs.
Green, Miss
Goadby, Mrs.
Guion, Mrs.
Gillies, D. G. Mrs.
Guion
Gibson, J. R.
Garr, A. S.
Graydon, Joseph
Gray, W. F.
Greenwood, Mrs.
G. M.
Gordon & Talbot
Green, J. W.
Gates, Stedman & Co.
Griffin & Pulman
Green, Edward
Gregory, L.
Groshon, John
Gillespie, James, Mrs.
Gabaudon, A. W.
Glassford, R. W.
Green, James
Getty, R. P.
Gray, John A. C.
Grant, Charles E.
Gibson, James
Gardner, Thomas
Gregg, Mr.
Goeller, John M.
Gilroy, George
Gedney, S.
Gourlie, M.
Greig, J. S.
Gennin, J. N.
Gans, John
Gilman, Dr.
Geissenhainer, F. W., Revd.
Greenwood, H. B.
Goll, J. J.
Gage, William
Griffith, John

H.

Halsted, W. M.
Hoffman, L. M.

Hamersly, J. W.
Howland, G. G.
Howland, S. S.
Harsen, Jacob
Hussey, George
Hoadley, David
Hadden, David, & Sons
Hopkins & Weston
Hoffman, Martin
Hoyt, Henry S.
Howland, Samuel L.
Hatt, George, Revd.
Harris, John
Hatt, John A.
Harris, W. D.
Henderson, Alexander J
Hurd, Hiram
Hubbard, L. P.
Hume, Andrew
Horton, Jonathan B.
Holt, J. S.
Hickok, Preston
Howell, M. H.
Horn, James
Hogan, Thomas
Houghwout, S.
Hall, Joseph
Hyatt, Theodore
Hutchings, John
Hibbard, C. F. L.
Haff, Stephen
Harris, Charles J.
Howe, Bezaleel
Halsey, L. W.
Heydon, William
Humbert, William B.
Hazeltine, Leonard
Harvey, C. R.
Hurley, John
Horton, Richard, Revd.
Hepburn, J. C., M.D
Hall, Archibald
Hagadorn, John
Holbrook, E.
Hirshman, L.
Hobby, E. B.
Hallett, A. F.
Haight, Edwin
Hall, Andrew
Hatch, John
Hoyt, G. P. B.
Hutchinson, Benjamin
Holmes, Mr.
Hamersleys, Miss, The
Hubbard, A.
Hart, Mr.
Hanley, E.
Hart, John, M.D.
Hennell, Frederick
Hoyt, W. & O.
Howell, Albro
Hegadorn, John
Holmes, Eldad
Hubbard, R. T.
Holschler, Jacob
Herkman, N.
Hagan, Mrs.

Hammond, Miss
Harding, R.
Hart, H. & M.
Holbrook, E.
Hall, Valentine G.
Hurd, C. D.
Hatch, C. B.
Haines, H. B. Miss
Holmes, S. P.
Harbeck, John H.
Haight, E.
Hearn, G. A.
Hewes, Mrs.
Hyatt, Jacob
Haywood, Mrs.
Harvey, T. W.
Henry, S. L.
Hart, William J.
Hoyt, E.
Hearn, Mrs.
Hatfield, G.
Howard, Mr., by Mr. A. W.
  Spies
Harriot, Mr.
Horane
Hadley, R.
Hand, George
Hoyt, J.
Healey, Mr.
Hitchcock, W. R.
Hitchcock, C.
Hayward, William
H. K. B.
Halsted, A. L.
Harper, Fletcher
Hopkins, Mr.
Harper, John
H. B.
Hamilton, M. K.
H. C.
Hartley, R. M.
Hays, H. M.
Hecksher, Charles A.
Hosmer, Hoxie & Hubbard
Hyatt, Edward
Hilger, M.
Hawkins & Logan
Haydock, Robert
Houghton, E.
H. G. I.
Halstead, J.
Hamdeyum, F.
Horton, H. F.
Hamblin, F. N.
Hall, Mr.
Howell, J. S.
Hill, J. S.
Holt, Mr.
Hope, Thomas & Son
Hall, Mr.
Hopkins, T.
Hustace, John
Hield, J.
Hoyt, Gould
Hoyt, Lydig
Hodgkins, S. G.
Higgins, J. S.

3

LIST OF MEMBERS. (1849.

Hewlett & Holmes
Hunt, Wilson G.
Hopkins, Mr.
Hunter, Dr.
Hoppock, M. A.
Hayward, Mrs.
Hays, Mrs.
Hamersly, L. C.
Hopping, A. D.
Howell, C. & Co.
Howser, J. C.
Harrison, Mr.
Hind, J. J.
Hyer, Mrs.
Hall, E. Miss
Hunter, Mr.
Hossack, N. P.
Hoffman, J. L.
Hustace, Mr.
Hobart, Dr.
Harbnett, Mr.
Hoyt, Mr.
Henny, Philip
Hamilton, Mr.
Hunter, Dr.
Haight, N.
Hutton, Mr.
Hogg, Peter
Hilman, J. F.
Halsey, H. A.
Hardenburg, J. B.
Herrick, J.
Harris & Ockerton
Hill, John
Hyate, G. E.
Henderson, Mr.
Hazard, Samuel
Hoe, R. & R.
Hawley, Irad
Hancock, John
Hogencamp, John
Hoppell, F.
Hoagland, John S.
Hunt, Mrs.
Hendricks, Mr.
Hays, Mr.
Hebbard, H.
Houghout, E. V.
Heyn, E.
Hallock, W A.
Hatfield & Bertine
Houghwout, Simon
Havemeyer, G. L.
Hilbyn, J. B.
Hardt, Mr.
Halsey, Charles H., Revd.
Hallock, J. C.
Hitchcock, Mr.
Hall
Harris, E. C.
Hutchings, M. J.
Haydock, Wm.
Harvey, J.
Hindmarsh, Mr.
Hines, Mr.
Hindles, Mr.
Hoydt, Mr.

Hanmaker, Mr.
Holmes, A. B.
Hawks, Mrs.
Hunt, S. B.
Hotchkis, Jeremiah
Hall, A. B.
How, Mr.
Hunt, Mr.
Hemmon
Horsfield, R. T.
Harrison, Mr.
Howard, Mr.
Hart, Henry
Hart, David
Haws, George
Howland, B. J.
Herd, John C.
Howe, Calvin W.
Halsey, A. P.
Halsted, James M.
Haines, William A.
Huggins, Henry O.
Hone, John
Hubbard, T. R.
Hoffman, P. V.
Harris, T.
Hasbrook, Mr.
Haight, H.
Haydock, G. G.
Holt, Henry,
Hewlett, O. T.
Hewlett, Joseph
Haydock, H. W.
Hidden, E.
H. L. R.
H. A. P.
Hallock, Lewis, M. D.
Hewitt, W. H.
Hart, J. C.
Hubbard
Haskins, Elizabeth Mrs.
Hunter
Hicks, Miss
Hall, J. Prescott
Hastings
Henry, J. J.
Hammond, Judah
Hendricks, Mrs.
Hart, B S.
Hodgson, M. T. Mrs.
Holden, Horace
Haight, D. L.
Hall, Francis
Hoffman, Dr.
Herrick, J. B.
Hoppock, Ely
Harrison, C. J. Miss
Hutton, M. S. Revd.
Heyer, J. Mrs.
Hicks, Wm. T.
Holmes, L. H.
Houghton, Royal
Hoyt, John W.
Heuser, G. L.
Henderson, Howard
Hubbard, N. T.
Horn, James

Halsted, Schureman
Halsted, Samuel
Heath, L. C.
Hillman, William
Hennessy, D.
Hunt, M. M. Mrs.
Houghton, T. L.
Hepburn, Mrs.
Hutchinson, S.
Hurton, John H.
Hunter, Charles, E.
Hiler, S.
Hitchcock & Colvelnoni
Hayden, Thomas
Hubbs, George S.
Hunt, Zeba
Holstein, John
Halsey, S. R. & Co.
Hoff, J. C.
Hutchins, John
Hamilton, David H.
Haynes, True
Holman, Mr.
Hoey, John
Hausbroeck, Miss
Hass, Mr.
H. C. P.
Hoxie, J. Mrs.
Holstead, P. S. Mrs.
Held, A. H. M.
Hunt, Thomas & Co.
Hicks, J. H.
Horstman, Sons, & Dracker
Hunt, Wilson G. & Co.
Haskell & Merrich
Hayne, John
Havens, H. & Son
Henry, John
H. G. & Co.
Hoyt, S.
Hook, J. D. W.
H. & Co.
Habershaw
Heitkamp -
Hayden, N.
Hills, E.
Havemeyer, W. F.
Havemeyer, F. C.
Hopkins, N. F.
Hurd, J.
Herring, Silas C.
H. H. J.
Hunt, Jona.
Hall, Willis
Hoffman, M. Mrs.
Henderson, J. C.
Hertzel, Jacob F.
Harriot, James
Hurry, Edmund
Higgins, A. F.
Halsted, James
Hall, W. T.
Harned, Wm.
Herder, N. D.
Halsey, A.
Hall, C.
Hirshfield, H.

LIST OF MEMBERS.

Hart, H. E.
Hall, James W.
Hart, Robert
Howey, Thomas
Hunt, H. W.
Hinshelwood, R.
Hutchinson, Jane
Henry, Robert
Havemeyer, William
Hoe, Mr.
Havemeyer, Albert
Hutchinson, Ira
Havemeyer, C. H.
Halsey, E. C.
Hopper, H.
Halstead, L. W.
Horn, P. A.
Horton, A.
Holberton, J. W.
Holmes, C.
Hasbrouk, G. D.
Hays, Mr.

I. & J.

Johnson, John
J. W. H.
Joseph, Mr.
Jay, Ann Miss
Irvin, Richard
Jackson, Lewis E. by Revd. R. West.
Irving, P. P. Revd.
Ireland, William B.
Jones, Joshua
Jones, George
J. P. S. T.
Jones, Walter R.
Jervis, John B.
Jaffray, J. R. & Sons
Jaudon, S.
Johnston, William
Janes, W R.
Jacobs, Laban
Jones, Fitz Edwin
Jackson, Thomas
Jones, J. F.
Jenkins, J. J.
Ives, John, M. D.
Jeremiah, Thomas
Jackson, Luther
Jones & Co., S. T.
Johnson, H. W.
Janeway, William R.
J. H. & Co.
J. G. D.
Judson, C.
Jennings, Chester
J. C., M. & H.
Jones, Henry & Son
Johnson, Mr.
Johnson & Lazarus
Jergin, Lewis
Jones & Wilson
Janes, Edmond, Revd.
Jones, Mrs.

Just, John
Jones, Isaac
Jackson, A. J.
Ireland, Mrs.
Ireland, George
Jarvis, Mr.
Jenkins, T. W.
Johnson, Mrs.
J. P.
Judson, D.
Innis, Edward S.
Jackson, William H., M. D.
Jones, R. Mrs.
Jones, J. Wyman
J. N. C.
Jackson, Thomas
Jimmerson, R. J.
Jones, J. J.
Jennings, G. W.
Jones, D.
Ingersol, Chandler
Jarvis, Dr.
Jones, Birdsall & Rowland
J. T.
Jaques
Johnston, R. R.
Johnson, John
J. C. W.
Jackson & Mann
Johnson, George
Jones, G. F.
Johnson, Misses, The
Irving, L. G.
James, Mrs.
Irving, Mrs.
Janes, A.
Jordan, Emeline Mrs.
Jeroliman, H.
Jacobson, Dr.
Jenkins, Mr.
Jayne, A. A.
Irvin, Richard
J. H. A.
J. C.
J. S. H.
Jeremiah, P. E.
Jones, L. Revd.
Ingoldsby, F.
John St., 33, J. C.
Johnson, H.
J. L. S.
Jones, Henry
Jacot, Courvoiser & Co.
J. W.
J. M. W.
Johnson, E. A.
Ivison, H. Jr.
Jamerman
Jackson, G. N.
Jones, John
Isaacs, S. M. Revd.
Inman, J. H.
Johnson, H. F.
Jaques, Isaac
Ingersol, Mr.
Judah, S. N.
Jones, William B.

Johnson, H.
Johnson, L. L.
Jarvis, P.
Johnson, Mr.
Irving
James, Mr.
Inness, Mrs.
Inman
Johnson, J. H.

K.

Kipp, Leonard W.
King, James G.
Kennedy, D. S.
Kiley, Robert
Knapp, Shepherd
Kane, Delancey
Kendall, Isaac C.
Kelly, Joel
Kerney, James
Kirby, William
Kirby, Leonard
Kennedy, Thomas
Ketcham, Rogers & Bement
King, P. V.
Kemble, William
Knapp, E. & Cummings
Kirby, L. & V.
King, J. G.
Knox, E.
Kellogg, Mr.
Knox, Andrew
Kearsing, Mr.
Knapp, Mr.
Kirby, Leonard
Keeler, D. B.
Ketchum, Morris
Kearney, Edward
Kursheedt, Asher
Kelly, R W.
Knapp, James H.
Kipp, F. A.
Ketcham, Abel
Knipe, Wm.
Kirk, Mrs.
Kaysor, Mr.
Keys, John
Kellogg, S. O.
Kellogg, John D.
Ketchum, Philip
Kennedy, Thomas
Keys, David
Kearney, Mr.
Knighs, W. B.
Kent, William
King, C. W. Mrs.
Kingsland
Kelly & Meeks
Knipe, William
Kingsford, J. J.
Kenny, George
Kimball, Richard B.
Kingsland, D.
Kissam, Mrs.
Kingsbery, O. R.

LIST OF MEMBERS. (1849.

Kermit, Robert
Kingsby
Kissam & Keeler
King, William
Kirby, V.
Knowlton, D.
King, Rufus S.
Knapp, B. C.
Knapp, William H.
Ketcham, Treadwell
Kent, E. N.
Kenedy, William
Knapp, G. P.
Kinch, W.
Kissam, Dr.
Keyser, Dr.
Kerr, John
Karr, Dr.
Knapp, R.
Keiley, Philip
Kobbe, William
Kerney, James

L.

Lenox, James
Levington, Mrs.
Le Roy, Jacob
Laight, E. W.
Lord, D. Jr.
Le Roy, J. R.
Laight, W. E.
Lewin, Robert
Livingston, F. A.
L.
L. M.
Lottimer & Large
Lecount, V.
Lewis, R.
Lawrence, R.
Lippencott, Thomas
Lowerre, George W.
Ludlum, A. B.
Lefferts, Cornelius
Lee, Daniel F.
Leach, A. C.
Lewis, John
Lord, Benjamin
Longking, Joseph
Lockwood, William A.
Labagh, Isaac.
Long, N. R.
Lees, George
Ludlow, John R.
Lynes, S. C.
Loder, Benjamin
Lothrop, William K.
Lane, W. J.
Leary, J.
Lasak, F. W.
Lippet, Joseph F.
Lemoyne, A.
Lee, William P.
Lawrence, W. E.
Legh, C. C.
Little, A.

Lee, J. Jr.
Lindley & Mundy
Lee, D. F.
Ludlum, N.
Lowree, Seaman
Lowree, William
Loines, William H.
Lewis, James S.
Lewis, John W.
Lambert, Jeremiah
Lord, Mrs.
Lydecker, J. R.
Love, Thomas
Lamb, Francis
Le Roy, Benjamin
Lent, J. W. Mrs.
Loutrell, W. M.
Landry, F.
Ladd, George
Levey, J. L.
Labagh, John
Lawrence, Richard
Lewis, S. W.
Lee, B. A.
Lewis, T.
Lawrence, Mrs.
Lawrence, J. B.
Lote, S. G.
Lillie, William
Lay, J. C.
Ladd, Henry
Lees, James,
Lester, Andrew & Co.
L. W. & Co.
Lord, Warren, Salter & Co.,
Leeds, Samuel
Leland & Mellen
Lowe, Bauman
Lohman, Charles
Langlois, Mrs.
Lefman, Mr.
Lilinthall, Mr.
Liscomb, Mr.
Langdon, Mr.
Little, J. S.
Lawson, Miss
Ludlow, Mr.
Lockwood, Mr.
Legran, J. J.
Legran, J F.
Le Compte, Mr.
Le Compt, V.
Lininthall, C. & S
Lee, J. D.
Lampin, Mr.
Lindsay, Mr.
Lawrence & Veltman
Le Bouttilier, Thomas
Ladd, Mr.
Lilton, James
Levi, George
Lawrence, Mr.
Lane, G. W.
Livingston, M. Mrs.
Losee, Mr.
Lord, Rufus L.
Lydig, P.

Labah, Isaac
Lattan, Mr.
Lane, Nathan
Legrand, Mr.
Little, Samuel
Livesay, Jane
Lake, J S.
Lyles, Henry
Lindsay, Jared, M. D.
Lockwood, Roe
Lee, John H.
Lawrence, Joseph
Laveridge
Leupp, Charles M.
Livingston, A
Lawrence, Thomas Mrs.
Lorillard, Peter
Lady, A
Leeds, Samuel J.
Lathrop, Dwight
Lane, D.
Lahens, E.
Lowndes, Mrs.
Lowndes, Miss
Lowry, John
Leavenworth, Mrs.
Lentillon, E.
Lowndes, Thomas
Labatret, J. M. J.
Lewis, W. & W. H.
Layton, S. B.
L. S. M.
Lenox, James
Lawrence, William
Lathan, Joseph S.
Lay, Julia A.
Loose, Gilbert R.
Levy, Louis
Laroe, J. G.
Low, John
Lowry, John C. Revd.
Loweree, Mr.
Le Roy, Thomas Otis
Lord & Taylor
Lane, J. N.
Lockwood, F.
Lynes, William M.
Low, M. P.
Lightbody, John G.
Lounsbury, Susan
Lander, T. D.
Ludlum, William
Leach, Joseph
Lester, J. W.
Lorillard, Peter Jr.
Lynes, R.
Langan, Oliver
Ladd, John
Lathrie, J. B.
Lièvre, Eugene
Lee, David
Lawrence, Abraham R
Lord, Daniel D.
Lewis, G.
Lewis, Mrs.
Leavitt, Miss
Leverish, Mrs.

1849.) LIST OF MEMBERS. 45

La Motte, M.
Ludlam, H.
Lainbeer, Mrs.
Leonard, W. H. Mrs.
Lynch, Mr.
Lints, William
Lilley, William
Lee & Brewster
Lovett, James Capt.
Lamb, A.
Lane, N. B:
Leggett, A. A.
Leggett, William H.
Leeds, G. T.
Lang, S.
Lutzs, Brothers
Lord, J. C.
Long & Davenport
Little, Charles L.
Levy, W. H.
Lampert, H. H.
Large, J. G.
Lockwood

M.

Moore, N. F.
Minturn, Robert B.
Morgan, E. D.
Mackay, William
Maitland, R. Mrs.
Mortimer, Richard
Mead, Nathaniel, Revd., collection in 7th Street M. E. Church
Mackie, John
Morley, Isaac
M'Collom, George W.
Mott, William F., Jr.
Morgan, M.
Merritt, Ely & Co.
M. B., Mrs.
Miller, Horatio
Martyn
Murray, James B.
Mackay, W. A., by J. B. Collins
Munn, Stephen B.
Marshall, Charles H.
Mortimer, J., Jr.
Meeker, David
Moffat, David
Marshall, Benjamin, M.D.
McClaury, J., M.D.
McNaughton, A. P.
Martin, H. C,
McClain, O. D.
Martin, William
Murray, John
McCreary, John D.
Murphy, William
Montross, E.
Myers, John
Miller, J. C.
Morris, O. W.
Marsh, John R.

Merrick, Charles A.
Merrill, Charles
Morton, Robert
Murray, Alexander W.
Mollard, John
Merrill, Joseph
Millward, James
Messerole, A.
Miller, James S., M.D.
Mills, Abner
McPherson, Peter
Miller, Nehemiah
Mather, F. E.
Macy, William H.
Moran & Iselin
Moore, B. F.
Merewon & Co., G. B.
Macy, Charles A.
Morgan, D.
Millet, E. V.
Moore, Thomas D., Jr.
Milleroux, F.
M. T.
Middleton & Co.
McB. & L.
Mitchell, M.
Miller, Peter D.
M. & W.
Michel, Mr.
Milhan, Mr.
Martin Mulford
Milligan, W.
Mendell, Mr.
Murphy, John
Matthews, P. C. & L.
Mead & Belcher
Morgan, G. C.
M. L. & G.
Morgan, E.
Morley, Mr.
Morford, Mr.
Miller & Painter
Mayr, S.
Moore, Mr.
Muhle, Mr.
Morton
Miller, J. B.
Mulligan, Mr.
Maret, Mrs.
McIlwrath, T. J.
McMullen, Lewis
McMillen, Mr.
Moore, J. J.
Mettler
Meeker, W. E.
Man, J. P.
Merry, C. H.
Moreau, Mr.
Martin, J. B.
Moses, C.
Mott, J. C. & Co.
McKenna, John
Martin, P. N.
Morton & Allen
Moffat, William
Melio, Mr.
Morton, W. Q.

Mott, Mrs.
Mather, George
Mott, William F.
Macy, Josiah
Millbank, Samuel
Millbank, C. W.
Moore, J. L.
Murphy, John
Millbank, Samuel, Senr.
McCormick, Richard C.
Mollina, David
Macey, Isaac
McCoon, C.
Minturn, Sarah Mrs.
McCoskey, R.
Mitchell
Marsh, James
Maltbie
Morgan, Mrs.
Mollison, E.
McCurdy, R. H.
McVickar, John A., M.D.
Morris, Gerard W
Magie, David
Morris, A. E. Miss
McJimsey, J. M.
McKie, Thomas
Meyer, Henry
Markoe, T. H., M.D.
McKenzie, Mr.
McVickar, Mrs.
Meeks, James C.
March, Charles
Magill, James
Miles, A.
Morrison, David
Morris, L. B.
McCreary, John D.
Miller, William
McDonald, A.
Marcus
Mayhew, P. S.
Marston, Isaac
Michaels, Dr.
Milne, A.
May, David
Marks, Moses
Mitchels, Dr.
McKenzie, Mr.
Merchant, Mrs.
Moss, Mrs.
Moss, R. E.
Merrill, Manning
Merrill, Charles
Maubury, John
Marwedel, F.
McCue, Mrs.
Marsh, John R.
McCartin, Mr.
Myers, James
Marsh, John R.
Moore, James
McNespie, Captain
Mott, Mrs.
Murphy, Thomas S.
Metcalf, Mr.
Mowton, John

LIST OF MEMBERS. (1849.

McKinney, Mr.
Merritt, J. G.
Mount, Elizabeth
McDonald, Mr.
Merle, G.
Minuse, George F.
Murray, B. L.
Mathews, William
McGuire, B.
Moore, S. W.
Mattison, A. & G.
Miller, Eli
Matlock, Lucius C.
Maseman, N.
McKay, O.
McGee
Mayn, F.
Morris, M.
McCauley
Matile, Edward
Mosely, Mr.
Mathey, A.
Mason, S.
Miller, W. P.
Macey, W. H.
Maitland, A. L. Mrs.
McIlvane, Mrs.
Martin, C. J.
McEvers, P.
Mullen, T. E.
Moore, C. B.
McGee, Thomas M.
Marshall, Thomas W.
McCready, Mrs.
Monroe, John Mrs.
McNamee, R. M.
Mather, Ellen C.
Moxhet, Mr.
Mather, Eliza G.
Mather, Ellen L.
Mather, Laura
Morton, T. W. Mrs.
Mexey, James
Moss, Amos Mrs.
Munson, John
Maein, R.
Martin, Mr.
McKeon
Merritts, Miss, The
Morrison
McChain, John
Miller, Hiram
Moody
McComb, John
McLeod, Misses, The
Miles, Charles
Mills, Drake
McCreary, Mrs.
Martin, Samuel
Mackrell & Richardson
Morrell, Thomas
March, J. P.
Mead, J.
Mortimer, John, Jr.
Morrison, J. M.
McNeil, John H.
McFarlane, Thomas

Mason, Mary M.
Mooney, B.
Marsh, Samuel
Morrison, William
McKesson, John
Megary, A.
M. & L.
Mills, T. H. & Son
Morgan, J. L.
Martelle, A. & Co.
McLeod, D.
Morse, Richard C.
Minton, Charles
McLeod, A.
Milner, Dr. Mrs.
Macey, C. B.
Merserau, John W.
McGraw, John A.
Mumford, B A.
McCarron, Michael
Miller, Jonathan
Mitchell, J. F.
Martin, D. Randolph
Mann & McKimm
McKewan, John
Moses, D. B.
Miller, John R.
Many, Vincent
Meigs, H., Jr.
Mildeberger, M.
Morris, E.
Moore, S. B.
Meigs. M.
Moffat, Mrs.
Morris, DeWitt Clinton
Martin, William C.
Miller, George C.
McCrea, Mrs.
Moffat, James G.
McIntire, C. H.
Monroe, Eben.
Mason, J. M.
Mesler, William
Manzanedo, Mrs.
Moir, J. & W.
Mercer, E. H.
McNamara, M. S.
Martin, R. W.
Murphy, Mr.
Montgomery, S. J.
McKenzie, William
More, J. B.
Marshall, D. D. T.
Martin, William
McCaddin, B.
Moorehouse, Mr.
Mooney, E. C.
Marcus, Joseph
Muller, Jacob
Mackeys, William J.
Moffet, John
Mattison, T. H.
Manning, M. D. Mrs.
May, Mrs.
Marshall, William H.
Mrs. ———
Meakim, J. & A.

M. &. W.
Mails, A.
McLachlin, William
Munn, Stephen B.
Miller, Neh.
Miller, Jacob
Metzgar, Christian
Mills, Andrew
Mason, Mr.
Miller
Marshall, J. T.
Menzies, Mr.
Martin, Alfred
Maltby, Mr.
Mecklahan, Dr.
Munn, Mr.
Mauries, Mr.
Martin, Mr.
Mount, Mr.
Miller
May, E. W.
Miner, Mrs.
McAdams
March, Mr.
Massett, Mrs.
Mix, Mr.
Marshall
Myers, John K.
Maitland, Mrs.
McVickers, Mrs.
Morris, Mrs.
Mortimer, John H.
Murray, Robert L.
Murray, Mary

N.

Noble, John
Nitchie, H. A.
Norrie, A.
Naylor & Co.
Newbold, George
Nevins, R. H. & Co.
N. Y.
Newbold & Craft
Nicholson, John
Norcum, Frederick
Newell, D.
Nichols, C. L.
Nash, Lora
Nicholl, S. D.
Nesmith, John P.
Nash, Levi
Noble, Curtis
Newman, W. H.
Noyes, O. H. P.
Newton, J. W.
Naylor, Peter
N. F.
Negus, Mr.
Newbold, George
Nixon, N.
Norris, M.
Nelson, H. A.
Norris, N. T.
Newton, J.

1849.) LIST OF MEMBERS. 47

Newbold
Neilson
Noyes, William Curtis
Nye, Gideon, Jr.
Nevius, P. J., Jr.
Nevius, P. J.
Noyes, J. R.
Nostrand, C. Mrs.
Nash, William F
Nostrand, Mr.
N. N.
Newhardt, G.
Nanry, Charles M.
Newbould, Mrs.
Nicholl, S. B. Mrs.
Neeves, James
Niblo, Mr.
Nelson, William
Norton, C. L.
Nelson, R.
Norton, H. G.
Nichols, F. L.
Newall, G. T.
Neaby, F.
Newhouse, Benjamin
Nichols, William B.
Nicolson
Nicholson, Mr.
Newell
Neilson, John, Jr.

O.

Ogden, Benjamin, M.D.
Ogsbury, Francis W.
Owen, James
Oelrichs & Kruger
Oakley, W. F.
Orvis, Franklin H.
Oliver & Morgan
Otto, Madame
O'Meara, Mr.
O'Rourke, Mr.
Osborn, A.
O'Meara, J.
Olwell, J.
Ogden, Mr.
Osborn & Sears
Olwell, J.
Oliff, J. W., M.D.
Ortleys, Miss, The
Okill, Mrs.
Ogden, Henry
Owen, D.
O'Brien, John
Oakley, Mr.
Ogilvie, William
O'Keef, John
Ogden, Joseph
Ogden, M. L.
O'Brien, Mr.
Ogden, A.
Outhout, William
Ogden, J.
Ogden, N. G.
Ogden, E. D.

Olcott, John
Osborn, William
Orr, Mr.
Oakley, William
Oliphant, James
O'Farrell, Henry
Onderdonk, J. R.
O'Brien, William & John
Ogden, T. W.
Ogden, Miss
Osborn, H. S. Revd.
Orchard, Isaac, Revd.
Osborn, L. K.

P.

Post, Jehiel J.
Post, William B.
Prout, M. P.
Prime, Frederick
Pell, D. C. & W. & Co.
Pendleton, E. H.
Pickersgill, W. C.
Post, George D.
Pinkney, T. W.
Pearson, Adam
Prescott, J.
Pattison, Robert
Price, J. G.
Pease, J. W.
Phillips, S. B.
Peck, Nathan
Payton, E. H.
Place, Charles
Post, William
Peck, Gideon
Pattillow, Frederick
Pettit, B.
Parr, John
Pond, James O., M.D.
Patterson, S. P.
Pearsall, John
Phelps, Anson G.
Penfold, John
Penfold, Edward
Pou & Palanca
Priestley, J.
Prosser, Thomas
Platt, Jacob S.
Pike, D. B.
Pike & Son, Benjamin
Parks, J. B.
Parkhurst, Mr.
Pell, B.
Phelps, John J.
Powell, M. M.
Peugnet, H.
Platt, George
Price, Mr.
Packard, A. R.
Parker, H. A.
Phipps, James L.
Patton, Dr. Revd.
Post, J. W. Mrs.
Pringle, Thomas
Phillips, W. W.

Partridge, W.
Parker, J. M.
Pierson, S. H.
Pott, P.
Pike, M. S.
Purdy, A. B.
Porter, John
Putnam, N.
Putnam, N. Mrs.
Prindle, Mrs.
Pullen, S.
Post, E. & Co.
Powell, W. R.
Phillips, John P.
Parsons, Joseph
Post, A. T.
Porter, M. V.
Penney, John B.
Powles, Mr.
Pierce
Patterson, Mr.
Pollard, E. Mrs.
Phelps, Mr.
Palle, Mrs.
Pugsley, Mr.
Parker, Mr.
Pell, Mr.
Parsons
Page, P. P.
Pell, Alfred
Porter, Mortimer
Perigo, Ira, Jr.
Phillips, J. W.
Petrie, J. & A.
Palmer, John J.
Prime, Edward
Pearce & Co. George
Peck, Bradford & Beckmond
Perry, Thomas
P. & P.
Putnam, G.
Parks, L. W.
Potter, Ellis
Phyfe, Mr.
Patten, John
Phyfe, Duncan
Parker, C.
Park, Rufus
Painter, Mr.
Parmerlee, W.
Platt, Brush & Co.
Patrige, Mr.
Parish, Mr.
Pelly, Mrs.
Pachman, F.
Page, Mr.
Perrine, Mr.
Parsons, R.
Pierson, C. E., Dr.
Palmer, Mr.
Perago, Mr.
Phelps, Royal
Page, N.
Pine, Joseph
Prescott, J. M.
Paret, Mr.
Potter, Mr.

48 LIST OF MEMBERS. (1849.

Pike, Mr.
Purdy, J. B.
Pease, J. W.
Price, Thompson
Parsons, J. B.
Penfold, William
Purdy & Parker
Pryer, John
Paxson, S. C.
Pegg, Mr.
Prior, Mr.
Platt, E
Pinkney, T. W.
Post, A.
Pierce, James
Paton & Stewart
Pintard, Mrs.
Palmer, Cortlandt
Putnam, Tarrant
Phelps, Isaac N.
Phelps, George D.
Pell, Ferris
Parsons, Charles
Place, R. S.
Patterson, W. T.
Purdy, Jonathan
Pillow, W. H.
Polhamus, R. J.
Pope, Henry
Purdy, J. B.
Parshall, D. T.
Perine, P.
Perkins, A.
Parkhurst, Benjamin
Pray, David
Phillips, Col.
Palmer, Stephen
Pooton, Mr.
Phillips, Samuel
Pease, John
Patton, William
Pooley, Mr.
Prime, J. D.
Polhamus, John
Pomroy, J. B.
Peck, Mr.
Pratt, Mr.
Peet, H. S.
Peet, E. B.
Peet, J. L.
Potter, Mr.
Page, P. P.
Parshall, James L.
Patterson, William C.
Pearson, J.
Provoost, S. H.,
Primrose, J.
Price
Peter
Penchbeck, W. F.
Planten, Mr.
Parish, Henry
Phelps, A. G., Jr.
Palen, George
Paine, J.
Purdy, John
Parkin, Thomas

Pullman, Mrs.
Putnam, T. E.
Paton, William
Parker, J. C.
Paine, William H.
Parker, John
Pine, Misses
Payne, Mrs.
Price, A.
Prout, William
Pringle, A. Y.
Paterson
Peck, E.
Post, J. J.
Perry, Samuel
Pentz, G. W.
Packwood, Mr. or Mrs.
Polhemus, Abraham
Pell, Mrs.
Post, R.
Pryer, G. Mrs.
Pinckney, M. Mrs.

Q.

Quackenbosh, J. J.
Quackenbush & Bamber
Quincy, Charles E.
Quidoit, E. F.
Quin, Dr.
Quackenbush, B.

R.

Rogers, J. Smith, M. D.
Roosevelt, C. V. S.
Rogers, C. Miss
Remsen, S. A. Mrs.
Rogers, John P., by Dr. B. Ogden
Rogers, George Mrs., by Dr. B. Ogden
Roger, William
Redmond, William Mrs.
Ray, Robert
Riggs, E.
Redderow, John
Roosevelt, Mr.
Routh, H. L.
Rhinelander, W. C.
Ramsey, James R.
Ramsay, John
Rose, George W.
Ryers, T. R.
Redfield, J. H.
Rogers, James
Ryerson, Henry W.
Ruston, John
Randolph, A. D. F.
Ryer, C. B.
Rae, Robert
Roberts, Edward
Rudd, William
Redman, C. H.
Richards, William H.

Richards, Thomas P.
Rich, Josiah
Roome, Charles
Reed, Richard
Remsen, Mr.
Russell, Mr.
Robinson, B. F.
Robinson, Mr.
Russell, Mr.
Roome, H.
Ruton, Mrs.
Rolfe, Charles
Rickard, Mr.
Rogers, Arthur
Robhaus, Mr.
Redman, J. P.
Randell, J. & S.
Rabold, Daniel
Rogers
Rowley, John
Riley, Mr.
Ray, Robert
Roome, Charles
Rogers, C. Mrs.
Robenson, Mr.
Roosa, O.
Ruggles
Rangers, John
Richmond, Mr.
Rufut, Thomas
Rich, Thomas B.
Robinson, Edward Revd.
Rutgers, N. G.
Riley, Louisa
Redford, D. A.
Rutgers, N. G. Mrs.
Robinson, N.
Ross, D. S. Mrs.
Rigney, Thomas
Riggs, Babcock & Co.
Ross, Andrew
Robert & Williams
Reid & Sprague
Rose, William W.
R. S. B.
R. & P.
Robinson & Weir
Rusch, Escher
Rice, Mr.
Robinson, R. W.
Renwick, M. A. Mrs.
Roberts, D. S.
Romer & Riggs
Rhod, Daniel
Riley, S.
Rich, James
Riley, Mr.
Rogers, Mr.
Remsen, Mrs.
Rankin, W.
Robinson, R. F.
Rodman, J. F.
Richard, Mr.
Riley, Mr.
Randolph, S. F.
Redfield, W. C.
Redfield, J. H.

LIST OF MEMBERS.

Redfield, C. B.
Richards, Eliza
Randolph
Rapelye, G.
Riker, A.
Roberts, Charles
Roosevelt, J. Mrs.
Roosevelt, W.
Richards, Guy
Rhinelander, Mrs.
Rogers, J. K., M. D.
Rockwell
Romeyn, Samuel B.
Russell, Charles H.
Robinson, L.
Rachaud, Mr.
Roberts, Miss
Robertson, J. A.
Rachau, John A. F.
Rodgers, A. R.
Reed, Almet
Remsen, William
Richardson, Thomas
Robbins, George S.
Reichard, Frederick
Renwick, Miss
Ryerson, Mr.
Ranken, A.
Ryder, Edgar T.
Rodgers, Charles H.
Robbins, J. D.
Raynor, H.
Ryan, Maurice C.
Roberts, Samuel
Roberts, N.
Roberts, George
Robinson, William
Rodgers, B.
Rosenheim, Mr.
Roschild, S.
Randall, E.
Renoud, G.
Rider, George
Raper, Bogert
Robjohn, Thomas
Ritter, Joseph
Randall, N. G.
Rees, J.
Raymond, Mr.
Rose, Josiah, Jr.
Rolfe, Mrs.
Rader, M.
Rogers, R. S.
Raymond
Roberts, L. S.
Rivington
Rayter, W.
Ruggles, D. B.
Ray, W. G.
Rainsford, Mrs. & Miss
Rumsey, J. W. Mrs.
Roosevelt, S. W
Raymond, J. H.
Robson, G. Mrs.
Restuant, Mr. by Mr. Bloodgood
Rose, Mr

Raven, Mr.
Raynor, Samuel
Ranken, Mr.
Renwick, J.
Robertson, James
Rawdon, Freeman
Redman, C. H.
Ransom, J. H.
Rawdon, F.
Roshore, John
Ryder, S. H.
Read, Taylor & Co.
Rohe, J. A.
Reckard, S. B.
Russell, N. E.
R. & C.
R. & D.
Ratance & Gilley
Reid, George W.
Raymond, H. J.
Roosevelt, Samuel
Rudd, Joseph
Rodman, John
Reynolds, P.
Rowland, C. N. S.
Roche, Edward
Robinson, B.
Ryley, R. M.
Reemony, T. W.

S.

Sampson, Joseph
Spencer, William A. Capt.
Shields, G. W.
Stuyvesant, H. Mrs.
Skiddy, Capt. Mrs.
Smith, G., M. D
Skidmore, Samuel T.
Shieffelin, H. H.
Sheaf, J. F.
Stevens, John C.
Schermerhorn, Peter
Schermerhorn, Abraham
Suckley, Ruton
Schieffelin & Fowler
Sheldon, Henry
Schieffelin, P.
Sandford, Henry
Sturges, Jonathan
Sanderson, E. F.
Schermerhorn, Augustus Mrs
Stevens, John A.
Snow, Mr.
Storm, Walter
Sell, William P.
Sumner, Palmer
Sanxay, Joseph F.
Sharp, William
Sayer, John N.
Sparks, Samuel
Smith, W. D.
Steele, W.
Sperling, John G.
Sammis, J.
Smith, B. R.

Stansbery, James F.
Smith, Albert S.
Scott, William
Salter, Benjamin
Sheldon, Preston
See, Leander
Stout, Andrew V.
Smith, Wesley
Smith, Woodhull
Stelle, Nelson, M. D.
Spies, Adam W.
Speights, Charles
Strong, Thomas W.
Silleck, H.
Smith, Asa
Stebbins, William
Shaffer, Chauncey
Savage, C. C.
Skidmore, J.
Sheffield, Dudley
Sanatory Committee of the Board of Health, by R. T. Haws
Schoals, F. P.
Starr, N. W.
Smith, Mr.
Smilie, James
Still, G. S.
Spinington, A.
Starin, J. K.
Stokes, B. G.
Stevens, James H.
Scott
Sandford, Mrs.
Seguine, C.
Swift, H. A.
Sallsbury, H.
Smith, B. B.
Scott, A. M. L.
Starr, Charles, Senr.
Shepherd, D.
Stark, Andrew
Stewart, John
Stagg, Benjamin
Sherwood & Chapman
Steel, Dr.
Smith, Samuel
Smith, G. G.
Swazy, Isaac
Sprouls, S.
Shilman, F.
Storm, S.
Sperry, S. S.
Stevens, Mrs.
Starr, Charles, Jr.
Smith, William
Smith, G.
Seymour, Isaac N.
Slocum, William
Slocum, Frank
Smith, C. W.
Spycer, Mrs.
Sarracco, P.
Simons, Lewis
Swaine, Edward
Smith, Dr.
Sweet, G.

50 LIST OF MEMBERS. (1849.

Schmitz, A.
Souza, Theobald
St. John, Mrs.
Scudder, G. W.
Smith, Mr.
Scharbenberg & Sons
Scureman, Isaac
Secor, T. F.
Smith, Milton G.
Smith, William
Sterns, J. G.
Sheffield, D.
Spragg, Samuel
Slocum, Richard
Seaman, Conklin
Stewart, John M.
Skiddy, William
Simpson, Mrs.
Selleck, C. G.
Smith, Mrs.
Stoddard, Mr.
Sturenfildt, Mr.
Star, Mr.
Smith, Mr.
Spaulding, Mrs.
Spaulding, A.
Smith, Mr.
Smith, James W.
Simpson, Mr.
Saur
Skinner
Simpson, Mr.
Sloan, Thomas
Slosson, John
Smith, J. C.
Stewart, William Mrs.
Sherred, Mrs.
Shepherd, Mrs.
Stewart, J. J.
Schmelzel, J. B.
Skelly, E. Mrs.
St. John, L.
Street
Smith, Barnet
Sheridan, Edward
Sherman, D. R.
Shulthe, Charles
Shields, Mr.
Smith, Mr.
Skillman, Judge
Simpson, Solomon
Smith, Samuel J.
Smith, Peter
Spencer, Warner
Smith, J. G.
Secord, Joshua
Scwab, Mr.
Silverman, Mr.
Sammis, Daniel P.
Smith, Elias L.
Smith, C. E.
Slott, Alexander
Sneedeh, J.
Smith, Shadrach
Shave, Mr.
Sheldon, J.
Stevens, N.

Sherman, G. & J.
Stout, T.
Scott
Smull, Thomas
Scribner, Mrs.
Somerville, C.
Sears, R.
Simpson, I. B. & J.
Smith, John G.
Sparks, Samuel
Shaw, James
Smiley, D. C.
Scott. James
Spencer, William
Solomon, Dr.
Sather & Church
Stuker, E.
Seatin, John
Staples, S. P.
Stewart, Lispenard
Sandford, Edward
Smith, Cornelius
Stephenson, John
Stewart, Alvan
Strong, William K.
Sedgwick, Theodore
Stone, S. B.
Sanford, C
Snyder, Mrs.
Sutphen, John Mrs
Sproulls, Margaret Miss
Sproulls, Sarah Miss
Sproulls, Henry Master
Sawyer, R. Mrs.
Smith, Lemuel
Smith, Catharine Mrs.
Smith, C. E.
Shermer, R.
Stockwell, Mrs.
Sexton, Mr.
Schenck, C. C.
Squires, Mr.
Snedeker, Mr.
Simmons, H.
Sergent, Mr.
Scott, General
Suffern, Thomas
Smith, Sheldon
Stillman, T. B.
Scrymser, J.
Scofield, W. H.
Smith, Asa D. Revd.
Smith, Thomas
Seaman, S. M.
Staples, J.
Sacket, Mrs.
Stockbridge, J.
Somers, F.
Smith, William H. & Co.
Stamford Manufacturing Co.
Stringer & Townsend
Scheffelin, H. A.
Smith, L.
Spaulding, H. F.
Staples, Edward W.
Stryburg, Henry
S B. S.

Starr, W. H. & Co.
Shuster, J. F.
Stryker, C. C.
Sayre, J. N.
Scott, H.
Scovill, J. L. & W. H.
Smith, J.
Swicker
Slane & Burrell
Sherman, A. N., M.D.
Smith, Andrew
Swift, John H.
Stiles, Samuel
Schlesinger, F. S.
Sage, George E.
Smith, Thomas C.
Stokes, Henry
Sprague, J. H.
Scrymser, W. H.
Shelton, T. B., M.D.
Storm, Corn's.
Sheldon, H. A.
Skinner, T. H , Jr.
Sayory, C.
Scott, John D.
Steinle
Spring, Mr.
Sheldon, P.
Standley, William W.
Sarvin, David
Smith, A. P.
Steward, John & Co.
Saltus, Francis
Schuhardt, F.
Strong, George W.
Scribner & Coolidge
Schuhardt, Benjamin
Sacket, Belcher & Co.
Stone & Starr
Spies, Christ & Co.
Shipman & Ayres
Spencer, G. G.
Storm, Charles
Schlinger & Canely
Symington, James
Schmidt, J. W.
Sinillio, W. C.
St. John & Co. Charles
Sanxay, S.
Spooner, S.
Stebbins, Mr.
Sloan, Mr.
Spalding, W. E.
Saxton, Mr.
Stuart, R. L. & A.
Sanford, General
Seignett, Mr.
Sterling & Waller
Schermerhorn, P. A. Mrs.
Sturges, Jonathan
Shaddle, H. V.
Sagehorn, Mr.
Suydam, J. A.
Stevens, Robert L.
Stuart, C..
Seely, Mr.
Stevens, John C.

1849.) LIST OF MEMBERS. 51

Stuart, J. J.
Skillman, Mr.
Smith, Richard
Southart & Kissam
Schoot, Mr.
Strange, Mr.
Sears, Mr.
Silcock, Mr.
Swain, Mr.
Stansberry, J. S.
Stuart, William
Sheffield, Mrs.
Sinclair, W. T.
Scrymgeon, James
Sandheim
Smith, T. U.
Strong, Benjamin
Simonds, Mr.
Stuart, James
Smedburg, Mrs.
Stuart, Mrs.
Smith, J. M.
Sullivan, George
Skidmore, William B.
Spalding, Mr.
Schuyler, Messrs.
Sydam, Dr.
Slosson, Mr.
Smith, Mr.
Smith, W. D.
Smith, Mr.
Scott & Co. Charles
Stoppani, Mr.
Skinner, Mr.
Sherman & Stark
Seaman & Muir
Smith, James
Smith, Jess
Southack, J. W.
Sands, A. B.
Saxton, John
Sanford, M.
S. M.
Scott, William B.
Seymour, W. N.
Sweezy & Co. N. T.
Smith, C. D.
Smith, J. C.
Sewell, J. N.
Schencks, Miss
Stewart, A. T. & Co.
Swartwout
Stevens, B.
Schirmer, C. F.
Stone, Miss
Seymour
Smedes
Slocum
Starr, Mr.
Stephens, R. H., M.D.
Sabine, G. A.
Slosson, John, Children of
Spofford & Tileston
Swan, Caleb
Swords, George H.
St. John, Milton
Stevens, Byam K.

Secor, C. A.
Storer, George L.
Samson, A. W.
Stevens, Henry H.
St. John, C.
Skiddy, F.
Sherman, B. B.
Sherwood, S.
Suydam, J. A.
Sherwood, William
Sedgwick, Mr.
Stucken, Edward
Sandford, L. H.
Spear, Alva
Shepherd, T. S.
Story, Rufus
Surget, J.
Scribner, Abraham S.
Shoemaker, Abraham
Smith, John J.
Stout, A. V.
Simpson, W.
Seaman, G.
Simpson, W. & J.
Stohlman, Chs. F. E. Revd.
Short, John
Stilwell, William M. Revd.
Sice, C.
Scofield, P.

T.

Taylor, M.
Talbot, Charles N.
Thorne, Jonathan
Townsend, Elisha
Two Friends
Trimble, D.
Tredwell, Adam
Taylor, Thomas House Rev.
Tucker, D. N.
Terry, David Revd.
Thomson, John
Terbell, H. S.
Thomson, Mason
Taylor, Moses B.
Tracy, C.
Tucker, C. P., M.D.
Taff, Henry
Teller, Richard H.
Trafford, Abraham
Taylor, John
Thatcher, John P.
Tracy, George Manning
Thompson, W. J.
Terbell, Jeremiah
Tweedy, O. B.
Thomas & Co.
Templeton, Miss
Tappan, Lewis
Tweedy, E.
Toole, W. S.
Thompson & Stebbins
Thwing Brothers
Terry, S. H.
Tredwell, Mr.

Tryon, Mr.
Thompson, Mr.
Tucker, S. C.
Thompson, James
Thompson, Mr.
Tripp, Mr.
Taylor, Mr.
Thomas
Thomas, Mr.
Tuckerman, J.
Tarrant, James
Traggot, Mr.
Teats, Daniel
Taylor, J. D.
Tunison, Mr.
Terbell, S.
Talman, J. H.
Titus, W. H.
Thompson, Mr. Revd.
Tolenbach, Mr.
Thompson, Mr.
Truesdale, E. D.
Taylor, Mr.
Teets, Mr.
Tollidge, N.
Taylor, Mr.
Tracy, J. W.
Treadwell, George
Terbell, H. S.
Thorp, Henry S.
Thorp, A.
Tweed, R.
Tatham, Benjamin
Terry, Mr.
Thurston, C. M.
Tobias, Alfred
Tracy, S. F.
Tooker, John S.
Talmadge, J.
Townsend, W. H.
Taber, C. C.
Townsend, E.
Taylor, G. W.
Tillotson, J. C.
Titus, G. N.
Thayer, N.
Trowbridge, G. A.
Tinkham, Joseph
Tilton, William
Tweed, Richard, Jr.
Tappen, George, Jr.
Taylor, W. A.
Trainor, M.
Taaffe, William
Teixeira, D. J. Revd.
Titus, Charles F.
Tylee, Mrs.
Tripler, Mr.
Thatford, Mr.
Thompson, Asa L.
Tyler, Isaac
Tappen, Charles
Trafford, A.
Tappen & Burd
Tremper, Harman
Taylor, J. S.
Travers, Mr.

LIST OF MEMBERS. (1849.

Tapping, H.
Taylor, A. B.
Toal, Charles
Tieman, George
Thompson, T.
Tyng, Stephen H., D.D.
Tisdale, S. T. & Co.
Turell, W.
Taylor, R. Z.
Timpson, William
Tucker, F. C.
Thorn, W. K.
Thomson, John, M.D.
Taylor, Charles G.
Turner, Richard
Thomas, John
Tappen, G.
Thackerbury, D.
Townsend, John
Taylor, Morris
Townsend, S. P.
Thompson, W. B.
Tileston, W. H.
Tieman, J. W.
Tomlinson, T. E.
Truslow, William
Tillenghast, P.
Townsend, D. W.
Tracy, Irwin & Co.
T. S.
Tapscott, W. & J. T.
Thomas, A. B.
Trowbridge, H.
Thorp, H. S.
Tryon, F.
Torrey, Joseph
Tatam, J. R.
Tallman, A. S.
Tousley, Charles
Tenbroeck, R.
TenBrook, J.
Townsend, J. H.
Tucker, William
Talman, S. S.
Todd, William W.
Topham, William
Taylor, S.
Tappen, Mrs.
Turner, Mr.
Taylor, John W.
Tuowen, J. W.
Timpson, B.
Trowbridge, F. H.
Taylor, John
Thorn, M.
Tate, J. E.
Taylor, S. E.
Taff, Henry
Tripp, J. F.
Taylor, Mr.
Terry, Brothers
Taylor, J.
Town, Charles
Todd, Henry
Titus, James H.
Tappan, H. P. Profr.
Thorn, Jon.

U.

Upsdal & Pierson
Underhill, A. S.
Underhill, Walter
Underhill, J. S.
Underhill, Mr.
Ustick, Richard
U.

V.

Van Rensselaer, Alex.
Vanhook, W.
Van Allen, William
Van Nostrand, William A.
Van Dalsem, W. H.
Van Arsdale, Henry, M.D.
Van Winkle, William
Vermilye, W.
Vancycle, E.
V. A. H. & Co.
Van Benschoten, Mr.
Vassar & Co. M.
Van Antwerp, James
Van Waggenen & Tucker
Van Kleck, Mr.
Verplanck, G. C.
Vaughn, Mr.
Van Stader
Van Auken & Co.
Vidal, J. C.
Valentine, A. G.
Van Nortwyck, W. B.
Van Deusen
Varnum, J. B.
Van Winkle, Edgar S.
Vandervoort, J. B.
Van Wyck, H. L.
Van Santvoord, C.
Vandervoort, H.
Van Tuyl, B. S.
Vreeland, Mr.
Vaughan, George
Vantassel, Mr.
Vatel, Nicholas
Vermule, F., M.D.
Vermule, W., M.D.
Verplank, Samuel
Van DeWerken, E.
Vail, G.
Vernol, Mr.
Vail, A.
Vanderpool, A.
Van Duser, S.
Van Horn, C.
Van Buren, Mary Mrs.
Valentine, D.
Van Rensselaer, Alexander
Vermilye, Thomas E.
Van Wagenen, W F.
Valentine, Benjamin W.
Van Antwerp, S. Miss
Van Blankenstyne & Co.
Vandewater, J. & W.
Vernon, Thomas

Van Wartz, Henry, Jr.
Vermilye, W. R.
Van Nest, Abraham
Van Arsdale, John
Van Vleck, J. T
Van Doren, J.
Van Winkle, Abraham J.
Vreedenburgh, P.
Vandewort, M. A.
Vandewort, P.
Van Wagenen, William
Van Zant, J.
Van Houden, J.
Voorhis, Richard
Vliet, S.
Van Saun, Abraham
Van Saun, H. & Co.
Van Winkle, Edward H.
Valentine, H. M.
Van Buskirk, W.
Voris, H.
Vandevoort, D.
Valley, Dr.
Vandewater, J. E.
Van Winkle
Van Wick, Mr.
Vaniderstine, Mr.
Vreeland, Mr.
V. K
Van Buren, Abraham

W.

Wetmore, A. R.
Wilkes, Mrs.
Wilmerding, William E.
Webb, J. Watson
Wheelwright, Benjamin F.
Wright, Sturges & Co.
Walsh, Robinson A.
Walsh, John A. R.
Weeks, Edward A.
Weeks, R. D.
Wyeth, L. J.
Wood, Silas
Wainwright, E.
Wetmore, W. S.
Wolfe, John D.
Wood, William
Whitney, J. W.
Wiley, John
Whittemore, W. T.
Wolfe, Christopher
Woolsey, E. J.
Wiggins, W. H.
Woodward, Thomas
Wilbur, Charles
Wetmore, L.
Whittlesey, Henry
Wakeman, A.
Whittemore, Joseph
Warren, T.
Weir, James
Wheaton, William
Wentworth, Joseph W.
Wooster, Benjamin

1849.) LIST OF MEMBERS. 53

Waldron, C.
Wilson, J.
Wood, Henry
Williams, Erastus
Winter, E. T.
Weeks, D. C.
Wagstaff, William
West, Royal, Revd.
Warner, J. W.
Webster, D. A.
Ward, S. S.
Ward, L. B.
Walker, W. A.
Wetmore, William S.
Woodruff, L. B.
Walker, William
Winston, F. S.
Whitlock, William, Jr.
Waldo, Francis
Winslow, R. H.
Ward, James O.
Wolfe & Gillespie
Weeks & Douglass
Ward, W. C.
Wood, Frederick
Wallace, Weeks & Co.
Whitlock, B. M.
Waters, George C.
White, E.
W. C., Jr.
W. & B.
Walker, W. A.
White, F. & Co.
Wright
Wason, H.
Waterbury, Mr.
Walker, William
Wallace, William
Worthington & Sheffield
Witcheef, Henry
Whitlock & Harris
Wygans, E.
Wheeler, A.
Wilson, L. O.
Willis, Edward
Wait, Mr.
Willet, Miss
Wood, J.
Wray, Stephen
Waling, Mr.
Waller, Mr.
Wicksted, J.
White, W.
Walker, J.
Wilson, Mr.
Will, J. H.
Willson, Mr.
Woodward, Mr.
Weild, E.
Wilson, A. D., M. D.
Williams, A. G.
Weyman, Mrs.
Webster, Mr.
Warner, A.
White, Eli
Wright, William
White, Mr.

West, Mr.
Williamson, C. T.
Webb, Mr.
Wood, Mr.
Whitlock, Mr.
Williamson, Mr.
Williams, Mr.
Wakeman, A.
Webb, Mr.
Worley, Mr.
Walker, Mr.
Walker, Mr.
Woodworth, Miss
Wetmore, A. R.
Watts, Mrs.
Woolsey & Co.
Westervilt, J. A.
Williamson, D. D.
Williamson, J. A.
Williams, Richard
Wood, J., M. D.
Walton, E. L.
Whitmore, J. C.
Williams, Thomas, Jr.
Webb, Miss
Whitlock, Andrew
Willetts, Samuel
Willetts, Stephen
Willetts, R. R.
Watkiss & Kelley
Willitts, D. T.
Wetmore, P.
Willetts, E. P.
Woodward, Thomas
Wurts, John
Warner
Ward, Mrs.
Warren, Mr.
Woodhead, J.
Wetmore, S.
Wynkoop, F. S.
Wolcott, F. H.
Wolfe & Gillespie
Warren, Richard
Ward, Thomas, M. D.
Wisner & Phelps
Waggner, D. B
Weller, John
Weston, Edward
Wyles, John
Whitehead, John
Wetmore, N. Mrs.
Wilson, N.
Walker, George S.
Wilson, Mrs. D.
Wright, H. A. Mrs.
Whitewright, W.
Weisman, Augustus
Wardle, Thomas
Watkins, John L.
White, J. H.
Woods, E. Mrs.
Willson, E. & R. M.
Whitney, M. R.
Welch, William
Waterman, Mr.
Wilkins, James

Williams, Mr.
White, Edward
Waterhouse, Robert
Westerard, George W.
Weeks, Philip
Wattles, Mr.
Walker, Mrs.
Waller & Kreps
West, Joseph
Whithington, Lewis
Wagner, Mr.
White, Elizabeth
Woods, John
Ward, Adam
Wilson, William H.
Welford, Mr.
Walton, Ruth
Wing, Luman
Watson, Mrs.
Weeks, Absalom
Wagstaff, J. C. & Co.
Ward, L. B.
Wilkins, L. Denton
Wattemire, William W.
Wilkins, Denton
Weaver, B.
Williams & Hinman
Whalen, L. S.
Williams, Peter
Westfall, J. D.
Witherill, Mr.
White, Philip A.
Wood, John
Wells, John B.
Williams, R. S.
Wray, C.
Woolley
West, D.
Watt, William
Watson, J.
Walker, J. J.
Ward, O. D.
Worcester, H. Mrs.
Woodward, R. T.
Wagstaff, Mrs.
Watson, R. S.
Williams, B. Miss
Wheeler, A. H.
Wells, E. H. Mrs
Wells, A. Mrs.
West, C. E. Mrs.
W. Mrs.
Winter, Mrs.
Ward, Henry Dana
White, W.
Williams, R.
Williams, S. C.
Wilson, J.
White, Charles B.
Webb, William H.
Wheeler, E.
Wright, Neziah
White, J. T.
Weeks, Samuel
Walter, Mrs.
Ward, Isaac
Williams, C.

LIST OF MEMBERS. (1849

Waller, C. C. Mrs.
White, Henry, Revd.
Washburn, H. B.
Whiting, Charles
Wardell, M.
Ward, A. H.
Williams, C. P. & E.
Wm.
Wood, S. S.
Wetmore, L.
Windle, J. B. & Co.
Williams, P. H.
Woodward & Connor
Woods, D.
Woodhull, C. S.
W. H. & Co.
Wiley, John
Walker, S. G.
Wood, O. E.
Walton, W.
Williams, W. R.
Wells, N. M.
Winslow, L. C.
Warner, P. R.
Williams, John M.
Wicoff, Mrs.
Walsh, J. W.
Walduck, N. M.
Westervelt, Abraham D.
Wilson, J.
Warburton, W. F.
Wallace, J.
Wood, Benjamin
Wight, Richard
Wilson, E. B.
Worrall, H.
Williamson, S.
Wolters, H.
Walton, J. B.
Whitehorne, H.
West, William G.

Wooding, J. & A.
White, J.
Wallard, N. W.
Watterbury, F. W.
Witham, W.
Whitney, Mrs.
Westervelt, Mr.
Williston, J. S.
Wilson, Mr.
Wilcox, J. R.
Wainwright, E.
Wilson, M. P.
Weed, H. B.
Walker, Andrew
Woram, W.
Wise, Mr.
Williams, Jabes
Watts, Lewis H.
Whittemore, R. J.
Warren, James
Wilson, Harris
Westervelt, J. J.
Wardell, Mrs.
Wilson, B.
Weston, R. W.
Wildy, Mr.
Willer, S. Mrs.
Wilson, Mr.
Williams, J.
Washband, Mr.
Wilbur, Mr.
Williams, Mrs.
Ward, Mr.
Whaler, H. H.
Williams, Mr.
Wells, Mr.
White, Charles
Westbrook
Woolsey, Miss
Whittemore, Mr.
Welleton

Wickham, D. H.
Woodruff, Thomas T.
Wells, Mr.
White, R. H.
Wheeler, W. A.
Walker, Alexander
Withers, R.
W. A. S.
Waddington, W. D.
Whitlock, B. M.
Winston, F. S
Waldo, Samuel L.

Y.

Yelvertons & Fellows
Young, M.
Yates, Mrs.
Yates, C.
Young & Co. S. S.
Young, Abraham
Youle, G. W.
Yereance, R. S.
Young, E. M.
Young, G.
Youngs, David
Youngs, John
Young, D. S.

Z.

Zimmerman, J. C.
Zweck, Mr.
Zabriskie, G.
Zabriskie & Van Riper
Zongstreet, S.
Zabriskie, A. C.

SUPPLEMENT.

Augi, Job
Dwight, Edmund
Few, Miss
Few, Col.
Farmer, Mr.
Hoadley, David
Jay, Mrs. Wm.

Kipp, B. L.
Kipp, I. L.
Livingston, Mrs.
Lawrence, Isaac
McAuley, Mrs.
Newman, Caroline
Reeve, Henry

Russell, A.
Raphall, M. J. Rev.
Scuyler, P. G.
Stevens, John W.
Wood, Silas
Frelinghuysen, T.

CERTIFICATE OF INTENTION

TO INCORPORATE THE NEW-YORK ASSOCIATION FOR IMPROVING THE CONDITION OF THE POOR.

THE undersigned, being each and every of them of full age, and citizens of the State of New-York, desiring to associate themselves for the benevolent and charitable objects hereinafter expressed, that they may become a body politic and corporate, and be enabled to conduct the business of the Association in the City and County of New-York, according to the provisions of an " Act for the Incorporation of Benevolent, Charitable, Scientific, and Missionary purposes," passed April 12th, 1848, do for these purposes hereby certify,

I. That the name and title by which such Institution shall be known in law, is the "New-York Association for Improving the Condition of the Poor."

II. That the particular business and objects of such Association shall be the elevation of the physical and moral condition of the indigent ; and so far as is compatible with these objects, the relief of their necessities.

III. That the Board of Managers to manage the same shall consist of one President, five Vice-Presidents, one Treasurer, one Corresponding Secretary and General Agent, one Recording Secretary, the Chairman of each Advisory Committee, or as his proxy, some other member of said Committee, and four members to be chosen by said Board of Managers.

IV. That the following named persons shall constitute the Board of Managers for the first year, to wit : James Brown, President ; George

CERTIFICATE.

Griswold, J. Smyth Rogers, James Boorman, James Lenox, and Horatio Allen, Vice-Presidents; Robert B. Minturn, Treasurer; Robert M. Hartley, Corresponding Secretary and General Agent; Joseph B. Collins, Recording Secretary; together with the following elected Members and Chairmen of the Advisory Committees, namely: Stewart Brown, Frederick S. Winston, Erastus C. Benedict, John R. Ludlow, Daniel S. Briant, William Gale, Peter G. Arcularius, Abraham Fardon, Jr., Apollos R. Wetmore, Nicholas C. Everett, Calvin Tracy, James O. Pond, James Horn, Samuel P. Patterson, Lewis Chichester, Adam W. Spies, Thomas Denny, Luther Jackson, Stephen C. Lynes, and F. Ellsworth Mather.

In witness whereof, we hereunto have subscribed our names, in the city of New-York, this the eleventh day of December, in the year of our Lord one thousand eight hundred and forty-eight.

JAMES BROWN,	APOLLOS R. WETMORE,
GEORGE GRISWOLD,	NICHOLAS C. EVERETT,
J. SMYTH ROGERS,	CALVIN TRACY,
JAMES BOORMAN,	JAMES O. POND,
HORATIO ALLEN,	JAMES HORN,
ROBERT M. HARTLEY,	LEWIS CHICHESTER,
JOSEPH B. COLLINS,	ADAM W. SPIES,
STEWART BROWN,	THOMAS DENNY,
FREDERICK S. WINSTON,	LUTHER JACKSON,
DANIEL S. BRIANT,	STEPHEN C. LYNES,
PETER G. ARCULARIUS,	F. ELLSWORTH MATHER.
ABRAHAM FARDON, JR.	

Witness as to all the signatures,   D. F. CURRY.

City and County of New-York, [ss.]: On the eleventh day of December, A. D. 1848, before me came George Griswold, J. Smyth Rogers, Horatio Allen, Joseph B. Collins, Luther Jackson, Abraham Fardon, Jr., Lewis Chichester, Daniel S. Briant, Nicholas C. Everett, James O. Pond, Adam W. Spies, F. Ellsworth Mather, James Horn, Frederick S. Winston, Peter G. Arcularius, Stephen C. Lynes, Calvin Tracy, and Robert M. Hartley; and on the 12th day of December, A. D. 1848, before me came James Brown, Stewart Brown, and James Boorman; and on the 13th day of December, A. D. 1848, before me came Apollos R. Wetmore and Thomas Denny, to me known to be the same persons described in and who executed the foregoing instrument, who severally acknowledged that they executed the foregoing instrument, for the purposes therein mentioned.

D. F. CURRY, Commissioner.

I approve of the within Certificate, and allow the same to be filed.

H. P EDWARDS, Justice Supreme Court.

New-York, December 14, 1848.

STATE OF NEW-YORK, }
SECRETARY'S OFFICE, } Albany, Dec. 16, 1848.

I certify that the Certificate of Incorporation of the "New-York Association for Improving the Condition of the Poor," was received and filed this day in this office.

ARCH'D CAMPBELL,
Dept. Sec. of State.

THE SEVENTH ANNUAL REPORT

OF THE

NEW-YORK ASSOCIATION

FOR

IMPROVING THE CONDITION OF THE POOR,

FOR THE YEAR 1850.

WITH THE BY-LAWS AND A LIST OF MEMBERS.

ORGANIZED, 1843—INCORPORATED, 1848.

> "The quality of mercy is not strained;
> It droppeth as the gentle rain from heaven
> Upon the place beneath: it is twice blessed;
> It blesseth him that gives and him that takes."

NEW-YORK:
PRINTED BY JOHN F. TROW, 49, 51 & 53 ANN-ST.
1850.

PROCEEDINGS

AT THE

ANNUAL MEETING

OF THE

NEW-YORK ASSOCIATION FOR IMPROVING THE CONDITION OF THE POOR.

Held in the Hall of the Public School Society, Nov. 11, 1850.

———•●•———

In the absence of the President, GEORGE GRISWOLD, Esq., one of the Vice Presidents presided.

The Minutes of the last Annual Meeting were read by the Recording Secretary, and, on motion, approved.

The Treasurer presented his Annual Report, which was accepted, and ordered on file.

The Minutes of the Board of Managers, exhibiting their operations during the recess of the Supervisory Council, were read by the Corresponding Secretary, as their Annual Report to that body, and approved.

The Annual Report was read, accepted, and ordered to be printed under the direction of the Board of Managers.

On motion, the By-Laws were amended by inserting in the Fourth

Article, sixth line, "Second" Monday; and in the Twelfth Article, fourth line, a like alteration.

Voting by ballot having by resolution been dispensed with, the Association proceeded to the election of the following Officers, Managers, and Supervisory Council, for the ensuing year, after which the meeting adjourned.

OFFICERS, MANAGERS,
AND
SUPERVISORY COUNCIL.

President.
JAMES BROWN.

Vice Presidents.
GEORGE GRISWOLD,   JAMES BOORMAN,
J. SMYTH ROGERS, M. D.,   HORATIO ALLEN,
JAMES LENOX.

Treasurer.
ROBERT B. MINTURN.

Corresponding Secretary and Agent.
ROBERT M. HARTLEY.

Recording Secretary.
JOSEPH B. COLLINS.

Supervisory Council.
The first in order is the Chairman of each District Committee.

FIRST DISTRICT.
James C. Ramsey,
James Cruikshank,
Avery Brumley,
William Bogardus,
John Harris.

SECOND DISTRICT.
George W. Abbe,
Joseph F. Sanxay,
John N. Sayer,
William Sharp,
Charles Wilbur.

THIRD DISTRICT.
E. Cauldwell,
J. L. Baldwin,
E. L. Fancher,
W. D. Harris,
L. Wetmore,

FOURTH DISTRICT.
Abraham Fardon, Jr.,
Archibald Hall,
Hugh Aikman,
Charles Chamberlain,
John Gates.

FIFTH DISTRICT.
A. R. Wetmore,
William Forrest,
G. T. Cobb,
Wm. H. Richards,
Leonard Kirby.

SIXTH DISTRICT.
N. C. Everett,
Stephen Conover,
Daniel Fisher,
Frederick Lockwood,
John G. Sperling.

SEVENTH DISTRICT.
Stephen Cutter,
A. B. Ludlum,
J. Skidmore,
Thompson Price,
George Walsh.

EIGHTH DISTRICT.
Joseph B. Collins.
William Johnston,
John Endicott,
Charles C. Dyer.
O. D. McClain.

NINTH DISTRICT.
James O. Pond, M. D.,
James S. Miller, M. D.,
Thomas P. Richards,
Jeremiah Terbell,
Daniel French.

TENTH DISTRICT.
James Horn,
Joseph M. Bell,
Isaac Ford,
Pe er Alms,
H. Van Arsdale, M. D.

ELEVENTH DISTRICT.
S. P. Patterson,
R. H. Teller,
Abner Mills,
Peter McPherson,
Joel Kelly.

THIRTEENTH DISTRICT.
Lewis Chichester,
Thomas Kennedy,
John Pearsall,
Charles Merrill,
William A. Walker.

FOURTEENTH DISTRICT.
Adam W. Spies,
Robert Rae,
Alexander W. Murray,
William Post,
J. J. Jenkins.

FIFTEENTH DISTRICT.
Thomas Denny,
William G. Bull,
Joseph Lawrence,
Henry E. Davies,
James Marsh.

SIXTEENTH DISTRICT.
Luther Jackson,
Charles Roome,
L. B. Woodruff,
W. Vermilye,
H. K. Bull.

SEVENTEENTH DISTRICT.
S. C. Lynes,
James R. Gibson,
John Falconer,
Geo. Manning Tracy,
Thomas Jeremiah.

EIGHTEENTH DISTRICT.
F. E. Mather,
William Walker,
E. Holbrook,
J. W. Benedict,
John Campbell.

NINETEENTH DISTRICT.
O. W. Morris,
J. C. Miller,
M. W. Fox,
J. C. Hepburn, M. D.,
J. A. Cary.

Elected Members of the Supervisory Council.

J. C. Green,
Wm. S. Wetmore,
Jonathan Sturges,
William H. Macy,
Thomas Cock, M. D.,

E. J. Woolsey,
Peter Cooper,
John C Baldwin,
William B. Crosby,

George T. Trimble,
Lorin Nash,
John L. Mason,
Josiah Rich.

Elected members of the Board of Managers.

Stewart Brown.
John T. Adams,

Frederick S. Winston,
Erastus C. Benedict.

VISITORS,

Appointed by the Advisory Committee for the ensuing year.

FIRST DISTRICT.
John Harris,
Ralph Phinney,
James C. Ramsey,
George Hatt,
Wm. Frothingham.
Wm. Bogardus,
Calvin Wheelock, jr,
John Davidson.
Isaac Morly,
John Calvin Smith,
Avery Brumley.
David Meeker,
H. M. Baldwin,
John A. Hatt,
George Hatt, Sec'y.

SECOND DISTRICT.
Charles Wilbur,
Joseph F. Sanxay,
G. W. Abbe,

D. N. Tucker,
William Sharp,
John N. Sayer,
George Hatt, Sec'y.

THIRD DISTRICT.
Wm. A. Francis,
John Ramsay,
E. W. Page,
L. Wetmore,
Jas. Beatty,
W. D. Harris,
V. Lecount,
E. L. Fancher,
R. Lewis,
O. W. Norton Sec'y.

FOURTH DISTRICT.
Adam Pearson,
T. R. Kenney.
Alexander J. Henderson,

H. Whitlesey,
S. Fanning,
G. H. Traphagen, M. D.
L. F. Wheeler,
John Barry,
Hiram Hurd,
T. R. Ryers,
Martin Kingman,
H. Lockwood,
John Buxton, jr.
James R. Gedney,
T. H. Burras,
Henry Whittlesey, Sec'y.

FIFTH DISTRICT.
J. J. Greenough,
A. R. Wetmore,
Lemuel G. Evans,
T. V. Forster,
C. Adams,
O. W. Norton,

VISITORS.

A. Wakeman,
John Thompson,
H. S. Terbell,
R. Lawrence,
N. P. Hossack,
Wm. Van Allen,
V. Elliot.
Wm. Forrest,
J. H. Redfield,
David Terry,
J. F. Bridges,
Robert Pattison,
W. D. Smith,
S. S. Ward,
Robert Carter,
George T. Cobb,
P. Duryea,
J. E. Goddard,
W. Steele.
O. W. Norton Sec'y.

SIXTH DISTRICT.

William Ballagh,
Daniel Fisher,
John M. Clawson,
Benjamin Marshall, M. D.,
Frederick Lockwood,
J. McClaury, M. D.,
Moses B. Taylor,
Peter Burnett, M. D.
A. Florentine,
Geo. W. Lowere,
C. V. Rivenburgh, M. D.
Abraham Forbes,
Daniel A. Webster,
Samuel Baxter,
Benjamin B. Forbes,
Reub. S. Carpentier, M. D.
John G. Sperling.
Amzi Camp, Sec'y.

SEVENTH DISTRICT.

J. Sammis,
C. L. Nichols,
T. Warren,
J. B. Horton,
R. S. Place,
A. P. McNaughton,
G. Walsh,
B. R. Smith,
J. W. Goodwin,
J. P. Bremner,
H. C. Martin,
A. B. Ludlum,
B. G. Bruce,
Wm. A. Van Nostrand,
Andrew Lytle,
Stephen Cutler
Jona. B. Horton, Sec'y.

EIGHTH DISTRICT.

Joseph B. Collins,
O. D. McClain,
Isaac Gibson,

Daniel Conover,
James F. Stansbery,
Albert S. Smith,
Thomas Bailay,
William Johnston,
J. S. Holt,
Charles C. Dyer,
Louis J. Belloni,
Henry W. Ryerson,
C. P. Dakin,
P. A. Bogert,
John Endicott,
Edward Fields, M.D.,
John Gillelan,
Stewart E. Clark,
Darias Geer,
Frederick J. Coffin,
William Kirby, Sec'y.

NINTH DISTRICT.

John Ruston,
Joseph Houghton,
Nathan Peck,
Reuben Ayres,
Caleb C. Tracey,
Henry P. See,
H. W. Deems,
Walter Greenough,
C. P. Tucker, M. D.,
Benjamin F. Curtis,
William Martin,
William A. Foster,
Samuel J. Smith,
Welcome R. Beebe,
Leander See,
Thomas Fessenden,
Daniel F. Lee,
John Murray,
E. H. Payton,
John Carson,
George D. Cragin,
M. H. Howell.
John Ruston, Sec'y.

TENTH DISTRICT.

J. S. Reynolds,
Smith Downs,
Joseph M. Bell,
James Horn,
James Weir,
William Wheaton,
Andrew V. Stout,
Edward A. Fraser,
Corn. V. Clarkson, M.D.,
J. W. Sherwood,
Joseph W. Wentworth.
Hon. Van Ardsdale, M.D.,
Samuel Smith,
C. N. Churchwell,
Thomas Jackson,
Charles Place,
Edmund Anderson,
William C. Bradley,
John D. McCreary.
J. P. Lestrade, Sec'y.

ELEVENTH DISTRICT.

C. W. Hawkins,
Bennett Wilson,
Joel Kelly,
Thomas Hogan,
William Murphy,
W. E. Teall, M.D.,
John Lewis,
S. Houghwout,
Isaiah E. Stuckey,
William Bennett,
John Young,
Henry Taff,
John Camron,
J. Lewis,
John Reynolds,
C. Waldron,
Seth S. Chapin,
W. C. Barbour,
Joseph Hall,
James Price,
Moses Gardner,
S. C. Malory.
Grant Dubois, Sec'y.

THIRTEENTH DISTRICT.

Amos Bailey,
John Hutchings,
Samuel Fisk,
Elias Mills,
John R. Marsh,
George W. Bowne,
John Burr,
Charles A. Merrick,
Charles I. Harris,
Henry Wood,
Charles Merrill,
Isaac Abrams,
John W. Conover,
Abraham Trafford,
Francis Duncan,
Ferris Finch,
Andrew J. Case,
Erastus Williams,
Richard W. Moore,
Samuel Leech.
Noah Coe, Sec'y.

FOURTEENTH DISTRICT.

Bezaleel Howe,
Nelson Stelle, M. D.,
William Post,
Adam W. Spies,
Bezaleel Howe,
H. Miller,
William Johnson,
Charles M. Thomas,
Richard Brown,
Peter Carter,
J. J. Jenkins,
J. M. Howe, M. D.,
Aaron Hardman,
Thomas Fairweather,
Robert Rae,
Gideon Peck,

VISITORS.

Alexander W. Murray,
Daniel W. Teller.
William Gray, Sec'y.

FIFTEENTH DISTRICT.
George L. Storer,
Edward Vanderpool,
Frederick Pattillow,
John L. Fendall,
Rev. Isaac Orchard,
Henry Henshe,
Cornelius R. Disosway,
Benjamin Lord,
John Mollard.
Isaac Orchard, Sec'y.

SIXTEENTH DISTRICT.
H. K Bull,
Joseph Merrill,
J. A. Hubbard,
B. M. Fowler,
L. W. Halsey,
H. Dunn.
D. Coleman,
James Cowl,
Jacob Smith,
Asa Smith,
Thomas J. Burger,
John Taylor,
D. Chichester,
C. H. Tucker,
Joseph Longking,
D. S. Young,
John Parr,
S. Walling,
B. Pettit,

E. T. Winter, M. D.,
John Brady,
John Ives, M. D.,
William Heydon,
E. S. Yocom,
James F. Duff,
J. D. Adams,
James Kerney,
Richard Davies,
J. C. Hines,
J. F. Chamberlain.
Charles C. Darling, Sec'y.

SEVENTEENTH DISTRICT.
Henry McDougal,
R Albro,
James Duff,
C. H. Redman,
H. Griffin,
William B. Humbert,
William A. Lockwood,
J. S. Bowron, M. D.,
Ceorge Manning Tracy,
A. L Halsted,
Thomas Jeremiah,
William Stebbins,
Chauncey Shaffer,
James R. Gibson,
Jacob Aims,
James M. Cockcroft,
Henry Brown,
Isaac Labagh,
D. C. Weeks,
William Wagstaff,
D. T. Staniford.
Richard Horton, Sec'y.

EIGHTEENTH DISTRICT.
J. W. Benedict,
George L Hyslop.
Leonard Hazeltine,
J. C. Huntington,
James Armstrong,
J. H. Lyman,
Jacob L. Halsey,
Edward Roberts,
J. W Warner,
J. W. Oliver,
C. C. Savage,
J. B. Ballard,
W. A. Butler,
N. R. Long,
S. S. Wheeler,
J. B. Ballard, Sec'y.

NINETEENTH DISTRICT.
David E. Bartlett,
John C. Miller,
Abijah Pell,
Charles M. Lowerre,
Smith W. Bullock,
O. W. Morris,
Edward E. Rankin,
James W. Macomber,
Jotham Wilson,
John C. Parker,
John H. Moss,
John W. Patrick,
J. Wilson.
Enoch Mack, Sec'y.

BY-LAWS.

ARTICLE I.

Every person who becomes an annual Subscriber, a member of an Advisory Committee, or a Visitor, shall be a member of the Association.

ARTICLE II.

The President and Secretaries shall perform such duties as usually pertain to their office.

ARTICLE III.

The Treasurer shall give such security for the faithful performance of the trust reposed in him, as the Association may demand and approve. He shall take in charge all funds; keep an account of all receipts and disbursements; and pay all duly authorized demands. At the annual meeting, he shall render a particular and correct statement of all his receipts and disbursements to the Association. He shall also exhibit a summary report to the Board of Managers at their stated meetings, and whenever called upon by them for that purpose.

ARTICLE IV.

The Board of Managers shall have exclusive control of the funds of the Association, and authority to make By-laws; to fill vacancies; appoint all committees; and generally to adopt such measures as the objects of the Institution may require. It shall meet for the transaction of business, on the second Monday of every month; and the annual meeting of the Association shall be convened on the second Monday of

November, when the Board shall submit a report of its proceedings, and the officers and managers be chosen. In case of a failure to hold the specified meeting in November, a special meeting for the same purpose shall be convened in the course of the ensuing month.

ARTICLE V.

Special meetings of the Board of Managers and of the Supervisory Council, may be called by the Secretary, at the request of the President, or on receiving a requisition signed by five members. Two days' notice must be given of the time of meeting.

ARTICLE VI.

The Managers may at any time make such alterations in these By-Laws, as may be deemed necessary; provided they be not contrary to the Act of Incorporation, and that such alteration shall be submitted to the Board of Managers at least one meeting before the same is acted upon; and that it shall not be passed upon unless specified in the call of the meeting, and when a majority of the whole number of the Board of Managers is present.

ARTICLE VII.

An office shall be opened in an eligible situation, for the purpose of concentrating and diffusing all information pertaining to the Society's operations and objects, and for the transaction of its general business.

ARTICLE VIII.

It shall be the duty of the General Agent to devote himself with diligence and fidelity to the affairs of the Association.

ARTICLE IX.

The city shall be divided into eighteen Districts, each Ward forming a District; and the districts be subdivided into Sections. Each District shall have an Advisory Committee, to consist of five members; and each Section a Visitor.

ARTICLE X.

It shall be the duty of the Advisory Committee to divide their Districts into such Sections, as to apportion to each about twenty-five families requiring attention; endeavor to obtain suitable Visitors for each Section; supply vacancies which may occur; make the necessary arrangements for placing at the disposal of the Visitors food, fuel, and clothing, for distribution; and on some day in the first week of every month (excepting the meetings of July and August, which may be omitted in the discretion of the Committees), to convene all the Visitors of the Sections, for the purpose of receiving their returns, and conferring with them on the objects of their mutual labors. The Committees, moreover, shall duly draw upon the Treasurer for such proportion of the funds as may be appropriated to their Districts; they shall keep a strict account of all their disbursements, and only in extreme cases make donations of money; they shall monthly render an account of their expenditures to the Board of Managers; and in default of this duty, shall not be entitled to draw upon the funds of the Association. Each Committee shall appoint its own chairman, Secretary, and Treasurer, and shall transmit the Reports of the Visitors immediately after each monthly meeting, with any other information they may think desirable, to the General Secretary.

ARTICLE XI.

It shall be the duty of each Visitor to confine his labors exclusively to the particular section assigned him, so that no individual shall receive relief, excepting in the Section where he is known, and to which he belongs. The Visitors shall carefully investigate all cases referred to them before granting relief; ascertain the condition, habits of life, and means of subsistence of the applicants; and extend to all such kind services, counsel, and assistance, as a discriminating and judicious regard for their present and permanent welfare requires. And in case of sickness, it will be their duty to inquire whether there is any medical or other attendance needed; whether relief is afforded by any religious or charitable society; to provide themselves with information respecting the nearest Dispensary, and in all cases, when practicable, to refer applicants for aid to appropriate existing societies. When no other assistance is provided or available, they shall draw from the resources of this Association—not money, which is never allowed to be given, except with the consent of the Advisory Committee or a member thereof—but such articles of food, fuel, clothing, and similar supplies as the necessities of the case require. In all cases of want coming to the knowledge of the Visitors, they will be expected to perform the same duties, although no application has been made. It shall be their duty, moreover, to render a report of their labors, and also an account of all their disbursements, to their respective Committees, at the stated monthly meeting. No Visitor neglecting these duties will be entitled to draw on the funds of the Association.

ARTICLE XII.

The Board of Managers, the members of the Advisory Committees, and certain elected members, shall together constitute a Supervisory Council, whose duties shall be deliberative and advisory; and its annual meetings be held on the second Monday of November, in each year. Special meetings of this body shall be held, when called by the Board of Managers.

ARTICLE XIII.

It shall be the duty of the members of the Association to endeavor, in all suitable ways, to give practical effect to its principles; especially to discountenance indiscriminate alms-giving and street-begging; to provide themselves with tickets of reference; and instead of giving aid to unknown applicants, whose case they cannot themselves investigate, to refer such applications to the Visitor of the Section in which the applicants reside, in order that such cases may properly be inquired into, and, if deserving, relieved.

ARTICLE XIV.

The printed forms of tickets and orders for relief, shall be designated by the Board of Managers, and no other shall be used.

INCORPORATION.

CERTIFICATE OF INTENTION

TO INCORPORATE THE NEW-YORK ASSOCIATION FOR IMPROVING THE CONDITION OF THE POOR.

THE undersigned, being each and every of them of full age, and citizens of the State of New-York, desiring to associate themselves for the benevolent and charitable objects hereinafter expressed, that they may become a body politic and corporate, and be enabled to conduct the business of the Association in the City and County of New-York, according to the provisions of an "Act for the Incorporation of Benevolent, Charitable, Scientific, and Missionary purposes," passed April 12th, 1848, do for these purposes hereby certify,

I. That the name and title by which such Institution shall be known in law, is the "New-York Association for Improving the Condition of the Poor."

II. That the particular business and objects of such Association shall be the elevation of the physical and moral condition of the indigent; and so far as is compatible with these objects, the relief of their necessities.

III. That the Board of Managers to manage the same shall consist of one President, five Vice-Presidents, one Treasurer, one Corresponding Secretary and General Agent, one Recording Secretary, the Chairman of each Advisory Committee, or as his proxy, some other member of said Committee, and four members to be chosen by said Board of Managers.

IV. That the following named persons shall constitute the Board of Managers for the first year, to wit: James Brown, President; George Griswold, J. Smyth Rogers, James Boorman, James Lenox, and Horatio Allen, Vice-Presidents; Robert B. Minturn, Treasurer; Robert M. Hartley, Corresponding Secretary and General Agent; Joseph B. Collins, Recording Secretary; together with the following elected Members and Chairmen of the Advisory Committees, namely: Stewart

Brown, Frederick S. Winston, Erastus C. Benedict, John R. Ludlow, Daniel S. Briant, William Gale, Peter G. Arcularius, Abraham Fardon, Jr., Apollos R. Wetmore, Nicholas C. Everett, Calvin Tracy, James O. Pond, James Horn, Samuel P. Patterson, Lewis Chichester, Adam W. Spies, Thomas Denny, Luther Jackson, Stephen C. Lynes, and F. Ellsworth Mather.

In witness whereof, we hereunto have subscribed our names, in the city of New-York, this the eleventh day of December, in the year of our Lord one thousand eight hundred and forty-eight.

JAMES BROWN,	APOLLOS R. WETMORE,
GEORGE GRISWOLD,	NICHOLAS C. EVERETT,
J. SMYTH ROGERS,	CALVIN TRACY,
JAMES BOORMAN,	JAMES O. POND,
HORATIO ALLEN,	JAMES HORN,
ROBERT M. HARTLEY,	LEWIS CHICHESTER,
JOSEPH B. COLLINS,	ADAM W. SPIES,
STEWART BROWN,	THOMAS DENNY,
FREDERICK S. WINSTON,	LUTHER JACKSON,
DANIEL S. BRIANT,	STEPHEN C. LYNES,
PETER G. ARCULARIUS,	F. ELLSWORTH MATHER.
ABRAHAM FARDON, JR.,	

Witness as to all the signatures, D. F. CURRY.

City and County of New-York, [ss.]: On the eleventh day of December, A.D. 1848, before me came George Griswold, J. Smyth Rogers, Horatio Allen, Joseph B. Collins, Luther Jackson, Abraham Fardon, Jr., Lewis Chichester, Daniel S. Briant, Nicholas C. Everett, James O. Pond, Adam W. Spies, F. Ellsworth Mather, James Horn, Frederick S. Winston, Peter G. Arcularius, Stephen C. Lynes, Calvin Tracy, and Robert M. Hartley; and on the 12th day of December, A.D. 1848, before me came James Brown, Stewart Brown, and James Boorman; and on the 13th day of December, A.D. 1848, before me came Apollos R. Wetmore and Thomas Denny, to me known to be the same persons described in and who executed the foregoing instrument, who severally acknowledged that they executed the foregoing instrument, for the purposes therein mentioned.

D. F. CURRY, Commissioner.

I approve of the within Certificate, and allow the same to be filed.

H. P. EDWARDS, Justice Supreme Court.
New-York, December 14, 1848.

STATE OF NEW-YORK, SECRETARY'S OFFICE, } Albany, Dec. 16, 1848.

I certify that the Certificate of Incorporation of the "New-York Association for Improving the Condition of the Poor," was received and filed this day in this office.

ARCH'D CAMPBELL,
Dept. Sec. of State.

SEVENTH ANNUAL REPORT

OF THE

NEW-YORK ASSOCIATION FOR IMPROVING THE CONDITION OF THE POOR.

ON the recurrence of another Anniversary, the Seventh in the history of this Association, the Board of Managers would respectfully present their Annual Report.

During the labors of the year, now closed, nothing of unusual interest has transpired. The Institution has steadily pursued its wonted course, increasing, it is believed, in efficiency and public confidence, as its principles have become better understood and applied.

The first emotions of the Board on a review, are those of devout gratitude to Divine Providence for the continued prosperity of the Association, and of thankful acknowledgment to the numerous friends and donors, by whose pecuniary liberality its operations have been sustained.

Suitable thanks are also due to the Advisory Committees and Visitors, to whose faithful and efficient exertions, the organization is pre-eminently indebted for its usefulness and success. The great majority of these are no longer novices, likely to err in judgment, or to be deceived by the froward, the artful and designing, to the prejudice of the retiring and more deserving poor. Their long experience has made them quick and skilful to discern the seeming from the real; and so intelligently and judiciously to adapt the provisions of this charity, to whatever is peculiar in the physical and moral condition of each applicant, as that imposture may be detected and reproved, and all proper subjects participate in the important benefits which it aims to confer.

Among the prominent manifestations of interest in the Institution, the Board would not fail to record a bequest of *two thousand dollars*, by MISS S. DEMILT, deceased; also the announcement of a legacy of *two thousand dollars* by THOMAS FRISELL THOMPSON, Esq., deceased, both of this city. Fully appreciating these and similar testimonials of confidence in the Association, they are endeavoring to effect arrangements, by which the expressed wishes of the benevolent individuals who made these liberal bequests, shall be literally fulfilled.

To the Editors of the secular and religious press, during the past, as in former years, the Association has been greatly indebted; and to them, in behalf of the organization, the Board would renew their thanks. By their disinterested advocacy of this charity, not only has this great community been informed of its nature and objects, but by widely diffusing a knowledge of its principles and modes of action abroad, other communities have adopted the system, so that not less than ten of the principal cities in the United States are now enjoying its advantages.

One characteristic feature of the year's operations has been to *do more than hitherto for the permanent elevation of the indigent*. The sympathy which depresses character, while it disposes to relieve suffering, the Visitors understand, and sedulously endeavor to avoid. The disposition is not to do less pecuniarily, but more morally, by making alms not an end in itself, but the means of a higher and greater good, so that every outlay, by tending to improve the character and condition of the recipients, may at once diminish the number and prevent their increase. To save one family from falling into pauperism, or to rescue one from such a state and restore it to self-dependence, is obviously a greater private and public benefit, than would be the gratuitous support of such a family, to the end of life. And the Board have the satisfaction to report, as the statistics will show, that the number of such cases far exceed those of any preceding year.

But such results have not been attained without immense labor, nor are they under any circumstances unattended with difficulties. It is a great mistake to imagine that reforms are matters of course, or are always the reward of faithful effort. Pauperism is too stubborn and inveterate an evil to be remedied without the co-operation of those who suffer it. There are, it is true, many in the city, who, though industrious, frugal, and prudent, have, by reason of sickness, bereavement, and other unavoidable calamities, been reduced to want and suffering. There is nothing they more dread than the mortification and debasement of public relief, and nothing they more desire for themselves, and especially for their children, than to regain their former independence.— But despite of their best exertions, they are overtaken by want and need a helping hand. To such, the sympathy, counsel, and aid of the Visitor are most welcome. Seasonable relief comes without humiliating exposure. Their sinking spirits are revived, their energies are redoubled ; they are saved from sinking into that gulf of pauperism which they abhor, and from which recovery is so doubtful and difficult. But there are others, chiefly of foreign birth and mendicant habits, who are so degraded in spirit and wedded to debasement, that the task of interesting them in efforts so as to effect their own rescue, is well nigh hopeless. Those only know who have made the trial, how much of time, and means, and exertion, are sometimes expended on this abject class, without any seeming compensatory results. But even such are not abandoned in discouragement; for this would augment the number of the ignorant and depraved, and rivet upon the community the intolerable evils of a rapidly increasing pauperism. Some of this class have been reformed, and others may; but if parents are irreclaimable, it is not thus with their children. The offspring of the poor are as susceptible to kindness and to the impression of all good influences as the children of the rich. Consequently, among the most unpromising is found a vast field of usefulness; and the Visitors, improving the abundant facilities afforded for the moral and mental culture of the young, by the admirable systems of Sabbath and Public School instruction, are enabled to draw multitudes from ignorance and exposure to vice, and place them in circumstances the most favorable to their future virtue and respectability. Though all, in this respect, may not have been done which the deplorable condition of thousands requires; yet, in no previous year, has so much been effected to diminish juvenile mendicity, to check the growth of the pauper class, and to rescue those who had fallen into it.

Another prominent object in the labors of the year appears in the *more careful regulation of the amount and duration of relief.* In this particular no new principle has been introduced, for it has ever been a fundamental rule of the Association, not to give more than is necessary, nor to prolong relief beyond the duration of the necessity which calls for it. In former years, less attention was given to this rule than it merited; and injury to the beneficiaries, as also an unnecessary and burdensome increase of dependents and expenditure, were the consequences. But the evils of departing from so salutary a regulation, becoming increasingly manifest, special efforts the past year have been made for its more general observance ; and the results have been so beneficial, it is hoped such efforts will not relax until the operation of this important rule becomes universal. The Board are acquainted with no other system of relief on a large scale, in which the cautious principle referred to, is a constituent. It is not found in the out-door charity of our city authorities. A person, for example, registered by them at the beginning of a season, as entitled to aid, receives it to the end. This tends to pauperize the spirit and paralyze exertion, by engendering an habitual dependence on alms, rather than upon industry, and occasions an immense expenditure which might be avoided. Very different are the provisions and effects of this system. Relief to-day affording no pledge of a like supply to-morrow, the poor are constantly urged by the pressure of their necessities, to rely only upon their own efforts; and finding, if they fail to do this, they are left to suffer the consequences, the strong instinct of self-preservation stimulates them to the utmost diligence, and activity. Every desirable moral and physical result may be expected to follow in the train of such a system. And nothing less than such effects could be predicated of a system, that is founded on the divine law, which declares " If any man will not work, neither shall he eat."[*] And experience shows that this great law cannot be violated, by separating disobedience thereto from its appointed penalty, without encouraging that curse of populous communities, able-bodied pauperism. Every scheme of alms-giving, in short, is essentially defective, and will be rife with evils, that does not extend, restrict, and modify relief, according to the exigencies of each individual case.

[*] 2 Thes. iii. 10.

Another marked feature in the operations of the year, has been the effort *to diminish the number of those who habitually depend on alms.* It is well known to be the beneficent design of the Association, to elevate the poor to the condition of self-support, rather than to sustain them by charity. And there being great reason to fear that the relief of the same families, however deserving, from year to year, would militate against such a result, the principles of the Institution and the best interests of the class in question, alike required the use of such measures, as would tend to break up reliance on gratuitous aid, and urge all physically able, to earn their own subsistence. So important appeared the subject to the Board, that they caused a circular and an alphabetical list, containing the name and residence of more than twelve hundred such families, to be distributed among the Visitors, inviting their co-operation to effect such a reform, as the object in view required. They recommended that such families be visited in a friendly way, be reminded how long they have been aided, and that all able to work, be faithfully warned against depending upon this or any other charity. It was believed, if they could be induced to improve the season when expenses are diminished and labor most abounds, so as to save a small sum each week for deposit in the Savings' Bank, many would thereafter be able to subsist without alms, and a sense of self-respect and praiseworthy independence be promoted. Sufficient time has not yet elapsed to reveal the full effects of this movement, but enough has been developed to show that it was seasonable and proper, and will be attended with excellent results.

The Board in this connection would remark, that those who have long received the aid and kind attentions of the Association, without giving any evidence of improvement, thereby show their connection with a class that is not likely to be elevated by ordinary means, and some other mode of action with respect to them should be adopted. The nature of that action, the circumstances of each will indicate. It does not follow that all such persons should be denied relief; this, the design of the Association and the dictates of humanity may alike forbid. But as all experience, alas! shows that the evils of want and the cold hand of necessity must often be permitted to press on some descriptions of the poor, to spur them to exertion, so a very decided course has been recommended, when necessary, in order to arouse the indolent and thriftless, to the duty of self-maintenance.

As a corollary to these various labors, *there has been a striking diminution in the number of the dependent poor,* as compared with the previous year. During the year ending November 1st, 1849, 6672 families were relieved, containing 29,844 persons. In the course of the year just closed, but 5725 familes were aided, comprising 25,762 persons, thus exhibiting a decrease of 847 families, numbering 3,811 persons. The cause of this great disparity in the relief of two successive years, may in part be attributed to the prevalence of the cholera in 1849; but as will appear, this does not account for all the difference. Two processes being in operation to increase the relative number of the poor, it was, perhaps, a reasonable expectation that they would increase above the ratio of the population. Many of the rich and prosperous are removing from the city, while the poor are rapidly pressing in, especially by foreign emigration. In the three years and six months, preceding September 6th, 1850, the almost incredible number af 710.315 alien emigrants, landed at this port, exclusive of the multitudes of the destitute who arrived here by the ports of other States and the British Provinces. It is not known what per cent. of the above continue here, but it is certain that most of the provident, energetic class go into the interior, while the idle and thriftless chiefly remain. And though a special department has been formed for the care of indigent aliens, yet, as many of them refuse this provision and throw themselves on private charity, they greatly increase the aggregate of the needy, and become an oppressive burden to this Association. Notwithstanding, however, the immense influx of foreign immigrants, and the peculiar exposure of the city to pauperism, from this and other sources, it does not appear that the outdoor poor are increasing above the ratio of the increase of the inhabitants, but that they are actually *falling below it.* And though some have expressed their belief, that the tendencies of this Institution, however wisely conducted, were to augment the dependent class, the contrary appears to be the fact. To show, therefore, the fallacy of such opinions, which impliedly condemn as mischievous all organized charity, and to set at the same time, the influence of the Association, in this respect, in a true light, the following statistics of the relief granted by it since its formation, are subjoined. And let it be remembered, that it is not *a priori* reasonings, but facts and figures, which furnish a basis for all just conclusions on such subjects.

Year.	Families relieved.	Persons relieved.
In 1844	6,251	28,062
" 1845	5,737	25,816
" 1846	5,470	24,615
" 1847	5,580	25,116
" 1848	5,340	24,630
" 1849	6,672	29,844
" 1850	5,725	25,762

The foregoing statements may require a word of explanation. In 1844, the mechanism of a new organization was set in motion by persons unacquainted with its structure, and the numerous difficulties ever inseparable from a new enterprise, were unavoidably encountered. Under such circumstances, it is not surprising that relief was given more freely than a larger experience would justify. Hence it appears, that excepting the season of cholera, in 1849, more persons were aided in 1844, than in any other year since the establishment of the Institution. And it further appears, that as the principles on which relief should be given were better understood and applied, greater discrimination was exercised, so that the number aided in 1850 was *twenty-three hundred less* than in 1844. This result is the more encouraging and remarkable, because the increased thoroughness and expansion of the Association's labors, were least likely to overlook any proper subject of relief; and viewed in connection with the enormous increase of the population by foreign immigration during the same period, the fact is believed to be anomalous in the history of similar charities. It proves moreover, that the Association is not only preventing the spread of pauperism, as it promised to do, but is absolutely diminishing its actual and relative amount.

With such results, the Association has been content to adhere another year to the few well understood, and plainly defined objects for which it was originally organized, rejecting whatever might in any degree embarrass its operations, or endanger its usefulness and stability. It might, as it has often been urged to do, have entered upon a more diversified field of labor, by undertaking to diffuse a larger amount of moral influence, to adopt plans for the employment of the poor, and assume other responsibilities, besides those now contemplated. But admonished by the failure of so many similar attempts, in this and other cities, the necessity of great caution has been felt, and the determination avowed at the establishment of the Institution has ever been respected, to wit, that the co-operation of the public should be asked to no plan, the practicability of which was not reasonably certain, and which, if commenced, would not probably be attended by the desired results.

Seven years' experience has justified the wisdom of the course pursued, and induced a growing distrust of the clamor for the rights of labor, and pledges to supply it, as of doubtful utility. The Association professes not to meddle with the metaphysics of political economy, nor would the limit or the design of this Report, admit their discussion. But as providing employment for the poor is a subject of deep interest in itself, and to many, because of the connection observed to exist between physical condition and moral elevation, the Board deem it in place to submit a few considerations by which they have been governed, and which may tend to correct some of the popular mistakes on the subject.

It is evident that the resources of our city, however fully developed, can give employment only to a limited number. This fact discloses the origin of the difficulty with respect to labor. It consists simply in the concentration of a larger number in a locality, than such locality can employ. In other words, it is an excess of laborers beyond the demand, which inevitably diminishes the rewards of industry, and leaves many unemployed. Large cities, from the attractions which they present to adventurers, are constantly exposed to this evil, for which their own resources cannot, in the nature of things, provide an adequate remedy. Hence the uniform failure of all the oft-repeated attempts of the philanthropic, to furnish labor for the redundant population of such places. It is demonstrable, that beyond a certain limit, which limit is defined by what may be termed the law of reciprocity, there can be no demand for labor, because the community is supplied to its utmost capacity. It follows that the surplus laborers, if they remain, for the time being are doomed to idleness: and if without means to suffer the miseries of want, unless relieved by the hand of charity. Evidently no association of citizens is competent to change this state of things, by creating permanent employment beyond the actual demand. For such a result presupposes a sudden increase of capital, enterprise, commerce, manufactures, and, indeed, of all the elements essential to a state of unwonted prosperity, to an extent which shall put in requisition the labor of all the unemployed. All this too must be done and permanently sustained by artificial means, in direct opposition to those inflexible principles and natural processes, by which such results alone can be secured.

Nor does the difficulty end here. Admitting, for the sake of the argument, that the desired object was for once attained, and the thousands of the unemployed men, women and children in the city were provided with work, the knowledge of this fact would attract other thousands, equally needy and deserving; these supplied, others would press in, and so onward *ad infinitum*, always leaving the demand unsatisfied, and the community in as necessitous a state as it was before any thing was attempted.

The great number of the unemployed, moreover, aggravates the difficulty of providing relief. If there were but a few scores or a few hundreds in this destitute condition, their case might possibly be reached by the special exertions of the benevolent. But when they amount to thousands, of diverse occupations, as is generally the case in this city, to supply them with employment becomes a matter altogether too vast and complex to be undertaken by any association, however ample its resources.

Is it urged that temporary and not permanent employment is contemplated? In reply it may be said, that nothing less than permanent employment will meet the exigence; for here, there is always a large deficit of labor. But waiving the further consideration of this point, and admit that only temporary employment is required, this circumstance neither affects the premises nor the conclusions to which they lead. If all the existing wants of the community for labor are supplied, leaving a large surplus of unemployed persons, it does not appear how any association can create a new demand beyond this, even for a week or a month. If by the interference and special exertions of a third party, such information be given the needy as that they are enabled obtain temporary employment, this, it is obvious, would be a very different matter from creating a demand for labor; the result would merely prove, that the demand for labor previously existed, which demand would of itself eventually have put in requisition the services of the unemployed to the extent required, without any foreign agency whatever.

It is also found that deficiencies of labor are often aggravated by fluctuations of business, which suddenly and sometimes unexpectedly deprive many persons of employment.—But when such is the case, it is evident that the case itself is beyond the control of an association of private citizens, who must share themselves in the common disaster. When employment fails from this cause, the chief difference is that the suffering consequent upon it will be of shorter duration, and that time will work the remedy. All that can be done is to mitigate the force of the calamity, where it falls most heavily.—For to prevent such a state of things, or to reverse the results, and give employment to the unemployed when no demand exists for their labor, is evidently impracticable.

Without enlarging on these views, the course which should be pursued with respect to the *able-bodied unemployed poor* is clearly indicated. A wide distinction should evidently be made between them and the *impotent*. If the hale and vigorous cannot earn their subsistence here, they should earn it elsewhere. There should be no pledges of employment, which are generally deceptive and mischievous; and no proffer of comfortable alms-houses or of liberal out-door relief, to encourage them to remain. On the contrary, their own best interests, and those of the community, require that every proper motive and influence should be presented, and every practicable facility afforded to induce them to migrate.— And in order to effect this, we possess decided advantages over the crowded cities of the old world. There, they are obliged to provide local relief, because the rural districts are filled to their utmost capacity, and afford no outlet. It is very different in this country. If our cities are burdened with a population beyond the means of employment and subsistence, the country is ample, and abounds with all the essential elements of plenty and prosperity. Providence has bestowed upon us a vast extent of unoccupied territorial surface, with a fertile soil and genial climate, for the benefit of our fellow-men; and considerations of humanity, self-security and economy, alike urge us, so far as is practicable, to put the suffering and needy in possession of these advantages. And in order to effect this, the city should be stripped of the attractions it presents to this class; for while these exist, many of the able-bodied poor will remain, to become an intolerable tax and scourge to the community. The greatest kindness that can be shown them, is to cause them, if necessary, by rigorous measures, to choose the interior for their home, where, by honest industry, they may recover self-respect and independence, and become blessings instead of burdens to the country. This, it is believed, is the principle with respect to them, which should govern all the organized and unorganized charities of the city.

The Boston Employment Society, having discovered the utter inutility of seeking labor for the unemployed poor, where it could not be found, is now acting on the policy above suggested. To all unsuccessful applicants for work, the advice is to leave the city at once, and seek it in the interior. And more, there is reason to believe, have found relief by following this counsel, than in any other way. To deter persons, moreover, abroad, from coming to the city for that object, the Society published an official manifesto, earnestly recommending all the unemployed, who would avoid disappointment, and loss of time and money, not to hope for success in Boston. The inference from these facts is obvious. If true philanthropy renders such measures necessary in that city, it is much more important and necessary that a similar policy should be pursued in this, where the evil in question is experienced in a tenfold degree.

The impotent poor, and those who by unavoidable calamity require temporary aid, comprise a class with which all are so familiar, that little need be said about them. The same high authority which declares, "the poor shall never cease out of the land," also says, " thou shalt open thy hand wide unto thy poor brother ; thou shalt surely give him, and thy heart shall not be grieved when thou givest unto him."— Hence the claims of this class to kindness and sympathy is as equitable as their necessities are imperative ; and such claims carry with them the acquiescence of every benevolent heart. In the judicious relief of such, there is nothing artificial or hurtful—nothing which traverses or disturbs the beautiful designs or beneficent processes of nature so as to distemper society—nothing utopian or romantic, to undermine virtue or subvert right feeling—nothing that is exacting or compulsory, at which the heart revolts. On the contrary, Providence has provided an unfailing source of relief for all such, in one of the strongest and noblest of human instincts. It is a provision, moreover, which needs no importunity. All that it asks is, that it may be directed to proper objects ; and to select such objects, and provide a channel through which alms may flow to the needy of this class without perversion or abuse, is the design of this organization. How well it fulfils this design, let the records of the past decide.

If such a system of relief as this does not deserve confidence, in what other shall it be placed ? All will admit that, in dispensing charity, a distinction should be made between the virtuous and the vile, the industrious and the idle. How, then, and by whom, shall proper discrimination be exercised, and judicious relief be granted ? Shall unknown applicants be aided at our doors ? Such alms, in a great majority of cases, had far better be sunk in the sea, than be thus given to encourage vagrancy and street-begging, with all their appalling evils. Will the charitable visit the poor at their homes before relieving them ? Such a course, even if there was a disposition to do it, would be found utterly impracticable in this great city. It is a common artifice with the needy, and especially of impostors, not to seek relief in their own neighborhood, where their case can readily be examined, but in parts of the city so remote from their homes, that calling on them by those to whom they apply, is out of the question. But, unfortunately, there is little or no disposition to visit the poor before aiding them, or if in some instances attempted, the information obtained in a few hasty visits, particularly by the inexperienced, is too uncertain and defective to deserve confidence, so that with all their painstaking they are likely to be deceived, and pauperism in the end is promoted. The time was when fraud and deception were not, to the same extent as now, characteristics of our city poor, and aid could then have been given with less caution. But the immense influx of foreign mendicants of late years, has so generally deteriorated the character of the needy, that though many are now, doubtless, worthy of commiseration and aid, yet the only security against imposition is found in a *thorough system of personal investigation.*

And such is the system which this Association provides·

In the case of every strange applicant, whatever may be his story, or by whomsoever sent, personal investigation, except in very peculiar circumstances, invariably precedes relief. And this it is enabled to do, by its minute division of labor, numerous visitors, and methodical action, not only with surprising facility, but with the best practical results. Personal intercourse with the poor and their children, qualifies the visitor to act with intelligence and discrimination. If they are found worthy, he endeavors to extend relief, with such kindness and consideration as not to degrade, but so to elevate the recipients, physically and morally, as to save them from the humiliating necessity of receiving alms. If on the other hand the applicants are impostors, they will be detected; if idle and profligate, they will be earnestly reproved and counselled, with a view of improving their habits and amending their lives. It aims, in short, to accomplish a great social good, without the usual attendant evils; and possessing in a pre-eminent degree, as is believed, the essential requisites for the wise administration of charity in a large city, it asks the patronage of the benevolent, not as a perfect system, but as the best which human sagacity, with its present knowledge of the subject, can devise.

In order to keep pace with the rapid increase of population and growth of the city, the Board have found it necessary again to extend the Northern bounds of the Association so as to include the recently organized Nineteenth Ward.— The city is now divided into 317 sections, with a corresponding number of Visitors, being ten more than in the previous year. These are spread over the entire peninsula, extending from the Battery to Eighty-sixth Street, about six and a quarter miles; and from river to river, including a population of 450,000 souls.

As the Institution continues its operations without cessation throughout the year, the aggregate of the labors thus gratuitously performed, could it be stated, would appear incredible. Some idea of the amount may be inferred from the fact, that the statistical reports of these labors during the past year, fills nearly 4000 pages. But as the Association, with all its expansion, increase of Visitors, and multiform labors, carefully adapts its action to the various classes of the poor, and adopts every improvement which experience suggests, its operations continue to move on with progressive energy, economy, and effect.

The following is a tabular exhibit of the Monthly District Returns, from November 1st, 1849, to November 1st, 1850.

1849–50.	Number of Families Relieved.	Number of Persons do.	Number of Visits
November, . .	864	3,249	1,334
December, . .	2,225	8,267	3,580
January, . . .	3,926	14,825	6,490
February, . .	3,949	14,771	6,209
March, ...	3,381	12,686	3,281
April, ...	1,154	4,289	1,449
May, ...	592	2,234	871
June, ...	140	680	260
July, ...	131	564	243
August, . . .	182	764	276
September, . .	308	1,153	574
October, . . .	329	1,265	602

Receipts per contributions during the year, - $25,807 14
Disbursements for same period, - - - 23,821 99

Excess of contributions over disbursements, - $1,985 15

The Board having thus endeavored to condense into the limits of the Report, an outline of the year's operations, respectfully refer the subject, with all its interests, to the attentive consideration of the benevolent. Such cannot fail to observe that this organization is unlike every other, and that its claims to favor are correspondingly peculiar. Its action is not restricted to particular seasons, places, or persons; it undertakes no impracticable schemes, nor makes pledges it cannot redeem; it does not intrude on the natural sympathies and duties of relationship which God has wisely appointed for beneficent ends; nor supersede or interfere with existing charities. On the contrary, it overleaps all selfish, sectarian, and party objects, and becomes the friend, the ally, and coadjutor of all. It re-explores, indeed, the same ground, and having cared for those whom others may have overlooked, or that come not within their scope of relief, it passes beyond them, in its wider range, to other objects: it traverses every street, and lane, and alley, within the utmost bounds of this vast metropolis; it penetrates every cellar, and garret, and hovel, where the needy are found, and, without respect to difference of creeds, color, or country, ministers to all not otherwise provided for, in a way to benefit the recipient and promote the best interests of the community. It supplies, in a word, the acknowledged deficiencies in other charities, private, associate, and public; and, by its nicely adjusted machinery, numerous agents, and continuous action, furnishes a complete system of eleemosynary relief, which, if adequately sustained, will afford *an insurance against imposition and suffering from want,* to the extent it is or may be confided in, *for the entire city.*

But let it not be forgotten, that the Institution, with all its array of instrumentalities and self-sacrificing labors, is only the almoner of the benevolent. They have called it into existence, and on their bounty it depends for continuance. If the necessary means are supplied, it will do its appropriate work; if these are stinted or withheld, its operations, in like degree, will be crippled or fail, pauperism be increased, and an incalculable amount of suffering inevitably ensue. But better things are confidently anticipated, than such fears would indicate. It cannot be that the needy in a Christian community will be neglected, by the followers of Him, who, for our sake became poor, houseless, and dependent; and whose example and teachings show how deep, and tender, and abiding were the claims of the needy to his regard. For His sake thousands have liberally contributed for their relief; are there not other thousands who will do likewise? Waiving the *imperative duty* of giving, who would willingly forego the *privilege* of sharing in so noble a work? All above want, have something to spare for the less fortunate. Let each one give as God has prospered him, remembering who hath said, "With what measure ye mete, it shall be measured to you again," and "The blessing of him who was ready to perish shall come upon him; and the widow's heart sing for joy."

PRINTED FORMS USED BY THE ASSOCIATION.

Ticket of Reference for the use of Members.

Mr.   Visitor,
   No.   St.
is requested to visit
at No.

                                                           Member
                              N. Y. Association for
                        Improving the Condition of the Poor.

Visitor's Order.

   Mr.
   No.   St.
Please let
have the value of
in
                                184
                                                            Vis.
                              N. Y. Association for
                        Improving the Condition of the Poor.

Monthly Report.

Subjoined is a condensed plan of a Sectional Monthly Return. The original occupies a large page of foolscap, with appropriate columns, fifteen in number, which enable Visitors to give the following particulars of every family relieved. 1st. Name, residence, place of birth, sex, color, occupation, time in the city, number in family, and number of visits. 2d. Statements of character,—as being temperate or intemperate. 3d. Unavoidable causes of indigence, such as sickness, infirmity, or old age, with space for marginal remarks.

PRINTED FORM USED BY THE ASSOCIATION.

New-York Association for Improving the Condition of the Poor.

VISITOR'S MONTHLY REPORT OF SECTION No.   DISTRICT No.   DATED   184

☞ *A mark with a pen thus ,, in the columns, will point out the class to which the person named belongs.* ☜

FAMILIES RELIEVED. Always give full Name, and *male* Head of Family, if living.	RESIDENCE OF FAMILIES. — Which must be reported every month.	Foreigners.	Natives.	Colored Persons.	Males.	Females.	No. in Family.	No. of Visits.	KIND OF OCCUPATION.	Temperate.	Intemperate.	Sickness.	Misfortune.	Old Age.	AMOUNT EXPENDED. $	cts.	REMARKS.

Signed,   Visitor.

LIST OF MEMBERS.

Owing to inadvertence in the returns from some of the Districts, it is feared that the list of Members may not be perfectly accurate. The *amounts* received were duly credited, as may be seen by an inspection of the Treasurer's account, at the General Office. But as the names of some who contributed small sums did not accompany their donations, with all the efforts subsequently made to obtain them, the list may still be incomplete.

A.

Aspinwall, John
Astor, Wm. B.
Allen, Stephen
Andrews, Dr.
A Lady, by J. Smyth Rogers, M. D.
A Lady, by J. S. Aspinwall
Abbott, Isaac, per J. B. Collins
A Friend, by L. & E. D.
Alley, Saul
A Lady
Anthon, Dr. Rev.
A Friend
Ayres, Miss
Atwater, W. L.
Adams, John
A Friend, per Rev. C. C. Darling
Alsop, J. W.
Astor, J. J. Jr.
Abeel, John H.
Aspinwall, James S. & Mrs. Moore
Aymar & Co.
Allen, Horatio
Adams, John T.
Armstrong, George
Amerman, Richard
A Friend
Appleton, D. & Co.
Ahrenfeldt, D.
Aguiar, L.
Arkenburgh, R. H.
A Friend
Arnold, A.
Aitken & Miller
Ackerman Aldn.

Althause, S. B.
Allen, George
A Lady
Amerman, Wm. C.
Aitkin, Walter
Amerman, P.
Anderson, E.
Anthony, J.
Abrams, Jacob
Aikman, Hugh
Armstrong, M. & Son
Avery, J. W.
Allen, Wm. A.
Angle & Engle
Anthony, Mr.
Arnold, D. S.
Alger, Mr.
Alison, Mr.
Allen, Dr.
Anthon, J.
Arpin, P.
Allen, H.
Apgar, L.
Allan & Rose
Ambler, Dr.
A Friend
A. H. W. (cash)
Ashton, George
Aymar, Wm. & Co.
Ayers, J. N. & Co.
A Friend, per Mr Roome
A Friend
A Lady, per A. W. Murray
Abbe, G. W.
Adams, C.
Ayres, Reuben
Anderson, Edmund
Abrams, Isaac
Adams, J. D.
Albro, R.

Aims, Jacob
Armstrong, James
Aikman, Hugh
Aims, Peter
Ash, Joseph H.
Arnold, B. G.
Anderson, C. V.
Alford, S. M.
Ahles, George
Andrews, H. M.
Archer, Mr.
Allerton, Mr.
Alford, E. M.
Allen, Isaac
Ammerman, J. W.
Abeel, C.
Allison, Thomas
Anguish, James
Alexander, Isaac
Arnold, James
Armitage, Thos. Rev.
Amerman, J. W.
Appleby, Jacob A.
Aims, Peter
Anderson, H.
Anderson, Wm.
Andrus, R. C.
Acheson, Wm.
A Friend
Abel, C. A.
Ackland, John
Alcock, Mr.
Arcularius, George
Abrams, Mr.
Arenfield, Mr.
Atwill, John
Adams, Mr.
Allen, J.
Allen, Wm.

LIST OF MEMBERS. (1850.

Aikman, Robert
Avery, J. S.
Andrews, Benjamin
Aymar, John Q.
Aymar, Benjamin
Abbott, John S. C. Rev.
Andrews, S. W.
Aguirre, P. A.
Allen, George F.
Allen, W. M.
Abernethy, C.
Aspinwell, S. Mrs.
Arcularius, A. M.
Allen, Mr.
Anstice, Henry
Abbatt, W. M.
Albro, Richard
Allery, Mrs.
Allen, John
Atwater, Wm.
Adriance, Thomas M.
Averill, H.
Arcularius, P. G.
Adams, Wm.
Abbott, Gorham
Allen, D. B.
Atterbury, L. Jr.
Adams, J. T.
Alexander, H. M.

B.

Brown, James
Boorman, Johnson & Co.
Banyer, M. Mrs.
Boorman, James
Benedict, E. C.
B. C.
Brown, W. S. Mr. & Mrs.
Brown, Stewart
Bruce, George
Boorman, Robert
Baldwin, J. C.
Baldwin, Dibblee & Work
Benkhard, Mr.
Belmont, Augustus
Bronson, Arthur
Bull, W. G.
Ball, Tomkins & Black
Brevort, Miss
Bruen, A. M.
Benedict, J. W.
Benjamin, T. A.
Blackwell, J.
Brown, W. S.
Bunting, R. S.
Bedell, G. T. Rev.
Bartlett, Edwin
Burr, Isaac Mrs.
Beadle, Henry
B. T. A——t
Benedict, J. W.
Babcock & Culvert
Bergen, James
Bangs, N. Jr.

Berrian, W. D.
Bryce, J.
Brown, L. B.
Bogardus, William
Brumley, Avery
Baldwin, H. M.
Beatty, James
Barry, John
Buxton, J. Jr.
Burras, T. H.
Bridges, J. F.
Ballagh, Wm.
Burnett, Peter, M.D.
Baxter, Samuel
Bremner, J. P.
Bruce, B. G.
Bailey, Thomas
Belloni, Louis J.
Bogart, P. A.
Beebe, Welcome R.
Bell, Joseph M.
Bradley, W. C.
Bennett, William
Barbour, W. C.
Bailey, Amos
Bowne, George W.
Brown, Richard
Bull, H. K.
Brady, J.
Burger, Thomas J.
Bowron, J. S. M. D.
Benedict, J. W.
Ballard, J. B.
Butler, William A.
Bartlett, David E.
Bullock, Smith W.
Burr, John
Buloid, Robert
Ballagh, R.
Brennan, Owen W.
Boardman, John
Beach, Moses S.
Barton, William
Bushnell, O.
Brush, J.
Beebe, W. R.
Ball, James R.
Blackwell, J. M.
Breath, J.
Briggs, George
Baker, J. W.
Bartlett, A. H.
Bell, Thomas
Barmore, G. & H.
Banta, S.
Bassford, Abraham
Bush, R. J.
Bach, J. L.
Benson, C. S.
Barrow, James
Burch, H. B.
Busing, E. K.
Beebe, Philo V.
Burdett, H. C.
Bates, Mrs.
Bevier, J. H.

Bostwick, E. G.
Brownell, J. Sherman,
Buxome, V.
Bunn, M. T.
Bishop, D.
Brown, H.
Burdett, J.
Bebee, W. H.
Blondel, Charles
Brown, A. S.
Burnton
Brown, J.
Bond, W. S.
Benedict, S. H.
Balch, W. S.
Bleakly, Mrs.
Brett, P. M. Rev.
Boyce, J. R.
Boll, D.
Brower, L.
Beekman, J. W.
Benedict, J. H.
Burtman, A.
Babcock, N. H.
Bullock, Mr.
Belden, A.
Baldwin, C. P.
Brommer, John
Bishop, J. C.
Barr, Oliver
Blakely, J.
Burt, William
Burr, John
Boyd, Daniel
Baldwin, M. S. Mrs.
Boyle & Coleman
Baker, Mr.
Bennett, N. L.
Briggs, John
Bacon, F. S.
Black, John
Boerum, Jane
Brown, E. F.
Bettman, A. M.
Brohe, P. J.
Barnet, George
Bird, David K.
Baker, John R.
Butcher, John H.
Brown, T. W.
Bell, Joseph M.
Brady, Wm. C.
Barker, S.
Bartol, Samuel F.
Bradford, N. G.
Bruce, John T.
Bruce, Robert M.
Belcher, R. W.
Baldwin, Luther
Brush, J. E.
Brewster, Joseph
Belcher, Dr.
Baldwin, C. A.
Bond, G. W. M.D.
Barker, Joseph D.
Bean, B. S.

1850.) LIST OF MEMBERS. 39

Briggs, Mr.
Bush, George
Bell, Abraham
Beardsley, Mrs.
Bowden, Thomas
Brewer, Conrad
Bigler, D. Rev.
Burton, W.
Bowery Savings Store
Baldwin, Timothy
Bosch, Bernard
Baldwin. Gabriel M.
Bartholomew, J. H.
Bailey, J. H.
Beach, Susan Miss
Bradbrook, Mr
Baudoin, J.
Brown, J. F.
Beck & Co. J.
Brown, Nathan
Britton, John
Brissett, John
Bayley, Mr.
Barron, Thomas
Bloodgood, N.
Boyd, Wm.
Bailey, S. Mrs.
Bonnett, Mr.
Blackwell, Mr.
Burkhalter, R.
Bowden, A.
Brown, Samuel
Brower, J. L.
Bininger, Mr.
Brainard, G. W.
Bowden, Mrs.
Burger
Bruce, J.
Bingham, A.
Brinckerhoff, Mrs.
Bridges, D. F.
Birkbeck, George
Bachellor, Mrs.
Burhans, Samuel
Butler, S. C.
Bochaud. J.
Bethune. Mrs.
Butler, F.
Bunce, David
Bowman & Ebbetts
Boyce, J.
Blackmer, J.
Barker, I. S.
Bulkley, G.
Bird, M.
Buckman, Ezra
Bleecker, G. N.
Belknapp, E. S.
Baker, Dobel
Bulkley, E.
Barker, J. W.
Bird, J. Mrs.
Brooks, C. C.
Barstow, Samuel
Briggs, A. T.
Babcock, Nathan

Bidwell, M. J.
Burnham, G. W.
Blatchford, E. H.
Bage, Robert
Burgy, J. Henry
Brown, Richard
Blackett, John
Berger, F. E. Dr.
Bruce, George
Bishop, Japhet
Burrowes, Philip
Buck, Gurdon, Dr.
Beckwith, N. Marvin
Bushnell, Mrs.
Barrowes, C.
Brown, Silas
Bradford, Wm.
Butler, B. F.
Brooks, Horace
Bliss, J. C. Dr.
Buchanan, R. S.
Brown, W. H. Dr.
Beck, J. B. Dr.
Baldwin, E. Mrs.
Barry, G. R.
Baylis, Henry
Butterworth, J. F.
Bullard, P. Mrs.
Beekman, H.
Borrowe, J. H. M. D.
Breese & Elliott
Breese, Captain
Brevoort, J. C.
Bogert, C.
Buckland, A.
Bidwell, W. H. Rev.
Bonnett, P. R.
Bonney, B. W.
Bulkley, C. A.
Barrell, George
Brown, R. J.
Bacon, D. P.
Blois, S. M. D.
Browne, R. W.
Bulkley, H. D. M. D.
Brown, J. F.
Bogart, P. I.
Brooks, H.
Boorman, Robert, Jr.
Brewster, U. B.
Brush, Walter F.
Brown, W. H.
Bowne, Richard H.
Brown, Edgar
Burke, Michael
Bleecker, Jane, Mrs.
Bernard, A.
Backus, M. M.
Brouer, Jacob
Bogert, H. K.
Benedict. P. Mrs.
Bullus, Mrs.
Ballard, James
Bissell, John
Brady, A. C.
Brainard, D.

Badeau, P.
Bradley, J. N.
Butler, Henry Mrs.
Baker, James
Brooks, D. H. Mrs.
Buckley, J. L.
Butler, C.
Beekman, Wm. F.
Brumley, R.
Busteed, George W.
Baker, Susan
Bryce, Wm.
Barrett, W. C.
Boker, H.
Beckwith
Bacon, M. C.
Barnum, P. T.
Bartow, Edgar J.
Buck, W. J. & John Blunt
Bishop
Beers, C.
Brown & De Rossett
Bennett, M.
Benjamin, Wm. M.
Bangs, Platt & Co.
Bates, M. Jr.
Bate, T. & T. H.
Baldwin & Studwell
Barnes & Thayer
B. & W.
Brown
Burkholter, C.
Bloodgood, M.
Blackstone, W.
Blondell, Wm.
Banks, Martha
Bleakley, J. J. T. M.
Brinkerhoff, Walter
Barbour, James G.
Boutilier, Thos.
Birdsall, Samuel
Brower, Mr.
Born, Jacob
Brainard, A.
Buttle, S. S.
Beekman, J. W.
Benedict, S. W. Mrs.
Bonsell, R. W.
Brunner, Henry
Boyd, George
Bleakley, A.
Bruce, John M.
Bloomfield, Wm.
Bloomfield, E. S.
Benedict, Mr.
Berrian, C. A.
Burritt, Mrs.
Bernheimer, Mr.
Bussell, C.
Bussell, G.
Badeau, E. C.
Bruce, J. M. Jr.
Barnes, Joseph N.
Bach, Joseph
Brown, W. M.
Bensal, W. P.

LIST OF MEMBERS. (1850.

Bailey, S.
Bailey, Mr.
Brewster, J. B.
Blauvelt, D. T.
Bailey, Dr.
Bancroft, W. S.
Belloni, L. J.
Bayles, J.
Bogert, Wm. M.
Brannen, Peter
Bates, Ebenezer
Bates, Edwin
Berry, S. G.
Banta, Wm.
Barmore, A.
Brown, G. P. H.
Blank, T. J.
Banning, A.
Bell, Benjamin
Butterfield, W. H.
Buckmaster, Thos. O.
Brownson, W. W. Mrs.
Baird, Mr.
Barr, Simon
Bootman, E.
Bogert, P. A.
Block, E.
Becker, C. C.
Bunce, Nathaniel
Boddy, George
Bristol, W. B. & Co.
Banks, Theo.
Barker, D.
Brombacher, Jacob
Brooks, J. D.
Benedict. C. W.
Beach, E.
Bennett, William
Banner & Palmer
Bronson, Silas
Bunker, Mr.
Baitty & Welford
Brown, George
Brown, N
Brainard & Balcom
Belnap, A.
B. B.
Beach, Mr.
Booth, W.
Buckley, Mr.
Boyd & Wilkins
Boyd & Paul
Brown, N. N.
Blair, H. B.
Burkhalter, S.
Butler, F. M.
Bininger & Cozzens
Bryson, Mr.
Bouck, Mr.
Bonnet, D.
Baldwin, J. L.
Brooks, Mr.
Brodie, Mr.
Bunker, B. T.
Boyce, J.
Baker and Scudder

Belnap & Greggs
Bunn, W. C.
Brown A. & J.
Baines, Mr.
Brush, Platt
Bronson, Mrs.
Bronson, Mary Miss
Bronson, F.
Barclay, Anthony
Blunt & Syms
Blanco, B.
Burtus, S. A.
Borgew, Mr.
Bear, J.
Brennen, Mr.
Barker, Michael,
Brewer, Mr.
Bertine, Mr.
Bear, Isaac
Boardman, Mr.
Brodhead, Edgar
Brown, F.
Bergh, George R.
Betts, J. S.
Bullus, Mrs.
Babcock, F. H.
Brown, J. H.
Babcock
Brown, Wm. H.
Bushley, R.
Brewster, H.
Ballin & Sander
Beveridge & Co.
Bowne & Co.
Beal, Bush & Co.
Burritt, Francis
Bigelow, Richard
Blake & Brown
Blow & March
Burrell H. & Co.
Beers, Abner
Blackwell, Josiah, per A. W. Spies, Esq.
Bliss, Dr. Mrs.
Beals, S. J. Mrs.
Belden, Wm. Jr. Rev.
Burt, Brothers & Co.

C.

Collins, Joseph B.
Cruger, Harriet Douglas Mrs.
Collins, Stacy B.
Crosby, Wm. B.
Clark, R. Smith
Cash, left at Brown, Brothers C. A.
Cock, Thos. F. M. D.
Crosby, John P.
Costor, G. W.
Chauncey, Henry
Crane, D. B.
Cotheal & Co.
Currie, D. F.
Curtis, C,

Conklin, T. A.
Cauldwell, S. P.
Conklin, Jonas, by Conklin & Co.
Cooper, Peter
Cock, Thomas M. D.
Cockcroft, James M.
Coffin, Fredk. J.
Cauldwell, E.
Chichester, Lewis
Chamberlain, Charles
Conover, Stephen
Campbell, John
Curtis, Benjamin F.
Canfield, M.
Clark, B. G.
Carrington & Orvis.
Cox, Mr.
Carman, Mr.
Clickener, C. V.
Cromwell, H.
Cock, Thomas, M. D.
Chilton, Dr.
Campbell, Mr.
Cutting, F. B.
Carmer, C.
Colgate, George Mrs.
Colgate, C. C.
Clark, H.
Clearwater, Mr.
Chambers, W.
Curtis, Mr.
Cash
Cotton, R.
Cornwall, George
Clark, Avery
Conant, F. J.
Corn, A. M.
Church, J.
Cash, many
Christy, Thomas
Chelsea Cottage, 29
Cheesman, Joseph
Cairns, B. F.
Conklin, J.
Cornell, M.
Church, Austin
Chambers, J.
Cromwell, Daniel
Clark, John
Caswell, John
Cook, Levi
Cash, by many
Curtis, L. & B. & Co.
Crooks, R.
Clark, J. L.
Campbell, D. P.
Cassady, James
Chouteau, P. jr. & Co.
Culwest, J.
Coit, J.
Carter, Robert
Cobb, George T.
Clawson, John M.
Carpenter, R. S. M. D.
Cutter, S.

LIST OF MEMBERS.

Conover, Daniel
Clark, Stewart E.
Carson, John
Cragin, Charles A.
Clarkson, C. V.
Churchwell, C. N.
Cameron, John
Chapin, Seth S.
Conover, John W.
Case, A. J.
Carter, Peter.
Coleman, D.
Corol, J.
Chichester, D.
Chamberlain, J. F.
Cassabere, Henry A.
Cortelyou, Peter C.
Craig, J.
Clancey, Mrs.
Callender, Thomas L.
Constant, Mr.
Creveling, Dr.
Coffin, John
Conover, D. D.
Cotheal, H. L.
Child, Asa
Cummings, W. C.
Clinch, C. P.
Coulter, Samuel
Chamberlain, E.
Clayton, E. B.
Campbell, Freeman
Cornell, John H.
Coeke, Edward
Conover, G. A.
Crosby, O. H.
Connolly, Charles M.
Cox, Charles B.
Clark, Samuel
Cronk, S. W.
Carlin, John
Callahan, Mr.
Cooper, W.
Crolius, John
Clarke
Chesbro, A.
Camp, Henry.
Carpenter, W. B. C.
Conklin, J. W.
Clarke, Mrs.
Cable, Mrs.
Chace, Mr.
Claugus, Frederick
Clussman, Mrs.
Crane, Philander
Colt, A. H.
Clark, James
Cook, George
Curragher, John
Carrick, Mary
Coapman, John
Conway, James
Cook, James H.
Cook, Amelia
Craft, Andrew
Cornwall, John

Craig, Mrs.
Cassidy, B. M.
Conger, John
Chichester, Lewis
Cape, H. M. Mrs.
Camp, Catherine
Cockroft, J.
Cook, Ebenezer
Clarkson, C. V.
Churchwell, C. N.
Cooley, M E. Mrs.
Crumwell, D. Jr.
Campbell, Mrs.
Church, James C.
Clarke, A. B.
Clymer, Mrs.
Cooke, S. G.
Cook, George
Cheeseboro, Mrs.
Commeford, John
Coates, Joseph H.
Crane, J. J.
Contoit, John H.
Chichester, Aaron
Cochran, Mrs.
Canton, Nicholas
Chickering, Mr.
Collamore, E.
Cox, James
Chilson, Allen & Walker
Cahill, Mr.
Conover, Mr.
Cannon, C. J.
Cash. (Walker st.)
Chalmers, Dr.
Campbell, Mr.
Cornell, R.
Cammann, George P. M. D.
Corning, Mr.
Clark, A. H. Mr.
Clark, Mr.
Cochran, Mrs.
Copcut, Mr.
Crary, P.
Cary, Wm. F.
Cary, J.
Cropsy, Mr.
Cash (Clark).
Carter, R.
Camp. Mr.
Cook, J.
Clapp, John
C. B. C.
Conover, G. S.
Churchman, O.
Chichester, Abner
Carlisle, Mrs.
Clark, E. S.
Crittenden, H.
Colvill, Alfred
Coster, G. W.
Coster, H. A.
Coxhead, C. J.
Chesterman, J.
Clark, R. Smith
Collis, James

Coolidge, Henry
Clark, George
Carryl, N. T.
Carpenter, J. S.
Cuming, T. B.
Clark, R. M.
Clark, F. H.
Cronkhite, J. P.
Coddington, T. B.
Catlin, D. W. Mrs.
Cammann, O. J.
Cogswell, J. G.
Clark, Mrs.
Coles, J. W.
Cook, William
Clark, G. W.
Campbell, D.
Couch, William.
Craig. B. D. K.
Campbell, R.
Catterfield, W. T.
Cooper, M. S. Miss
Chrystie.
Carow, Isaac
Coggeshall, George
Chauncey, William
Codwise, D.
Comstock, J. Mrs.
Crane, Theodore
Cornell, Samuel M.
Collins, Robert B.
Collins, Charles
Crane, Augustus
Corwin, O.
Creighton, F.
Clayton, Charles H.
Curtis, C. E.
Chardavoyne, William
Carveil, Mrs.
Church, L. H.
Calhoun, William
Cash, by several
Coe, D. B. Rev.
Crasto, M. G.
Coe, C. A.
Cheever, George B. Rev
Carpenter, W. F.
Colgate, Robert
Curtis, Joseph
Coggill, H.
Clark, Edward
Cromwell, C. T.
Chegaray, H. D.
Cockran, Samuel
Carter, L. Rev.
Cooper, Brothers
Cushman, J. H. H
Conner, James
Comstock, L. S.
Coffin, Mrs.
Colgate, M.
Crary, Mrs.
Cleland, J.
C. D. H.
Cooper, Peter

LIST OF MEMBERS. (1850.

Cock, E. & W. & Co.
Clark & West
Cash, many
Canfield, D. W.
Constant, Samuel S.
Centor, A. H.
C. G. P. & T.
Crane, Rufus E.
Collis, A. H.
Culver, D.
C.
Curtis, P. A.
Collins, G. C.
Clay, G.
Colt, S. Mrs.
Currie, Mr.
Chichester, G.
Clark, James
Clinton, Doctor
Cornell, T. F.
Creighton, John
Clark, Mathias
Curtis, G. H.
Cook, Mr.
Cornell & Amerman
Cook, W.
Cox, Dr.
Cummings, Mr.
Civil, Anthony
Carpenter, W. C
Coles. C.
Combes, John
Clark, M.
Comes, W. D
Clark, Daniel
Cooper, F. W
Curtis, Edwin
Connah, John
Carpenter, N. H
Camerden, Henry
Clark, A.
Carpenter, Mrs.
Collamore, Davis
Collard, J. P.
Crowen, Thomas J.
Cameron, James
Cook, John
Cramsey, J. D.
Crassous, F.
Carpenter, Mr.
Campbell, Mrs.
Caton, Dr.
Cooper, Mr.
Crane, J. B.
Cook, W. E.
Clarkson, James I. G.
Cox, Richard Rev.
Corey, Mrs.
Cook, George H.
Coleman, Hiram
Cornell, Mrs.
Chamberlain, Charles
Church, Charles M.
Clark, H.
Cludius, Charles
Candee, E. W

Cromwell & Birdsell
Carle, John jr.
Christopher, R.
Cooledge, George F.
Chardavoyne, W. & T.
Craft, John
Corwith, D. Mrs.
Chattiler, M.
Convoy, Michael
Coggleshall, George D.
Cauldwell, E. Miss
Coughtry & Dougherty
Con, Charlotte, Mrs.
Clark & Austin

D.

Donaldson, James
Delano, Warren, jr.
De Peyster, F.
Dennistoun, Wood & Co.
De Forrest, B. & Co.
Douglas, William
Douglas, George
Depeyster, S. M. C.
Dawson, B. F.
Davis, D. H.
Dutilh & Cousinery
Dutilh, E.
Day, Henry
Delafield, E.
De Rham & Moore
Dubois, Cornelius
Demilt, S.
Demilt, E.
Denny, Thos.
Davies, Henry E
Decker, Thomas
Day, A. E.
Door, W. S. Mrs.
Dodge, S. N.
Davison, Geo. W
Dittenhoeffen, E.
Dare & Webb
Deromus, Peter
Devlin, Charles
Decker, Charles N.
Dando, Stephen
Deitz, John
Dayton, M. P.
Davis, John M.
Duckworth, Mr.
Denmarest & Co.
Durye, Mr.
Duryea, Mr.
Doscher, J.
Dayton. W. H.
Deveau, J. A.
Devoe, Mr.
Donevan, Mr.
Dewing, L. C.
Dodge, Mrs,
Danforth, M. J.
Downing, A. C.
Doroner, S. P.

Dennis, S. A.
Denvill, William
Dwight, John
Degraw, Mrs.
Deraismes, Mr.
Drew, Robinson & Co.
Day, J.
Dean, Thomas
Durbrow, J.
Dean, John
Dole, Nathaniel
Davidson, John
Duryea, P.
Dyer, Chas. C.
Dakin, C. P.
Deems, H. W.
Dorons, Smith
Duncan, Francis
Disosway, C. R.
Dunn, H.
Darling, C. C. Rev.
Duff, J. F.
Davies, R.
Duff, James
Dodd. J. B. M. D.
Dwight, Henry Jr.
Delano, F. A.
Dickson, S. H.
Dambmann, C. F
Dorr, F. F.
Deming, B.
Dewitt, T. Rev.
Durand, A. B.
Dustan, S. Mrs.
Dawson, William
Draper, J. W. M. D
Drake, J. M.
Detmold, Wm. M. D
Deruyter
Donnelly, T.
Day, Benjamin, H.
Deforest, L. Mrs.
Duke, Wm. S.
Donelson, Catharine
Dibble, W. W.
Dodge, Wm. E.
Deen & Thornton
Downer, E.
Dietz, W. H.
Dobbins, C. Mrs.
Dougherty, William
Drake, J.
Dominick, J. W. Jr.
Duffie, C. R. Rev.
De Forest, W W.
Davies, J. M. Jones & Co.
D. N. T. & J. F. S.
D. G. H.
Deitz, Brothers & Co.
D. & B.
D. M.
D. E. S.
Dodd, F.
Dunderdale, W.
Delluc & Co.
Dickie, Mrs. P.

1850.) LIST OF MEMBERS. 43

Dellinger, C.
Dussenbury & Miller
Dickinson, James, Mrs.
Dupuy, E.
Day & Newell
Duncan, James
Del Vecchi, Mr.
Demarest, Daniel
Dodworth, A.
Dufour, L.
Dufour, Mr.
Downs, H.
Dorsey, J. Miss
Dubois, Dr.
Dyckman, Mr.
Dudley, W. J.
Devoe, Daniel M.
Drucker, G. Mrs.
Davis, John
Demarest, Henry & Co.
Demarest, R.
Dodge, Mr.
Devlin, Mr.
Doubet, Mrs.
Dodworth, H. B.
Dodworth, Mrs.
Deguerre, Joseph F.
Dickinson, J. S.
Delapierre. C. B.
De Forest, H. G.
Dana, P. Mrs.
Dickinson, Charles M. D.
Darling, D. S.
Demerest, Abraham
Dodge, S. V.
Dickinson, B.
Dolbear, Mrs.
Degraw, J.
Demerest, David T.
Demerest, W. J.
Dowling, J.
Dunshee, H. W.
Drew, D. F.
Dudley, M.
Duff, James
Dougherty, Mr.
Davis, S. A.
Dickson, James
Duncan, F.
Dairs, Joseph
Diverman, Mr.
Decker, James H.
Dennis, Oliver
Dolner, H.
Dodd, John M.
Drake, B. M. D.
Doughty, S. S.
Dunn, A. Mrs.
Durning, Charles E.
Diettenhoefer, Isaac
Dame, W. H.
Dunshee, Samuel
Dieckman, J. H.
Delprat, J. C.
Doolittle, A.
Davies, Abraham

Delapierre, B.
Daniel, E. O.
Dubois, Mr.
Dalrymple, A.
Duncan & Son, J.
Dixson, J.
Divine, J.
Delafield, Joseph
Drake, Mr.
Denison, C.
Drake, Mrs.
Door, C.
Dunham & Co.
De Puga, Mr.
Dash, Mrs.
Demilt, Miss
Dominick, J. W. Sen.
Dominick, Elizabeth
Day, Mahlon
Dennistoun, Mr.
Denike, A.
Decker, Alfred
Devoe, W. L.
Degrove, Quincy C.
Douglass, J. H. M. D.
Downes, A. Mrs.
Dunlap, T.
Dayton, W. P.
Dean, Henry

E.

Eno, A. R.
Edgar, William
Elder, George
Emmet, T. A.
Edicott, W.
Earl, A. L.
Engs, Philip W.
Eaton, A.
Ely, E. H.
Endicott, Mrs.
English, C. R.
Elsbury, Isaac
Eveleth, M. W. Mrs.
Ewen, Daniel
Eveleth, Emma
Eversly, Charles
Ely, M.
Eagle, Henry Mrs.
Earl, A. T.
Eaton, J. A.
Eaton, W. S.
Eiseman, A.
Ellison, Capt.
Ellsworth, E.
Embury, Mr.
Eastman, J. S.
Eaton, D. C.
Eggleston, Thomas
Emmett, Robert
Edgar, D.
Easton, Charles
Ely, E. C.
Ensign, E. H.

Elles, K. S.
Everitt, C. L.
Earle, John H.
Easton, Charles
Eagle, Henry Jr.
Eggert, D. & Son
Engle, J. & S.
Everdell
Eldridge, E. K.
Eaton
Elsworth, Henry
Engle, S. S.
Elderd, Miss
Earl, Miss
Ely, George
Emons, John
Etienne, D. G
Egan, David D.
Eldridge. N. T. Mrs.
Effray, Felix
Egleston & Battell
Edwards, Alfred
Evans, Thomas
Evans, M. Miss
Erk, Charles
Elliot, Mr.
Elsworth, C.
Ewen, Mr.
Eastman, Mrs.
Evelyn. M.
Everett & Brown
Erving, G. W.
Ellet, William H.
Escher & Rusche
Evans, L. G.
Elliot, V.
Endicott, John
Everett, N. C.

F.

Fardon, Abraham, Jr.
Furguson, Edward
Fearing & Hall
Faile, J. H.
Field, B. H.
Fiedler, Ernest
Few, Mrs.
Frost & Hicks
Ferguson, John
Ferguson, S. F.
Foster, F. G.
Field, E. W. & Co.
Falconer, John
Forgay, William
Folsom, George
Fellows, Wadsworth & Co.
Figaniere, Henry C. De La
Francis William A.
Fonda, A. P.
Forbes, William
Fisher, C. W.
Ficht, F. H.
Farrell, J. & T.
Flint, Mr.

LIST OF MEMBERS. (1850.

Fox, Charles
French, Richard
Friend,
Fenn, Gaius
Faulkner, J. C.
Francis, C.
Fisher, F.
Fox, G. H.
Fair J. & G.
Forster, C.
Fowler, J.
Fuller, L. F.
Farnham, G. W.
Fish, Mr.
Fanning, Solomon
Frances, N.
Fitzgerald, Mr.
Fowler, Mr.
Fitz, Mr.
Field, J.
Faginer, Daniel
Faxon, Mr.
Fabrequetts, E.
Freeman, N. P.
Franklin, Morris
Fisher Henry
Fieldman, J. S.
Fuller, Dudley B. & Co.
Frothingham & Beckwith
Ferris, A. Morton
Fleming, John B.
Folke, Mrs.
Fox, G. S.
Fonerden, E. M. Mrs.
Frothingham, W.
Fancher, E. L.
Francis, W A.
Fanning, Solomon
Foster, T V.
Forrest, William
Fisher, Daniel
Florentine, Abraham
Forbes, A. G.
Forbes, B. B.
Fields, Edward, M. D.
French, Daniel
Foster, William A.
Fessenden, Thomas
Fraser, Edward A.
Fisk, Samuel
Finch, Ferris
Fairweather, Thomas
Pendall, John L.
Fowler, B. M.
Ford, Isaac
Frost, Mrs.
Field, Peter
Fish, W. Mrs.
Frazee, Abraham
Frye, Jed.
Ferris, J. G.
Forrest, A. P.
Fairbank, D.
Freeman, C.
Fowler, Charles
Fitch, G. S.

Fosdick, R. B.
Fellows, Mrs.
Front, St.
Flint, James
Foe, P.
Friend
Freeman, James
Freeman, Wm.
Forester, Mrs.
Forester, Charles
Fowler, D. S.
Frisk, Dr.
Ford, Isaac
Field, Robert M.
Field, Josiah
Foster, Wm. R.
Fraser, E A.
Foulke, Thomas
Firth, Horatio E
Fanning, T.
Ferris, Mr.
Fatman, Mrs.
Frye, Isaac
Fowler, H. P.
Freeman, Norman
Falkner, J.
Fisher, R.
Frink, J. B.
Ferris, Dr.
Finch, Amos
Freeborn, Wm. A.
Field, Edward
Freeman, W. G. U.S.A
Franklin, R. L.
Fehrman, D.
Findlay, J. B.
Fiedler, Ernest
Foster, James Jr.
Fowler, Joseph
Fraser, Wm.
Fisher, G. H. Rev.
Freelan, R. J.
Fisher, John T.
Fuller, Mrs.
Fellows, James
Frost, Samuel
Fellows, Wm. M.
Flemming, Thomas
Finn, A. T.
Frazer & Everett
Frizbee, M. J.
F. D.
F. L.
Ferguson, T. M.

G.

Griswold, George
Green, John C.
Graves, E. Boonen
Graves, E. Boones Mrs.
Grinnell, Henry
Grosvenor, Seth
Grinnell, Moses H.
Goodhue & Co.

Griswold, John
Grant & Barton
Green, Horace, M. D.
Giraud, Jacob P.
Greenway, J. H. & Co.
Gans, Mrs.
Gould, Charles
Gregory, J. B.
Godfrey, Pattison & Co.
Greenway, W. W. T.
Gillman, W. S.
Green, Mary & Lucy, Mrs
per L. Jackson
Gedney, James R.
Greenhough, J. J.
Goddard, J. E.
Gibson, Isaac
Gillelan, John
Geer, Darius
Greenhough, Walter
Gardner, Moses
Griffin, H.
Gibson, James R.
Goodwin, J. W.
Gibbes, T. S.
Gaul, Laura M.
Goelet, Robert
G. N. L.
Gill, John
Gordon & Talbot
Green, Joseph W.
Gale, William
Genin, J. N.
G. W. A.
Gilbert, Colgate
Gunther, C. G.
Gilmartin, D.
G. & P.
Gray, John A. C.
Grant, Charles E. Cap.
Gedney, S.
Gray, John
Gibson, James
Galley, Miss
Gregg, Mr.
Greenwood, M.
Gregan, John
Grim, M. D.
Gordon, Robert
Gilroy, G.
Ginochie, J. B.
Gilman, Dr.
Gardner, Wm. C
Gann, John
Goodrich, Henry
Goldsmith, H.
Guillandett, Emily
Garvey, Wm. M.
Goodwin, E. & Brother
Gedney, J. R.
Griffin, N. P.
Gray, John A.
Green, Alonzo
Guthrie, J. B.
Gilsey, Mr.
Greenleaf & Kinsley

1850.) LIST OF MEMBERS. 45

Glen, Mr.
Goss, Mr.
Gibson, Mr.
Greenwood, Mr.
Gray. S. F.
Groom, Mr.
Gibert, N.
Gritman, Mr.
Goldsmith, Dr.
Grace, Mr.
Grocery
Gottker. J. H.
Grant, Mrs.
Goddard, Wm. C.
Gourlie, A. T.
Guibart, Mr.
Gilles, W.
Guedin, J.
Guion, W. H.
Gowdy, H.
G. A. H.
Gen. D. W.
Gates, John
Gemmel, James
Gray, John
Gillmartin, John G.
Gescheidt, Anthony, M.D.
Gilbert, John S.
Getty, Robert
Gifford, James N.
Groshon, John
Green, Edward
Gillespie, J.
Gray, Nathaniel
Greene, James
Griffin, T. T,
Greenough, W.
Greeley, H.
Gamage, Mr.
Griffiths, J. M.
Gould & Williams
Goodrich, E. B.
Greig, Lucretia
Galvan, Daniel
Gumbs, E. Mrs.
Goodsman, Mrs.
Gray, Neil
Gardiner, William
Glover, Mr.
Griffiths, William
Griffin, Thos. B. M. D.
Graham, John R.
Goadby, Thomas
Green, Thomas
Grice, C. C.
Giraud, Joseph
Gray
Griffing, Solomon
Grant, F. S.
Griscom, J. H. M. D.
Gillespie & Co.
Goodwin, Jacob W.
Griswold, Mrs.
Green, W. R.
Goddard, G. C.
Gallatin, James

Griffin, Francis
Gibson, J. Mrs.
Gustine, M. A. Mrs.
Givan, J. Mrs.
Gallatin, A. R.
Green, S. & M. Misses
Gelston, M.
Gunning, T. B.
Glover, R.
Gillman, S.
G. C.
Guion, Mrs.
Greens, Misses, the
Goadby, William, Mrs.
Garr, Andrew S.
Gibson, J. R.
Gilman, W. C.
Gray, E. C.
Guion, J. H.
Gray, Wm. F.
Gandy, S.
Gerard, J. W.

H

Halsted, Wm. M.
Halsted, Wm. M. and others
Hosmer & Hubbard
Hunt, Thomas & Co.
Holmes, Silas
Hitchcock, W. R.
Hitchcock, Cyrus
Hoffman, L. M. & Co.
Hammersley, J. W.
Hazen, C. D.
Hadden, D. & Son
Harsen, Jacob, M. D.
Huston, David
Howland, B. J.
Hone, John
Hoffman, P. V.
Hyatt, E. P.
Hammersley, Lucretia
Hammersley, Elizabeth
Hoffman, R. H.
Harris, Wm. Mrs.
Hicks, John H.
Hartley, Robert M.
Hicks, Wm. M.
Hubbard, J. A.
Halsey, L. W.
Heyden, Wm.
Hines, J. C.
Humbert, W. B.
Halsted, A. L.
Hyslop, George L.
Hazeltine, L.
Huntington, J. C.
Halsey, Jacob L.
Holbrook, E.
Harris, Mr.
Hall & Son
Hart, Solomon
Hoppock, M. A.
Hustace, Mr.

Hopkins, Mr.
Hollis, Mr.
Hammersly, L. C.
Hale & Hemrod
Hoyt, Henry
Hope & Co.
Hild, Mr.
Hope, A.
Healy, Mr.
Houghland, Mr.
Hoyt, Mr.
Howell & Son
Holin, Mr.
Hodgkins, J. G.
Harsison, Mr.
Hoyt, Gould
Hunter, Dr.
Hutchler, J. B.
Houghwout, S.
Holmes, Mr.
Hotchkiss, Jeremiah
H. H. W.
Hillyer
Havemeyer, G. L.
Hines, J. C.
Hunt, Wm. S.
Halsted, R. F.
Harring, J. S.
Hinricks, C. F. A.
Hays, H. M.
H. L. R. & S.
Hoppock, Eli
Haggerty, Draper & Sons
Hudson, Mrs.
Henry, John
Howe, C. W. Mrs.
Hoyt, E.
Hoogland, A.
Hall, Chase Mr.
Harris, John
Hatt, George, Rev.
Hatt, John A.
Harris, W. D.
Henderson, A. J,
Hurd, Hiram
Hall, Archd.
Hosack, N. P.
Horton, J. B.
Holt, J. S.
Houghton. Joseph
Howell, M. H.
Horn, James
Hawkins, C. W.
Hogan, Thomas
Hall, Joseph
Hutchings, John
Harris, Charles I.
Howe, Baraleel
Howe, J. M. M. D.
Hardman, Aaron
Heinshe, Henry
Hooper, Mr.
Heath, Aaron B.
Hammersley, M
Havemeyer, F. C.
Havemeyer, W. F.

LIST OF MEMBERS. (1850.

Herring, S. C.	Hamersley, Lucretia &	Halsted, John O.
Hopkins, N. F.	Elizabeth, Misses	Halsted, O.
Hunt, John	Hughes, Thomas	Houghton, E.
Harriot, James	Heustis, Mr.	Harper, F.
Henderson, J. C.	Howe, J. M.	Halsted, A. L.
Hoffman, Murray,	Hagan, P.	Haight, R. K.
Hurry, Edmund	Harman, Philip	Hall, Valentine G.
Hurd, John R.	Hashagen, H.	Holmes, S. P.
Holdrich, H.	Hodg, W. D.	Heney, Mr. S.
Hunt & Heron	Harris, John	Haight, E.
Haxtun, Mrs.	Harriot, J. A.	Henry, T. S.
Hale, James W.	Hadley, Ritter,	Harris, George
Hart, H. E.	Hitchcock & Leadbeater	Horstman, Sons & Drucker
Hirshfield, Herman	Howell, Mr.	Haskell & Merrick
Holden, Samuel	Hill, John	Hayden, N.
Hovey, H. R.	Harrison, Henry	Hallsted, Benjamin
Hart, Robert	Himes, Mr.	Havens, H.
Hall, W. S.	Hunter James	H. S. B.
Herder, N. D.	Hosack, Mrs.	Hoyt, J. K.
Hoadley, L. A.	Hamilton, Alexander	Hunt, Edwin
Hutchings, Mrs.	Hobart, Dr.	Heckscher, Chas. A.
Higgings, L.	Hunter, Mrs.	Halsey, A. P.
Higgins, J.	Haight, Miss	Hageman, A. B.
Harned, Wm.	Halsey, Mr.	Henry, Robert
Hunt, W. G.	Hardenberg, Mr.	Hearn, Brothers
Hull, J. C.	Horton, Mr.	Havemeyer, William
Hoole, J.	Hagerman, Mr.	Havemeyer, C. H.
Hepburn, J. C. M. D.	Herrick, Mr.	Halsey, E. C.
Howell, William	Hamilton, Mrs.	Houghwout, E. V.
Heyter, Richard	Hagadon, Mr.	Hutchinson, J.
Hartman, Augustus	Hyslop, R	Herbert, J.
Hutchins, John	Hogg & Delamater	Havemeyer, Albert
Hunt, Zeber	Hustace, Mary	Hutchings, E. W.
Holstein, John	Hawley, Irad	Hoe, James H.
Husted, Mrs.	Hewlett, O. T.	Hunter, C. F.
Hussey, C. Mrs.	Haydock, H. W.	Hays, John
Hughes, Henry	Hancock, John	Hoagland, J. S.
Hamilton, D. H.	Hoe & Co. R.	Houghton. E.
Hoey, John	Hedden, E.	Hunter, Mrs.
Halsey, Stephen	H. A. P.	Hudson, Mr.
Hobby, Mr.	Harrison, C. J. Miss	Higgs, Robt. W.
Harger. James	Hoffman, Wickham	Hall, T. Mrs.
Hardenburgh, H.	Heyer, J. Mrs.	Hall, T.
Hibbert, C. F. L.	Hayward, Henry	Hays, W. B.
Helmont George	Harrison, Jane Miss	Hasbrouk, G. D.
Halsey, Jeremiah	Holmes & Co.	Hogencamp, John
Hoffman, M. Mrs.	Hubbard, N. T.	Hasbrouk, Mr.
Hoe, R. & Co.	Herrick, J. B.	Higgins, John
Haight, Edwin M.	Hall, Francis	Hall, Mr.
Horn, James	Hodgson, J. W.	Haskins, Mrs.
Halsted, S.	Hutton, M. S. Rev.	Hilliker, W. W.
Heath, L. C.	Hopkins, E. N.	Harris, Mrs
Haws, Robt. T.	Houghton, R.	Hallock, Wm. A. Rev.
Halsted, Samuel	Howes, M.	Hoppell, F.
Hains, Francis	Holden, Horace	Horan, Mr.
Hillman, William	Hall, J. Prescott	Hubbard
Hennessy, D.	Hill, T	Hoyt, W. & Co.
Hepburn, S. Mrs.	Hendricks, F. Mrs.	Hyatt, Geo. G.
Hurten, John H.	Hook, C. G.	Holmes, Eldad
Healey, E.	Hargous, P. A.	Hickman, John
Hunt, M.	Hargous, L. E.	Hasey, Alonzo
Houghton, T. L.	Halsted, C. O.	Hart, J. Dr.
Hunchinson, S.	Hay, Allen & Co.	Heckmann, Arnold
Howard, Sarah M.	Hallock, Lewis, M. D.	Hagadorn, John
Hayden, Peter	Harper, S. B.	Harding, Richard
Hutchinson, Benjamin	Hull, James S.	Hicks, C. C.

1850.) LIST OF MEMBERS, 47

Han, Peter
Harris, M. E.
Hambers, C.

I. & J.

Jay, Ann Miss
Jaffray, J. R. & Sons
Johnson, John
Jay, J.
Johnston, John S.
Irvin, Richard
Jaudon, S. Jr. & Co.
Jay, John
Jay, Matilda
Jay, Elizabeth
J. R.
Jones, Birdsall & Roland
Johnsons & Lazarus
J. A. K. by A. Longking, through Rev. C. C. Darling
J. A. K. by Mrs. Longking
Jackson, Luther
Ivison, H.
Johnson, E. A.
Jones, A.
James, Mrs.
Irwin, William
Jenkins, Richard
Jones, David
Jarvis, Dr.
Jackson, Thomas
Jenkins, J. J.
Jacobs, W. B.
Jacobson, Richard S.
Johnson, Austin
Josephi, Mr.
Janes, E. S.
Isaacs, Mr.
Judson, Mr.
Ireland, Mrs.
J. S. F.
Just, John
Ireland, George
Irleand, George, jr.
Jenkins, T. W. Mrs.
Johnstone, Mrs.
Judson, D.
J. B.
Innes, E. S.
Johnson, J. D.
Jones, Isaac
Johnson, F. U. M. D.
Jackson, W. H. M. D.
Irving, A. S. Mrs.
Johnson, Bradish
Jones, J. I.
Iselin, J. A.
Jervis, J. B.
Jones, John A.
Ingham, T.
Johnson, A.

Jones, J. Q.
Johnson, S. Mrs.
Jones, E. S. Miss
Jeremiah, Thomas
J. J. C.
J. E. F.
Jackson, John
Jones, L.
Irving, J. T.
Jones, George F.
Jackson, Lewis E.
Janes, A.
Johnson, Misses the
J. P. C.
Jesup, T. S.
Jackson, H.
J. W. H.
Ingoldsby, F.
J. V.
Journey, A. jr. & Co.
J. H. & Co.
J. M. M.
J. O. W.
Johnson, H.
J. C. & Co.
J. L. M.
Jenning
J. & L. D.
Jackson, George R.
Jones, John
Jacobus, David
Isaacs, S. M. Rev.
Johnson, Henry
Jones, W. B.
Jeffers, W. H.
Jones, Mrs.
Imman, John H.
Joice, Samuel
Johnson, J. C.
Johnson, Robert R.
Jackson & Many
Johnson, Mr.
Jones & Wise
Johnson, Mr.
Jackson, W. H.
Irving, Theodore
Jaques, D. R.
Johnson, J. W.
Illius, C.
Johnson, H. W.
Jones, B. T. & Co.
Jackson, Letitia Mrs.
Ireland, William B.
Jay, William Mrs.
Johnson, Austin, per E. Mack
Jenkins, J. Foster
Jube, J. B.
Johnston, William
Jackson, Thomas
Johnson, William
Ives, J. M. D.
Jeremiah, Thomas
Jenkins, J. J.

K.

King, P. V.
Kearney, P. R.
Ketchum, Rogers & Bement
Kemble, Mr.
Knapp, Speherd
Kennedy, David S.
King, James G.
Kermit, R.
Kissam, Mrs.
Kenny, T. R.
Kelly, Joel
Kearney, J.
Kingman, Martin
Kennedy, Thomas
Kirby, Leonard
Kelly, Patrick, Alderman
Kelly, David
Kirby, V.
Knowlton, Dr.
Kortright, Mrs.
King, R. S.
Kemp, N.
Knapp, W. H.
Keavny, P.
Kearney, J.
Kyle, Mrs.
Ketchum, Philip
Kennedy, Thomas
Keeps, Henry
Keys, John
Kipp, F. A.
Knapp, Jas. H.
Kingman, H. W.
Knipe, William
Kohler, Mrs.
Kearsing, Mr.
Kaufman, Mr.
Katenhorn
Kummel, H. E.
Keeler, D. B.
Kissam, R. S. M. D.
Kirby, B.
Kersheedt, Asher
Kearney, E.
Ketchum, H.
Knox, J. M.
Kinsley, Hudson M. D.
Kinney, George
Kimball, Richard
Kingsland, D.
Kingsford, John I.
Kent, William Mrs.
Kingsland, D. & A.
King, William
Kipling, R.
Kutre, E. F.
Kipp, Leonard, W.
Kenedy, William
Kinch, William
Kissam, J. B.
Kitchen, George H.
Knapp, Mr.
Karr, D.

LIST OF MEMBERS. (1850.

Kalischie, Theodore
Kearney, P.
Kellogg, J. W.
Kidder, J. B.
Kofft, Christian H.
Kinney, T. R.
Katen, Mr.
Knox, E.
King, A. G. Mr.
Knapp, C.
Keeman, George
Knapp, G. Lee & Palen
Killian, J. A.
Kailay, Mr.
Keys, C.
Koop, Fischer & Co.
Knapp, E. & Cummings
Kip, B. Livington

L.

Lennox, James
Laight, W. E.
Lennox, Jennet Miss
Lennox, H. A. Miss
Lord, Daniel
Lord, D. D.
Le Roy, Jacob
Lottimer & Large
Livingston, M. & W.
Livingston, Mrs.
Low, J.
Lawrence, Joseph
Laight, E. W.
Lee, James & Co.
Le Roy, J. R.
Lefferts, Mrs.
Lynch,
Le Roy, E.
Lord, R. L.
Lynes, S. C.
Leland & Mellen
Loder & Co.
Lord, Samuel P.
Lord, Warren, Salter & Co.
Lawrence, Isaac
Leggett, A. A.
Lillie, William
Library, Committee
L. T.
Lewis, Mrs.
Lecount, V.
Lewis, R.
Lockwook, H.
Lawrence, R.
Lockwood, Frederic
Lowerre, Geo. W.
Ludlam, A. B.
Lytle, Andrew
Lee, Daniel F.
Lewis, John
Lewis, J.
Leech, Samuel
Lord, Benjamin
Longking, Joseph

Lockwood, William A.
Labagh, Isaac
Lyman, J. H.
Long, N. R.
Lowerre, Charles M.
Long & Davenport
Lawrence, Mrs.
L. F.
Lord & Taylor
Lamport, H. H.
Lang, S.
Lord, J. C.
L. C. P. L. S. G. W.
L. B.
Loines, William H.
Lowerre, Seaman
Ludlum, N.
Lewis, John W.
Lowerree, W.
Lambert, Jeremiah
Lewis, James S.
Loutrell, W. M.
Lamb, Francis
Lord, Mrs.
Lewis, Mr.
Lane, Adolphus
Lipselt, H.
Lent, J. W. Mrs.
Love, Thomas
Lord, John N.
Levy, S. J.
Le Roy, T. O.
Lockwood, F.
Lightbody, John G.
Lorrillard, Peter
Lane, J. A.
Littell, E. B.
Littell, H. B.
Lester, J. W.
Ludlum, A. B.
Leach, Joseph
Lounsbury, Mrs.
Langon, Oliver
Lamphere, Mr.
Lee, J.
Lilenthal
Langdon, T W.
Little, C. S.
Lynch, P.
Langlois, Mrs.
Larned, Mr.
Ludlum, N. S.
Lockwood, W.
Lecompte, V.
Lecompte, N.
Lilenthal, Mr.
Legran, A.
Leddy & Sheridan
Lawson, Miss
Ludone, H.
Little, J.
Lany, Mr.
Lewis, Mr.
Leise, F.
Lathrop, W. M.
Lawrence, J. Mrs.

Leonard, W. B.
Lawrence, R.
A. Lawrence, S.
Livingston, Mrs.
Longstreet, Samuel
Legrave, Mr.
L. & H.
Lees, J.
Lownds, Thomas
Libby, Robert & Demorin
Lynch, James
Loder, Benjamin
Lothrop, William K.
Leggett, S. M.
Leary, James
Leggett, A.
Lee, A. P.
Lawrence, W. E.
Lane, P. H.
Le Moynes, A.
Leigh, C. C.
Lewis, Samuel
Leake, C. J.
Labagh, Ellen Mrs.
Littell, Andrew
Lindley & Mundy
Lee, J.
Loweree, C. W.
Lourie, J. C. Rev.
Lawrence, William
Lyon, Eliphalet
Loper, Charles S.
Leasladler, Thomas
Lamb, Benjamin S.
Levy, Louis
Labatut, J. M.
Ludlow, C. L.
Layton, J.
Laug, Robert
Larkin, Daniel A.
Lawson, George
Leonard, J.
Ladd, Mr.
Litton, James
Lane, G. W.
Livingston, H. A.
Lane, Mr.
Lydig, P.
Lee, L.
Livesay, Mrs.
Linsey, Jared
Lyles, Henry jr.
Lowery, John
Livingston, J. R. jr.
Laboyteaux, P.
Langdon, W.
Langdon, Mrs.
Livingston, L.
Laurie, John
Leeds, H. H.
Lentilhon, E.
Lippincott, H. H. Mrs.
Lowndes, R.
Low, M.
Lawrence, M. Mrs.
Livingston, A.

1850.) LIST OF MEMBERS. 49

Lockwood, Roe
Lovett, James, Capt.
Lamb, H.
Lewin, R.
Lee, David
Lawrence, R. M
Lyman, J. H.
Leonard, W. H.
Ludlow, Mrs.

M.

Minturn, Sarah, Mrs.
Minturn, Robt. B.
Metcalf, J. W.
McWharton, Mrs.
Morgan, E. D.
Munn, Stephen B.
Murray, John R.
Murray, Mary Miss
Minturn, Edward
Mackay, Wm. per J. B. Collins
Morris, Lewis
Maitland, Robert, Mrs.
Morewood, Geo. B. & Co.
Mills, Drake
Moran & Iselin
Moore, Nathaniel F.
Mott, Wm. F. Jr.
McIlvain, B. R.
Miller, J. Mrs.
Mason, John L.
McLeod, William, Rev.
Morris, O. W.
Mather, E. F.
Macomber, James W.
Moore, C. C. Prof.
Munn, Samuel
Morgan, Wm. A.
McFarland, T. M.
Moses, Lorenzo
Meeks, J. C.
Miller, James
Massett, B. W. C.
Mattlem, Wm. D.
Mels, Mr.
Middlefield & Cohen
Marvin, Mr.
Murford & Vermilye
McRinstry, Charles
Morgan, H. F.
Middleton & Co.
Morley, J.
McAuley, Margaret
McGrath, George
Maury, M.
McVicker, Edward
McCurdy & Aldrich
M'Neil, J. H.
Macomber, Mr.
Marrienne, B. F.
Meeker, David
Marshall, Benjamin, M. D.
McClaury, J. M. D.
3

McNaughton, A. P.
Martin, H. C.
McLain, O. D.
Martin, Wm.
Murray, John
McCreary, John D.
Murphy, Wm. M.D.
Malory, S. C.
Mills, Elias
March, John R.
Mirrill, Charles
Merrick, Charles A.
Moore, Richard W.
Miller, H.
Murray, A. W.
Mollard, John
Merrill, J.
McDougal, Henry
Miller, John C.
Moss, John H.
Miller, James S. M.D.
Mills, Abner
McPherson, Peter
Marshall, Mr.
McGee, J.
Murphy, Mrs.
McKenzie, Wm.
Merrill, W. H.
Matteson, T. H.
McArthur, Mr.
Marius, Joseph
Moelich, S.
Merklee, John
Marshall, Wm. H.
Mooney, E. C.
Marsh, M. L.
Murray, Mr.
Miller, James
Miller, Mrs.
Moore, Mr.
Miller, R. H.
Mitchell, John
Mathews, W.
McGinnes, Robert
Miller, E.
Merle, G.
Mathey, A.
Mattison, A. & J.
Miller, W. P.
Murray, R. L.
Merritt, J. G.
Moore, S. W.
Morrison, D.
Moore & Co.
Moseman, N.
McDonald, Henry
Meinell, B. & Co.
Matlock, S. C.
Moore, Mrs.
Menstal
Michol, Mr.
Mead & Belcher
McMillan, Mr.
Martine & Co.
Meeks, J.
McWharton, A.

Mulford & Martin
McCoy, Mr.
Meary, O.
McLauchlin, Mr.
More, D. L.
Meeker, Mr.
Miller & Parsons
Morgan, Mr.
Moses, C.
Mount, Elizabeth
Marshman, B.
Miller, J.
Mather, W. L.
McCabe, Mr.
Miller, O.
Merritt, A.
McBride, Mr.
Miller, A.
Mills, Abner
Mills, Andrew
McMillan, Mrs.
McCleod, Mr. Rev. D. D.
March, P. S.
Martin, A.
Miller, Silvanus
Man, A. P.
Mead, William
McCune, H.
Mortimer, John, Jr.
M. A. G.
McComb, J.
McCreery, Mrs.
McArthur, Mrs.
Miles, C.
March, J. P.
Martin, S.
Mackrell & Richardson
Miles, Wm. B.
Morrison, J. M.
McCullum, R.
McLeod, Helen
McLeod, Eliza Miss
Maas, Herman
Murry, M.
Meehen, Isaac
Mason, M. W. Mrs.
Morris, R. S. M.D.
Mead, L. M.
Maitland, Robert L.
Meacy, C. A.
Macy, W. H.
Maghee, Thos. H.
McCready, Mrs.
Maden, Cristoval
Maycock
M. Mrs.
Marshall, Mrs.
Mather, Ellen, P.
Mather, Eliza G.
Mather, Ellen L.
Mather, Laura W.
Marsh, Samuel
McKesson, John
Merrill, N. W.
Mortimer, John, Jr.
Morrison, Wm.

LIST OF MEMBERS. (1850.

Marelle & Cobelman
Manchester, James
McM.
Meyer, E.
Munn, Stephen B.
Martin, Wm. C.
Miller, George C.
Meakin, John
McIntire, C. H.
Mesber, Wm.
Muffett, James G.
McCrea, Robert Mrs.
Metcalf, A. W.
Mills & Thompson
Morrison, James
Marshall, D. D. T.
Moir, W.
May, Mrs.
Monroe, E.
Moorehouse, S.
Morse, Mr.
Martin, R. W.
Martin, Peter
McNamara, M. S.
Miller, J. B.
Mettchell, John
Manning, Mrs.
McCadden, Henry
Malone, James
Melliss & Ayres
Moulton, John
Murphy, T. S.
Morris & Cummin
Morse, Richard, C.
McGaw, John A.
Minton, Charles
Mumford, B. A.
Milnor, E. Mrs.
Mace, J.
Moses, D. B.
Mitchell, J. F.
McCarron, Michael
McMichael, John
Mersereau, John W.
McKewan, John
Mason, J. M.
Martin, D. Randolph
Mildeberger, J. A.
Mildeberger, C.
Meigs, Henry, Jr.
Moller, Peter
Mason, F. Jr.
McIntyre, W. N.
Many, Vincent W.
Miller, J. R.
Maltby, Mr.
Meigs, C. A.
Morris, E.
Maze, Catharine
Moore, S. V. R.
Maloy, R. S.
McLaghlin, Alexander
Morrison, David
Menck, William
Murray, Mr.
Macleland, Mr.

McNespie, Captain
Mott, Mr.
Mayhew, P. S.
McCartin, B.
Milne, A.
McCue, Mrs.
Michaelis, Dr.
Matthews, Mrs.
Moore, James
Myers, James
Moger, Simeon
Mather, E.
Marwedell, Mr.
Marks, D.
Morand, Augustus
Mouburg, John
Marks, Mr.
McKenzie, John
Moore
Marsh, John R.
Miller, Amand
Merrill, Charles
Merrill, Manning
Moore, Thomas
Moss, R. E.
Mellen, David
Magill, James
McCreary, John
Miles, A.
Morris, L. B.
McGeah, John
Moore, Henry
McDonald, Alexander
Mathews, S. R.
Mapes, Mr.
McClairy, J. M.D.
Meir, Robert
Morton & Bremner
McDonoghue
Michel, Frederick
Morrison, David
McGuire, John
Morgan, George
McGay, Isaac
McGregory, Mrs.
Morrison & Allen.
Morris, Mr.
Morton, J.
Maxwell, Mrs.
Mullegan Mr.
Moore, J. C.
McAuley, Samuel
Mott, Joseph
Mott, William
Martin, J. B.
Manley, Mr.
Merrill, Mr.
Moreau, Mr.
Merry, C. H.
Mettler, Mr.
McMullin, Louis
McMullin, W.
Millegan, W. E.
Mortimer, J. H.
Mason, J. L. Mrs.
Mott, W. F.

Mather, G.
Millbank, S.
Millbank, Isaac M.
Millbank, S. jr
Macey, Josiah
Moore, J. L.
Morgan, M.
Mortimer, R.
Mackinzie, G.
Miller, Horatio
McNamee, T.
Mitchell, W.
McJimsey, J. M.
Morris, G. W.
Marsh, James
Mathews, D. A.
Morris, A. Mrs.
Magie, D. jr.
May, Antoine
Mason, Henry
Miller, G. & H.
Moore, S. M.D.
Merwin, T. T.
Mount, A. R.
Morgan, Mathew
Mease, C. B.
Mead, M. Mrs.
Maltby, O. E.
Morgan, J. J.
McCoon, C.
Mann, F.

N.

Nicholson, John
Noble, John
Newbold, George
Nevins, R. H. & Co.
Neilson, John, sen.
Nicoll, S. T. & Co.
Nesmith & Co.
Norton, C. L.
Noyes, W. Curtis
Nash, Lora
Nelson, Edward D.
Naylor, P.
Nickols, F. L.
Newell, G. T.
Nash, William F.
Nostrand, Egbert
Noyes, Isaac R.
Nostrand, Charity
Neeves, James
Newman, E. H.
Newcom, Mr.
Newton, Isaac
Norris, R. T.
Nelson, H. A.
Nichols, W. S.
Neilson, J. M.D.
Nye, G. M D.
Nevius, P. I. jr.
Nevius, P. I.
Nash, S. P.

1850.) LIST OF MEMBERS. **51**

Newbold, T. H.
Nunns, R.
Nelson, William
Nitchie, H. A,
Neilson, A. B.
Newhouse, B.
Newton, N.
Nash, F. Henry
Nanry, Charles M.
Needhards, C.
Norton, Mr.
Nicolson, John
Newell, D. C.
Newton, J. W.
Noyes, O. & P.
Noyes, C.
Napier, Thomas
Norton, O. W.
Nichols, C. L.

O.

Ogsbury, F. W.
Oebrich & Kruger
Ogden, T. W.
Ogden, John
Ogden, N. G.
Ogden. J. G.
Olcott, E. N.
Ogden, E. C.
Onderdonk, Levi
Odell, Mr.
Ogilvie, William
Ogden, Mr.
Olding, Henry
Ostrander, G.
Overton, R. C.
O'Donoghue, M.
O'Hara, James
Ogden & Co.
Osborn & Sears
Ortleys, Misses
Okill, M. Mrs.
Oakley, T. J. Mrs.
Oothout, William
Olmsted, John
Oakley, W. B.
Orr. David
Ogden, J. T.
Oothout, Miss
Odell, Mr.
Otto, Madame
Ooterweir, Mr.
Overhiser, A.
Onderdonk, J. R.
Ogden, G. M.
Okell, William
Orger, G. D.
Owen, James
O'Brien, Wm. & John
Oswald, Samuel Rev.
Orchard, Isaac Rev.
Oliver, J. W.

P.

Post, W. B.
Phelps, Anson G.
Parish, Henry
Pike, Benjamin, jr.
Porter, Robert
Platt, George
Powell, M. M.
Pearson, S. H.
Pentz, Wm. A. F.
Patten, W.
Peugnet, H.
Peugnet, L.
Price, C. W.
Patridge, William
Post, W.
Pringle, Thomas
Phillips, W. W.
Pott, Frances
Parker, Benjamin
Pray, H.
Peet, H. P.
Peet, J. L.
Peet, E.
Pell, Abijah
Pell, Charles
Peet, E. B.
Potter, Mr.
Pettegrew, Mr.
Prague, David
Pease Johu
Philips, Samuel
Pootan, William
Pomroy, J. B.
Pearsall, Robert
Potter, Mr.
Phillips, J. J.
Platt, J. A.
Prime, J. D.
Patterson, S. Q.
Polhamus, John
Peck, J. B.
Prime, J. D.
Parsons, Charles
Pearsall, John
Parker, Asa
Patterson, W. T.
Purdy, J.
Parker, Samuel
Place, J. K.
Perine, O.
Post, Jeheil J.
P. W.
Prout, William F.
Pine, Joseph
Price, Abel
Peterson, R. E.
Pitman, C.
Purdy, Emery
P. J.
Potter, Ellis A.
Perago, Mr.
Pearsons, Mrs.
Pierson, Dr.
Palmer, B.

Prescott, J. M.
Patterson, R.
Penford, William
Paxson, S C.
Patrick, Richard
Place, R. S.
Platt, E.
Prior, Mr.
Platt, E. L.
Pinkney, T. W.
Peck, Gideon
Pattillow, Frederick
Parr, J.
Pettit, B.
Pell, Abijah
Parker, John C.
Patrick, John W.
Price, Thompson
Pond, James O., M.D.
Pearsall, John
Pease, J. W.
Phyfe, J. M.
Papham, W. H.
Peters, C. J. M.D.
Parker, G. P.
Putnam, T.
Pond, L. S.
Post, G. D.
Pearsall, F. W.
Peet, E.
Post, A. C. M.D.
Plum, G. T.
Purdy. A. S. M.D.
Phelps, J. J.
Platt, Nathan C.
Pell, Ferris
Phelps, George D.
Porter, Mortimer
Patridge, Charles
Post, J. M.
Platt, G. W.
Palmer, J. J.
Purdy, J. F.
Phelps, T. W. Mrs.
Pendleton, E. H.
Patten, J. H.
Pearson, J. Green
Polhemus, Abraham
Peck, E.
Pell, James K.
Perry, Samuel
Packwood, S. Mrs.
Pryer, M.
Purdy, A. S.
Phelps, Royal
Phelps, Anson G. Jr.
Pell, James R.
Palon, George
Paine, John
Prime, Edward
Paine, W. H.
Patterson, James A.
Parker, Mrs.
Payne, Mrs.
Pittis, Mrs.
Pine, E.

52   LIST OF MEMBERS.   (1850.

pou & Palanca
penfold, John
penfold & Schuyler
poppenhussen, C.
platt, Jacob S.
pike, B. & Son
palee, R. N.
pike, D. B.
porter, John
putnam, B. Mrs.
pierson, J. P.
phraner, W.
platt, John
popham, William
putnam, Dr.
pool, Mrs.
parish, James
post & Young
pullen, S.
patchman, F. W.
powell, Mr.
pearson, S. T. Mrs.
pascall, Mr.
phillips, Jonas B.
parcells, A.
page, P. P.
pryer, T.
phelphs, William
pearson, Adam
planten, Henry
peck, E. & E.
patterson, W. C.
pinchbeck, W. F.
primrose, James
prall, J. P.
Phillips, Wells
Peck, G. A. P.
Parshall, J. L.
Pottitgen, M.
Putnam, G. P.
Patridge, W. M.
Palmer & Newcom
Parker, Charles
Phyfe, Duncan
Parks, S. W.
Patton, Mr.
Peet, Mr.
Potter, F.
Provost, S. H.
Phillips J.
Parkhill, S.
Parker, M.
Pollard, Mrs.
Pearse, A. F.
Pugsley, T.
Pollock, James
Pollock, J. K.
Pistor, P. F.
Painter, W. R.
Poins
Phillips, J. W.
Phelps, Royal
Potter, Mr. per Mr. Salter.
Putnam, O. C.
Post, Ralph per Mr. Horton.
Petrie, J. & A.

Pierce, George & Co.
Pardy, J.
Post, J. J.
Prime, F.
Pearl Street
Prosser, Thomas
Perrego, Ira, jr.
Parker, D.
Patten, Thomas
Pell, D. C. W. & Co.
Phillipe, L.
Phinney, Ralph
Page, E. W.
Pearson, Adam
Pattison, Robert
Place, R. S.
Peck, Nathan
Payton, E. H.
Place, Charles
Price, James
Post, William

Q.

Quackinbush, B.
Quinn, J. A.
Quidort, Mr.
Quiggin, Mrs.
Quinby, Brothers
Quimby, E.
Quincy, C. E.
Quackinbush, Mrs.
Quackinbus & Bambre

R.

Rogers, George Picton
Rogers, John Mrs. per Dr. B. Ogden
Rogers, J. Smyth M. D.
Russell, W. C.
Rogers, Catherine
Rosevelt & Son
Rhinelander, W. C.
Ray, Robert
Richardson, Watson & Co.
Remsen, H. R.
Richards, Guy
Russell, Charles H.
Rashau, J. A. F.
Robbins, G. S.
Raymond, Henry J
Reid, George R.
Renard, Jules
Riley, Louisa A. Miss per J. B. Collins
Rexford, D. A.
Rutgers, N. G.
Roosevelt, James Mrs.
Reading, R. A.
Redmond, W. Mrs.
Renwick, J.
Reiss, Brothers, & Co.
R. H. T. Mrs.
Roosevelt, C. V. S.

Rich, Josiah
Reynolds, James S.
Rourke, M. O.
Romer, J.
Romain, W. H.
Runnells, Mr.
Robinson, M.
Robbins, A. F.
Richardson, Oliver
Riley, A.
Roome, Charles
Riddle, C.
Russell, Theodore
Rockwell, C. D.
Richards & Starling
Roger, J.
Riggs, E.
Rigmun, Theodore
Rose, William W.
Reeve, Henry
Raphel, Morris Jacob Dr.
Robinson, Edward D. D.
Rowe, J. W.
Russell Archibald
Ramsey, James C.
Ramsey, John
Ryers, T. R.
Redfield, J. H.
Rivenburgh, C. V. M.D.
Ryerson, H. W.
Ruston, John
Reynolds, J. S.
Reynolds, John
Rae, Robert
Redman, C. H.
Roberts, Edward
Richards, Thomas B.
Richards, Wm. H.
Roome Charles
Rankin, Edward E. Rev.
Rowell, Charles S.
Rauch, John H.
Randale, John
Robinson, B.
Rudd, Joseph
Reynolds, P.
Rowland, C. N. S.
Roche, Edward
Ritter, W.
Radcliffe, C.
Rogers, Caroline M
Roberts ——
Russell, R.
Ramsay, David
Remson, John
Richard, Mrs.
Ringgold, J.
Rumney, Mrs.
Rosenfiler, M. H.
Rumsey, J. W.
Renny, James
Ryer, E. B.
Ryan, Maurice
Randall, E.
Reed, Nathan
Richter, John

1850.] LIST OF MEMBERS. 53

Reilly, B. O.
Riker, J. L.
Robinson, William
Rider, George
Roberts, George
Rowland, Jonathan
Rosenburgh, Isaac
Rodgers, P.
Rapalye, George
Reeps, Henry
Roberts, Nathan
Rapelyea, George
Ryerson, J. B.
Russell, Hiram
Rogers, C. H.
Ryder, Edgar T.
Raynor, H.
Riker, A. jr.
Redgate, Edmund
Rose, Mrs.
Rankin & Ray
Raynor, S.
Rich, Stephen A.
Roberts, P.
Riley, Mr.
Rogers, A.
Rich, Mr.
Randolph, Jeremiah
Redfield, W. C.
Rankin, Daniel
Remson, Mrs.
Rodman & Co.
Rappelye, George
Ritch, H. L.
Randolph.
Riker, A.
Read, T. T.
Ray, W. G.
Renard, Jules
Ruggles, Mrs.
Remsen, H. R.
Remsen, W.
Robert, C. R.
Ray, M. Mrs.
Reed, Almet
Renwick, Miss
Ranken, A.
Ryerson, J. A.
Roberts, M. Mrs.
Ross, J. H. M.D.
Riggs, Alfred, M.D.
Richards, E. B. Mrs.
Romaine, S. B.
Rhinelander, M. Mrs.
Rogders, J. Kearney, M.D.
Roach, P. R.
Roberson, James
Rawden, F.
Redman, C. H.
Russell, Mrs.
Repan, A. B.
Remington, J.
Robbins, R. A.
Russell, N. C.
Rozynhowskie, J. K.
Read, Taylor & Co.

Ross, Andrew
R. H. & Co.
Rallhaus, P.
Robbins, J. J.
Robertson, G. O.
Richard, S. B.
Roberts, Mr.
Rickard, J. W.
Reeve, S. B.
Reynolds, Mrs.
Ryckman, Mrs.
Reid, Mrs.
Robert, J. H.
Requa, Austin
Rodh, David
Russell, John
Rosenbaum, Mr.
Rozenblatt, A.
Ryckman, Mrs.
Ruthhault, J.
Rolfe, Charles
Rice, Henry
Rader, M.
Rees, J.
Reese & Hoyt
Rafferty & Leask
Rockwell, J. S.
Rodgers, R. P.
Roberts & Reese
Rose, J.
Raymond, A.
Ray, D. M.
Roshore, Mr.
Robinson, B. S.
Rendell, Jesse
Ransom, J. H.
Rowland, James
Renwick, Mrs.
Russell, Mr.

S.

Spencer, Wm. A. Capt.
Sampson, Joseph
Schermerhorn, Peter
Schermerhorn, Augustus Mrs.
Sturges, Jonathan
Siffkin & Ironsides
Schuchhardt & Gebhard
Schermerhorn, Banker & Co
Stewart, John
Stevens, R. S.
Suffern, Thomas
Sturges, Bennett & Co.
Stuart, R. L. & A.
Schieffelin, Brothers
Sheaf, T. F.
Stevenson, J. F.
Sabine, Dr.
Saltus & Co.
Skidmore, S. T.
Swords, Charles R.
Swords, M. H. Mrs.
Schieffelin, P. & Co.
Spofford, P. Jr.

Stewart, David
Schieffelin, H. M.
Sullivan Street Methodist
  Church, by W. H. Ferris
Sheldon, H.
Smith, B. R.
Stansbery, James F.
Smith, A. S.
Salter, Benjamin
See, Henry P.
Smith, Samuel J.
Smith, R.
Sears, S.
Schott, S.
Southart & Kissam
Stewart, J. J.
Skell, R.
Swift & Briggs
Strange, E.
Slawson, Mr.
Stevens, John C.
St. John, Raymond & Co.
Sumner, Mr.
Shyler & Grundy
Smith, W.
Shurman, Mr.
Summers, A. B.
Southworth, J.
Sterns, Mr.
Sheffield, Mr.
Seaman, Conklin
Smith, W. H. Mrs.
Storer, George L.
Scudder, Egbert
Simpson, E.
Smith, Fletcher Mrs.
Stokes, H. Mrs.
Sloan, Thomas G.
Smith, Wm. Jr.
Skiddy, Wm.
Stewart, John M.
Salter, Mrs.
Salmon, H. H.
Spaulding, J.
Spaulding, A.
Stuart, J. S.
Serow, Henry A.
Serrell, Mr.
Smith & Bertine
Scrymser, James
Saltus, Francis
Scribner & Coolidge
Sherman & Stark
Seaver, B. F.
S. T. R.
Seymour, A. B.
Spies, Christ & Co.
Spencer, George G.
Spooner, S.
Shepherd, Mrs.
Sherrod, S. Mrs.
Smith, J. C.
Smith, H. N.
Smith, Gilbert, M.D.
Smith, John C.
Sanscay, Joseph F.

3*

LIST OF MEMBERS. (1850.

Sharp, Wm.
Sayer, John N.
Smith, W. D.
Steele, W.
Spirling, John G.
Sammis, Joel
Swan, Caleb
Scott, J. W. M.D.
Stucken, E.
Sampson, C.
Sandford, L. H. Judge
Suydam, J. Mrs.
Stimpson, Dr.
Sprague, Roswell
Sheldon, F.
Swan, E. H.
Stevens, B. K.
Swan, B. L. Jr.
Stevens, B.
Scribner, Charles
Strang, Theodosius
Sherman, B. B.
Speir, G. M.
Sturges, T. T.
Starr, Nathan
Shegogue, J. H.
Smedes, E. S. Mrs.
Southmayd, A.
Suydam, D. R.
Stevens, A. W.
Smith, Augustus, M.D.
Suckley, Rutsen
S. R. G. Mrs.
Seymour, E. P. Mrs.
Stillman, T. B.
Sackett, A. M.
Shad, Mrs.
Scofield, W. A.
Smith, Asa D. Rev.
Sutherland, Wm.
Schuyler, Mrs.
Stone, George C.
Somers, F.
Smith, Wm. Alexander
Sedgwick, Theodore
Smith. Sheldon
Schenck, Wm. J.
Strong, W. K.
Smith, Samuel G.
Smith, C.
Sommer, S.
Stone, R. C.
Smith. Wm. H. & Co.
Smith & Peters
Staples, George W.
Schieffelin, B.
Schieffelin, James L.
Spaulding, H. J.
Stamford, Man. Co.
St. Jurgo Rivera
Strybing, Henry
Smith, T. & Co.
Stringer & Townsend
S. R.
S. B. S.
S. A. S.

Smith, John J.
S. R.
Scovill Manufacturing Co.
Shuster
Smith, Torry & Co.
Storrs, Charles
Scharfenberg & Luis
Salsburgh, Henry
Seguine, C.
Starr, Charles Jr.
Starr, Charles sen.
Scott, A. M. L.
Spyoer, Miss
Stratton, James L.
Southmayed, Horace
Story, John
Smith, S. C. Mrs.
Stansbery, E.
Sommer, Joseph
Sharp, Mr.
Saracco, Mons.
St. John, M. C.
Sommerville, Mrs.
Seymour, J. N.
Smith, Dr.
Seymour, John F.
Sherwood & Chapman
Steele, Dr.
Southmayed, S. C.
Straus, Simon
Smith, Mr.
Sinclair, William T.
Sanger, Z.
Silcock, John J.
Smith, Wm.
Smith, Geo.
Storme, S.
Satterthwait, John B.
Simons, L.
Stevens, W.
Smith, James
Seaman, Mr.
Souza, N.
Stevens, J.
Sperry, T. S.
Sill, H.
Swaine, Miss
Smith, G. G.
Sather & Church
Sherman, G. & J.
Simpson, John
Smull, Thomas
Smith, Edward
Sparks, Samuel
St. John, Lewis
Smith & Ely
Sears, Robert
Smith, Elizabeth
Sommerday, Mrs.
Scott, Thomas
Smith, John
Stiles, Elijah
Sten
Suydam, J. A.
Saxton, Mr.
Sloan, W.

Stebbins, Mr.
Stewart, Mr.
Spencer, M.
Seignette, Mr.
Southwick & Tupper
Smith & Barker
Sterling & Morgan
Skinner, Mr.
Sanford, General
Stout, A. V.
Shoemaker, Abraham
Shipman, A. D.
Stohlmann, C. F. E. Rev.
Stillwell, W. M. Rev
Schaefer, Philip
Sickels
Short, John
Stanley, A.
Scott, Mrs.
Sloane, John
Smith, E.
Smith, Charles E.
Sammis, L. M.
Samon, John G.
Spier, Louis
Selpho, William
Smith, J. S.
Staples, J.
Scott, L.
Steinsierk, Charles
Sneckner, John
Squire, S. P.
Schenck, M. Mrs.
Schenck, C.C.
Smith. C. W.
Stuyvesant, Sarah Mrs.
Squire, B. S.
Seaman & Muir
Sheffield, Mrs.
Schmelzel, John B.
Schmelzil, George J.
Symes H.
Shumway, Mr.
Scrymgeour, J.
Strong, Benjamin
Smith, James
Seligman, H. A.
Skidmore, W. B.
Sears, W. S.
Smith, C.
Slauson, A.
Smedburg, J. R. Mrs.
Story, John
Sill, H, W.
Schuyler, R.
Spalding, Mr.
Swift, Mr.
Saxton, John
Saxton, Baldwin
Stuart, J.
Smith, James
Sweezy & Co., N. T,
Scott, W. B.
Seymour, W. N.
Southark, J. W.
Sands, A. B.

1850.) LIST OF MEMBERS. 55

Smith, Jesse
St. John, C.
Sherwood, W.
Sarles, H.
Shepard, B.
Stevens, H. G.
Stagg, Benjamin
Stevens, H. H.
Swords, George H.
Sedgwick, R.
Stanton, T. B.
Skiddy, Francis
Schermerhorn, J.
Stoppani, Charles G.
Sweeney, H., M.D.
Stiles, Samuel
Sagory, C.
Sherman, Dr.
Stokes, B. G.
Swift, John H.
Smith, Andrew
Schlesinger, F. S.
Scrymser, William H.
Stokes, Henry
Sprague, J. H.
Sturges, E. J.
Sandford, P. Mrs.
Sage, G. E.
Sage W. B.
Stephens, James W.
Senior, E. H.
Stagg, John
Spring, Gardiner, jr.
Seaman, Henry J.
Scott, John D.
Schoals, F. P.
Still, G. S.
Smillie, J.
Steinle, F.
Sheldon, P.
Stanley, William W.
Smith, J. Lee
Shults, P. J.
Sackett, C. D.
Sprague, J. A. Mrs.
Sarvin, David
Starr, N. W.
Suydam, Lambert
Schmidt, H. J.
Sheridan, T.
Stoner, H.
Shofford, Y. A.
Sturges, S. B.
Schoonmaker, Mrs.
Smith, H. A.
Seabury, Mrs.
Schultz, Charles
Smith, J. G.
Smith, Peter
Stickley, Charles L.
Simpson, Solomon
Shields, Charles
Spencer, Warner
Smith, C. E.
Stopenhagen, Ernest
Suydam, H.

Sammis, D. P.
Smith, E. L.
Schwab, Mr.
Sommers, William
Sneeden, J.
Silverman, Jacob
Selligman, M.
Smith, Shadrach
Smith, Miss
Silver, James
Shipman, William
Smith, Samuel
Scott, Alexander
Story, Rufus
Scribner, Abraham S.
Seyman, G.
Simpson, William
See, Leander
Stout, A. V.
Sherwood, J. W.
Smith, Samuel
Stuckey, J. E.
Stelle, Nelson, M.D.
Spies, Adam W.
Storer, Geo. L.
Smith, Jacob
Smith, Asa
Stebbins, Wm.
Shaffer, Chauncy
Staniford, D. T.
Savage, C. C.
Sharp, Wm.
Skidmore, J.

T.

Titus, James H.
Treadwell, Adam
Third Associate Presbyterian
  Church, Charles Street
Tinkham, Captain
Two members, through A.
  W. Murray, Esq.
Talbot, C. N.
Taylor, Moses
Tiffany, Young & Ellis
Trimble, George T.
Tucker, D. N.
Traphagin, G. H.
Thompson, John
Terbeil, H. S.
Terry, David Rev.
Taylor, Moses B.
Tucker, C. P. M.D.
Teall, W. E. M.D.
Taff, Henry
Trafford, A.
Thomas, Charles M.
Teller, Daniel W.
Taylor, John
Tucker, C. H.
Tracy, Geo. Manning
Terbell, Jeremiah
Teller, R. H.
Tracey, C. C.

Townsend, D. Y.
Tracy, Samuel F.
Tucker, P. C.
T. S.
Templeton, Mrs.
Tracy, Charles
Thorp, A.
Tilden, William
Thomson, J. M.D.
Taylor, George W.
Tracy, Irwin & Co.
Tomes, Francis & Son
Tisdale, S. T. & Co.
Trimball, Mr.
T. S. H.
Tapscott, W. & J. T.
Tapscott, James T.
Trowbridge, Henry
Tucker, William
Talman, Stephen S.
Tomes, Mrs.
Todd, Ira
Thwing, C.
Tait, Mrs.
Thomas, E.
Thompson, J. B.
Trowbridge, F. H.
Towle & Son
Thilman, F.
Titus, Mrs.
Tate, Isaac E.
Tracy, S. P.
Taylor, John
Tappan, Mrs.
Thompson, T.
Thorn, Charles E.
Tapping, Henry
Tryon, E. W.
Thompson, S.
Tenny, R.
Thenot, Mr.
Tuttle & Co.
Tuckerman, Joseph
Tucker, T.
Tarrant, Doctor
Tilton
Taylor, A.
Tripp, E. H.
Turner, J. B.
Taff, H.
Terry, Brothers
Turner, S. H. D.D.
Tompkins, Ray
Terret, H. N.
Teet, Mr.
Tweedy, O. B.
Thomas & Co.
T. & H.
Thompson, John
Thompson, Thomas F.
Terret, J. C. Rev.
Tappan, H. P. Prof.
Townsend, David
Thomas, Charles K.
Townsed, W. U. Mrs.
Townsend, D. W.

Townsend, J. H.
Tilletson, Mrs.
Talmage, J. V.
Tallman, Abram S.
Toursey, C.
Tenbroek R.
Thompson, Mr.
Treacy, P.
Taylor, J. S.
Titus, Charles F.
Tyter, Isaac
Tylee, Mrs.
Timpson, Judge
Tappen & Burd
Tappen, Charles
Taylor, W. R.
Thatford, Joseph
Tremper, Harman
Trafford, Abraham
Tiebout, Nicholas
Trowbridge, George A.
Tweed, R.
Tappen, George
Townsend, J.
Taylor, George
Tilton, John J.
Thomas, Griffith
Tyson, William
Tappen, T.
Thompson, Mrs.
Tracy, J. W.
Tayler, John
Tolrige, T.
Thomas, Mr.
Talman, J. H.
Terbell, H.
Terbell, J. H.
Titus, W. H.
Thompson, Mr.
Taylor & Sons
Tracy, F.
Truesdale, Mr.
Thorp, H. S.
Tweed, R.
Terry, N. M.
Tatham, Benjamin
Thurston, W. W.
Thorndicke, Mrs.
Trenor, John M.D.
Thompson, D.
Tooker, J. S. Mrs.
Townsend, J. R. Mrs.
Titus, G N.
Thorne, Jonathan
Talmage, James
Townsend, W. H.
Townsend, T. J.
Thurston, C. M.
Treadwell, S.
Taylor, W. B.
Tallman, G D.
Townsend, S. P.
Truslow, William
Tillinghast, P.
Thompson, W. B.
Tucker, Cath.

Thompson, A.
Three dollars.

U.

Underhill, A. S.
Underhill, J. S.
Underhill, William
Ubsdell & Pearson
Underhill, A
Ustick, Richard.

V.

Van Gahan, Mr.
Vermilye, W. R.
Van Nest, Abraham
Vredenburgh, F.
Van Vleck, I. T.
Van Arsdale, John
Van Nest, John
Vandervoort, P.
Van Waggenen, William
Vergue, Delia
Vorhis, Richard
Van Hauden, John
Van Buren, J.
Van Wart, Mr.
Vreeland, Mrs.
Vermule, F.
Vermule, W. M.D.
Vandevort, Henry
Van Tassall, C.
Van Rensselaer, Alexander
Van Ingen, A.
Verplanck, Gulian C.
Van Auken, Mrs.
Van Auken, James
Vought, Mr.
Vaughn, G.
Van Woert, J.
Van Schaick, P. C.
Van Ranselaer, J. M.D.
Van Hook, William
Van Zandt, P. P.
Vermilye, W M.
Van Santvoord, C.
Van Wyck, R. L.
Van Winkle, E. S.
Van Ortwick, W. B.
Van Wagenen, W. F.
Van Antwerp, S. Mrs.
Vail, A.
Van Horn, C.
Vanderpool, A.
Vandewater, T. & W.
V. B. & Co.
Vliet, S.
Vanderhoof, Mr.
Vermillya, Mr.
Van Saun, Henry
Vanderbeck, William
Veltman, Mrs.
Venebles, R.
Van Buskirk, W. J.

Van De Worker, 1.
Van Blankensteyn & Heinemann
Vale, G.
Van Benschoten J.
Van Waggenen & Tucker
Vassar, M. & Co.
Van Kleck & Co.
Vanderheyden, Mrs
Van Wagenen, R. D.
Van Horn, A. M.
Van Allen, William
Van Nostrand, William A.
Van Arsdale, Henry
Vanderpool, Edward
Van Arsdale, H. M.D.
Vermilye, W.

W.

Wetmore, A. R.
Wetmore, W. S.
Wolf, John D.
Wythe, L. J.
Whiting, Augustus
Wood, William
Williams, Edgar
Wolfe & Gillespie
Western, E.
Wolfe, Charles
Wright, Miss
Wright, Sturges & Shaw
Walker, Alexander
Wetmore, E.
Wainwright, R.
Wheelright, B. F.
Weeks, Edward A.
Wainwright, William Rev.
Weeks, R. D.
Woolsey, E. J.
Winston, F.S.
Wheelock, Calvin
Wilbur, Charles
Wetmore, L.
Whittelsey, H.
Wheeler, L. F.
Wakeman, A.
Ward, S. S.
Webster, Daniel A.
Warren, T.
Walsh, G.
Weir, James
Wheaton, William
Wentworth, J. W.
Wilson, Bennet
Waldron, C.
Wood, Henry
Williams, Erastus
Walling, S.
Winter, E. T. M.D.
Wagstaff, William
Warner, J. W.
Wheeler, S. S.
Wilson, J.
Walker, William A.

LIST OF MEMBERS.

Woodruff, L. B,
Walker, William
Wilson, Jotham
Wilson, John
White, P. A.
Wiley, L.
Wygant. Mr.
Wells, Wait
Worthington & Shufeldt
Waldo, W.
Wallace, Miss
Wolf, Leo Dr.
Wood & Mabbatt
Wiggins, J.
Wray, S.
Walling, H. & Co.
Woefeenstein, J. W.
Win'ant & Sephton
Wegen, Mr.
Wareby, O.
Wood, A. A. L.
Wright, Mr.
Wilson, W. S.
Waller, J. A.
Williams, Mrs.
Waite, Alfred
Warren James
Walton, J.
Walton, W.
Walton, A. Mrs.
Walton, L. Miss
Walton, M. A. Miss
Westervelt, John J. V.
Wilbur, M.
Willard, Mrs.
Wood, J. C.
Wilson, B. M.
Wandell, B. C.
Woodruff, L. B.
Wilson, William H.
Warren, S.
Weilstein, J.
Waller, W. R.
Whiting, Charles
Ward, O. D.
Whitlock, Augustus & Co.
Wolcott, F. H.
Ward, Joseph
Week, Kelly & Co.
Williams, F. B.
Whitmore, J. F.
White, K. H.
Woodruff, Thomas T.
Wilson, A.
W. B. jr. & Co.
White, S. B.
Watts, Mrs.
West, Mr.
Williams, C. T.
Williams, F.
West street (182)
Wilcox, Mr.
Wall, Mr.
Whitlock, William
White, E.
Warner, Mr.

Ward, S. S.
Wilkes, Mrs.
Wood, Mr.
Woolsey & Co.
Wood, J. M.D.
Westervelt, J. A.
Whitmore, J. C.
Willets, Samuel
Willets, R. R.
Willets, Stephen
Willets, E. P.
Webb, Miss
Wetmore, P.
Walton, E. L.
Willets, D. T.
Woodward, Thomas
Williams, Thomas
Williams, R.
Watkiss, Lewis
Whitlock, Andrew
Woodhull, Mrs.
Wetmore, P. M.
Wendle, J. D.
Weller, John
Wilmurt, T. A.
Wyles, J.
Winslow, R. H.
Walker, J. L.
Watson, J. M.D.
Walsh, A. Robertson
Whitehead, John
Wells, A.
Wilmerding, W. E. jr.
Ward, Thomas, M.D.
Wilks, M.
Whittemore, Timothy
Wright, J.
Wisner, W. H.
Wilson, A. M. Mrs.
Ward, John
Ward, H. H.
Wright, C. Mrs.
Woodhead, J.
Waddington, W. D.
Ward, W. G. Mrs.
Woodward, J. S.
Webb, William H-
Withers, R.
Wells, L. W.
Ward, Isaac
Wright, Helen Mrs.
Williams, C.
W. A. B.
Wilber, N. B.
Wright, Neziah
White, John T.
Willett, E. M.
Williamson, B.
White, Charles B.
Weeks, Samuel
White, Henry
Walker, William
Watson, John
Winston, F. S.
Waddell, William C. H.
Woodford, O. C.

Watson, W.
White, F.
Wheaton, A.
Whitney, M. R.
Ward, H. D.
Wells, L. W.
W. T. M.
Ward, A. H.
Walworth & Nason
Wichelhousen, R. & S.
W. O. (by Kessam & Keeler)
W. & C.
W. V.
Wagner, George
Williams, C. P. & E.
W. H. & Co.
Woolsey, F.
Wendell, J. D.
Wilson, David
Wilson, W. M.
Wight, R.
Wilson, E. B.
Woram, William
Williams, Samuel
Wood, B.
Wadleigh, J. Mrs.
Wright, William
Walton, J. B.
Windle, George B.
Watkins, William S.
Williamson, S.
White, Archibald
Whiting, Winslow L.
White, John T.
Wilson, R. M.
White, J.
Winterton, S.
Winship, A. L.
Wainright, Mr.
Wooding, J. & A.
Ward, C. Mrs.
White, William
Weston, George S.
Wise, M.
Woodworth, D. A.
Windsor, Mr.
Wood, Mrs.
Wright, Alexander
Wilson, O. H.
Wood, James L.
Wood, William
Wells, J. B.
Williams & Hinman
Westfall, J. & D.
Wheeler, L. F.
Wintringham, J.
Wray, Christopher
Wood, M. Q.
West, D.
Witherell
Whyte, John
Warren, H. M.
Warmsley, Edward
Worrell & Co.
Wilkes, George
Walker, S. G.

LIST OF MEMBERS. (1850.

Williams, W. R.
Woodward, W. A.
Wood, O. E.
Ward, R. M.
Wheeler, Z.
Whitney, W. E.
Ward, W. C.
Wells, M. M.
Williams, W. R.
Wicoff, Mrs.
Williams, J. M.
Warner, P. R.
Wallace, J.
Woodhouse, Captain
Williamson, H. W.
Westervelt, James
Watson, John
Walduck, R. M.
Westervelt, Jacob
Wood, J.
Wilson, John
Williams, S.
Wood
Ward, L. B.
Wilkins, Denton
Wilbur, Mr.
Webber, Mrs.
West, Joseph
Waterbury, William
White, Edward
Walker, Mrs.
Weeks, Philip
Wallace, J. P.

Wing, Mrs.
Woods, John
Ward, Adam
Withington, Lewis
Wood, Alonzo D.
Wing, L. B.
Wilford. Mr.
Wagner, James
Walton, Ruth
White, William
Williams, Erastus
Wiggins, Louis Y.
Wood, James
Weisman, A.
Whitewright, W.
Weeker, H.
Wardle, Thomas
Watkins, John L.
Willard, Martin
Welch, William
Wheaton, W.
Wagstaff & Co. J. H.
Williams, Roger
Williams, Maria Mrs.
Williams, S. C.
White, William W.
White, William
Woodruff, Thomas T.
Weil, George P.
Waldron, Eliza Mrs.
Walker, R. S.
Woodford, J.
Walker, J. & D.

Warriner, D. C.
Witters, William
Wilson, Dr.

Y.

Young, E. M.
Young, Abraham
Youle, G. W.
Young & Co. T. S.
Young, William
Yates, A. E. Mrs.
Young, W.
Young, George
Yerance, Richard
Youdale
Young, Mr.
Young, W.
Young, W. C.
Yelverton & Fellows
Young, John
Young, D. S.

Z.

Zinck, Theodore,
Zerfass, John
Zerega, A.
Zebriskie & Van Riper
Zimmerman, J. C.
Zabriskie, A. C.

THE
EIGHTH ANNUAL REPORT

OF THE

NEW-YORK ASSOCIATION

FOR

Improving the Condition of the Poor,

FOR THE YEAR 1851.

WITH THE BY-LAWS AND A LIST OF MEMBERS.

ORGANIZED, 1843—INCORPORATED, 1848.

"The quality of mercy is not strained;
It droppeth as the gentle rain from heaven
Upon the place beneath; it is twice blessed;
It blesseth him that gives and him that takes."

NEW-YORK:
PRINTED BY JOHN F. TROW, 49 ANN-STREET.
1851.

PROCEEDINGS

AT THE

ANNUAL MEETING

OF THE

New-York Association for Improving the Condition of the Poor.

Held in the Hall of the Public School Society, Nov. 10, 1851.

James Brown, Esq., President, in the chair.

The Minutes of the last Annual Meeting were read by the Recording Secretary, and, on motion, approved.

The Treasurer presented his Annual Report, which was accepted, and ordered on file.

The Minutes of the Board of Managers, exhibiting their operations during the recess of the Supervisory Council, were read by the Corresponding Secretary, as their Report to that body, and approved.

The Annual Report was read, accepted, and ordered to be printed under the direction of the Board of Managers.

Voting by ballot having by resolution been dispensed with, the Association proceeded to the election of the following Officers, Managers, and Supervisory Council, for the ensuing year, after which the meeting adjourned.

OFFICERS, MANAGERS,

AND

SUPERVISORY COUNCIL.

President.
JAMES BROWN.

Vice Presidents.
GEORGE GRISWOLD, JAMES LENNOX,
JAMES BOORMAN, HORATIO ALLEN,
A. R. WETMORE.

Treasurer.
ROBERT B. MINTURN.

Corresponding Secretary and Agent.
ROBERT M. HARTLEY.

Recording Secretary.
JOSEPH B. COLLINS.

Supervisory Council.
The first in order is the Chairman of each District Committee.

FIRST DISTRICT.
James C. Ramsey,
James Cruikshank,
William Bogardus,
John Harris,
William Frothingham.

SECOND DISTRICT.
George W. Abbe,
Joseph F. Sanxay,
William Sharp,
Charles Wilbur,
Dan. N. Tucker.

THIRD DISTRICT.
E. Cauldwell,
J. L. Baldwin,
E. L. Fancher,
W. D. Harris,
L. Wetmore.

FOURTH DISTRICT.
Abraham Fardon, Jr.,
Archibald Hall,
Hugh Aikman,
Charles Chamberlain,
John Gates.

FIFTH DISTRICT.
A. R. Wetmore,
G. T. Cobb,
William H. Richards,
Wm. Steele,
David Terry.

SIXTH DISTRICT.
N. C. Everett.
Stephen Conover,
Daniel Fisher,
Frederic Lockwood,
Peter Burnett, M. D.

SEVENTH DISTRICT.
Stephen Cutter,
Thompson Price,
George Walsh,
Joseph R. Skidmore,
B. G. Bruce.

EIGHTH DISTRICT.
Joseph B. Collins,
John Endicott,
Charles C. Dyer,
O. D. McClain,
J. S. Holt.

NINTH DISTRICT.
James O. Pond, M. D.,
Jacob S. Miller, M. D.,
Thomas B. Richards,
Jeremiah Terbell,
Daniel French.

VISITORS. (1851.

TENTH DISTRICT.

James Horn,
Joseph M. Bell,
H. Van Arsdale, M. D.,
E. A. Fraser,
Thomas Jackson.

ELEVENTH DISTRICT.

S. P. Patterson,
R. H. Teller,
Abner Mills,
Peter McPherson,
Joel Kelly.

THIRTEENTH DISTRICT.

Lewis Chichester,
Thomas Kennedy,
John Pearsall,
Charles Merrill,
Wm. A. Walker.

FOURTEENTH DISTRICT.

Alexander W. Murray,
Robert Rae,
William Post,
J. J. Jenkins,
H. Miller.

FIFTEENTH DISTRICT.

Thomas Denny,
Wm. G. Bull,
Joseph Lawrence,
James Marsh,
Adon Smith.

SIXTEENTH DISTRICT.

Luther Jackson,
Charles Roome,
L. B. Woodruff,
W. Vermilye,
H. K. Bull.

SEVENTEENTH DISTRICT.

S. C. Lynes,
James R. Gibson,
John Falconer,
George Manning Tracy,
Thomas Jeremiah.

EIGHTEENTH DISTRICT.

F. E. Mather,
William Walker,
E. Holbrook,
J. W. Benedict,
Adam W. Spies.

NINETEENTH DISTRICT.

M. W. Fox,
J. C. Hepburn, M. D.,
J. C. Miller,
D. E. Bartlett,
Charles S. Pell.

TWENTIETH DISTRICT.

J. F. Chamberlain,
James Reeve,
J. P. Ostrom,

Charles H. Rusher,
W. J. Peck.

Elected Members of the Supervisory Council.

J. C. Greene,
Wm. S. Wetmore,
Jonathan Sturges,
Wm. A. Macy,
George T. Trimble,

E. J. Woolsey,
Cyrus Curtis,
John C. Baldwin,
William B. Crosby,
Thomas Cock, M. D.

Wm. G. Bull,
Lorin Nash,
J. T. Adams,
F. S. Winston,
Jasper Corning.

Elected Members of the Board of Managers.

Stewart Brown,
John T. Adams,

Peter Cooper,
Erastus C. Benedict.

VISITORS,

Appointed by the Advisory Committee for the ensuing year.

FIRST DISTRICT.

John Harris,
John McIntire,
James C. Ramsey,
George Hatt,
W. Frothingham,
William Bogardus,
Calvin Wheelock,
John Davidson,
John Calvin Smith,

Hollis E. Jewell,
H. M. Baldwin,
John A. Hatt,
George Hatt, Secretary.

SECOND DISTRICT.

Charles Wilbur,
Joseph F. Sanxay,
G. W. Abbe,
D. N. Tucker,

William Sharp,
John L. Watkins,
George Hatt, Secretary.

THIRD DISTRICT.

R. S. Gould,
John Ramsay,
A. L. Stimson,
L. Wetmore,
A. Taylor,

VISITORS.

W. D. Harris,
V. Le Compt,
R. Lewis,
E. L. Fancher,
   Edward Pratt, Secretary.

FOURTH DISTRICT.

Adam Pearson,
T. R. Kenney,
A. J. Henderson.
H. Whittlesey,
Solomon Fanning,
G. H. Traphagen, M.D.,
L. F. Wheeler,
Silas C. Smith,
Hiram Hurd,
T. R Ryers,
M. E. Kingman,
H. Lockwood,
H. G. Leask,
T. H. Burras,
   Henry Whittlesey, Sec'y.

FIFTH DISTRICT.

J. J. Greenough,
A. R. Wetmore,
L. P. Evans,
T. V. Forster,
Peter Mood,
John Tradguskis,
William Van Allen,
Wm. B. Eager, M.D.,
H. S. Terbell,
John Cook,
N. P. Hossack,
R. Burkhalter,
V. Elliot,
E. W. Page,
J. H Redfield,
David Terry,
J. F. Bridges,
R. Pattison,
W D. Smith,
P. Duryee,
A. W. Chamberlain,
G. T. Cobb,
H. A. Halsey,
James Litton,
Charles Selden,
William Steele,
   Edward Pratt, Secretary.

SIXTH DISTRICT.

William Ballagh,
Daniel Fisher,
John M. Clawson,
Benjamin Marshall, M. D.,
Frederic Lockwood,
William Jervis,

Moses B. Taylor,
Peter Burnett, M. D.,
Abraham Florentine,
George W. Lowerre,
C. V. Rivenburgh, M. D.,
Andrew Hume,
Samuel N. Burrill,
Samuel Baxter,
John P. Ware,
Reuben S. Carpentier, M.D.,
Richard Tritton,
   Amzi Camp, Sec'y.

SEVENTH DISTRICT.

M. N. Terry,
Charles M. Decker,
T. Warren,
J. B. Horton,
R. S. Place,
A. P. McNaughton,
G. Walsh,
B. R. Smith,
J. W. Goodwin,
William Gurney,
J. P. Bremner,
Joseph R. Skidmore,
B. G. Bruce,
Joel Sammis,
Andrew Lytle,
S. Cutter,
   Jonathan B. Horton, Sec'y.

EIGHTH DISTRICT.

Joseph B. Collins,
O. D McClain,
Isaac Gibson,
Daniel Conover,
James F. Stansberry,
Albert G. Smith,
Thomas Bailey,
J. W. Kellogg,
J. S Holt,
Charles C. Dyer,
Lewis J. Belloni,
Henry W. Ryerson,
C. P. Dakin,
P. A. Bogert,
John Endicott,
Edward Fields, M. D.,
John Gillelan,
Luke Kelly,
Darius Geer,
Stephen Austin,
   William Kirby, Sec'y.

NINTH DISTRICT.

John Ruston,
W. E. Kidd,
Charles Tousley,
Reuben Ayers,

Caleb C. Tracy,
Henry P. See,
H. W Deems,
Joseph Houghton,
C. P. Tucker, M. D.,
Reuben R. Wood,
William Marten,
William A. Foster,
Simon Shindler,
A. Chesebro,
Leander See,
Thomas Fessenden,
Daniel F. Lee,
John Murray,
E. H. Payton,
John C. Carson,
Charles A. Cragin,
M. H. Howell,
   John Ruston, Sec'y.

TENTH DISTRICT.

C. C. St. John,
Wm. Clymer,
Joseph B. Bell,
James Horn,
James Wier,
William Wheaton,
Andrew V. Stout,
Edward A. Fraser,
C. V. Clarkson, M. D.,
J. W. Sherwood,
Joseph W. Wentworth,
Henry Van Arsdale, M. D.,
Samuel Smith,
James K. Place,
Thomas Jackson,
Charles Place,
Edmund Anderson,
William C. Bradley,
Thomas Holman,
   J. P. Lestrade, Sec'y.

ELEVENTH DISTRICT.

C. P. Hawkins,
Grant Dubois,
Joel Kelly,
Thomas Hogan,
Wm. Murphy, M. D.,
S. W. Andrews,
Benjamin Dean,
Simon Houghwout,
Isaiah E. Stuckey,
William Bennett,
John Young,
William Barker,
Gilbert Leggett,
William Romain,
C. Waldron,
Grant Dubois,
John Myers,

VISITORS.

W. K. Tattersall,
W. H. Denny,
Moses Gardner,
H. P. Hibbets,
   Grant Dubois, Sec'y.

THIRTEENTH DISTRICT.

Amos Bailey,
John Hutchings,
Oliver Powell,
Elias Mills,
John R. Marsh,
Shadrach Smith,
John Polhamus,
John Burr,
Henry Wood,
Charles Merrill,
Isaac Abrams,
T. C. Gould,
P. C. Shaver,
Abraham Trafford,
Francis Duncan,
J. D. Prime,
N. N. Bennett,
Erastus Williams,
J. T. Klots,
Oliver Brainard,
Wm. S. Brown,
   Noah Coe, Sec'y.

FOURTEENTH DISTRICT.

Bezaleel Howe,
Nelson Stelle, M. D.,
William Post,
Richard Brown,
Bezaleel Howe,
William Johnston,
William Gray,
C. B. Pearson,
J. M. Howe, M. D.,
H. Miller,
Nehemiah Lounsberry,
J. J. Jenkins,
Thomas Fairweather,
Robert Rae,
Peter Carter,
Gideon Peck,
Alexander W. Murray,
Daniel W. Teller,
   William Gray, Sec'y.

FIFTEENTH DISTRICT.

George L. Storer,
Isaac Orchard,
Charles Sullivan,
Henry Holman,
Josiah Dodge,
Isaac Orchard,
Henry Swords,
C. R. Disosway,
Benjamin Lord,
John Mollard,
   Isaac Orchard, Sec'y.

SIXTEENTH DISTRICT.

H. K. Bull,
B. M. Fowler,
W. Phillips,
J. M. Hubbard,
Marks Cornell,
Stephen Merritt,
G. Whitely,
D. Coleman,
J. Cowl,
J. Smith,
A. Smith,
T. J. Burger,
J. Taylor,
D. Chichester,
C. H. Tucker,
J. Longking,
E. S. Yocom,
J. D. Adams,
L. D. Beatty,
J. C. Hines,
   C. C. Darling, Sec'y.

SEVENTEENTH DISTRICT.

James Duff,
R. Albro,
C. H. Redman,
H. Griffin,
W. B. Humbert,
George Shop,
Thomas M. Beare,
George Manning Tracy,
A. L. Halsted,
Richard W. Moore,
W. A. Lockwood,
J. R. Gibson,
John Sloat,
M. Vanderhoof,
J. W. Metcalf, M. D.,
R. Horton,
John Young,
Wm. Wagstaff,
J. A. Weisse, M. D.
D. S. Staniford,
   Richard Horton, Sec'y.

EIGHTEENTH DISTRICT.

J. W. Benedict,
G. L. Hyslop, M. D.,
L. Hazeltine,
J. C. Huntington,
Brainard Kent,
A. R. Plumley,
Edward Roberts,
Charles Irving,
E. T. Winter, M. D.,
L. Ranney, M. D.,
C. C. Savage,
J. B. Ballard,
W. A. Butler,
A. R. Long,
S. S. Wheeler,
James Armstrong,
   J. B. Ballard, Sec'y.

NINETEENTH DISTRICT.

John Voorhis,
John C. Miller,
Abijah Pell,
D. E. Bartlett,
Smith W. Bullock,
J. O. Shoonmaker,
N. Wilson,
James W. Macomber,
H. McCoun,
John C. Barker,
W. P. Moss,
Luther Lee,
J. Wilson,
   Enoch Mack, Sec'y.

TWENTIETH DISTRICT.

Francis F. Cook,
L. W. Halsey,
R. Matherson,
J. Parr,
Franklin Gregg,
Francis Buckley,
James Muir,
E. T. Winter, M. D.,
A. U. Lyon,
J. Coddington,
William Heydon,
J. F. Duff,
James Kearney,
George E. Myers.

BY-LAWS.

ARTICLE I.

EVERY person who becomes an annual Subscriber, a member of an Advisory Committee, or a Visitor, shall be a member of the Association.

ARTICLE II.

The President and Secretaries shall perform such duties as usually pertain to their office.

ARTICLE III.

The Treasurer shall give such security for the faithful performance of the trust reposed in him, as the Association may demand and approve. He shall take in charge all funds; keep an account of all receipts and disbursements; and pay all duly authorized demands. At the usual meeting, he shall render a particular and correct statement of all his receipts and disbursements to the Association. He shall also exhibit a summary report to the Board of Managers at their stated meetings, and whenever called upon by them for that purpose.

ARTICLE IV.

The Board of Managers shall have exclusive control of the funds of the Association, and authority to make By-laws; to fill vacancies; appoint all committees; and generally to adopt such measures as the objects of the Institution may require. It shall meet for the transaction of business, on the second Monday of every month; and the annual meeting of the Association shall be convened on the second Monday of November, when the Board shall submit a report of its proceedings, and the officers and managers be chosen. In case of a failure to hold the specified meeting in November, a special meeting for the same purpose shall be convened in the course of the ensuing month.

ARTICLE V.

Special meetings of the Board of Managers and of the Supervisory Council, may be called by the Secretary, at the request of the President, or on receiving a requisition signed by five members. Two days' notice must be given of the time of meeting.

ARTICLE VI.

The Managers may at any time make such alterations in these By-Laws, as may be deemed necessary; provided they be not contrary to the Act of Incorporation, and that such alteration shall be submitted to the Board of Managers at least one meeting before the same is acted upon; and that it shall not be passed upon unless specified in the call of the meeting, and when a majority of the whole number of the Board of Managers is present.

ARTICLE VII.

An office shall be opened in an eligible situation, for the purpose of concentrating and diffusing all information pertaining to the Society's operations and objects, and for the transaction of its general business.

ARTICLE VIII.

It shall be the duty of the General Agent to devote himself with diligence and fidelity to the affairs of the Association.

ARTICLE IX.

The city shall be divided into twenty Districts, each Ward forming a District; and the districts be subdivided into Sections. Each District shall have an Advisory Committee, to consist of five members; and each Section a Visitor.

ARTICLE X.

It shall be the duty of the Advisory Committee to divide their Districts into such Sections, as to apportion to each about twenty-five families requiring attention; endeavor to obtain suitable Visitors for each Section; supply vacancies which may occur; make the necessary arrangements for placing at the disposal of the Visitors food, fuel, and clothing, for distribution; and on some day in the first week of every month (excepting the meetings of July and August, which may be omitted in the discretion of the Committees), to convene all the Visitors of the Sections, for the purpose of receiving their returns, and conferring with them on the objects of their mutual labors. The Committees, moreover, shall duly draw upon the Treasurer for such proportion of the funds as may be appropriated to their Districts; they shall keep a strict account of all their disbursements, and only in extreme cases make donations of money; they shall monthly render an account of their expenditures to the Board of Managers; and in default of this duty, shall not be entitled to draw upon the funds of the Association. Each Committee shall appoint its own Chairman, Secretary, and Treasurer, and shall transmit the Reports of the Visitors immediately after each monthly meeting, with any other information they may think desirable, to the General Secretary.

ARTICLE XI.

It shall be the duty of each Visitor to confine his labors exclusively to the particular Section assigned him, so that no individual shall receive relief, excepting in the Section where he is known, and to which he belongs. The Visitors shall carefully investigate all cases referred to them before granting relief; ascertain the condition, habits of life, and means of subsistence of the applicants; and extend to all such, kind services, counsel, and assistance, as a discriminating and judicious regard for their present and permanent welfare requires. And in case of sickness, it will be their duty to inquire whether there is any medical or other attendance needed; whether relief is afforded by any religious or charitable society; to provide themselves with information respecting the nearest Dispensary, and in all cases, when practicable, to refer applicants for aid to appropriate existing societies. When no other assistance is provided or available, they shall draw from the resources of this Association—not money, which is never allowed to be given, except with the consent of the Advisory Committee or a member thereof—but such articles of food, fuel, clothing, and similar supplies as the necessities of the case require. In all cases of want coming to the knowledge of the Visitors, they will be expected to perform the same duties, although no application has been made. It shall be their duty, moreover, to render a report of their labors, and also an account of all their disbursements, to their respective Committees, at the stated monthly meeting. No Visitor neglecting these duties will be entitled to draw on the funds of the Association.

ARTICLE XII.

The Board of Managers, the members of the Advisory Committees, and certain elected members, shall together constitute a Supervisory Council, whose duties shall be deliberative and advisory; and its annual meetings be held on the second Monday of November, in each year. Special meetings of this body shall be held, when called by the Board of Managers.

ARTICLE XIII.

It shall be the duty of the members of the Association to endeavor, in all suitable ways, to give practical effect to its principles; especially to discountenance indiscriminate alms-giving and street-begging; to provide themselves with tickets of reference; and instead of giving aid to unknown applicants, whose case they cannot themselves investigate, to refer such applications to the Visitor of the Section in which the applicants reside, in order that such cases may properly be inquired into, and, if deserving, relieved.

ARTICLE XIV.

The printed forms of tickets and orders for relief, shall be designated by the Board of Managers, and no other shall be used.

Incorporation.

CERTIFICATE OF INTENTION

TO INCORPORATE THE NEW-YORK ASSOCIATION FOR IMPROVING THE CONDITION OF THE POOR.

THE undersigned, being each and every of them of full age, and citizens of the State of New-York, desiring to associate themselves for the benevolent and charitable objects hereinafter expressed, that they may become a body politic and corporate, and be enabled to conduct the business of the Association in the City and County of New-York, according to the provisions of an "Act for the Incorporation of Benevolent, Charitable, Scientific, and Missionary purposes," passed April 12th, 1848, do for these purposes hereby certify,

I. That the name and title by which such Institution shall be known in law, is the "New-York Association for Improving the Condition of the Poor."

II. That the particular business and objects of such Association shall be the elevation of the physical and moral condition of the indigent; and so far as is compatible with these objects, the relief of their necessities.

III. That the Board of Managers to manage the same shall consist of one President, five Vice-Presidents, one Treasurer, one Corresponding Secretary and General Agent, one Recording Secretary, the Chairman of each Advisory Committee, or as his proxy, some other member of said Committee, and four members to be chosen by said Board of Managers.

IV. That the following named persons shall constitute the Board of Managers for the first year, to wit: James Brown, *President;* George Griswold, J. Smyth Rogers, James Boorman, James Lenox, and Horatio Allen, *Vice-Presidents;* Robert B. Minturn, *Treasurer;* Robert M. Hartley, *Corresponding Secretary and General Agent;* Joseph B. Collins, *Recording Secretary;* together with the following elected Members and Chairmen of the Advisory Committees, namely:

Stewart Brown, Frederick S. Winston, Erastus C. Benedict, John R. Ludlow, Daniel S. Briant, William Gale, Peter G. Arcularius, Abraham Fardon, Jr., Apollos R. Wetmore, Nicholas C. Everett, Calvin Tracy, James O. Pond, James Horn, Samuel P. Patterson, Lewis Chichester, Adam W. Spies, Thomas Denny, Luther Jackson, Stephen C. Lynes, and F. Ellsworth Mather.

In witness whereof, we hereunto have subscribed our names, in the city of New-York, this the eleventh day of December, in the year of our Lord one thousand eight hundred and forty-eight.

JAMES BROWN,	APOLLOS R. WETMORE,
GEORGE GRISWOLD,	NICHOLAS C. EVERETT,
J. SMYTH ROGERS,	CALVIN TRACY,
JAMES BOORMAN,	JAMES O. POND,
HORATIO ALLEN,	JAMES HORN,
ROBERT M. HARTLEY,	LEWIS CHICHESTER,
JOSEPH B. COLLINS,	ADAM W. SPIES,
STEWART BROWN,	THOMAS DENNY,
FREDERICK S. WINSTON,	LUTHER JACKSON,
DANIEL S. BRIANT,	STEPHEN C. LYNES,
PETER G ARCULARIUS,	F. ELLSWORTH MATHER.
ABRAHAM FARDON, JR.,	

Witness as to all the signatures, D. F. CURRY.

City and County of New-York, [ss.]: On the eleventh day of December, A. D. 1848, before me came George Griswold, J. Smyth Rogers, Horatio Allen, Joseph B. Collins, Luther Jackson, Abraham Fardon, Jr., Lewis Chichester, Daniel S. Briant, Nicholas C. Everett, James O. Pond, Adam W. Spies, F. Ellsworth Mather, James Horn, Frederick S. Winston, Peter G. Arcularius, Stephen C. Lynes, Calvin Tracy, and Robert M. Hartley; and on the twelfth day of December, A. D. 1848, before me came James Brown, Stewart Brown, and James Boorman; and on the thirteenth day of December, A. D. 1848, before me came Apollos R. Wetmore and Thomas Denny, to me known to be the same persons described in and who executed the foregoing instrument, who severally acknowledged that they executed the foregoing instrument, for the purposes therein mentioned.

D. F. CURRY, *Commissioner.*

I approve of the within Certificate, and allow the same to be filed.

H. P. EDWARDS, *Justice Supreme Court.*

New-York, Dec. 14, 1848.

STATE OF NEW YORK, SECRETARY'S OFFICE, } *Albany, Dec.* 16, 1848.

I certify that the Certificate of Incorporation of the "New-York Association for Improving the Condition of the Poor," was received and filed this day in this office.

ARCHIBALD CAMPBELL,
Dept. Sec. of State.

Eighth Annual Report

OF THE

NEW-YORK ASSOCIATION FOR IMPROVING THE CONDITION OF THE POOR.

The Board of Managers, in presenting their Eighth Annual Report, would gratefully acknowledge the kindness of Divine Providence during another year, and their obligations to the friends and patrons of the Institution, by whose pecuniary liberality and co-operation its labors have been sustained.

It will be seen that the name of a lady heads the list of subscribers with the generous donation of *one thousand dollars*. Distinguished as she is, for enlarged practical benevolence and purity of character, it is unnecessary that her name should appear in annual reports in order to find a place among the estimable of the earth. The Board refer, therefore, to the donation, not with the expectation of augmenting her well-deserved fame, but to express their sense of the gratitude which so generous an act claims, from all who are interested in the objects of this Association.

The Board would not omit to notice in this review, the breach which death has made in their number during the year. With sincere grief they record the decease of J. Smyth Rogers, M. D., the second Vice President of the Institution, who died in this city after a lingering illness, on the 30th of March.

Dr. Rogers was among the earliest projectors of this Association, and one of its most assiduous and devoted friends. His counsels, labors, and warm-hearted philanthropy in this relation were invaluable. Though often suffering from infirm health that would have justified an occasional intermission of his labors, yet while strength permitted, he declined no services which might promote the Institution's efficiency and usefulness. Charity being in him a deep-seated religious principle, he never wearied in well-doing, and the lively interest which he felt in sustaining and perfecting this peculiar system of relief, only ceased with his life.

In no previous year have the objects contemplated by the Institution been more thoroughly and energetically carried out; while enlarged experience has tended to develop more fully the necessity of such an organization in order to meet the peculiar wants of this great and growing metropolis. And so sadly has the character of the poor deteriorated of late years in this city, from the immense influx of foreigners, many of them being of the most thriftless, degraded class, with whom begging is a trade, nothing less thorough, it is believed, than the counteracting influence of such an Association as this could check the growth of pauperism, or prevent the community from being overrun by swarms of the idle and dissolute.

The Institution having now been eight years in operation, ample opportunity has been given by appeals to experience to separate the practical from the theoretical, so as to combine into a consistent whole whatever afforded the assurance of producing the best practical effects. That it is adapted to its objects, is increasing in usefulness, and is becoming more and more extensively appreciated by the public, is most satisfactorily shown, not only by the results, but also by the annual increase of its friends and patrons.

The Board, in view of the Association's duties and responsibilities, have during the past year endeavored to direct its efforts to such objects, as in their judgment most required attention, and would best subserve the interests of the poor and of the city. Among the more prominent of these may be noticed :

I. *The exercise of increased discrimination in giving relief.* To dispense aid judiciously is one of the most important, as it is also one of the most difficult duties. Yet to fail in this, is not only injurious to the recipient by removing the proper incentives to self-reliance, but to the community by augmenting the number of the idle and dependent. So very numerous, however, are the expedients of the worthless and lazy to obtain gratuitous relief, that the utmost energy and vigilance are constantly required to circumvent their fraudulent impositions. But with the superior advantages of this system for the detection of the unworthy, thousands of them are driven every year to the alternative either of starving or of earning their own support. Probably in no previous year has the Association been more successful in diminishing the number of the habitually dependent. The Report of 1850 showed, that notwithstanding the immense influx of foreign emigrants and the peculiar exposure of the city to pauperism from this and other sources, the indigent needing relief that year, were *twenty-three hundred less* than in 1844. And during the year just closed, although the causes of pauperism have not abated in activity, the number requiring aid has not only fallen far below the ratio of the increase of population, but as the returns show, was numerically less by three hundred and twenty-five families, containing *twelve hundred and sixty persons*, than in 1850. This encouraging result is mainly attributable to two causes: first, the sounder discrimination which the enlarged and comprehensive experience of the Visitors qualified them to exercise; and second, the decisive course pursued, in urging upon all the able-bodied poor, here suffering for employment where it cannot be obtained, to seek it elsewhere in the vast inland, where it abounds.

II. *More decisive measures than heretofore have been adopted in respect to the debased poor.* These, unhappily, are too numerous and dangerous a class to be allowed to increase, without special efforts to reduce their number. Their indolent and vicious habits are so firmly established, that they are not likely to be changed, except under a course of powerful and effective treatment. They generally have not only an insuperable aversion to labor, but also to the Alms-House, because of its salutary privations and restraints. They love to clan together in some out-of-the-way place, are content to live in filth and disorder with a bare subsistence, provided they can drink, and smoke, and gossip, and enjoy their balls, and wakes, and frolics, without molestation. Instead of putting their children to school, or to some useful trade, they are driven out to beg, pick up fuel, sweep the street crossings, peddle petty wares, &c., that they may themselves live lazily on the means thus secured. This is the class of parents whom the Chief of Police informs us, " send forth their offspring to practices of theft and semi-bestiality—selling the very bodies and souls of those in whom their own blood circulates, for the means of dissipation and debauchery." And these, as we learn from the same authority, are " the vagrant and vicious children, of both sexes, who infest our public thoroughfares, hotels, docks, &c.—who are growing up in ignorance and profligacy, only destined to a life of misery, shame and crime, and ultimately to a felon's doom."

Experience has shown with respect to this grossly immoral class of parents, that little is to be hoped from any reformatory efforts in their behalf. It is obvious, moreover, that so long as such parents are suffered to train up their children in dissolute habits, juvenile depravity, despite of every effort, will increase and abound. The trite maxim, "Begin at the beginning," is the only true philosophy in this matter. To keep such families together, either by occasional relief or employment, is to encourage their depravity, and would not only be unkind to them, but most pernicious in its consequences to the community. These nurseries of indolence, debauchery, and intemperance, are moral pests of society, and should be broken up. The inmates, in the absence of a more suitable provision, should be sent to the Alms-House—the sick, if there are any, to the Hospital—the children to be educated and apprenticed, and the able-bodied adults set to work, under such discipline and regulations, as would tend to correct their habits, and oblige them to earn their own subsistence. It is obvious that this Association, having no police powers, can do but little effectively, for a class requiring such treatment. All that it can do, it is now effecting; it discourages their vicious courses, by withholding gratuitous relief, and, by appropriate moral means, endeavors to improve their character. But were the decisive course above recommended, pursued by the proper authorities, with a few families in each Ward, others, it is believed, would take warning from their example, and a vast amount of street begging and vagrancy, not only be prevented, but many of like character be deterred from coming to the city. The truth cannot be too often nor too deeply impressed, that juvenile depravity, already enormous, will continue to increase, and daily assume a more alarming and inveterate form, while the offspring of these vicious parents—children worse than orphans—are subjected to their corrupting influence.

III. *Special efforts have been made to establish an organized system to benefit the children of the poor.* So manifest was the necessity of some effective measures in behalf of this class, that previous to the startling disclosures of the police department, public attention had been called to the subject, and the Legislature memorialized for some new enactments in relation to it. And this Association, ever watchful to improve every opportunity of doing good that comes within its appropriate sphere, appointed a committee consisting of seven Managers, early in October, 1849, for the purpose of taking into consideration the expediency of establishing some permanent institution for that object. This committee enlarged its number by inviting the co-operation of several gentlemen, distinguished for intelligence and philanthropy, who, after mature deliberation, recommended the forming of an institution, differing in some of its features from any before projected, for the benefit of the friendless, neglected, and vicious children, which abound in this city. The recommendation being approved, application was made to the Legislature for an Act of Incorporation, but without success, until the last special session of that body, when corporate powers were conferred on the new institution, by the title of the "New-York Juvenile Asylum." The new organization is soon expected to commence its labors, under very favorable auspices.

IV. *More has been done for the permanent relief of the indigent sick than in former years.* It was obvious on the most cursory review, that medical provision had hitherto neither kept pace with other city charities, nor yet with the rapid growth and increasing wants of the inhabitants. In 1830, with a population of 202,000 souls, there were three dispensaries; in 1850, with a population of 515,000, the number of public dispensaries had not been increased; consequently the northern part of the city above Fourteenth street, which as much required such a provision as any other, was entirely unprovided for. As early as 1845, the attention of the Board was called to the vast amount of suffering among the sick poor, occasioned by the absence of proper medical provisions; and for several years the Association furnished medicines and medical attendance gratuitously to the most abject and needy, at an annual expenditure of about five hundred dollars. But as the peculiar care and medication of the sick, fell without the scope of its design, and having no funds that could legitimately be applied to the object, this aid was necessarily discontinued And as neither the Common Council, nor the Alms-House Department, have in their official capacity the power to establish public dispensaries, the duty of founding these institutions necessarily devolves upon the voluntary action of private citizens.

In view of these facts, the Committee of the Board having the matter in charge, called select meetings of the residents in the destitute district, on the 19th of February, and also on the 7th March, when, after a full consideration of the subject by each meeting, they successively resolved, "That it was expedient to establish a Medical Dispensary for the benefit of the indigent sick, in the northeastern part the city." Pursuant to this resolution, the Committee intrusted with the work, prosecuted it with such energy and success, that a Certificate of Incorporation, duly executed and approved, was filed with the Clerk of the City and County of New-York, March 26th, and with the Secretary of State, March 27th. Having thus accomplished the purposes of its formation, the preliminary local committee was dissolved, and the management of the new institution was assumed by its Corporate Managers, who, on the 8th day of April, 1851, adopted a code of by-laws, elected their officers, and appointed the standing committees.

Liberal subscribtions for the new Dispensary commenced among the Officers and Managers of this Association, which were increased by others. The institution was denominated the "Demilt Dispensary," in consequence of the munificent donation of five thousand dollars, from a benevolent gentleman, "as one of the Residuary Legatees of the Demilt family." The Committee say, "Without such encouragement they might have been unable to accomplish any result worthy of note;" and they close a very satisfactory report of their proceedings with the assurance that the Demilt Dispensary will be well endowed, efficiently and ably conducted, and they trust that ere long it will not only become a useful, but a model institution.

It is proper to remark, that in accordance with the recommendation of their Committee, the design of the Board included the founding of two Dispensaries, but one of which has yet been established. For the organization of the other, to be located in the northwestern part of the city, *one thousand dollars have been pledged*, and the work will be commenced when sufficient funds justify the undertaking. And these, it is believed, would not long be wanting, if our benevolent citizens were acquainted with the urgent necessities of the indigent sick in that rapidly populating portion of the city. For however strong the claim of other charities, all instinctively know and feel that the sick poor should not be neglected. When Providence takes from them the ability to labor, it lays on others the obligation of ministering to their wants. O, who that sympathizes in "the afflictions of the afflicted," and would do them good, can in any other way so certainly and permanently benefit them, as by generous donations to such an object?

V. *Special efforts have been made to diffuse sound practical views, in respect to the nature and objects of this charity.* This great city presents an ample, but a very difficult field for the exercise of benevolence. Being the commercial metropolis of the Western world, whither the tide of European emigration most strongly sets, it is peculiarly exposed to an inundation of foreign paupers. Nearly 2000 vessels, having an aggregate of more than a million of tons burthen, are employed in bringing passengers to this port. Of the vast crowd of immigrants thus arriving, the larger part bring with them the means of reaching their destination in the interior, where, by their industry and energy, they become valuable acquisitions to the country. For the relief of the less fortunate, who from any cause are needy and suffering, a fund is provided by a tax upon ship-owners, which is prepaid by the passengers themselves. But, notwithstanding this provision, the destitution among us requiring charitable aid is chiefly imported. According to the county official returns, the number of paupers chargeable to the State during the past year, amounted to 104,399; and during the same period, the alien emigrants in the State chargeable to the Emigration Department, were officially reported to be 50,000, making the whole number relieved 154,399. Of the State paupers, but 45,116 were natives, while 59,283 were foreigners, to which add the before-named 50,000 recent emigrants, and the result shows that 119,283 foreigners, or more than 70 per cent. of the whole number of paupers relieved or supported were from foreign countries, and 45,116, or less than 30 per cent., were natives. Startling as this exhibit may appear, in view of the enormous emigration of the past ten years, it was to be expected. From January 1st, 1842, to October 1st, 1851, 1,417,871 emigrants have arrived at this port alone; and as this city winnows from the immense mass the most infirm, improvident and thriftless, who remain here to subsist on alms, and augment the number of the indigent, it is not surprising that so undue a proportion of the dependent among us are foreigners. Dividing the destitute of the city into eight parts, but one part, or an eighth of the whole number, would be American. While these remarkable facts strikingly illustrate the disinterestedness of our municipal charities, they also show that poverty here is of so unnatural a growth, that most of our alms-giving institutions might be disbanded, but for the necessities of the foreign poor.

We may not doubt that the evictment of tenantry from estates, and the wholesale shipment of parish dependents, are now and long have been a part of the economic arrangements in Europe, and especially in Ireland, in order to rid the wealthy of the burthen of their support. But if we see much inhumanity in such an unscrupulous expatriation of the poor, and injustice to ourselves by such a systematic invasion of our country by the indigent, we should not imitate the example we condemn, by suffering those thus thrown upon our shores to perish by our neglect.

And yet, the liberal course which has hitherto been pursued by the Association in respect to these classes of the poor, has brought upon it, the Board regret to say, the censure of some donors. The complaint is, that a large part of the Institution's expenditures are bestowed upon persons of foreign birth, and chiefly of the Roman Catholic faith, while persons of the same faith are generally unwilling to contribute to its funds.. They do not complain of the poor who have no ability to give, but of the rich among them, who, having ample means, yet refuse to contribute of their means to this charity, by which their poor are so greatly benefited; and hence, the foreign poor of that denomination, are chiefly relieved and supported by Protestant funds. Such, in brief, is the substance of the charge, the truth of which cannot be disputed; but as it is preferred in a tone which implies that the principles admitting such a distribution of alms are unsound, the Board feel called upon for such an explanation, as, they trust, will make the duty of such a distribution more obvious than it may now appear. The subject is not without difficulties; but these difficulties, they believe, exist less in the subject itself, than in the medium through which it is viewed. If the origin and objects of this Association are impartially examined, and the mutual ties and dependencies by which Providence designs to unite in one brotherhood the entire family of man, are recognized, they confidently cherish the hope that the principles on which the Institution bestows alms will be approved by every unbiassed mind. Without further introduction, they remark:

First. That previous to the establishment of this charity, all the alms-giving societies in this city were organized for the benefit of specified classes, which left all that were not included in these classes, to beg or suffer unrelieved, unless they availed themselves of public charity. Hence our streets were filled with vagrants and mendicants, and the wants of the poor became so urgent, as frequently to require the volunteer exertions of our citizens in different wards and localities, every winter for their relief. The absolute necessity, in short, of a permanent provision, commensurate in extent to the relief of all the poor in the city not otherwise provided for, was universally felt and acknowledged, by all informed on the subject. To meet this want, this Institution was formed, being expressly for the benefit of all the indigent in the city, irrespective of every sectarian or national distinction; and on this clearly defined basis, appeals were subsequently made for co-operation and funds, which were generously and confidingly responded to by thousands of our citizens, who became members of the Association, and liberally contributed for its support. Having, therefore, been organized under these circumstances for such objects, it is imperatively bound to abide in entire strictness to these objects, and carry into effect its promulged principles. It has no right to limit or restrict its charities in any way contrary to the conditions it has publicly expressed. If it should withhold alms from any on account of peculiarities of faith, or country, or for any other pretext which involves a departure from avowed principles, the organization would virtually be dissolved.

Second. Although the Association is designed for the benefit of all the poor in the city not otherwise provided for, it does not follow that all who apply will receive aid, for almsgiving is not recognized as the only or the most important charity. The Constitution says that it shall be granted only so far as is compatible with the physical and moral elevation of the indigent. And as these latter important results may be endangered by indiscreet relief, the Institution does not blindly dispense its favors, but requires of its Visitors careful discrimination. If the applicant, however, has no other resource, and after careful examination is found to come within the scope of the Association's objects, the Visitor is under moral obligation to give such relief as it has pledged itself to bestow. In such cases, to make sect or birth a disqualification for alms, would not only be unjust to the individual, and a direct violation of the Constitution of the Association, but, if generally carried into effect, would defeat one of the leading objects of the Institution, inasmuch as seven-eighths of the poor it was designed to relieve, would thus be excluded from its benefits.

Third. The views of the Association which appear to be entertained by the complainants, do great injustice to its disinterested and elevated character. A better knowledge of its principles, would have shown them that it regards every man as a neighbor and brother, and prompts to the exercise of kindness and beneficence to all. It overleaps all denominational and national considerations, and within its appropriate sphere is as free as the air and sunshine. It was formed on the divine model which admits of no such contracted limitations; and it is manifest that any system inferior to this would not have adequately provided for the poor of this great community. Whoever, therefore, admits the authority of the model, should also admit the claims of the principle here recognized and founded upon it, for it is of universal and perpetual obligation. And let it be remembered, that in it there are no conflicting requisitions. It does not hold a man responsible for his neighbor's faith or conduct; but it does hold him responsible, if having the opportunity and ability to give, it sees him suffering and withholds relief.

Such, in brief, is an outline of some of the more prominent measures, to which the Board have specially directed their attention during the past year. The effects, it is believed, have been to subserve the interests of the poor, and to promote the general welfare and security of the community. They have tended, moreover, to remove difficulties, awaken new interest in the subject, and to disprove the manifestly erroneous opinion entertained by some, that the evils inseparable from gratuitous relief more than counterbalance its advantages. In such fallacies as these, some pseudo-philanthropists find an apology for their own selfishness and inaction, while they would persuade others that there is a mistake in those clear and often repeated injunctions of Scripture, which inculcate kindness and sympathy for the indigent. But however specious may be the objections urged against the command to do good unto all men, at all times. as we have opportunity, it still remains, and ever will remain in all its binding force and obligation, making our ability in this relation, the measure of our duty and responsibility. And in this, as in every other scriptural precept, Divine wisdom justifies itself to human experience, by showing that well directed exertions, to ameliorate the condition of the poor, are never expended in vain.

In respect to the arrangements of the organization, it may be remarked, that in order to conform with the recent division of the Sixteenth District into two Wards, another District has been formed. The new District, numerically the Twentieth, has been subdivided into sixteen sections, and includes the area northward from Twenty-sixth Street to Fortieth Street, and from the Sixth Avenue to the Hudson River. It has also been necessary to alter the bounds of some sections, and add seven new ones, so that the present number is three hundred and twenty-four.

Each of these sections, it should be remembered, has its appropriate visitor, whose noble employment it is to explore, in person, the habitations of the poor, in order to sympathize with the suffering and forsaken, counsel the vicious and erring, elevate the depressed, and minister to the needy, according to their actual wants. Who that appreciates the rewards of such an employment, or has experienced the secret joy which expands the bosom in assuaging human misery, would not covet such a service? Yet such a service among the multitudinous variety of poor in this city, is not performed without incredible self-sacrifice and toil. That men, indeed, can be found in this busy metropolis, who will engage and persevere with unwearied fidelity for years in such a work, should at once inspire us with gratitude to God, and confidence in man. Such endeavors to relieve, enlighten, and reclaim our poorer brethren, we are assured are more pleasing to Him than any other. And if, as we may not doubt, it is by such and kindred agencies, that He designs to ameliorate the condition of the poor, they properly demand our best energies, and deserve all they demand.

1851.)   EIGHTH ANNUAL REPORT.   29

The following is a tabular exhibit of the Monthly District Returns, from November 1st, 1850, to November 1st, 1851:

1850–51.	Number of Families Relieved.	Number of Persons Relieved.	Number of Visits.
November, . .	801	3,088	1,215
December, . .	2,167	8,158	3,072
January, . .	3,643	14,293	5,312
February, . .	3,838	15,147	4,811
March, . . .	3,021	12,000	3,485
April, . . .	1,463	5,849	1,587
May, ...	462	1,837	596
June, ...	265	1,060	292
July, ...	192	768	201
August, . . .	241	964	352
September, . .	389	1,556	489
October, . . .	548	2,192	864

Disbursements during the year ending October 31st, $33,656 95
Receipts for the same period, - - - - - 32,327 31

Balance due the Treasurer, - - - - - $1,329 64

As benevolence will ever vindicate itself, and maintain its own place among the highest of human virtues, the Board deem it unnecessary to say any thing in its behalf. They are willing to leave the entire duty of contributing for eleemosynary re-relief, to the "willing generosity, the spontaneous and unforced sympathies of our nature." This, they believe, is a broad and firm ground of confidence. "Nature," says one of the deep thinkers for the poor, "has made compassion one of the strongest and steadiest of our universal instincts. It were an intolerable spectacle, even to the inmates of a felon's cell, to behold one of their number in the agonies of hunger; and rather than endure it, they would share their own scanty morsel with him." Much more intolerable would it be for the virtuous and humane, to witness the indigence, suffering and wretchedness of this great city, and withhold relief. Relief will therefore be given, but if impulsively, without investigation, knowledge or discrimination, who can estimate the perversions of such charity, the waste of means, or the mischiefs, disorder, and wretchedness that would inevitably ensue? It is obvious there must be system, intelligence, and discrimination, in order to a wise and efficacious distribution of alms in this vast community. This being admitted, the Board feel that it is unnecessary to commend this system for distributing such relief, to those acquainted with it, now comprising so large and increasing a number of our most intelligent and devoted philanthropists; for experience has shown that such acquaintance affords the surest guaranty of their continued co-operation and aid. The chief embarrassment hitherto has not arisen out of a want of liberality among those familiar with the Institution, but from the difficulty of diffusing such a knowledge of its principles as to excite general interest, and unite the great mass of our citizens in its support. If all on whom the poor have claims, could be persuaded to examine the Association for themselves, its design, mode of action and results, this system of relief would ere long, they believe, become the channel of charity for the city; and thus, happily, be instrumental in fulfilling some of the highest obligations of humanity, and in saving the community from the wretchedness, the expense, and the peril of a vagrant, indigent, and vicious population.

> "Give alms: the needy sink with pain;
> The orphans mourn, the crushed complain
> Give freely: hoarded gold is curst,
> A prey to robbers and to rust.
> Christ, through his poor, a claim doth make,
> Give gladly, for thy Saviours's sake."

Association for the Improvement of the Condition of the Poor in Account with Robert B. Minturn, Treasurer.

1851.				1851.		
Oct. 31	To Amounts expended from Oct. 31, 1850,	$33,656 95		Oct. 31	By Amounts received per donations and collections from Oct. 31, 1850,	$32,327 31
					" Balance,	1,329 64
		$33,656 95				$33,656 95
1851.						
Oct. 31	To balance as debt of Association due the Treasurer,	$1,329 64				

The undersigned hereby certify that they have examined in detail the above account and find it correct and properly vouched, showing a balance due the Treasurer of thirteen hundred and twenty-nine and sixty-four hundredths dollars.

JOSEPH B. COLLINS, } *Auditing Committee.*
FREDERICK S. WINSTON,

New-York, Nov. 6, 1851.

PRINTED FORMS USED BY THE ASSOCIATION.

Ticket of Reference for the use of Members.

Mr.   Visitor,

    No.   St.

is requested to visit

at No.

                                                     Member

                              N. Y. Association for
                          Improving the Condition of the Poor.

Visitor's Order.

Mr.

No.   *St.*

Please let

have the value of

in

                          184

                                                      Vis.

                              N. Y. Association for
                          Improving the Condition of the Poor.

Monthly Report.

Subjoined is a condensed plan of a Sectional Monthly Return. The original occupies a large page of foolscap, with appropriate columns, fifteen in number, which enable Visitors to give the following particulars of every family relieved. 1st. Name, residence, place of birth, sex, color, occupation, time in the city, number in family, and number of visits. 2d. Statements of character,—as being temperate or intemperate. 3d. Unavoidable causes of indigence, such as sickness, infirmity, or old age, with space for marginal remarks.

PRINTED FORM USED BY THE ASSOCIATION.

New-York Association for Improving the Condition of the Poor.

VISITOR'S MONTHLY REPORT OF SECTION No.   DISTRICT No.   DATED   184

☞ *A mark with a pen thus ,, in the columns, will point out the class to which the person named belongs.*

FAMILIES RELIEVED. — Always give full Name, and *male* Head of Family, if living.	RESIDENCE OF FAMILIES. — Which must be reported every month.	Foreigners.	Natives.	Colored Persons.	Males.	Females.	No. in Family.	No. of Visits.	KIND OF OCCUPATION.	Temperate.	Intemperate.	Sickness.	Misfortune.	Old Age.	AMOUNT EX- PENDED. $	cts.	REMARKS.

Signed,   Visitor.

List of Members.

Owing to inadvertence in the returns from some of the Districts, it is feared that the list of Members may not be perfectly accurate. The *amounts* received were duly credited, as may be seen by an inspection of the Treasurer's account, at the General Office But as the names of some who contributed small sums did not accompany their donations, with all the efforts subsequently made to obtain them, the list may still be incomplete.

A.

Aspinwall, J. L.
Allen, Horatio
Aspinwall, W. H.
Allen, Stephen
Alley, Saul
Astor, Wm. B.
Astor, J. J.
Allen, G. F.
Aldrich, H. D.
Abernethy, C.
Anderson, S. W.
Aguirre, P. A.
Aspinwall, S. Mrs.
Aymar, J. Q.
Arcularius, George
Adams, Crowel
Atwill, John
Adams, John T.
Abbatt, I.
A. C. D.
A Friend, by J. Donalson
Aymar & Co.
Anthon, Dr. Revd.
Adams, John
Abeel, John H.
A Friend
Anonymous
A Friend, by G. W. Strong.
Auten, J. W.
Andrew, H. Mrs. & family.
Ashton, George
Alsop, J. W.
Allen, J
Aikman, R.
Avery, J. S.
Anderson, John H., M. D.
Abel, C. A.
Albro, Benjamin
Anderson, Wm.

Avery, E. L.
Acheson, Wm.
Austin, G.
Allen, C. G.
Austen, David
Austen, John H.
Anderson, E. J.
Arcularius, P. G.
Abbott, G. D.
Atterberry, Mr.
Aitkin & Miller
Althause S. B.
Atwater, W. L.
Ackerman, James
Allen, Jonathan W.
Ammerman, Wm. C.
Alexander, Wm.
Anthony, J,
Anderson, Mrs.
Allen, George
Ammerman, P.
Anderson, E.
Ayres, Albert
Alford, S. M.
Allen, Wm. B.
Allen, John
Ayres, O.
Andrews, George
Alford, E. M.
Allen, Isaac
Andrews, J. E.
Alexander, Isaac
Arnold, J.
Abeel, C. Miss
Allison, Thos. H.
Amerman, John W.
Anguish, James
Appleton, D. & Co.
Althof & Ahlborn
Ahrenfeldt, C.
Alvord, C. A.

Aguiar, L.
A. W. M.
Atwater, Wm.
Allen, W. M. A.
Anderson, C. V. & J.
Ash, James H.
Allen, John
Allen, Gilbert
Abbatt, Wm. M.
Anstice, Henry
Aims, Jacob
Arcularius, A. M.
Arnold, B. G.
Averell, Horatio
Adriance, Thos. M.
Atwater, Wm.
Albro, Richard
Anderson, Hiram
Ackerly, R. C.
Allan & Rose
Adams, C.
Allen, T. E.
Apgar, Levi
Alcock, Dr.
Allen, C., M.D.
Arpin, Paul
Anthon, John
Allison, Michl.
Arnold, D. S.
Avery, J. W.
Armstrong, M.
Ahrens, G.
Asche, Henry
Aikman, Hugh
A Friend
Allen, Wm. A.
Angell, Engel & Hewitt
A. F. Jr.
Ayres, Mary, pr. C. C. Darling
Abbe, George W.

LIST OF MEMBERS. (1851.

Aikman, Hugh
Austin, Stephen
Ayres, Reuben
Anderson, Edmund
Andrews, S. W.
Abrams, Isaac
Albro, R.
Armstrong, James
Adams, J. D.

B.

Banyer, Mrs. M.
Brown, James
Boorman, James
Brown, Stewart
Benedict, E. C.
Boorman & Johnston
Bruen, A. M.
Bull, Wm. G.
Burr, Isaac Mrs.
Bronson, A. Mrs.
Bruce, George
Bolton, J., M. D.
Burrows, P.
Beadell, Henry
Belmont, A.
Bange, Henry
Bonnev, B W.
Bliss, T. E.
Bussing, J. S.
Bonnett, P. R.
Bloodgood, N.
Baylis, H.
Bedell, G. T. Rev.
Butterworth, J. F.
Bullard, P. Mrs.
Bininger, A.
Beekman, H.
Buck, G., M. D.
Brush, S.
Bristed, C A.
Borrowe, J. H., M. D.
Breese, S. L. Capt.
Breese & Elliot
Brown, E J.
Ball, Tompkins & Black
Bishop, T.
Blain, Mrs.
Beekman, W. F.
Baldwin, Dibblee & Work
Brown, R. J.
Bogert, C.
Buckland, A.
Bidwell, M. J.
Blatchford, E. H.
Bage, R.
Burgy, J. H.
Bradford, W.
Butler, B. F.
Bacon, D. P.
Bouchard, J.
Bushnell, O.
Beckwith, N. M.
Bliss, J. C. M. D.
Brown, W. H., M. D.

Bruen, M. Mrs.
Barrell, G.
Brown, J. F.
Brown, R.
Brooks, M. C.
Burr, M.
Browne, R. W.
Baudoine, C. A.
Beck, James & Co.
Brown, Nathan
Biggar, J. B.
Britton, D.
Bailey, Wm.
Barron, Thomas
Boyd, Wm.
Bowdoin, G. R. J.
Bonnell, Mr.
Blackwell, Wm. B.
Bunce, David
Bowman & Ebbits,
Burkhalter, R.
Bethune, Mrs.
Burdett, Charles
Bowden, Andrew
Black, Mrs.
Boyce, J.
Burrell, S. & J.
Bush R. I.
Brown, J. L.
Brainerd, G. W.
Brinckerhoff, Mrs.
Bridges, J. F.
Butter, T. C.
Burhams, Samuel
Batchelor, Mary Mrs.
Brown & Ogden.
Bull, H. K., by Rev. C. C. Darling.
Banks, Mark
Boyd & Paul
Borden, Wm.
Brodhead, Edgar
Babcock, F. H.
Born & Schuchardt
Blow & March
Blake & Brown
Bigelow Richard
Blake & Duyckinck
Burrell & Co. H.
Benjamin & Co. W.
Burritt, Ira
Beales & Brush
Bent, Brothers & Co.
Bowne & Co.
Bingham, L. S.
Brennen, P.
Belknap, E. S.
Baker, Dobel
Bird, Mathew
Bulkley, G.
Bulkley, E.
Barstow, Samuel
Bowen, A. S.
Buckman, E.
Brooks, E.
Briggs, A. T.
Brooks, John

Bacon, John E.
Blackmer, J.
Buckanan, Mrs.
Bell, Abraham
Bloodgood, Wm.
Brown, Andrew
Brown, N. Mrs.
Baldwin, S. Mrs.
Bigler, D. Rev.
Bouyee, Anthony
Bartholemew, F. H.
Belden, Wm. jr. Rev.
Bard, J. M.
Bush, George
Baker, T.
Bergen, J.
Brady, Wm. C.
Bell, Joseph M.
Bradford, A. W.
Barker, Stephen
Bruce, John T.
Bruce, R. M.
Busche, Frederick Rev.
Belcher, H. W.
Baldwin, C. A.
Baldwin, Luther
Belcher, E , M. D.
Burr, E. W.
Bean, B. L.
Brooks, Horace
Butler, Chs. Mrs.
Brown, E. M.
Bradley, J. N.
Butler Wm. H. V.
Bryce, Wm.
Bruen,
Brumley, R.
Brooks, Joshua
Barry, T. F.
Brown, Mrs.
Borst, Mr.
Barton,
B & C
Bloodgood, M.
Burkhalter, C.
Bruce, John M.
Backstone, Willis
Beekman, Jas W.
Banks, Martha
Blondell, Wm.
Born, Jacob
Birdsall, Samuel
Brower, J. D.
Bonsall, R. W.
Bodinier, J. V., M. D.
Benedict, S. W.
Buttle, S. S.
Brinkerhoff, W.
Bleakley, J. T. M.
Burritt, Mrs.
Berrian C.
Bleakley, A.
Brainerd, A.
Bruce John M. jr.
Becket, John
Burger, E. H.
Badeau, E. C.

1851.) LIST OF MEMBERS. 37

Bloomfield, E. S.
Bevenbroick, A.
Bernheimer & Co.
Back, Joseph
Barnes, Joseph N.
Bowles, James
Bugsell, C.
Bussell, George
Brunner, Henry
Blauvelt, D. T.
Bancroft, W. S.
Binse, L. B.
Brewster, J. B.
Bogart, C.
Bloomfield, Wm.
Burdge, Ira Mrs.
Banta, Wm.
Bootman, E.
Brown, Mr.
Bell, Benjamin
Buckmaster, Thos. O.
Bussell, Mr.
Brownson, Mrs.
Bensell, W. P.
Brown, Wm. M.
Brown, J. H.
Bock, E.
Brinck & Russell
Barton, Wm.
Burnham, Elizabeth Mrs.
Beebe, W. R.
Breath, James
Barmore, G. & H.
Beebe, Philo V.
Brown, Chs. P.
Bishop, Dwight
Bell, Thomas
Bussing, C. K.
Beadleston, Eben.
Burges, W. F.
Brush, James E.
Bartlett, A H.
Bollis, E. L.
Bassford, Abm.
Blackwell, J. M.
Berdett, Jacob
Back, J L.
Benson, C. S.
Banta, S.
Burdett H. C.
Burch, H. B.
Bush, Richard T.
Bunn, M. Y.
Battersby, J. Mrs.
Barrow, James
Bates, Mrs.
Bostwick, C. J.
Bevier, J. H. Rev.
Brown, H.
Brownell, J. S.
Baxter, J. C.
Bush,
Brintnall, E. M.
Brown, Anson S.
Bond, W. L.
Burnton,

Brown, James T.
Brockner, W.
Benedict, S. H.
Bogert, Albert
Brown, C.
Bogart, J C.
Belden, D.
Balch, W. S. Rev.
Berdan, Mr.
Brooks & Cummings
Brown, Charles
Bohen, W. B.
Bennett, John
Brown, G. W.
Brown, Garret
Billings, Dr.
Bergen, Abm. L.
Burris, Mr.
Burdsall, Hosea
Bear, Henry
Bunnell, A,
Burdsall,
Brommer, John
Baldwin. C.
Boyle & Coleman
Bausher, Henry
Bell, Mrs.
Barr, O.
Brown, G. W.
Burke, Wm.
Barton, Joseph
Brown, E. D.
Boyd, Daniel
Bennett, N. L.
Burr. J
Baldwin, B. S., Mrs.
Bacon, Francis
Baker, John H.
Butcher, John H.
Brenley, J. E.
Bower, T.
Barnum P. T.
Barton, Edgar J.
Barnes & Pharo
Brown & De Rosset
Bennett, M.
Bangs, Bro's. & Co.
Bishop, Victor
Benjamin, Wm. M.
Bates, T. & T. H.
Bishop,
Baldwin, Studwell & Fisher
Brett, T. F.
Brewer, Wm.
Bostwick, Z.
Buchanan,
Bennett, Wm.
Braisted, Thos. H.
Brooks, J. T.
Barnes, J. N.
Brennen, Owen W.
Buloid, R.
Benedict. A. C.
Brush, Walter F.
Brewster, U. B.
Brown, W. H.

Boorman, R.
Bowne, Richard H.
Burke, Michael
Booth, W. A.
Bleecker, Jane Mrs.
Brouwer, Jacob
Bridgeman, Eli
Babcock, G. Mrs.
Bogart, Henry K.
Bernard, A.
Beesley, Isaiah
Ballard, James
Bissell, John
Badeau, P.
Berrian, W. D.
Blunt & Syms
Brady, M. D.
Barlett & Wilford
Brigham, Mr.
Bronson, Silas
Brush, Platt
Brower, A.
Baker, Scudder & Co.
Barnes & Mackay
Boyce, Mr.
Ballard, R. Mrs.
Buskey, Joshua, M. D.
Butts, G. S.
Beach & Phillips
Baldwin, J. L.
Bunker, B. F.
Bonnett, Mrs.
Brinkerhoff, W. C.
Beal, J. H.
Boyd, Mr.
Butler, S. C.
Bininger & Cozzens
Blair, H. B.
Burkhalter, Stephen
Brown, Albert
Brown, Geo. L.
Brown, Silas
Brown, H. S.
Boyd & Paul
Boyd & Wilkins
Beach, Clark & Co.
Berry, House
Booth, J. C.
Beebe, Wm.
Baldwin & Sexton
Bronson, Mary Miss.
Blanco, B.
Bunce, Nathaniel
Birdsall, Thos. W.
Brooks, George
Banks, Thos.
Brombacker,
Busted, George Washington
Beers, Abner
Broadway Post Office
Bogardus, Wm.
Baldwin, J. L.
Burnett, Peter, M. D.
Bruce, B. G.
Bell, Joseph M.
Bebee, Judge

LIST OF MEMBERS. (1851.

Bartlett, D. E.
Benedict, J. W.
Bogardus, Wm.
Baldwin, H. M.
Burras, T. H.
Burkhalter, R.
Bridges, J. F.
Ballagh, Wm.
Baxter, Samuel
Bremner, J. P.
Bruce, G. B.
Bailey, Thos.
Belloni, L. J.
Bogert, P. A.
Bradley, W. C.
Bennett, Wm.
Barker, Wm.
Burrill, S. N.
Burr, John
Bennett, N. N.
Brainard, Oliver
Brown, W. S.
Brown, Richard
Burger, T. J.
Beatty L. D.
Beare, T. M.
Ballard, J. B.
Butler, W. A.
Bullock, Smith W.
Bulkley, Francis
Bailey, Amos

C.

Crosby, Wm. B.
Collins, Joseph B.
Cock, T. F., M. D.
Carson, Jacob, M. D.
Clark, W. M.
Conklin, Jonas
Curtis, Cyrus
Cromwell & Birdsall
Cruger, Harriet Douglas Mrs.
Clark, R. Smith
Coster, G. W.
Coster, H. A.
Chesterman, J.
Colles, James
Cary, S. T.
Cammann, O. J.
Catlin, D. W.
Currie, W.
Callender, W. S.
Chastelain, J.
Coddington, T. B.
Clark, G.
Carpender, J. S.
Cuming, T. B.
Clark, J.
Crittenden, H.
Conant, F. J.
Cook, Z.
Colwill, A.
Cooke, W.
Clarke, G. W.

Coman, L. D.
Clay, G.
Cogswell, J. G.
Clark, Mrs.
Coltamore & Co.
Cash
Cox, J.
C. A. W. & Co.
Cahill, Mr.
Clune, Anna
Carr, James
Chapen, L. B.
Coles, J. U. Mrs.
Couch, W.
Coxhead, C. J.
Campbell, D.
Catterfield, W. F.
Cash
Clay, E. P.
Campbell, Matthew
Cunningham, Mr.
Camann, G. P., M.D.
Cornell, G. J.
Coleman, Mrs.
Corning, W. B.
Cook, Israel
Cochran, Mrs.
Copcutt, J. & F.
Coit, Henry
Cropsy, James
Carey, W. F.
Carter, R.
Conner & Winser
Conover & Wooley
Canfield, E. H.
Carryl, N. T.
Crapo, Samuel A.
Christy, Thomas
Constant, S. S.
Cornell, M.
Church, John B.
Cash
Church, Austin
Cummings, J. P.
Crane, D.
Crane, H. D.
Crosby, John P.
Cassiday, James
Clark, Joseph L.
Condit, Noble & Co.
Choutau & Co. P.
Cook, Levi
Chauncey, Henry
Cash
Crooks, R.
Coit, Henry A.
Curtis, L. B.
Clark, E. S.
Cary, J. A.
Cash
Clap, John
Carlisle, Mrs.
C. B. C.
Cash, (Several)
Corwith, Cath. S.
Cohen, Mrs.

Cromwell, W. D.
Carroll, James, M. D.
Cox, Joseph
Crane, John J , M. D.
Corwin, M. Mrs.
Coates, Joseph H.
Coey, Wm. John
Contoit, John H.
Cash
Cape, H. M. Mrs.
Cook, Ebenezer
Christopher, R.
Cockroft, James M.D.
Cromwell, Daniel
Camp, C. Mrs.
Church, F.
Clarkson, C. V. M D.
Cort, N. L.
Conklin, H.
Clarke, A. B.
Chamberlain, M.
Creagh, W.
Crawford, Wm.
Cooke, S. G.
Caswell, John
Coe, Charles A.
Colgate, Robert
Chegary, Madam
Comstock, L. S.
Coffin, J. P.
Coggill, Henry
Crary, Mrs.
Curtis, Joseph
Carey, John Jr.
Carpenter, U. F.
Cooper & Brothers
Campbell, Robert
Cromwell, Mr.
Cheever, Geo. B. Rev.
Campbell, John
Coles
Curtis, P. A.
Constable, James M.
Collins, G. C.
Clinton, Dr.
Clark, James
Currie, J. H.
Curtis, Edwin
Curtis, Geo. H.
Chilton, B. A.
Clark, Mathias
Collamore, D.
Cornell & Ammerman
Cornell, T. J.
Campbell, Mrs.
Clarke, M.
Carpenter, N. H.
Clarkson, Jas. G.
Cook, Wm. E.
Cook, John
Clark, Alexander
Church, Wm.
Cooke, George H.
Campbell, A. E. Revd.
Cornell, H. Mrs.
Carpenter, A. G.

1851.)　　　　　LIST OF MEMBERS.　　　　　39

Cameron, James
Coles, Corns.
Combs, John
Cox, Dr.
Chippendale, Mrs.
Carpenter, Mrs.
Camerden, J.
Campbell, W. S.
Cowles, Henry B.
Campbell, Freeman
Charraud, John
Clarke, Thomas
Childs, Asa
Cook, Edward
Coleman, E. W.
Cummings, Thomas
Clinch, C. P.
Coulter, Samuel
Chamberlin, E.
Clark, S. M.
Church, C. L.
Connolly, Chas. M.
Cox, Chas. B.
Camp, H.
Carlin, J.
Cunningham, W. J.
Cornell, J. H.
Conklin, J.
Cash
Chesebro, A.
Cronk, S. W.
Cash
Creighton, John
Clarke, J. A.
Clarke, W.
Chapman, Robert
Cox, Mrs.
Christie, B.
Codwise, David
Curtis, Charles
Chesebrough, Dr.
Collins, Wm.
Cook, Mr.
Conger, John
Chapin, L.
Clussman, Mrs.
Clark, James
Cook, Alderman
Cash
Clement, A. M.
Currahger, Captain
Cook, A. H. Miss
Carrick, Mrs.
Craig, Mrs.
Cornwall, J.
Crane, Philander
Chichester, Lewis
Cooper, Peter
Clark & West
Canfield, D. W.
Cash
Chamberlain, Jacob
Chambers, J. & Foster
Centre, A. H.
Collis, A. H.
Clayton, A. T.

Cocker, James & Co.
Crane, Rufus E.
C. F. A. H.
Culver & Corry
Church, C. M.
Cassebeer, H. A.
Creveling, Dr.
Cash
Cash
Cortelyou, P. C.
Cornell, J. B. & W.W. & Co.
Coffin, John
Clancy, Mrs.
Conant, W. A.
Carpenter, G.
Campbell, D. P.
Cash (Several)
Chauncey, Wm.
Codwise, D.
Campbell, Wm. W.
Chambers, James
Church, L. H.
Crane, Augustus
Crane, Theodore
Collins, Robt. B.
Collins, Charles
Crane, John J.
Creighton, Frederick
Corwin, Oliver
Cornell, Willis & Co.
Collins, John
Cahoone, H.
Chardavoyne, Wm.
Coe, D. B. Revd.
Campbell, J. D.
Crommeline, J.
Coon, Richard
Campbell, Solomon
Clark & Austin
Cragin, G. D.
Clark, A. H.
Chapin, Mr.
Crowell & Stratton
Crocheron D.
Close Aaron
Cash
Cock, Thomas M.D.
Chilton, Dr.
Cutting, F. B.
Cromwell, Henry
Crozier & Wallace
Comstock, Mr.
Clark, J. M.
Cable
Cash
Coggeshall, Geo. D.
Coolidge, Brothers
Cauldwell, E. Miss
Carle, John, Jr.
Craft, John
Clark, H.
Chattilon, J.
Chamberlain, Chas.
Currie, N.
Cash, through Revd. J. P. Lestrade

Coughtry & Dougherty
Conkling, Mr.
Chambers, T. W.
Cruikshank, James
Cauldwell, E.
Cobb, G. T.
Conover, Stephen
Cutter, Stephen
Chamberlain, J. F.
Cock, Thomas, M. D.
Cooper, Peter
Cook, John
Chamberlain, A. W.
Clawson, J. M.
Carpenter, R. S., M. D.
Camp, Amzi Revd.
Conover, Daniel
Chesebro, A.
Carson, J. C.
Cragin, C. A.
Clarkson, C. V. M. D.
Carter, Peter
Cornell, Marks
Coleman, D.
Cowl, J.
Chichester, D.
Cook, Francis
Coddington, J.
Clymer, Wm.

D.

Douglas, George
Douglas, Wm.
Donaldson, James
Derham & Moore
Dutilth & Co.
Dean, Thomas
Deleno, W. Jr.
Delafield, E., M. D.
Depeyster, F.
De Ruyter, J.
Dinsmore, W.
Dambmann, C. F.
Davison, E.
Dorr, G. B.
Decoppett, L.
De Witt, T. Revd.
Dorseville, Mrs.
Denny, Thomas
Davies, H. E.
Dean, H.
Dwight H. Jr.
Davis, G.
Davies, J. M.
Durand, A. B.
Dustan, S. Mrs.
Dayton, W. P.
Dubois, C.
Detmold, Dr.
Dubois, Mr.
Dalrymple, J.
Duncan & Son, J.
Del Hoyo Frances
Davenport, Rufus

LIST OF MEMBERS. (1851.

Dean, W. E.
Delafield, Joseph
Denison, Charles Jr.
Dunham, H R.
Deraismes, J.
Dash, D. Mrs.
De Puga, Manuel
Dwight, John
Dennis, S. A.
Duncan, E. M.
Dunn, Hugh S.
Depeyster, S. M. C.
Depeyster, Jas. F.
D. T.
De Forrest, Geo. B.
De Alfaro. N.
Davis, D. A.
De Bois & Vandervoort
Dennistown, Wood & Co.
Delmonico, Joseph
Drew, Robinson & Co.
Day, J.
Dibblee & Co. H.
Diamond. N.
Devoe, W. L.
Day, Mahlon
Decker, Alfred
Dominick, J. W.
Dennistoun, Mr.
Denike, A.
Duryee, Jacob
Doolittle, A., M. D.
Devins, John
Dieckmann, John H.
Davis, J. W.
Dunshee, Samuel
Delprat, John C.
Durning, Chas. E.
Drake, Benjamin, M.D.
Dodd, John M.
Dunn, A. Mrs.
Durbrow, E.
Dittenhoefer, Isaac
Desroches, J.
Drummond, M. J.
Dudley, J. G.
Dean & Thornton
Dodge, Wm. E.
Dickinson, Mr. Revd.
Dellinger, C.
Delluc & Co.
Dickie, Patrick
Dickson, Jas. Mrs.
Damarest, Daniel
Dupuy, Mr.
Day & Newell
Duncan, James
Dodworth, A.
Del Vechio
Dubois, Abram, M. D.
Dubreuel, Mons.
Dessoir, J.
Demarest, Henry
Devoe, D. M.
Dufour, Lawrence
Davis, John

Dudley, W. S.
Demarest, R.
Dodge, Samuel
De Mott, Mr.
Dyckman, W. N.
Dean, Thomas
Downs, Hugh
Day, A. E.
Dorr, W. S. Mrs.
Decker, Thomas
Dickinson, J A.
Dickinson, Chas., M. D.
Dana, Mrs.
De Forrest, H. G.
Davis, S. N.
Demerest, Abm.
Danforth, J.
Dolbear, Mrs.
Degraw, J
Demerest, W. J.
Dunshee, Henry W.
De la Vergne. G. W.
Dowling, J. Revd.
Deveau, Selleck & Co.
Delamontagnie, Edward
Davis, E R.
Davenport, J.
Devoy, Mich.
Delany, David
Dewing, L. C.
Denny, W. H.
Dougherty, Mr.
Duff, James
Davis, Joseph
Dickson, James
Dowe, John J.
Degrove, E. W.
Dennis, Mr.
Duncan, Francis
Dem It
Dater, Miller & Co.
Douglas, George
De Forest, Wm. W.
Davis, John M. & Jones
Dollner & Potter
Delapierre, C B
Davids & Black
Dietz, Brothers & Co.
Droz, H. E.
Dodd, Freeman
Dubois F. & Co.
D. O. C.
Doubleday. U. F.
Delluc & Co.
Depeyster, Mr.
De Forest, L. Mrs.
Duke, Wm. S.
Day, B. H.
Dibblee, W. W.
Donaldson, Mrs.
Doscher, Mr.
Duryee, Peter
Duryee, Mary A. C.
Doran, Mr.
Demarest & Joralemon
Duckworth, M. H.

Davison & Bell
Dusenbury, Wm. Cox
Doremus, Peter
Dodge, Samuel N.
Devlin, Charles
Deming, B. W.
Dittenhoffer, E.
Decker, Charles A.
Duer, Judge, per P. P. Irving
De Forest, G. B.
Dyer, Chas. C.
Davis, Henry E.
Davidson, John
Duryee, P.
Decker, Chas. N.
Dakin, C. P.
Deems, H. W.
Dubois. Grant
Dean, Benjamin
Denny W. H.
Duncan, Francis
Dodge, Josiah
Dissosway, C. R.
Darling, C. C. Revd.
Duff, James
Duff, J. F.

E.

Edgar, Wm.
Eaton, D. C.
Emmett, R. jr.
Egleston, T.
Emmett, T. A.
Elsworth, Wm.
Escher & Rusch
Everett & Brown
Eno, A. R
Eastman, S. J.
Ewing, D.
Elderd, Henry
Elleau, Francis
Everett, C. L.
Earle, John H.
Eagin, John H.
Evarts, Wm. M.
Eagle, Henry
Elsworth, Henry
Engle, S. S.
Earle, Miss
E. & M.
Ely, George
Egan, David D.
Emmons, J. A.
Effray, F.
Eldridge, N. T. Mrs.
Etienne, D. G.
Elder, George
Eaton, Augustus
Engs, P. W.
Earle, A. L.
Edwards, R C.
Earle, Sylvester
Endicott, Mrs.

LIST OF MEMBERS.

Endicott. W.
Emeny, William
Edwards, G. W.
Eveleth, Emma
Eggert D. & Son
Engle, J & S.
Everdell, Wm.
Ely, A. L.
E. O. & Co.
Easton, Charles
Edgar, James A.
Ely, E. C.
Ellis, K S.
Ensign, E. H.
Ellsworth, E.
Eliot, Mr.
Eggleston & Battelle
Evans, Mr.
Ely, Smith jr.
Edwards, A.
Everett, N. C.
Endicott, John
Evans. L. P.
Edgar, W. B., M. D.
Elliot, V.

F.

Ferguson, Edward, by John Ferguson
Ferguson, Samuel T.
Fardon, Abraham jr.
Faile, F. G.
Fiedler, Ernest
Fleming, J. B.
Folger, R. W.
Field, B. H.
Finn, A. T.
Few, C. Mrs.
Field, E.
Frear, A.
Furness, W. P.
Foster, J. jr.
Fowler, J.
Fowler, T. O.
Freeman, L. A.
Fisher, R.
Fontane, F. A.
Fisher, J. G.
Ferris, L C , M. D.
Finch, Thomas
Feldmann, J. G. W,
France, James
Furman, P. H.
Fairbanks, C.
Franklin, M.
Faxon, Wm.
Fabrequettes, E.
F. B.
Flenry, J. A.
Freeman, N. B.
F.
Fisher & Fellows
Foulke, Thomas
Frothingham & Beckwith

Foster. J P. Girard
Fuller, Dudley
Foster, Thomas R.
Frost & Hicks
Fearing & Hall
Flynn, James
Fox, H. M.
Fink, John
Freeborn, W. A.
Ferris, N.
Freeborn, J. F.
Forrester, G.
Frey, Isaac
Fanning, Edward
Ferguson, James
Farrell, E.
Foster, W. W.
Field, Josiah
Fisher & Bird
Floyd, B W.
Fraser, E. A.
Fourett, Wm.
Fox, George S.
Frost, Samuel
Fulton, George
Fisher, Geo. H.
Ferguson, Thomas M.
Fonda, A. P.
Fraser, Wm.
Farrington, J. D.
Fowler, J.
Fisher, Charles W.
Forrester, Robert
Ficht, John H.
Fink, M.
Forrest, A. P.
Fish, C. Mrs.
Flint, Cyrus
Frazee, Abm.
Freeman & Shear
Freeman, C.
Foot, T. C.
Ferris, J. G.
Fairbank, Dexter
Fitch, G. S.
Fowler, C.
Fellows, Mrs.
Fox & Oothont
Folsom, Charles J.
Fitzpatrick,
Fowler, John H.
Fancher, David
Fitch, Mr
Foster, Benjamin
Field, J.
Ferris,
Fanshaw, W. H.
Freeman, Wm.
Freeman, James
Fowler, D. S.
Forester, Charles
Freund, H.
Freund, V.
Fellows & Co.
Fellows, Louis S. & Schell
Fellows, W. M.

Flemming, Thomas
Field, Cyrus W. & Co.
Fraser & Everett
Frisbie, M. J.
Frey, W. H. & Bros.
Freely, Bernard
Frost, Mrs.
Foote, C. B.
Falconer, John
Forbes, John E.
Fisher, Joseph
Francis, C. S.
Ferris, H. N.
Fuller, Mr.
Fowler, J. O.
Foster. Dr.
Fair, John & George
Fowler & Odell
Fox, E.
Foster, J.
Frances, Mr.
Frances, W. A.
Fox, G H.
French, Richard
Fenn, G.
Francis, N. Mrs.
Fanning, Solomon
Fox, Charles
Fish, Daniel
Faulkner, J. C.
Frothingham, Wm.
Fancher, E. L.
Fisher, Daniel
French, Daniel
Fox, M. W.
Frothingham, W.
Fancher. E. L.
Fanning. Solomon
Forster, T. V.
Fisher, Daniel
Florentine, Abm.
Fields, Edward, M. D.
Foster, W. A.
Fessenden. Thos.
Fairweather, Thos.
Fowler, B. M.

G.

Griswold, George
Goodhue & Co.
Grosvenor, Seth
Green, John C.
Graves, Boonen & Co.
Griswold, John
Griswold, N. L. Mrs.
Gallatin, A. R.
Gelston, M.
Gould, C.
Giraud, J. P.
Gordon, A. R.
Gallatin, J.
Gilbert, C.
Gregory, J. G.
Green, W. G.

Greenway, E. M.
Greenway, J. H.
Green, H., M D.
Gould, E. S.
Griffin, F.
Gunning, T. B.
Goupil & Co.
Gould, H.
Groom, H.
Green, T. T.
Graham, James L.
Greenly, George
Goddard, James E.
Giraud, Joseph
Gurnee, Benjamin
Gourlie, A. T.
Gibbs, R. M.
Gans, M.
Gamage, Jane E.
Green, Elizabeth
Greeley, Horace
Goldschmidt, L.
Gaylor, C.
Gray, J.
Griffin, Solomon
Griffin, J. F.
Gant, F. S.
Guion, Mr.
Griscom, John H., M. D.
Gantz, John J.
Gilley, F. W.
Goadby, Thomas
Griffin, Thos. B., M. D.
Green, James
Geery, J. & W.
Grovestein, James H.
Gardiner, Wm.
Gramlend, C.
Grinnell, Moses H.
Gibbs, R. M.
Givan, Mrs.
Gibbs, T. S.
Gaul, L. M. Mrs.
Gray, John A. C.
Gray, John
Gardner, Samuel J.
Gibson, James
Gedney, Sylvanus
Gallier, John
Gregg, James J.
Greenwood, H. B.
Gilliardy, A.
Gilman, Dr.
Gilman, Dr. Mrs.
Ginochio, J. B.
Gardner, W. C.
Goldsmith, H.
Gilroy, George
Gardner, Mrs.
Grant, Charles E.
Gunn, A. N., M. D.
Gilbert, John S.
Groshon, John
Gregory, L.
Green, Edward
Gunther, C. Godfrey

Gillespie, James
Gabaudon, A. W.
Griffin, Thos. T.
Greenough, Walter
Gibbins, R.
Gaynor, H.
Glassford, F. Mrs.
Gerrard, G. W.
Grandy, W.
Grey, Mr.
Gardner, James
Gregory, W. A.
Gobles, Albert W.
Gutenburg, Mr.
Godfrey, Mr.
Gregor, Mr.
Graham, Alexander
Gould & Williams
Griffith, J. M.
Goodrich, E. B.
Goodsman, Thomas
Grumbs, Elizabeth Mrs.
Green, J. W.
Gunther, C. G. & Sons
Gordon & Talbot
Gennin, J. N.
Guiden, J.
Gilbert, C.
Gale, Wm.
Griffin & Pulman
Gilmartin, D.
Garrelly, J. G.
Gemmel James
Gescheidt Dr.
Guion, W. H.
Gowdy, H.
Guion, Mrs.
Green, Miss
Goadby, Wm. Mrs.
Greyden, Joseph
Gilman, Wm. C.
Garr, A. S.
Guion, J. H.
Gale, A. H. & Co.
Griffin, Wm. P.
Gustine, Mrs.
Gandy, E. Mrs.
Gurney, J.
Gulick & Holmes
Gillis, W.
Greason, John
Gibson, James
Greenwood, I. J.
Gray, Dr.
Gibert, Mr.
Gibson, Wood
Goss, H. H.
Gilbert, Prentis & Tuttle
Greenleaf & Kinsley
G. L. K. & P.
Griffin, P. N.
Green, Alonzo
Guthrie, J. B.
Goodwin, Eli
Green, Misses, per L. Jackson

G. A. H.
Greeley, Horace
Gates, John
Gibson, James R.
Gould, R. S.
Greenough, J. J.
Goodwin, J. W.
Gurney, Wm.
Gibson, Isaac
Gillelan, John
Geer, Darius
Gardner, Moses
Gould, T. C.
Gray, Wm. Rev.
Griffin, H.
Gregg, Franklin

H.

Hunt, Thomas & Co.
Halsted, W. M.
Hayes, H. M.
Hubbard, M.
H. L. Mrs. by W. E. Laight, Esq.
Hitchcock, W. R.
Hadden, David
Hoffman, L. M.
Hammersly, J. W.
Hartley, Robert M.
Hamilton, A. Jr.
Hoppock, Ely
Hopkins, E. N.
Hecksher, C. A.
Henderson, H.
Hart, J.
Holden, H.
Henry, J. J.
Houghton, R.
Hunt, E.
Howes, M.
Holmes, S.
Hyatt, E.
Howland, B. J.
Herrick, J. B.
Hall, F.
Higbie, N. T.
Hutton, M. S. Revd.
Habicht, C. E.
Harrison, C. J. Miss
Hoffman, W. Mrs.
Heyer, J. Mrs.
Hayward, H.
Harrison, J. Miss
Hicks, Wm. M.
Hoffman, P. V.
Hunter, W. C. Mrs.
Hill, T.
Howland, J.
Hone, J.
Holmes & Co.
Hayes, H.
Hook, C. G.
Hueston, S.
Hitchcock & Leadbeater

LIST OF MEMBERS.

Hill, John
Hines, James
Harrison, Henry
Herzog, Ignacio
Heard, John, M. D.
Hunter, James
Hosack, Alex., M. D.
Hall, Alfred
Hustace, Wm.
Hyslop, Robert
Hall, Thomas
Hoyt, Jesse
Hunter, Dr. Mrs.
Hudson, Mrs.
Halsey, H. A.
Henry, Philip
Hiscox, J. D.
Hegeman, Wm.
Herrick, Josiah
Hasbrouck, J. L.
Hogg, Peter
Hobart, Wm., M. D.
Hobart, D.
Holmes, A. B.
Hilger, M.
Havemeyer, G. L.
Hitchcock, U. L.
H. H. W.
Hunt, W. S.
Hall, A. B.
Honier, C. E. P.
Haggerty, Draper & Jones
Hendricks, Brothers
Hardt & Co.
Halstead, Mr.
Hoyt, E.
Hunt & Co. Wilson G.
Hull, John C.
Hogg, Thomas
Hepburn, J. C., M.D.
Hewlett, O. T.
Hancock, John
Hoe, R. & R.
Hawley, Irad
H.
Harmer, C. G.
Hoffman, E.
Hues, Thomas
Hunn, John
Harriot, John H.
Horn, James
Hains, Francis
Hellman, Wm.
Heath, L. C.
Hennesey, D.
Haws, Robt. T.
Healey, E.
Hurtin, John H.
Hunter, E. L.
Houghton, T. L.
Hepburn, S. Mrs.
Hill, John
Haight, J. L.
Heard, Charles
Hutchinson, S.
Holbrook, Ephraim

Hall, Valentine G.
Hains, E. Mrs.
Harbeck, Wm. H.
Harms, Mr.
Haight, R. K.
Halsey, A. P.
Henry, Robert
Havemeyer, C. H.
Hutchinson, Ira
Havemeyer, Wm.
Hutchings, E. W. & W.
Herbert, J.
Halsey, E. C.
Havemeyer, Albert
Hallock, James C.
Hunter, C. F.
Houghland, John S.
Hall, James F.
Hearn, Brothers
Hewitt & Moorton
Hoagland, W. C.
Hedges, James E.
Hays, John
Hasbrouck, B.
Hasbrouck, G. D.
Hogencamp, John
Howser, J. C.
Haskins, Ann
Higgs, R. W.
Hilliker, W. W.
Hunt, Mrs.
Hollenbeck, Solomon
Hull, J.
Havemeyer, Wm. F.
Havemeyer, F. C.
Herring, Silas C.
Hopkins, N. F.
Hurd, J. R.
Havemyer, D. M.
Hall, Willis
Henderson, John C.
Hunt, J.
Harned, Wm.
Herring & Ryer
Haxtun, Mrs.
Harriot, James
Hallet, J. H.
Hurry, Edmund
Hirsfield, Hermann
Hunt, H. G.
Hart, Robert
Harker, Abel
Huse, John B.
Hay, Mrs.
Haggenback, George
Hall, James W.
Higgins, L. & J.
Hovey, Mrs.
Hicks, W. H.
Hertzel, J. F.
Haddock, W. J.
Hansen George
Herder, N. D.
Holden, Samuel
Hobart
Holden, Samuel

Hutchings, Jane
Hoffman, Mary
Hall, Wilbur
Hunt, H. W.
Horatio, S.
Houghwont, Simon
Hiscock, Mr.
Hanigan, Bernard
Haight, John
Holmes, D. L.
Harvey, Francis
Haight, D. T.
Hopkins, E.
Hart, Felix
Hedden, John
Hutchens, John
Hoffman & Schubeel
Hoffman, M. Mrs.
Hunt, Zeber
Halsey, S. R.
Hoey, John
Hobby, E. B.
Harger, J.
Holstein, John
Hildberghawser, H.
Harmance, Mr.
Hussey, C. F. Mrs.
Hoe, R. & Co.
Helmont, George
Hunt, Thomas
Hurlbut, Sweetser & Co.
Haskell, Merrick & Bull
Hayden, P. & T.
Haydes, John E. Sons
Heyer, E. P. & Co.
Haviland, D. G.
Henry, John & Co.
Hart, Lucius
Hanna & Beebe
Halsted, Benjamin
Hook, J. D. W.
Hoe, R. & Co.
Hall, F. C.
Hneseman & Co.
Halse, W. & Co.
Hoyt, J. K.
Heitkamp, C.
Hutchler, J. V.
Heath, Aaron B.
Hammersley, Miss
Hodges, P. H.
Hitchcock, Cyrus
Halsted, C. O.
Hoge, Wm.
Hay, Allen & Co.
Hallock, L.
Hull, J. S.
Harper, S. B. Mrs.
Harper, John
Harper, Fletcher
Hyatt, Stephen
Heurtley, R. W.
Halsted, A. L.
Houghton, E.
Hitchcock, J. R.
Halsted, Samuel

44 LIST OF MEMBERS. (1851.

Hidden, Mrs.
Haight, Nicholas
Herreman, Mrs.
Hunt, W. L.
Hoagland, J. M.
Hurd, A. T.
Hodgkins, T. G.
Hall, G. R.
Hammeisley, L. C.
Hutchins, Mr.
Hyer, Sarah Mrs.
Held, John
Harper, Mr.
Henry, Mr.
Hopkins, H. & J.
Hoppock & Son
Hopkins, M.
Hoyt, L. M.
Hyall, Geo. E. L.
Harding. R.
Heyer, E.
Hicks, Chas. C.
Hart, H. & M.
Hasey, Alonzo
Hart, J. C.
Hall, Archibald
Halsey
Hoyt, Ralph Revd.
How, Calvin W, Mrs.
Harris, John
Harris, W. D.
Hall, Archibald
Holt, J. S.
Holbrook, E.
Hepburn, J. C., M. D.
Hogencomp, Daniel
Hatt, Geo. Revd.
Hatt, John A.
Harris, W. D.
Henderson, A. J.
Hurd, Hiram
Hosack, N. P.
Halsey, H. A.
Hume, Andrew
Horton, J. B.
Houghton, Joseph
Howell, M. H.
Holman, Thos.
Hawkins, C. P
Hogan, Thomas
Houghwout, Simon
Hibbets, H. P.
Hutchings, John
Howe, Bazaleel
Howe, B.
Howe, J M.
Holman, Henry
Hubbard, J. M.
Hines. J. C.
Humbert, W. B.
Halsted, A. L.
Horton, Richard Revd.
Hyslop, G. L., M. D.
Hazeltine, L.
Huntington. J. C.
Halsey, L. W.

Heydon, Wm.
Hammersley, J. W.

I & J.

Jay, Ann, Miss
Jay, Elizabeth Clarkson Miss
Jay, Susan Matilda Miss
Ireland, Wm. B.
Johnston, John
In Memory of a Donor
Jaffray & Sons J. R.
Irving, Richard M.
Jones, J. A.
Johnson, Mrs.
Iselin, J. A.
Innes, E. S.
Jay, W.
Jones, J. Q.
Irving, J. T. Mrs.
Irving, G. Mrs.
Johnson, B.
Ingham, T.
Johnson, S. Mrs.
Jones, J. C.
Jones, J.
Jones, E. R Mrs.
Jones, E. S. Miss
Jones, E. L.
Isaacs, S. J.
Ireland, Sophia Mrs.
Ireland, Geo. Jr.
Ireland, Geo.
Johnson, J. W.
J. M. Tr.
Jung, J. W.
Jones & Co. S. T.
Johnson, Henry
Jones, Morris
Jacobson, Richard S.
Jarvis, W. S.
Jackson, T.
J. P. J.
Janes, Adrian
Jones, Geo. F.
Jackson, Lewis E.
Jenkins H. T.
Johnson, Mrs.
Jones,
Jackson, G. R.
Jones, John
Jacobus, D.
Jacobus, C. C.
Jeffirs, W. H.
Isaacs, S M. Revd.
Jones, W. T.
Johnson, Henry
Jones, W. B.
Ivison, H.
Johnson, Edward A.
Jones, A.
Jacobson, Frederick
Jackson, Saml. L.
Jarvis, J.

Johnston, L. L.
Jones, Miss
Jackson, Moses B.
Johnston, James
Jarvis, J.
Jolly, Mr.
Irwin, Wm.
Jones, D.
Jenkins, R.
Ingersoll, Chandler
Ingoldsby, F.
J. W. Q.
J. L. R.
Jacot C. & Co.
J. A. G.
Ingersoll, J. D.
Johnston, D. & S.
Jackson & Many
Jeremiah, Thos.
Johnson, J. A.
Jones, L. Revd.
Johnson, J. K.
Jenkins, E. O.
Jones, A. S.
Jennings & Co.
Johnson & Lazarus
Johnson, Wm.
Jones, Rowland & Co.
Johnson, R. R.
Johnson, Austin, by Mr. E. Mack
Irving, P. P.
Jackson, Thomas
Jenkins, J. J.
Jackson, Luther
Jeremiah. Thos.
Jewell, Hollis E.
Jervis, Wm.
Johnston, Wm.
Irving, Chas.

K.

Kennedy, D. S.
King, A. G.
King, P. V.
Koop, Fischer & Co.
Kermit, R.
Knapp, Shepherd
Ketchum, H.
Kearny, E.
Kurshedt, A.
Knox, J. M.
Kissam. M. A. Miss
Kane, D.
Kissam, R. S., M. D.
Kinsley, H., M. D.
Kirby, V.
King, John
Kemble, Wm.
Kemp, Peter
Kaup, E. & Cummings
King, N. T.
Keeler, D. B.
Kimball, H,

1851.) LIST OF MEMBERS.

Keyser, John	Lawrence, Joseph	Lane, George
Knapp, James H.	Lord, R. L.	Lyons, Emanuel
Kipp, F. A.	Le Roy, Jacob	Livingston, Mary
Knipe, William	Laight, E. W.	Loss, Francis H.
Kingsland, A. C.	Laight, W. E.	Lurget, Jacob
Kipp, Leonard W.	Laverty, H.	Lillie, Wm.
Kipp, B. Livingston	Livingston, M. & W.	Lester, J. W.
Kemp, R. C.	Livingston, M.	Lounsbury, N.
Knapp, P. B. & G. P.	Lane, D.	Legrand, Wm.
Kennedy, W.	Livingston, J. R.	Lee, David
Kissam, Dr.	La Barbierre, A.	Lane, Wm. G.
Kellogg, J. W.	Low, N.	Lawrence, R. M.
Kinch, Wm.	Livingston, L.	Lathrop, F. S.
Knapp, Wm.	Lane, J.	Lathrop, Mrs.
Kidder, J. B.	Langdon, W.	Lyman, J. H.
Kellock, James	Lefferts, J. L. Mrs.	Lawrence, G. N.
Ketcham, T.	Lanier, J. F. D.	Ludlum, J. & L.
Knowlton, D.	Low, J.	Le Couteulx, A.
King, Rufus S.	Lentilhon, E.	Leverich, Mrs.
King, Wm.	Larkin, T. O.	Luis, Frederick
Knapp, R.	Lamson, C.	Lewis, John W.
Kimbell, M. T. C.	Lowery, J.	Loweree, W.
Knapp, Wm. H.	Leeds, H. H.	Le Boutillier, Thos.
Kelly, Joel	Lawrence, M. Mrs.	Loines, Wm. H.
Killan, Alexander	Livingston A.	Loweree, Seaman
Knouse, Mr.	Leeds, S.	Ludlum, Nicholas
Keely, P.	Livingston, F. A. Mrs.	Lynes, Samuel
Kidder, S.	Lockwood, Roe	Lambert, Jeremiah
Kennedy, Thomas	Luther & Hampton	Lane, A.
Ketchum, Philip	Little, A.	Lewis, J. S.
King, Wm. G	Ladd, W. F.	Love, T.
Kissam & Keeler	Loosey C. T.	Loutrel, Wm. M.
King, William	Leonard, J. Mrs.	Lent, James W.
Knoepple, Wm. H.	Little, J. P.	Lewis, Mr.
Kellog, A. W.	Litton, James	Lamb, Francis
Kiggins, H.	Lane, G. W.	Lange, Conrad
Kingman, M. E.	Lee, W. H.	Lockwood, J. L.
Kelly, David	Lattan. Lewis	Loder, Benjamin
Kreps, Henry	Lane, Nathan	Lothrop, W. R.
Kingsland, D.	Lawton, Mr.	Lester, Andrew & Co.
Kinney, George	Labagh Isaac	Leigh, Chs. C.
Kimball, Richard B.	Lydig, P.	Lawrence, M. E.
Knapp, C.	Livingston, M. Mrs.	Le Moyne, A.
King, J. G.	Lawrence, R.	Lee, W. P.
Knox, E.	Leise, F.	Lee, S. L.
Kingsland, R.	Leonard, W. B.	Leary, James
Kenney, T. R.	Legget A. A.	Lane, W. J.
Kirkman, J.	Lawrence, D. L. by Mr. Og-den	Leggett, Abraham
King, John, by J. Longking.		Leverett, J. S.
Kelly, Joel	Lottimer & Large	Lockhart, Thos.
Kennedy, Thos.	Lewin, M.	Lippett, J. F.
Kingman. M. E.	Logan, David	Littell, Andrew
Kellogg, J. W.	Loder & Co.	Lee, J. jr.
Kelly, Luke	Lord, Warren & Salter	Lindley & Mundy
Kidd, W. E.	Leland & Mellen	Lent & Jemerson
Kirby, Wm.	Lowndes, Thomas	Lyons, James
Klots, J. T.	Langdon,	Leggett, J. L.
Kent, Brainard	Lawrence, F.	Lyons, S. L.
Kearney, James	Lane & Mangam	Lewis & Woodruff
	Livesay, Mrs.	Little, J. W.
	Lane, J. A.	Lyon, Eliphalet
L.	Lyles, Henry jr.	Lord & Taylor
	Linsly, J , M. D.	Litchfield & Co.
Lenox, James	Ludwig, Henry	Levy, Mark & Bros.
Lind, Jenny Miss, by John Jay, Esq.	Leo, Ansel Rev.	L. B. B.
	Leavy, John	Lang, L.

LIST OF MEMBERS. (1851.

Lord, J. C.
Long & Davenport
Little, Charles S.
Leonard & Wendt
Lewis M. &. W. H.
Lockwood, H. M.
Lynch, James
Lindeman, Wm.
Lyman,
Lamb, Anthony
Lasak, F. W.
Livingston, R. C. Mrs.
Leavenworth, N.
Lake, E. E.
Loines, Sarah
Lee, Mrs.
Lamphear, J. C.
Lillenthral & Co.
Lecompte, N.
Le Compte Vincent
Ludlum, N. S.
Lagrave, A. F.
Lagrave, J. J.
Leddy & Sheridan
Linneman, H.
Larned, Wm., M. D.
Langlois, Mrs.
Lillenthal, Mr.
Liscomb, Mr.
Luers & Jurgens
Langdon, Mr.
Lee, J.
Lathrop & Ludington
Lawson, Miss.
Littell E. B. & Co.
Le Roy, T. O. Co.
Ludlum, Wm.
Lightbody, G. Mrs.
Londoner, H.
Lounsberry, Mrs.
Lockwood, H.
Lawrence, Isaac
Lord, D. D.
Lockwood, Frederic
Le Compt, V.
Lewis R.
Leask, H. G.
Liton, James
Lowerre, G. W.
Lytle, Andrew
Lee, D. F.
Leggett, Gilbert
Lestrade, J. P. Rev.
Lounsberry, N.
Lord, Benjamin
Longking, J.
Lockwood, W. A.
Long, N. R.
Lee, Luther
Lyon, A. U.

M.

Minturn, Robert B.
Minturn, Sarah Mrs.
Minturn, Edward
Munn, Stephen B.

Mills, Drake
Moran & Iselin
Metcalf, J. W.
Moore, Mrs. by J. L. Apinwall
Mott, Wm. F. jr.
Moore, Nathl. F.
Morgan, H. T.
Murray, Mary Miss ⎫
Murray, John R.   ⎬
Mortimer, R.
Morgan, M.
Murray, J. B.
Marshall, C. H.
Miller, W. S.
McCurdy, R. H.
McVicker, C. Mrs.
Moir, J.
Mead, M. Mrs.
Mackenzie, G.
McNamee, T.
Mitchell, W.
Munkitbrick, A.
Marie, C.
Morris, A. Mrs.
Magie, D. Jr.
May, A.
Mann, F.
Morris, G. W.
Marsh, J.
Mount, A. R.
Morgan, J. J. Mrs.
McCoon, C.
Miller, S. Mrs.
Montford & Co.
Maunder, Wm.
Morrison & Allen
Mass, Godfried
Morton. John
Maxwell, Mrs.
Mulligan, Mr.
Martin, J. B.
McAuley, Charles
Mott, W. & J. C.
Merry, C. A.
March, P. S.
Martin, A.
Menzies Wm
M. T.
Miller, W. T.
Mott, J. H.
Meritt, Miss
McMullen, T.
Mackay, A.
Middleton & Co.
Maitland, Phelps & Co.
Mellis & Ayres
McClune, Thos. & Co.
Morewood & Co., G. B.
Martin, W. R.
Merrett, B.
McDonald, A. B.
Morrison, David
McCotter, A.
Macomber, J. W. Rev.
Mott, W. F.
Macy, Josiah

Moore, J. L.
Mather, G.
Milbank, Jeremiah
Milbank, Samuel Jr.
Milbank, Isaac M.
Morgans, Morgan
Milbank, Samuel Sr.
Motly, J. C.
Mott, John W.
Murphy, James
M.
McLaughlin, Wm. G.
Morton & Bremner
Morrison, David
Morris, L. B.
Miles, A.
McKee, J.
McCreary, J. D.
Moore, H
Mead, John H.
Mapes, S. S.
Maitland, Robert L.
Macy, Wm. H.
Macy, Chs. A.
Mead, W.
Marshal, T. W.
Merl, Chs.
Morris, J. L.
Morris, E. Mrs.
Macomb, A. S.
Mitchell, Mrs.
McLawrin, W. S.
Martin, Wm. C.
Miller, J. C.
Meakim, John
Moffet, James G.
Morris, Agnes
Morris, Lewis
McIntire, C. H.
Morrison, James
Munroe, E.
McCrea, R. Mrs.
Miller, J. E.
Marshall, Wm. H.
Mesler, Wm.
Morton & Murray
Marshall, M.
Murphy, G. S.
May, Mrs.
Martin, R. W.
Moir, J. & W.
Manning, Mrs.
Miller, J B.
Martin, Peter
Mooney, E. C.
Mitchell, John
Marsh, Mr.
McDongall, W.
Miller, Mrs.
Marrius, Joseph
Mitchel, Mr.
Moffitt, Mrs.
Moorhouse, Mr.
Meeks, Mr.
Malony, P.
McGee, J.
McGaw, John A.

LIST OF MEMBERS.

Macy, C. B.
Mace, John
McCarron, Michl.
Mason, J. M.
McKewan, John
Mersereau, J. W.
Mumford, B. A.
Mitchell, J. V.
Moller, Peter
Moller, Wm.
Martin, D. R.
McGay, James
McLachlan, Alex.
Milnor, Eleanor Mrs.
Meigs, Henry Jr.
Many, V. W.
McCready, B., M. D.
Maltby, E.
Moore, S. F.
Meigs, C. A.
McAdams, George
Miller, E.
Morris, E.
Maze, Abraham
Miller, Samuel R.
Mott
Malloy, R S.
Milligan, G. M.
McMullan, P. J.
Miller & Shaurman
Miller, Alderman
Mills, Abner
Miner, Noble G.
Medtzger Christian
Mather, W. L.
Mckinsie, A. W.
Miller, A.
Mank, H.
Moran, Mr.
Moore, C. W.
McPherson, P.
Mackrell & Simpson
Moreau, Frederick
Merrill, Charles
Merril, Manning
Mayheu, P. S.
Michaelis, Dr.
Milne, Alex.
McCartin, Bernard
Marsh, John R.
Moss, Reuben E.
Marwedell, F.
Mouberry, John
Mather, E. W.
Miller, Gilbert
Martin, R.
Myers, James
McKenzie, Mr.
Moore, James
Mathews, Mrs.
Miller, Amand
Marsh, Samuel
McKesson, John
Merrill, N. W.
Martin & Lawson
Meyer
Moore & Baker

Moore, Daniel
Martelle & Holderman
Mason, L Jr.
Mortimer, John, Jr.
Mills, J. M.
M.
Meyer, E.
Merrill, N. W
Morrison, Daniel
McCaddin, Henry Jr.
Morris & Cummins
Murphy, Thos. S.
Malone, James
Mealis, Lewis
McComb, John
Mortimer, John Jr.
McLeod, Misses The
Miles, Charles
Miles, Wm. B.
Morrison, J. M.
McIntyre & Young
Mitchell, John W.
Murray, Robert I.
Murray, Mary
Moreau, John B.
Meeker, Isaac
Mackrell & Richardson
Martin Samuel
Mead, R.
McCullum, A.
Mitchell, J. S. Rev.
Mason, W. Mrs.
Morris, R. L.
Milkman
Meday, C. H.
Mease, Mrs.
M. K. H.
Moses, C.
Maine, J. M.
Miller, G. & Co.
Martin, A.
Morford & Vermilye
McAlister, Dr.
McMurray, R.
Mathews, James
McCall, Mr.
Martin & Witcheef
Mowbray, R. & J.
Metler, Wilson
Mills, E. J.
Mead, Belcher & Titus
Merritt, J. G.
Marshman, B.
Matteson, A. & J.
Merle, George
Morrell T.
McGrorty, Wm.
Murray, R. L.
Mathey, A.
Mi'ler, Wm. P.
Matlack, S. C.
Mathews, Wm.
Moseman, Nash
Marsh,
Moore,
McDonald, Henry
McLeod, Wm.

Mulenburgh, Wm. A. Rev.
McKay, Wm.
McClain, O. D
Miller, Jacob S., M. D.
Mills, Abner
McPherson, Peter
Merrill, Chs.
Murray, A. W.
Miller, H.
Mather, F. E.
Morris, O. W.
Miller, J. C.
Macy, W. H.
Mason, J. L.
McIntire, John
Mood, Peter
Marshall, Benj. M. D.
McNaughton, A. P.
Marten, Wm.
Murray, John
Murphy, Wm., M. D.
Myers, John
Mills, Elias
Marsh, John R.
Mollard, John
Merritt, Stephen
Moore, Richard W.
Metcalf, J. W., M. D.
Macomber, J. W.
McCoun, H.
Moss, W. P.
Matherson, R.
Muir, James
Myers, George E.
Mack, Enoch
Marsh, James

N.

Noah, M. M.
Nesmith & Co.
Noble, J.
Newbold & Craft
Nicholl, S. T. & Co.
Niblo, William
Nevins, D. H.
Noyes, W. C.
Nash, S. P.
Nevius, P. J. Jr.
Nevius, P. J.
Neilson, W.
Neilson, J., M. D.
Newman, E.
Noonan, P. H.
Newell, D. C.
Nicoll, Henry
Noyes, O. H. P.
Newton, J.
Nelson, H. A.
Norris, R. T.
Negus, Thomas
Neeves, James
Noe, B. M.
Noe, C. L.
Nostrand, C. Mrs.
Nevins, R. H.
Nash, Lorin

48   LIST OF MEMBERS.   (1851.

Napier, Thos.
Newbold, George
Nixon, R
Nash, F. H.
Newhouse, Benjamin
Newton, N.
Noe, John C.
Norton, C. & L.
Nelson, Edmund D.
Nelson, Geo. P.
Newton, James W.
Nichols, Wm. B.
Nagles, C.
Newell, G. S.
Nicols, Dr.
Nash, W. F.
Northrop, C. B.
Nostrand, E.
Nelson, Wm.
Newman, A. G.
Nordburger, S. D.

O.

Ogden, Elizabeth Mrs.
Ogden, Benjamin, M. D.
Ogden, Henry
Ogsbury, Francis W.
Ogden, Henry Capt. U. S. N.
Ogden, T. W.
Oliphant, R. M.
Owens, James
Osborn, W. W.
Ogden, M.
Oelrich & Kruger
Osgood, S. Revd.
Okil', M. Mrs.
Oothout, H.
Olcott, H. W.
Ortleys, Misses
Overton, R. C.
Oakley, T. A. Mrs.
Oakley, Mr.
Ogden, John
Onderdonk, Levi
Ogden, J. G. Jr.
Oakley, James B.
Ogden, P. K.
Overhieser, A.
Ogilvie, Wm.
Ogden, M. H.
Oppenhiem, J. M. & Co.
Oothout, Wm.
Owen, Daniel
Olliffe, Wm. L., M. D.
Olwell, J. & M.
Osborn, Abner
O'Meara, James
O'Meara, C.
Orvis, F. H.
Osborn & Sears
Ogden, John F.
Orchard, Isaac Revd.
Ostrom, J. P.

P.

Post, W. B.
Post, G. D.
Palmer, J. J.
Pendleton, E. H.
Prall, Mrs.
Patridge, C.
Parker, W, M. D.
Phelps, G. D.
Phelps, J. N.
Platt, N. C.
Porter, M.
Putnam, T.
Peet, E.
Post, A. C., M. D.
Platt, G. W.
Phyfe, J. M.
Peters, C. J., M. D.
Parker, G. P.
Potter, E.
Page, D.
Pierson, C. E., M. D.
Paillet, Henry
Pfeiffer, C. F.
Pike, Benjamin
Pugsley, T.
Prime, Frederick
Petrie, J. & A.
Phillips, J. W.
Phelps, Dodge & Co.
Pierce & Co. George
P. J, N.
Peet, Edward
Peet, Edmond, B.
Pell, Abijah
Pell, Chas. S.
Pease, W. J.
Price, Thomson
Penfold, Wm.
Paxson, C. S.
Peck, H. W.
Page, F. P.
Pryer, James
Prior, Mr.
Polhamus, H. A.
Pinkney, T. W.
Platt, J.
Palmer, John
Paxton, John R.
Purdy, S.
Pecare, Jacob
Pfeiffer, D., M. D.
Parker, Asa
Patterson, W. T.
Perry, Samuel
Parker, S.
Purdy, Jonathan
Place, J. K.
Pershall, D. T.
Phelps, S. T.
Polhamus, M. Mrs.
Pilcher, Jas. M.
Purdy, J. B.
Peck, A. L.
Pettegrew, Thos. A.

Proud, D.
Parker, C. M.
Phelps, Anson G. Jr.
Prime, Edward
Paine, J.
Parker, J. C. Mrs.
Purdy, John
Parkin, T.
Pell, Mrs.
Pettigue, John
Parsells, A.
Powell, W. R. Mrs.
Parish, James
Patchman, F. W.
Putnam, Mrs.
Porter, John H.
Pirsson, J. P.
Post & Young
Piggot, Samuel
Platt, George
Potter, S. B.
Purling, Levi
Phelps, W. H.
Pearson, S. H.
Powell, Wm. H.
Patton, Wm. Revd.
Powers, L.
Palmer, A. W.
Pearse, A. F.
Pentz
Price, C. W.
Post, Washington
Peugnet. Louis
Peugnet, H.
Pound, Jesse Revd.
Partridge, Wm.
Pringle, Thos.
Phillips, Dr. Revd.
Pierce, J. H.
Parker, B.
Pray, Henry
Prall, H. R.
Price, J. B.
Phillips, M.
Parkhill, Samuel
Patterson, S. P.
Phillips, John
Post, S S.
Powell, Mr.
Prague, D.
Parsons, Charles
Pootan, Wm.
Platt, J. A.
Phillips, Samuel
Polhamus, John
Prime, J. D.
Pease, John
Pope, Henry
Pomroy, J. D.
Pratt, John R.
Peck, J. B.
Phillips, J J.
Pearsall, J. Alderman
Penfold & Schuyler
Phelps, Anson G.
Penfold, J.

LIST OF MEMBERS.

Paret, John
Prosser, Thos. & Son
Paton
Pappenhusen, C.
Patrick, R. & Co.
Pike, D. B.
Purlee, R. N.
Palmer, S. H.
Parkhurst
Pike, Benjamin Jr.
Peck, E.
Porter, Robert
Pierce, G. & Co.
Peck, Elisha
Pell, J. K.
Packwood, Mary Ann Mrs.
Post, Ralph
Pryer, G. Mrs.
Porter, J. S.
Purdy, A. S., M. D.
Pickens, Daniel
Polhemus, A.
Putnam & Co.
Place, Charles
Peet, M. S.
Proddow & Beach
Potter, Ellis
Phyfe, D.
Painter, W. H.
Park, Rufus W.
Parker, Charles
Partridge, T. M.
Partridge, J. R.
Palmer & Newcomb
Pearson, A.
Paterson, N. C.
Planter, Henry
Page, P. P.
Price, Thompson
Pond, James O., M. D.
Pearsall, John
Post, Wm.
Peck, J. W.
Pratt, Edward
Pearson, Adam
Page, Enoch W.
Pattison, R.
Place, R. S.
Payton, E. H.
Place, Charles
Powell, Oliver
Polhamus, John
Prime, J. D.
Pearson, C. B.
Peck, Gideon
Phillips, W.
Plumly, A. R.
Pell, Abijah
Parker, J. C.
Parr, J.
Place, James K.

Q.

Quincey, C. E.

Quincy, J. W.
Quinby, Brothers
Quackinbush, B.
Quinn, J. A.
Quidoit, E. F.
Quackenboss & Bambre

R.

Remsen, Susan A.
Roosevelt, C. V. S.
Rogers, J. Smyth, M. D.
Rhinelander, W. C.
Ray, Richard, Mrs.
Rogers, G. P.
Robinson, N.
Robbins & Son G. S.
Remsen, H. R.
Richards, Guy
Rashau, J. A. F.
Russell, W. H
Roosevelt, J. Mrs.
Reed, A.
Ryerson, J. A.
Reese, J. Jr.
Ray, W. G.
Remsen, W.
Riggs, A., M. D.
Ray, M. Miss
Romaine, S. B.
Rodgers, J. K., M. D.
Roach, P. R.
Richards, E.
Rudderow, J. & Co.
Richmond, George
Roberts, P.
Reilly, S. S.
Rae, John
Rich, J. V.
Roome, Mr.
Randolph, S. F.
Rankin & Co.
Rogers, Mr.
Ray, Robert
Roome, W. J.
Read, Jehiel
Riley, Asher
Rogers, J. E.
Richardson, O.
Rogers, J.
Ruderow & Co. J.
Rutgers, N. G.
Rogers, Henry
Rogers, C.
Ruddy or Raddy, Mrs.
Roosevelt & Son
Reeve, Henry
Robinson, Edward, D. D.
Routh, H. L. & Co.
Roberts, Spencer & Co.
Rigney, Thomas
Rose, Wm.
Richardson & Co. E.
Rankin, Edward, E. Revd.
Rumsey, J. W.

Riker, J. H.
Ritch, H. L.
Riker, A.
Randolph, Mr.
Rollinson
Raynor, Samuel
Requa
Rose, Henry
Rankin & Ray
Rang, Robert
Ryder, Edgar T.
Rogers, C. H.
Reynolds, Lucy
Raynor, Hiram
Robinson, E. C.
Rising, Mrs.
Rickard, J. W.
Reynolds, E. B. Mrs.
Roberts, Stephen
Ryckman, Mrs.
Russell, John
Requa, Austin
Roffe, Mrs.
Robinson, Mrs.
Rothharett, Jacob
Rodh, David
Robb, Mrs.
Roe, Ann
Ruton, Mrs.
Reid, Julia Mrs.
Robert, J. H.
Rothaus, Mr.
Reid, Geo. W.
Rodgers, T.
Randle, John
Roe, E. W.
Rudd, Joseph
Reynolds, P.
Rowland, C. N. S.
Raymond, H. J.
Ritter, W.
Rosenfield, M. H.
Raydon, Benjamin
Roach, C. H.
Russell, R.
Rushard, Mrs.
Ramsey, David
Renshaw, J. B.
Riley, John
Rimson, John
Reed, G.
Rowland, W. F.
Rich & Bliss
Rothchild, Mr.
Romain, W. H.
Russell, Mr.
Rolin, Mr.
Riblett, W.
Riker, Daniel
Randall, E.
Riker, John L.
Richter, D. A.
Robinson, Henry
Reed, Nathan
Rapelye, George
Rodgers, B.

3

LIST OF MEMBERS. (1851.

S.

Rosenbemch, Mr.
Roberts, Nathan
Roberts, George
Robinson, Wm.
Rowlank, Jonathan
Ryerson, Mr.
Raper, Bogert M.
Read, Taylor & Co.
Ross, Andrew
Raymond & Fullerton
Rich & Knowlton
Rankin, D. & Co.
Reynolds, C. T.
Rohe, J. A.
Russell, N. E.
Rosselet, P. A.
Rader, M.
Roberts & Rees
Rauch, John, H.
Rowell, Chas. S.
Rawdon, Freeman
R. S. B.
Robertson, James
Redman, C. H.
Ruggles, H. J.
Russell, Jane Mrs.
Rogers, S. S. Mrs.
Rait, Robert
Romer, John
Read & Brothers
Read, M. P.
Rates, Mr.
Rainhard, Starling & Co.
Ransom & Co.
Read, G. W. & J.
Renwick, M. A.
Reeys & Hoyt
Rees, James
Rose, J.
Rafferty & Leask
Rogers, R. P.
Rockwell, Charles
Ross, J. H., M. D.
Roosevelt & Son
Rogers, Henry
Rogers, C.
Ramsey, J. C.
Richards, W. H.
Richards, Thos. B.
Rae, Robert
Rusher, Chas. H.
Rich, Josiah
Roome, Chas.
Ramsey, John
Ryers, T. R.
Redfield, J. H.
Rivenburgh, C. V., M. D.
Ryerson, W. H.
Ruston, John
Romain, Wm.
Redman, C. H.
Roberts, Edward
Ranney, L., M. D.
Reeve, James

Sturges, Jonathan
Spencer, Wm. A. Capt.
Siffkin & Ironside
Skidmore, Samuel T.
Stevens, Horatio G.
Sampson, Joseph
Schermerhorn, Peter
Snow, G. W
Smith, U. J.
Staples, G. W.
Strong, E. A.
Sturges, T. T.
Scribner, C.
Sherman, R. B.
Stewart, L.
Strong, C. E.
Sandford, J. S.
Spier, J. M.
Stuecken, E.
Sanford, L. H. Hon.
Spencer, J. S.
Sedgwick, R.
Schermerhorn, A.
Stout, A. G.
Scott, J. W., M. D.
Sherwood, S.
Swan, C.
Smith, J. O., M. D.
St. John, C.
Suydam, J. Mrs.
Sprague, R.
Schermerhorn, A. Mrs.
Schermerhorn, Miss
Sabine, G. A., M. D.
Swan, E. H.
Swan, B. L.
Stevens, B. K.
Swan, B. L. Jr.
Stevens, B.
Southmayd, A.
Seymour, M.
Skinner, T. H. Rev.
Sarles, H.
Stevens, H. G.
Stagg, B.
Sus, A. W.
Simpson & Kemp
Smith, Isaac & Co.
Saxton, Warren
Seaman & Muir
Stewart, Charles
Sheffield Mrs.
Schmelzel Geo.
Scanlan Hugh
Shumway, James
Scrymgeour, James
Smith T. U.
Swift, E. H.
Smedburgh, G. T. Mrs.
Stuart, Joseph
Skidmore, W. B.
Schmidt, H. J. Rev.
Sagehorn, Henry
Sears, W. S.

Smith, C.
Smith, J. McCune, M. D
Smith, W. D.
Skillman, J.
Smith, J. E.
Stuart, J.
Schuyler P. J.
Sill, Henry
Storey, John
Srong, Benjamin
Syms, W.
Savage, J. W.
Salmon, H. H.
Smith, G. W.
Scheman, G.
Schieffelin. P. & Co.
Smith, Alex. W.
Stewart, R. L. & A.
Schermerhorn, Banker & Co.
Stevens & Son, J.
Schieffelin, H. M. & Fowler
Shelden, Frederick
Strong, G. W.
Smith & Denton
Smith, M.
Seymour, W. N.
Schrff, Mrs.
Stewart, David
Schieffelin, H. H.
Stebbins, Russell
Smythe, Henry
Scribner & Coolidge
Spies, Christ & Co.
Syz, Irminger & Co.
Schuchardt & Gebhard
Stewart & Co., J.
Swarez, J. L.
Sherman, B. P.
Seaver, B. F.
Smith, John Calvin
Smith, S. T.
Sheriden, Thomas
Stoner, Harriet
Schoonmaker, Mrs.
Smith, Wm. A.
Saxton, John
Sands, A. B.
Smith, James
Southark, J. W.
Sweezy, N. T. & Co.
Smith, Jess
S. S. S.
Sherman & Co.
Strong, Thos. W.
Steinzieck, Charles
Squire, S. P.
Sammis, A. D. B.
Smith, C. W.
Stohlman, C. F. E. Rev.
Smith, J. M.
Spencer, Wm.
Schenck, C. C.
Schenck, John W.
Scott, L.
Shannon, W.
Staples, J.

1851.) LIST OF MEMBERS. 51

Schench, Mercy Mrs.
Simpson, Wm.
Stout, A. V.
Seaman, George
Simpson, Wilson
St. John, L.
Stillwell, W. Rev.
Scofield, P.
Seaman, W. S.
Schaeler, P.
Sands, D. H.
Sherwood, S. W.
Short, John
Schaider, John
Seise, Catharine
Sloan, Wm.
Smith, Wm. Alex.
Smith, Cornelius
Smith, Sheldon
Sanford, Edward
Strong, W. K.
Staples, S. P.
Schenck, Wm. J.
Smith, S. A., M. D.
Skiddy, Wm. Mrs.
Skiddy, F.
Stone, R. C.
Schoals, F. P.
Smith,
Sommer, S.
Sanderson, E. P.
Suydam,
Speir, F.
Scharfenberg, Wm.
Sequine, C.
Starr, Charles Sen.
Starr, Charles Jr.
Spycer, Mrs.
Southmayed, Horace
Stratton, James L.
Scott, W.
Scott, A. M. L.
Stark, A. Mrs.
Southmayd, S. C.
Smith, S. C.
Simmons, Louis
Stansbery, E.
Sharp, R.
Sarracco, Pierre
Sanger, Z.
Smith, James
Stevens, Wm.
Sherwood & Chapman
Steel, Dr.
Sinclair, W. J.
Swain, Misses The
Stanford, Robert
Sillcock, Mr.
Smith, Wm.
Stevens, J. Mrs.
Storm, S.
Smith, George
Sommerville, Mrs.
Sommer, Joseph
Seymour, J. N.
Seymour, J. H.

Smith, D., M. D.
Seymour, Mrs.
Smith & Crane
Smith, C. W.
Stiles, Samuel
Sagory, Chs.
Sherman, Dr.
Seaman, Henry J.
Schlesinger, F. S.
Smith, Andrew
S. R.
Senior, E. H.
Stokes, Henry
Sheppard, George, G.
Stokes, B. G.
Sage, George E.
Slosson, J.
Stewart, James
Sheldon, Preston
Sprague, J. H.
Stagg, John
Sandford, P. Mrs.
Scott, J. D.
Spencer, W. G.
Shutts, P. J.
Soper, Abraham
Sullivan, C.
Scudder, Linus
Sage, W. B.
Smith, Pascal B.
Spencer, Mark
Smillie, J.
Stilt, G. S.
Stephens, J. H.
Steinle, Fred.
Sackett, C. D.
Stanley, Wm.
Sutton, George
Scudder, W. H.
Sarvin, David
Smith, J. Lee
Struthers, J.
Salisbury, John S.
Sykes, L. A.
Smith, John C. T.
Shelton, T. B., M. D.
Skinner, T. H. Jr., Rev.
Scrymser, Wm. H.
Sanford, M. B.
Sydam, Lambert
Smith, J. P.
Spencer, O. F.
Stillman, Allen & Co.
Sibell, George
Sudlow & Siney
Stearns, J. C.
Summers, A. B.
Smith, Milton
Sheffield, D.
Seaman, C.
Schutz, L.
Sanford, N.
Spellman, Mr.
Squires, Captain
Seely, J. F. Rev.
Shannon, Samuel

Shields, C.
Smith, H. A.
Strohmeiere, F.
Stickney, C. L.
Shipman, Wm.
Shelden, Wm. H.
Smith, C. E.
Summers, Wm.
Stott, Alex.
Suydam, H.
Smith, E. L.
Smith, Shadrach
Silverman, Jacob
Sammis, D. P.
Schultz, Mr.
Smith, Peter
Silver, James
Smith, Samuel
Sueeden, J.
Smith, Wm. H. & Co.
Strang, Adriance & Co.
Smith, Lemuel
Schieffelin, James L.
Schieffelin, B.
Strybing, Henry
Sanford, H. J.
Spaulding, H. F.
Scovill Manufacturing Co.
Smith, Deey & Eddy
Stringer & Townsend
S. A. T.
S. B. F.
Smith, T. & Co.
S. B. R.
Schiffer, S. & Bros.
Stoneall,
Spiker S. & Co.
Sloan H. S.
Stoppani, C. G.
Smith, C.
Sweeny, Hugh, M. D.
Suckley, Rutsen
Stuyvesant, Ellen Mrs.
Stillman, T. B.
Sturges, Bennet & Co.
Scrymser, J.
Smith, John J.
Sampson, Mrs.
Sackett, A. M.
Sackett, J. R.
Secor, T.
Snow, G. T.
Shipman, S. D.
Stalker, Thomas
Stillwell, R.
Smith, A. D.
Scudder, E.
Snacken, Mrs.
Staniford, D. F.
Shoemaker, J.
Suydam, J. A.
Spalding, W. E.
Sloan, W.
Stebbins, Wm.
Suydam, Reed & Co.
Skeel, R.

LIST OF MEMBERS. (1851.

Sowza, Mr.
Schott, Mr.
Sears, H.
Skinner, H.
Smith, Richard
Sanford, General
Sayre, Mrs.
Seignette, Mr.
Sterling & Walton
Suydam, S. A.
Stevens, R. L.
Smith, W. D.
Stillwill & Brown
Stevens, John C.
Strange & Co.
St. John, S. H.
Suydam, J. R.
Southart & Kissam
Serrell, J. J.
Southwich & Tupper
Schermerhorn, August. Mrs.
Smull, Thos
Simpson, J. B. & G.
Somerville, Andrew
Sather & Church
Sears, Robert
Smith, Elizabeth Mrs.
Somerby, Mrs.
Scott, Thomas
Staniford, D. T.
Sharp, A. H.
Seymour, W. N.
Sheafe J. F.
Shieffelin, H. H.
Sanxay, J. F.
Sharp, Wm.
Steele, Wm.
Skidmore, J. R.
Spies, Adan W.
Smith, John Calvin
Stimson, A. L.
Smith, S. C.
Smith, W. D.
Selden, Charles
Smith, B. R.
Skidmore, J. R.
Sammis, Joel
Stansberry, J. F.
Smith, Albert G.
See, H. P.
Shindler, Simon
See, Leander
St. John C. C.
Stout, A. V.
Sherwood, J. W.
Smith, Samuel
Stuckey, Isaiah E.
Smith, Shadrack
Shaver, P. C.
Stelle, Nelson, M. D.
Storer, George, L.
Sullivan, Charles
Smith, J.
Smith, A.
Shop, George
Sloat, John

Staniford, D. T.
Savage, C. C.
Swords, Henry
Schoonmaker, John O.
Smith, Adon

T.

Titus, James H.
Taylor & Co., Moses
Tredwell, Adam
Tweedy, O. B.
Talbat, C. N.
Townsend, W. H.
Taylor Brothers
Talmadge, H. F.
Tillotson, J. C.
Thorndycke, J.
Thomas, J. A. Col.
Tooker, J. S. Mrs.
Townsend, J. R. Mrs.
Treadwell, S.
Trenor, J, M. D.
Thompson, D.
Taylor, W. B.
Tallman, S. S.
Tinson & Co., R. N
Tilly, John R.
Truesdale, E. D.
Taylor, John
Toldridge, Barnett
Taylor, J. D.
Talman, J. F.
Terbell
Treadwell, C. R.
Titus, Wm. M.
Toole, W. S.
Tracy, F. A. Mrs.
Taylor, John & Sons
Tilden, L. W.
Thompson, W. A.
Trippe, J. F.
Terry, Brother
Taylor, Lyman
Treadwell & Gould
Thompson, J.
Thomas
Trimble, Mr.
Totten, Joseph
Tweed, R.
Thorp, H. S.
Terry, M. N.
Tatham, Benjamin
Tappen, G.
Taylor, Isaac
Tyson, Wm.
Thompson, Samuel B.
Tripp, Charles
Thomas, Griffith
Tweed, Richard
Tappen, George Jr.
Townsend, Elihu
Templeton, Mrs.
Townsend, Effingham

Thompson, John, M. D.
Thorp, A.
Tracy, Charles
Taylor, R. S.
Talman, Stephen S.
Topham, Wm.
Tomes, Mrs. Sen.
Thompson, Major
Thwing, C. & E. W.
Tracy, S. P.
Trowbridge, F. H.
Tate, J. E.
Thorn, Wm.
Towle, Thomas
Thomas, E.
Tapan, John
Ten Brook, J.
Tallman, A. S.
Talmadge, Fredk. A.
Townsend, J. H
Tousley, Charles
Turner, D.
Thompson, James
Taff, Henry
Teller, R. H.
Tupper, C. H.
Trumpy. C.
Taylor, J. C.
Tiebout, N.
Tylee, J. Mrs.
Titus, C. F.
Tappen & Burd
Thetford, Joseph
Tremper, Harman
Trempard, Samuel
Trafford. Abm.
Timpson, Judge
Taylor, John
Tappen, Chas.
Tracy, Irvin & Co.
Trowbridge. Henry
Tapscott, W. & J. T.
Tucker, James W.
Thorburn, J. M. & Co.
Thompson, Thomas
Thomas, Thomas
Townsend, S. P.
Tisdale, Saml. T. & Co.
Thompson, G. W. Mrs.
Truslow, Wm.
Tillinghast, P.
Thompson. A.
Tilden, William
Taylor, J. B.
Thompson, James
Tenny, James
Tiffany, Young & Ellis
Thomas, Mr.
Tucker, J. C.
Tarrant, Dr.
Taylor, A.
Trippe, E. H.
Tilton, S.
Tucker, T. C.
Topping, H.
Tieman, George

1851.)　　　　　　　LIST OF MEMBERS.　　　　　　　53

Teal, Charles
Thorn, Charles E.
Thorn, Jonathan Mrs. per A.
　W. Murray
Thruston, R. H.
Thruston, C. M.
Tucker, D. N.
Terry, David Revd.
Terbell, Jeremiah
Teller, R. H.
Tracy, Geo. M.
Trimble, G. T.
Taylor, Moses B.
Triton, Richard
Taylor, A.
Traphagen, G. H., M. D.
Tradguskis, John
Terbell, H. S.
Terry, M. N.
Tracy, C. C.
Tucker, C. P.
Tousley, Charles
Tattersal, W. K.
Teller, D. W.
Trafford, Abm.
Taylor, J.
Tucker, C. H.

U

Upson, Stephen
Underhill, A. S.
Underhill, J. S.
Ustick, Richard
Ubsdell, Peirson & Co.
Underhill, A.
Underhill, Wm.

V.

Van Hook, W.
Van Winkle, E. S.
Vernon, E.
Van Wyck, H. L.
Van Antwerp, J.
Van Santvoord, C
Vandervoort. J. B.
Vermilyea, W. M.
Van Zandt, P. P.
Van Nortwitch, W. B.
Van Duesen, D.
Van Auken, Mrs.
Vaughn, Mrs.
Voorhies, W. L.
Verplanck, G. C.
Vermilye, W. R.
Van Rensselaer, Alexander
Van Wagenen, Richd. D.
Vail, H. N.
Van Tuyl, A.
Vandervoort, H.
Van Tuyl, B.
Vail, Aaron
Vanderpool, A.

Van Duzer, S.
Vendenheuven, Mary
Van Norden, Wm.
Van Saun, Henry
Vliet, S.
Vermillya, J.
Vandervoort, Dr.
Van Winkle, Dr.
Vredenburgh, Peter
Van Nest, Abm.
Van Vleck, J. T.
Vredenbergh, P.
Van Nest, P.
Vandervoort, P.
Vandervoort, Mrs.
Van Arsdale, John
Van Nostrand, J.
Van Nest, John
Van Hein, George
Van Valen, J. D.
Van Saun, S. J.
Van Wagenen, Wm.
Van Dyck, P.
Vreeland, J.
Voorhis, Richd.
Van Deusen, S.
Van Houden, John
Van Cleef, John T.
Van Winkle, J.
Van Pelt
Van Cott, Gabriel
Vreeland, Jacob
Vermule, Wm., M. D.
Vermule, Field, M. D.
Van Deventer, J. & W.
Van Nest A. R.
Van Blankestyne, & Co.
Vernon, Thomas
Vanderbilt, Wm. S.
Von Glahn, H.
Van Wagenen, W. F.
Valentine, D. T.
Van Antwerp, S. Mrs.
Van Orden, Mr.
Van Kleck & Co.
Van Auken, B. H.
Van Waggenan, Mrs.
Van Benschoten, J.
Van Wyck, Mr.
Vassar, M. & Co.
Vernol, Mr.
Van De Werker, E.
Vale, G.
Van Blankenstyne & Heine-
　mann
Van Arsdale, H., M. D.
Vermilye, W.
Van Allen, Wm.
Vanderhoof, M.
Voorhis, John

W.

Wetmore, A. R.
Wetmore, W. S.

White, Robert, Jr.
Whiting, Augustus.
Wainwright, Ely
Wolf, John, D. by Capt.
　Wm. A. Spencer
Walsh & Mallory
Ward, A. H.
Wheelright, B. F.
Wisner, W. H.
Willis, W.
Wilson, A. M. Mrs.
Woodruff, M. P.
Wright, J.
Walker, J. Mrs.
Winslow, R. H.
Watson, J., M. D.
Wyles, J.
Wilmerding, W. E. Jr.
Ward, T., M. D.
Ward, J.
Ward, H. H.
Wilks, M.
Waddington, W. D.
Ward, W. G. Mrs.
Weller, J.
Wilks, M.
Whitehead, J.
Winslow, T. S.
Whittemore, T.
Waller, R.
Woodhead, J.
Wilmurt, T. A.
Wagner, D. B.
Wood, W.
Williamson, D. A.
Woodward, J. S.
Wetmore, P. M.
Woodford, J. C.
Williams & Stevens
Wood, W. S.
Walker. J. & D.
Withers, Wm.
Whitthus, J. D.
Wilson, A. D., M. D.
White, S. B.
Warner, Abm.
Whitlock. Wm. Jr.
White, Eli
West, Wm.
Wiskeman, Philip
Welstein, J.
Wilcox, W. J.
Wilkes, George, M. D.
Wood, D.
Ward, S. S.
Wright, A.
Wray, Stephen
Winston, F. S.
Waller, Josuah A.
Wilson, B. M.
Williams, P. H. & W.
Wilbur, M.
Woodruff, L. B.
Walton, W.
Wood, J. N.
Ward, R. M.

White, Charles
Wilson, W. S.
Walton, M. A. Miss
Whittemore, J.
Wood, J. C.
Walton, S. Miss
Wells & Co.
Woolsey, E. J.
White, Robert H.
Wetmore & Cryder
Wolcott, F. H.
Wawzer, Miner & Co.
Warburg, E.
Welchman, J. W.
Williams, F. B.
Weeks & Co. W.
Wolf & Gillespie
Whitlock, Augustus
Wells, Brothers
Ward, L. B.
Wood, Isaac, M D.
Westervelt, J. A.
Williams, Richard
Willets, Robert
Willets, Stephen
Willets, Samuel
Whitmore, J. C.
Walton, E. L.
Webb, J. B.
Watkiss, Lewis
Webb, Mrs.
Willets, E. P.
Wetmore, Mary
Woodward, Thomas
Williams, Thomas
Willets, T., M. D.
Woolsey, C. W. Mrs.
Weeks, Samuel
Williams, M. Mrs.
Walter, G.
Williams, R.
Weisman, Augustus
Wicker, Henry
Wardle, Thomas
Willard, M.
Wheaton, Wm.
Welsh, Wm.
Wentworth, O. R.
Wright, John
Wetmore, Saml.
Watson, John
Walker, Wm.
Watt, Wm.
Walker, John
Walker, T. E.
Woodford, O. P.
Weir, S. E.
Wagstaff, Mrs.
Western, Mrs.
W. L. J.
Woram & Haughwout
Williams, S. T.
Wilson, D.
Wood, B.
Walton, J. B.
Wight, Richard

Weed, W. H.
Wooding, J.
Ward, Miss
Wise, M.
Wilson, F.
White, John J.
Wood, David
Weston, G. S.
Wainright, E.
Wickstead, J. W.
Wickens, George
Winship, A. L.
Winterton, Mr.
White, Wm.
Wight, Jas. W.
Wilson, Wm.
Watkins, C. S.
Woodworth, D. A.
White, Arch.
White, John
Wood, D. Mrs.
Walker, James
Wooding, James
Woodward, W. A.
Walker, S. G.
Williams, Wm. R.
Wood, O. E.
Whitney, W. E.
Williams, Thos.
Wells, H. M.
Ward, W. C.
Williams, W. R.
Wilson, M.
Wheeler, Z.
Wycoff, Mrs.
Williams, J.
Williamson, J.
Woodward, Samuel
Warner, P. R.
Woodhouse, Capt.
Westervelt, James
Whittaker, W. B.
Wallace, James
Westervelt, Jacob
Walduck, R. M.
Wilson
Wilson, M.
Webb, William H.
Williams, Jabez
Wood, A. L.
Wessing, James
Woolvering, Josiah
Wright, D. D.
Willett
Warren, Mr.
Watson, Mr.
Wells, Mrs.
West, Joseph
Welling, Mr.
Walker, Mrs.
Withers, R.
White, Edward
Welford, Mr.
Ward, Adam
Williams, Erastus
Wing, Luman

Withington, Lewis
Wallace, J. R.
Weeks, George
Wiggins, W. H.
Walworth, Nason & Guild
Worwerck, W.
Wichelhausen, Recknagle & Schwab
Waldron & Ilsley
W. H. E. & M.
Williams, C. P. & E.
Wood & Hughs
Woolsey, John
Wagner, G. & Co.
W. J. C.
W. B.
Watkins, John L.
Woodhull, C. S.
Wells, O. P., M. D. by Rev. C. C. Darling
Wray, Christopher
Wilson, O. H.
Wilkes, George
Worrall & Co.
Withers, R.
White, Chas. B.
Williams, C.
Wright, Neziah
Washburn, H. B.
White, John T.
Ward, Isaac
Willet, E. M.
W. H. S.
Whitewright, Wm.
Waterbury, Mary Ann Mrs
Wheeler & Co.
Wyman, J. G.
Webster, B. C.
Waller, W. R.
Wells & Kirk
Wood & Mabbit
Wiggins, James
Wallace, Miss
Waldo, S. L.
West, W. G.
Whedon, Dr.
Wait, Mr.
Worley, Nathan
Wood & Gibson
Wygant, E.
Willis, Edward
Wetmore, L. M.
Williams & Hinman
W. A. B. & Co.
Westfall, J. & D.
Wintringham, J.
Warren, H. M.
Wheeler, L. F.
Walmsley, Ed.
West, Daniel
Whyte, John
White, P. N.
Wood, J. L.
W.
Wright, Sturges & Shaw
Weeks, Edward A.

LIST OF MEMBERS.

Walsh, Mallory & Co.
Wilbur, Chas.
Wetmore, L.
Walsh, George
Walker, Wm A.
Woodruff, L. B.
Walker, Wm.
Woolsey, E. J.
Wheelock, Calvin Jr.
Walkins, J. L.
Whittelsey, Henry
Wheeler, L. F.
Ware, J. P.
Warren, T.
Walsh, G.
Wood, R. R.
Weir, James
Wentworth, J. W.
Waldron, C.
Wood, Henry
Williams, Erastus

Whitely, G.
Wagstaff, Wm.
Weisse, J. A., M. D.
Winter, E. T., M. D.
Wheeler, S. S.
Wilson, J.
Wilson, N
West, H. P.

Y.

Yates, A. E. Mrs.
Young, W.
Yates, B. S.
Young, Wm.
Yelverton & Fellows
Young, T. S.
Young, Henry
Yates, C.
Yongs, G.

Youle, George
Young, E. M.
York, Mrs.
Young, David
Young, Frederick
Youle, Geo. W.
Young, John
Yocum, E. S.

Z.

Zerega, A.
Zabriskie, A. C. & Co.
Zabriskie, C.
Zimmermann, A.
Zinck, Theodore
Zeigler, G. F.
Zabriskie, O. Mrs.
Zabriskie, A. C.

THE

NINTH ANNUAL REPORT

OF THE

NEW-YORK ASSOCIATION

FOR

Improving the Condition of the Poor,

FOR THE YEAR 1852.

WITH THE BY-LAWS AND A LIST OF MEMBERS.

ORGANIZED, 1843—INCORPORATED, 1848.

"The quality of mercy is not strained;
It droppeth as the gentle rain from heaven
Upon the place beneath; it is twice blessed;
It blesseth him that gives and him that takes."

NEW-YORK:
PRINTED BY JOHN F. TROW, 49 ANN-STREET.
1852.

PROCEEDINGS

AT THE

ANNUAL MEETING

OF THE

New-York Association for Improving the Condition of the Poor.

Held in the Hall of the Public School Society, Nov. 8th, 1852.

George Griswold, Esq., Vice-President, in the chair.

The Minutes of the last Annual Meeting were read by the Recording Secretary, and, on motion, approved.

In the absence of the Treasurer, the Auditing Committee presented his Annual Report, which was accepted, and ordered on file.

The Minutes of the Board of Managers, exhibiting their operations during the recess of the Supervisory Council, were read by the Corresponding Secretary, as their Report to that body, and approved.

The Annual Report was read, accepted, and ordered to be printed under the direction of the Board of Managers.

Voting by ballot having by resolution been dispensed with, the Association proceeded to the election of the following Officers, Managers, and Supervisory Council, for the ensuing year, after which the meeting adjourned.

OFFICERS, MANAGERS,
AND
SUPERVISORY COUNCIL.

President.
JAMES BROWN.

Vice Presidents.
GEORGE GRISWOLD, JAMES LENOX,
JAMES BOORMAN, HORATIO ALLEN,
A. R. WETMORE.

Treasurer.
ROBERT B. MINTURN.

Corresponding Secretary and Agent.
ROBERT M. HARTLEY.

Recording Secretary.
JOSEPH B. COLLINS.

Supervisory Council.

The first in order is the Chairman of each District Committee.

FIRST DISTRICT.
James C. Ramsey,
James Cruikshank,
William Bogardus,
John Harris,
John Davidson.

SECOND DISTRICT.
George W. Abbe,
Joseph F. Sanxay,
William Sharp,
Charles Wilbur,
Dan. N. Tucker.

THIRD DISTRICT.
E. Cauldwell,
J. L. Baldwin,
E. L. Fancher,
W. D. Harris,
V. Le Compt.

FOURTH DISTRICT.
Abraham Fardon, Jr.,
Archibald Hall,
Hugh Aikman,
Charles Chamberlain,
John Gates.

FIFTH DISTRICT.
A. R. Wetmore,
J. H. Redfield,
N. P. Hosack,
Marcus Mitchell,
David Terry.

SIXTH DISTRICT.
N. C. Everett,
Stephen Conover,
Daniel Fisher,
Frederic Lockwood,
Peter Burnett, M. D.

SEVENTH DISTRICT.
Stephen Cutter,
George Walsh,
B. G. Bruce,
J. L. Moore,
Thomas Warren.

EIGHTH DISTRICT.
Joseph B. Collins,
John Endicott,
Charles C. Dyer,
O. D. McClain,
J. S. Holt.

NINTH DISTRICT.
James O. Pond, M. D.,
Jacob S. Miller, M. D.,
Thomas B. Richards,
Jeremiah Terbell,
Daniel French.

VISITORS. (1852.

TENTH DISTRICT.

James Horn,
Joseph M. Bell,
H. Van Arsdale, M. D.,
E. A. Fraser,
Thomas Jackson.

ELEVENTH DISTRICT.

Abner Mills,
Peter McPherson,
Joel Kelly,
Michael Devoy,
David L. Young.

THIRTEENTH DISTRICT.

Lewis Chichester,
Thomas Kennedy,
John Pearsall,
Charles Merrill,
Wm. A. Walker.

FOURTEENTH DISTRICT.

Alexander W. Murray,
William Post,
J. J. Jenkins,
H. Miller,
Richard Brown.

FIFTEENTH DISTRICT.

Thomas Denny,
William G. Bull,
Joseph Lawrence,
James Marsh,
Adon Smith.

SIXTEENTH DISTRICT.

Luther Jackson,
Charles Roome,
L. B. Woodruff,
H. K. Bull,
J. P. Cumming.

SEVENTEENTH DISTRICT.

S. C. Lynes,
James R. Gibson,
George Manning Tracy,
Thomas Jeremiah,
James W. Metcalf, M. D.

EIGHTEENTH DISTRICT.

F. E. Mather,
Wm. Walker,
J. W. Benedict,
Adam W. Spies,
J. H. Earle.

NINETEENTH DISTRICT.

J. W. Rumsey,
J. C. Miller,
D. E. Bartlett,
W. G. Mackay,
William E. Davis.

TWENTIETH DISTRICT.

J. P. Ostrom,
James Reeve,
J. F. Williams.
Charles H. Rusher,
J. W. Miller,

Elected Members of the Supervisory Council.

J. C. Greene,
Wm. S. Wetmore,
Jonathan Sturges,
Wm. A. Macy,
George T. Trimble,

E. J. Woolsey,
Cyrus Curtis,
John C. Baldwin,
William B. Crosby,
Thomas Cock, M. D.,

Wm. G. Bull,
Lorin Nash,
Capt. Wm. A. Spencer,
F. S. Winston,
Peter Cooper.

Elected Members of the Board of Managers.

Stewart Brown,
John T. Adams,
Jasper Corning,
Erastus C. Benedict.

VISITORS,

Appointed by the Advisory Committee for the ensuing year.

FIRST DISTRICT.

John Love,
Enoch W. Page,
John McIntire,
John Harris,
J. C. Ramsey,
George Hatt,
Alexander Ferguson,
William Bogardus,
A. L. Stimson,
Calvin Wheelock, Jr.,

John Davidson,
John Calvin Smith,
Peter Allyn,
H. M. Baldwin,
George Hatt, *Secretary.*

SECOND DISTRICT.

Charles Wilbur,
Joseph F. Sanxay,
George W. Abbe,

D. N. Tucker,
William Sharp,
John L. Watkins,
George Hatt, *Secretary.*

THIRD DISTRICT.

R. S. Gould,
Volney Elliot,
James W. Dunning,
Richard B. Lewis,

VISITORS.

A. Taylor,
W. D. Harris,
V. Le Compt,
R. Lewis,
E. L. Fancher,
  Edward Pratt, Secretary.

FOURTH DISTRICT.

Henry Whittlesey,
A. Pearson,
Thomas Wallace,
A. J. Henderson,
H. Whittlesey,
G. H. Traphagen, M.D.,
Charles M. Decker,
E. H. Sands, M.D.,
Hiram Hurd,
T. R. Ryers,
M. E. Kingman,
H. Lockwood,
Wm. A. Brusle,
S. Fanning,
T. H. Burras,
  Henry Whittlesey, Sec'y.

FIFTH DISTRICT.

T. V. Forster,
A. R. Wetmore,
Marcus Mitchel,
Peter Mood,
B. Barney, M.D.,
Moses Christy,
William Van Allen,
Wm. B. Eager, M.D.,
H. S. Terbell,
John Cook,
N. P. Hosack,
Charles Mason,
James H. Matthews,
L. G. Evans,
J. H. Redfield,
David Terry,
Robert Pattison,
John E. Jackson,
John A. Kennedy,
Thomas E. Smith,
John M. Wilcox,
William Jackson,
J. S. Hoagland,
H. A. Halsey,
Charles Selden,
James Litton,
  Edward Pratt, Secretary.

SIXTH DISTRICT.

Noah Worrell,
Daniel Fisher,
John M. Clawson,
Benjamin Marshall, M.D.,
Frederick Lockwood,
Wm. Jervis,

Moses B. Taylor,
Peter Burnett, M D.,
Abraham Florentine,
George W. Lowerre,
Benjamin Marshall, Jr. M.D.
Andrew Hume,
Samuel N. Burrill,
Samuel Baxter,
John P. Ware,
Reuben S. Carpentier, M.D.,
Richard Tritton,
  Amzi Camp, Secretary.

SEVENTH DISTRICT.

W. Rowell,
N. P. Beers,
T. Warren,
J. B. Horton,
R. S. Place,
A. P. McNaughton,
G. Walsh,
B. R. Smith,
William Kerr,
J. L. Moore,
B. F. Eaton,
Charles Roberts,
B. G. Bruce,
Joel Sammis,
Edmund Farrel,
Stephen Cutter,
  Jonathan B. Horton, Sec'y.

EIGHTH DISTRICT.

Joseph S. Holt,
O. D. McClain,
Samuel Winterton,
Daniel Conover,
James F. Stansberry,
James Clark,
Thomas Bailey,
J. W. Kellogg,
Samuel P. Sherwood,
Charles C. Dyer,
Louis J. Belloni,
Henry W. Ryerson,
C. P. Dakin,
Luke Kelley,
John Endicott,
Edward Fields, M.D.,
John Gillelan,
John Nichol,
Darius Geer,
James V. Freeman,
  William Kirby, Secretary.

NINTH DISTRICT.

J. B. Ferguson,
W. E. Kidd,
O. T. Wardell,
W. H. Knapp,
Ira C. Pierson,

Henry P. See,
Henry W. Deems,
A. Demarest,
William Bogert,
Thomas Ackenback,
William Marten,
Wm. A. Foster,
J. Ruston,
A. Chesebro,
Leander See,
M. Allison, Jr.,
Daniel F. Lee,
John Murray,
J. C. Baxter,
John C. Carson,
Charles A. Cragin,
M. H. Howell,
  Lewis E. Jackson, Sec'y.

TENTH DISTRICT

A. L Bogart,
Wm. Clymer,
Joseph B. Bell,
James Horn,
James Wier,
Wm. Wheaton,
Andrew V. Stout,
Edward A. Fraser,
C. V. Clarkson, M.D.,
J. W. Sherwood,
Joseph W. Wentworth,
Henry Van Arsdale, M.D.,
Samuel Smith,
James K. Place,
Thomas Jackson,
Charles Place,
C. N. Decker,
William C. Bradley,
Thomas Holman,
  J. P. Lestrade, Sec'y.

ELEVENTH DISTRICT

C. P. Hawkins,
J. V. D. B. Fowler,
Joel Kelly,
Thomas Hogan,
Wm. Murphy, M.D.,
John Cameron,
E. H. Kimbark, M.D.,
D. C. Smith,
James Wissing,
Charles Wooster, Jr.,
John Young,
William Barker,
Gilbert Leggett,
Peter Squire,
Cornelius Waldren,
James Jones,
John Myers,
Emery Van Tassel,
Moses Gardner,
James Little,
James Price,

VISITORS. (1852.

George Winslow,
Ardon Mead,
J. W. Schuler,
William Brown,
Edward Roberts,
Grant Dubois, Sec'y.

THIRTEENTH DISTRICT.

William F. Nash,
John Hutchings,
J. F. Cook,
J. E. Stillwell,
John R. Marsh,
G. W. Shannon,
I. A. Clark,
John Burr,
Henry Wood,
Charles Merrill,
E. Falconer,
P. C. Shaver,
Abraham Trafford,
Francis Duncan,
G. D. Smith,
M. H. Stebbins,
Erastus Williams,
J. T. Klots,
H. S. De Grove,
J. Brown,
Noah Coe, Secretary.

FOURTEENTH DISTRICT.

Nehemiah Lounsberry,
Nelson Stelle, M.D.,
Wm. Post,
Richard Brown,
Bezaleel Howe,
Wm. Johnston,
John Leavy,
C. B. Pearson,
J. M. Howe, M.D.,
H. Miller,
Henry P. West,
J. J. Jenkins,
Thomas Fairweather,
Nelson Sammis,
Peter Carter,
Gideon Peck,
Alexander W. Murray,
James Knox,
William Gray, Sec'y.

FIFTEENTH DISTRICT.

George L. Storer,
Isaac Orchard,
Charles Sullivan,
Henry Holman,
Josiah Dodge,
Henry Swords,
C. R. Disosway,
Benjamin Lord,
John Mollard,
Isaac Orchard, Sec'y.

SIXTEENTH DISTRICT.

R. Cole,
B. M. Fowler,
W. Phillips,
J. M. Hubbard,
Marks Cornell,
Stephen Merritt,
S. Bridger,
G. Whitely,
H. Jones,
J. Cowl,
J. Smith,
A. Smith,
T. J. Burger,
D. Chichester,
Wm. Heydon,
D. Irwin,
J. D. Adams,
D. L. Beatty,
J. C. Hines,
C. C. Darling, Sec'y.

SEVENTEENTH DISTRICT.

James Duff,
R. Albro,
C. H. Redman,
H. Griffin,
W. B. Humbert,
I. G. Worrall, M.D.,
R. Reed,
W. J. Barnes,
Geo. Manning Tracy,
D. T. Staniford,
A. L Halsted,
R. W. Moore,
Geo. Shopp,
S. D. Washburn, M.D.,
James R. Gibson,
John Slote,
John Patterson,
J. W. Metcalf, M.D.,
E. West, M.D.,
James Phair,
John Young,
A. Green,
W. A. Carrington, M.D.,

J. K. Johnson,
D. T. Macfarlan,
Richard Horton, Sec'y.

EIGHTEENTH DISTRICT.

J. W. Benedict,
G. L. Hyslop, M.D.,
L. Hazeltine,
John N. Power,
B. Kent,
Edward Johnson,
Edward Roberts,
Charles Irving,
E. T. Winter, M.D.,
James France,
John Clark,
C. C. Savage,
J. B. Ballard,
W. A. Butler,
N. R. Long,
L. Ranney, M.D.,
James Armstrong,
J. B. Ballard, Sec'y.

NINETEENTH DISTRICT.

Walter G. Mackay,
John C. Miller,
J. O. Schoonmaker,
Moses J. Decker,
John A. Cormack,
D. E. Bartlett,
N. Wilson,
H. McCoun,
J. N. Shaffer,
John C. Parker,
Jacob Dunn,
Charles Johnson,
Jotham Wilson,
Enoch Mack, Sec'y.

TWENTIETH DISTRICT.

John G. Sewell, M.D.,
L. W. Halsey,
R. Mathison, M.D,,
J. Parr,
Franklin Gregg,
Francis Buckley,
C. F. Church,
E. T. Winter, M.D.,
J. F. Williams,
Robert Gibbons,
Wm. Heydon,
J. F. Duff,
J. N. Husted, M.D ,
Wm. Pringle,
Richard Hayter, Sec'y.

OFFICE OF THE ASSOCIATION, Public School Building, Second Story, 148 Grand street, corner of Elm.

BY-LAWS.

ARTICLE I.

EVERY person who becomes an annual Subscriber, a member of an Advisory Committee, or a Visitor, shall be a member of the Association.

ARTICLE II.

The President and Secretaries shall perform such duties as usually pertain to their office.

ARTICLE III.

The Treasurer shall give such security for the faithful performance of the trust reposed in him, as the Association may demand and approve. He shall take in charge all funds; keep an account of all receipts and disbursements; and pay all duly authorized demands. At the usual meeting, he shall render a particular and correct statement of all his receipts and disbursements to the Association. He shall also exhibit a summary report to the Board of Managers at their stated meetings, and whenever called upon by them for that purpose.

ARTICLE IV.

The Board of Managers shall have exclusive control of the funds of the Association, and authority to make By-laws; to fill vacancies; appoint all committees; and generally to adopt such measures as the objects of the Institution may require. It shall meet for the transaction of business, on the second Monday of every month; and the annual meeting of the Association shall be convened on the second

Monday of November, when the Board shall submit a report of its proceedings, and the officers and managers be chosen. In case of a failure to hold the specified meeting in November, a special meeting for the same purpose shall be convened in the course of the ensuing month.

ARTICLE V.

Special meetings of the Board of Managers and of the Supervisory Council, may be called by the Secretary, at the request of the President, or on receiving a requisition signed by five members. Two days' notice must be given of the time of meeting.

ARTICLE VI.

The Managers may at any time make such alterations in these By-Laws as may be deemed necessary; provided they be not contrary to the Act of Incorporation, and that such alteration shall be submitted to the Board of Managers at least one meeting before the same is acted upon; and that it shall not be passed upon unless specified in the call of the meeting, and when a majority of the whole number of the Board of Managers is present.

ARTICLE VII.

An office shall be opened in an eligible situation, for the purpose of concentrating and diffusing all information pertaining to the Society's operations and objects, and for the transaction of its general business.

ARTICLE VIII.

It shall be the duty of the General Agent to devote himself with diligence and fidelity to the affairs of the Association.

ARTICLE IX.

The city shall be divided into twenty Districts, each Ward forming a District; and the districts be subdivided into Sections. Each District shall have an Advisory Committee, to consist of five members; and each Section a Visitor.

ARTICLE X.

It shall be the duty of the Advisory Committee to divide their Districts into such Sections, as to apportion to each about twenty-five families requiring attention; endeavor to obtain suitable Visitors for each Section; supply vacancies which may occur; make the necessary arrangements for placing at the disposal of the Visitors food, fuel, and clothing, for distribution; and on some day in the first week of every month (excepting the meetings of July and August, which may be omitted in the discretion of the Committees), to convene all the Visitors of the Sections, for the purpose of receiving their returns, and conferring with them on the objects of their mutual labors. The Committees, moreover, shall duly draw upon the Treasurer for such proportion of the funds as may be appropriated to their Districts; they shall keep a strict account of all their disbursements, and only in extreme cases make donations of money; they shall monthly render an account of their expenditures to the Board of Managers; and in default of this duty, shall not be entitled to draw upon the funds of the Association. Each Committee shall appoint its own Chairman, Secretary, and Treasurer, and shall transmit the Reports of the Visitors immediately after each monthly meeting, with any other information they may think desirable, to the General Secretary.

ARTICLE XI.

It shall be the duty of each Visitor to confine his labors exclusively to the particular Section assigned him, so that no individual shall receive relief, excepting in the Section where he is known, and to which he belongs. The Visitors shall carefully investigate all cases referred to them before granting relief; ascertain the condition, habits of life, and means of subsistence of the applicants; and extend to all such kind services, counsel, and assistance, as a discriminating and judicious regard for their present and permanent welfare requires. And in case of sickness, it will be their duty to inquire whether there is any medical or other attendance needed; whether relief is afforded by any religious or charitable society; to provide themselves with information respecting the nearest Dispensary, and in all cases, when practicable, to refer applicants for aid to appropriate existing societies. When no other assistance is provided or available, they shall draw from the resources of this Association—not money, which is never allowed to be given, except with the consent of the Advisory Committee or a member thereof—but such articles of food, fuel, clothing, and similar supplies as the necessities of the case require. In all cases of want coming to the knowledge of the Visitors, they will be expected to perform the same duties, although no application has been made. It shall be their duty, moreover, to render a report of their labors, and also an account of all their disbursements, to their respective Committees, at the stated monthly meeting. No Visitor neglecting these duties will be entitled to draw on the funds of the Association.

ARTICLE XII.

The Board of Managers, the members of the Advisory Committees, and certain elected members, shall together constitute a Supervisory Council, whose duties shall be deliberative and advisory; and its annual meetings be held on the second Monday of November, in each year. Special meetings of this body shall be held, when called by the Board of Managers.

ARTICLE XIII.

It shall be the duty of the members of the Association to endeavor, in all suitable ways, to give practical effect to its principles; especially to discountenance indiscriminate alms-giving and street-begging; to provide themselves with tickets of reference; and instead of giving aid to unknown applicants, whose case they cannot themselves investigate, to refer such applications to the Visitor of the Section in which the applicants reside, in order that such cases may properly be inquired into, and, if deserving, relieved.

ARTICLE XIV.

The printed forms of tickets and orders for relief, shall be designated by the Board of Managers, and no other shall be used.

Incorporation.

CERTIFICATE OF INTENTION

TO INCORPORATE THE NEW-YORK ASSOCIATION FOR IMPROVING THE CONDITION OF THE POOR.

THE undersigned, being each and every of them of full age, and citizens of the State of New-York, desiring to associate themselves for the benevolent and charitable objects hereinafter expressed, that they may become a body politic and corporate, and be enabled to conduct the business of the Association in the City and County of New-York, according to the provisions of an "Act for the Incorporation of Benevolent, Charitable, Scientific, and Missionary purposes," passed April 12th, 1848, do for these purposes hereby certify,

I. That the name and title by which such Institution shall be known in law, is the "New-York Association for Improving the Condition of the Poor."

II. That the particular business and objects of such Association shall be the elevation of the physical and moral condition of the indigent; and so far as is compatible with these objects, the relief of their necessities.

III. That the Board of Managers to manage the same shall consist of one President, five Vice-Presidents, one Treasurer, one Corresponding Secretary and General Agent, one Recording Secretary, the Chairman of each Advisory Committee, or as his proxy, some other member of said Committee, and four members to be chosen by said Board of Managers.

IV. That the following named persons shall constitute the Board of Managers for the first year, to wit: James Brown, *President;* George Griswold, J. Smyth Rogers, James Boorman, James Lenox, and Horatio Allen, *Vice-Presidents;* Robert B. Minturn, *Treasurer;* Robert M. Hartley, *Corresponding Secretary and General Agent;* Joseph B. Collins, *Recording Secretary;* together with the following elected Members and Chairmen of the Advisory Committees, namely: Stewart Brown, Frederick S. Winston, Erastus C. Benedict, John R. Ludlow, Daniel S. Briant, William Gale, Peter G. Arcularius, Abraham Fardon, Jr., Apollos R. Wetmore, Nicholas C. Everett, Calvin Tracy, James O. Pond, James Horn, Samuel P. Patterson, Lewis Chichester, Adam W. Spies, Thomas Denny, Luther Jackson, Stephen C. Lynes, and F. Ellsworth Mather.

In witness whereof, we hereunto have subscribed our names, in the city of New-York, this the eleventh day of December, in the year of our Lord one thousand eight hundred and forty-eight.

JAMES BROWN,	APOLLOS R. WETMORE,
GEORGE GRISWOLD,	NICHOLAS C. EVERETT,
J. SMYTH ROGERS,	CALVIN TRACY,
JAMES BOORMAN,	JAMES O. POND,
HORATIO ALLEN,	JAMES HORN,
ROBERT M. HARTLEY,	LEWIS CHICHESTER,
JOSEPH B. COLLINS,	ADAM W. SPIES,
STEWART BROWN,	THOMAS DENNY,
FREDERICK S. WINSTON,	LUTHER JACKSON,
DANIEL S. BRIANT,	STEPHEN C. LYNES,
PETER G. ARCULARIUS,	F. ELLSWORTH MATHER.
ABRAHAM FARDON, JR.,	

Witness as to all the signatures,   D. F. CURRY.

City and County of New-York, [ss.] : On the eleventh day of December, A. D. 1848, before me came George Griswold, J. Smyth Rogers, Horatio Allen, Joseph B. Collins, Luther Jackson, Abraham Fardon, Jr., Lewis Chichester, Daniel S. Briant, Nicholas C. Everett, James O. Pond, Adam W. Spies, F. Ellsworth Mather, James Horn, Frederick S. Winston, Peter G. Arcularius, Stephen C. Lynes, Calvin Tracy, and Robert M. Hartley; and on the twelfth day of December, A. D. 1848, before me came James Brown, Stewart Brown, and James Boorman; and on the thirteenth day of December, A. D. 1848, before me came Apollos R. Wetmore and Thomas Denny, to me known to be the same persons described in and who executed the foregoing instrument, who severally acknowledged that they executed the foregoing instrument, for the purpose therein mentioned.

D. F. CURRY, *Commissioner.*

I approve of the within Certificate, and allow the same to be filed.

H. P. EDWARDS, *Justice Supreme Court.*

New-York, Dec. 14, 1848.

STATE OF NEW-YORK, } *Albany, Dec.* 16, 1848,
SECRETARY'S OFFICE,

I certify that the Certificate of Incorporation of the "New-York Association for Improving the Condition of the Poor," was received and filed this day in this office.

ARCHIBALD CAMPBELL,
Dept. Sec. of State.

Ninth Annual Report

OF THE

NEW-YORK ASSOCIATION FOR IMPROVING THE CONDITION OF THE POOR.

EVERY organization which embodies within itself principles and objects important to the well-being of community, has a work to perform, on which it may confidently expect the Divine blessing. In the arduous mission undertaken by this Association, the Board of Managers would gratefully acknowledge the favors of Providence hitherto manifested towards it, and with a deepening sense of dependence, humbly seek the same assistance and guidance in future.

The labors of the year just closed, appear to justify the remark, that the objects and operations of the Institution lose nothing by the lapse of time, of their original interest or importance.

It is a no less beautiful than beneficent provision for the poor and afflicted, that there are always hearts to sympathize in their sorrows, and hands to relieve their necessities. And thus will it ever pre-eminently be, where the humanizing influences of Christianity prevail. While other gifts and graces shall vanish away, " Charity," we are divinely assured, like the Being from whom it emanates, " never faileth."

Several causes have transpired during the year to augment the claims on the Association for relief. Among these may be noticed, the unusual length and severity of the past winter, which materially increased the expenses of living, while it deprived thousands of their customary employment. Also, the unprecedented influx of destitute emigrants, who, though having no legitimate claims on this charity, were extensively relieved to save them from suffering. Add to these the increase of needy applicants growing out of a wider knowledge of this source of relief, and we satisfactorily account for the enlarged aid and expenditure of the past year.

But while the claims have increased, it is a gratifying circumstance that the number of donors has also materially increased; and if the receipts have not augmented in the same ratio, it is to be attributed neither to diminished liberality, nor to a failure of interest in the object, but mainly to the fact that an expenditure much beyond that of the previous year was unexpected, and therefore the means were unsolicited. It is probably not too much to say, that the leading practical principles of the Association, have spread wider and struck deeper their roots each succeeding year, eliciting to an unwonted degree the charities of this great city, and given to them a direction, a system and an efficacy unknown before.

Marked changes are transpiring in the social condition of the people, which become more apparent every year. The laboring population, constituting a large part of the community, appear not to obtain a proportionate share of the growing prosperity around them. This, we scarcely need say, is the result of those irresistible laws of supply and demand, which no body of men, however sagacious or philanthropic, is competent to control. It were as untrue as unjust to imagine that there are combinations among the wealthy to oppress labor for their own advantage. On the contrary, it is the competition of labor with labor that reduces its value and starves the laborer. Labor preys upon itself by surfeiting the demand. Qualifications being equal, the lowest bidder is employed, both as a matter of interest and of necessity, in order to enable the employer to compete with his rivals. Double the supply of laborers, and in the strife for employment compensation would be ratably reduced; diminish the supply one half, and remuneration would advance in the same ratio. Such appears to be the natural law of supply and demand, which cannot be interfered with, without aggravating the evils it may be the purpose to remedy.

But while the law which governs labor may not be unwisely tampered with, much may be done to mitigate the pressure where it falls most heavily, and in distributing labor where it is wanted, and will meet with a fair reward. This is the only way by which labor can recover its dignity and maintain the balance of power which is its natural right.

That is neither the happiest condition of society, nor most consonant to our institutions, or to the best interests of individuals or communities, where the poor are degraded to the earth, and the rich elevated to palaces; but, where the disparity of wealth is least and social equality the greatest. As the tendencies to these extremes are generated by a too great concentration of labor in our cities, the corrective found in its better organization and diffusion, should, so far as practicable, be applied; and for this, our country with its millions of unoccupied acres, affords admirable facilities. When these, however, cannot be made available, it is the part of Christian beneficence, by ameliorating the condition of labor, to remove the causes of estrangement and distrust, so as to unite in harmonious social relations, those whom Providence has bound together, in mutual ties and dependencies.

Applications for relief, having for the reasons before named been unusually numerous, corresponding care and discrimination have been required, both in granting and withholding it, in order that the funds might be expended so as to effect the greatest practicable amount of good. It is but small praise to say, that the Visitors in the discharge of their arduous, unobserved and unobtrusive duties, involving immense sacrifices of time and convenience—often requiring personal exposure at all hours and seasons, amid scenes and circumstances most trying—have been found faithful. These labors are voluntary and gratuitous, yet in many instances, talent and influence have been devoted to the work which money could not purchase. Nor can we doubt as to the principle by which the laborers in such a field are animated. There is but one that can inspire them. Bearing the broad seal, "by their works ye shall know them," we can neither mistake its nature nor its source.

APPLICANTS FOR AID.

Of the applicants for aid, it may be supposed that many are reluctantly, yet necessarily rejected. It is the design of the Association to aid all for whom no other provision is made. Were it the purpose to relieve all irrespective of such a provision, then other charities would be superseded, the alms-house might be demolished, and every other form of alms-giving, public, private, and associate, cease. But this being for obvious reasons neither desirable nor practicable, it is important that the action of the organization in this particular should be clearly understood.

In the list of exceptions may be included,

First, Incorrigible mendicants, the wilfully improvident, the indolent who will not work, and the intemperate, on whom neither counsel, nor kindness, nor alms, after faithful trial, have availed to recover from their wicked, wasteful and ruinous courses. Such being referred to public relief, are left to learn wisdom in the school of experience, for they will learn in no other. In regard to such, there is a command from God, "If a man will not work, neither shall he eat."

Second, All persons who have relatives able and willing to relieve them—for it would not be right to interfere with those reciprocal claims and obligations founded in affinity, which have both a divine and human sanction.

Third, All who have become so pauperized in spirit by long continued vagrancy, or other causes, that there is no hope of inciting them to self-support, and to aid whom would foster a great social evil.

Fourth, All that have legitimate claims on other sources of relief, which can be used for their benefit; for it is not the design of the Institution to supersede existing available charities.

Fifth, All persons who from any cause are likely to be entirely and permanently dependent on charity; because, if these should be relieved, the entire funds of the Association would soon be exhausted in the support of a permanent list, and its primary objects—the elevation of the moral and physical condition of the poor—be defeated. Such persons should become an in-door public charge, which is far preferable to dependence on incidental relief.

Sixth, All recent emigrants who have claims on the Emigration Department; because the said department is obligated by law to care for such persons, if needy, for five years after their arrival, and are provided with means for this purpose. Consequently, every dollar expended on such by the Association, would be an improper appropriation of so much of its funds, which have been intrusted to it for other objects.

By refusing aid to the foregoing description of persons, none are necessarily left to suffer. Even those who obstinately persist in their vicious courses, have a resource in alms-house relief. The Association, in making these exceptions, is governed by such humane and economical considerations, as have important moral and social bearings, both on the individuals concerned and the public. To be less discriminating and rigid, would in many instances violate the Divine law; the Institution would become the enemy rather than the friend of humanity, and produce mischiefs that would counterbalance its benefits.

APPLICANTS RELIEVED.

After so thorough a sifting, let it not be supposed that but few entitled to aid remain. Far from this is the fact. During the year, 6559 families were relieved, containing 29,515 persons. Hence it appears, that excepting the season of cholera in 1849, (when the number was 299 greater), more were aided last year than in any other since the establishment of the Institution. And it may be noticed, that the aggregate stated, is the actual number relieved, there being no repetition, as often happens, in this class of statistics. The persons aided consisted chiefly,

First, Of indigent widows and deserted wives with young children—a very numerous class—who, in struggling to support and properly train their families, were often overtaken by want, and as often assisted and also counselled in the management of their affairs, with the rational expectation that such attentions and aid might not only save them from degradation and vice, but prove the means eventually of introducing them into society, as self-dependent, industrious and useful citizens.

Second, Of educated and even accomplished females, of whom there are hundreds in the city, who have been reduced from comfortable, perhaps affluent circumstances to dependence, and are now without the ability of earning their subsistence. They, unfortunately, answer to the description of those who "cannot dig, and to beg are ashamed." Many of them have been mentally and morally cultivated, but are physically feeble, because too delicately reared; and being uninstructed in any useful art or employment, because labor was considered degrading, now find, that though willing and anxious for some honorable means of earning a livelihood, have neither strength nor skill to engage in remunerative occupations. They are, in short, the victims of a mistaken education, and by a life of humiliation and want, are suffering the severe penalties of parental pride and folly. How many, alas, are thus brought to eat the bitter bread of dependence, perhaps of dishonor, who by a more rational training, might on a reverse of fortune, have turned their attainments to good account, and become a blessing instead of a burden to themselves and others! This, however, is not the place to dilate on the evils which grow out of the mistakes in female education and the irrational customs of society. Let it here suffice to remark, that the relief of this class is often accompanied by such efforts as result in interesting respectable families in their behalf, whose sympathy and assistance are better suited to meet their peculiar wants than organized charity.

Third, Females, once in comfortable circumstances, who have been reduced to poverty by the death or misfortunes of their husbands and relatives, or by other causes. Wives of shipmasters or other sea-faring men, and such as have sick and bedridden husbands or children. Widows of tradesmen or mechanics, having children and, perhaps, aged fathers and mothers depending upon them for support. These are mostly American born, from the great middle class, and are generally deserving of commiseration and aid.

Fourth, The sick and bereaved generally, who by their misfortunes have been brought to temporary want. This class is very numerous, and has drawn largely on the sympathy and assistance of the Association. Sickness and death bring unutterable sorrow where they enter, whether it be into the hovels of the poor or the mansions of the opulent. But these afflictions are sadly aggravated by poverty, where there are none to pity or to succor. The Visitors of this Charity, alas, are familiar with scenes of sickness, suffering and want, little known to the wealthy and prosperous. To such abodes they are welcomed as messengers of mercy. They minister to the necessities of the feeble, the languishing and dying, while they endeavor to mingle in the cup of bitterness such solaces and consolations as may tend to mitigate their woe. Such is not a factitious indigence; and it is a noble mission to be instrumental in its relief.

Fifth, Those who have been accustomed to provide their own support, and prefer self-dependence to reliance on alms; but being reduced to want by unavoidable causes require temporary aid. The increased emigration from Europe in late years, has operated adversely to the interests of the native laboring and mechanic classes in this city, both by crowding them out of employment, and diminishing the rewards of industry. Needy foreigners accustomed to live upon less than our own countrymen, are enabled to produce articles cheaper, and to work for lower wages. With the increase of laborers, the standard of comfortable subsistence has not only been depressed, but wages must continue to fall as competition increases. A considerable part of our bakers, carpenters, cabinet-makers, shoemakers, tailors, &c., are Germans; many of the stone-cutters, masons, pavers, cartmen, hackmen, &c., are Irish. Hence, thousands of the native population, once in productive occupations, now earn so scanty and precarious a subsistence, that a slight increase of expenses or interruption of their usual income by sickness or other causes, subjects them to want and suffering. Past experience has abundantly shown in respect to this class, both male and female, that the danger to be apprehended for them is, that after buffeting awhile with the difficulties of their condition, they will accept of alms-house relief, rely upon it, lose their self-respect, and descend from the respectable and independent position they had previously maintained, to that of the vagrant pauper class. Thus, without the preventive action of this Association, pauperism and mendicity would, as in former years, continually increase by large accessions from this class, and no subsequent exertions likely to be made, would avail to effect their rescue from it. Though now unreached by other instrumentalities, they are within the reach of this Institution; and by cutting off this prolific source of pauperism, the aggregate of the evil will be constantly diminishing, until eventually, few will be found dependent upon public charity, except imported paupers, and those who from imbecility or bodily infirmity are incapable of providing their own support.

Sixth, Recent emigrants and those having claims on other charities. This class of persons, for the reasons before stated, has no claims for assistance from this organization. Yet many of them, having been referred to their proper sources of relief, on failing to receive aid, have fallen back on this Institution. The Visitors, pitying their extreme destitution, gave what was designed for temporary relief. But the success of some applicants encouraging others, the rush for relief often defied control, so that large numbers have been aided by us who belong not to us. Visitors having passed the line of separation between proper and improper persons, lose sight of it, and find it difficult to stop while there are subjects to relieve. Meanwhile, the Emigration establishment, the Alms House department and others, finding that the cases neglected by them are cared for by this Association, one strong incentive to fidelity on their part is removed, and they are encouraged to throw upon this charity, so far as it is willing to bear it, the support of all the out-door poor in the city.

CLAIMS ON OTHER CHARITIES.

The Board feel called upon to refer to this subject with some particularity, because hitherto it more than any other has embarrassed the Visitors and also the legitimate action of the Association.

This Institution is publicly pledged to extend *transient or temporary aid* to persons having claims on other sources of relief, provided there is risk of suffering, until they can be notified thereof, so that such relief may be made available for the needy. What is meant by such a provision? Evidently, not that this Association should assume the charge of all cases of distress which might be thrown upon it by the delinquency of other charities. If the neglect or delinquency of other institutions is to be the measure of our duty, we may soon have all the poor in the city to provide for; and not only be thrown into a position utterly at variance with our objects, but which it will be impossible for this Association to sustain. Relying on the good faith of other institutions, we humanely promised assistance to those having claims upon them, until they could be informed of the facts, when our responsibility towards such cases would cease. This is all that is meant by temporary assistance to the persons in question. Beyond this we cannot go without defeating our own ends, and assuming a weight of responsibility, which would inevitably crush the Institution.

In order to avoid such results and better enable the Association to accomplish its objects, the Board have published in the Directory of the present year, a few plain rules for the guidance of Visitors in the cases referred to, which, with a new arrangement of cards of reference provided for applicants, will, it is believed, remove most of the difficulty hitherto experienced in respect to them. These rules, in effect, provide that persons ineligible to assistance from this Association, shall be referred to their appropriate relief, by a card, which assigns the reason why such relief is denied; also a duplicate thereof, which members should require applicants to show, when they affirm that the Institution has refused them aid. The complaints of unrelieved applicants who have been sent to this charity, should not, therefore, be listened to, until they produce a card from the Visitor; *for a card of this kind is always given to unrelieved applicants,* which, if exhibited, will explain why they were not relieved; and if unproduced, a proof that they have been attended to. In either case, the action of the Visitor and the reason for it, will be made known. The rules in question have been inserted in the Directory, because that document being preserved for reference, and more widely distributed than any other of the Association's publications, they will there be always accessible, both to Visitors and members.

In this connection, it may be both useful and interesting to mention a few particulars relating to different classes of the needy.

It may be preliminarily remarked, that most of the destitution is among foreigners. If the relieved were divided into eight parts, as near as can be estimated, four parts would be Irish, three German and miscellaneous, and but one part American.

If divided according to religion, it would be found that at least three-fourths of those asking aid are Roman Catholics, while the remainder are mostly indifferent to the claims of the gospel, and unconnected with any Protestant religious society. It also deserves notice, that while the rate of mortality is generally less among the comparatively rich than the poor, it is greatest among the Irish, being according to recent estimates, as compared with the German, nearly as two to one.

OCCUPATION, ITS DIFFICULTIES AND DEFECTS.

The subject of occupation also claims attention, because of its direct bearing on the condition of the poor. In all our Atlantic cities, more than half the needy are Irish and German; but whether foreigners or natives, the men requiring aid are generally without mechanical skill, mostly mere day laborers, who have been accustomed only to the rudest and humblest employments. The women of the same class, are like the men in these respects, with the additional disadvantage of finding less demand for their services, and less wages. It is true, moreover, of both, that they are generally too far advanced in life, to acquire much profitable dexterity in those handicraft operations, which even in youth, when the habits are most pliant, require an apprenticeship of years. But little, evidently, can be done to increase the productiveness of this class of laborers; yet some have vainly imagined in respect to the women, that they could be so improved in the art of sewing and other appropriate female occupations, as to command for them employment and good wages. But were this practicable, as experience has proved it not to be, yet the promised result cannot be realized while there is so large a surplus of such labor in the market. All correct inductions from facts, would have demonstrated the fallacy of such an expectation, anterior to experiment.

The result of special inquiries directed to the occupations of the poor, show, that of the foreigners relieved, more than *three-fourths* are common laborers, among the men, and washers, house-cleaners, sewers, &c., among the women, there being about an equal proportion of each. In other words, they are mostly persons who have been trained to no trade or regular employment, and having little skill in any, are forced to accept of such as is offered. Hence, during the busy season, the men work about the wharves, or as diggers, hodmen, &c., and the women as rough washers, house-cleaners, coarse sewers, or in any other rude work they can find to do. Such occupations being, at best, irregular and precarious; and the women, especially, being poorly qualified even for these, it is not surprising that they have but little work and small wages, or that they often need extraneous aid. But to such, relief is cheerfully given, when sobriety, activity, cleanliness, and proper instruction and training of children can be induced, or where there are other satisfactory indications, that the attentions and assistance bestowed will not be perverted, so as to weaken the incentives to virtuous industry.

But in this city, where there is so large a redundance of

labor, even the possession of industrial skill affords no guaranty either for employment or good wages. Here are probably more than twelve thousand seamstresses, whose dependence for a livelihood is on the needle in its various applications for the clothing trade; about two thousand cap sewers, and several thousand shoe binders, exclusive of numerous other thousands, who in different ways "ply the polished shaft" for support. Take the case of one of these females for an illustration. The prices paid usually range so low, that with steady work and long hours, the most expert sewer can make but a scanty living. This, as elsewhere shown, is in consequence of the rivalry of the employed among themselves, and not the fault of the employer. "Every person in every business, has to compete with every other person in the same business; and no business man will blame himself or his neighbor, for laying in his goods at the lowest rates. This principle pervades all mercantile operations. The difficulty exists in the fact, that there are more laborers of this class pressing on the market than the market can absorb.

"Another serious difficulty grows out of the ever fluctuating operations of commerce in this metropolis. At certain seasons there is a demand for the labor of thousands, which does not exist at another. Either then the compensation for labor during the season of activity must be redundant, or the operatives must receive extraneous aid in periods of dulness to sustain them during its continuance. And if they are deficient in economy and thrift, as often happens, the result must be privation and suffering. These ebbings and flowings are perennial. To provide artificial employment in such cases, would tend to discourage those habits which are essential to success and self-dependence. It would, moreover, so augment the supply of articles, as to lower the price of similar goods, and consequently, by diminishing the compensation to that class of operatives, increase rather than diminish the amount of suffering. It is in vain to say that the surplus products might be sold elsewhere. For such is the searching activity of enterprise, that every available market is already sought out and supplied as soon as discovered."

But while the limits of this Report forbid the Board to enlarge on such particulars, they would be inexcusable in omitting among the causes of poverty, the mention of one so prominent as is *Intemperance*. It is scarcely necessary to say, that this vice to which the poor are here so much exposed, is beyond all others productive of want and suffering. To show how widespread and fearful are its ravages, we need neither refer to statistics nor number its victims, for the sufferings from this cause are the constant burden of our Visitors' reports. Intemperance is peculiar in this. It is both a moral and physical malady, whose necessary and inseparable effects are to impoverish and debase. Most other causes of indigence are incidental and outward, and leave energy and integrity unimpaired; nay, their very pressure may nerve the oppressed to successful resistance. But intemperance, itself a vice, is the grand instigator and ally of other vices, and enervates while it pollutes. Producing, moreover, idleness, recklessness and improvidence, what hope is there for its infatuated victims, who not only dig for themselves the pit which ingulfs them, but fearfully multiply want and wretchedness, by dragging down their families into like ruin? Nor is their condition the less deplorable because of their own producing. We would not exclude from the broad circle of benevolence, the weakest or wickedest human being; yet philanthropy itself must despair of the moral and physical elevation of the inebriate, except by first recovering him from the vice which is the cause of his debasement and poverty.

From the foregoing review, it appears that intemperance, indolence, and improvidence, the over stocked condition of the labor market, and the continued influx of needy emigrants, are among the chief causes of destitution in this city.

FOREIGN EMIGRATION.

So important is this subject in its relations to the social condition of the city, and yet so imperfectly understood, that the Managers, at the risk of exceeding the usual limit of their Report, feel themselves called upon to submit a fuller statement in regard to this class of the needy than they have yet presented.

The great experimental system for the care of emigrants arriving at this port, which has now been in operation more than five years, has little chance amid more exciting subjects, of receiving the attention its importance demands. Few, probably, of our citizens, are fully aware of the changes to which the provisions for that object have been subjected, the abuses which have existed, the remedies applied, or of the difficulties that have embarrassed the establishment of the present system. Deeply interesting, however, as is each of these topics to the legislator, philanthropist, and to the population generally, the Board are constrained by the limits of this Report to waive their consideration, in order to present such a view of the present legal provision for emigrants arriving at this port, as is imperatively required of them in the official relations they sustain to the destitute.

Emigrants, in respect to their sources of relief, may be divided into two classes. First, those who by long residence are entitled to Alms-house aid; secondly, recent emigrants, who, if needy, have claims on the Commissioners of Emigration.

It has been the uniform policy of the law, to require shippers' bonds and other securities, that the alien emigrants brought by them into this port, should not within a given time become a public charge, or in commutation of such bonds, the payment of a stipulated sum. In 1847, an act was passed, establishing a new department, designed to provide more effectually for destitute emigrants of this class, and to create a fund sufficient for their maintenance. A close examination, however, of these various provisions, show that no tax hitherto imposed on shippers or emigrants, has indemnified this city for the pecuniary outlay incurred by it for their benefit.

Under the old law, it was supposed that the risk of aliens becoming a public charge, would cease after *three years,* and the tax imposed was consequently designed to cover that period. But when the new department came into power, the term was extended to *five years,* with an assessment graduated according to the estimated risk on each alien passenger. Experience, however, has demonstrated that the hazards have been uniformly underrated; for the fund thereby accruing, though economically disbursed by an efficient executive Board, composed of leading merchants and gentlemen eminent for business ability and integrity, has been found greatly deficient, and the department is now deeply in debt.

But does the risk of foreigners becoming paupers cease after a period of *five years,* or render them as capable of self-support as the native population? By no means. If this were so, how does it happen that while they constitute but about *one-third* of the inhabitants, more than *three-fourths* of the paupers are foreigners? If after the lapse of *five years,* emigrants were not more likely to become dependent than the native population, there would be two native paupers to one foreign. But the indisputable fact is, as verified by the records of this Association and the statistics of our public institutions, that there are, at least, *three* paupers of foreign birth to *one* American. It appears, therefore, that the legislation on this subject is based on principles that are essentially false, and that its effects are most injurious and oppressive to our citizens. It evidently accomplishes neither of its threefold objects—*adequate provision for the destitute,—the suppression of vagrancy, nor pecuniary indemnity for the support of foreign paupers.* On the contrary, the tendencies of the laws are to deluge this city with imported mendicants and vagrants, and to load the population with taxes for their support. These facts are clearly shown by the following statistics of our public charities.

The number of persons relieved in this city, by the Alms-house department, during the year ending December 31st, 1851, was as follows :—

In the Alms-house, 2,783, of whom 78 per cent. were foreigners.
 Bellevue Hospital, 5,342, " 82 " "
 Penitentiary, 3,450, " 75 " "
 City Prison, 21,279, " 71 " "
 Lunatic Asylum, 441, " 72 " "
 Randall's Island, 2,087, " 75 " "
 Out-door Poor, 42,872, " 73 " "
 Work-house, 965, " 75 " "

 Total relief, 79,732, of whom 75 per cent. or 59,799 were foreigners.*

During the same year (1851), the number of persons relieved by this association was 27,022, three-fourths of whom were of foreign birth. Allowing that one-half of this number was aided by the Alms-house, also that those dependent on the numerous city charitable societies—private alms-giving and street-begging—classes of poor not before enumerated, amount to 20,000 persons, and we have the following result :—

   Alms-house Relief, 79,732
   City Association, 13,511
   Other Charities, 20,000
     Total, 113,243

Of the above total 75 per cent., or 84,925 persons are of *foreign birth, who have been in the country more than five years*, and for whose support the emigration laws furnish no indemnity

---

* In the above return, the *nativity* of those relieved in the Penitentiary and on Randall's Island not being given in the official reports, they have been rated according to the general average.

whatever; and are consequently maintained by a direct tax upon our citizens of about $500,000 a year. During the same year, 85,036 emigrants who had been here *less than five years*, were relieved by the Commissioners of Emigration, at a cost of $480,000; but of these no account is made, because they create their own fund while chargeable to that department. It is unnecessary to enlarge on this view of the subject; for what stronger proof of the inefficiency of the law can be conceived, than the foregoing figures and facts present?

But there is another aspect of the subject which deeply concerns this Association and the public, that should not be overlooked. It has been shown that more than 84,000 emigrants, either needy or depraved, are now quartered on this city, with little hope while they live of their removal; and it is to be feared that the present number, under the existing laws, will materially increase. Of the 1,041,238 foreigners who arrived at this port, during the five years preceding the 5th of May, 1852, until the end of that period, not one could become a public charge because of their claims on the Emigration Department. But as the first five years of the law's limitation of relief from that source have terminated, the destitute will henceforth be thrown upon the public, and a gradual increase of the dependent may be daily expected. What that increase will be, is, at present, problematical; but if with the comparatively trifling amount of immigration, previous to 1847 the statistics exhibit 84,000 foreigners in this city, who are chiefly paupers or criminals, depending on public support, it appears within the range of probability, that in future years, if no legal preventive is applied, they will augment in a ratio corresponding with the recent immense influx of immigrants. In that case, who can estimate the physical and moral evils that will be entailed upon the city? Other things being equal, taxes will increase, property depreciate, industry be robbed of its rights, and idleness, with her prolific progeny of mischiefs, outnumbering the workers, may be expected to overrun the community with vice and profligacy.

As the country at large will be benefited by a healthy emigration, that should be encouraged. But as it is not less certain that emigration of an opposite character will be detrimental, such an evil, if possible, should be averted. With the acknowledged mistakes of many European governments before us, in respect to legal charity, we are solemnly admonished to avoid unsound views and unwise legislation, especially when the consequences are so fearful. Considerations the most weighty, at once patriotic and philanthropic, urge us to guard most sedulously against the contamination and curse of a vicious pauper population. And as most of the swelling tide of emigrants which is pouring into the United States, enter at the port of New-York, upon this city devolves, in a peculiarly important sense, the duty of protecting itself, and so far as is practicable, the nation, against the influx of this terrible evil. Whatever advantages may generally result to the country from such accessions to the population, the disadvantages are mostly felt at the great point of debarkation. The worst part of the refuse class which is thus thrown upon our shores, here clan together and remain in the city, nor can they be persuaded to leave it. These mostly consist of imbecile and thriftless parish paupers and dependents, the former inmates of poor-houses and even of prisons, who being unwilling or unable to gain an honest subsistence any where, have been sent here, in order to rid the country from which they come of their support, and who become a burden and a nuisance from the moment of their arrival. Many of them are afflicted with pestilential diseases, more or less developed, which, as they wander about in search of shelter, are disseminated through the city to the manifest detriment of public health, and to the destruction of life. During the past year, nearly 80,000 persons of this class, exclusive of those in the Alms-house and Emigration Hospitals, were gratuitously attended and prescribed for by three of our City Dispensaries.

Among, however, the most annoying and reproachful consequences of this overwhelming rush of indigent emigrants, are the swarms of incorrigible vagrants which are allowed to overrun the city. Work they do not want, even if it could be obtained. To beg is their privilege and profession. They are every where found most pertinaciously demanding alms—many of them not as a favor, but seemingly as a right, and as if it were the duty of our citizens to give them an unearned support. If relief from this intolerable nuisance is sought from the Almshouse authorities, they promptly disclaiming all jurisdiction over recent immigrants, refer the complainants to the Emigration Department, to which they legally belong. But application to that department brings no redress, for the immigrants, rather than comply with the conditions of relief exacted by it, choose to become beggars and vagrants, and to throw themselves on the charities of the community. Hence the city is thronged with this class of mendicants. The general State law against vagrancy, in respect to them, appears to be a nullity; for in no instance, to the knowledge of the Board, has it been enforced against this class of persons. The existing laws, in short, are such, that between the Alms-house and Emigration Department, the city, to its disgrace, has no effective legal protection from this description of vagrancy and its attendant evils. All that this Association can do is, to enter its earnest protest against their continuance, and invoke legislative interference. In no other way is it responsible for the prevalence of this type of pauperism; for possessing no police powers, it is without authority to act in the premises.

But manifestly deplorable as are the results of existing legal provisions for the emigrant, the Board would not imply that such results were contemplated by the Legislature or are desired by the Commissioners of Emigration. The design of the revised laws, was to protect more effectually the destitute strangers among us, and guard the community against an increase of pauperism. Nor can it be supposed that those intrusted with the execution of the laws have in view any other than the same beneficent object. As the experience, however, of more than five years, has demonstrated the inefficiency of the legislative provision for this purpose, should not the public be governed by the convictions thus forced upon it, and in sober earnestness demand such a revision of the laws as, with the practical knowledge now acquired, would secure the results desired and originally contemplated?

REMEDIAL MEASURES.

It obviously pertains to the Legislature rather than to this Board to determine what modification of the Emigrant laws will better adapt them to their object, and what provisions and appliances on the part of the Emigration Department will be requisite to give them effect. As the nature of the evils, however, appears to suggest a remedy, the Board may be excused for expressing the belief, first, that if the bonds now given by owners or consignees of passenger vessels for five years, should hereafter be required for a term of ten years; and secondly, if the bonds now commuted for one dollar and fifty cents, should not hereafter be commuted for less than three dollars for each alien emigrant, some of the worst consequences incident to the present system would be removed. Among the advantages which might be expected from such a modification of the laws, may be noticed—

First.—The introduction of a more select class of emigrants into the country. And is not such a result both desirable and practicable? We cannot arrest the progress of immigration, nor would we if we could. The industrious and worthy should be encouraged to come. The vast, unoccupied regions of the fertile west are wide enough for them and for us. We may not doubt that Providence has reserved this land as an asylum for the down-trodden and oppressed of other countries, nor that such will continue to flow in upon us for an indefinite period to an indefinite amount. The immigration from ill-fated Ireland, which has hitherto more than doubled that from all other countries, must soon begin to diminish from actual exhaustion. But what are the seven millions of that country as a source of immigration compared with the German population of forty millions, of France with thirty-five millions, Italy with twenty-two millions, Belgium, Holland, and Prussia with twenty-three millions, to say nothing of the more northern nations of Europe, from all of which emigration is increasing with rapid strides, and may be expected to increase, in coming years? What else, indeed, could be looked for? There, despotism is tightening its bands and becoming more exacting; taxes are augmenting; the extremes between wealth and poverty are widening; and personal liberty is becoming more and more abridged. Intolerable oppression or voluntary expatriation, being the only alternatives for multitudes, westward to this land of freedom and plenty, as if moved by a divine impulse, the great ocean of humanity directs its course; and who shall stay its progress, or say to the swelling tide, "Hitherto shalt thou come, and no farther?" With such prospects of future immigration before us, all that is practicable by adequate legislation should be done, to guard the community against its attendant evils.

Second.—The proposed modifications of the law would operate both preventively and remedially. Were shippers compelled to give available bonds that no alien passenger landed by them should become a public charge for ten years after their arrival, they would be careful to bring only such as were likely to earn their own support. Or if such bonds were commuted by the payment of three dollars for each passenger, the fund thus created might indemnify the community for the expense of such as should need relief. This might diminish the profits of the shipper. But is it right that he should be benefited at the cost and annoyance of all the rest of the community? Is it right that he should be rewarded for bringing vice and beggary and pestilence into the country? It might diminish immigration; but is not this the very thing desired in respect to the indolent, the vicious, and depraved? The country will not be enriched nor morally benefited by the importation of vice and beggary. Better have fewer emigrants of the right class, than to be overrun with those who would be a burden and a curse to the community. Nor can it be supposed that such a regulation would be adverse to the true interests of commerce in this city. The acknowledged advantages of New-York as a port of debarkation, and again of divergence to all parts of the interior, would, it is believed, in future as hitherto, notwithstanding the proposed restriction, command for it the preference of the best class of emigrants.

In this connection it may be remarked, that the future teems with hope for the oppressed of other lands who make this their home, provided they improve the facilities for moral and physical elevation, which here abound for the benefit of those who are sufficiently considerate to turn them to account. But it should not be forgotten, that the same defects of character, with the consequent ignorance and unthrift which degraded many in their own country, will, if unremedied, condemn them to a like condition in this. No change of outward circumstances, however favorable, no securities, no regulations, no benevolent arrangements, however ample or energetic, without a radical improvement of character, will keep them here from becoming objects of charity or the inmates of our alms-houses and prisons. Hence we see why our public and private charities are so generally monopolized by foreigners, and our penitentiaries chiefly filled by persons of the same class; and why miscellaneous relief is so impotent in eradicating pauperism. Such charities leave the source of evil unreached, or by their misapplication strike deeper its roots. "Were the world morally better, it would be physically happier." And it is owing to the neglect of the harder and more thankless task of morally elevating the poor, that so large an amount of benevolent effort only aggravates the evils it would remove.

INCIDENTAL OPERATIONS.

It appears appropriate to the objects of this Report, to notice briefly the progress of other organized Charities which have derived their origin from this Association.

First.—THE DEMILT DISPENSARY. This Institution was organized the past year, and is making very encouraging progress in the accomplishment of its objects. The Board of Managers have published their first Annual Report, from which it appears that a site for the Dispensary building has been purchased at the northwest corner of Second Avenue and Twenty-third street, for the sum of $6,000. Contracts have also been made, and an edifice is in course of completion, 92 feet by 44, three stories, which will combine beauty and utility, at a cost including land of about $30,000. Meanwhile the Managers have not been inattentive to the immediate necessities of the sick. For nearly a year past medicines have been dispensed gratuitously, and three capable physicians employed to visit every sick person who might require their services in the District. The Managers say that the importance and value of such an Institution in that part of the city can be scarcely overrated. It not only carries help and comfort to the indigent sick, and is instrumental in banishing disease and guarding the poor and the community generally from the ravages of pestilence, but it brings to light the moral wants and the social and physical condition of a class which would otherwise be unreached.

Second.—THE NORTHWESTERN DISPENSARY. The establishment of another Medical Dispensary, as originally contemplated by the Board and suggested in their preceding Annual Report, has been partially effected and is now progressing. It is designed for the benefit of the indigent sick, in a large and rapidly populating portion of the city, hitherto inadequately supplied with such a provision. Having commenced under encouraging auspices with an efficient Board of Managers, it is soon expected to take its place among the permanently useful institutions of the city. In behalf of this important and interesting object, funds are now earnestly solicited. Its success in its commencement must entirely depend on the liberality of an enlightened and benevolent public; and it is believed, to none more deserving their confidence as a wise, humane and necessary charity, can their benefactions be applied.

Third.—THE JUVENILE ASYLUM. This Institution, also referred to in a previous Report, embracing objects of the highest importance to public morals, to individual character, and to the enduring interests of the community, has enlisted, as it deserves, a large share of public sympathy, and is endeavoring to obtain by voluntary contributions, the sum required by law, in order to draw an equal sum from the Public Treasury. About three-fourths of the necessary amount has been subscribed; and as the Institution offers an opportunity for a permanently useful charitable investment, such as every benevolent person might desire, it is commended to their confidence with the hope that the deficient funds may be speedily supplied.

Fourth.—PUBLIC BATH AND WASH HOUSE. This Establishment, claiming a kindred origin with the foregoing, is located in Mott street, near Grand, and has been in operation for the past ten months. Combining every convenience for bathing, washing and ironing, at charges so low as to bring its advantages within the reach of all, it greatly contributes to the health, comfort and cleanliness of the classes for whom it was designed. Being the first of the kind erected in this country, the enterprise was an experiment; but as the best evidence of its usefulness, is its appreciation by the laboring population, judged by this test, the results are most satisfactory. An increase of such establishments in different sections of the city, would scarcely fail to augment the health and comfort of large masses of the industrious class. The cost of the present one, including ground, was about $40,000.

Increase of Sections and Visitors. Owing to the migratory habits of the poor and rapid increase of population, particularly in the upper Wards, changes in the area of some sections, and an increase of their number, has again been rendered necessary. The city is now divided into 337 sections, with a corresponding number of visitors, being thirteen more than in the previous year. These are spread over the entire peninsula, extending from the Battery to Eighty-sixth street, about six and a quarter miles; and from river to river, including a population of 550,000 souls.

Subjoined is a summary statement of the District Relief from November 1st, 1851, to November 1st, 1852:

Number of District, or Ward.	Number of Families Relieved.	Number of Persons Relieved.	Number of Visits.
1	1068	4272	1356
2	194	776	253
3	219	876	293
4	634	2536	823
5	1153	4612	1517
6	1262	5048	1592
7	1132	4528	1453
8	1637	6548	2043
9	995	3980	1314
10	889	3556	1130
11	1864	7456	2304
13	1455	5820	1803
14	1413	5652	1750
15	654	2516	780
16	1647	6588	2010
17	1806	7224	2203
18	987	3948	1152
19	485	1940	610
20	1179	4716	1487

NINTH ANNUAL REPORT.

The following is a tabular exhibit of the Monthly District Returns, from November 1st, 1851, to November 1st, 1852:

1851-52.	Number of Families Relieved.	Number of Persons Relieved.	Number of Visits.
November,	970	3,880	76
December,	2,895	11,580	3,839
January,	4,501	18,004	5,883
February,	5,067	20,268	6,159
March,	3,905	15,620	4,631
April,	1,037	4,148	1,221
May,	559	2,236	684
June,	233	932	287
July,	121	484	128
August,	188	752	189
September,	477	1,908	515
October,	741	2,964	810

Receipts during the year ending Oct. 31, - - $34,577 95
Disbursements for the same period, - - - 33,865 07

Balance, - - - - - - - - $712 88

The bequest of $2000, noticed in a previous report, by Thomas Frisell Thompson, Esq., deceased, was paid into the Treasury during the year, and in compliance with the wish of the bequeather, has been invested as the "Frisell Fund," the interest only being used in promoting the objects of the Association.

A liberal bequest of $10,000, has also been made during the year, by the late Ephraim Holbrook, Esq., the payment of which being contingent, it is not likely soon to be realized.

The Board in noticing this bequest by their deceased associate and fellow-laborer, would bear testimony to their high sense of his many excellent qualities and virtues, as a friend, philanthropist and Christian. He was long connected with this Institution, as a member of the Advisory Committee in the Eighteenth District, where by the faithful discharge of official duties, he greatly contributed to its success, in alleviating the sufferings, and in ministering to the wants of the destitute. But, a good man's deeds outlive him; and such deeds appertain to the life of their late esteemed friend. His benevolent acts will long be remembered with gratitude, and the fragrance of a useful life embalm his memory.

In presenting the foregoing statement of the year's operations, it will be observed that the Board has departed somewhat from the studied brevity of previous reports. This has been necessary in order to meet the reiterated demand of the public, for more minute information in respect to the causes of indigence, the occupation, nativity and character of applicants, etc., and also a fuller exposition of the principles by which the Association is governed, in dispensing and withholding relief. Possessing superior facilities for obtaining correct knowledge on topics of this kind, it appears right that something should be gathered up from so vast a field, and added to the common stock; especially is this desirable for the information of moral economists, philanthropists, and the friends of the poor generally who desire it, and cannot in a population so numerous and wide-spread as our own, by personal inquiries, procure it for themselves. If the length of the document requires any other vindication, it is found in the increased benefits likely thereby to result to the indigent; for sympathy in their behalf can only be awakened, as the nature of their necessities, and the means of their alleviation, shall be made known.

Long, however, as is this Report, its limits compel the Board to exclude several topics, and many suggestions and reflections, which it was their desire to present. To those who are familiar with the objects of the Institution, and have watched its progress, it is unnecessary to speak of results; and upon others unacquainted with its nature and design, who admit the necessity of some adequate provision for the needy, they would respectfully urge a careful examination of this system, as practically developed by its previous labors, and set forth in its published documents and reports.

In surveying the past from this position, which the Association has toiled for years to attain, if it should appear that all has not been accomplished which the sanguine anticipated and desired, yet enough, it is believed, has been done to satisfy every reasonable expectation, and to inspire larger hopes for the future. While nothing has transpired to impair confidence in the principles of the organization, or in the practicability of its objects, the suggestions of experience have done much in adapting means to ends, so as to augment its efficiency in the attainment of proposed results. Acting upon the knowledge thus gained, and relying upon the progressive intelligence and co-operation of the benevolent, the Board with firm faith in its increasing usefulness, would commit the Institution, to the leadings of Providence, in all that pertains to its future direction and support.

In conclusion, the Board feel that the duty of caring for the poor is so obvious and absolute, that any extended appeal in behalf of this Charity, would here be misplaced. So far as almsgiving is concerned, it is merely the almoner of the benevolent. Whatever contributions are made, it is pledged to disburse among the needy within its bounds, at all times and seasons. And nine years' operations show that it has not undertaken an impracticable task. What isolated efforts could not do, is done with proper intelligence, discrimination and effect, by a minute division of labor among its *three hundred and thirty-seven* Visitors, who for this purpose are distributed at convenient distances, all over the city. If adequate means are furnished, it affords a guaranty that the poor shall not be left to suffer; if these are withheld, as it has no other resource than these voluntary offerings, extensive suffering will inevitably ensue. The experience, however, of past liberality forbids apprehension for the future, while it encourages the expectation of such enlarged contributions, as will at once meet the growing necessities of the augmenting population, and enable the organization greatly to extend its sphere of usefulness. And why should not such hopes be fully realized, when with the increasing wealth and prosperity of this metropolis, there is also an increased disposition to diffuse the accumulations of wealth to advance and ameliorate the condition of humanity? Such being, in the order of Providence, among the signs of the times, the Board devoutly thanking God therefor, would take courage, and with new zeal address themselves to their arduous work.

Association for the Improvement of the Condition of the Poor in Account with Robert B. Minturn, Treasurer.

1852.			1852.		
Oct. 31.	To Amounts expended from Oct. 31, 1851,	$33,865 07	Oct. 31.	By Amounts received per donations from Oct. 31, 1851,	$34,577 95
	To Balance,	712 88			
		$34,577 95			$34,577 95
			1852.		
			Oct. 31.	By Balance at credit of Association,	$712 88

The undersigned hereby certify that they have examined in detail the above account, and find it correct and properly vouched, showing a balance in the hands of the Treasurer of seven hundred and twelve eighty-eight hundredths dollars, on the 31st Oct., 1852.

JOSEPH B. COLLINS, } *Committee.*
THOS. DENNY,

New-York, Nov. 5, 1852.

PRINTED FORMS USED BY THE ASSOCIATION.

Ticket of Reference for the use of Members.

Mr.   Visitor,

   No.   St.

is requested to visit

at No.

                                              Member

N. Y. Association for
Improving the Condition of the Poor.

Visitor's Order.

   Mr.

   No.   St.

   Please let

   have the value of

   in

                          184

                                               Vis.

N. Y. Association for
Improving the Condition of the Poor.

Monthly Report.

Subjoined is a condensed plan of a Sectional Monthly Return. The original occupies a large page of foolscap, with appropriate columns, fifteen in number, which enable Visitors to give the following particulars of every family relieved. 1st. Name, residence, place of birth, sex, color, occupation, time in the city, number in family, and number of visits. 2d. Statements of character,—as being temperate or intemperate. 3d. Unavoidable causes of indigence, such as sickness, infirmity, or old age, with space for marginal remarks.

PRINTED FORM USED BY THE ASSOCIATION.

New-York Association for Improving the Condition of the Poor.

VISITOR'S MONTHLY REPORT OF SECTION No.   DISTRICT No.   DATED   184

☞ *A mark with a pen thus ,, in the columns, will point out the class to which the person named belongs.*

FAMILIES RELIEVED. Always give full Name, and *male* Head of Family, if living.	RESIDENCE OF FAMILIES. Which must be reported every month.	Foreigners.	Natives.	Colored Persons.	Males.	Females.	No. in Family.	No. of Visits.	KIND OF OCCUPATION.	Temperate.	Intemperate.	Sickness.	Misfortune.	Old Age.	AMOUNT EXPENDED. $	cts.	REMARKS.

Signed,   Visitor.

List of Members.

Owing to inadvertence in the returns from some of the Districts, it is feared that the List of Members may not be perfectly accurate. The *amounts* received were duly credited, as may be seen by an inspection of the Treasurer's account, at the General Office. But, as the names of some who contributed small sums did not accompany their donations, with all the efforts subsequently made to obtain them, the list may still be incomplete.

A.

Astor, Wm. B.
Anderton, Ralph L.
Astor, J. J. jr. Mrs.
Astor, J. J. jr.
Aspinwall, W. H.
Alley, Saul
Aspinwall, J. A.
Adams, John
A Lady, (by E. W. Laight)
Anthon, Rev. H.
Allen, Stephen
Alsop & Chauncey
Andrew, H. Mrs. & family
Allen, G. F.
Aymar, J. Q.
Alsop, J. W.
Auffen, Ordt, Hessenberg & Co.
Aymar & Co.
A. W.
Ayres, Robert
Adams, Sturges & Co.
Adams, J. T.
Anderson, C. V. & J.
Alexander, James W.
Auten, J. W.
Abernethy, C.
Abbatt, J.
Averill, A.
A Friend
A Lady
A Friend (S. A.)
Aycrigg, B.
A Gentleman
A.
Anderson, H.
Abeel, John H.
Averell, Wm. J.

Arcularius, A. M.
Abbott, Wm. M.
Aimes, Jacob
Auchmuty, Mrs.
Anstice, Henry
Adams. H. W.
Allen, Gilbert
A Few Friends, Jackson, Mississippi
Allen, Horatio
Abbe, George W.
Allyn, Peter
Akenback, Thomas
Adams, J. D.
Albro, R.
Armstrong, James
Allison, M. Jr.
Aldrich, H. D.
Ashton, George
Anderson, S. W. Mrs.
Aguirre, P. A.
Aspinwall, S. Mrs.
Aitkin & Miller
Althause, S. B.
Ackerman, James
Abrams & Johnson
Anthony, J.
Arrowsmith, G. L. Mrs.
A Lady
Archer
Allard, N. W.
Alexander, J.
Apel, Mrs.
Anderson, E.
Austin
Allison, Miss
Anderson, John, jr.
Asey, Geo. W.
Austin, Wm. B.
Atkinson, W.

Andrus & Sears
Arnold & Southworth
Austen, Mr.
Allen & Rose
Apgar, L.
Allison, Michael
Allen, C. C., M. D.
Arnold, Dr.
Allison, C.
Alcock, Dr.
Arcularius, Geo.
Alcock, H.
Atwill, John
Adams, W.
Aymar, Wm.
Ardenburg, R. H.
Ayatt, Theodore
Arthur & Burnett
Anderson, John
Averill, J. Otis
A. F. H.
Adams & McChesney
A. R. & M.
Averell, H.
A. F. K.
Appleton, D. & Co.
Ahlborn, J.
Aquiar, L. H. F.
Atwater, Wm.
Arcularius, A. M.
Ascham, John
Arkenburgh, R. H.
Albro & Hoyt
A. D. C.
Alvord, C.
Amos, Thomas
Ackenback, George
Allen, John
Archer, T. H.
Allen, W. P.

LIST OF MEMBERS. (1852.

Allen, J. K.
Alcock
Ames, Samuel
Albro, Benjamin
Albert
Acheson, W.
Anderson, Hiram
Anderson, L. B.
Anderson, Wm.
Alford, Edwin M.
Amerman, J. W.
Allen, Isaac
Andrews, J. E.
Abeil, C. Miss
Arnold, Jas.
Alexander, Mr.
A German Friend
A Freeborn Irishman
Ackerly, R. C.
Albro & Brothers
Allen, Geo. C.
Allen, Henry
Aird, Thos.
A Friend
Ash, J. H., jr.
Aunch, Louis
Anthony, E.
Alvord, A. A
Abbott, Gorham D.
Anderson, E. J.
Adams, H. C.
Anthony, N. K.
Atterbury, L. jr.
Agnew, A. M. L.
Arcularius, P. G.
Alexander, H M.
Armstrong, M. & Sons
Anderson, A.
Avery, J. W.
Allen, Wm. A.
Angell, Engell & Hewitt
Aldrich, J. V. C.
Aikman, Hugh
Asche, Henry
A Lady
Andrews, Wm. D.
Allen, John
Aikman, Robert
Avery, J. S.
Allen A.
Allen, Mrs.
A Lady, by J. Orchard

B.

Banyer, M. Mrs.
Brown, James
Brown, Stewart
Boorman, James
Brown, Smith Mrs.
Bruen, A. M.
Boorman, Johnston & Co.
Belmont, Augustus
Beadel, Henry
Bruce, George
Benedict, E. C.

Burr, Isaac Mrs.
Bronson, F.
Bange, Henry
Burnham, G. W.
Butler, B. F.
Bronson, A. Mrs.
Burrows, Philip
Bell, Jacob
Blunt & Symes
Brown, William Smith
Brown, A. N.
Bull, W. G.
Beekman, W. F.
Brown, J. M.
Brown, Alexander Mrs.
Borst, John B.
Brush, Mr.
Benjamin, F. A.
Bartlett, Washington A.
Boorman, Robert
Bull, H. K.
Buchanan, R. M.
Buckley
Bayard, Robert
Bowne, Robert
Bowne, Richard H.
Birdsall, Thos. W.
Butterworth, J. T.
Beadell, G. T. Rev.
Blunt, George
Ball, Black & Co.
Barclay, Anthony
Bronson, Silas
Bronson, Miss
Benkard, James
Barron, James
Burdett, Charles
Baldwin, Adams & Co.
Baldwin, Starr & Co.
Barnum, P. T.
Burnham, E. Mrs.
Buckley, Charles A.
Bailey, N. P.
Blanco, R.
Bleecker, Jane
Buller, F. E.
Brown, Chas. E.
Beebe, Chas. E.
Beebe, Wm. J.
Berrian, W. D.
Betts, S. R.
Babcock, J. C. Mrs.
Bogart, Henry R.
Bement, P. R.
Bogardus, Wm.
Burnett, Peter, M.D.
Bruce, B. G.
Bell, Joseph M.
Brown, Richard
Baldwin, John C.
Bliss, Jas. Mrs. Dr.
Banks, Mark, (two donations
Beach, Brothers, (Advertis
Beers, Abner
Bolton, J. M.D.
Bonney, B. W.
Bussing, J S.

Bonnett, P. R.
Bloodgood, N
Butterworth, J. F.
Bullard P. Mrs.
Bininger, A.
Beeckman, H.
Bange, Fredk.
Breese, S. L. Capt.
Breese & Elliott
Brodie, A. O.
Brown, E. J.
Bogert, C.
Bogert, J. L.
Burges, J. Henry
Bradford, W.
Bronson T. for Sister.
Brown, R. J.
Bacon, D. P.
Bouchaud, J. Miss
Bushnell, O
Buchanan, R. S.
Barrell, George
Brown, J. F.
Bishop, Japhet
Brooks, M. C.
Bussing, E. J.
Browne, R. W.
Broadway Post Office
Brown, Richard
Blackstone, W.
Bloodgood, M.
Bruce, John M.
Burkhalter, C.
Banks, Martha Mrs.
Beekman, J. W.
Boyce, Gerardus
Brougham, John
Beekman & Co.
Brinckehoof, Walter
Bonsale, R. W. S.
Bogert, S. G.
Bleakley, Andrew
Birdsall, S.
Bleakley, Judge
Blauvelt, D. T.
Barnes, J. N.
Bishop Dwight
Bartholomew, J. R.
Bloomfield, E. S.
Bloomfield, W.
Burgen, E. H.
Badeau, E. C.
Bowman, Geo.
Bach, Jos.
Bancroft, Mr.
Boggs, J. L.
Brown, W. M.
Brown, G. H.
Buckmaster, T. O.
Bussell, R.
Bull, Miss
Bootman, E.
Belknap, Mrs.
Brownson, Mrs
Borger, John J.
Brown, John S.
Beadman, Jas.

1852.) LIST OF MEMBERS. 51

Beckett, John
Backus, M. M.
Brower, J. D.
Bogert, C.
Burr, Mrs.
Brown, David
Bouton, Alderman
Brigham & Miller
Barbour, Wm. C.
Burdsell, Hosea
Brown, George
Brooks & Cummings
Bertine, Robert
Boutell, A.
Bear, Isaac
Bauer, Henry
Birkner, J.
Brigg, Joseph
Baker, J. B.
Boyd, W. B.
Bartley, Mr.
Burrows, C. D.
Brower, Garret
Bennett, J. L.
Brady, James
Becknel, Joseph
Bartlett & Welford
Boyd & Paul
Boyd & Wilkins
Brown, Palmer & Dwight
Brainard, Geoffroy & Co.
Brown, H.
Brown, Silas
Broadhead & Storm
Booth, J. C.
Baker & Scudder
Beach, L. D.
Bearns & Co.
Brown, A.
Baker, A.
Boyce, John
Brooks, N. L.
Blair, H. B.
Burkhalter, Stephen
Butler, F. M.
Boyd, John
Beadel, John H.
Bunker, T. E.
Bunker, E. S.
Bevridge, John
Brinckerhoff, Miss
Bryson, Peter
Baldwin & Sexton
Brady, John
Brown, N. & J.
Britten, Mr.
Black, Thos.
Burhans, Samuel
Birkbeck, George
Burrell, Samuel
Brown, J. S.
Baudoine, Chas. A.
Boyce, J.
Brown, John L.
Brown, Sarah Mrs.
Brez, Paul

Bullus, Dr.
Brush, Platt
Bowden, A. & Sons
Bunce, O.
Barber, F.
Burkhalter, R.
Backwell, W. B.
Bonnell, D.
Bailey, Mrs.
Bowdoin, G. R. J.
Bailey, Wm.
Black, J.
Butterfield, Major
Bethune, Mrs.
Bowden, A.
Beck, James & Co.
Brown, Thomas
Brinckerhoff, J. L. Mrs.
Burroughs, Mr.
Brainard, G. W.
Brissel, John
Boyd, John N.
Bartlett, D. E.
Boorum, Cornelius
Briggs, J. R.
Blow & March
Blake & Brown
Babcock, Milnor & Co.
Burt, Brothers & Co.
Brower & Co. J. H.
Benjamin, W. & Brothers.
Barnes, Dunnell & Co.
Beach, Henry A.
Brown, Thos. E.
B. & R.
Bodmer, Henry, jr.
Boyd. J. J.
Baker & Duychinck
Bock & Ingliss
Bullock & Locke
Brown, W. A.
Burlew, R.
Bradford & Richmond
Baker, H. T.
Brockelman, T. & J.
Brown, L. B.
Brown & De Rosset
Bangs, Brothers & Co.
Bennett, M.
Bishop, V.
Bate, T. & T. H.
Bishop T. E.
B. & S.
Baldwin & Many
Benjamin, M. M.
Barrett, Nephews & Co.
Brooks, H. J.
Braisted, F. H.
B. & P.
Baldwin & Studwell
Burr, H. L.
Bradshaw, A.
B. P. & Sons
Baker, J. W.
Burdett, H. C.
Breath, James

Beach, John C.
Barmore, G. & H.
Bell, Thos.
Brush, Caleb, jr.
Brush, J. E.
Banta, S.
Bassford, A.
Burgess, W. F.
Bartlett, A. H.
Bush, R. I.
Bach, J. L.
Burdett, Jacob
Barrow, James
Bishop, D.
Brown, C.
Benson, C. S.
Brown, Anson
Bostwick, Mrs.
Baxter, J. C.
Brown, H.
Bogert, Jacob C.
Bunn, M.
Belden, David
Brownell, J. Sherman
Bower, Israel
Bowron, Joshua W., Jr.
Brown, J. T.
Bogert, Wm.
Bond, W. S.
Berrien, R. P., Jr.
Burch, H. B.
Benedict, S. H.
Bogert, A.
Berdan, John
Bates, Mrs.
Balch, W. S.
Burnton, Mr.
Bruce, Robert M.
Bradford, V. G.
Belden, Wm., Jr.
Bodine, J. M
Brady, Wm. C.
Bell, Joseph M.
Baldwin, N. B.
Barker, G.
Briggs, W.
Baker, G. A., Mrs.
Brewer, John
Baker, Thos.
Bostwick, Z.
Boyle, E. J.
Bernstein, Zion
Bernstein, Isaac
Belcher, Henry
Barns, A. W.
Barker, A.
Bell, M., Mrs.
Brown, J.
Boyle & Coleman
Brommer, John
Briggs, E. F.
Bauscher, H.
Brown, E. D.
Bennett, N. L.
Barton, Joseph
Baker, Peter C.

LIST OF MEMBERS. (1852.

Boyd, Daniel
Burr, John
Briggs, Isaac V.
Burke, Wm.
Baldwin, M. S., Mrs.
Bettman, Mr.
Brown, M., Mrs.
Burt, L. A.
Bowyee, Anthony
Bush, George
Bartholomew, F. H.
Bell, Abraham
Bigler, D.
Bloodgood, Wm.
Bowery Saving Store
Bean, B. G.
Bruns, Thos.
Bean, B. W.
Bell, R. & W. McLachlan
Betts, J. S.
Burr, Francis
Barkley, Wm. N.
Butterworth, H. H.
Brown, S. C.
Boyd, John S.
Babcock, Francis
Blakesley, A. W.
Bergh, G. R.
Brown, J. H.
Boardman, Mrs.
Bishop, C. P.
Barnes, Mrs.
Barnes, J.
Benher, N.
Babcock, Mr.
Boardman, W.
Benedict, A. C.
Bennett, Wm.
Buloid, R.
Brennan, Owen C.
Ballagh, M. & R.
Belter, J. H.
Bebee, Wm.
Barnes, J. N.
Barr, J. T.
Boardman. John
Bigelow, Richard
Brown, E. M.
Butler, Charles, Mrs.
Brooks, Hiram
Britton, W. A.
Beers, J. D.
Butler, H. V.
Bromley, E.
Bradley, J. N.
Baker, James
Bryce, William
Barritt, Mrs.
Bennett, David L.
Brooks, Joshua
Busteed, George W.
Barton, Mrs.
Brusley, Mrs.
Banks, Theo.
Brahe, A. H.
Brombacher, J.

Burtus, S. A.
Barker, Daniel
Badger, Mr.
Bush, Joseph
Brush, Cornelius
Bowen, A. S.
Belknap, E. S.
Baker, Dobel
Bulkley, George
Bird, M.
Barstow, Samuel
Buchanan, Mrs.
Briggs, A. T.
Brooks, J.
Bucknam, E.
Brower, Jacob
Bridgman, E.
Brown, Paul S.
Brown, M. C.
Burk, M.
Blackfan, J.
Booth, W. C.
Banks, T.
Buckley, J. L.
Bernard, A.
Belcher, R.
Bissell, J.
Brady. A. C.
Barien, Mrs.
Bearns, W. F.
Baker, Wm.
Bull, H. K.
Benedict, J. W.
Bartlett, D. E.
Baldwin, J. L.
Baldwin, H. M.
Brusle, Wm. A.
Burras, T. H.
Barney, B., M. D.
Burrill, Samuel N.
Baxter, Samuel
Beers, N. P.
Bailey, Thos.
Belloni, Louis J.
Baxter, J. C.
Bogart, A. L.
Bell, Joseph B.
Bradley, Wm. C.
Brown, Wm.
Burr, John
Brown, J.
Bridger, S.
Burger, T. J.
Beatty, D. L.
Barnes, W. J.
Ballard, J. B., Rev.
Butler, W. A.
Bartlett, D. F.
Buckley, Francis
Bogart, Wm.

C

Cruger, Harriet Douglass, Mrs.
Collins, Joseph B.

Crosby, Wm. B.
Cock, Thos. F., M. D.
Cock, Thomas, M. D.
Clark, R. Smith
Chauncey, Henry
Cottenet, F.
Caswell, John
Chester, W. N.
Curtis, C.
Curtis, S.
C. R. by H. Rogers
Coster, G. W.
Coster, H. A.
Cary, S. F.
Case, W. S.
Catlin, D. W.
Cunningham, J. B.
Coit, H. V.
Crosby, J. P.
Crane, D. B.
Cotheal & Co.
Cornell, M.
Cook, T. F., M. D.
Cromwell, Edward
Cotheal, A. J.
Center, Mr.
C. D.
Collins, S. B.
Chauncy, W. & Co.
Crane, D. P.
Chouteau, P., Jr., & Co.
Cook, Levi & Co.
Chouteau, P.
Chesterman, J.
Colles, James
Cary, S. T.
Cammann, O. J.
Carleton & Co.
Cooper, Peter,
Crowell, Adams & Co.
Cutting, F. B.
Cunningham, James
Cary, W. E.
Cary, W. F.
Colden, D. C., Mrs.
Contoit, John H.
Cheesebrough, M., Mrs.
Coe, Charles A.
Clapp, John
Cochran, S.
Chamberlain, J. F.
Carter, Walter
Comstock, S. R.
Carpenter, G.
Campbell, D. P.
Collins, R. B.
Cruikshank, James
Cauldwell, E.
Chamberlain, Charles
Conover, Stephen
Cutter, Stephen
Cummings, J. P.
Corning, Jasper
Christy, Moses
Cook, John
Camp, Amzi, Rev.

1852.) LIST OF MEMBERS. 53

Clawson, John M., M. D.
Coe, Noah, Rev.
Cornell, Thos. F. (Clothing)
Chamberlain, J. F., (by C. C. Darling
Curtis, Joseph
Catlin, D. W.
Callender, W. S.
Chastelain, J.
Cronkhite, J. P.
Clark, G.
Carpenter, J. S.
Cuming, T. B.
Clark, J.
Collins, Mrs.
Clark, E. S.
Crittenden, H.
Conant, F. J.
Cook, Zebedee
Colvill, A.
Clarke, G. W.
Coman, L. D.
Cobb, J. N.
Cogswell, J. G.
Coolidge, H.
Coles, J. U., Mrs.
Couch, W.
Colvil
Campbell, D.
Catterfield, W. F.
Cash (several)
Currie, J. H.
Cooley, F.
Constable, J. M.
Chichester, G.
Cornell & Amerman
Clark, M.
Compton, Alderman
Cornell, T. F.
Collamore, Davis
Cargill, N., Mrs.
Cragin, G. D.
Craig, J. J.
Carpenter, N. H.
Clayton, A. T.
Clark, P. P., Mrs.
Clark, Alexander
Curtis, S.
Connor, C. A.
Civill, Anthony
Camerden, Mrs.
Chatterton, S. S.
Cameron, Miss
Cook, Geo. H.
Chester, J. N.
Cornell, H.
Clark, Dr.
Cromwell, A., Mrs.
Cook, J.
Cropsey, J.
Cockren
C., Mrs.
Codwise, David
Clark, C. W.
Colyer, Wm.
Curtis, Charles

Chapin, J., M. D.
Clark, Jacob
Collins, Wm.
Croker, Henry
Cornwell, R.
Conklin, Nelson
Cheesman, G. B.
Cheeseborough, Dr.
Churchill, Samuel
Church, Andrew
Cornish, J.
Clark, Mr.
Colbum, Thos.
Carter, Robert
Cash
Clark, A. H.
Carpenter, A. G.
Cornell, S. M.
Clark, L. E.
Clark, H. F.
Close, A.
Crocheron, D.
Cummings, Collins & Co.
Cain, J. H. & Co.
Constantine, Mrs.
Cromwell, Henry
Carman, R.
Chamberlain, E.
Chilton, Doctor
Coffle, Mr.
Cash
Conner & Winser
Conover & Woolley
Copcut, J.
Cochran, Mrs.
Cook, Israel
Conner, J.
Collamore, E.
Chickering, Mr.
Cucks, James
Cox, J. & I.
Cahill, S.
Cammann, G. P., M. D.
Cornell, R. C.
Cox, Dr.
Chalmers, Dr.
Clark, Mr.
Clay, E. B.
Campbell, M.
Cash & Black
Civill, T.
Constantine, J. N.
Copcut, John
Coit, H.
Charlott, Mr.
Carr, James
Campbell & White
Clark & Saxton
Clarendon, Miss
Church, Chas L.
Creighton & Edwards
Cornell, W. W.
Camp, Henry
Conklin, P. S.
Conklin, E. F.
Christie, J.

Colt, S.
Clark, J. A.
Clarke, Wm.
Cox, Mrs.
Cape, H. M., Mrs.
Conklin, C., Mrs.
Cockcroft, James, M. D.
Cook, Ebenezer
Cort, N. L.
Clyde, Mrs.
Campbell, M. E., Mrs.
Carr, J.
Church, James C.
Cromwell, Daniel
Cromwell, Daniel, Jr.
Cash
Cassidy, B.
Clarkson, C. V.
Cumings, James
Coggeshall, James
Cummings, S. N.
Cox, A. E
Cheevers, H. T., Rev
Chapin, Lyman
Clussman, C., Mrs.
Cram, Philander
Craig, Sarah, Mrs.
Clark, James
Cook, Alderman
Cook, A. K., Miss
Case, A. J.
Currahger, Capt
Cornwell, J.
Chichester, Lewis
Cunningham, James
Conger, John
Corwin, A.
Crane, John J., M. D.
Cash
Clayton, E. B.
Coey, W. J.
Cock, C. J.
Carryl, N. T.
Christy, Thos.
Camfield, E. H.
Church, J. B.
Cutter, Mr.
Chichester, W. J.
Clarke, Peter
Crane, D.
Curry, D. J.
Carpenter, J. S.
Cannan, Wm. H.
Conklin, Isaac
Crawford, C.
Cook, Alanson
Clark, Jas. S.
Cargill, Miss
Cash
Conklin, J. W.
Curtis & Co., L. & B.
Cerf, Beer, May & Co.
Cousinery, F.
Coffin, E.
Callender, W.
Corning, J.

LIST OF MEMBERS. (1852

Care, Burnett & Co.
Carey, P. G.
Cheeseborough, Silsby & Co.
Cunningham & Osborn
Condit & Noble
Crooks, R.
Cash (A.)
Caesar & Pauli
Cash (C.)
Cash (B.)
Ceballs, P.
Cassidy
Clark & West
Congreve, C. M.
C. A.
C. M. H.
Chandler. Job & Foster
Constant, S. S.
Center, A. H.
Cocker, James & Co.
Carson & Hard
Corwin, Daniel W.
C. T. A. H.
Chapman, L.
Charity
Celleallo
C. V. H.
Coffin, W. J.
Culver & Corry
Coosh, A. & Co.
Clark & Bailey
Crocker, Hall & Stow
Charruaud, John J.
Conover, G. A.
Connolly, Chas. M.
Campbell, Freeman
Cook, R. S.
Child, Asa
Campbell, W. S.
Cummings, A.
Chamberlain, E.
Clark, S. M.
Clowes, J. W.
Cummings, Thomas
Cornell, John H.
Clinch, Charles P.
Cunningham. Wm. J.
Coulter, Samuel
Coleman, E. W.
Cook, Edward
Clinton, Alexander
Cox, Charles B.
Chesebro, Albert
Coles, W. H.
Crouch, Miss
Cole, Isaac
Cornel, J. M.
Cassebeer, H. A.
Church, C. M.
Creveling, Dr.
Conant, W. A.
Conover, S.
Campbell, R.
Chevalier, J. D.
Columbian Foundry
Cornell & Nesbitt

Cash
Curtis, Joseph
Cutting, Fulton
Cheever, George B. Rev.
Cochran, S.
Coffin, J. P.
Curtis, P. A.
Cleland, Gilbert
Carpenter, U. F.
Colgate, S.
Carey, John, Jr.
Clarkson, Dr. Jr.
Crabtree, E.
Colgate, Robert
Crane, J. J.
Chave, W. G.
Chegary, Madame
Cromwell, C. T.
Crogham, Mrs.
Chappel, Mrs.
Chester, E. W.
Cooper & Brothers
Currier, N.
Cooledge, George F. & Co.
Carle, John, Jr.
Craft, J.
Contrell, Joseph
Chamberlain, Chas.
Canton Tea Co.
Coughtry & Dougherty
Cauldwell, E., Miss
Chichester, A.
Case, J. B.
Christopher, R.
Clapp, John
Clarke, H.
Civil, Acton
Carlisle, Mrs.
Corwith, Mrs.
Codwise, D.
Cromwell, W. D.
Chardevine
Chauncey, P. H.
Chambers, J. Mrs.
Campbell, W. W.
Coe, D. B.
Chesebrough, E.
Carpenter, Dr.
Cahoon, Mrs.
Carrott, M.
Cummings, Wm. A.
Church, C. H.
Castle, John
Carpentier, Reuben S., M.D.
Conover, Daniel
Clark, James
Cheesbro, A.
Carson, John C.
Cragin, C. A.
Clymer, William
Clarkson, C. V., M.D.
Cameron, John
Cook, J. F.
Clark, J. A.
Carter, Peter
Cole, R.

Cornell, Marks
Cowl, J.
Chichester, D.
Carrington, W. A., M.D.
Clark, John
Cormack, John A.
Church, C. F.

D

Demilt
Douglass, George
Donaldson, J.
Dawson, B. F.
Dennistoun, Wood, & Co.
Deleno, Warren
Delano. W. Jr.
Davis, D. H. & Co.
D. T.
Dutilh & Co.
Denny, Thomas
Day, M.
Dunning, C.
De Forrest, G. B.
D.
Deronge, Moran & Co.
Depeyster, James F.
Dean, Thomas
De Ruyter, John
De Rahm, H. C.
Dibble, Work & Moore
Dibble, H. E. & Co.
Dowley, J.
Dale & Wright
Dows & Co.
Durand, John & Co.
Durand, C.
De Forrest, W. W., & Co.
Davies, John M. & Jones
Dater, Strang & Co.
Duncan, W. Butler
Depeyster, F.
Delafield, Edward
Decker, Alfred
Decker, C. N.
Dubois, Grant
Dakin, C. P.
Deems, H. W.
Demarest, A.
Darling, C., C. Rev.
Duer, John
Dehon, T.
Davison, E.
Dorr, G. B.
Decoppet, L.
De Witt, T. Rev.
Davies, H. E.
Dean, H.
Durand, A. B.
Dustan, S., Mrs.
Dubois, C.
Detmold, Dr.
Dobbs, Edwin, per C C Darling
Dickie, Patrick

1852.) LIST OF MEMBERS. 55

Dupuy, Eugene
Day & Newell
Delluc & Co.
Dessoir, J.
Demarest, Daniel
Dillinger, C.
Dibben, Henry
Del Vecchio
Dodworth, A.
Durcon, James
Dean, Thomas
Dusenbury, Jas.
Donington, Ogden
Dieden, Mrs.
Dibblee, Wm.
Dudley, W. G.
Demarest, R.
Dugro, Anthony
Decker, Wm. J.
Dela Montagnie Edward
Dodge, Charles
Devoe & Sellick
Devoy, M.
Dally, Joseph
Davenport, John
Davis, E. V.
Dougherty, W.
Dow, M. F.
Docherty & Pearson
Dayton, M.
Doscher, C.
Darling, Mr.
Duryea, Peter
Deitz, G. F.
Duckworth, M. H.
Demarest & Jeroloman
Davison, A. M.
Davison, Jane
Dalrymple, Alexr.
Duncan & Sons
Darling, Mr.
Donnelly, James
Del Hoyo Francis
Delafield, Dr.
Denison, Chas.
Dunham, H. R. & Co.
De Gonge, Mr.
De Puga, Mr.
Dow, Mr.
Deraismes, John
Dixon, J. D.
Donaldson, Jas.
Dally, John
Dudley, M.
Douglass, James B.
Delmonico, Joseph
Douglass, C. S.
Dambmann, C. F.
Delaunay, V.
Day, J.
Dwight, A. T.
Dollner & Potter
D. E.
Delafield, W.
Dayton, Sprague & Co.
D. & K.

Dunscomb, E., Cook & Co.
De Suz, L. P.
Delapierre, Chs. B.
Draper, C. E.
Dart, R. & N.
Dubois, Francis & Co.
Droz, H. E.
Deitz Bro. & Co.
Davids & Black
Dunderdale, Forbes
De Forest, H. G.
Danna, R. P., Mrs.
Demarest, A.
Dolhear, E., Mrs.
Degraw, J.
Dodge, S. V.
Dowling, Dr., Rev.
Donelson, Wm.
Dodd, John M.
Drake, Benjamin
Dun, A., Mrs.
Duryee, Levi
Dittenhoefer, Isaac
Delapierre, B.
Donaldson, James
Doughty, Samuel S.
De Camp, Catty
Davis, Jas.
Doughty, J. H.
Dickson, James
Decker, Joseph
Dowe, John J.
Dunshee, Samuel
Davis, C.
Doolittle, A., M. D.
Douglas, Joseph, M. D.
Dickson, J. R.
Danforth, Mr.
Doremus, Peter
Dennis, S. A.
Davis, S.
Duncan, E. W.
Demarest, Mr.
Denham, J.
Dolan, Wm.
Demarest, Silas
Darling, S. E.
Dymock, Wm.
Dominge, F.
Dodge, Mrs.
Dodge, W. E.
Douglass, Benjamin
Dudley, J. G.
Duncan, W. T. H.
Douglass
Dwight, E.
Dickinson, Dr., Rev.
Dash, Bowie
Dean & Thornton
Dodge, J. N.
Decker, C. N.
Deromas, Peter
Davies, J. M.
Dennistown, Mr.
Denike, A.
Damott, Wm. H.

Dominick, J. W.
Dewitt, J., Mrs.
Delapierre, C. B.
Dennison, C. L., Mrs.
Dodge, John T.
Dibblee, Thos. B.
Dominick, A. E.
Deleplaine, J. F.
Dean, J. E. P.
Dexter, A.
Davidson, John
Dyer, Charles C.
Devoy, Michael
Davis, Wm. E.
Dunning, James W
Decker, Chas. M.
Duncan, Francis
De Grove, H. S.
Dodge, Josiah
Disosway, C. R.
Duff, James
Decker, C. N.
Decker, Moses J.
Dunn Jacob
Duff, J. F.

E

Eyre, Henry & Co.
Eno, Amos R.
Edgar, William
Elsworth, H.
Eno, Mahony & Co.
Edgar, John A.
Earle, John H.
Eastman, Sheldon & Townsend
Everett & Brown
Ely, E. C.
Ely, A. K.
Everett, N. C.
Endicott, John
Earle, J. H.
Elliot, Volney
Eager, W. B.
Evans, L. G.
Eaton, B. F.
Eaton, D. C.
Emmett, R., Jr.
Eggleston, T.
Emmettt, T. A.
Engle, S. S.
Elmore, Mr.
Earle, Miss
Edwards, D. & Co.
Egan, D. D.
Ely, George
Ensign, J. E.
Eldridge, Mrs.
Elmore, D. M.
Eshamner, John
Elliot, John H.
Ellis, Thomas
Earle, Thomas
Elsworth, H.

LIST OF MEMBERS.   (1852.

Elliott, W.
Elder, George
Embury, Peter
Emmons, Henry
Ewen, Edward
Escher & Reusch
Escheverin, M.
Escoriaza
Engler, Chas.
Eggert, D. & Son
Ellis, R. & T. P.
Engle, J. & S.
Elphinstone, W. H.
E. S.
Everdell, Wm.
English, W. C. R.
Engs, P. W.
Endicott, Mrs.
Everitt, C. L.
Eveleth, Emma
Elderd, Henry
Eaton, J. A.
Eaton, W. S.
Elleau, F.
Elder, A.
Edward
Egins, J. H.
E. P.
Evarts, Wm. M.
Ely, Smith
Evans, John
Ellis, J. A.
Ellis, Benjamin
Eggleston & Battelle
Edwards, Alfred
Ewing, D.
Easton, Chas.
Ensign, E. H.
Ellis, K. S.
Engle, J.
Earle.

F

Faile, Thos. H.
Ferguson, Edward
Fardon, Abraham, Junr.
Fiedler, Ernest
Fearing & Hall
Fleming, J. B.
Ferguson, S. F.
Fowler, F. R.
Foster, A. & Sons
Fairbanks & Co.
Field, B. H.
Foster, J. Junr.
Fellows, Van Arsdale & Cooper
Fellows, Louis & Schell
Field, Cyrus W., & Co.
Fellows & Co.
Frost & Hicks
Forgay, Wm.
Few, C., Mrs.
Female Guardian Society
Ferris, Geo. B.
Fowler, B. M.

France, James
Fairweather, Thomas
Frear, A.
Furniss, W. P.
Fowler, T. O.
Florence & Harpel
Fisher, Geo. H., M. D.
Frazer, Wm.
Funda, A. P.
Farnham, Geo. W.
Forbes, Wm.
Friend to Cause
Flemming, J., Mrs.
Fox & Oothout
Folsom, Charles J.
Fitz, Henry
Foster, Benjamin
Fanchnor, John
Fowler, John H.
Foot, H. B.
Ferris, C.
Field, Jude
Fisher, Henderson & Co.
Francis, C.
Forbes, J. H.
Fuller, L. F.
Fowler, J. O.
Farquar, A,
Forster, James
Francis, N.
Farr, J. & G.
Furman, P. H.
Finch, Amos
Frazer, J. H.
Freeman, N. A.
Ferris, J. H.
Ferris, Dr.
Fieldman, J. G. W.
Fisher, J G.
Friend, J. J.
Flynn, James
Folger, R. W.
Freeman, Pliny
Foster, Thos. R.
Fuller, Dudley B.
Foulke, Jas., Jr.
Fisher, Joseph
Friend
Felt, W.
F. H. M.
Fleming, Thos.
Finn, A. T.
Frisbie, M. J.
Frazer & Everitt
Fox, E.
Fraser, T.
Frey, W. H. & Brother
Flint, Cyrus
Fish, E., Mrs.
Furman, Samuel
Fitch, G. S.
Frazee, Abraham
Freeman, N., Mrs.
Frink, Samuel E.
Ferris, John G.
Fairbank, D.
Foster, Wm. M.

Friend
Foote, T. C.
Field, Robert M.
Field, Josiah
Foster, W. R.
Fraser, E. A.
Freedman, Solomon
Faulkner, Wm.
Ferguson, Asa
Freeman, Jas.
Freeman, Wm.
Flanders, Elijah
Freedgen, Henry
Freund, V.
Folger, R. B., M. D.
Forester, Chs.
Frien, J.
Fatman, Joseph
Ford, Isaac
Finch, Nathaniel
Fabrequettes, Eugene
Francis, W. A.
Faxon, W.
Flannagan, J. R.
Fisher, Henry
Fleming, Robert
Fink, Mr.
Franklin, M.
Frost, M., Mrs.
Foster, Wm. G.
Frost, Samuel
Forrest, Wm.
Furnald, F. P.
Forbes, H. D., Mrs.
French, R.
Frish, D.
Friend
Fox, Charles
Fox. Geo.
Faulkner, J. C.
Fanning, S.
Francis, A.
Freeborn, W. A.
Ferris, N.
Freeborn, J. A.
Frost, H. P.
Fancher, E. L.
Fisher, Daniel
French, Daniel
Ferguson, Alexander
Fanning, S.
Forster, T. V.
Florentine, Abraham
Farrell, Edmund
Fields, Edward, M. D.
Freeman, J. V.
Ferguson, J. B.
Foster, Wm. A.
Fowler, J. V. D. B.
Falconer, E.
Few, Miss.

G

Griswold, George
Grinnell, Moses H.
Graves, Boonen & Co.

LIST OF MEMBERS.

Goodhue & Co.
Grosvenor. J.
Grosvenor, Seth
Green, John C.
Green, L. & M., Misses
Gilman, W. S.
G. A. H.
Griswold, John
Gans, Meyer
Griffin, George
Goddard, George C.
Gallatin, A. R.
Gallatin, J.
Grant & Barton
Gibbes, R. M.
Giraud, J. P.
Griswold, N. L., Mrs.
Gregory, J. G.
Greenway, J. Henry
Green, H., M. D.
Gillelan, Edward H.
Goodwin, Eli
Gilman, Wm. C.
Guion
Guion, Maria, Mrs.
Guion, W. H.
Gale, A. H. & Co.
Glover, Chas. S.
Groot
Gear
Gustine, M. A. Mrs.
Goadly, Mrs.
Gibbons, Robert
Gould, Charles
Grimly, Mrs.
Gibbes, T. S.
Gates, John
Gibson, James R.
Gould, R. S.
Gardner, Moses
Griffin, H.
Green, A.
Gregg, Franklin
Gibbons, Robert
Gillelan, John
Geer, Darius
Gray, William, Rev.
Green, Miss
Gilbert, C.
Green, W. G.
Gunning, T. B.
Gelston, M.
Gamage, J. E., Miss
G. A. H.
Gardner, Sam'l J.
Gibson, James
Gaylord, J. H.
Gidney, S.
Greer, Henry C.
Geisenhaimer, Mrs.
Gantz, John
Grosz, Michael
G. C. K.
Gridley, Edward
Good, Mrs.
Green, Chas. E.

Gregory, James
Gregory, W. A.
Gardner, James
Goetre, F. A.
Gormley, W.
Godfrey, E. J.
Gould, J. M.
Gurney, J.
Green, G. T.
Girard, H.
Gulick, W.
Gould, H. A.
Greason, John
Glen, Mr.
Gibson, Wood
Gordon, P.
Gilbert, Nicholas
Greenleaf & Kins'ey
Greenwood, John
Gerschel, C.
Guiber, John
Graham, Jas. L.
Goupil & Co.
Geib & Jackson
Green, Thos. T.
Green, Dr.
Grice, Charles
Gillies, W.
Giraud, J.
Grandmain, E.
Griffin, Miss
Gihon, John
Greenway, E. M.
Giro, Emanuel
Gomez, R. M.
Gray & Garwin
Green, J. W.
Gunther, C. G. & Sons
Guedin, J.
Gordan & Talbot
Genin
Gibbert, C.
Gale, Wm.
Griffin & Pullman
Gross, Francis
Grant, Charles E.
Gregory, L.
Griffith, Charles
Green, Edward
Groshon, John
Gunn, A. N., M.D.
Gaberdon, R. W.
Griffin, Thos. T.
Gillespie, James
Greenough, W
Glassford, Mrs.
Gaynor, H.
Gardiner, Wm.
Godine, F.
Giffing, David S.
Goodkind, W.
Griffiths, J. M.
Garrabranth, Wm.
Goodsman, Thos.
Gardner, Henry
Graves, Edward

Grumbs, E., Mrs.
Goadby, Thos.
Griffeths, W.
Gerrey, R. N. W.
Gallagher, John
Gilbert, J. S.
Gourlie, A. T.
Grant, M. O., Mrs.
Gray. Mrs.
Gibbons, J.
Green, Jas.
Ganty, George W.
Glffon, Jas. N.
Gordon, Wm.
Gentle & Wilder
Gemmel, James
Gescheidt, A., M.D.
Givan, Mrs.
Gaul, Mrs.
Gage
Gregory, Mrs.
Goldsmith, Mrs.
Gansy, Mrs.
Green, Alonzo
Guthrie, J. B.
Gray, J.
Gant, F. S.
Griffin, Solomon
Grayden, Samuel
Graydon Joseph
Greenwood, Mrs.
Griffin, M. M., Mrs.

H

Harsen, Jacob, M.D.
Hicks, Wm. T. & Co.
Hewitt, Lees & Co.
Hitchcock, W. R.
Holbrook, E.
Hoyt, Gould
Hamilton, Alexander, Mrs.
Harris, Evans & Co.
Hoppock, Ely
Hunt, Thos.
H. R., by H. Rogers
Hoffman, L. M.
Halsted, W. M.
Hicks, Wm. M.
Hoge, W. & Co.
Hadden, David
Haggerty, John
Halvetius
Holden, Horace
Howland, G. G., Mrs.
Hurry, John J.
Hamersly, Mr.
Hamersly, Mrs.
Hunt, Thomas, & Co.
Huskell, Merrick & Bull
Hunt, Wilson, G., & Co.
Henry, Josiah J.
Hayes, H. M.
Heckscher, C. A.
Henderson, H.

3*

LIST OF MEMBERS. (1852.

Howland, J.
Hopkins, E. M.
Hoppock, M.
Horn, James
Havemeyer, W. F.
Herring, Silas C.
Havemeyer, F. C.
Havemeyer, D. M.
Hurd, John R.
Hall, Valentine G.
Hagadom, Wm.
Haggerty, Green & Co.
Hoge, Wm.
Hitchcock, Cyrus
Hoople, W. H.
Halsted, C. O.
Holmes, S. P.
Hiddon, E.
Hallock, L., M.D.
Harper, John
Hyatt, S.
Hook, J. D. W.
Harris, John
Halsted, A. L.
Hoyt, Mrs.
Harper, Samuel
Hitchcock, Mrs.
Hunt, H. D.
Holzdeber, John
Hendricks, A.
Halsey, H. A.
Hume, Andrew
Horton, Jonathan B.
Howell, M. H.
Holman, Thos.
Hawkins, C. P.
Hogan, Thomas
Hutchings, John
Howe, Bezaleel
Howe, J. M., M.D.
Hart, John
Hasbrouck, A. B.
Hunt, E.
Hughes, Harriet, Miss
Hedden, F., Mrs.
Howe, Calvin W.
Howès, M.
Hyatt, E.
Howland, B. J.
Herrick, J. B.
Hall, Francis
Higbie, N. T.
Hutton, M. S., Rev.
Harison, C. J., Miss
Heyward, H.
Hoffman, P. V.
Hall, J. Prescott
Holmes & Co.
Hayes, H.
Hook, C. G.
Halsey, A. P.
Herbert, J.
Hall, James F.
Halsey, E. C
Harrison, J.
Hewitt & Morton

Hovencamp, John
Hartley, Robert M.
Hedden
Hasbrook, Mr.
Hasbrouck. G. D.
Hirst, E.
Hallock, A.
Hart, John
Hasbrouck, F., M.D.
Hahn, H.
Hern, Brothers
Hutchings, W.
Havemeyer, A.
Hall, Thos.
Hunt, Mrs.
Howser, J. C.
Hacltlander, Henry
Hiscock, Freeman
Haughwout, S.
Hoft, John
Hopkins, E. A.
Harrison, Thomas
Hatfield, Gilbert
Hedding, John
Halenbeck, Peter
Hicks, William
Hart, B.
Harris, E. T.
Haith, Mr.
Hackett, Mr.
Hunt, Wilson J.
Hagerty, Green & Co.
Hoyt, J.
Hoagland, J. M.
Hurd, A. T.
Hall & Ruckle
Hodgkins, J. G.
Healy, Mr.
Hope, A. S. & Co.
Halsted, Jacob
Hall, Jas.
Hart, Jas.
Hopkins, H. B.
Hamersly, Andrew
Held, John
Hope, T. S., & Co.
Hyatt, T.
Husted, Mrs.
Hurton, Miss
Halsey, H. A.
Hill, John
Hitchcock & Leadbeater
Hunter, James
Hosack, A, E., M D.
Hustace, Wm.
Hall, A.
Henry, Philip
Hyslop, Robert
Hoyt, Jesse
Hasbrook, J. L.
Horton & Tweedy
Hegeman, Wm.
Herrick, J.
Hulse, T.
Harrison, A.
Hobart, W. H., M.D.

Hobart, Dayton
Hull, G. L.
Hull, J. C.
Hepburn, J. C.
Hubbell & Pattee
Hardt & Co.
Henequin, & Co, H.
Hall, G. L.
H.
Hazard Powder Company
Hosford, F. J.
Hubbell, N. T.
Hendricks & Bros.
Hoose, Frederick
Hayden, P. & T.
Hyde, J. James
Heyer, C. P. & Co.
Hurlbut, W. W.
Haviland, D. G.
Halsey, W. & Co.
Hatch, C. B. & Co.
Halsted, B.
Huesmann & Co.
Holmes
Hoe R. & Co.
Hawley, James H.
H. S. T. & Co. (At.)
H. J. J. & Co.
Henderson, John C.
Hunt, Jonathan
Hall, W. C.
Hudelburgh, M.
Hutchinson, Ira
Hallett, J. H.
Herring & Ryer
Hopkins, N. F., Mrs.
Harriott, James
Hunt, H. G.
Harned, Wm.
Hale, Jas. W.
Huse, John B.
Hoxie, N. B.
Haddock, W. J.
Hasbrouck, J. A. H.
Higgins, L. & J.
Hirshfield, H.
Hall, W. T.
Hart, Robt. H.
Holden, Samuel
Hertzel, Jacob F.
Hustace, J.
Hatfield, R. G.
Herder, N. D.
Hutchings, Jane, Mrs.
Hunt, H. W.
Hendrick, T.
Hume, Thos.
Hoogland, A.
Hull, J.
Halsted, S.
Hyer, John
Heath, L. C.
Huey, M. M.
Hill, M., Mrs.
Hillman, W.
Hillman, G. W.

LIST OF MEMBERS.

Hamilton, W. A.
Hadley, John S.
Harrison, V. P.
Homan, R. S.
Hunter, C. E.
Hampton, A.
Haggart, James
Haws, R. J.
Healy, E.
Hiser, H.
Hicks, Benjamin W.
Hutchinson, S.
Hunt, Zeber
Herrer, Louisa
Hutchens, John
Hoffman, M. Mrs.
Hoffman & Scherbert
Herman, A. S.
Hoey, Peter
Halsey, Jeremiah
Halsey, S. R.
Holstien, John
Hoe, R. & Co.
Hussey, C. F.
Hobby, E. B.
Harger, John
Holmes, Sarah, Mrs.
Heller, Wm.
Hamilton, David
Hawes, L. P.
Hewlett, G. T.
Hoffman, E.
Hadley, Ritter
Havemeyer, Geo. L.
Hunt, S. B.
Hegeman, John
Halsted, J. W.
Howard, George
Hockman, Wm.
Haight, B. J.
Hines, J. C.
Hyslop, David
House, Mrs.
Horton, C.
Hamersley, Misses
Hodges, P. H.
Hutschler, J V.
Houghton, Elijah
Heath, Miss
Harbeck, Wm. H.
Haines, W. A.
Hoadley, David
Hedges, Miss
Hamlin, F. V.
Hilton, Archd.
Hyde, S. T.
Harteen, Mr.
Holmes, Adrian
Hurry, Edmund
Hearne, G. A.
Hazard, Mr.
Hasey, A.
Hall, Archibald
Harding, R.
Hazen, J.
Hart, H. & M.

Hyatt, George E.
Henenschire, Alfred
Hart, J. C.
Hewlett, O. T.
Hoe, R. & R.
Hancock, John
Haydock, Robt.
Harmer, C. G.
Harding, W.
Harriman, O.
Havens, A. C.
Hill, B. M.
Howard, G. H.
Harris, John
Harris, W. D.
Hosack, N. P.
Holt, J. S.
Hait, George, Rev.
Henderson, A. J.
Hurd, Hiram
Hoagland, J. S.
Horton, Richard, Rev.
Holman, Henry
Hubbard, J. M.
Halsey, L. W.
Heydon, Wm.
Hyslop, G. L., M.D.
Hazeltine, L.
Hayter, Richard, Rev.
Husted, J. N.
Hines, J. C.
Humbert, W. B.
Halsted, A. L.
Hayden, Nathaniel
Hammersly, Mrs.
Hammersly, J. W.

I & J.

Jay, Ann, Miss
Jay, Elizabeth Clarkson
Jay, Susan Matilda
Jaffray, J. R. & Sons
Johnston John (Estate)
Jones, J. J.
Jones, J. Colford Mrs.
Ingoldsby, F.
Johnson, B.
Johnson & Lazarus
Ireland, Sophia Mrs.
Ireland, Wm. B.
Ireland George
Ireland, George Jr.
Irvin, Richard
Jay, John
Jones, Rowland & Co.
Johnson, Bradish
Jones, Isaac
Jones, E. S. Miss
Johnson, S. Mrs.
Jones, W. R.
J. M. D.
J. W. W.
J. G. G.
Johnson, Austin
Jackson, Thomas

Jenkins, J. J.
Jeremiah, Thomas
Jackson, Luther
Jackson, John E.
Jackson, Wm.
Jervis, Wm.
Jackson, Thomas
Jones, James
Irwin, D.
Johnson, J. K.
Johnson, Edward
Irving, Charles
Johnson Charles
Jones, H.
Johnston, Wm.
Jackson, Lewis E.
Jenkins, J. J.
Jenkins, J Foster, M. D.
Iselin, J. A.
Jones, J. Q.
Irving, G. F. Mrs.
Irving, J. T. Mrs.
Jacobus, David
Jones, John
Jeffers, W. H.
Jacobus, C. C.
Johnson, H. F.
Jones, Mrs.
Jones, M. Miss
Janes, David
Ingersoll, S.
Jimmerson & Co.
Jackson, L.
Jarvis, James
Jones, J. F.
Johnson, James
Jaushee, W. H.
Jennings, W. T.
Johnson, J. W.
Johnson, W. S.
Jennings & Co. W. T.
Jones, H.
Janes, Edmund S., Rev.
Isaacs, S. I.
Janes, C. M
Jung, John W.
Judson, Curtis
Ivernois, B.
J. M. F.
J. E. F.
Jewell, Harrison & Co.
J. W. Q.
Journeay, A. Jr. & Co.
J. D. J.
J. J. B.
Johnson, E. A.
Jacobson, Frederick
Johnson, J. J.
Jones, B.
Ireland, T. D.
Jackson, Thomas
Jube, John P.
J. W.
Johnson, George W.
Irwin, Wm.
Jenkins, Richard

60   LIST OF MEMBERS.   (1852,

Johnson, Wm.
Jarvis, J.
Jayne, A. A.
Jennings, M. J.
Jacobus, J.
Johnson, Wm.
Irwin, David
Jaques, D. K.
Johnson, S. R.
Jones, S. W.
Jackson, W. W.
Isaacs, W. M.
Jolly, Isaac
Jenkins, T. F.
Jackson & Many
Janes, A.
Johnson, W. Mrs.
Jenkins, Henry T.
Jones, Edward S.
Johnson, R. & Son
Irvine, Mrs.
Jacques, E. J.
Jeremiah, T.
Jung, T. C.
Jordan, A. L.
Jackson, Mr.
Jones, A. H. Mrs.
Johnson
Johnston, J. R.
Jones, Mr. Rev.

K.

Kennedy, D. S.
Ketcham, Rogers & Bement
King, Peter V.
Kip, L. W.
Kane, Delancy
Kimble, Wm.
Kelly, R. W.
Knapp, Shepherd
Kipp, B. Livingston
King, James G.
Kelly, Robert
Kirby, L. & V. & Co.
King, J.
Kermit, Robert
Kaup, E & Cummings
Kerr, Wm.
Kinney, George
Kimball, R. B.
Kelly, James
Kuyler, A.
Kuypers, S. M.D.
Kerr
Keeler, W.
Kissam, L.
Kipp, S. & A. Brown
Knox, Cahoun & McClintock
Kelley, Joel
Kennedy, Thomas
Kingman, M. E.
Kennedy, John A.
Kerr, Wm.
Kirby, Wm.

Kellogg, J. W.
Kelley, Luke
Kidd, W. E.
Knapp, W. H.
Kimbark, E. H. M.D.
Klots, J. T.
Knox, James
Kent, B.
Kean, Ann
King, John, per C. C. Darling
Ketchum, H.
Kearney, E.
Kurshedi, A.
Kirby, L.
Knox, J. M.
Kissam, R. S., M. D.
Kinsley, H., M. D.
Kirby, V.
Kissam, D. Doct.
Kennedy, W.
Kerr, John
Kinck, Wm.
Karr, Mrs.
Kidder, Mr.
Kellock
Kelly, Joel
King, John
Killen, A.
Kimbark, E. H., M. D.
Knouse, Charles
Kelly, Philip
Kingsland, A.
Knox, P. H.
Kattenhorn & Roman
Koster, M.
Knapp, C. & Co.
King, A. G.
Kennedy, J. A.
Kelley, F. M.
Koop, Fischer & Co.
Kissam & Keeler
King, Wm.
Kiggings & Kellogg
Knoepfel, H. W.
K. & S.
Ketcham, T.
Knowlton, D.
King, Rufus S.
King, J. B.
Kemp, Wm.
Knapp, W. H.
Knapp, James H.
Kipp, F. A.
Ketcham, E. C.
Knipe, Wm.
Kirkman, J.
Keys, John
Knower, E. D.
Ketcham, Philip
Kennedy, Thomas
Knauth, Theodore
Ketchum, E., Mrs
Keyser, Mary
King, Wm.
Keys, D.

Kelly, Daniel
Knapp, James

L.

Lenox, James
Lenox, Misses, The
Lorillard, Peter
Laight, E W.
Lawrence, Joseph
Langdon, W.
Laight street, 28
Lord, Rufus L.
Le Roy, Jacob
Lord, Daniel
Livingston, Mrs.
Loeschigk, Wesendonck & Co.
Loder, B.
Lawrence, Richard,
Laight, W E.
Livingston, M & A.
Leavenworth, H.
Lane, W. J.
Lottimer & Large
Lee, James & Co.
Lowrie, Walter
Livingston, C. R.
Lord & Taylor
Lydig, P.
Laverty, H.
Larkin, T. O.
Lane, J.
Low, N.
Livingston, Maturin
Livingston, Mortimer
Lawrence, Isaac
Leary, John
Loomas, E., Mrs.
Leavy, John
Lynes, S. C.
Le Compt, V.
Low, J.
Lownds, R.
Lentilhon, E.
Lamson, C.
Lane, D.
Lawrence, A. H., Mrs
Lowery, J.
Livingston, A.
Livingston, J. R.
Le Barbier
Livingston, L.
Leeds, S.
Leggett, A. A.
Le Boutillier, Thomas
Lambert, J.
Lockwood, R.
Ludlum, N.
Love, Thomas
Loines, W. H.
Loutrell, W. M.
Lent, George
Lowber, Mr.
Levy, K.

1852) LIST OF MEMBERS. 61

Lowery, Seman
Largent, M.
Little, E. B.
Levy & Jones
Luhrs, A. & N.
Lugar, S. G.
Leggett, Joseph
Little, S. W.
Lyons, Samuel
Lewis & Woodruff
Lathrop & Luddington
Lamphier, J. P.
Leary & Co.
Lilienthal & Co.
Long, J. A.
Le Compte, V.
Le Compte, Nicholas
Legrave, J.
Legrave, A.
Ludlum, N. S.
Little, C.
Langdon, T. W.
Lynch, P.
Liscom, H. P.
Lilienthal, L.
Luther & Hampton
Little, A.
Lee, W. H.
Levins, Mr.
Leonard, Miss
Little, E. P.
Litton, James
Lane, N.
Latton, L.
Low, John
Lyon, A. M.
Leckie, Wm.
Lester, A. & Co.
Lee & Case
Lord, J Couper
Lawrence, F.
Lownds, Thomas
Ludlow, E. H.
Lawrence, E. N.
Lord, Samuel P.
Litchfield & Co.
Lippincott. H. A., Mrs.
Ludlum, Henry
Lehmaier, Brothers
Loder & Co,
Litchfield, Jervis, & Co.
Lenhmann, Charles
Leverick
Lord, J C.
Locke, John D.
Long & Davenport
Lovett. Southwick & Co.
Little, Charles S.
Lang, L.
Liese, Frederick
Leonard & Wendt
Leon, H.
L. B. R.
Lewis, P. & H. & Brother
Lothrop, Wm. K.
Lane, George W.

Leet, Allen N.
Leary, James
Leigh, C. C.
Leonard, M G.
Lowerie, Wm.
Latting, J. J.
Lee, J. A.
Lee, W. P.
Lee, John, Jr.
Lewis, J. W.
Long, Mr.
Loewenthal, Simon
Leggett, A.
Lawrence, W. E.
Little, A.
Lewis, J. S.
Laird, J. M.
Lombard, L. L.
Loss, Francis H.
Lester, Jo eph W.
Leweck & Cahn
Lorre, S. A.
Lounsbury, N.
Lane, George
Lay, G. C , Mrs.
Lother, Thomas
Lyon, Eliphalet
Levy, Louis
Lowe, B.
Leonard, W. B.
Livingston, Mr.
Lynch
Longstreet, Samuel
Lovejoy, Reuben
Lewis, W. &. N. S. C.
Lynch, James
Lindeman, Wm.
Lockwood, F.
Lee, Laniel
Libby, D.
Lane, M. H.
Lee, David
Leverich, Mrs.
Lawrence, G. N. L.
Laqueer, R.
Lathrop, Mrs.
Le Coutch la de Cumont, A.
Lanier, J. B.
Lawrence, R. & A. R.
Lee. G., Knapp & Palen
Le Roy, T. O. & Co.
Littell, E. B. &. Co.
Lightbody, John G.
Lockwood, H.
Lander, T. D.
Ludlum, W.
Livesey, Jane, Mrs.
Lawrence, Richard
Lewis, Charles D.
Lyon, S. L.
Lyon, S.
Lane, J. A.
Lyles, Henry
Leveridge, J.
Lamb, Anthony
Leeds, Gurdon J.

Lewis, Dr.
Lewis. Isaac
Livingston, Schuyler
Livingston, R. C.
Lefferts, Marshall
Lineathall, Dr. Rev.
Lane, R.
Livingston, Mrs.
Lee, W.
Link, Mrs.
Lockwood, Frederick
Love, John
Lewis, Richard B.
Lewis, R.
Lockwood, H.
Litton, James
Lowerre, George W.
Lee, Daniel F.
Lestrade, J. P., Rev.
Leggett, Gilbert
Little, James
Lounsberry, Nehemiah
Lord, Benjamin
Long, N. R.
Lord, Daniel D.

M.

Minturn, Sarah, Mrs.
Munn, Stephen B.
Minturn, Robert B.
Moore, N. F.
Murray, John R.
Murrey, Miss
Moran & Iselin
Mali, H. W. T. & H.
M. T.
Merritt, Bliss & Co.
Mooney, Edward, Mrs.
M'Namee, T.
Morgan, M.
Murray, J. B.
Marsh, James
Miller, H.
Mackay, W.
Morgan, H. T.
Mackay, A.
Mortimer, R.
Martin, William C.
Meakim, John
McCall & Strong
Marsh, Samuel
Maitland, Robert, Mrs.
Maitland, Robert L.
Morse, Sidney E.
Macy, Josiah
Mott, Willi m F.
Mitchell, W., & Blair
Moore, Mrs.
M'Vicar, Mrs.
Mott, W. F., Jr.
Mortimers & Gawtry
Merritt, Miss (per A. W Murray)
Mitchell, J. W., Mrs.

LIST OF MEMBERS. (1852.

Mann, E. J.
Morris, Mrs.
Miller, Hiram
Murray, John
Murphy, William, M. D.
Myers, John
Mead, Ardon
Marsh John R.
Mollard, John
Merritt, Stephen
Moore, R. W.
Macfarlan, D. T.
Mack, Enoch, Rev.
McCoun, H.
Mathison, R.
McPherson, Peter
M'Curdy, R. H.
Mackie, John
Mechanics' Shirt Store
McIlvaine S. R.
M., William
Meday, C. H.
Marshall, Charles H.
McVicker, C. Mrs.
Moir, J.
Mead, M. Mrs.
Mackenzie, G.
Mitchell, W.
Minton, S. C., Mrs.
Morris, A. Mrs.
Magie, D., Jr.
Morris, G. W.
Mount, A. R.
Mann, E. J.
Mathews, George
Meffet, James G.
Munroe, Alfred & Co.
McRey, Mrs.
Miller, Mrs.
Martin, Mr.
Morrison, J.
Martin, R. W.
Monroe, Ebenezer
Morton & Murray
May, Mrs.
Marshall, M.
Mesler
Miller, J. B.
Montgomery, S. J.
McFarlan, A.
Moorehouse, Mr.
Morris, S. P.
Maverick
Mooney, Mr.
McCalden, William
Marshall, W. H.
Miller, G. B. Mrs
McKinley, Mrs.
Mitchell
McIntire, C. H.
McClane, Mr.
Maverick
Mills, Abner
Mallory, S. C.
McPherson, P.
Myers, S. P.

Mackrell & Simpson
McLelland, Thomas
Mills, Andrew
Miller, A.
Metzker, Christian
Moreau, F.
Morgan, James
McCrary, J. D.
McCrary, H.
Martin, Dr.
Mott, B.
Mank, H.
Mather, W. H.
McKennie, D.
McGruger, P.
M. & T.
Mead, Belcher & Co.
Martin, Mulford
Mills & Co.
Muirheid & Clark
Michol, M.
Main & Adams
Miller, G. J. & Co.
Mabbat, S. R.
Martin, A. A.
Marsh & Northrop
Morford & Vermilye
Mettler, Wilson
Miner, Israel
Mowbray, J. M.
Meeks, J. & I. W.
McKenny, John
McWhorten, A.
Mass, G.
Morton, John
Martin, Edward
McLaren, William,
Merry, C. H.
Mott, J. C. & Co.
Morrison & Allen
McLaughlin, Daniel
Moore, William M.
Maunder, William
McAuley, Charles
Maxwell, Mrs.
Martin, W. A.
Martins, John B.
Maxwell, Mr.
McMurry, R.
Main, R. W.
Mettler, Samuel
Martin, D. R.
Morton, W. Q.
Mortimer, F. R.
Moore, J. C.
Mott, Mr.
McAuley, Mrs.
McDonald, A. B.
Merrick, David
Menck, William
Meigs, J. T.
Monee, Mary A. Mrs.
Moller, Sands & Riera
Meads & Co.
Morewood, George B.
Macy, C. A.

Meliss & Ayres
Moore, T. D.
Meeker, Herbert & Perkins
McKenzie. R.
Maghee, Thomas H.
Muller, A. H.
M. & A.
Miner, A. B.
Massie & Mitchell
Middleton & Co.
Mitchell, M.
M. & I.
Merrill, N. W.
McKesson, John
Mason & Law
Martin & Lawson
Morrison, William
M. & H.
Moore & Baker
Morgan, James L.
Morgan, A. U.
M. Thomas
McLeish, Allen
Moller, William
Man, Robert J.
McGaw, John A.
McLachlen, Alexander
McCarren, Michael
Meyers, John S.
Mason, J. M.
McGay, James
McKimm, W. R.
Mumford, B. A.
Miller, E.
Merserau, J. W.
Mitchell, J. T.
Meigs, H. Jr.
McCready, B., M. D.
Meigs, C. A.
Maltbie, E.
Many, Vincent W.
McKewan, John
Moore, S. V. R.
Moore, E. D.
Maze, Abraham
Maxwell, James T.
Miller, S. R.
Malloy, R. S.
McKernan, D.
Miles, W. B.
Marven, John B.
Muford, T. N.
Miles, A.
Man & Son
Moore, Henry
Munson, Robert
McDonough, T. R.
McKee, J.
McDonough, S. Mrs.
Morrison, Abraham
McCartin, B.
Mayhew, Mr.
McCarrick, Mrs.
Michalis, Dr.
Monholland, John
McCue, M. Mrs.

1852.) LIST OF MEMBERS. 63

Moore, James
Moores, C. W.
Merrill, Chas.
Merrill, M.
Moss, R. E.
Marmedell, F.
Mead, Mrs.
McKenzie, John
Mather, Elihu
Moubry, John
Myers, Jas.
Marsh, John R.
Misplee, S. Mrs.
Misplee, S.
McLoughlin, M. B. Mrs.
Martin, R.
Morrison, David
Miller, Humphry
McClaury, James, M.D.
Mix, Isaac, Jr.
McGay, Isaac
McGraw, N.
Morton & Bremner
Morgan, Henry
Menzies, Wm.
Martin, Alfred
Moses, Lorenzo
Moore, Alfred
Murray, Wm.
McGrath, George
Miner, F. S.
Morrison, M. E. Miss
McFadden, W. J.
Munson & Wright
McLeod, J. N.
Murphy, Thos. S.
Morrison, David
McCaddin, H.
Mealio, L.
Miner & Havens
McGrath, Judge
Macy, W. H.
Mulligan, J.
Mitchell, E. Mrs.
Markoe, T. M., M.D.
Mead, Wm.
Maghee, J. H.
Mildeberghei, C. Mrs.
Martin, P.
Marshall, Thos. W.
Morris, J. L.
McCready, Mrs.
Murray, John B.
Merle, Charles
Mowton
Madison Ave. Pres. Church
Myers, John K.
Miller, W. P.
Mattison & Isham
Morrell, Thos.
Mathey, A.
Moore, S. W.
Meyer, E.
Marsh, B.
Moffatt, David
Merle, G.

McKenny, Thos. R.
Matthews, Wm.
Mannherty, Wm.
Mullins, D.
McAlpine, D. H.
Moore, J. L.
McDowell, Joseph
Millbank, Samuel
Millbank, J.
Mott, J. W.
Morgans, Morgan
Martin, Sheldon
McNorman, D. C.
Mott, W. T., Jr.
Mortimer, John, Jr.
McComb, John
Miller, Sidney G.
Macomber, Edward
McLeod, Misses
Miles, Chas.
McAllister, Mrs.
McCollum, Mrs.
McCormick, Patrick
Milnor, Chas. E.
Murray, Robt. J.
March, Nathaniel
Morrison, J. M.
March, J. P.
May, Thos P.
Martin, Samuel
Miles, Wm.
Mead, R., Jr.
McCreary, John D.
Morris, Dr.
Morris, E.
Manchester, Jas.
Macfarlan, T.
Messerole, A.
Middlebrook, S. Mrs.
Mason, M. W. Mrs.
Mathison, R.
Millward, J.
Mitchell, Marcus
Moore, J. L.
McClain, O. D.
Miller, Jacob S., M.D.
Mills, Abner
Merrill, Charles
Murray, Alexander W.
Miller, H.
Marsh, James
Matcalf, J. W. M.D.
Mather, F. E.
Miller, J. C.
Mackay, W. G.
Miller, J. W.
Macy, Wm. A.
McIntire, John
Mood, Peter
Mason, Charles
Matthews, J. H.
Marshall, Benjamin, M.D.
Marshall, Benj. Jr., M.D.
McNaughton, A. P.
Marten, Wm.

N

Niblo, Wm.
Nevins, R. H.
Nevins, D. H.
Nevius, P. I., Jr.
Noyes, Curtis W.
Newhouse, B.
Newton, N.
Neagles, Mrs.
Neil, Mrs.
Nash, T. H.
Nichols, Dr.
Newman, E. H.
Newcomb, Mrs.
Neefus, P. W.
Nesmith, John P.
Nicoll, S. T.
Nevius, P. I.
Nevins, G. P.
Noyes, O. H. P.
Negus, T. S.
Newbury, W. B.
Naylor & Co.
Nelson, Wm.
North, Brothers
N. J Jr. & Co.
Norton, C. L.
Nelson, E. D.
Norwood, A. S.
Nelson, J. P.
Nagle, C.
Nichols, Wm. B.
Newell, G. T.
Nostrand, C. Mrs.
Nichols C. L. Mrs.
Nietsch, Chas. F.
Newton, Chas. F.
Nash, Wm. F.
Nostrand, Edward
Northrop, C. B.
Negus, Thomas
Neeves, Jas.
Nichols, Jas.
Newell, D. C.
Nash, S. P.
Nash, Stephen
Newell, Mr.
Norris. Noah
Nash, L.
Naylor, P.
Napier, Thos.
Norris, R. T.
Newton, J.
Nash, Lora (Foreman o Sheriff's Jury)
Noble, J.
Newbold, George
Nathan, Edward
Nichol, John
Nash, Wm. F.
Nash, Lorin

O.

Ogsbury, F. W.

LIST OF MEMBERS. (1852.

Osgood, J. Rev.
Okill. M. Mrs.
Oothout, H.
Oelrich & Co.
Obermaier, Isaac
Osborne, Abner
Overhiser, A.
Ostrand, Chas.
Orr, R. B.
Orvis, F H.
Oakly & Fox
Oiwell & Co.
O'Meara, J.
O'Rourke, P.
Otto, Henry
O'Brien John
Ogden & Co.
Ostrander, C. P.
Olyphant's Sons
O. L. & T. Co.
Owen, James
Oppenheim, J. M.
Oothout, W.
Onderdonk, Levi
Oakley, J. B.
Olmsted, C.
Osborn, B. W.
Odell, J. A.
Osborn, W. W.
Ostrander, G.
Olliff, Wm.
Oldring, H. J.
Orchard, Isaac, Rev.
Ogden, H. M.
Ogilvie, Wm.
O'Brien, W.
O'Rorke, James, M.D.
Osborne, C. F.
Oakey, Daniel
Ogden, E. D.
Owen, D.
Owen, E. H.
Oakley, T. J. Mrs.
Owen, James, Mrs.
Ogden, P. T.
Ockerhausen, A. F.
Owen, Thomas
Ortley, The Misses
Ogden, Henry
Ogden, H. W., Capt. U.S.N.
Oakland, Michigan
Ogden, Ludlow, Mrs.
Ogden, T. W.
Ogden, R. H.
Ogden, Alfred
Owens
Ostrom, J. P
Ogden, J. W.

P.

Pendleton, E. H.
Phalen, James
Parker, Willard, M.D.
Post, G. D.

Palmer, J. J.
Palmer & Newcomb
Phelps, R.
Porter, M.
Phillips, J. W.
Pell, A.
Pell, Walden
Potter, J. A.
Phillips, Lewis
Parsons, A. B. Mrs.
Parsons, W. B.
Pickersgill, W. C.
Penfold & Schuyler
Penfold, John
Phelps, Anson G., Jr.
Pease & Murphy
P. S. (West Point)
Page, P. P.
Peyser, D. M.
Pell, James K.
Pierce, George & Co.
Pond, James O., M.D.
Post, Wm.
Pratt, Edward, Rev.
Pattison, Robert
Place, R. S.
Pierson, Ira C.
Place, J. K.
Parker, John C.
Power, J. N.
Phair, Jas.
Patterson, John
Phillips, W.
Price, James
Pearson, C. B.
Peck, Gideon
Parr, J.
Pringle, Wm.
Patridge, C.
Phelps, G.
Phelps, J. N.
Putnam, T.
Phelps, J. J.
Platt, N. C.
Peet, E.
Post, A. C., Dr.
Platt, G. W.
Phyfe, J. M.
Peters, J. C., M.D.
Post & Young
Putnam, Betsey
Phalon, Mr.
Pirsson, J. P.
Porter & Fairchild
Price, James
Peck, E. Mrs.
Piggott, Mr.
Pool, Mrs.
Parsles, Abrm.
Parker, Mrs.
Parrish. Jas.
Perry, Mrs.
Pachtmann, F. W.
Princk & Russell
Patterson, S. P.
Pearson, E.

Palmer, Abraham A.
Powers & Schoonmaker
Peterschen, John
Parr, John
Philips, John P.
Price, James
Phillips, John I.
Post, A. K.
Prentice, Thomas
Price, Wm.
Putnam & Co.
Partridge, S. M.
Paynlee, J. G.
Proddow & Beach
Patton & Co.
Paynter, W. P.
Park, R. W.
Packer, Chas.
Phyfe, Duncan
Potter, F.
Peet, Munson S.
Pfirrmann, C. & J. P.
Potter, Ellis
Ponsot, George
Paillet, Henry
Pierson, Dr.
Patrullo, Andrew
Pfeiffer, C. F.
Peet, J. Lewis
Peet, Edward
Peet, E. B.
Peet, H. B.
Potter, Mrs.
Peet, H. P.
Peet, H. P. Mrs.
P. A.
Prescott, J. M.
Palanca, R.
Pavenstedt E.& Schumacher
P. & V. D.
P. A. B. & C.
Patterson, Almy
Poag, John
Patterson & Price
Plume, George T.
Perry, Samuel
P. & M.
P. H. & D.
Pettibone, A. H.
Picot, M. A.
Pine Street (36)
Pattison, James
Prentice, J. H. & Co.
Peckham, A. G.
Paton & Co.
Paret, John
Pool, Pentz, & G 'n
Prosser, Thos. & Son
P. & J.
Perlee, R. N.
Pike, D. B.
P.
Pixley, A.
Parkhurst
P. D.
Petrie, James S.

1852.) LIST OF MEMBERS. 65

Platt, George
Price, E. V.
Pentz, W. A. T.
Price, Wm.
Parker, John A.
Pearse, A. F.
Portington, H.
Post, Washington
Peugnet, H.
Pearson, S. H.
Potter, S. B.
Pray, Henry
Prall, H. R.
Phillips, Dr.
Price, C. W.
Parker, Benjamin
Parker, A.
Patterson, H. A. & Bros.
Pell, R. M.
Parmalee, S. N. Mrs.
Polhemus, Margt. Mrs.
Parker, Samuel
Place, E. B.
Perine, P.
Place, Jas. K.
Pearson, C. B.
Panne, E. H.
Peacock, E. T.
Pope, Henry
Prague, D.
Pearsall, Robt.
Pootan, Wm.
Pratt, John R.
Parsons, C.
Prankard, John B.
Prime, J. D.
Peck, J. D.
Polhamus, John
Pease, John
Pomroy, J. B.
Powers, T.
Prout, Wm. F.
Pecare, Jacob
Paxton, J. R.
Palmer, John
Pollock, Jas.
Pistol, Philip F.
Peck, Henry W.
Pugsley, T.
Patton, Wm. Rev.
Pierce, Abm. Mrs.
Page, T.
Pike, Benjamin, Jr.
Porter, Robert
Pierce, George
Phelps, Wm.
Pell, W.
Paine, J.
Prime, Edward
Pomroy, A. H.
Parkins, Thomas
Purdy, John
Post, J. A. Mrs.
Parker, J. C.
Pettigrew, John
Phelps, Anson G.

Phelps, T. W.
Pearson, Adam
Planten, H.
Patterson, Wm. C.
Price, David W.
Phillips, Samuel
Price, Thompson
Pryer, James
Poillon, Richard
Pinkney, T. W.
P. W.
Place, R. S.
Patrick, Richard
Platt, E.
Page, P. P.
Platt, J.
Penfold, Wm.
Polhamus, H. A.
Prior, Mr.
Polhamus, A.
Post
Perry, Samuel
Packwood, M. A; Mrs.
Pentz, Adam P.
Pryn, John
Palmer, C.
Pomroy, Mrs.
Prentiss, Rev. Dr.
Purdy, Dr.
Porter
Place, Charles
Pearsall, John
Pearson, A.
Page, E. W.

Q.

Quinby, Brothers
Quackinbush, David
Quackinbush, A. S.
Quackinbush, B.
Quinn, Jas. A.
Quackenbos, M. M.

R

Roosevelt, C. V. S.
Roosevelt & Son
Riveira & Baldwin
Rudderow, J. & Co.
Reynolds, Mrs.
Robertson, J. A.
Russell, A.
Ray, Robert
Rogers, G. P.
Rogers, John, Mrs., by Dr. B. Ogdon
Robinson, Nelson
Robbins & Son, G. G.
Rhinelander, W. C.
Remsen, Henry R.
Ray, Richard
Richards, Guy
Russell, C. H.

Rashaw, J. A. F.
Roosevelt, J. Mrs.
Russell, W. H.
Rigney, Thomas
Read, Taylor & Co.
Rogers, T.
Ray, Richard Mrs.
Rees, Brothers & Co.
Redman, Charles H.
Russell, Mrs.
R...., Sarah
Rogers, E.
Robinson, Edward
Reeve, Henry
Ross, J. H., M.D.
Roth, W., M.D.
Reed, A.
Reese, J. Jr.
Ray, W. G.
Remsen, Wm.
Riggs, A., M.D.
Renwick, James
Renwick, M. A.
Ray, Mary, Miss
Robert, J. R.
Romain, S. B.
Robert, M. Mrs.
Russell, W. H
Rich, S. A.
Robins, J.
Roux, A.
Robert, J. H.
Russell, John
Roshore, John
Requa, Austin
Rocksfellow, Rufus
Reed, Julia, Mrs.
Rikeman, Rachel, Mrs.
Russell
Roberts, Dr.
Ringold, J. P.
Rodh, David
Robinson, Mrs.
Rowe, W.
Robins, C. L.
Roberts, George
Riley, Francis O.
Rothchild, B.
Rosman, N.
Robinson, P.
Ransom, J. H.
Rianhard, Starling, & McMurdie
Radcliff, F. E.
Randel, J.
Rait, Robert
Rosenbaun, M.
Russell & Dunham
Rosenbock, Mr.
Riley, S. T.
Ritters, Wm.
Riggs, A.
Rogers, John
Romer, John
Randell, Henry
Rankin & Co.

LIST OF MEMBERS. (1852.

Redfield, W. C.
Roberts, P.
Ryder, S. H.
Randolph, J. F., Jr.
Randolph, J. F.
Rich, James
Redfield, J. H.
Reade street, No. 3
Rowland, Mr. Rev.
Rankin, E. E.
Rumsey, J. W.
Rodewald, Brothers
Redmond, Wm.
Richardson, E.
Rainer & Downer
Rose, W. M.
Rushton, Joseph
Rosenheim & Brother
Recknagle & Schwab
Ross, Andrew
Robbins & Brother
Russell, N. E.
Rich, Josiah
Raynolds, C. T.
Raymond & Fullerton
Rohe, J. A.
R. H. A.
Rosselot, P. A.
Rozat
Richards & Johnston
Raymond, H. I.
Reynolds, P.
Reid, George W.
Roosevelt, S.
Rudd, Joseph
Roe, O. W.
Rowland, C. N. S.
Rogers, James T.
Robbins & Van Ostrand
Roach, P. R.
Ritter, W.
Rosenfield, M. H.
Russell, R.
Ramsey, David
Remsen, John
Riley, John
Rumnay, Mrs.
Rogers, C. H.
Ryder, Edgar T.
Richards, Richard
Raynor, J.
Raynor, H.
Robins, David
Revnolds, Lewis
Robinson, E. C.
Rhodes, Martha, Mrs.
Reynolds, J. S.
Reeve, S.
Randall, E.
Riker, Daniel
Robinson, Mr.
Robinson, Wm.
Russell, Hiram
Reed, Nathaniel
Richter, Daniel
Rosenburg, I.

Rodgers, B.
Rosenbrat, S. S.
Roberts, N.
Riker, John L.
Raper, B W.
Raynor, Samuel
Rankin & Ray
Rockwell, Charles
Rush, H. B.
Riley, Asher
Roome, Charles
Ruthven, James
Robinson, H. W.
Ranney, E W.
Rodgers, George A.
Rojas, P. T.
Reed, Wm.
Rogers, Mr.
Roberts & Rees
Rader, M.
Rauch, John H.
Rowell, C S.
Rosevelt, S. W.
Russell
Rising, Mrs.
Robinson, Douglass, Mrs.
Rockwell, J. S.
Reese & Hoyt
Rose, J. Jr.
Rafferty & Leask
Rodgers, P. P.
Randolph
Riker, A.
Roe, F. A. & Co.
Rosenblat
Ritch, H. L.
Ramsey, James C.
Redfield, J. H.
Richards, Thomas B.
Roome, Charles
Rumsey, J. W.
Reeve, James
Ruston, J.
Ryerson, H. W.
Roberts, Charles
Rusher, C. H.
Ryers, T R.
Rowell, W.
Roberts, Edward
Redman, C. H.
Reed, R.
Ranney, L., M.D.

S.

Spencer, Wm. A., Capt.
Skidmore, Samuel T.
Schermerhorn, Peter
Sampson, Joseph
Schermerhorn, Augus's, Mrs.
Suydam, Reed & Co.
Stevens, R. L.
Stevens, John L.
Stevens, John
Schuyler, Misses, The
Syms, S. R.

Siffkin & Ironside
Schuchardt & Gebhard
Schermerhorn, Banker & Co.
Saltus, Frances
Spies, Christ & Co.
Stone, W. W.
Stone & Starr
Smith, W. H. & Co.
Smith, Samuel G.
Smith, Lemuel
St. Jurgo, Rivera
Strang, Adriance & Co.
Slosson, John
Shenfe, J F.
Suarez, L. S.
Smith, Cornelius
Staples, Seth P.
Schenck, W. J.
S. W. D.
S.
Scheiffelin, H. M.
Stewart, R. L. & A.
S. A R., by H. Rogers
Strong, George A.
Sturges, Jonathan
Smith, W. Alexander
Schieffelin & Brothers
Stevens, John A.
Sheldon, F.
Sheldon, H.
Swords, C. R.
Schieffelin, P. Haines & Co.
Shepherd, E. F.
Sabine, Dr.
Sanford, M.
S. A. F.
Swan, Caleb
Southart & Kissam
Setlington, H. D., & L. Russell, Mount Airy, Highland County, Va.
Scott, John W., M.D.
Schermerhorn, John
Swords, M. H.
Sweeny, Dr.
Stuyvesant, P. G., Mrs.
Stuyvesant, G.
Smith, Henry
Staniford, D. T.
Shopp, George
Slote, John
Savage, C. C.
Schoonmaker, J. O.
Shaffer, J. N
Sewell, John G., M.D.
Stevens, Alexander H., M.D.
Scott, John W., M.D., per C. C. Darling
Smith, U. J.
Scribner, C.
Strong, C. E.
Sandford, J. S.
Sandford, L. H.
Sedgwick, W. E.
Stout, A. G.

1852.)   LIST OF MEMBERS.   67

Smith, Adon
St. John, C.
Suydam, J., Mrs.
Sprague, R.
Shiff, Mrs.
Stevens, B. K.
Swan, B. L., Jr.
Stevens. B.
Starr, N.
Southmayd, A.
Suydam, D. R.
Seymour, M.
Scribner, U. R.
Stagg, B.
Simpson, A.
Seguine, C.
Scharfenberg & Luis
Strauss, Simon
Smith, S. C., Mrs.
Scott, W.
Spies, Adam W.
Steele, Wm., M.D.
Spycer. Mrs.
Starr, Charles Jr.
Smith & Crane
Scott, Alexander
Sherwood & Chapman
Simonds, Louis
Smith, A. S.
Stephens, J.
Shultz, Mrs.
Scudder, Mrs.
Smith, Dr.
Stephens, Mrs.
Stebbins, Mrs.
Silcox, J. J.
Seymour, J. F.
Sharrock, Dr.
Seymour, Isaac N.
Stoffard, Rodman
Skidmore, Stephen H.
Stillman, Allen & Co.
Sperry, John
Simonson, T.
Sybell, W. E.
Sudlow & Siney
Sybell, George
Sterns, J. G.
Smith, Milton G.
Simonson, C. M.
Summers, A. B.
Savage, James O.
Savage, Peter
Sprague, Samuel
Stillman, Hall
Smith, Samuel G.
Sawin, Henry & Co.
Squires, Capt.
Sheffield, Dudly
Spellman, W. B.
Stukey, E.
Sybell, B. B.
Scuts, Louis
Sanford, Nathan
Sloper, C. S.
Shultz, Louis

Seaman, C.
Smith, C. E.
Smith, R.
Skeel, R. W.
Suydam, James
Salsbury & Co.
Smith, Dean, & Eddy
Stebbins & Co.
Smith, S. B.
Sagehorn & Kornahrens
Schoot, George
Solomons, Mr.
Solomons & Hart
Sloane, Wm.
Sears, H.
Smith, Richard
Skinner, H. N.
Stockbridge, B.
Sumner, P.
Suydam, S. A.
Serrell, L.
Strange & Brother
Sears & Hyde
Smith & Barker
Seignett, A.
Schafer, Dr.
Smilee, Dr.
Sayr, Mrs.
Sanford, General
Stellings, Mr.
Schmelzel. G.
Smith, J. E.
Skillman, Joseph
Sears, Wm.
Smith, H. J.
Simonton, R.
St. John & Raymond
Slawson, A.
Smith, J. McCune, M.D.
Smith, E.
Swift, E. H.
Smedburgh, Mrs.
Stuart, J. J.
Stuart, J.
Smith, W. D.
Symms, W.
Smith, James
Sherman, George E.
Smith, T. U.
Strahlheim, S.
Smith, S. T.
Sanger, L.
Sampson, George G.
Scrymser, James
Stuart, J. M.
Scheuer, Joseph
Smythe, F. A.
Snow & Heartley
Shipman, C. H.
St. John, Milton
Schwendler, Frederick
Syz, Irminger & Co.
Sage, R. F.
Schulten, J. W. & Hurd
Stewart, Thomas J.
Smith, N. Denton

Spencer, G. G.
Sus, A. W.
Stalker, Thomas
Sandford, H. J.
Staples, George W.
Schieffelin, James L.
Schieffelin, B.
Spaulding, H. F.
Swift, Hurlbut & Co.
Schiffer, S. & Brother
Strybing, Henry
Scoville Manufacturing Co.
Stringer & Townsend
Sunder, G.
Smith, T. & Co.
Stokes, Henry
Sweetzer, J. A.
S. A S.
S. B. S.
Smith, J. S.
Sillecks
Sill & Thomson
Smith, Thomas T.
Schuster, P. F.
Starr, Fellows & Co.
S. F. & Co.
Struller, Louis
Schulting, H.
S. E.
Simon, John R.
Sawyer & Hobby
Smith, E. L.
Stranger
Smith, Pascal B.
Sagory, Charles
Stiles, Samuel
Stiles, J. C.
Southmayd, Horace
Sherman, Doctor
Sage, G. E.
Schlesinger, F. S.
Scrymser, W. H.
Soper, Abraham
Senior, E. H.
Sandford, P. Mrs.
Seaman, H. I.
Scudder, Linus
Spencer, Mark
Sheppard, G. G.
Stagg, John
Shutts, P. J.
Sage, W. B.
Suydam, Lambert
Syz, F. G.
Storms, W. J.
Stokes, B. G.
Sykes, L. A.
Secor, Z.
Southmayd, S. C.
Smith, Charles
Seaman, H. J.
Stewart, James
Sutton, George
Scudder, W. H.
Stainle, Frederick
Skinner, T. H., Rev.

LIST OF MEMBERS. (1852.

Scott, J. D.
Smillie, James
Stephens, J. H.
Sacket, C. D.
Stitt, George S.
Shannon, William
Sarvin, David
Sanford, M. B.
Sterens, A.
Stark, J. M.
Stark, Mrs.
Salisbury, John S
Stanley, William W.
Spencer, O. F., Jr.
Seaman, J. F.
Simpson, William
Scribner, A. S.
Stout, A. V.
Smith, Noah
Smith, R. E.
Stanly, A.
Smith, J. J.
Short, John
Summervill, M.
Schoot, C.
Seabury, J. L.
Stickney, Charles
Shields, Charles
Smith, H. A.
Smith, James R.
Schultz, Charles
Smith, H. F.
Smith, C. E.
Summers, William
Suydam, Henry
Smith, E. L.
Sammis, D. P.
Smith, Shadrach
Silverman, Jacob
Sheldon, Henry
Smith, Peter
Silver, James
Sharot, A. H.
Sneeden, John
Shipman, William
Stickney, C. L.
Squire & Brother
Schoot, L.
Staples, J.
Strong, T.
Smith, J. T. S.
Selpho, William
Smith, C. W.
Sammis, A. D. B.
Scarf, George
Schenck, C. Mrs.
Schenck, J. W.
Schenck, C. C.
Spencer, W.
Seymour, J. K.
Stoddart, Alexander
Stewart, J. M.
Sherman, Gardiner
Sutherland, William
Shotwell, Mr.
Smilie, W. C.

Smith, Floyd
Salisbury, W. D.
Spaulding, J.
Stebbins, Mrs.
Shannon, R. W.
Stevens, Mrs.
Scudder, Salmon
Schell, H. S.
Spinner, Samuel
Stephenson, A. G. Mrs.
Smith, William H.
Smith, James T.
Spence, F.
Sanford, Charles
Stoughton, William B.
Stouvend, T. B.
Smith, C.
Sloan, Henry S.
Stoppani, C. G.
Schaffer, C. N.
Shaw, James M.
Skiddy, William
Sanderson, E. F.
Smith, Sheldon
Suydam, C.
Smith, J. Augustus, M. D.
Stone, R. C.
Strong, J. W. K.
Smith, George G.
Satterlee, G. C.
Speir, G. M.
Skiddy, William
Scott, W. B.
Sherman, W. B.
Scheiffelin, Richard L.
Schoals, F. P.
Summers, Sebastian
Stansbury, Mrs.
Smith, F. H.
Scheiffelin, S. S. Miss
Scheiffelin, Helen M. Miss
Suydam, J.
Smull, Thomas
Scott, Thomas
Smith, Silas C.
Sather & Church
Simpson, J. B. & I.
Schwartz, Theo.
Spitzer, S.
Somerville, A. & M.
Summerhay, Mrs.
Smith, James
Saxton, John
Southack, J. W.
Sterling, Frederick A.
Sheldon, Preston
Seymour, W. N. & Co.
S. S. S.
Sands, A. B.
Snow, W. G.
Staniford, D. T.
Secor, T. F.
Sackett, A. M.
Shipman, S. D.
Smith, Isaac T.
Sackett, J. R.

Sutton, Silas
Stillwell, R.
Stewart, C. L.
Snediker, William
Smith, Walter M.
Scudder, Mr. Rev.
Smith, J. J.
Smith, Asa D., Rev.
Sanxay, John F.
Sharp, William
Smith, Adon
Stimson, A. L.
Smith, John Calvin
Sands, E. H.
Smith, Thomas E.
Seldon, Charles
Smith, B. R.
Sammis, Joel
Stansberry, J. F.
Sherwood, S. P.
See, H. P.
See, Leander
Stout, A. V.
Sherwood, J. W.
Smith, Samuel
Squire, Peter
Smith, D. C.
Schuler, J. W.
Stillwell, J. E.
Shannon, G. W.
Shaver, P. C.
Smith, G. D.
Stebbins, H. M.
Stelle, Nelson, M. D.
Sammis, Nelsen
Storer, George L.
Sullivan, Charles
Swords, H.
Smith, J.
Smith, A.

T.

Titus, James H.
Thorne, J. Mrs.
Trimble, George T.
Talbot, C. N.
Two Ladies, (F.)
Tiffany, Young & Ellis
Tarrant, James
Terbell, H. S.
Tweedy, O. B.
Tredwell & Gould
Tomes, Francis & Son
Tweedy, B.
Tredwell, Adam
Trenor, J.
T. M. R., by H. Rogers
Trow, J. F.
Taylor, George
Tracy, George Manning
Taylor, Moses B.
Trafford, Abraham
Taylor, C. G.
Tillotson, J. C.

LIST OF MEMBERS.

Thorndycke, J.
Tooker, J. S. Mrs.
Thorne, J.
Townsend, J. R. Mrs.
Treadwell, S.
Thurston, R. H.
Thompson, D.
Taylor, W. B.
Tallman, S. S.
Tilden, William
Trueman, J. S.
Tompson, Major
Thwing, C. & E. W.
Terry, D.
Titus, Erastus, Mrs.
Taylor, Mrs. and Mother
Thorn, W.
Tracy, Emily, Mrs.
Tate, (427 Broadway)
Towle & Son
Tripp, Mrs.
Taylor, J. C.
Teller, R. H.
Taff, Henry
Taff, David J
Tupper, C. W.
Tomlinson, J.
Taylor, Elizabeth
Thaooerner, C.
Trumpey, C.
Trech, Mr.
Tenney, I.
Titus, E.
Tripp, Mr.
Taylor, A.
Tucker, J. C.
Taylor, James
Tilton, S.
Tyson, William
Tredwell, E.
Tupper & Beebe
Tracy, M. C.
Terbell, Ruth, Mrs.
Tayntor, Asa
Truesdell, E. D.
Teets, Philip
Taylor, John
Tilley, W. R.
Tinson, R. N.
Taylor, J. D.
Tunison, G. D.
Titus, William M.
Tillotson, J.
Toole, W. S.
Trainor, Thomas
Thompson, John
Thompson, James
Terret, Mr.
Trumper, Peter
Taber Silence.
Thomas, C. W. & A.
Talman
Thompson, Jonathan
Trimble, M.
Terry, Samuel H.
Trevor, Mr.

T. P.
Tomes, Francis & Son
Tapscott, W. & J. T. & Co.
Trowbridge, Henry
Tiemann, D. F. & Co.
Tredwell, George C. & Co.
Taylor, Theodore B.
Tasker, William
Taft, A. H.
T. L.
Trow, William
Tabile, J. H.
Ten Brook, J.
Thurston, Charles C.
Townsend, J. H.
Tallmadge, F. A.
Tallman, Ab'm I.
Tousley C.
Trainor, D.
Tompkins, William B.
Thatford, Thomas
Timpson, C. B.
Tiebout, N.
Titus, Charles F.
Trafford, A.
Tylee, John
Tappen & Burd
Torrence & Tuttle
Taylor, John
Taylor, Isaac
Tappen, G.
Taylor, Isaac, Jr.
Tows, W. R.
Tucker, T. W.
T. W. C.
Turner, Professor
Thompson, William A.
Taggart, J. W., Rev.
Thorp, Edmund
Tyrrel, Caleb
Thompson, John
Thorn, Ebenezer
Thompson, J. B.
Thetton, T. B.
Templeton, Mrs.
Townsend, E.
Tucker, F. C.
Thorp, A.
Thomson, John, M. D.
Thorp, George W.
Timberlake, L.
Thompson, G. W.
Thorne. Mr.
Tracy, Charles
Townsend, Mrs.
Townsend, Miss
Tieman, George
Thorn, A. E.
Toal, Charles
Tatham, Benjamin
Tweed, R.
Thorp, H. S.
Truslow, James L.
Tillinghast, T.
Thompson
Truslow, William

Tallmadge, N. F.
Trugillo, M.
Tileson, William H.
Trotter, John
Thompson, G.
Thompson, A.
Torry, J.
Townsend, S., M. D.
Taylor, J. B.
Thayer, Warren
Thomas, George
Terry, David, Rev.
Taylor, A.
Tucker, D. N.
Traphagen, G. H., M. D
Terbell, Jeremiah
Terbell, H. S.
Tritton, Richard

U.

Underhill, James W.
Ubsdell & Pierson
Underhill, W , Jr.
Underwood, Joshua
Uhl, J.
Ustick, Richard
Underhill, J. S.
Underhill, Walter
Underhill, W. S.

V

Van Rensselaer, Alexander
Valarquez, Mariam
Van Winkle. E. S.
Van Wyck, H. L.
Van Antwerp, J.
Van Santvoord, C.
Vandervoort, J. B.
Vermilye, W. M.
Van Zandt, P. P.
Van Nostwick, W. B.
Van Hook, W.
Vliet. Simon
Van Saun, Ab.m.
Van Winkle, Dr.
Van Orden, Mr.
Valentine, Mrs.
Venables, Richard
Van Saun, H.
Van Pelt, S. S.
Van Kleek & Co., W. H.
Van Auken, B.
Vanduser, John, 231 Washington street.
Vassar, M.
Van Benschoten, J.
Voorhies, W.
Van Auken, Mrs.
Vought, Samuel
Verplanck, Gulian C.
Vose, Chas. L.
Van Antwerp

LIST OF MEMBERS. (1852.

Van Deventer, Jacob G.
Van Nest, A. R.
Vorwerck, C. W.
Vail, W.
Vernons
Van Nest, Abm.
Vreedenburgh, Peter
Van Vleck, J. T.
Vandervoort, P. L. Mrs.
Van Nest, Peter
Van Vest, John
Van Dalen, Jacob
Van Wagenen, Wm. T.
Van Nostrand, J.
Van Saun, Samuel
Van Winkle, J.
Van Haudon, J.
Van Dyck, P.
Vandervort, W.
Vantuyl, A P.
Vogelsang. Henry
Vanarsdale, Peter, M.D.
Vancott, John
Valentine, C.
Valentine, J. C.
Vanarsdale, Henry, M D.
Vermule, Warren, M.D.
Vermule, Field. M.D.
Vreeland, Jacob M.
Vermilye, W. R.
Van Wyck, J. T.
Vanderbilt, Wm. S.
Vail, A.
Vanderpool, A.
Van Duser, S.
Van DeWerken, E.
Vale, A.
Vernol, L. & T.
Van Blankenstein & Heineman
Van Wagenen, Rich. D.
Van Rensselaer, D. J. Mrs.
Van Wagenen W. F. Mrs.
Van Schaick, P. C. Mrs.
Van Antwerp, S. Mrs.
Vanderhoof, J. T.
Vermilye, Thos , Rev.
Valentine, B. W.
Van Buren, J.
Valentine
Vanderbilt
Voorhis, Richard
Van Arsdale, H., M.D.
Van Allen, Wm.
Van Tassel, Emery

W

Willets, Samuel
Wetmore. A. R.
Wright, Sturges & Shaw
Ward, Augustus
Ward, A. H.
Wetmore, Samuel

Wolfe & Gillespie
Whittelsey, J. P.
Wolfe, J. D.
Wyeth, L. J.
Walker, Joseph
Whitlock, Wm.
Watson, John
White, E.
Walker, Wm.
Walsh, A. Robertson
Wheelwright. B. F.
Webb. Wm. H.
Westervelt & Mackay
Whiting, A.
Wolfe, Christopher
Whitlock & Co.
Wainwright, E.
Wells, Miss
Wallace, Miss
Watts, A. Mrs.
Weeks, E. A.
Wood, Isaac
Warden, Wm. & Alex. Lee, Patterson,The little Brothers, Georgia
W. A. B. & Edgar
Washburn, H. B
Wright, A. H.
Wagner, John
Wilson, Jane
Williamson, W.
Whittlesey, Heary
Winterton, Samuel
Wier, James
Wheaton, Wm.
Wentworth, J. W.
Waldron, Cornelius
Wissing, James
Wooster, Chas.
Winslow, George
Wood, Henry
Williams, Erastus
West, H. P.
Whitely, G.
Worral, I. G.
Washburn, S. D.
West. E.
Winter, E. T., M.D.
Wilson, N.
Wilson, Jotham
Williams, J. F.
Walsh, J. W.
Wilson, A. M. Mrs.
Woodruff, M. P.
White, Robt., Jr.
White, Robert H.
Winslow, R. H.
Wilkes, H.
Waller, R.
Whitehead, J.
Winslow, T. S.
Whittemore, T.
Woodhead, J.
Woodruff, T. T.
Ward, T., M. D.
Ward, John

Ward, H. H.
Wilkes, M.
Waddington, W. D.
Ward, W. G.
Weller, John
Wagner. D. B.
Williamson, D. A.
Wetmore, P. M.
Woram & Dalley
Woodruff, A.
Wood, Benjamin
W. K.
Wilson, Daniel
Williams, S. T.
Waters, Horace
Ward, Miss
Wilkey, W. F.
Wright, Richard
Woolsey, John
Walton, J. B.
Wood, Mr.
Williamson, Jas.
Williams, Frederick
Wooding, Julius
White, John
White, Wm.
Walkins & Co.
Wise, M.
Western, Mr.
Wickstead, J. J.
Wickens, Obed.
Wooding, Jas.
Wood, Mrs.
Wight, James W.
Willet, J. C. & Co.
Wake, William
Watterbery, Joseph
Wagenberen, Conrad
Walker, Wm.
Watts, Henry H.
Wallace. J. P.
Wright, D. D.
Watson, W. S.
Wising, James
Woodford, O. P.
W. P. & R.
Wyman, J. G.
Webster, C. B.
Wheaton, W.
Welsh & Paine
Whitehead & Brothers
Wygant, Edward
Worley, N.
Walton & Sterling
West & Caldwell
Wyck, Chas.
Wemmell, Peter
Watson, Mrs.
Wicksted, Mrs.
Walker, Alexander
Ward, Sylvanus
Webb, John
Woodford, J.C.
Williams, J. B.
West, Wm.
Welstein, J.

West, Z.
Wiskemann, P.
Wilson, A. D., M.D.
Winne, J. D.
White, S. B.
Wallis, J. G.
Wiggins, Jas.
Wood, E. A.
Warner, Abram.
Ward, L. B.
Wing, N. S.
Wilkins, N. D.
Wanzer, Minor & Co.
Ward, J. O.
Wolcott, F. H.
W. A.
Williams, W. P.
Whitney, J. S.
Warburg, E.
Wallace, Wicks & Co.
Winkley, H.
Williams, F. B.
Wyckoff, Son & Co.
W. H. W.
Wood & Hughes
Weld, A.
Williams, O. P. & E.
Wilson, Hawksworth, Ellison & Moss
Wetmore, L.
Wallach, Willy
Wagner, George
Woods, David
Wendel
Woodhull, G. C.
W. & O.
Woodward, W. A.
Wood, O. E.
Williams, Wm. R.
Warner, Peter R.
Wells, H. M.
Wetherspoon, James
Williams, T.
Wheeler, Z.
Waring, Chas. B.
Williams, W. R.
Williams, John M.
Waterbury, A. G.
Woodward, S.
Walsh, Thos. S.
Wyckoff, Mrs.
Woodhouse, Capt.
Welford, C.
Whittaker, Wm. B.
Wilson, John
Westervelt, James
Wisner, B D.
Wicker, Henry
Weismann, Augt.
Walton, Isaac
Wilson, J.
Wild, W.
White, M.
Wilsey, J. G.
Wilsey, Mary, Mrs.

White, A. L., M D.
Whiteer, Chas. W., Rev.
Waydell, J. H. & F.
Weber, Edmund
Williams, M. W.
Welsh, Wm.
Wing, L. B.
West, Joseph
Williams, Erastus
Westlake, Chas. G.
Walker, Mrs.
White, Edward
Woods, John
Weeks, George
Welling, John T.
Ward, Adam
Withington, Lewis
Weeks, S.
Woodworth, Francis C.
Weed, J. W.
Woodworth, A. M. Mrs.
Willson, E.
Wilbur, M.
Walton, W.
Walton, M. Miss
Walton, S. Miss
Wilson, B. M.
Woodruff, Judge
Winslow, Wm.
Waller, James
Wallace, John
Wright, Mrs.
Whittemore, H. S.
Wylie, Robt. L.
Wixon, Samuel
Wheeler, H. H.
Wilcox, J. T.
Wray, John
Williams, G. H.
Warsback, Geo. C.
Wray, Christopher
Worral & Co.
Wilkes, George
White, Norman
Woodward, R. T.
Wyckoff, Henry S.
Waddell, Wm. C. H.
Walker, John J.
Walker, T. E.
White, L J.
W. L. J.
Weir, T. E.
Weston, Mrs.
Watt, Wm.
Warren, H. M.
Whittingham, J.
Williams & Hinman
Williams, Richard S.
Wood, James L.
Westfall, J. & D.
Woodford, O. W
Wheeler, L. F.
Whyte, John
West, Daniel
White, P. A.

Williams, C. F.
Wood, M. Q.
Willets, E. P.
Webb, J. B.
Webb, Mrs.
White, W. C.
Westervelt, J. A.
Whitmore, J. C.
Willets, D. T.
Walton, E. L.
Woodhull, Mrs.
Waring, Samuel J.
Williams, Thos.
White, J.
Willets, Stephen
Willets, R. R.
Watkins, Lewis
Williams, C.
Wells, L. W.
Winthrop, B. R.
Withers, R.
White, Charles B.
Wright, Neriah
White
Weller, Mrs.
Watkins, John L.
Whiting, C.
West, C E.
Willet, Edward M.
Wilbur, Chas.
Walsh, George
Walker, W. A.
Walker, Wm.
Woodruff, L. B.
Williams, J. F.
Woolsey, E. J.
Winston, F. S.
Wheelock, Calvin, Jr.
Walkins, John L.
Wallace, Thos.
Wilcox, John M.
Worrell, Noah
Ware, John P.
Warren, T.
Walsh, G.
Wardell, O. T.

Y.

Yates, A. E. Mrs.
Youngs, George
Young, John
Young, David L.
Young, C. L.
Yosterphen, Peter
Young, F.
Yanenbaumn, J.
Yvelin, H. & Son
Yelverton & Fellows
Youngs, li. J.
Yznaga & Etiebien
Young, E. M.
Youle, G. W.
Youngs, W.

Young, Henry
Yates, C.
Young, John
Young, Wm.
Young, Hiram

X.

Zerrega, A.
Zabriskie, Mrs.
Zabriskie & Van Riper
Zipcey, Jacob
Zellner, Charles

Zinck, T.
Zabriskie, C. A.
Zimmerman, Miss
Zeigler, G. F.
Zabriskie, C., Jr.
Zabriskie, Martin

THE

TENTH ANNUAL REPORT

OF THE

NEW-YORK ASSOCIATION

FOR

Improving the Condition of the Poor.

FOR THE YEAR 1853.

WITH THE BY-LAWS AND A LIST OF MEMBERS.

ORGANIZED, 1843—INCORPORATED, 1848.

"The quality of mercy is not strained;
It droppeth as the gentle rain from heaven
Upon the place beneath; it is twice blessed;
It blesseth him that gives and him that takes."

NEW-YORK:
JOHN F. TROW, PRINTER, 49 ANN STREET.
1853.

PROCEEDINGS

AT THE

ANNUAL MEETING

OF THE

New-York Association for Improving the Condition of the Poor.

Held in the Chapel of the New-York University, Washington Square, Nov. 8, 1853.

GEORGE GRISWOLD, Esq., Vice-President, in the chair.

The meeting was opened with prayer by the Rev. Dr. Dewitt.

The Minutes of the last Annual Meeting were read by the Recording Secretary, and on motion, approved.

In the absence of the Treasurer, the Auditing Committee presented his Annual Report, which was accepted and ordered on file.

An Abstract of the Annual Report of the Board of Managers was read by the Corresponding Secretary.

The following resolution was then moved by Horatio Allen, Esq.:

Resolved, That the Report now read be accepted, printed, and circulated under the direction of the Board of Managers.

Seconded by the Rev. Dr. Tyng, with an able and eloquent address, urging, with great variety of argument and felicity of illustration, the almost peculiarly American idea of elevating the dependent and degraded to the dignity of self-support and respectable life, as was the avowed design of this institution. He argued that the root of all pauperism in this country is intemperance; and in this view he urged, that until the Association becomes "an absolutely aggressive Association for an assault on the whole fabric of intemperance, it can never effectually and permanently alleviate the condition of the poor."

The following resolution was submitted by A. R. Wetmore, Esq.:

Resolved, That the Visitors of the Association, to whose self-denying labors it mainly owes its success, are entitled to the grateful acknowledgments of the friends of the poor in this community; and that while they carefully guard against a misapplication of charitable aid, they be encouraged to persevere in their philanthropic exertions to improve and elevate those whom it is their privilege to relieve.

Seconded by the Rev. Dr. Adams, who, in supporting the resolution, pronounced a high eulogium on those disinterested and self-denying labors, which, according to the law pervading all human action, necessarily subjected those employed in doing good to some form or modification of suffering; and who, though they do not feel the need of such remuneration, are entitled to the thanks and gratitude of the community. He strongly commended the efforts of Christian philanthropy to elevate its objects, as in striking contrast with the deteriorating effects of impulsive relief; setting forth in eloquent and impressive terms the Good Samaritan, as the model of Christian charity; also, the motives to increased zeal in prosecuting the work, and the hopes to the city, in the multiplication of systematic agencies, governed by Christian principle.

The resolution was then put and carried unanimously.

All the exercises of the occasion were of a highly interesting and encouraging character.

Voting by ballot having, by resolution, been dispensed with, the Association proceeded to the election of the following Officers: Managers, and Supervisory Council for the ensuing year, after which the meeting adjourned.

OFFICERS, MANAGERS,
AND
SUPERVISORY COUNCIL.

President.
JAMES BROWN.

Vice-Presidents.
GEORGE GRISWOLD,   JAMES LENOX,
JAMES BOORMAN,   HORATIO ALLEN,
A. R. WETMORE.

Treasurer.
ROBERT M. MINTURN.

Corresponding Secretary and Agent.
ROBERT M. HARTLEY.

Recording Secretary.
JOSEPH B. COLLINS.

Supervisory Council.
The first in order is the Chairman of each District Committee.

FIRST DISTRICT.
James C. Ramsey,
James Cruikshank,
William Bogardus,
John Harris,
John Davidson.

SECOND DISTRICT.
George W. Abbe,
Joseph F. Sanxay,
William Sharp,
Charles Wilbur,
Dan. N. Tucker.

THIRD DISTRICT.
W. R. Jones,
J. L Baldwin,
W. D. Harris,
Ervine H. Tripp,
Charles Van Wyck.

FOURTH DISTRICT.
Abraham Fardon, Jr.,
Archibald Hall,
Hugh Aikman,
Charles Chamberlain,
John Gates.

FIFTH DISTRICT.
A. R. Wetmore,
J. H. Redfield,
N. P. Hosack,
Marcus Mitchell,
L. G. Evans.

SIXTH DISTRICT.
N. C. Everett,
Stephen Conover,
Daniel Fisher,
Frederick Lockwood,
Peter Burnett, M. D.

SEVENTH DISTRICT.
John H. Griscom, M. D.
Stephen Cutter,
B. G. Bruce,
Thomas Warren,
R. S Place.

EIGHTH DISTRICT.
Joseph B. Collins,
John Endicott,
Charles C. Dyer,
O. D. McClain,
J. S. Holt.

NINTH DISTRICT.
James O. Pond, M. D
Jacob S. Miller, M. D.
Thomas B. Richards,
Jeremiah Terbell,
Daniel French.

TENTH DISTRICT.

James Horn,
Joseph M. Bell,
H. Van Arsdale, M. D
E. A. Fraser,
Thomas Jackson.

ELEVENTH DISTRICT.

Abner Mills,
Joel Kelly,
Michael Devoy,
David L. Young,
Andrew Storms.

TWELFTH DISTRICT.

R. C. Andrus,
W. H. Colwell,
H. Patterson,
J. O. Higgins,
E. H. Brown.

THIRTEENTH DISTRICT.

Lewis Chichester,
Thomas Kennedy,
John Pearsall,
Charles Merrill,
William A. Walker.

FOURTEENTH DISTRICT.

Alexander W. Murray,
William Post,
J. J. Jenkins,
H. Miller,
Richard Brown.

FIFTEENTH DISTRICT.

Thomas Denny,
William G. Bull,
Joseph Lawrence,
James Marsh,
Adon Smith.

SIXTEENTH DISTRICT.

Luther Jackson,
Charles Roome,
L. B. Woodruff,
H. K. Bull,
J. P. Cumming.

SEVENTEENTH DISTRICT.

S. C. Lynes,
James R. Gibson,
Thomas Jeremiah,
James W. Metcalf, M. D.
Jonathan K. Johnson.

EIGHTEENTH DISTRICT.

F. E. Mather,
William Walker,
Adam W. Spies,
J. H. Earle,
Nathaniel Hayden.

NINETEENTH DISTRICT.

O. W. Morris,
J. W. Rumsey,
J. C. Miller,
William E. Davis,
C. C. Tracy.

TWENTIETH DISTRICT.

J. P. Ostrom,
James Reeve,
Charles H. Rusher,
J. W. Miller,
H. McLean.

TWENTY-FIRST DISTRICT.

J. W. Benedict,
J. Stevenson,
Edward Roberts,
Henry E. Quinan,
J. B. Brewster.

TWENTY-SECOND DISTRICT.

A. M. Lyon,
J. C. Hepburn, M. D.
J. A. Van Riper.
J. Ives, M. D.,
A. T. Serrell,

Elected Members of the Supervisory Council.

J. C. Greene,
Jonathan Sturges,
William A. Macy,
George T. Trimble,
E. J. Woolsey,

Cyrus Curtis,
John C. Baldwin,
William B. Crosby,
Thomas Cock, M. D.,
William G. Bull,

Lorin Nash,
Capt. Wm. A. Spencer,
F. S. Winston,
Peter Cooper,
Robert Ray.

Elected Members of the Board of Managers.

Stewart Brown,
John T. Adams,

Jasper Corning
Erastus C. Benedict.

VISITORS

Appointed by the Advisory Committees for the ensuing year.

FIRST DISTRICT.

John Love,
H. P. Hyde,
John McIntyre,
John Harris,
J. C. Ramsay,
George Hatt,
Alexander Ferguson,
William Bogardus,
A. L. Stimson,
Peter Allyn,
John Davidson,
John Brown,
Calvin Wheelock, Jr.
H. M. Baldwin.
George Hatt, Secretary.

SECOND DISTRICT.

Charles Wilbur,
Joseph F. Sanxay,
George W. Abbe,
D. N. Tucker,
William Sharp,
John L. Watkins.
George Hatt, Secretary.

THIRD DISTRICT.

H. S. Terbell,
Volney Elliot,
James W. Dunning,
Richard B. Lewis,
Thomas McLaughlin,
Vincent Le Comte,
Ervin H. Tripp,
Robert Lewis,
Wright Gillies.
Edward Pratt, Secretary.

FOURTH DISTRICT.

David Moffat,
Thomas Wallace,
A. J. Henderson,
H. Whittlesey,
G. H. Traphagen,
Charles N. Decker,
E. H. Sands, M. D.
Hiram Hurd,
T. R. Ryers,
M. E. Kingman,
Edward Blackford,
William A. Brusle,
Solomon Fanning,
Thomas Bristol.
Henry Whittlesey, Sec'y.

FIFTH DISTRICT.

T. V. Forster,
A. R. Wetmore,
Marcus Mitchell,
Peter Mood,
George Walker,
Moses Cristy,
William Van Allen,
William B. Eager, M.D.
N. P. Hosack,
John Cook,
C. J. Mason,
James H. Matthews,
L G. Evans,
J. H. Redfield,
Nathan Brown,
Robert Pattison,
John E. Jackson,
John A. Kennedy,
Thomas E. Smith,
Benjamin F. Clark,
Jacob La Wall,
H. A. Halsey,
William G. West,
Richard Ritter.
Edward Pratt, Secretary.

SIXTH DISTRICT.

Noah Worrell,
Daniel Fisher,
John M. Clawson,
William Buttre,
Frederick Lockwood,
William Jervis,
Moses B. Taylor,
Peter Burnett, M. D.
Abraham Florentine,
George W. Lowerre,
James B. Wyckoff, M.D.
Andrew Hume,
Samuel N. Burrell,
Samuel Baxter,
John P. Ware,
Joseph N. Parker,
Richard Tritton.
Amzi Camp, Secretary.

SEVENTH DISTRICT.

William Rowell,
N. P. Beers,
T. Warren,
J B. Horton,
R. S. Place,
Samuel R. Cutter,
Charles J. Harris,
P. A. Woods,
E. Falconer,
A. B. Ludlum,
William Lane,
Charles Roberts,
B. G. Bruce,
John C. Graham,
Lewis Watkiss,
Roosevelt G. Secor.
Jonathan B. Horton, Sec'ry.

EIGHTH DISTRICT.

Joseph S. Holt,
O. D. McClain,
William Alexander,
Daniel Conover,
James F. Stansbury,
James Clark,
James Winterbottom,
John S. Hoagland,
Samuel P. Sherwood,
Charles C. Dyer,
Louis J. Belloni,
Henry W. Ryerson,
C. P. Dakin,

VISITORS. (1853.

Thomas Housworth,
John Endicott,
Edward Fields, M. D.
John Gillelan,
John Nicol,
Darius Geer,
James Freeman.
William Kirby, Sec'ry.

NINTH DISTRICT.

J. B. Ferguson,
W. E. Kidd,
O. T. Wardell,
Abraham Maze,
Ira C. Pierson,
Henry P. See,
Henry W. Deems,
J. W. Bush,
William Bogert,
Thomas Ackenback,
William Marten,
William A. Foster,
J. Ruston,
J. B. Huse,
M. Allison, Jr.
C. J. Jones,
John Murray,
F. M. Lane,
John C. Carson,
Charles A. Cragin,
M. H. Howell.
Lewis E. Jackson, Sec'ry.

TENTH DISTRICT.

J. W. Lester,
Edmund Anderson,
Joseph M. Bell,
James Horn,
James Wier,
William Wheaton,
E. A. Fraser,
Henry Wicker,
C. V. Clarkson, M. D.
James P. Tibbits,
Henry Moore, Jr.
Henry Van Arsdale, M. D.
Samuel Smith,
James K. Place,
Thomas Jackson,
Charles Place,
C. N. Decker,
William C. Bradley,
Thomas Holman.
J. P. Lestrade, Sec'ry.

ELEVENTH DISTRICT.

C. P. Hawkins,
Joel Kelly,
Thomas Hogan,
William Murphy, M. D.
John Cameron,

R. A. Barry, M. D.
D. C. Smith,
Eneas Elliot,
Edwin G. Griswold,
John H. Smith,
William Barker,
Gilbert Leggett,
Cornelius Waldron,
Peter Squire,
John Meyers,
Nathan Sanford,
Moses Gardner,
James Little,
Alexander McVey,
George Winslow,
Augustus Brainerd,
J. W. Schuler,
William Brown,
George H. Dawson,
John H. Bulen, Sec'ry.

TWELFTH DISTRICT.

James McKean,
John Rollins,
Wm. H. Colwell,
John Greaves,
Doctor Tanner,
R. C. Andrus,
W. S. Carman,
J. L. Ambler,
William Porter,
J. S. Hickson,
Captain Dean,
John Lowery.
J. L. Ambler, Sec'ry.

THIRTEENTH DISTRICT.

William F. Nash,
John Hutchings,
J. F. Cook.
J. C. Egbert,
John R. Marsh,
John R. Smith,
J. A. Clark,
John Burr,
Henry Wood,
Charles Merrill,
E. Falconer,
P. C. Shaver,
Abraham Trafford,
Francis Duncan,
G. D. Smith,
Adonijah Brummell,
Samuel Trenchard,
Willet S. Robbins,
A. H. Sharot,
J. Brown.
David Russell, Sec'ry.

FOURTEENTH DISTRICT.

Nehemiah Lounsberry,
Henry P. West,

William Post,
Richard Brown,
Bezaleel Howe,
William Johnston.
John Lindmark,
C. B. Pearson,
Alfred Goodell,
Humphrey Miller,
George Brandon,
J. J. Jenkins,
James Montgomery,
Nelson Sammis,
Peter Carter,
Gideon Peck,
Alexander W. Murray,
James Knox.
William Gray, Sec'ry.

FIFTEENTH DISTRICT.

George L. Storer,
Charles Sullivan,
Henry Holman,
Josiah Dodge.
Isaac Orchard,
David Stevens,
C. R. Disosway,
Benjamin Lord,
John Mollard
Isaac Orchard, Sec'ry.

SIXTEENTH DISTRICT.

R. Cole,
W. Phillips,
J. M. Hubbard,
Marks Cornell,
Stephen Merritt,
S. Bridger,
G. Whitely,
R. F. Halsted,
J. Cowl,
H. Jones,
A. Smith,
T. J. Burjer,
D. Chichester,
Wm. Heydon,
D. Irwin,
J. D. Adams,
D. L. Beatty,
E. & D. Crane.
C. C. Darling, Sec'ry.

SEVENTEENTH DISTRICT.

James Duff,
R. Albro,
C. H. Redman,
H. Griffin,
W. B. Humbert,
I. G. Worrall,
J. Phair,
J. K. Johnson,
E. Harris, M. D.

D. T. Staniford,
James Duff, Jr.
R. W. Moore,
G. Shopp,
S. D. Washburn, M. D.
James R. Gibson,
A. Green,
Francis Duncan,
A. L. Halsted,
J. W. Metcalf, M. D.
E. West, M. D.
J. Young,
G. W. Greene,
J. Crosby,
R. Horton,
D. T. Macfarlane.
Richard Horton, Sec'ry.

EIGHTEENTH DISTRICT.

L. Hazeltine,
C. Wolcott,
H. S. Blackett,
N. R. Long,
G. J. Hamilton,
J. B. Ballard,
Henry Day,
William Allen Butler,
C. C. Savage,

R. H. Lievesley,
J. B. Ballard, Sec'ry.

NINETEENTH DISTRICT.

Charles Smithson,
James Hatfield,
Benjamin Place,
J. C. Parker,
William E. Davis,
J. C. Miller,
C. C. Tracy,
J. Reese,
Enoch Mack, Secretary.

TWENTIETH DISTRICT.

John G. Sewall, M. D.
R. Gibbens,
William Donaldson,
J. F. Williams,
Franklin Gregg,
C. H. Buckley,
P. Gordon,
E. T. Winter, M. D.
J. McIntyre,
A. B. Chadwick, M.D.
James Demarest,

J. Armstrong,
J. N. Husted, M. D.
J. Erskine,
Richard Hayter, Sec'ry.

TWENTY-FIRST DISTRICT.

Edward Roberts,
William Bowen,
E. T. Winter, M. D.
T. D. Porter,
W. B. Bibbins, M. D.
L. Ranney, M. D.
J. W. Benedict,
J. France,
J. C. Hines.
J. B. Ballard, Sec'ry.

TWENTY-SECOND DISTRICT.

A. T. Serrell,
E. H. Munson,
S. Fleet,
Philip Dunn,
A. J. Haines,
David Grinsted,
William Ellis,
Jotham Wilson.
Enoch Mack, Sec'ry.

OFFICE OF THE ASSOCIATION, *Bible House, No.* 39 *Third floor, entrance on Eighth-street.*

1*

BY-LAWS.

ARTICLE I.

EVERY person who becomes an annual Subscriber, a member of an Advisory Committee, or a Visitor, shall be a member of the Association.

ARTICLE II.

The President and Secretaries shall perform such duties as usually pertain to their office.

ARTICLE III.

The Treasurer shall give such security for the faithful performance of the trust reposed in him, as the Association may demand and approve. He shall take in charge all funds; keep an account of all receipts and disbursements; and pay all duly authorized demands. At the usual meeting he shall render a particular and correct statement of all his receipts and disbursements to the Association. He shall also exhibit a summary report to the Board of Managers, at their stated meetings, and whenever called upon by them for that purpose.

ARTICLE IV.

The Board of Managers shall have exclusive control of the funds of the Association, and authority to make By-Laws; to fill vacancies; appoint all committees; and generally to adopt such measures as the objects of the Institution may require. It shall meet for the transaction of business on the second Monday of every month; and the annual meeting of the Association shall be convened on the second

Monday of November, when the Board shall submit a report of its proceedings, and the officers and managers be chosen. In case of a failure to hold the specified meeting in November, a special meeting for the same purpose shall be convened in the course of the ensuing month.

ARTICLE V.

Special meetings of the Board of Managers, and of the Supervisory Council, may be called by the Secretary, at the request of the President, or on receiving a requisition signed by five members. Two days' notice must be given of the time of meeting.

ARTICLE VI.

The Managers may at any time make such alterations in these By-Laws as may be deemed necessary; provided they be not contrary to the Act of Incorporation, and that such alterations shall be submitted to the Board of Managers at least one meeting before the same is acted upon; and that it shall not be passed upon unless specified in the call of the meeting, and when a majority of the whole number of the Board of Managers is present.

ARTICLE VII.

An office shall be opened in an eligible situation for the purpose of concentrating and diffusing all information pertaining to the Society's operations and objects, and for the transaction of its general business.

ARTICLE VIII.

It shall be the duty of the General Agent to devote himself with diligence and fidelity to the affairs of the Association.

ARTICLE IX.

The city shall be divided into twenty-two Districts, each Ward forming a District; and the districts be subdivided into Sections. Each District shall have an Advisory Committee, to consist of five members; and each Section a Visitor.

ARTICLE X.

It shall be the duty of the Advisory Committee to divide their Districts into such Sections as to apportion to each about twenty-five families requiring attention; endeavor to obtain suitable Visitors for each Section; supply vacancies which may occur; make the necessary arrangements for placing at the disposal of the Visitors food, fuel, and clothing for distribution; and on some day in the first week of every month (excepting the meetings of July and August, which may be omitted in the discretion of the Committees), to convene all the Visitors of the Sections, for the purpose of receiving their returns, and conferring with them on the objects of their mutual labors. The Committees, moreover, shall duly draw upon the Treasurer for such proportion of the funds as may be appropriated to their Districts; they shall keep a strict account of all their disbursements, and only in extreme cases make donations of money; they shall monthly render an account of their expenditures to the Board of Managers; and in default of this duty, shall not be entitled to draw upon the funds of the Association. Each Committee shall appoint its own Chairman, Secretary, and Treasurer, and shall transmit the Reports of the Visitors immediately after each monthly meeting, with any other information they may think desirable, to the General Secretary.

ARTICLE XI.

It shall be the duty of each Visitor to confine his labors exclusively to the particular Section assigned him, so that no individual shall receive relief, excepting in the Section where he is known, and to which he belongs. The Visitors shall carefully investigate all cases referred to them before granting relief; ascertain the condition, habits of life, and means of subsistence of the applicants; and extend to all such kind services, counsel and assistance, as a discriminating and judicious regard for their present and permanent welfare requires. And in case of sickness, it will be their duty to inquire whether there is any medical or other attendance needed; whether relief is afforded by any religious or charitable society; to provide themselves with information respecting the nearest Dispensary, and in all cases, when practicable, to refer applicants for aid to appropriate existing societies. When no other assistance is provided or available, they shall draw from the resources of this Association—not money, which is never allowed to be given, except with the consent of the Advisory Committee or a member thereof—but such articles of food, fuel, clothing, and similar supplies, as the necessities of the case require. In all cases of want coming to the knowledge of the Visitors, they will be expected to perform the same duties, although no application has been made. It shall be their duty, moreover, to render a report of their labors, and also an account of all their disbursements, to their respective Committees, at the stated monthly meeting. No Visitor neglecting these duties will be entitled to draw on the funds of the Association.

ARTICLE XII.

The Board of Managers, the members of the Advisory Committees,, and certain elected members, shall together constitute a Supervisory Council, whose duties shall be deliberative and advisory; and its annual meetings be held on the second Monday of November, in each year. Special meetings of this body shall be held, when called by the Board of Managers.

ARTICLE XIII.

It shall be the duty of the Members of the Association to endeavor, in all suitable ways, to give practical effect to its principles; especially to discountenance indiscriminate alms-giving and street-begging; to provide themselves with tickets of reference; and instead of giving aid to unknown applicants, whose case they cannot themselves investigate, to refer such applications to the Visitor of the Section in which the applicants reside, in order that such cases may properly be inquired into, and, if deserving, relieved.

ARTICLE XIV.

The printed forms of tickets and orders for relief, shall be designated by the Board of Managers, and no other shall be used.

Incorporation.

CERTIFICATE OF INTENTION

TO INCORPORATE THE NEW-YORK ASSOCIATION FOR IMPROVING THE CONDITION OF THE POOR.

THE undersigned being each and every of them of full age, and citizens of the State of New-York, desiring to associate themselves for the benevolent and charitable objects hereinafter expressed, that they may become a body politic and corporate, and be enabled to conduct the business of the Association in the City and County of New-York, according to the provisions of an "Act for the Incorporation of Benevolent, Charitable, Scientific, and Missionary purposes," passed April 12th, 1848, do for these purposes hereby certify,

I. That the name and title by which such Institution shall be known in law is the "New-York Association for Improving the Condition of the Poor."

II. That the particular business and objects of such Association shall be the elevation of the physical and moral condition of the indigent; and so far as is compatible with these objects, the relief of their necessities.

III. That the Board of Managers to manage the same shall consist of one President, five Vice-Presidents, one Treasurer, one Corresponding Secretary and General Agent, one Recording Secretary, the Chairman of each Advisory Committee, or, as his proxy, some other member of said Committee, and four members, to be chosen by said Board of Managers.

IV. That the following named persons shall constitute the Board of Managers for the first year, to wit: James Brown, *President;* George Griswold, J. Smyth Rogers, James Boorman, James Lenox, and Horatio Allen, *Vice-Presidents ;* Robert B. Minturn, *Treasurer;* Robert M. Hartley, *Corresponding Secretary and General Agent;* Joseph B. Collins, *Recording Secretary;* together with the following elected Members and Chairmen of the Advisory Committees, namely: Stewart Brown, Frederick S. Winston, Erastus C. Benedict, John R. Ludlow, Daniel S. Briant, William Gale, Peter G. Arcularius, Abraham Fardon, Jr., Apollos R. Wetmore, Nicholas C. Everett, Calvin Tracy, James O. Pond, James Horn, Samuel P. Patterson, Lewis Chichester, Adam W. Spies, Thomas Denny, Luther Jackson, Stephen C. Lynes, and F. Ellsworth Mather.

In witness whereof we hereunto have subscribed our names, in the city of New-York, this the eleventh day of December, in the year of our Lord one thousand eight hundred and forty eight.

JAMES BROWN,	APOLLOS R. WETMORE,
GEORGE GRISWOLD,	NICHOLAS C. EVERETT,
J. SMYTH ROGERS,	CALVIN TRACY,
JAMES BOORMAN,	JAMES O. POND,
HORATIO ALLEN,	JAMES HORN,
ROERT M. HARTLEY,	LEWIS CHICHESTER,
JOSEPH B. COLLINS,	ADAM W. SPIES,
STEWART BROWN,	THOMAS DENNY,
FREDERICK S. WINSTON,	LUTHER JACKSON,
DANIEL S. BRIANT,	STEPHEN C. LYNES,
PETER G. ARCULARIUS,	F. ELLSWORTH MATHER,
ABRAHAM FARDON, JR.	

Witness as to all the signatures,   D. F. CURRY.

City and County of New-York, [ss]: On the eleventh day of December, A. D. 1848, before me came George Griswold, J. Smyth Rogers, Horatio Allen, Joseph B. Collins, Luther Jackson, Abraham Fardon, Jr., Lewis Chichester, Daniel S. Briant, Nicholas C. Everett, James O. Pond, Adam W. Spies, F. Ellsworth Mather, James Horn, Frederick S. Winston, Peter G. Arcularius, Stephen C. Lynes, Calvin Tracy and Robert M. Hartley; and on the twelfth day of December, A. D. 1848, before me came James Brown, Stewart Brown, and James Boorman; and on the thirteenth day of December, A. D. 1848, before me came Apollos R. Wetmore and Thomas Denny, to me known to be the same persons described in and who executed the foregoing instrument, who severally acknowledged that they executed the foregoing instrument, for the purpose therein mentioned.

D. F. CURRY, *Commissioner.*

I approve of the within Certificate, and allow the same to be filed.
H. P. EDWARDS, *Justice Supreme Court.*
New-York, Dec. 14, 1848.

STATE OF NEW-YORK, SECRETARY'S OFFICE, } *Albany, Dec.* 16, 1848.

I certify that the Certificate of Incorporation of the "New-York Association for Improving the Condition of the Poor," was received and filed this day in this office.

ARCHIBALD CAMPBELL,
Dept. Sec. of State.

Tenth Annual Report

OF THE

NEW-YORK ASSOCIATION FOR IMPROVING THE CONDITION OF THE POOR.

THE Board of Managers of the New-York Association for Improving the Condition of the Poor, herewith respectfully submit their Annual Report.

The Institution having completed the tenth year of its organization, it appears not less appropriate than profitable, at this point of its history, to retrace its previous labors, in order to ascertain how nearly it has fulfilled its original design, and what are the teachings of experience in respect to its future action.

The original design of the Association, it should be observed, was not to supersede existing charities, but, by co-operating with them, to supply what was necessary to complete an organized system of aid for all the needy not otherwise provided for, so as to afford an insurance against imposition and suffering from want, to the extent it should be made the channel of relief, for the entire city.

Before this Institution was formed, a noble emulation prevailed, as at present, among the benevolent in their attentions to the poor, which was evinced by the numerous organizations for the benefit of particular classes of the indigent. But it was evident from the results, as an immense work was left unaccomplished, that their modes of relief were defective. There were still vast numbers for whom there was no charitable provision; pauperism steadily increased above the ratio of the population, though the flow of foreign immigration was then scarcely felt; the streets were filled with mendicants; the benevolent annoyed with applications for aid; and importunate impostors often obtained the assistance which was designed only for the truly needy and deserving. The prevailing defects in dispensing charity may be thus summarily stated:

First, Want of discrimination in giving relief. There being no adequate arrangements by which it was possible to learn the character and condition of applicants, no sound discrimination could be exercised in distributing aid. The societies, of course, were subjected to constant imposition, and large sums were so misapplied as to create more want than they relieved.

Second, The societies, acting independently of each other, was another fruitful source of evil. Having no concert of action or reciprocation of intelligence between them, they were ignorant of each other's operations; and artful mendicants so turned this ignorance to their own advantage, as often to obtain aid from many of the societies at the same time, without detection. The most undeserving, consequently, received the largest amount of assistance, and were thus encouraged in dissolute and improvident habits; while the better class of the needy not only obtained less aid, but often far less than their necessities required, and the benevolent would have bestowed, provided such a knowledge of their character and circumstances had been possessed, as a better system would have conferred.

Third, The existing organizations made no adequate provision for personal intercourse with the recipients of alms at their dwellings, nor for such sympathy and counsel as tended to encourage industrious and virtuous habits, or foster among them a spirit of self-reliance   The final and prospective end of all true charity was consequently unattained, inasmuch as in addition to other defects, they failed to provide for the permanent physical and moral improvement of those their alms relieved.

Fourth. It appeared, moreover, that the *legal provision* for the poor, having no reference to the causes of pauperism, was so administered as to increase its amount; and it appeared equally certain, that no such provision could embrace all the objects of private benevolence, or supersede its efforts; and after the law had done its utmost, a vast work would remain undone, which could not be performed either by isolated individuals or separate independent organizations.*

Although the principles and modes of operation adopted in respect to this defective condition of our charities have long been before the public, it may not be improper here to remark, that it has been the purpose of the Association, in avoiding the mistakes or imperfections of previous plans of relief, to adapt itself to whatever is peculiar in the social character and progressive exigencies of our population, so as to make this one of the most effective voluntary organizations for the aid of the needy, the tempted, and the fallen, which the sagacity of the Board, with its present knowledge, could devise.

In carrying out this purpose, it is a matter of encouragement and gratulation, that, after ten years' experience, the Board have been unable to discover any defects in the plan

* Vide Report of 1845.

of the organization, or in the soundness of its principles. It is true that it has attained a higher and clearer conception of its arduous duties and responsibilities, but it has not been able to improve on itself, except as its efficiency has been augmented by the means employed in obtaining results. Its mode of action may be briefly considered under three aspects.

First, As establishing an *effective system of eleemosynary relief*, for the city. And this it does, not only by removing all apology for the promiscuous aid of unknown persons, by furnishing the means of correct information in respect to them, but also by providing a channel through which the charities of the benevolent may flow to the needy with the utmost practicable discrimination, economy, and effect. By this system a position is gained which commands a full view of the whole field of labor, so as to bring into distinct recognition the actual condition and character of every indigent applicant. Thus it is enabled to sympathize with the suffering, encourage the desponding, detect imposture, and extend to the needy appropriate relief.

Second, *It is preventive*.. The teachings of Inspiration and human experience alike affirm, that the " destruction of the poor is their poverty." The tendency of indigence is often to make men reckless and desperate. Thousands of persons in this city being brought every year, often by unavoidable causes, to abject want, their great danger is, that after a few ineffectual struggles with the difficulties of their condition, they will seek almshouse relief, lose their self-respect, become, perhaps, vicious or debased by crime, or so pauperized in spirit that their subsequent recovery to self-support is nearly hopeless. Yet how small an expenditure of means and efforts, timely and judiciously applied, would probably have saved them from wretchedness and degradation! Such means and efforts it is the office of this Association, through its almost ubiquitous agencies, to bestow. Being conversant with poverty in all its phases, and penetrating its very depths and recesses, to aid the helpless, and to infuse new life and energy into the dejected, the results justify the belief, that in no other way has its exertions been more useful or successful than in the preventive. The happy effects, as will hereafter appear, are shown in the gradual diminution of the number of the dependent in proportion to the population. And though no specific enumeration in the returns give prominence to the facts, there is satisfactory evidence that a vast amount of settled and permanent pauperism has thus been prevented.

Third, It is remedial. This city, unfortunately, is peculiarly exposed to a class of persons, who have been the inmates of foreign poor-houses, or the subjects of parochial relief, where such inveterate habits of pauperism have been formed, that they come here with the settled expectation of an unearned support, and become a burden and an annoyance from the moment of their arrival. There are others, also, of foreign birth, who from the ease with which they can impose on the credulity of the benevolent, and obtain aid from organized private and public charity, fall into like degrading habits. Though abundantly able to labor, they are idle, vagrant, and vicious; many of them given to theft and intemperance, and subsist by prowling about the streets, and preying upon the earnings of the frugal and industrious. Steeped in ignorance themselves, and indifferent to the obligations of public and private duty, what better could be expected of them in their domestic relations, than their utter neglect of the proper training of their offspring, and their encouragement in habits most demoralizing and ruinous? Hence the swarms of " street children" among us, which is a synonyme for all that is most deplorable and dangerous in the elements of our social organization.

Fourth, It is discriminating. The general action of the Association in regard to applicants, has been so fully set forth in previous reports, that more than a brief synopsis in this place, is deemed unnecessary. In giving and withholding aid, it is governed by the common sense principle, which requires a difference of management, according to difference of circumstances and character. What would be harsh and indiscreet in some cases, is just the treatment which humanity and prudence require, in others. It appears in place here to remark, that there is nothing which the great mass of the poor more generally need, than a friend to counsel, encourage and direct them. Hence, whatever other means may be employed for their benefit, discriminating, judicious, personal influence, is at once the most simple, natural, and efficacious. If any instrumentality can do them good, it is the confiding, friendly intercourse of the educated with the uneducated, the virtuous with the vicious, when it earnestly seeks the rescue of the degraded and wretched, by the exercise of those kind offices, and agencies, which Christian sympathy inspires. If any thing can soften and subdue the obdurate and unyielding, it is the persevering attention of disinterested benevolence in their behalf. Patient kindness, in effect like the rod with which Moses drew living waters from the rock at Meribah, works miracles in transforming character, and elevating the degraded to respectable life. Such, at least, in respect to certain classes of the poor, has been the experience of this Association. By diffusing among the suffering and neglected through the noiseless, unobserved, and unobtrusive agency of its numerous Visitors, the warm sunlight of benevolent affection and interest, thousands there is reason to believe—nay, there is arithmetical evidence of the fact—have in past years, either been prevented from falling into settled habits of pauperism, or recovered therefrom, to honest industry and self-support.

As against able-bodied pauperism, in all its multiform manifestations and effects, whether among children or adults, this Association is now, and has ever been, most determinedly opposed, it has earnestly labored both by preventive and remedial measures, for its suppression. This has, as was expected, especially in so heterogeneous and varying a populalation like our own, not only proved a very difficult work, but one which requires a somewhat diversified course of action. For as the artful and designing are detected in one mode of deception, ever fruitful in expedients, they resort to another; and so numerous are their artifices and evasions, that besides the exercise of constant vigilance, new means must be employed from time to time, to guard the community against their impositions. Of all the forms, however, which pauperism assumes, that affecting the children of vicious pauper parents, is the most lamentable and unmanageable, and has consequently required the most comprehensive and energetic measures for its correction. Notwithstanding all the effort and influence the Institution had brought to bear upon this evil, it became so alarmingly prevalent, that a special organization, clothed with new legal powers, was deemed indispensable to its suppression. Hence the origin of the "Juvenile Asylum," an offshoot of this Association, noticed in a previous report, which has been chartered, and is now in effective operation. But even more than this, in the way of legal provision, was considered necessary to arrest the progress of an evil so widespread and inveterate. The Board being decidedly of the opinion, that it is not only the just right, but the imperative duty of the State, in a matter so vitally affecting the public welfare, to enforce by legal enactment, the proper care, training, and instruction of neglected children, united with others, during the past year, in memorializing the Legislature, for a law to that effect. In accordance with the application, at the recent Extra Session of that Body, a general law was passed, authorizing the arrest of vagrant and truant children, on the complaint of any citizen before a magistrate, to be so disposed of as that the State itself should assume the position and responsibility of parent to such children, in order to be so educated, as to secure their usefulness, and promote the well-being of society. While to give the law effect, is one of the obvious duties of every citizen—an earnest co-operation with the official authorities for that end, appeared to be so obviously required of this Association, that the Board caused a copy of the Act to be sent to each Visitor, accompanied by a circular, urging them to a faithful enforcement of its provisions, in all proper cases. What the results will be, can only be known by trial; but as it is one of those progressive measures, aiming at prevention of evil by tearing up the " seed-crop of crime," now so much demanded by the social necessities of this community, its operation can scarcely fail to be salutary in various ways. Its direct effect will be to benefit neglected children; it will exercise a happy reflex influence on reckless parents, by inciting them to a better care of their offspring; and by its restraints on juvenile vagrancy and mendicancy, tend to dry up those polluted and polluting streams of youthful depravity, which have so long defiled our city.

During the past year, moreover, the Association adopted a rule of relief, directly bearing upon the instruction of the class of children in question, which it is believed will be useful in its results, and should receive a brief notice.

It was in effect resolved, that the attention of Visitors be specially directed to the Education of the children of such families as applied to the Association for aid; and in order to facilitate this important object, that blank certificates be furnished, to which the Visitor should require such families to obtain the signature of the teacher, affirming that their children of suitable age, had attended school, during the week preceding the application.

In respect to the foregoing rule, it may be remarked, that one of the primary causes of poverty as well as crime, is the want of *education and moral culture;* and as these advantages are least valued where most needed, parents of this class usually allow their offspring to grow up as ignorant and debased as themselves, and of course, as unfitted for a higher condition. Troops of such children may be seen wandering about our streets, filthy, and ragged, begging for morsels of bread, exposed to vices, in which they early become adepts; and advancing from smaller to greater crimes, often complete their miserable career in the penitentiary. Or if crimes are avoided which would subject them to the penalties of the law, it is notorious that many of them become incorrigible vagrants, and through life, a burden and pest to society. Such being the facts, have not the children of the poor strong claims upon this Association? If left to their parents, or themselves, how certain it is, that they will augment the pauperism, crime, and wretchedness, of the community! In the view of the Board, therefore, such families should be visited with the determined purpose to bring, if practicable, into our day and Sabbath schools, all the children of suitable age to receive instruction. This would tend to extinguish juvenile mendicity, and confer one of the greatest blessings upon the poor and upon the community.

It was not, however, designed that the foregoing regulation should be so construed that non-compliance therewith would, in every case, bar the otherwise deserving and well-disposed from gratuitous relief. Sickness, and other unavoidable causes of which the Visitor is a competent judge, may sometimes prevent the required attendance. But if no such causes exist, and parents wilfully neglect, or obstinately refuse to conform to a requisition so important to the best interests of the children and of the community, then it becomes the duty of the Visitor to withhold from such parents the benefits of the Association.

But among the objects claiming the attention of the Board during the year, none have deserved or received more careful consideration, than that relating to the *sanitary condition of the laboring classes.* This subject was early regarded as one coming legitimately within the scope of the Association's designs; and its first plan for giving it practical effect, involved the idea of a distinct organization, which, in order to show the practicability of the scheme, should erect one or more model houses. The investigations, preparatory to the intended prosecution of the work, furnished information, from which was elaborated the plan for a kind of building, which, it was believed, would combine such improvements as the objects in view required. But this scheme, originally suggested by its alleged utility in some European cities, was after mature consideration rejected, as unadapted to the wants and circumstances of this city. The designs, however, were lithographed, and extensively distributed among capitalists and builders (whose attention was called by an accompanying circular to the subject) and were probably not less useful in this way, than if the original purpose had been consummated.

From that period may be dated the first direction of public attention to the habitations of the laboring classes in this city, and to the building of a new order of tenant houses, expressly for their use. Some of these houses combining many improvements, numbers were thereby greatly benefited, and from so promising a beginning, much that would be advantageous was expected in future. But after a time, an unlooked for deterioration in the character of the buildings was manifested. Many were erected on so contracted and penurious a scale, as to be inferior as it respects the essentials of a dwelling to the old buildings whose places they were intended to supply. While increase of wealth adorned our city, improved its business facilities, and multiplied the mansions of the opulent, it was increasingly evident that the accommodations indispensable to the health, comfort, and morals of the poor, had failed to keep pace with their rapidly increasing necessities; and that the evils consequent upon this failure, must steadily augment, unless special efforts were made to remove the causes. As something definite should be immediately attempted in this direction, after mature deliberation, it was resolved to appoint a committee, to inquire into the sanitary condition of the laboring classes, and the practicability of devising measures for improving the comfort and healthiness of their habitations, with instruction to report the result of their investigations to the Board. That Committee, after a laborious inquiry, made their first report on the 10th of October, which was accepted and ordered to be printed, as has since been done in a pamphlet of thirty-two pages, from which full particulars may be obtained. The publication of that document, just issued, is too recent to show what will be the effect of its disclosures and suggestions; but in the judgment of the Board, the subject itself, in its relation to the classes in question, is surpassed by no other in importance; for the subsequent improvement of their condition, both physically and morally, will greatly depend upon the reforms that may be made in their dwellings and inn-door life.

Of specific results, during the year, it is not the design of the Board to speak. Such is the nature of the organization and its labors, that the good effected can neither be put in tabular form nor embodied in any Report, however extended or minute. The burden of each of the more than 4000 Monthly Reports of the Visitors, has been of good achieved or evil prevented. Each of the more than 25,000 visits to the poor, the forlorn and wretched, have been errands of mercy and relief. But what figures will truthfully reveal the amount of these influences, or the benefits to the lone widow and orphans, " dropping as the gentle dew from heaven, upon the earth beneath," through the 337 sectional Visitors, distributed over the city? The results may be faintly shadowed forth by the facts and statements the Board are privileged to present; and more than this will not be attempted. It being their earnest conviction that the Association is adapted to its objects, and that these objects Christian philanthropy approves, it is encouraged to toil on, animated by the assurance that as the Institution has hitherto been instrumental in conferring substantial blessings upon the city—with the Divine favor upon its efforts; for time to come, it will steadily increase in usefulness.

It was to be expected that poverty in this city would have increased *above* the ratio of the growth of the population, inasmuch as the accessions thereto consisted chiefly of needy emigrants from abroad. Facts, on the contrary, show that the general ratio of such increase has actually fallen *below* the growth of the inhabitants, which is conclusive proof that preventive and remedial influences have been effectively at work. How far this Association has contributed to so encouraging a result, it may not be practicable to determine; it is, however, demonstrable that the number aided by it, instead of augmenting as was anticipated, has diminished, both relatively and numerically, being less at present than eight years ago. In 1845, with 375,232 inhabitants, the Institution relieved 5,737 families, containing 25,816 persons. After that period, the tide of emigration set in with such force, as to add in the following seven years to the permanent population of the country nearly a million and a half of human beings. What proportion of this vast number took up their abode in this city, cannot be accurately ascertained; but it is certain, as shown by the late census, that 144,284 persons were added to our resident population in five years, making the aggregate 515,507 souls, of whom

237,795 were of foreign birth. If, as there is no reason to doubt, the same ratio of increase has continued to the present time, from births, accessions from the country and from abroad, then the present population cannot be less than 600,000. It is therefore demonstrable, that if the needy entitled to aid from this charity had augmented in a corresponding degree, instead of relieving the past year, as shown by the returns, but 5,468 families, or 269 less than in 1845, the increase would have been 3,472, or the total families relieved the past year, 9,272. The statistics of the Association consequently exhibit a decrease of this class of the dependent in eight years, as compared with the population, of more than 60 per cent., so that the actual number is at present 269 families less, numbering about 1600 persons, than in 1845. Probably no other city on earth would have borne so large an emigration with so little detriment. Foreigners have continued to flow in like currents of air; but there is a recuperative power in our free institutions and vast country which is a legitimate source of hope—both to ourselves in this commingling of races, and also to the exiles, who make this the land of their adoption. However these facts may strike the public mind, it is a matter of gratulation to the Board, that it can point to results so unequivocal and full of encouragement.

It is gratifying, moreover, to observe, how many new schemes of Christian benevolence not originally contemplated, have been called into operation, through the humble agency of this Institution. It would be unjust to itself, and to other benevolent organizations which owe their origin to it, to overlook the importance of their co-operation in the great work of ameliorating the condition of the poor in this city; for all, rightly viewed, are co-laborers and parts of a single plan, aiming to attain a common object. Of these may be named,

First, THE DEMILT DISPENSARY, which having overcome the difficulties usually incident to a new enterprise, has now, with encouraging prospects of increasing efficiency, taken its place among the permanently useful institutions of the city.

Second, THE NORTH-WESTERN DISPENSARY, more recently organized, which by the amount of good it has already accomplished, furnishes a proof that such an institution was needed, and an earnest of what may be expected in future.

The position of both these Institutions is such, that if they meet the wants of the indigent sick, in the growing population around them, they must necessarily be energetic and progressive. Their importance in their respective localities can scarcely be overrated. In ministering to the sick poor, they not only perform an imperative work of mercy, and become conservators of public health, but by restoring to the disabled the ability to labor, and consequently of self-maintenance, they at once cease to be a burden to others, and contribute to the resources and well-being of the community. Surely, no kinds of benevolent effort are more deserving of sympathy and support, than those which relate to the sanitary condition of the people.

Third, THE JUVENILE ASYLUM. This noble charity, since the last Report, has realized by voluntary contributions the sum required by law, in order to draw an equal amount from the public treasury. It is now, consequently, in possession of $100,000, to enable it to carry out its novel and interesting objects. In January last, it opened a House of Reception for friendless boys, of whom it has about two hundred in charge, and is at present engaged in efforts to obtain within the county an eligible site, whereon to erect a permanent edifice for its operations.

Fourth, PUBLIC BATH AND WASH-HOUSE. The character of this institution, and the results thus far, are forcibly expressed in the following extract from its last Report : " Since the day of opening, the experience brought by time, has only served to convince the Committee, that the necessity for such public accommodation for bathing and washing, in this vast metropolis, was no idle fancy, but that it then existed, as indeed it still exists, to an untried and unimagined extent. The good that has been realized, is shown by the record of its daily and weekly statistics, and by the substantial and unaccustomed benefits, and the great and hitherto unattainable comforts economically bestowed upon the different classes of society."

This Institution has been established at a cost of about $42,000. In the first year of its operation, there were 80,375 bathers, and 10,038 washers.

The changes which have transpired in respect to the number of the poor in some wards, may deserve a passing notice. It has before been shown that the relief during the past year was less than the aggregate of 1845. The following exhibit indicates the nature of the changes referred to:

Wards.	Families Relieved.	Families Relieved.		
I.	In 1845 . 390	In 1853 . 939	Increase .	549
VIII.	In 1845 . 1,604	In 1853 . 1,103	Decrease .	501
XI.	In 1845 . 1,092	In 1853 . 1,189	Increase .	87
XVII.	In 1845 . 731	In 1853 . 1,601	Increase .	870

The above may serve as an illustration. While in some wards the poor have more than doubled, in others they have decreased nearly in a corresponding ratio. The actual relief, as before stated, is less than it was eight years since, though the population in that time has augmented more than 65 per cent.

By these changes the First Ward, for example, which a few years since was chiefly the abode of the opulent, is now computed to contain 15,000 needy persons. Such an extraordinary increase of the indigent in the lower part of the city, who are too poor to pay a physician, and too remote from a dispensary to obtain gratuitous medical aid, evidently required some new dispensary arrangements. The Board, therefore, addressed a communication to the Trustees of the New-York Dispensary, suggesting the establishment of a branch institution at some eligible point south of their present location. What measures to supply the deficiency that excellent charity will adopt have not yet transpired; but its past unwearied devotedness to its philanthropic work affords a guaranty that it will do all that humanity requires for the benefit of the indigent sick within its proper territorial limits.

Increase of Districts and Sections. As the Association had not deemed it expedient in previous years to extend its limits beyond Eighty-sixth street, which is the northern boundary of the Nineteenth Ward, the Twelfth, or out-of-town ward, was consequently left in charge of an independent organization, which was formed the past year. But so many were the disadvantages to the public and to the needy by this arrangement, that the Board were induced, on the application of the Twelfth Ward Advisory Committee, to form a new district, by incorporating that Ward into this organization. By this large addition of territorial area, the Association now covers the entire island, from river to river, and from the Battery to King's Bridge, a length of about fifteen miles. The Eighteenth and Nineteenth Wards, moreover, having, by a recent act of the Legislature, been divided so as to form two new Wards, the Directory has been made to conform to this arrangement. The number of Districts consequently is now 22; and 20 new Sections having been added, the present total is 357.

The following is a tabular exhibit of the monthly district returns from November 1, 1852, to November 1, 1853:

1852–53.	Number of Families Relieved.	Number of Persons Relieved.	Number of Visits.
November . .	706	2,324	1,923
December . .	1,811	7,244	2,911
January . .	3,609	14,436	4,766
February . .	3,890	15,560	5,579
March . . .	3,181	12,724	3,969
April . . .	1,245	4,980	1,952
May . . .	520	2,080	944
June . . .	225	900	802
July . . .	134	536	368
August . .	184	736	480
September .	251	1,004	339
October . .	460	1,840	602

The following is an exhibit of the aggregate relief, *without repetition*, which is unavoidable in the foregoing table, to wit:

Number of different families relieved from Nov. 1,
   1852, to Nov. 1, 1853 5,468
Number of persons 24,606
Number of visits 25,203

  Receipts for the same period . . . $31,359 16
  Disbursements   "   . . 29,692 57

  Excess of receipts over disbursements $1,666 59

Indiscriminate relief and its consequences having been the burden of previous reports, it is with regret the Board are again constrained to urge its consideration upon their fellow-citizens. It being, however, one of the chief causes of able-bodied pauperism among us, and also one of the chief obstructions to its removal, they would be unfaithful to their trust if they failed to repeat, in a definite and intel ligible form, the teachings of experience on this subject, or ceased to warn the public against a practice so rife with pernicious consequences. And this course is the more necessary, because the results of impulsive, indiscriminating almsgiving, are generally neither suspected nor anticipated.

Causes, eluding ordinary observation, often travel a long way before their effects are discovered; yet their ultimate development may not be the less mischievous or certain. To give alms to an unknown beggar in the street may appear a humane, or, at least, a harmless act. But traced to its consequences in a vagabond mendicant population, preying upon the property and disturbing the peace of the community, it is a flagrant social offence. To relieve a strange child at the door may be regarded as meritorious; seen, however, in its results—neglected education and the vagrancy and crime which often lead to temporal and eternal ruin—and it stands out as a high misdemeanor, which admits of no justification.

It is the nature of indiscriminate charity to infuse into the mind of its subjects the belief that they have *a right* to subsistence, independent of their own earnings. And while many professed friends of the poor practically sanction this absurdity, is it surprising that voluntary pauperism should abound despite all the efforts for its suppression? Where, then, is the remedy for this terrible evil, if it be not found in enforcing the primitive terms on which man's subsistence was promised—"*In the sweat of thy face thou shalt eat bread?*"[*]—not otherwise; and this law has never been abrogated. It is the appointment, not of man, but of God. It bears the impress of infinite wisdom, and is safest and best; for labor is not only essential to happiness, but the parent and guardian of virtue. Hence there was a blessing con-

[*] Gen. 3 : 19.

cealed under the apparently austere condemnation of the race to toil. Every man has a right to the products of his own industry; to nothing more, except as Providence takes away the ability to labor; and for such the same beneficent Power which imposed the law of labor provides, by positive commandment, not only repeatedly enjoined, and most strenuously urged in Scripture, but also by the compassionate interest which it instinctively awakens in the hearts of others for their relief. Nature thus echoes the teachings of Revelation on this subject, showing that it has its foundation in man's constitution; and just so far as individuals or associations succeed in conforming to these principles, they will be instrumental in reducing the voluntary pauperism of the city, while experience proves that every divergence from them tends to its increase.

Though it appears to be one of the simplest of self-evident propositions, that to encourage evil is not the way to suppress it; that to give alms to those about whom we know nothing, is to offer a premium to vagrants, and make it their interest to beg; yet how slow are those who but half comprehend the subject, to learn these palpable truths, and to act upon them. While it is the reiterated dictate of experience, of Christianity, and of common sense, "that if a man will not work, neither shall he eat,"[*] these pseudo-philanthropists say that the man shall eat. While it is an abiding law of Providence that the obstinately indolent, thriftless, and vicious should be left to the bitter retribution which is the divinely-appointed result, the morbidly benevolent, regardless of this law, inconsiderately subordinate to their own impulses the highest interests of the individual and of the community, by stepping in between folly and its cure; and, irrespective of character, bestow upon the lazy, the vagrant, and

---

[*] 2 Thes. 3 : 10.

the vicious, that which should only be for the solace of the suffering, the relief of the unfortunate and infirm, or the reward and encouragement of struggling poverty.

There was a period in the history of our city charities when, from the absence of available facilities, reliable information in respect to mendicants could not be obtained, so that there would be risk of suffering, provided none but investigated cases were relieved. That period happily passed away with the establishment of this institution. Being organized for the express purpose of meeting the charitable wants of the community, its arrangements and agencies have been specially adapted to the actual exigencies of the population, both rich and poor, however concentrated or diffused. Its three hundred and fifty-seven visitors, distributed over the city, are so many tangential points between the benevolent and the needy. All persons referred to them who live between the Battery and Harlem River, the Association, if sustained, is publicly pledged to care for, promptly, discreetly, humanely, according to the actual merit or demerit of each applicant. Ten years' experience has tested the efficacy of this system. Thousands of our most respectable and wealthy families have found, that so far as they have withheld indiscriminate alms at their doors and elsewhere, and made this Institution the channel of their charities, they have not only been saved from annoying applications, while all proper subjects have been effectively relieved, but also that able-bodied vagrancy has been diminished in the same ratio. It appears evident, therefore, that by the general co-operation of our citizens in such a plan, the cure of this description of pauperism and its attendant evils is as plain and practicable as the practice and its mischiefs are notorious and disgraceful. Let it not be encouraged and fostered, and it will be starved out. Forced to capitulate to its own necessities, it will be glad to resort to labor for its support. On the other hand, it is evident that this great social evil can neither be prevented nor remedied without the co-operation described. Why, then, should there not be this concurrent effort, especially when it is found that the *moral degradation* of those who are the subjects of indiscriminate aid is incomparably greater and more lasting than the physical inconveniences from which they are thus temporarily removed?

But on these and kindred topics, however interesting or important, the limits of this Report will not permit the Board to enlarge. In conclusion, therefore, they would only add, that while the Association, on a critical review of its own measures and action, is deeply conscious of having done less than it desired, it yet has the satisfaction to know that it has been dispassionate and earnest in its purpose, and has largely aided in promoting the well-being of those it was instituted to benefit. What, then, is required of it in future, but to modify its action by the experience of the past, and to conform its labors to those changes which time may develope and circumstances render expedient? The work before it is vast, momentous, and difficult, requiring patience, sympathy, and unfaltering perseverance; but, if wisely directed, its rewards are commensurately certain in the ultimate attainment of great and good results. Its grand mission being the physical and moral elevation of the poor by such methods as practical wisdom suggests and the principles of moral and economic science approve, why should there not be strong faith both in its objects and issues? Voluntary pauperism is a reproach to humanity, a disgrace to civilization, and a curse to any community. That it should be uprooted, as an exotic, alike foreign to our country and institutions, is not less certain than that the truly needy and unfortunate shall ever be with us as a Providential trust, to be kindly and discreetly cared for. The duty of laborious, self-sacrificing charity for such grows out of our relations to them as children of a common Parent, "who maketh the poor and the rich." Charity is indeed an element of our moral nature, identified with our own religious hopes, and inseparable from spiritual Christianity. Our obligations, therefore, " to consider the needy," and to " pity the afflictions of the afflicted," will ever remain until the "poor cease out of the land," and a paradisean state be restored.

And it is a cause of devout gratitude to God, and of gratulation to the Board, that these obligations have been felt and acknowledged by so many of their fellow-citizens. That amid the pressing and alluring occupations of this great city so many have volunteered to discharge the arduous and responsible duties of visitors to those "who cannot recompense them again." That so many, moreover, have given "out of their abundance," and others even "out of their deep poverty," for the relief of those poorer than themselves; so that it may in truth be said, "the high and low, the rich and poor, together" have, in the support of this Association, blended their commiseration and aid. The difficulty experienced is not to awaken the sympathy of those acquainted with the Institution, for such are its steadfast patrons; but so to diffuse a knowledge of its objects among the charitable who are uninformed of its nature and design, as that they also may appreciate its claims on their confidence and support. Next, therefore, to their own interest in this charity, the greatest favor the friends of the poor can confer upon it, is to excite a like interest in its behalf in the circles of their acquaintance; for its usefulness must ever be in proportion to its universality. Make this the channel of almsgiving for the city, and helpless distress will be relieved, the depressed elevated, the abuse of compassion prevented, and vagrancy and mendicity dried up at their source.

Association for Improving the Condition of the Poor in Account with Robert B. Minturn, Treasurer.

1853.				1853.		
Oct. 31.	To Amounts expended from Oct. 31, 1852,	$29,692 57		Oct. 31.	By Amounts received per donations from Oct. 31, 1852,	$31,359 16
	To Balance,	1,666 59				$31,359 16
		$31,359 16		1853.		
				Oct. 31.	By Balance at credit of Association,	$1,666 59

The undersigned Committee hereby certify that they have examined the foregoing account, find it correct, and properly vouched, showing a balance in the hands of the Treasurer on the 31st of October, of sixteen hundred and sixty-six dollars and fifty-nine cents.

JOS. B. COLLINS, } Committee.
THOS. DENNY,

New-York, Nov. 5th, 1853.

PRINTED FORMS USED BY THE ASSOCIATION.

Ticket of Reference for the use of Members.

Mr.   Visitor,

  No.   St.

is requested to visit

at No.

                                               Member

N. Y. Association for
Improving the Condition of the Poor.

Visitor's Order.

  Mr.
  No.   St.
Please let
have the value of
in

                      18

                                          Vis.

N. Y. Association for
Improving the Condition of the Poor.

Monthly Report.

Subjoined is a condensed plan of a Sectional Monthly Return. The original occupies a large page of foolscap, with appropriate columns, fifteen in number, which enable Visitors to give the following particulars of every family relieved. 1st. Name, residence, place of birth, sex, color, occupation, time in the city, number in family, and number of visits. 2d. Statements of character,—as being temperate or intemperate. 3d. Unavoidable causes of indigence, such as sickness, infirmity, or old age, with space for marginal remarks.

PRINTED FORM USED BY THE ASSOCIATION.

New-York Association for Improving the Condition of the Poor.

VISITOR'S MONTHLY REPORT OF SECTION No.   DISTRICT No.   DATED   18

☞ *A mark with a pen thus ,, in the columns, will point out the class to which the person named belongs.*

FAMILIES RELIEVED. — Always give full Name, and *male* Head of Family, if living.	RESIDENCE OF FAMILIES. — Which must be reported every month.	Foreigners.	Natives.	Colored Persons.	Males.	Females.	No. in Family.	No. of Visits.	KIND OF OCCUPATION.	Temperate.	Intemperate.	Sickness.	Misfortune.	Old Age.	AMOUNT EX-PENDED. $	cts.	REMARKS.

Signed,   Visitor.

List of Members.

Owing to inadvertence in the returns from some of the Districts, it is feared that the List of Members may not be perfectly accurate. The *amounts* received were duly credited, as may be seen by an inspection of the Treasurer's account, at the General Office. But as the names of some who contributed small sums did not accompany their donations, with all the efforts subsequently made to obtain them the list may still be incomplete.

A.

Astor, Wm. B.
Anderton, Ralph L.
Astor, J. J. jr. Mrs.
Astor, J. J. jr.
Aspinwall, W. H.
Aspinwall, J. L.
Adams, John
A Friend, by Brown, Brother & Co.
Alley, Miss
Aspinwall, L. E. Mrs.
Adams, C. & Co.
Ash, Joseph H.
Anderson & Combs
Aymar, John Q.
Aymar & Co.
Alsop, Joseph W.
Andria & Co.
A. W. & Co.
Adams, J. T.
Adams & Sturges
Ayres, Robert
Anthon, H. Rev.
Abbatt, Wm. M.
Abeel, Joanna, Miss
Alexander, James W. D.D.
Allen, G. F.
Andrew, Henry, & family
Averill, A.
Auffmordt, Hessenberg & Co.
Aymar, Wm.
A Delinquent
A Friend
Allard, Mrs.
Acker, Mrs.
Asche, Henry
Allen, Horatio

Allen, R.
Avery, H. M.
Abbatt, J.
Abbe, George W.
Allyn, Peter
Allison, M. jr.
Ackenback, Thomas
Anderson, Edward
Ambler, John L. Rev.
Andrews, R. C.
Adams, J. D.
Armstrong, J.
Alexander, Wm.
Arnoux, A. & G.
Adams, William
Atkins, John
Anderson, Hiram
Atchison, Mr.
Allen, Mrs.
Agate, J. B.
Arnold & Southworth
Allan & Rose
Apgar, L.
Allen, T. E.
Allison, C.
Alcock, Doctor
Allen, C. M.D.
Allison, Michael
A Friend
Abel, C. A.
Ackland, John
Albro & Brothers
Anthony, E.
A Friend
A Lady
Allen, Isaac
Amerman, J. W.
Allison, Thos. H.
Alford, Edwin M.
Abeel, C. Miss
Allen, G. C.
Acken, Isaac

Angevine, O.
Ayres, J. W.
Allen, Henry
Aird, Thomas
Ameling, T. A. Mrs.
A Friend
Aldrich, H. D.
Allen, W. M.
Aymar, B.
Aikman, Robert
Andrews, Wm. D.
Allen, John
Ashfield, A.
Austin, W.
Arnold, A. & Co.
Aitkin & Miller
A. T.
Abrams & Johnson
Anthony, J.
Allen, James
Anderson, E.
Arras, C. Mrs.
Aymar
Ayers, Reuben
Amos, Thomas
Ashley, S. S.
Ackenback, George
Archer, Isaac H.
Allen, John K.
Andrews, H.
Anthony, Mr.
Adams, W.
Arthur, W. H. & Co.
Almy, Pattison & Co.
A Friend
Alexander, F.
Alden, P.
Averill, J. Otis
Arnold, B. G.
A. C. R. & Co.
A. S.
Ayres, S. P.

LIST OF MEMBERS. (1853.)

A Friend
Attler
Abernethy, Charles
Appleton, D. & Co.
Atwater, W.
Amburger, C. W. & Co.
Alvord, C. A.
Austen, J. B.
A. & H. S. T. & Co.
Arcularius, A. M.
Averill, W. J.
Allen, Gilbert
A Lady
Albro, R.
Anstice, Henry
Auchmuty, Mrs.
Aims, Jacob
Adriance, Thomas M.
Arpin, P. Mrs.
Alvord, A. A.
Alexander, H. M.
Abbott, G. D.
Atterbury, Lewis, jr.
Anthony, A. K.
Anderson, E. J.
Agnew, Alexander M.
Alford, S. M.
Aspinwall
Anderson, C. E.
Adams, P. C.
Andrews, M. H.
Armstrong, M. & Sons
Anderson, A.
Aikman, Hugh
Aldrich, John V.
Allen, Wm. A.
Avery, James W.
Allerton, George W.
Arkenburgh, R. H.
Allerton, A. M.
Allerton, Charles H.

B.

Boorman, James
Brown, James
Brown, Wm. Smith
Banyer, M. Mrs.
Bronson, A. Mrs.
Burr, Isaac, Mrs.
Boorman, Johnston & Co.
Berrian, Mrs. Rev. by J. H.
 ̄ Weston
Beers, Abner
Bull, William G.
Bruen, A. M.
Brown, Stewart
Bronson, F. as Executor
Bronson, F.
Belmont, A.
Bridge, John
Bruce, George
Burr, J.
Blanco, B.
Butler, B. F.
Buckley & Co.

Beadel, Henry
Burnham, G. W.
Beadell, G. T.
Buckman, A. F.
Broadway Post-Office
Buckman, R. S.
Boorman, Robert
Brush, Walter F.
Barnum, P. T.
Baldwin, Starr & Co.
Bliss, Briggs & Douglass
Benkard, James
Blunt & Syms
Bronson, Miss
Banker, Edward, & Son
Baldwin, Adams & Co.
Beebe & Co.
Bowne, Robert
Bishop, Japhet
Blair, J. W.
Brown, Alexander, Mrs.
Butler, F. E.
Ball, Black & Co.
Banks, Mark
Brown, Albert
Bronson, S.
Barclay, Anthony
Barron, Thomas
Brooks, Horace
Borst, John B.
Bulkley, C. A.
Bronson, G. C.
Bange, Henry
Brisley, William J.
Brush, S. L. & Co.
Brown, M. Miss
Butler, F. E.
Bogardus, Wm.
Baldwin, J. L.
Brown, John
Baldwin, H. M.
Blackford, Edward
Bruslee, Wm. A.
Bristol, Thomas
Beesley, Isaiah
Brown, Nathan
Burnett, Peter, M.D.
Buttre, Wm.
Burrill, Samuel N.
Berry, J. F.
Baudoine, C. A.
Beck, James, & Co.
Bulpin, George, & Co.
Brodie & Co.
Brown, N. & J.
Bayley, William
Boyd, William
Brougham, Mr.
Bagley, Mrs.
Bonnett, D.
Brinkerhoff, Mrs.
Brush, P.
Burrell, John
Brez, Paul
Brown, Mrs.
Bush, R. J.
Bogardus, Mr.

Black, Thomas
Burhaus, S.
Butler, S. C.
Bowden, Andrew
Bowden, A. jr.
Burrell, Samuel
Baldwin & Sexton
Brower, A.
Bailey, J. D.
Barker & Philips
Birkbeck, George
Brower, J. L.
Brainard & Co.
Bullus, R. S. M.D.
Belzer, John
Bennet, N. L.
Butcher, Z.
Bradford, N. G.
Barker, N.
Bradley, Wm. C.
Belden Wm. Rev.
Baldwin, J. L.
Blake & Brown
Brady, M. B.
Becknell, J. J.
Beach, Harvey
Brown, Silas
Brown, H. L.
Burger, W.
Boyd & Wilkin
Boyd & Paul
Baker, Scudder & Co.
Bigelow, Mr.
Boyce, John
Bogart, A. L.
Beach, Mr.
Beaumont, J. P.
Bunker & Co.
Bunker, B. F. & Co.
Bryson, P. M.
Bevridge, J. & Co.
Beadel, J. H.
Butler, S. or T.
Brown, S. & Co.
Bellamy
Belknap & Griggs
Broadhead & Storms
Baibre, J.
Binninger & Cozzens
Bush, George
Bartholomew, J. H.
Bell, Abm.
Bouyee, A.
Bloodgood, William
Bruns, Thomas
Burt, L. A.
Brown, Mary
Baldwin, Mr.
Bowery Savings Store
Barnes, J. N.
Bennett, William
Boardman, John
Benedict, A. C.
Brennen, Owen C.
Barr, Alderman
Bauscher, Henry
Brommer, John

1853.) LIST OF MEMBERS. 45

Baldwin, M. Mrs.
Boyle & Kelly
Brown, John H.
Boyd, Daniel
Billinge, Mr.
Burke, William
Burr, John
Briggs, Isaac V.
Buchanan, R. M.
Blow & March
Bell, Richard
Boyd, John S.
Blakesly, A. W.
Bradford, A. W.
Butterworth, S. F. Mrs.
Bond, Thomas
Borden, William
Brown, Harvey
Betts, John S.
Barkley, J. T.
Bass, S. W.
Buckham, George
Brown, John H.
Babcock, Francis
Boardman, Norman
Bergh, George R.
Bridgeman, Andrew
Bradley, Mrs.
Bryant, Mrs.
Babcock, Edward
Barrows, Edward
Barnes, Daniel
Beecher, Nelson
Bennett, J. H.
Bolton, J. M.D.
Bonney, B. W.
Bussing, J. S.
Bonnett, P. R.
Bloodgood, N.
Ballard, P. Mrs.
Bininger, A.
Beeckman, H.
Brown, E. J.
Bogert, C.
Blatchford, E. H.
Burges, Henry J.
Bradford, W.
Brown, R. J.
Bacon, D. P.
Bouchard, E. Miss
Bushnell, O.
Bliss, J. C. M. D.
Buchanan, R. S.
Barrell, G.
Browne, J. F.
Burrowes, P.
Brooks, M. C.
Brown, R. W.
Bayliss, Henry
Bulkley, George
Bulkley, E.
Baker, Dobel
Belknap, E. S.
Briggs, A. F.
Buchanan, Mary, Mrs.
Brooks, J.
Barstow, Samuel

Bird, M.
Brower, Abraham
Barrow, H. H.
Brinkerhoof, Mr.
Buckley, M.
Beekman & Company
Bloodgood, M.
Blackstone, W.
Burkhalter Charles
Brinkerhoff, W.
Brower, J. D.
Bonsall, R. W. S.
Birdsall, S.
Bernheimer, Simon
Bloomfield, W.
Berrian, J. & C.
Bebee, William H.
Brown, W. M.
Bancroft, W. S.
Barnes, J. N.
Bogardus, Abraham
Burger, E. H.
Beckett, John
Blauvelt, D.
Borger, John J.
Broome-street, 460
Bogert, C.
Bootman, E.
Brownson, Wm. Mrs.
Bell, M.
Boggs, J. L.
Badeau, C. C.
Buckmaster, T. O.
Broger, M.
Brinckerhoff, Jacob
Briggs, George
Burnham, E. Mrs.
Breath, James
Baker, S. W.
Barmore, G. & H.
Burdette, H. C.
Banta, S.
Burgess, W. F.
Bartlett, A. H.
Bassford, A.
Brunner, William
Bush, R. T.
Benson, C. S.
Barrow, James
Bishop, D.
Butler, Henry
Bliven, Charles
Burdett, J.
Burkhalter, Stephen
Belden, D.
Bach, J. L.
Backus, J. S. Rev.
Bunn, Mrs.
Brown, J. T.
Button, J. J.
Brenley, I. E.
Bogert, Jacob C.
Brodie, John
Berdan, Mrs.
Bowron, J. W.
Battersby, J. C.
Banta, M.

Bogert, Albert, jr.
Brown, Anson S.
Bell, Thomas
Burnton, Mr.
Burritt, Francis
Brown, Charles E.
Brookman, H. D.
Burt, Brothers, & Co.
Bourry, D'Ivernois & Co.
Beach, D.
Benedict, S. W.
Barrett, N. P. H.
Brown & Dimock,
Burlew, R.
Bullock J. & J. B. Lock
Blow & March
Babcock & Co.
Bogert, S. G.
Brown, Thomas E.
Bernheimer Brothers
Beck, E. & Kunhardt
Baker & Duyckinck
Bigelow, Richard
Boyd, J. J.
Brown
Betman
Brockelman, S.
Beach, M. J.
Butterfield
Burrell, H. & Co.
B. M. C.
Benjamin, Wm. jr. & Co.
Buck & Inglis
Bunker & Van Boskerck
B.
Bacon
Burdsall, H.
Bell, Jacob
Brigham & Miller
Barber, W. C.
Bunce, Jeremiah S.
Bell, Mr.
Brooks & Cummings
Bouton, E.
Bear, Isaac
Boutelle, John A.
Brown, Lewis B.
Bangs, Brothers & Co.
Barrell, Nephew & Co.
Baldwin & Many
Baldwin, Studwell & Fisher
Bennett, M.
Buck, Swift & Seaman
Brown & De Rossett
Bishop, V.
Bishop, Mr.
Burr, Henry L.
Berger & Walter
B.
B. & S.
Bate, Thomas H.
Bean, D. S.
B. F. B.
Brown
Baker, J. A.
B. M
Bunce, G. H.

LIST OF MEMBERS. (1853.

B. & E.
Birdsall, W. jr.
Bleeker, Jane, Mrs.
Bogart, H. R.
Babcock, J. C. Mrs.
Brown, Paul S.
Brouwer, Jacob
Bruce, J. M.
Bangs, Lemuel
Banks, Theodore
Burke, M.
Brady, A. C.
Benedict, Mr.
Bissell, John
B. M. H.
Boy, P. W.
Butler, Charles
Beers, J. D.
Bigelow, Richard
Bailey, N. P.
Brown, E. M.
Bramwell, J.
Britton, W. A.
Bird, George
Bradley, J. N.
Butler, H. V.
Baker, James
Bryce, W.
Benjamin, W. M.
Burrit, G.
Bushnell, William
Bennett, J. L.
Brooks, Joshua
Busteed, George W.
Boyd
Ballow
Barton, C.
Bourn, Francis
Burdick, Perrin
Budd, Mrs.
Barnes, J.
Buck, J. W.
Bullock, C.
Boyce, Mrs.
Brown, Mrs.
Barrett, George
Baker, Henry
Banks, Theodore
Brahe, A. H.
Brombacher, Jacob
Burtis, James A.
Barker, Daniel
Badger, A. H.
Bush, Joseph
Beekman, J. C.
Bacon, S. C. Mrs.
Boll, Mr.
Black, Andrew
Brock, Miss
Brower, L.
Burucker, Mr.
Boorum, Mr.
Blachman
Benedict, Isaac H.
Burnett, Peter, M. D.
Bulen, John H.
Baxter, Samuel

Bruce, B. G.
Beers, N. P.
Belloni, Louis J.
Bush, J. W.
Bell, Joseph M.
Bradley, Wm. C.
Barry, R. A. M. D.
Barker, William
Brainerd, Augustus
Brown, Wm.
Brown, E. H.
Burr, John
Brown, J.
Brown, Richard
Brandon, George
Bridger, S.
Bull, H. K.
Burger, T. J.
Beatty, D. L.
Blackett, H. S.
Ballard, John B. Rev.
Butler, Wm. Allen
Buckley, C. H.
Bowen, William
Benedict, J. W.
Brewster, J. B.
Brummell, Adonijah
Bibbins, W. B. M. D.
Bogert, William
Benedict, E. C.
Baldwin, J. C.

C.

Cruger, Harriet Douglas, Mrs
Crosby, Wm. B.
Clark, R. Smith
Conklin, T. A.
Conklin, John
Collins, Joseph B.
Cutting, Fulton
Corning, Jasper
Clapp, J.
Center, E. C.
Clarkson, Matilda, Mrs.
Coates, Joseph H.
Case, A. S.
Coster, G. W.
Clark, Ed.
Corwin & Co.
Cotheal & Co.
Campbell, W. W.
Coolidge & Young
Crosby, J. P.
Cook, Zebedee
Collis, J.
Chesterman, James
Crane, D. B.
Chambers, Thomas
Cleaveland & Co.
Cotheal, A. J.
Cochran, Samuel
Cottenet, F. & Co
Coit, Henry A.
Curtis, L. & B. & Co.
Cousinery, F. & Co.

Cook, Levi & Co.
Chauteau, P.
Cary, W. F.
Condit & Noble
Congreve, Charles
Cooper, Peter
Carpenter, J.
Caswell, John
Colden, Mrs.
Cary, W. H.
Cunningham, James
Cammann, Doctor
Copcut, J. & F.
Chesebrough, M. Mrs.
Contoit, John H.
Carryl, N. T.
Cammann, O. J.
Campbell, G. W.
Coolidge, Henry
Coster, H. A.
Cornwell, W. K.
Cash, A Lady
Cock, Thos. F. M. D.
Cock, Thos. M. D.
Comstock, M. D.
Collins, R. B.
Collins, S. B
Cruikshank, James
Cauldwell, E.
Chamberlain, Chas.
Cristy, Moses
Cook, Jno.
Clark, Benjamin F.
Camp, Amzi Revd.
Conover, Stephen
Clawson, John M.
Cutter, Stephen
Cutter, Samuel R.
Collamore, E.
Cox, J. & I.
Cahill, S.
Cocks, James
Cash, (several)
Connelly, James
Cox, Doctor
Chalmers, Doctor
Campbell, A.
Cogswell, Miss
Cropsey, J.
Constantine, A. & R.
Cornell, G. C.
Campbell & White
Coit, Henry
Cameron, Mr.
Cunningham, Wm.
Christie, P. R.
Collins, John
Chattelin, John
Coggeshall, Mrs.
Cape, H. M. Mrs.
Cash
Cape, J. J.
Cash, (J. W.)
Clyde, Mrs.
Campbell, Mrs.
Carter, Thomas
Conklin, Mrs.

1853.) LIST OF MEMBERS. 47

Conger, John
Cockcroft, James, M. D.
Cumings, James
Cox, Mrs.
Carpenter, G. W.
Carter, Robert
Cornel, S. L.
Clark, A. H.
Cash, (by several)
Collins, Cummings, & Seaman
Corlies, J. W.
Chilton, Doctor
Cromwell, H.
Carman, R.
Comstock & Co.
Cummings, Robert
Clark, H. F.
Close, H.
Corwin, Abel
Clayton, E. B.
Crane, John J. M. D.
Cash.
Coey, W. J.
Chilson, Richardson & Co.
Church, C. M.
Campbell, Robert
Columbian Foundry
Cassibeer, H. A.
Conover, S.
Cornell & Nesbitt
Caffrey, Geo. W.
Chapin, L.
Clussman, C. L. Mrs.
Craig, Mrs.
Cook, James H.
Clark, James
Crane, Philander
Case, A. J.
Currahger, Capt.
Croft, Joshua
Chichester, Lewis
Christy, Thomas
Constant, S. S.
Chichester, Wm. S.
Cable, Walton
Cash
Coddington, Mr.
Church, John B.
Carpentier, J. S.
Cummings, J. P.
Curry, D. F.
Clark, George
Conover, S. jr.
Coburn, R. H.
Conklin, Isaac
Cheesman, O.
Crane, Benjamin F.
Cabrera, T.
Clark, J. A.
Clark, Thos. J. G.
Coles, C.
Clark, F. G.
Connor, James E.
Carey, John
Chapman, George
Cowl, James

Clark, Mrs.
Clark, James S.
Cypher, W. J.
Carson, G. W.
Clark, L. G.
Cummings, James P.
Cummings, Wm. A. Mrs.
Clark, John
Cassedy, James
Coles, A. P.
Cook, E. G.
Cargill, Thos. S.
Claggett, M.
Cogswell, Henry
Conklin, H.
Conacher, John
Cooper, John
Cranna, George
Clark, George
Carter, Walton
Campbell, James
Clark, P.
Catlin, D. W. Mrs.
Callender, S.
Chattelain, J.
Cuming, T. B.
Clark, J.
Collins, Miss
Clark, E. S.
Conant, T. J.
Clarke, G. W.
Cobb, J. N.
Coles, J. W. Mrs.
Couch, Wm.
Catterfield, W. F.
Corwith, Mrs.
Clark, H. C.
Cauldwell, Mrs.
Cock, E. &. W. & Co.
Close, J. B.
Cock, Geo. E.
Cromwell, Edward
C. S. R.
Chase, Henry
Cromwell, Richard
Clark, H.
Christopher, R.
Cauldwell, E. Miss
Cludius, Chas.
Cromwell, A. Mrs.
Currie, John H.
Cone, S. H.
Cornell, T. F.
Clark, Alexander
Cook, J.
Clarke, James
Cargill, A. Mrs.
Cragin, G. D.
Craig, J. J.
Crowen, Thos. J.
Cooley, F.
Clayton, A. J.
Cohen, B. A.
Crosby, C. W.
Civill, Anthony
Clarke, M.
Cook, Geo. H.

Cameron, Miss
Campbell, W. S.
Campbell, F.
Clark, Edward P.
Conover, G. A.
Clark & Coleman
Clinton, Doctor
Clowes, J. W.
Cummings, Thos.
Creighton & Edwards
Cumings, A.
Childs, Asa
Cornell, John H.
Cook, Edward
Chrystie, J.
Cunningham, W. J.
Coulter, Samuel
Coleby, H.
Cook, R. S.
Chesebro, Albert
Cotheal, H. L.
Coles, W. H.
Crocker, Wm. A.
Collier, Thos.
Chamberlin, E.
Clarke, Wm.
Colt, Mrs.
Cox, Mrs.
Cash, (by several)
Cerf, Beer, May & Co.
Coit, Henry
C. E. N.
Crabtree, W. F.
Collomb, Felix
Crooks, Ramsey
Carr, Burnett & Co.
Chesebrough, Silsby & Co.
Caesar & Pauli
Coffin, E.
C. A. S. & Co.
Curtis, Cyrus
Curtis, F. & Co.
Cassidy, T.
Collins, Charles
Cook, Joseph J.
Carhart, G. B.
Codwise, D.
Clark, C. W.
Colyer, W.
Curtis, Charles
Columbe, Thos.
Chapin, R. S. M. D.
Chesebrough N. H. M. D.
Crane, Rufus E. & Co.
Chandler, J. & Foster
Cash
Crocker, James & Co.
Center, A. H.
Comstock, A. & W. S.
Chapman, L.
Craft, P.
Corwin, D. W.
Clark, L. E.
C. W.
C. & H.
Culver, David
Coit, S.

LIST OF MEMBERS. (1853°

Chardavoyne, Mrs.
Cromwell, Wm. D.
Chanler, Mrs.
Clark M. P.
Campbell, J. jr.
Chambers, J. Mrs.
Cahoone, Wm.
Clinch, L. H.
Coe, D. B.
Crumbie, James
Chandler, J.
Collins, J. W.
Collord, G. W.
Cooper, Charles
Culver, J. W.
Clarke, L. H.
Cantrell, Saml.
Crane, E. Miss
Cowan, James
Colgate, Robert
Cheever, Geo. B. Rev.
Colgate, George, Mrs.
Curtis, Joseph
Curtis, P. A.
Comstock, William
Carpenter, U. F.
Crane, Theodore
Curtis, J. L.
Carey, John, jr.
Chigary, W. D.
Coster, D. J. Mrs.
Campbell, W. W.
Croghan, Mrs.
Cooper & Brothers
Chave, Wm. G.
Chambers, Talbot W.
Carlin, John
Cutler, P. Y.
Crane, D.
Cronk, S. W.
Cook, John, Mrs.
Carpenter & Co.
Cooper, Mr.
Camp, T. D.
Coyle, J. jr.
Crosby, F. J.
Cade, Mrs.
Cutler, Grace
Coughtry & Dougherty
Carrill, N.
Carle, John, jr.
Crap, J.
Chamberlain, Charles
Canton Tea Company
Cable, Mrs.
Cornell, Mr.
Clark, Mrs.
Coolidge, Geo.F. & Brother
Close, David
Contrell, Joseph
Currier, Nathaniel
Conover, Daniel
Clark, James
Carson, John C.
Cragin, Charles A.
Clarkson, C. V. M. D.
Cameron, John

Colwell, W. H.
Chichester, Lewis
Cook, J. F.
Clark, J. A.
Carter, Peter
Cummings, J. P.
Cole, R.
Cornell, Marks
Cowl, J.
Crane, E.
Crane, D.
Crosby, J.
Chadwick, A. B. M. D.
Carman, W. S.
Chichester, D.
Courier & Enquirer,

D.

Douglass, George
Dean, Thomas
De Forrest, W. W.
Durand, C.
Denny, Thomas
Davies, J. M. Jones & Co.
Delafield, Edward, M. D.
Dean & Thornton
Derham & Moore
De Peyster, F.
Deruyter, John
Dubois & Vandervoort
Delafield, E.
Davis, D. H.
Day, M.
De Forrest, G. B. & Co.
Donation, a fund from }
  Journal of Commerce }
D. T.
Donaldson, J.
Dennison, L.
De Peyster, Susan M. C.
  Miss
Duer, John
Decker, Alfred
Dubois, H.
Dibblee, Work & Moore
Dibblee, H. E. & Co.
Dowley, John
Draper, Simeon
Dale, James G.
De Launey, Iselin & Co.
Duncan, W. B.
Dows & Cary
Dickie, Patrick
Dunham H.
Dwight, John & Co.
Davidson, John
Dunning, James W.
Decker, Charles M.
Darling, C. C. Rev.
Dyer, Charles C.
Dakin, C. P.
Deems, Henry W.
Devoy, Michael
Dawson, George H.
Dean, Captain
Duncan. Francis

Dodge, Josiah
Disosway, C. R.
Duff, James, jr.
Duff, James
Day, Henry
Davis, W. E.
Dunn, Philip
Demarest, James
Donaldson, William
Dalrymple, Alexander
Duncan, J. & Sons
Davison, Mr.
Delhoyo, F.
Davenport, R.
Dean, W. E.
Delafield, Doctor
Drake, Mrs.
Denison, Charles, jr.
Dejonge, Mr.
Depuga, Mr.
Deraismas, John
Dailey, John
Dixon, Mr.
Dodd, John M.
Dunn, Mrs.
Dung, Albert
Drake, Benjamin
Drummond
Derby, L. L.
Doyton, W. H.
Dotscher, C.
Duckworth, Nelson
Duckworth, M. H.
Daitz, G. F.
Duryea, P.
Demilt & Vreeland
Draper, Clark & Co.
Dunshee, Samuel
Davis, C.
Doolittle, A. M. D.
Dickson, J. R.
Doughty, J. H.
Dickson, James
Dairs, Joseph
Decker, Joseph
Dayton, Isaac
Demarest, S. D.
Down, Samuel
Dominick, F.
Delamater, John
Downing, A. C.
Downer, S. P.
Donohue, Mr.
Denman, Alderman
Demarest, P. P.
Doremus, P.
Davis, Mr.
Dennis, S. A.
Denham, John
Deming, Mr.
Devling, Francis
Dymock, William
Dainty, Jonathan
Dodge, William H.
Dolan, William
Dominge, E. Mrs.
Dunn, Hugh S.

1853.) LIST OF MEMBERS. 49

Day, Charles
Dyer, Thomas
Draper, John
Day, Mrs.
Dehon, Theodore
Davison, E.
Dorr, G. B.
De Coppet, L.
Detmold, W. M. D.
De Witt, T. Rev. Dr.
Douglass, H. J. M. D.
Davis, H. E.
Dean, Henry
Durand, A. B.
Dustan, S. Mrs.
Dayton, W. P.
Dubois, C.
Dwight, Edmund
Dewing
Dayton, S.
Deniston, William
Denike, A.
Derrickson, E. J.
D. R. S.
Dellinger, C.
Dupuy, Eugene
Delluck & Co.
Demarest, Daniel
Delgado, F. P.
Devoe, Daniel M.
Duncan, James
Dieden, John
Dusenberry
Douglass, John
Dudley, W. J.
Dean, Thomas
Dodworth, H. B.
Dominge, P. E.
Danforth, Mr.
Dana, R. P. Mrs.
Dickie, E. P.
Demarest, Abraham
Delano, J. W.
Doran, J.
Degrau, J.
Dodge, S. V.
Davy, Thomas
Donelson, Wm.
Delmonico, Joseph
D. B. & Co. per N. D. D.
Dunscomb & Barnstorff
David & Henriques
Duncan & Burdett
Dayton, Sprague & Co.
Day, J.
Dyke
Dord C. & Co.
Dennistoun, F.
Dollner & Potter
De Luz, J. P.
Deeker, J. W.
Delamontagnie, E.
Dickinson, W. W.
Dunbar, George C.
Douglass, George
Delano, Frederick A.
Dillon, R.

Deitz, Brothers & Co.
Draper
Droz, H. E.
Dubois, Francis
Davis, C. & J.
D.
D. & C.
Dane
Dodd F.
De Forrest, Lockwood, Mrs.
Day, B. H.
Donaldson, Catharine
Dodge, John T.
Delapierre, C. B.
Dominick, E.
Dibblee, Mrs.
Duggan, B.
De Forrest, H. G.
Dodge, Wm. E.
Delprat, John
Dash, John B.
Dwight T.
Day, Henry
Ducas, M.
Dignan, Patrick
Davis, Martha
Dodge, J. N.
Durkee, C. N.
Doremus, Peter
Drees, W.
Dengledain, Mr.
Dougherty, Andrew

E.

Edgar, William
Earle, John H.
Egleston, Thomas
Elsworth, H.
Eyre, Henry
Eno, Amos R.
Eastman, A. L.
Engle, J. & S.
Everett & Brown
Emmet, T. A.
Eaton & Vernon
Everst, George H.
Elliot, Volney
Everett, N. C.
Eager, W. B. M. D.
Evans, L. G.
Endicott, John
Elliot, Eneas
Egbert, J. C.
Erskine, J.
Ellis, William
Egan, D. D.
Ellsworth, William
Embury, Peter
Edinger, Herman
Earle, Thomas
Ellsworth, H.
Evelyne, H.
Enzelbruch, J. C.
Elder, A. M. D.
Esler, Edward

Emerson, J. M.
Eaton, D. C.
Emmett, T. A.
Ewen, D.
Elliot, John
Edwards, Robert
E. P. D.
Edwards, D.
Engles, S. S.
Ely, George
Effray, F.
Eldridge, Mrs.
Ensign, J. L.
Engs, P. W.
English, W. C. R.
Endicott, Mrs.
Edwards, G.
Escher & Rush
Ewen, John
Engler, Charles
Elkins, T.
Eggert, D. & Sons
Ellis, R. & T. P.
Ely, N. K.
Ely, A. L.
Elphinstone, W. H.
Erhard
Everdell, William
Ely & Keese
E.
Easton, Charles
Ensign, E. H.
Everitt, C. L.
Ellis, R. S.
Ely, N. C.
Ebbets, Daniel
Evarts, Wm. M.
Elliott, M. E. Mrs.
Erskine, John
Eastman, Mr.
Earle, Cornelius
Ely, Smith
Evaus, John
Egglestone & Battelle
Ellis, J. A.
Ellis, B.
Edwards, Alfred
Ely, R. S.

F.

Fleming, J. B.
Few, Catharine, Mrs.
Foster, James, jr.
Fergusen, S. F.
Fergusen, E.
Field, B. H.
Fardon, Abraham, jr.
Fiedler, Ernest
Faile, Thomas H.
Field, Cyrus W. & Co.
Frost & Hicks
Foster, Thomas R.
Folger, R. W.
Fellows & Cooper
Fellows & Co.

3

Fellows, Lewis S. & Schell
Foster, F. G.
Fowler, F. R.
Forgay, William
Fowler, T. O.
Fish, Col. Mrs.
Fisher, Daniel
Florentine, Abraham
Falconer, E.
Ferguson, Alexander
Fanning, Solomon
Forster, T. V.
Fields, Edward, M. D.
French, Daniel
Freeman, James
Ferguson, J. B.
Foster, Wm. A.
France, J.
Fleet, S.
Freeman, Norman
Fisher, J. G.
Ferris, J. H.
Ferris, Doctor
Fieldman, J. G.
Favre, C. F.
Finch, A.
Fuller, Mr.
Field, Robert M.
Field, Jonah
Floyd, B. W.
Foster, W. R.
Fink, E.
Fraser, E. A.
Freedman, S.
Francis, C.
Frasee, Mrs.
Farrar, J. D.
Francis, C. S.
Foster, H. L.
Fisher & Cushing
Fuller, L.
Furman, S. A.
Fowler, J. O.
Foster, J.
Fair, J. G.
Ford, J.
Fatman, Joseph
Frier, Isaac
Foster, George
Freeman, James
Freeman, William
Forgay, William
Flanders, Elijah
Folwell, Nathan
Freund, O.
Flynn, Edward
Finch, Ferris
Forrester, Charles
Franklin, Morris
Francis, Wm. A.
Flagg, A. C.
Faxon, W.
Fox, G. H.
Finch, Sanderson & Co.
Fleury, James A.
Fleming, Robert
Freeman, N. P.

Fowler, John, jr.
Fisher, Henry
Ferguson & Brother
Fleming, J. B.
Frear, Alexander
Field, B. H.
Freeborn, W. A.
Francis A. Mrs.
Freeborn, J. F.
Fox, R. N.
Ferris, O. L.
Francis, N. Mrs.
Fisher, George H.
Frazer, William
Farnham, G. W.
Fleming, Mrs.
Fowler & Sons
Forbes, William
Freeman, Wm. C.
Fish, E.
Ferris, J. G.
Ford, E.
Freeman, C.
Frazee, Abraham
Furman, C.
Flint, C.
Freeland, S.
Fairbank, D.
Foote, T. C.
Fitch,
Fuller, Dudley B.
Francia, Gomez & Co.
Frost, Samuel
Foulke, Joseph
Fox & Polhamus
Fisk, J. M.
Fowler, John & Talmage
Fiancier, A. P.
Fisher, Joseph
Fuller, W. B.
Fox & Oothout
Folsom, Charles J.
Fowler, John H.
Fitz, H.
Ferris, E.
Fansher, Wm. H.
Frisbie, M. J.
Fleming, Thomas
Freeman, D. C.
Finn, A. T.
Fraser & Everitt,
F. C.
Fox, E.
Frey, W. H. & Brother
Fischell,
Frasee, P. A.
Foulke, Thomas
Fisher, Joseph
Fanning, T.
Freeman, J. C.
Falls, W. H.
Frost, Samuel
Frazer, T.
Frost, M.
Fust, Mr.
Fox, P.
Friend

French, Richard
Fanning, S.
Fish, Daniel
Friend
Fox, Charles
Fox, George
Faulkner, J. C.
Foey, P.
Fanning, J.

G.

Griswold, George
Green, John C.
Gallatin, A. R.
Grinnell, Moses H.
Griswold, John
Gihon, John
Graves, Boonen & Co.
Goodhue & Co.
Grosvenor J.
Grant & Barton
Gibbes, R. M.
Griswold, George, jr.
Geraud, J. P.
Gelston, M.
Greene, D. H.
Griffin, G.
G. C. & C.   box 1753
Goodwin, Eli
Gold Piece
Gould, Charles
Greenway, J. H.
Gilbert, Clinton
Gilpin, John
Gaw, A. Mrs.
Grosvenor, Seth
Groesbeck, Brothers
Gillet, Augustus I.
Gillies, Wright
Gates, John
Gray, Wm. Rev.
Gillilan, John
Geer, Darius
Griswold, Edwin
Gardner, Moses
Greaves, John
Goodell, Alfred
Gibson, James R.
Green, A.
Griffin, H,
Greene, G. W.
Gibbens, R.
Gordon, P.
Grinsted, David
Griscom, John H. M. D.
Graham, John C.
Gregg, Franklin
Goupil, Mr.
Greene, Thomas T.
Godonoy, Mr.
Gurney, Mr.
Grice, Charles C.
Gammond, Mr.
Greenly, George
Graham, John

LIST OF MEMBERS.

Geraud, Mrs.
Gillespie, J. M.
G. M. T.
Green, Mrs.
Gardnier, Mr.
Godine
Gage, Sloanes & Dater
Gilsey, P.
Green, G. D.
Gilbert & Tuttle
Gillies, Wright
Gibson, Wood
Glen, Mr.
Greenleaf & Kinsley
Geery, J. N. W.
Griffiths, Mr.
Goadby, Thomas
Gilpin, Lucy, Mrs.
Green, James
Geschidt, Doctor
Gumbs, E. Mrs.
Goodsman, Thomas
Gillies, Wm. R.
Gardner, Henry
Griffiths, J. M.
Groesbeck, Brothers
Gilman, Wm. S.
Glentworth, J. B.
Gall, John J.
Grant, M. O. Mrs.
Genin, Mr.
Goldsmidt, Mrs.
Glover, Ralph
Green, James
Green, Wm. A.
Gentle & Wilder
Gunning, E.
Garfield, Miss
Giraud, J. P.
Gallatin, James
Gilbert, Clinton
Griswold, N. L. Mrs.
Gregory, J. G.
Green, W. C.
Greenway, J. H.
Gunning, T. B.
Gelston, Maltbie
Gray, John A.
Gray, J.
Graydon, Samuel
Gillespie, James L.
Gale, William
Graff, John A.
Gardner, Samuel J.
Gross, Michael
Gordon, R.
Gedney, Sylvanus
Ganse, J.
Gray, John
Gridley, Edward
Gregory, L.
Gabaudan, A. W.
Gunn, A. N. M. D.
Griffiths, Charles
Green, Edward
Groshon, John
Gray F. C.

Gorman, Walter
Griffin, S.
Glassford, F. Mrs.
Gillespie, James
Goodliff, T.
Graydon, J. W.
Gignoux, C.
Goldsmith, J.
Gibbs, Wm. S.
Gregory, W. A.
Godfrey, E. J.
Gardner & Blake
Gregory, James
Gunther, C. G. & Sons
Guiden, J.
Green, Joseph W.
Gordon & Talbot
Gilbert, C.
Green, Miss
Graydon, Mrs.
Goadby, Mrs.
Geer, D. W.
Gale, A. H. & Co.
Greenwood, Mrs.
Goold, E. L.
Gresham, Mr.
Gray, E. C. Mrs.
Greenway, E. M.
Greenway, Wm. W. T.
Gansley, Shephard
Gilbert, F. R.
Gibbes, T. S.
Gratacap
Grestice, Mrs.
Gibson, J.
Gregory, E. W.
Gardner, D.
Green, Alonzo
Guthrie, J. E.
Guest, H. B.
Gillett, Mrs.
Gaintz, Mrs.
Good, Mrs.
Gray, John A.
Greerz, Miss

H.

Harsen, Jacob, M. D.
Hitchcock, W. R.
Halsted, W. M.
Hewitt, Lees & Co.
Harris, Evans & Co.
Hedges, C. Miss
Holbrook, E. Mrs.
Hall, Valentine G.
Heckscher, C. A.
Hopkins, E. M.
Hunt, Thomas & Co.
Herrick, J. B.
Hoppock, Ely
Henderson, H.
Howland, John
Harper & Brothers
Hoge, William
Hall, Dana & Co.
Hayes, H. M.

Hennequin, H. & Co.
Handford & Brothers
Hunt, Wilson G. & Co
Haskell, Merrick & Bull
Havemeyer, W. F.
Havemeyer, F. C. H.
Havemeyer D. M.
Herring, S. C.
Hamersly, J. W.
Hamersly, Mrs.
Hurry, J. A.
Harrison, Miss
Hartley, Robert M.
Hodges, A. C.
Hoffman
Hadden, D.
Hoffman, L. M.
Hopkins & Co.
Henry, Joshua A.
Harrison, Mrs.
Holden, H.
Heming, A.
Hume, Andrew
Horton, J. B.
Horton, Richard, Rev.
Hyde, H. P.
Harris, W. D.
Harris, John
Hatt, George, Rev.
Henderson, A. J.
Hurd, Hiram
Hayter, Richard, Rev.
Hosack, N. P.
Hall, Archibald
Halsey, H. A
Harris, Charles J.
Holt, Joseph S.
Hoagland, John S.
Housworth, Thomas
Huse, J. B.
Howell, M. H.
Horn, James
Holman, Thomas
Hawkins, C. P.
Hogan, Thomas
Higgins, J. O.
Hickson, J. S.
Hutchings, John
Howe, Bezaleel
Haight, Edwin M.
Heller, W.
Hoffman, Mrs.
Haughwort & Durley
Hilger, M.
Hyatt, E.
Halsted, J. W.
Hunt, William S.
Heard, J. S. M. D.
Hageman, John
Hitchcock, U. L.
Higgins, A. F.
Havemeyer, George L.
Hillyer, John B.
Howard, George
Hicks, Mr.
Hunt, Mrs.
Haight, Rev. Dr.

LIST OF MEMBERS. (1853.

Hamilton, P. P.
Holdridge, J. Rev.
Howell, C.
Hockman, William
Hard, N. G.
Hall, A. B.
Hopper, S.
Hewitt, H. N.
Hermeanu, Mr. Rev.
Hopper, A. D.
Hasbrouck, A. B.
Howes, M.
Heyward, H.
Howland, B. J.
Hall, Francis
Higbie, N. T.
Hutton, M. S. Rev.
Harrison, C. J. Miss
Hatt, J. Prescott
Holmes & Co.
Hayes, Horace
Hook, C. G.
Hoe, R. R. & Co.
Haydock, Robert
Hawley, J.
Hanford, P.
Haydock, H. W.
Hall, Daniel K.
Hewlett, Oliver T. Mrs.
Hewlett, Joseph
Harmer, Charles
Hait, John W.
Hall, Thomas
Herbert, J.
Halsey, E. C.
Hall, James F.
Howell, Mrs.
Hovencamp, John
Hasbrouck, G. D.
Haise, J.
Howser, J.
Halleck, W. A.
Hasbrouck, Doctor
Hart, John I.
Hunt, Mrs.
Hitchcock & Leadbeater
Humphreys & Peterson
Hill, John
Hyke, Mr.
Heilbeck, Mr.
Hawes, W. E.
Hosack, A. E. M. D.
Harvey, Mrs.
Hunter, James
Hardenburgh, J. B. Rev.
Hyslop, R.
Henry J. Mrs.
Henry, Philip
Husted, Mrs.
Huston, Mrs.
Harrison & Jones
Halsey, H. A.
Harrison, Mrs.
Hasbrook, J. L.
Herrick, J.
Hyatt, Thaddeus

Hunter, C. E.
Hagarth, James
Henry, J. G.
Hamilton, W. A.
Homan, R. S.
Hullemiron, H.
Hunt, Mr.
Hampton, Mrs.
Hyatt
Hadley
Hall, General
Hagerty, Green & Co.
Hall, Thomas
Herrick & Koster
Haws & Hinsdale
Halsted, Mr.
Harrison, W.
Haley, J. J.
Houston, J.
Hodgkins, T. G.
Hall, Rucker & Co.
Hope & Co.
Hammersley, L. C.
Hammersley, Mrs.
Hall, G. L.
Hall, J.
Hopkins, H. & J.
Hopkins, Francis
Hoppock & Mooney
Hustace, John
Hawes, L.
Hewlett, G. T.
Hadley, R.
Hurlburt, C. T.
Hutchler, J. V.
Hammersley, the Misses
Horton, Charles
Houghton, E.
Hodges, P. H.
Heath, Mrs.
Hunt, Seba
Hutchins, J.
Hoffman & Shubart
Halsey, S. R.
Hoey, Peter
Hoe, R. & Co.
Holstein, John
Harger, J.
Hasbrook, B. H.
Hutchings, William
Hern, Brothers
Hedden, C. H.
Hurd, J. R.
Hutchinson, Ira
Hall, C. Mrs.
Harriott, James
Hatfield, R. G.
Heidelback, M.
Henderson, John C.
Hunt, John
Hays, C.
Harned, Wm.
Higgins, L. & I.
Haddock, W. J.
Herring, S. C.
Hertzel, J. H.

Huse, John B.
Hoffman, Miss
Hirshfield, H.
Hume, Alexander
Hale, J. W.
Hart, Robert H.
Holden, Samuel
Herder, N. D.
Hunt, H. W.
Hall, W. T.
Hutchinson, V. or T.
Hoagland, A.
Hendrix, Isaac
Harcous, Brothers & Co.
Hill, Hyde & Co.
Hyatt, E.
Haggerty, Jones & Co.
Hyde, D. C. & Co.
H. P. Co.
Hoxie, J. jr.
Hubbard, N. T.
Hubble & Pattee
Hostage, Francis
Hawkins & Logan
Hoguet & Dias
Haydock, R.
Hooze, Frederick
Harvey, Willard
H. S. H.
H. T. B.
Hamilton
Horn, B. C.
Hopkins, E. A.
Harrison, T.
Haft, John
Hatfield, G.
Hart, Felix
Hyser, Jacob
Helenbeck
Heckett
Hall, A. A. & Brother
Hoyt, E. T.
Hayden, P. A. T.
Haviland, Brother & Co.
Holden, James C.
Hyde, J. E.
Heyer, Edward P. & Co.
Hunter, R. H.
Hook, J. D. W.
Hodgeman, D.
Henry, John, & Co.
Hoyt, S. & Co.
Hatheway, F.
Halsey, W. & Co.
H. J. B.
Hoyt, W. & O.
Henricks, Charles A
Hallstead, B.
Holmes
Hewett, H. T.
Huesmann
Hatch, C. B. & Co.
Horn, C. V.
Hicks, Wm. T. & Co.
H. J.
Harrison, H.

1853.)   LIST OF MEMBERS.   53

Hitchcock, Cyrus
Hotchkiss, Wm. B.
Hoople, Wm. H.
Huntington, Mr.
Hull, J. S.
Hay, Allan & Co.
Hyde, Joseph
Hart, Lucius, Mrs.
Harriman, O.
Harper, S. B. Mr. & Mrs.
Hitchcock, E.
Hart, James, sen.
Hillman, Samuel, Mrs.
Hutchings, S. B. Mrs.
Hamlin, P. V.
Herrick, Elias H.
Harbeck, J. H.
Harbeck, Wm. H.
Hurry, Edmund
Hayton, M. A.
Hunt, H. D.
Holmes
Hilton, Archd.
Hyde, S. T.
Heister, J.
Harris, Mr.
Hanks, Mr.
Hettrick, M. H.
Hatch, Alexander
Hart, J. C.
Hasey, Alonzo
Hall, Archibald
Harding, R.
Hazen, John
Hart, H. & M.
Hayatt, George E. L.
Hepburn, J. C.
Hull, J. C.
Hyatt, Mr.
Hilmer, C. D
Holden, Miss
Hill, Charles H.
Hoyt, Mr.
Howard, Joseph W.
Hurenschmidt, Alfred
Helmich & Schmidt
Howard, S. W.
Hayen, J. H.
Hendee, C. M. by J. L. Baldwin
How, Calvin W.
Hall, Henry C.
Holman, Henry
Hubbard, J. M.
Halsted, R. F.
Heydon, Wm.
Humbert, W. B.
Harris, E. M. D.
Halsted, A. L.
Hayden, Nathaniel
Hazeltine, L.
Hamilton. G. J.
Hatfield, James
Husted, J. N. M. D.
Hines
Hepburn, J. C. M. D.
Haines, A. J.

I. & J.

Jay, Ann, Miss
Ireland, Wm. B.
Jay, Elizabeth Clarkson, Miss
Johnson, E. T.
Jaffray, J. R. & Sons
Irvin, Richard
Jay, John
Jones, Rowland & Co.
Jones, George
Jones, George F.
Jones, J. J.
J. M. W.
Irving, R.
Jones, Isaac
Jones, C.
Johnson & Lazarus
Jones, F. M. & Co.
Janes, Beebe & Co.
Jones, J. C. Mrs.
Jenkins, J. Foster, M. D.
Isham, W. B.
Johnson, Austin
Jones, W. R.
Jackson, John E.
Jackson, Lewis E.
Jervis, William
Jones, C. J.
Jackson, Thomas
Johnston, Wm.
Jackson, Luther
Irwin, D.
Jones, H.
Jeremiah, Thomas
Johnson, J. K.
Ives, J. M. D.
Johnson, Jonathan K.
Janes, Revd. Mr.
Jackson, Mrs.
Jackson, J. A.
Ireland, George
Ireland, George, jr.
Ireland, Sophia, Mrs.
Johnson, T. D.
Jennings & Co.
Ivison, E.
Johnson, W. S.
Jenkins, J. J.
Jenkins, E. W.
Jackson & Many
Johnson, G. W.
Irwin, Wm.
Jenkins, Richard
Jervis, J.
Jervis, John B.
Johnson, Wm.
Johnson, S.
Johnson, Saml. R.
Irwin, David
Johnson, J. W.
Jacobus, C. C.
Jones, S. W.
Jackson, Wm. H.
Jenkins, Thos. F.
Jaques, D. K.
Jones, J. A.

Jones, J. Q.
Jay, Wm.
Jones, E. R. Mrs.
Jones, Miss
Jennings, J. E.
J. L.
Jones, John
Jacobus, D.
Jeffers, W. H.
Jones, M. R.
Jones, Ann, Mrs.
Johnson, E. A.
Jennings, S. H.
Jacobson, F.
Johnson, J. J.
Jessup, B. T.
Jung, John W.
Judson, Curtis
I. W. W. & Co
J. C. H.
Jee, Carmer & Co.
Jewells, Harrison & Co.
Jones, D.
Jarvis, J.
Jackon, J. L.
Jimmerson & Beers
Jones, J. F.
Jones, Mr.
J. W. Q.
Journay, A. Jur. & Co.
J. L. R.
J.
J. P. S.
J. C. M.
Jeremiah, Thomas
Jeremiah, T. F.
Jung, T. C.
Jones, A. H.
Jones, L.
Jones, A. S.
Jenkins, R. F.
J. S.
Johnson, M.
Irving, J. T. Mrs.
Irving, Gabriel T. Mrs.
Innes, Edward S.
Jones
Ives, Enos
Irving, Wm.
Johnson, W. F.
Johnson, R. & Son
Jamison, Chas. M. Revd.
Johnston, Robt. J.
Irvine, Mrs.

K.

Ketchum, Morris
King, Peter V.
Kirby, L. W. & Co.
Kemble, Wm.
Knapp, Sheppard
King, James G. & Sons
Kip, B. Livingston
King, John A.
Kennedy, D. S.

LIST OF MEMBERS. (1853.

Kirby, L & V. & Co.
Kingman, M. E.
Kennedy, John A.
Kirby, Wm.
Kidd, W. E.
Kelly, Joel
Knox, James
Kip, Mr.
Knapp, James
Ketchum
Ketchum, E. C.
Keeler, E.
Keep, H.
Knapp, Cyrus
Kattenhorne & Romaine
Kelly, R. L.
Kennedy & Hill
Kennedy, J. A.
King, W. F.
Kennedy, Thos.
Kelly, Wm.
Keys, J. & J. D.
Kellogg, H. L.
Korn, F.
Keyser, Mary, Mrs.
King, Wm.
Knox, Calhoun & M'Clintock
Kemp, Mrs.
King, Wm. Mrs.
Kettell, Thos.
Ketchum, Enoch
Ketchum, Hiram
Kearney, E.
Kersheept, A.
Knox, J. M.
Kissam, M. Miss
Kane, Delancy
Kissam, R. S. M. D.
Kinsley, H. M. D.
Kingman, H. W.
Kornahrens, H.
Kissam, James, M. D.
Kinch, W.
Kerr, John
Kimball
Knight, Fenn. Mrs.
Katzenstein, J.
Ketcham, T.
Knowlton, D.
King, R. S.
Kemp, Wm.
King, J. B.
Knapp, W. H.
Kohnstaum, S.
Koop, Fischer & Co.
Kelly, F. M.
K. & W.
Keeley, Philip
Killen, A.
Knouse, Chas.
Kissam & Keeler
Kiggins & Kellogg
King, W.
Knoepfel, W. H.
K.
Kissam, Miss
Kearsing, Ann L. Mrs

Kinney, George
Kimball, Richard B.
Kelly, James
Knebel, Henry
Kuypers, Doctor
Kirk, T.
Kirk, Mrs.
Kirkland, Chas. P.
Keeler, D. B.
Keeler, J. R.
King
Kearney, James
Karsch, John
Kisler
Knapp, G. L. & Palen
Kerr, Wm.
Kapp, James
Kirkman, J.

L.

Lenox, James
Lawrence, Joseph
Lorillard, Peter
Leroy, J.
Lawrence, Isaac
Lord, J. Couper
Larkin, T. O.
Lottimer, Large, Ellery & Co
Lanier, J. F. D.
Livingston, M. & W.
Livingston, M.
Leavenworth, Mr.
Lane, Josiah
Laight, H.
Laight, W. E.
Lord, Daniel
Lee, David
Lawrence, Richard
Livingston, M. Mrs.
Low, Nicholas
Lord, Rufus L.
Lydig, P.
Loder, Benjamin
Lockwood, Le Grand
Lathrop, W. K.
Lawrence, A. A. & Co.
Loeschigk, Wessendok & Co
Lindmark, John
Lynes, S. C.
Lord, Benjamin
Long, N. R.
Livesley, R. H.
Lyon, A. M.
Leary & Co.
Luther & Hampton
Leonard, J. Mrs.
Litton, J.
Lattan, Lewis
Lavery, Richard & Co.
Lounsberry, N.
Lathrop & Ludington
Lilenthall, Miss
Leavitt & Allen
Long, J.
Le Compt, Nicholas

Le Compt, Vincent
Ledron, M.
Lagrave, J. G.
Lagrave, A.
Ludlow, Mr.
Lee, J.
Langlois, Mrs.
Liscomb, H. P.
Lee, W. H.
Lewis, R. B.
Langdon, T. W.
Lindeman, Wm.
Lockwood, F.
Lynch, James
Lovejoy, Reuben
Loss, A.
Luroh, Ford
Lent, L. B.
Lyon, Eliphalet
Lowther, T.
Libby, J. S.
Lord & Taylor
Lester, Andrew & Co.
Lowe, Bauman
Ladd, Wm. F.
Lawrence, Wm. R.
Longstreet, Saml.
Leonard, Wm. B.
Livingston, Vanbrugh
Ludlam, John
Luckey, F. G.
Livingston, Mrs.
Little, C. S.
Livingston, L.
Low, James
Lamson, Charles
Lane, David
Livingston, A.
Livingston, J. R.
Le Barbier, A.
Livingston, L.
Leeds, Samuel
Livingston, C. R. Mrs.
Lefferts, H.
Livesay, Jane
Lyon, S.
Lyon, Ezekiah
Lyle, Henry, jr.
Lord, W. G.
Lane, J. A.
Lewis, C. D.
Leveredge, J.
Le Boutillier, Thos.
Ludlum, N.
Lowerre, S.
Loines, W. H.
Lent, George
Love, Thos.
Lawson, James
Lee, Jane A.
Lee, Wm. P.
Lowerre, Wm.
Lane, Geo. W.
Leet, Allen N.
Leigh, Chas. C.
Lawrence, W. E. & Co
Lee, J. jr.

Leonard, M. G.
Lamson, E. O.
Lewis, John W.
Lowenthal, S.
Lane, Mr.
Leggett, Abraham
Latting, John J.
Lee & Case
Loeback, Wm. & Schepler
Louis, Ritzs & Co.
Lord, J. Couper
Lester, A. & Co.
Livingston, Cochran & Co.
L. M. & J.
Ludlow & Mailett
Lyon, A. M.
Lowndes, Thomas
Lenzmann, Charles
Ludlum & Pheasants
Litchfield, Jervis & Co.
L.
Langdon
Lahmoier, Brothers
Loder, L. B.
Lent & Mulford
Little, E. B.
Levy, John
Lawrence, W. B.
Lewis & Woodruff
Lyons, Samuel
Lord, John C.
Litchfield & Co.
Leverich
Long & Davenport
L. S. & Co.
Leverett, J. L.
Little, Chas. S.
Lang, L.
L.
L. H. & M.
Leise, F.
L. H.
Leonard & Wendt
Leaird, Alexander
Livingston, Schuyler
Leeds, G. I.
Luqueer, F. S.
Lane, N. B.
Lefferts, M.
Lane, Adolphus
Lowden, S. M.
Lillie, John
Lalor, Martin
Laurence, R. M.
Le Couteulx, A. & Counant
Lord, D. D.
Le Roy, Robert
Lawrence, George N.
Leverich, S. A. Mrs.
Lathrop, D. Mrs.
Lawrence, D. L.
Lee, Oliver H.
Lettle, J. T.
Loomis, Jacob
Lyderhen, G. P.
Lewis, Hiram
Le Roy, Thos. O. & Co.

Little, E. B. & Co.
Lightbody, Jno. G.
Lockwood, H. & Co.
Lander, J. D,
Ludlum Wm.
Lowerré, C. W.
Low, Misses, the
Lackey, Mr.
Lehman, Mr.
Le Ecluse, T.
Leggett, A. A.
La Wall, Jacob
Love, John
Lewis, Richd. B.
Le Comte, Vincent
Lewis, Robert
Lestrade, J. P. Revd.
Lockwood, Frederick
Lowerre, George W.
Ludlum, A. B.
Lane, Wm.
Lane, F. M.
Lester, J. W.
Little, James
Leggett, Gilbert
Lowery, John
Lounsberry, Nehemiah

M.

Minturn, Robert B.
Minturn, Sarah, Mrs.
Melliss, J. F.
Murray, Miss
Maitland, Robert L.
Marsh, L.
Miller, Geo. C.
Moran, & Iselin
Mali, H. W. T. & H.
Moller, Sand & Riera
Morans, Brothers
Mooney, Edward, Mrs.
Minturn, Edward
Morgan, Matthew
Murray, J. B.
Morris, G. W.
Marsh, James
Miller, W. S.
Mount, A. R.
Magie, D.
Mortimer, R.
Mott, Wm. F.
Macy, Josiah
Martin, W. C.
Maitland, R. Mrs.
Munn, Stephen B.
Mann, E. G.
Morgan, H. T.
Martin, Daniel
Mott, Wm. F. jr.
Mackay, W.
Marvin, A. S.
Moore, N. F.
Mason, Sidney
Morris, O. W.
Mauray, M.

Mackie, J.
Moring, G.
Mack, E. Revd.
Matthews, James H.
Mood, Peter
Mitchell, Marcus
Moffat, David
McLoaghlin, Thomas
McIntire, John
McClain, O. D.
Miller, Jacob S. M. D.
Maze, Abraham
Marten, Wm.
Murray, John
Moore, Henry, jr.
Mills, Abner
Murphy, Wm. M. D.
McVey, Alexander
Meyers, John
McKean, James
Merrill, Charles
Marsh, John R.
Murray, Alexander W.
Miller, Humphrey
Montgomery, James
Mollard, John
Merritt, Stephen
Moore. R. W.
Metcalf, J. W. M. D.
McFarlan, D. T.
Mather, F. E.
Miller, J. C.
Mackay, W. G.
Miller, J. W.
McIlvaine, B. R.
McMartine, P.
Markoe, G. M. M. D.
Marshall, J. W.
McCready, Ann
McElrath, T.
Morse, R. C.
Martin, P.
Martine, Theodore
Mathews, Albert
Miller, J. W.
Middleton. Richard E.
Meyrick, Thomas R.
Morris, Mrs.
McLean, Henry
Marsin, Alexander
Mandeville, Samuel
Mathews, Daniel A.
Moffet, Mrs.
Molan, Edward
Malone, Ellen
McGregor, Susan
Moore, D.
Miller, W. P.
Mattison & Isham
Morrell, Thomas
Mathy, A.
Moore, S. W.
McAlpine, D. H.
Morford, S. D.
Megie, E.
Marsh, B.
Maffat, David

56   LIST OF MEMBERS.   (1853.

Merle, G.
McKenny, Thomas R.
Mathews, Wm.
McDonald, A. B.
Morrell, J. B.
Mobra, Mr.
McNeal, Mrs.
Moathe, F.
McDonald, Henry
Mullins, D.
Mechanics' Guard of Ninth Ward, by James P. Isaacs
McIlvaine, B. R.
McCrea, R. Mrs.
Morris, E. C.
Morris, Lewis
Morris, Wm.
Munson, E. P.
Montgomery, James
McIntyre, J.
Macy, Wm. A.
Marti, Rio & Co.
McFarlin
Massie. W. O.
M. E.
Moses, D B. & W.
McChesney, R. D.
Moore, T. D.
Mills, Andrew
Mackrell & Simpson
Mills, Abner
McKenzie, W. & D.
Montanye, J. D.
Morrell, A. W.
Morgan, James
Mather, L.
McCreary, J. D.
Meyer, Julius
Mason & Law
Martin & Lawson
Meyer, F. W.
Morgan, Joseph L. & Co.
Morrison, Wm.
Mayor, A.
Messenger, Thomas
Moore & Baker
Meyer, E.
Morgan, A. W.
Mainerre, B. F.
Muller, Charles
Marsden
M. & P.
Morse, J. D.
McComb, J.
McCullum, Rebecca, Mrs.
Mead, Ralph, jr.
Mease, Charles B.
Martin, R. W.
Morrison J. M.
Mead, F.
March, J. P.
Miles, C.
Mackrell & Richardson
Munroe, Henry
Munn, O. D.
Miller, R. B. Miss
Miller, M. E. Miss

Moreau, Mr.
Martin, George W.
Mitchel, Roland
Mead, E.
Morris, Mrs.
Money, Mrs.
McKeen, Joseph
Minor, C.
Molana, Mrs.
Mead, William
Myers, John L.
Mulligan, John
Morrell, Thomas
Mildeberger, Christopher, Mrs.
Macy, W. H.
McGee, J. H.
Martin, P.
Murray, J. B.
Marshall, W. H.
Morton & Murray
Miller, J. B.
Morrison, James
Moffet, James G.
Martin, Samuel
McIntire, C. H.
Merry, C. H.
Meday, C. H.
Monroe, Ebenezer
Morris, Lewis
Mesler, William
Montgomery, S. J.
Mix, J. jr.
Marshall, M.
Maeder, J. G.
Morris, S. P.
Macfarlane, Andrew
Mooney, E. C.
Morehouse, Stephen
Morrison, L. M.
Miller, Mrs.
Martin, M.
Moir, J. & W.
Marvin, Mrs.
Millers, Mrs. family
Merritt, Miss
McGaw, John A.
Moller, William
McLachlan, Alexander
Mechanics' Guard of Ninth Ward
McIntire, W. N.
McCarron, Michael, Rev.
Mitchell, J. F.
Mason, J. M.
Mersereau, J. W.
Meigs, Charles A.
Mumford, B. A.
Many, Vincent W.
Meigs, Henry, jr.
Maltby, E.
McCready, B. W. M. D.
Millspaugh, P.
Morewood, A. S.
McGay, James
McKewan, John
Miller William A.

Moore, T. B. R.
McKimm, W. R.
Miller, E. Mrs.
Mott, John H.
Maze, Abraham
Merklee, G. F.
Melich, A. D.
Macy, C. A.
Monroe, William
Mailer & Lord
Morewood, George B.
Melliss, & Ayres
Mitchell & Pate
Middleton & Co.
McCarthy & Allen
Muller, Adrian H.
Murch & Co.
Meagher, Thomas H.
McKenzie, J.
Mayhew, P. S.
Morgan, H.
Menzies, Wm.
Martin, Alfred
Moore, Alfred
McGrath, George
Mettler, Wilson
Miller, E. H.
McMartin, A. J. Mrs.
Merrill, Wm. H.
McBride, Abraham
Moore, Richard
Maxwell, A.
Marsh, M. L.
Mowatt, E. A. Mrs.
Meyer, T. A.
Mills, E. S.
Massett, Mrs.
Martindale, S. Rev.
McDougal, Matthew
Montgomery, Robert
Merrill, Joseph
Moriarty, J. D. Mrs.
McCullum, Mrs.
Mason, Mr.
McCann, D.
McVicar, Edward
McCord, G.
Moses, L.
McFarland, Thomas
McKenna, D.
McLeod, S. B. Wylie, M. D.
Miner, F. S.
McCurdy, R. H.
McEvers, J. Mrs.
Mead, M.
McKenzie, G.
McNamee, T.
Mitchell, W.
Morris, Anne
Morris, Henry
Milbank, Samuel
Moore, J. L.
Mott, J. W.
Morgans, Morgan
Martin, Shelden
Macy, Josiah G.
Miles, Wm.

LIST OF MEMBERS.

McClure, A.
Miller, J. G.
Mellen, A.
Moller, Peter
Morris, L. B.
Mather, G.
Munroe, Alfred & Co.
Meakin, John
Morrison, John
Maas, G.
Morton, John
Maxwell, Mrs.
Martin, J. B.
Martin, W. A.
McAuley, Charles
Maunder, William
Morton, W. Q.
Miller, S.
McLaren, Wm. Rev.
Mott, Josiah C.
Mott, William
Mortimer, J. H.
McKee, Joseph
Morrison, Abraham
Marvin, John B.
Mott, M.
Mumford, W. or T. N.
Moore, Mr.
Maxwell, W. A.
McDowell
M. W.
Miles, Wm. B.
McNamee, Richard
Michol, M.
Muirhead & Clark
Mead, Belcher & Co.
Martin, Mulford
Martin, D. R.
Main & Adams
Morgan, J. K.
Miller, G. J. & Co.
Mott, Weaver & Richardson
Merrill, Henry
Marsh & Northrup
Martin, A. A.
McLaughlin, Thomas W.
McMurray, R.
Main, R. W.
Mortimer & Gawtry
Mowbry, R. S.
Meeks & Co.
McClaury, J. M. D.
Morrisson, Mr.
McKinstry, R. jr.
Morehead, James
Morrison & Orr
Murphy, Thomas F.
Miner & Stevens
Malone, James
McCaddin, H.
Mealio, Daniel
McGrath, Judge
McCartin, B.
Michaelis, Doctor
Merrill, Charles
Merrill, M.
Moore, James

Martin, Patrick
Morand, Augustus
Marmedell, F.
Moores. Charles W.
Moss, Harriet N.
Metzger, Charles
Myers, James
Marberry, J.
Marsh, John R.

N.

Nevins, R. H.
Nevins, D. H.
Niblo, William
Noyes, W. Curtis
Nicoll, S. T. & Co.
North, Wm. H.
Nesmith, John P.
Norton, Butler & Hoyt
Naylor & Co.
Newbold, George
Nash, Lora
Noble, J.
Napier, Thomas
Naar, Mrs.
Noonan, P. H.
Noe, C. L.
Nostrand, Mrs.
Neistep
Nunns & Clark
Niles, Mr.
Negus, Thomas
Neeves, James
Nash, William F.
Northrop, C. B.
Nostrand, Elbert
Nason, Joseph
Newell, D. C.
Neilson, William
Norris, Mrs.
Nevius, P. I. jr.
Neilson, J. M. D.
Newton, Isaac
Norris, R. T.
Newhouse, Benjamin
Newell, R.
Nash, F. H.
Newton, N.
Nelson, Edward D.
Norton, C. L.
Nagle, C.
Newcomb, Colin, Mrs.
Neilson, Wm. H.
N. C.
Nevins, G. P.
Nevius, P. I.
Newberry, W. B.
N. L.
Negus
Nichols, E. S.
Nash
Nelson, William
Neely, E. A. Mrs.
Noah, Mr.

Niles, Mrs.
North, A.
Nash, S. P.
Neilson, J.
Nesbit, James
Newcomb, Mrs.
Neilson, N. F.
Nichol, John
Nash, W. F.

O.

Ostrander, C. V. B.
Ogden & Co.
Onderdonk, E.
Ostrander
Odell, Mrs.
Osborn, B. W.
Olwell, J. M.
Osborn, A. P.
Otto, H.
O'Rorke, James, M. D.
Owen, D.
Olliff, William
Oldring, Henry
Ogilvie, William
Ogden, H. M.
O'Sullivan, J. L.
Osborne, Mrs.
Ogden, E. D.
Ogden, J. D. M. D.
Owens, William
Oliver, A. M.
Oakley, Nathaniel
Osgood, Samuel, Rev.
Oothout, Henry
Ortley, M.
Owen, Thomas
Owens, Daniel S.
Owen, G. B.
Oakley, J. B.
Olcott, J. N.
O. L. & T. Co.
Owen, James
O'Donnel, John
Ostrand, C.
Oothout, William
Oppenheim, J. M. & Co.
Orange, A.
Oakley, T. J. Mrs.
Owen, E. W. Mrs.
Ogden, G. M.
Ostrom, J. P.
Ogden, R. T.
Ockerhausen A. F.
Owen, Thomas
Ogden, John T.
Ogden, T. W.
Ogsbury, F. W.
Olyphant's Sons
Ogden, H. Capt.
Oelrich & Co.
Okill, M. Mrs.
Orchard, Isaac, Rev.
Ostrom, J. P.

3*

P.

Phalen, James
Post, G. D.
Phelps, Anson G. Jr.
Post, Wm. B.
Prall, M. A. Miss
Parker, C. M.
Parish, Susan M. Mrs.
Phillips, J. W.
Phelps, Dodge & Co.
Phelps, J. J.
Parker, Doctor
Paton & Stewart,
Palmer, J. J.
Post, A. C., M. D.
Phelps. I. N.
Phelps, Royal
Prime, E.
Parker, C. C. Rev.
Pell, A.
Pickersgill, W. C. & Co.
Penfold, John
Pease, J. W. & Co.
Petrie, James S.
Parkin, Doctor
Polhamus, A.
Putnam, G. P.
Platt, N. C.
Partridge, C.
Parker, W., M. D.
Peet, E.
Platt, G. W.
Pierce, G. V. & Co.
Pattison, Robert
Pratt, Edward, Rev.
Parker, Joseph N.
Place, R. S.
Pond, James O. M. D.
Pierson, Ira C.
Place, James K.
Place, Charles
Porter, William
Pearsall, John
Post, William
Pearson, C. B.
Peck, Gideon
Phillips, W.
Phair, J.
Place, Benjamin
Porter, T. D.
Parker, J. C.
Patterson, H.
Palmer, B.
Patrullo, A.
Ponsot, G.
Paillet, Mr.
Pike & Co.
Place, E. B.
Pearson, C. B.
Panne, E. H.
Polhamus, Mrs.
Patterson, E. C.
Pratt, R. F.
Palmer & Newcomb
Place, Charles
Parks, R. W.

Parker C.
Painter, W. R.
Painter, J. G.
Peet, M.
Paine, Elijah
Potter, Ellis
Paulson, Leonard
Phyfe, D.
Paton & Co.
Pecare, Jacob
Powers, Thomas
Prout, W. F.
Peterson, W. T.
Publes, B. K.
Pike, B. jr.
Peck, J. B.
Peck, E. & E.
Porter, R.
Prague, D.
Parsons, Charles
Pope, Henry
Pearsall, Robert
Pootan, Wm.
Polhamus, John
Pomroy, J. B.
Prankhard, J. B.
Pearsall, Alderman
Pollock, James
Pugsley, T.
Peck, H. W.
Pistor, P. F.
Peck, G. M.
Pollock, John
Parker, Moses
Pearce, E. A.
Pickering, Thomas
Paradise, J. W.
Pierce, Mrs.
Pollock, James
Philips, Simon
Post, P. J.
Purroy, J. B.
Patton, Wm. D. D.
Phyfe, J. W.
Peters, J. C. M. D.
Patrick, Richard
Page, P. P.
Poillon, Richard
Platt, E.
Price, Thompson
Price, David W.
Place, R. S.
Platt, J.
Provost, J. H. Mrs.
Pinckney, J. W.
Philips, Samuel
Polhamus, H. A.
Penfold, Wm.
Pegg, R.
Pettee, D. L.
Parsons, C. S.
Post & Young
Putnam, Albert
Pirsson, J. P.
Phalon, Edward
Parker, James
Pachtmann, J. W.

Parsell, A.
Patterson, Knapp & Co.
Parrish, J.
Platt, George
Plum, J. M.
Pearse, A. F.
Price, E. V.
Portington, H.
Pray, Henry
Phelps, W. H.
Powers, L.
Post, W.
Philips, W. W.
Parson, S. H.
Parker, J. A.
Porter & Fairchild
Parker, B.
Prescott, J. M.
Palanca, R.
Peck, E.
Pettibone, H. A.
Patteson, James
Peck, G. M.
Perry, Samuel
Patterson, J. A.
Plume, George T.
Pawling, Levi
Pyatt & Walker
Purley, Charles
Powers & Schoonmaker
Pierson, Edwin
Peterkin, John
Phillips, J. P.
Patterson, Wm.
Price, James
Perine, B.
Parsons, W.
Parr, John
Parkill, Samuel
Peckham, Alfred G.
Paret, John
Poole, Pentz & Goin
Prosser, Thomas & Son
Palen, William
Pike, D. B.
Perlee, R. N.
Packwood, Mrs.
Post, Ralph
Perry, S.
Paine, Wm. H.
Pentz, A. P.
Phillips, J. D.
Pryer, G.
Pinckney, M.
Patterson, David, Mrs.
Pentz, B. J. Mrs.
Paine, John
Philips, Lewis
Pomroy, A. H.
P.
Parker, J. C.
Purdy, John
Paxson, S. C.
Peck, Wm.
Post, James
Peabody, Mrs.
Pearson, Adam

LIST OF MEMBERS.

Paterson, W. C.
Peet, Edward
Peet, E. B.
Peet, J. Lewis
Peet, H. P. Mrs.
Peet, H. P.
Pell, Chas. F.
Pell, Abijah
Pratt, Mrs.
Potter, Mrs.
Planten, H.

Q.

Quackenboss & Hamilton
Quackenboss, H.
Quackenbush, A. S.
Quackenbush, B.
Quinn, J. A.
Quimby, E. E.
Quackenbos, M. M.
Quincy, C. E.
Quain, Mrs.
Quinan, Henry C.

R.

Roosevelt, C. V. S.
Rhinelander, W. C.
Roosevelt, J. A. & I.
Robinson, Nelson
Robertson, J. A.
Ray, Robert
Rogers, G. P.
Richards, Guy, Capt.
Roosevelt, J. Mrs.
Remsen, H. R.
Renwick, J.
Rogers, C. H.
Rachau, J. A. F.
Robbins, G. S. & Son
Ray, R.
Rutgers, N. G.
Remsen, Mr.
Reeve, Henry
Russell, C. H.
Russell, W. H.
Robert, M. Mrs.
Reid, George W.
Rigney, Thomas
Read, Taylor & Co.
Rogers, C. B.
Rushton, Clark & Co.
Ramsey, James C.
Russell, David
Ryers, T. R.
Redfield, J. H.
Ritter, Richard
Rowell, Wm.
Ryerson, Henry W.
Richards, Thomas B.
Rusten, J.
Rollins, John
Robbins, Willet S

Roome, Charles
Redman, C. H.
Rumsey, J. W.
Rusher, C. H.
Roberts, Edward
Ranny, L., M. D.
Reeve, James
Reese, J.
Roberts, Charles
Richmond, George
Roberts, P. & Co.
Reilly, S. S.
Rosenfelt, Mr.
Rich, James
Randolph, J.
Robinson, Mrs.
Rogers, A.
Rogers, John
Randal & Co.
Ruckman, E.
Rockwood & Co.
Rhodes, Mrs.
Rosenbaum, S.
Rosenbener, J.
Reeve, S.
Robinson, E. C.
Raynor, H.
Robbins, Mrs.
Ryder, E. T.
Reynolds, Mr.
Rogers, Mrs.
Read, J. & Co.
Rainhart, Starling & Co.
Rockwell & Winton
Reed, A.
Rourke, P.
Raynor, Samuel
Rankin, A. & Co.
Rush, H. B.
Roberts & Reese
Rauch, John H.
Reynolds, Mr.
Riker, Daniel
Robinson, William
Robinson, Henry
Richter, D. A.
Randall, E.
Rodgers, B.
Rodgers, M. Mrs.
Rosenblatz, S. S.
Ryerson, J. B.
Roome, Charles
Riley, Asher
Ruthven, D. & J.
Rodgers, Joseph
Read, J.
Rowe, Mrs.
Rodgers, J. K. Mrs.
Robinson, H. W.
Rowe, Peter
Reilly, Edward
Ranney, E. W., M. D.
Robinson, Henry
Rodgers, George A.
Richmond, Robert
Raybold, Daniel
Roosevelt, Mr. Revd.

Ruyter, F.
Rodgers, B. J.
Richardson, Mr.
Russell, A.
Reese. J. Jr.
Ray, W. G.
Remsen, Wm.
Riggs, A., M. D.
Renwick, James
Renwick H. H.
Robert, C R.
Romaine, S. B.
Rich, H. L.
Riker, A.
Runyon, M. T.
Ritter & Besson
Rich, S. A.
Robins, J.
Roux, A.
Rowe, Wm. Jr.
Rickard, John
Russell, J R.
Roshore, John
Requa, A.
Reid, Julia, Mrs.
Ralph, John
Rodh, David
Raymond, H. J.
Roosevelt, S.
Reynolds, P.
Rogers, T.
Ritter, Miss
Randolph, Mrs.
Richards, Thos. B.
Richards, J.
Robbins & Van Ostrand
Roe, E. W.
Rudd, Joseph
Rowland, N. S.
Romer, J.
Rosenfield, M. H.
Roach, C. H.
Russell, R.
Ramsey, David
Remsen. John
Rodewald, Brothers & Co.
Routh, H. L. & Sons
Redmond, William
Richardson, E. & Co.
Rose, Wm. W.
Richards & Co.
Root, R. C. & Anthony
Ramee & Downer
Raymond & McMurray
R. Y. & Co.
Romain, W. H.
Rossman, N.
Rugg, W. G.
Rossman, S.
Rothschild, S.
Robinson, P.
Roberts & Brother
Raynolds, C. T.
Recknagel & Schwab
Rich, Josiah
Rosselot, P. A.
Ross, Andrew

Raymond & Fullerton
Rankin & Co.
Rohe, J. A.
Reckard, S. B.
R. H. & Co.
Ransom, J. H.
Russell, J. G. Mrs.
Robins, Mrs.
Ressoz, John W.
Rogers, Wm. J.
Randall, John
Robinson, D. Mrs.
Russell, S P.
Russell. N. E.
Ridley, J.
Rodgers, J. N.
Reeve, J.
Ragland, Mrs.
Rodney, Hannah
Russell, Alfred
Rives, N.
Rockwell, J. S.
Rees, J.
Reese & Hoyt
Ross, J. Jr.
Rafferty & Leask
Rodgers, R. P.
Rumsey, J. W.
Rankin, Edward E.
Rockwell, S. D.
Raymond, A.
Robinson, E., D. D.

S.

Spencer, W. A. Capt. U. S. N
Sturges, Jonathan
Shipley, Joseph, Wilmington, Del.
Schuffelin & Fowler
Siffkin, Ironsides & Co.
Surplus subscription to the Lemnon Fund, by Henry, Smith & Townsend
Seymour, W. N.
Smith, W. A.
Skiddy, F.
Schermerhorn, W. C.
Schiffelin, P. & Co.
Schermerhorn, A. Mrs.
Stewart, R. L. & A.
Stevens, R. L.
Stevens, John C.
Sampson, Joseph
Suckley, Rutsen
Schieffelin, H. M.
Sheafe, J. F.
Skiddy, Francis
Schieffelin. S. S. Miss
Schiefflin. H. M. Miss
Sparks, S.
Scuchardt & Gebhard
Strong & Smith
Steward, John, jr. & Co.
Smith, Lemuel
Stuyvesant, P. G. Mrs.

Smith, Cornelius
Staples, Seth P.
Schneck, Wm. S.
Suydam, Charles
Sanford, Edward
Saltus, Francis
Stone, Wm. W.
Spies, Christ & Co.
Stillman & Allen
Smith, W. H. & Co.
Strang, Adriance & Co.
Skidmore, S. T.
Swan, Caleb
Schieffelin, S. A.
Staples, S.
Schieffelin, H. H.
Seymour, M. L.
Strong, A. E.
Schermerhorn, E. H.
Strong, George W.
Suydam, J. Mrs.
Shiff, Mrs.
Snow, G. M.
Sabine, G. A., M. D.
Sherwood, S.
Swords, C. R.
Swords, M. R.
Stout, A. G.
Schuyler, G. L.
Stewart, J. M.
Suydam & Reed
Smith, Adon
Spies, Adam W.
Secor, Rosevelt G.
Stimson, A. L.
Sanxay, Joseph F.
Stanford & Co. D. R.
Schmelzel, George
Shannon, Mr.
Smith, Thos. U.
Sill, W. H.
Stuart, J.
Smedburg, Mrs.
Swift, E. H.
Stevens, A.
Smith, J.
Smith, James
Symes, W.
Slawson, A.
Sears, N. T.
Simonson, Richard
Sampson, G. H.
Smedes & Shroder
Smith, J. E.
Smith, S. B.
Shaw, R T.
Smith, W. D.
Scribner, A.
Smith, H.
Smith, J. J.
Simpson, W.
Seaman, S. C.
Seuffort
Smith, Noah
Scott, Mrs.
Stout, A. V.
Suydam, A.

Sloan, H. S.
Saunders, A. & J.
Smith, Dean & Edy
Smith, J. J.
Solomon & Hart
Sloan, W. & J.
Smith & Knapp
Stebbins & Co.
Sluyter, W. R. & Co.
Sears, Adrianna & Pratt
Skeel, R. W. & Co.
Shaw, John
Southart & Kissam
Schott, G. S.
Sage, J. M.
Steele, W.
Stockbridge, Mr.
Sears, H.
Storm, J. K.
Smith, Richard
Skinner, H. N.
Serrell, John
Suydam, S.
Sears, J. R.
Sterling & Walton
Seabury, W.
Spear, G. M.
Smith, C. W.
Smith, John T. S.
Schenck, E. Mrs.
Staples, Joseph
Strong, T. W.
Sammis, A. D. B. Mrs.
Schenck, C. C.
Scarff, George
Selpho, Wm.
Schenck, J. W.
Squire & Brother
Stoppani, Chas. G.
Spitzer, S.
Smith & Conant
Shields, C.
Smith, James
Sneeden, J.
Summers, Wm.
Sammis, D. P.
Smith, S.
Silver, James
Silverman, James
Smith, Elias L.
Smith, H. F.
Stickney, C. L.
Schwab, Mr.
Smith, C. E.
Shipman, Wm. M.
Sharot, A.
Stone, Geo. E.
Smith, W. H.
Shaw, Thomas
Shotwell, Wm.
Salmon, H. H.
Smith, Daniel Drake
Smillie, W. C.
Sutherland, Wm.
Smith, N. H.
Sturges, Wm.
Sherwood, Emily, Mrs.

LIST OF MEMBERS.

Swift, H. A.
Stanley, Joseph
Spaulding, J. Revd.
Smith, Washington
Smith, G. W.
Schwerin, M.
Still, George S.
Smillie, George
Sutton, Charles
Smith, James B.
Stebbins, Mrs.
Stoddard, Wm. A.
Stoughton, Wm. B.
Schmidt, H. J.
Seaman, Mrs.
Stouvenal, John B.
Spence, James
Schwartz, A.
Spinner, Samuel
Searing, Alfred
Smith, James T.
Stansbury, James
Sherwood, Luman
Seaman, R. S., M. D.
Seybel, F.
Seal, J. S.
Salisbury, W. D.
Sfender, A.
Strong, C. E.
Sandford, J. S.
Stusken, E.
Sedgwick, W. E.
Scott, J. W., M. D.
Subscriber to N. Y. Observer
Smith, Adon
St. John, Chauncey
Sprague, R.
Stevens. B. K.
Swan, B. L. jr.
Stevens, B.
Starr, Nathan
Suydam, D. R.
Sarles, H.
Sands, A. B. & D.
Saxton, John
Southack, John W.
Sweezy, N. T. & Co.
Strong, Mr.
Smith, Samuel
Smith, H.
Shelden, Martin
Skaden, Joseph C.
Smith, James
Scharfenberg & Luis
Seguine, C.
Sherwood & Chapman
Starr, Charles, jr.
Spycer, R. Mrs.
Simons, Louis
Smith, S. C. Mrs.
Sharrock, Wm. M. D.
Schermerhorn, John
Stebbins, Mrs.
Sillcock, J. J.
Somerville, Mrs.
Storm, S.

Smith, C. W.
Scudder, Mrs.
Seymour, J. N.
Skarren, Mrs.
Sandheim, Lewis
Smith & Crane
Scott & Clark
Shuster, J. G.
Sage, W. B.
Stiles, Samuel
Slosson, John
Sealy, W. A.
Skinner, T. H. Rev.
Sheldon, S. G.
Smillie, James
Sherman, Doctor
Shults, T. J.
Soper, J. C.
Spencer, M.
Sage, George E.
Sheppard, G. G.
Stokes, Henry
Syz, J. G.
Southmayd, A.
Southmayd, Horace
Savage, George W.
Scudder, Linus
Sykes, L. A.
Scott, John D.
Smith, Pascal B.
Storms, W. J.
Steinle, F.
Smith, E. Mrs.
Stewart, James, M. D.
Stephens, James H.
Stokes, B. G.
Sutton, George
Suydam, Lambert
Shannon, W.
Scudder, Wm. H.
Senior, E. H.
Stoutenburgh, D.
Scudder, A. H.
Sarven, David
Sacket, E. D. Mrs.
Storms, Wm. P.
Stevens, James
Smith, Charles
Stone, Starr & Co.
Schulten, J. W. & Hurd,
Smythe, H. A.
Sackett, Belcher & Co.
Spencer, G. G.
Snow, G. T.
Swazey, H. B.
Scrymser, J.
Sterling
Stursberg, A.
Smith, G. A.
Scheur
Sage, R. V.
Shipman, C. H.
Skeel, R. R.
Smith, N. Denton
Stonebridge, J. & W.
Stalker, Thomas
Stark, J. M.

S.
Syz, Irminger & Co.
St. John, Milton
Sardy, John B.
S. F. C.
S. B. B.
Sperry, John
Summers & Calkins
Simonson, Charles M.
Stickney, Charles L.
Sibell, W. E.
Stearns, John G.
Savage, James P.
Scutts, Lewis & Co.
Sprague, Samuel
Smith, C. E.
Sandford, S. N.
Spelman, W. B.
Strybing, Henry
Schieffelin, James L.
Schieffelin, B.
Staples, G. W.
Sewall. J. N.
Scoville Manufacturing Co.
Smith, T. & Co.
Swift, Hurlbut & Co.
Stamford Manuf. Co.
Schiffer S. & Brother
Stringer & Townsend
Schieffelin, S. A.
S. B. S.
Silleck,
Sheffield, J. B.
Smith, Edmund A.
S.
Simon, J. R.
Shuster, P. F.
Sanderson, G.
Sawyer & Hobby
Sanford, M. B.
S. F. & Co.
Spruce-street, No. 12.
Secor, T. F.
Stillman, T. B.
Staniford, D. T.
Stuyvesant, Mrs.
Smith, Milton G.
Stuyvesant, G.
Smith, James E.
Stillman, Richard
Skinner, R. O.
Smith, D. Mrs.
Smith, Isaac T. Mrs.
Staats, Mr.
S. L. & C.
Stillheimer, I.
Smith, C. H.
Saunderson, E. F.
Smith, Sheldon
Smith, Augustine, M. D.
Strange, E. B.
Skiddy, William
Smalwood, John L.
Sherman, W. B.
Scott, Wm. B.
Suydam, H. jr.
Spies, Adam W.

Strong, W. K.
Stone, R. C.
Schieffelin, R. L.
Satterlee, G. C.
Smith, Cornelius F.
Schoals, F. P.
Smith, Thomas C.
Snedicor, John D.
Sommer, S.
Spier, G. M.
Smith, Henry B.
Simons, N. H.
Stone, H. G.
Stewart, Wm. R.
Smith, Daniel H.
Safford, Mrs.
Somers, T. S.
Smith, Mr.
Secll, Aris
Smull, Thomas
Scott, Thomas
Sather & Church
Simpson, J. B. & J.
Schwartz, Theodore
Spitzen, S.
Smith, Silas C.
Somerville, A. & M.
Safford, B.
Smith, S. T.
St. John, Mrs.
Sheridon, Thomas
Stower, Mrs.
Sparks
Sanger, L.
Sather, P.
Smull & Healy
Stout, Richard
Sears, Robert
Stephenson, John
Skinner, by J. L. Baldwin
Sampson. A.
Sharp, William
Sands, E. H. M. D.
Smith, Thomas E.
Stansbery, James F.
Sherwood, Samuel P.
See, Henry P.
Smith, Samuel
Smith, D. C.
Smith, John H.
Squire, Peter
Sanford, Nathan
Schuler, J. W.
Storms, Andrew
Smith, John R.
Shaver, P. C.
Smith, G. D.
Sharrott, A. H.
Sammis, Nelson
Storer, George L.
Sullivan, Charles
Stevens, David
Smith, A.
Staniford, D. T.
Shopp, G.
Savage, C. C.
Smithson, Charles

Sewell, John G. M. D.
Stevenson, J.
Serrel, A. T.

T.

Tilley, W. R.
Taylor, John
Tuttle, G. W.
Thompson, John
Terrett, H. N.
Tunison, Mr.
Titus, James
Tabor, Augustus
Truesdell, Mr.
Taylor, A.
Taylor, John
Trowbridge, G. A.
Tully, Doctor
Thompson, James
Tenny, James
Thompson & Mills
Trigg, G. P.
Tredwell, E.
Tucker, J. C.
Taylor, J.
Tripp, E. A.
Tyson, W.
T. B. R.
Tappen, George
Tows, Mrs.
Tappen & Burd
Trafford, Abraham
Tylce, John
Tully, M. C. M. D.
Torrance & Tuthill
Turner, Samuel H.
Thomson, Maron
Tucker, Joseph
Terry, Brothers
Tucker, T. W.
Thwing, C. & P. W.
Taylor, Robert
Thomson, Wm. A.
Thompson, D. B.
Thomson, J.
Taggart, J. W. Revd.
Tobias, Mrs.
Thompson, John
Tyrrel, Mrs.
Taylor, C. G.
Treadwell, S.
Trenor, J. M. D.
Thurston, R. H. Mrs.
Thompson, David
Talman, S. S.
Tweed, Robert
Thorp, H. S.
Tremper, H.
Terry, N. M.
Tallman, S. S.
Terry, David, Revd.
Tate, J. E.
Thomas, E
Taylor, A. Mrs.
Tremper, J. H.

Titus. E. Mrs.
Taylor, J. Mrs.
Thomas, David
Thorn, W.
Ten Brook, J.
Thorp, George W.
Townsend, J. H.
Therasson, L. F.
Tallman, Abm. S.
Trenope, John
Thomas & Achelio
T.
T. N.'
Trimble, Merrett
Thomas, C. W. & A.
Turner, E. T.
Torrey, Wm. A.
Tompkins & Co.
Taylor, Richards & Co.
Taylor, J. C.
Taff, Henry
Tomlinson, Isaac
Taff, David
Tanenbamer, Isaac
Trumpy, E.
Tapscott, W. & T. & Co.
Tieman, D. F.
Thompson & Roselet
Trowbridge, H. & Co.
Tuttle & Bailey
Tyler, A.
T. V. B.
T. B. T.
Tallmage, Henry F.
Thompson, W. B.
Truslow, Wm.
Thompson, A.
Tileston, Wm. H.
Trotter, J.
Townsend, D. Y.
Tillinghast, P.
Townley, J. H.
Taylor, W. B. jr.
Terpeny, Nathaniel, Mrs.
Templeton, Mrs.
Townsend, W. H.
Townsend, Effingham
Taylor, R. L.
Trowbridge, H.
Tucker, F. C. jr.
Thompson, G. W.
Tiffany, T. A.
Thompson, J. M. D.
Thorp, A.
Trask, C. H.
Timpson, W.
Tracy, C.
Taylor, Robert
Thayer, W.
Tieman, George
Thorn, A. E.
Thilemann, Frederick
Taylor, Mrs.
Thorn, Charles E.
Titus, James H.
Talbot, C. N.
Trow, J. F.

LIST OF MEMBERS.

Tiffany, Young & Ellis
Tracy, Irving & Co.
Thorn, Jonathan, Mrs.
Taylor, Moses
Tweedy, O. B.
Tuckerman, J. & L.
Tredwell & Gold
Two Friends, by J. Lenox
Townsend, John R. Mrs.
Townsend, Charles A.
Townsend, R. H. L.
Tatham, Benjamin
Thurston, R. H. Mrs.
Toal, Charles
Tillotson, J. C.
Torrey, Joseph
Taylor, Moses B.
Tritton, Richard
Tucker, D. N.
Tripp, Irvin H.
Traphagen, G. H. M. D.
Terbell, H. S.
Terbell, Jeremiah
Tracy, George Manning
Tibbets, James P.
Tanner, Doctor
Trafford, Abraham
Trenchard, Samuel
Tracy, C. C.
Trimble, George T.

U.

Underhill, Doctor
Underhill, J. S.
Underhill, G.
Ubsdell, Peirson & Co.
Unknown
Underhill, W.
Underhill, W. S.
Uhe, J.
Uhl, Anna
Underhill, J. W.
Ustick, Richard

V.

Van Wagener, R. D.
Vail, A.
Van Wych, H. L.
Van Waggener, Richard
Van Auken, B. H.
Vermilyea, W. R.
Van Hook, Wm.
Van Nest, Abraham
Verplank, G. C.
Van Rensselaer, Alexander
Van Wyck, Charles
Van Allen, Wm.
Van Arsdale, Henry, M. D.
Van Riper, J. A.
Vaughn, Mrs.
Vancott, J.
Van Norton, Mr.
Van Benschoten, J.

Vassar & Co.
Van Kleek & Co.
Von Gahn, H.
Vermule, Doctor
Vreeland, J. M.
Van Wyck, John T.
Van Winkle, E. S.
Van Wyck, H. L.
Van Antwerp, J.
Van Santvoord, C.
Vermilye, W. M.
Van Zandt, P. P.
Van Nortwich, W. B.
Vandevoort, J. B.
Van Norman, Doctor
Valentine, S. T.
Vliet, S.
Van Winkle, E. H.
Vradenburg, Mary
Van Hoynigen
Vredenburgh, Peter
Van Brunt, T.
Vandenburgh, J.
Van Vleek, J. T.
Van Nest, John
Van Saun, S. J.
Van Wagenen, Wm.
Van Houden, J.
Vandervoort, Mrs.
Van Dyck, P.
V. P. & Co.
Voight, Millington & Co.
Vanderburgh, S. G. E.
V. M.
Van Cott, W.
Van Pelt, J. J.
Vail, Walter
Van Nest, Abrm R.
Vanwerck, C.
Vernon, Brothers
Vanderwort, Charles
Voght, T. & Co.
Van Wagenen, W. F.
Van Antwerp, Mrs.
Voorheis, A.
Valentine, D. S.
Vanderhoof, J. T.
Vickers, James
Van Duzen, S.
Vandevoort, Henry
Voorhis, Mr.
Vanderbelt, W. G.
Venables, Mrs.
Vanderwerken, E.
Vale, G.
Vernol, L. & T.
Van Blankenstein & Hinneman
Van Nostrand, J.
Valentine, Peter

W.

Wetmore, A. R.
Walsh, A. Robertson
Ward, A. H.

Wheelright, B. F.
Winslow, R. H.
Wood, A.
Whittemore, F.
Woodhead, J.
Ward, H. H.
Wetmore & Cryder
Wainwright, E.
Walsh, Mallory & Co.
Ward, L. B.
Wetmore, W. S.
Whitney, A
Woolsey, E. D.
Whiting, A.
Wolfe, Charles
Whittelsey, J. P. Wallingford, Connecticut
Wolfe, J. D.
Wood, Isaac
White, Robert, jr.
Whitmore, L. (Bushwick)
Weston, Mr. Rev.
Wyckoff, S.
Wilks, Miss
Willett, Samuel
Willets, R. R.
Willets, D. T.
Willets, E. P.
Willets, Stephen
Ward, H. H.
Wood, O. E.
Williams, Wm. R.
Wyeth, Leonard J.
Wolf, Gillespie & Co.
Whitlock, Wm. jr.
Walker, Joseph
Webb, W. W.
Withers, Reuben
Wells, L. W.
White, Charles B.
Wetmore, Samuel
Walker, William
Watson, John
Ward, Warren
Wheelock, Calvin, jr.
Wilbur, Charles
Watkins, John L.
Wallace, Thomas
Whittelsey, Henry
Walker, George
West, Wm. G.
Worrell, Noah
Wyckoff, James B. M. D.
Ware, John P.
Winston, F. S.
Williams, J. F.
Warren, Thomas
Woods, P. A.
Watkiss, Lewis
Winterbottom, James
Wardell, O. T.
Wier, James
Wheaton, William
Wicker, Henry
Walsh, George
Walker, Wm. A.
Woodruff, L. B.

LIST OF MEMBERS. (1853.

Waldron, Cornelius
Winslow George
Wood, Henry
West, Henry P.
Whitely, G.
Worrall, J. G.
Washburn, S. D. M. D.
West, E. M. D.
Walker, William
Wolcott, C.
Winter, E. T. M. D.
Wilson, Jotham
Woolsey, E. J.
Williams & Stevens
Woodford, Mr.
Wyman, J. G.
Wilson, Mrs.
Wemell, Peter
Whitlock, M
Wilton, William
Wilson, A. D. M. D.
White, S. B.
Ward, S.
Wood, D.
Westein, J.
West & Cauldwell
Wilson, Mr.
West, W.
Wallis, Mr.
Ward, E.
Wotton, J. A.
Whiticar, C. H.
Willard, M.
Weisman, Doctor
Wiley, John
Waterbury
Woodford, O. P.
Wilson, L. O.
Wells, John
Webster, B. C.
Waring, H. & Co.
Wray, C.
Wait, Wells & Co.
Wood & Mabbat
Wheaton Mr.
Wygant, E.
Wiggins, James
Welsh & Paine
Wheeler, Doctor
Wilson & Goll
Wallace, W.
Worly, Mr.
Woodworth, A.
Weeks, S.
Wilson, G.
Walter, J. F.
Wray, Christopher
Worrell & Co.
White, Edward
Withington, Lewis
Woods, John
Walker, Mrs.
Williams, Erastus
Whittemore, J.
Ward, Adam
Weeks, George
Warren, James

Winslow, James
Williams, P. & M.
Webster, Horace, L. L. D.
Winslow, L. C.
Wilson & Brown
Wood, J. N.
Wellstood, John G.
Winslow, William
Waller, J.
Woodruff, Marcus P.
Williamson, C. T.
Westervelt, E.
Wilson, Bird, Rev.
Wines, John C.
Wray, John
Wheeler, H. H.
Weston, George S.
Williams, W.
Walton, William T.
Williams, G. H.
Wilson, B. M.
Wragg, W.
Williams, T. D.
Wixon, Samuel
Whittemore, H. S.
Westbrook, Samuel
Winepalts, Harman
Woodruff, L. B.
Westervelt, S. P.
Wells, O. P. M. D.
Wilson, A. M. Mrs.
Watson, J. M. D.
Wilkes, Henry
Waller, Robert
Whitehead, John
Winslow, T. S.
Whittemore, T.
Woodhead, J.
Ward, T. M. D.
Ward, John
Waddington, W. D.
Weller, John
Wagner, D. B.
Woodward, J. S.
Wetmore, P. M.
Williams, T. jr.
Woodhull, Mrs.
Webb, A. J.
Warring, Samuel J.
Westervelt, J.
White, William C.
Whitemore, H.
Wood, William
Westlake, A. W.
Wood, S. M.
Wilkie, J.
Walton, E. L.
Warring, S.
Wood, B.
Wilson, Daniel
Williams, S. T.
Wilkey, W. F.
Ward, James
Wortendyke, C. R.
Woolsey, J.
Wight, R.
Wooding, J.

Wise, M.
Wickstead, J. J.
Wescott, Isaac
Walton, J. B.
Wight, James W.
Williams, F. W.
Wooding, James
Walker, S. G.
Woodward, W. A.
Wilson, W. M.
Woodruff, W.
Waring, C. B.
Wicoff, Mrs.
Wells, N. M.
Williams, M.
Williams, W. R.
Wheeler, Z.
Warner, P. R.
Ward, W. C.
Williamson, H.
Walsh, T. S.
Winans, W. W.
Woodward, Samuel
Woodhouse, P. Capt.
Wisner, D. B.
Wilson, Morris
Wilson, William, M. D.
Waterbury, A. G.
Winant, S.
Westervelt, B. J.
Wilson, Mrs.
Wheeler, Edward
Welford, W.
Ward, James O.
Wanzer, Minor & Co.
Wetherspoon & Kingsford
Wiggins, William H.
Wisner & Philips
Whiting, W. E.
Wagner, George & Co.
Warburg, Edward
Wright, John B.
Whitney, J. J.
Wallace, James P.
Williams, E. H.
Wyckoff & Hazen
Wright, William P.
Williams, F. B.
W. D.
W.
West Street
Wooster, C.
Wissing, James
Waterbury, Joseph
Wright, D. D.
Windeluff, Lewis
Wilson, James
Windeluff, Claus
Wheeler, William A. & Co.
West, E. G.
Windle, W. B.
Warren, J. & T.
Williams, C. P. & E.
Williams, J. G.
Wheeler, F. G.
Wilson, Hawksworth, Ellison & Moss

LIST OF MEMBERS.

Weld, A.
Wetmore, L.
Wells
Woods, D. & Co.
Wood & Hughes
W.
Wendle, W. D.
Walloch, Willy
Woods
W. & Co.
W. C. G.
Winthrop, B. R.
Winham, A. jr.
Williams, C.
Way, Thomas B.
Whitewright, William
White, H. L. Mrs.
Whyte, John
Washburn, H. B.
Wm. W.
Whiting, Charles
Warner, W. F.
Williams, Samuel
Waller, W.
White, Norman
Woodward, R. T.
Wetton, T. B.
Williamson, D. A.
Waterman, William
Wycoff, H. S. Mrs.
Walker, J. J.
Walker, T. E.
Waddell, William C. W.
Washburn, N. J.
Watt, William
Walton, W.

W. L. J.
White, Campbell P.
Walton, M. Miss
Williams, J. F.
Wayland, Mrs.
Wright, A. H.
Waterman
W. H.
Willard, Martha
Warren, H. M.
Whittingham, J.
Williams & Hinman
Williams, Richard S.
Wood, James S.
Woodford, O. W.
Wheeler, L. F.
Whyte, John
West, Daniel
White, P. A.
Williams, C. F.
Wood, M. Q.
West, Mrs.
Webber, Mrs.
White, Mrs.
Wills, Mrs.
Wilson
Wood, James L.
Westfall, J. & D.
Walmsley, Edward
W. R. W.

X.

X. X.

Y.

Youle, George W.
Youngs, W.
Young & Ward
Yates, A. E. Mrs.
Yates, M. Mrs.
Young, E. M.
Yelverton & Fellows
Yznaga, A.
Youngs, D. L.
Young, Frederick
Young, C. L.
Young, Hiram
Young, N.
Young, Henry
Yelverton, John P.
Yates, C.
Yereance, Richard
Young, J.
Young, David L.

Z.

Zimmerman, Miss
Ziegler, G. F.
Zebley, J. F.
Zinck, Theodore
Zabriskie, C. A.
Zerega, A.
Zabriskie, A. C.
Z. & Y.
Zimmerman, Adam
Zipcy, Jacob
Zabriskie, C. jr.

APPENDIX.

A Summary Statement of the Objects and Principles of the Association, for the Information of Members and Visitors.

The design of this Association is the elevation of the moral and physical condition of the indigent: and, so far as is compatible with this design, the relief of their necessities.

Every person who becomes an annual subscriber or a Visitor, is a member of this Association.

The following is an abstract of the fundamental rules by which it is governed:

1. To regard each applicant for relief as entitled to charity, until a careful examination proves the contrary.
2. To give relief only after a personal investigation of each case, by visitation and inquiry.
3. To relieve no one excepting through the visitor of the section in which he lives.
4. To give necessary articles, and only what is immediately necessary.
5. To give what is least susceptible of abuse.
6. To give only in small quantities in proportion to immediate need; and of coarser quality than might be procured by labor, except in cases of sickness.
7. To give assistance at the right moment; not to prolong it beyond the duration of the necessity which calls for it; but to extend, restrict, and modify relief, according to that necessity.
8. To require of each beneficiary abstinence from intoxicating liquors as a drink; of such as have young children of proper age, that they be kept at school, except unavoidable circumstances prevent; and to apprentice those of suitable years to some trade, or send them to service. The design being to make the poor a party to their own improvement and elevation, the wilful violation of disregard of these rules, shall debar them from further relief.
9. To give no relief to recent emigrants having claims on the Commissioners of Emigration, except in urgent cases for two or three days, or until that department can be informed of such cases, when the responsibility of this Association towards them shall cease.
10. To give no aid to persons who, from infirmity, imbecility, old age, or any other cause, are likely to continue unable to earn their own support, and consequently to be permanently dependent, except in ex-

treme cases for two or three days, or until they can be referred to the Governors of the Alms-house.

11. To discontinue relieving all who manifest a purpose to depend on alms, rather than on their own exertions for support, and whose further maintenance would be incompatible with their good and the objects of the Institution.

12. To give to those having claims on other charities, a card directing them thereto, which indicates thereon, why such relief was refused by the Association; also a card, a duplicate thereof, which the member should require the applicant to produce, when he affirms that the Association has denied him relief.

As it would be impracticable to give a detailed exposition of the foregoing rules in this Directory, members and others are referred for this purpose, to the Visitor's Manual, and other published documents and Reports.

Most of the rules will, doubtless, commend themselves at once to approval. As it respects others, the propriety of which may appear less obvious, the following brief explanations are offered.

In the 9th Rule, recent emigrants are not considered proper subjects of relief, because the Commissioners of Emigration are obligated by law to care for such persons, if needy, for five years after their arrival, and are provided with means for this purpose. Consequently, every dollar expended on such cases by the Association, would be an improper appropriation of so much of its funds, intrusted to it for other objects.

In the 10th Rule, the permanently dependent are not regarded as proper subjects, because if these should continue to be relieved, the entire funds of the Association would soon be exhausted in the support of a permanent list; and its primary objects—the elevation of the moral and physical condition of the poor—be defeated. Such persons should become an in-door public charge, which is far preferable to reliance on incidental relief.

The 11th Rule refers to those who have become so pauperized in spirit by long continued vagrancy or gratuitous relief, or so debased by other causes, that there is no hope of inciting them to self-support, and to aid whom, would encourage vice and indolence, and foster a great social evil.

The 12th Rule especially interests members, inasmuch as its observance will always inform them, if an applicant is denied relief, the reason of such denial. The complaints of unrelieved applicants who have been sent to the Association, should therefore not be listened to, until they have produced a card from the Visitor; for a card assigning the reason of refusal *is always given to the unrelieved applicant*, which, if produced, will show why he was not relieved; and if unproduced, a proof that he has been attended to. In either case, the member will thus be made acquainted with the action of the visitor, and the reason for it.

Two or three important results involved in the observance of the foregoing Rules, deserve notice. *First,* by refusing aid to the persons described, none are necessarily left to suffer. Even those who obstinately persist in their vicious courses, and cannot be relieved by this charity without injury to them and to the community, still have a resource in the legal relief to which they are referred, so that all are cared for. *Second*, the Association does not supersede existing charities, but so far as is practicable, makes them available to those for whom they are designed. *Third*, that it is governed by such humane and economical considerations, as have most important moral and social bearings on the individuals concerned, and the public.

☞ Visitors in complying with the foregoing Rules, should carefully direct their attention to such particulars, bearing on the different classes indicated therein, as will qualify them for an intelligent and judicious discharge of their highly important and responsible duties.

☞ The attention of members is also called to the said Rules, and their co-operation with the Visitors most earnestly solicited; for without it, the great and difficult work in which the Association is engaged, cannot be effectually accomplished.

☞ Applications are not unfrequently made at unseasonable times, and hours, by professedly homeless, needy persons, for immediate relief, or for the means of procuring lodging for the night; and those applied to are often at a loss how to dispose of such cases. Generally such persons are impostors, and artfully urge their appeal under circumstances which preclude investigation, and are most likely to induce relief. If unknown, they should not be aided, but sent to one of the nearest Station Houses, which are always open for their reception. The following is a list of the Station Houses in the different parts of the city.

First.—52 Trinity Place and at Franklin Market.
Second.—70 Beekman-street.
Third.—38 Barclay.
Fourth.—9 Oak.
Fifth.—49 Leonard.
Sixth.—Halls of Justice, Centre-street.
Seventh.—Foot of Gouverneur.
Eighth.—Prince, corner of Wooster.
Ninth.—Jefferson Market.
Tenth.—Essex Market.
Eleventh.—Union Market.
Twelfth.—Harlem.
Thirteenth.—Attorney, corner of Delancy.
Fourteenth.—Centre Market.
Fifteenth.—220 Mercer.
Sixteenth.—West 29th st., between 7th and 8th Avenues.
Seventeenth.—48 Sixth-street.
Eighteenth.—East 29th st., between 4th and 5th Avenues.
Nineteenth.—Yorkville and 8th Avenue, corner West 48th street.
Twentieth.—West 35th st., between 8th and 9th Avenues.

To the District Secretaries and Visitors of the New-York Association for Improving the Condition of the Poor.

NEW-YORK, *October*, 1853.

GENTLEMEN:—In compliance with the instructions of the Board of Managers, I herewith transmit for your use, a copy of "An Act to provide for the care and instruction of idle and truant children," passed April 12th, 1853, which is as follows:

The People of the State of New-York, represented in Senate and Assembly, do enact as follows:

1. IF any child, between the ages of five and fourteen years, having sufficient bodily health and mental capacity to attend the public schools, shall be found wandering in the streets or lanes of any city or incorporated village, idle and truant, without any lawful occupation, any justice of the peace, police magistrates, or justices of the district courts, in the City of New-York, on complaint thereof by any citizen on oath, shall cause such child to be brought before him for examination, and shall also cause the parent, guardian, or master of such child, if he or she have any, to be notified to attend such examination. And if, on such examination, the complaint shall be satisfactorily established, such justice shall require the parent, guardian, or master to enter into an engagement in writing, to the corporate authorities of the city or village, that he will restrain such child from so wandering about, will keep him or her on his own premises, or in some lawful occupation, and will cause such child to be sent to some school at least four months in each year, until he or she becomes fourteen years old. And such justice may, in his discretion, require security for the faithful performance of such engagement. If such child has no parent, guardian, or master, or none can be found, or if such parent, guardian, or master refuse or neglect, within a reasonable time, to enter into such engagement, and to give such security, if required, such justice shall, by warrant under his hand, commit such child to such place as shall be provided for his or her reception, as hereinafter directed.

2. If such engagement be habitually or intentionally violated, an action may be brought thereon, by the overseers of the poor, or either of them, of such city or village, in the name of the corporate authorities thereof, and on proof of such habitual or intentional violation, the plaintiff shall recover therein a penalty of not more than fifty dollars

with costs. And thereupon, the magistrate or court, before whom such recovery shall be had, shall by warrant commit such child to the place so provided for his or her reception, as aforesaid.

3. The corporate authorities of every city and incorporated village shall provide some suitable place for the reception of every child that may be so committed, and for the employment of such child in some useful occupation, and his or her instruction in the elementary branches of an English education, and for his or her proper support and clothing. Every child so received shall be kept in such place until discharged by the overseers of the poor, or the commissioners of the alms-house of such city or village, and may be bound out as an apprentice by them or either of them, with the consent of any justice of the peace, or any of the aldermen of the city, or any trustee of the incorporated village where he may be, in the same manner, for the same periods, and subject to the same provisions, in all respects, as are contained in the first article and fourth title of the eighth chapter and second part of the Revised Statutes, with respect to children whose parents have become chargeable on any city or town.

4. The expenses of providing and maintaining such place for the reception, clothing, support, and instruction of such children shall be defrayed in the same manner as charges for the support of paupers, chargeable upon such city or village; and the corporate authorities of every city and village shall certify to the board of supervisors of the county, at their annual meetings, the amount necessary for said purposes, which amount the said supervisors shall cause to be levied and collected as part of the taxes for the support of the poor, chargeable to such city or village.

5. It shall be the duty of all police officers and constables, who shall find any child in the condition described in the first section of this act, to make complaint to a justice of the peace, as provided in the said section.

6. The fees of justices for services performed under this act shall be the same as allowed by law in cases of vagrancy, and shall be paid by the city or village in which they were rendered.

7. This act shall take effect immediately.

You scarcely need be reminded, that the education and religious instruction of the children of the poor, and their subsequent apprenticeship to some occupation or trade, so as to qualify them in after life to become useful and industrious citizens, were among the earliest objects to which the attention of the Association was directed. And it will be fresh in your recollection, that the Board of Managers, last winter, solicited your special efforts to induce the attendance at school of the children of suitable age, whose parents applied to this Institution for aid. Now, the foregoing law not only strengthens our hands in this good work, but encourages us to renewed exertions by the assurance that, in the judgment of the Legislature, we have not overrated the importance of the subject.

The act in question is believed to be wise in its provisions, and beneficent in its objects. The necessity of providing by law for the organization and support of public schools, is universally conceded, since experience has shown that it is not safe to leave an interest so vital to the welfare of society, to the sense of duty or public spirit of individuals.

Public Schools having been thus provided, it follows that attendance upon them, in certain cases, should be made obligatory. For it is clear that schools can be of little benefit to those who cannot or will not attend them. If the parent is intemperate, incompetent, or indifferent to the education of his children, the law should take his place, and see that they are properly trained. If he is avaricious, and desires to make gain out of the tender bones and sinews of his offspring, to the entire neglect of their mental and moral culture; or if he is reckless and unprincipled, and, as is common in this city, sends out his children to beg or steal, that he may lazily subsist on the means thus obtained; it is right and expedient that the State should protect itself against such evils, while it enforces the just claims, and promotes the best interests of the unprotected.

Why is it that the neglected children of our city have so long furnished the class which endangers life and property among us, and tenants our prisons and penitentiaries? It is because mere moral influence, opposed by parental authority, has been incompetent to effect their recovery; and because previous legislation had shrunk from its high duty in respect to them. The law, which is so omnipotent concerning adults, whose stringent provisions reach our modes of living,—which regulates the steamer, the rail-car, the stage-coach,—the markets which supply our food,—polices our streets, and ordains in what kind of houses we shall not live; which, with almost unlimited power, binds and unbinds the marriage tie, interferes between man and man, husband and wife, brother and sister,—has, until now, failed to extend its protecting care over unprotected and neglected children.

But this anomaly in legislation no longer exists. Our State has the merit of being foremost in this great work of reform, and of thus establishing for itself a lasting memorial of its wisdom and beneficence. By assuming the place of a parent to its helpless children, and undertaking their training, it raises them from the degradation of their previous condition to one of equality with the other pupils of our public schools, while it saves such pupils from the dread of debasement by intercourse with them.

The Legislature, be it observed, has now done all that it can consistently do. It has framed the machinery, and put it into our hands. But that machinery will be useless lumber, or fail to effect its purpose, except it be put into operation. Any citizen can do this, by causing the arrest of these unfortunate or vicious children, and placing them under the control "of any justice of the peace, police magistrate, or justices of the district courts," who are bound to take cognizance thereof, and care for all such cases. While this, however, is the duty of every citizen, it is in a peculiar sense obligatory on this Association, because of its relations to the poor and their offspring, and its superior facilities for acting with proper intelligence and efficiency through its numerous Visitors, in respect to all requiring their interference; also, by co-operating with the public officers, whose imperative duty it is to attend to all such children as are described in the foregoing Act.

The Board would therefore respectfully urge on Visitors a faithful enforcement, in all proper cases, of the foregoing law; also, the carrying out of the March Circular, in respect to the children of such families as apply to the Association for relief. For by the joint operation of these measures, there is ground to expect that much of the juvenile vagrancy and mendicity of the city will be corrected, and invaluable benefits thereby accrue to the community, and to an interesting yet dangerous, and hitherto almost hopeless, class of our population.

By order of the Board.

Respectfully yours,
R. M. HARTLEY,
Secretary.

POVERTY, U. S. A.
THE HISTORICAL RECORD

An Arno Press/New York Times Collection

Adams, Grace. **Workers on Relief.** 1939.

The Almshouse Experience: Collected Reports. 1821-1827.

Armstrong, Louise V. **We Too Are The People.** 1938.

Bloodworth, Jessie A. and Elizabeth J. Greenwood.
The Personal Side. 1939.

Brunner, Edmund de S. and Irving Lorge.
Rural Trends in Depression Years: A Survey of Village-Centered Agricultural Communities, 1930-1936. 1937.

Calkins, Raymond.
Substitutes for the Saloon: An Investigation Originally made for The Committee of Fifty. 1919.

Cavan, Ruth Shonle and Katherine Howland Ranck.
The Family and the Depression: A Study of One Hundred Chicago Families. 1938.

Chapin, Robert Coit.
The Standard of Living Among Workingmen's Families in New York City. 1909.

The Charitable Impulse in Eighteenth Century America: Collected Papers. 1711-1797.

Children's Aid Society.
Children's Aid Society Annual Reports, 1-10.
February 1854-February 1863.

Conference on the Care of Dependent Children.
Proceedings of the Conference on the Care of Dependent Children. 1909.

Conyngton, Mary.
How to Help: A Manual of Practical Charity. 1909.

Devine, Edward T. **Misery and its Causes.** 1909.

Devine, Edward T. **Principles of Relief.** 1904.

Dix, Dorothea L.
On Behalf of the Insane Poor: Selected Reports. 1843-1852.

Douglas, Paul H.
Social Security in the United States: An Analysis and Appraisal of the Federal Social Security Act. 1936.

Farm Tenancy: Black and White. Two Reports. 1935, 1937.

Feder, Leah Hannah.
Unemployment Relief in Periods of Depression: A Study of Measures Adopted in Certain American Cities, 1857 through 1922. 1936.

Folks, Homer.
The Care of Destitute, Neglected, and Delinquent Children. 1900.

Guardians of the Poor.
A Compilation of the Poor Laws of the State of Pennsylvania from the Year 1700 to 1788, Inclusive. 1788.

Hart, Hastings, H.
Preventive Treatment of Neglected Children.
(Correction and Prevention, Vol. 4) 1910.

Herring, Harriet L.
Welfare Work in Mill Villages: The Story of Extra-Mill Activities in North Carolina. 1929.

The Jacksonians on the Poor: Collected Pamphlets. 1822-1844.

Karpf, Maurice J.
Jewish Community Organization in the United States. 1938.

Kellor, Frances A.
Out of Work: A Study of Unemployment. 1915.

Kirkpatrick, Ellis Lore.
The Farmer's Standard of Living. 1929.

Komarovsky, Mirra.
The Unemployed Man and His Family: The Effect of Unemployment Upon the Status of the Man in Fifty-Nine Families. 1940.

Leupp, Francis E. **The Indian and His Problem.** 1910.

Lowell, Josephine Shaw.
Public Relief and Private Charity. 1884.

More, Louise Bolard.
Wage Earners' Budgets: A Study of Standards and Cost of Living in New York City. 1907.

New York Association for Improving the Condition of the Poor.
AICP First Annual Reports Investigating Poverty. 1845-1853.

O'Grady, John.
Catholic Charities in the United States: History and Problems. 1930.

Raper, Arthur F.
Preface to Peasantry: A Tale of Two Black Belt Counties. 1936.

Raper, Arthur F. **Tenants of The Almighty.** 1943.

Richmond, Mary E.
What is Social Case Work? An Introductory Description. 1922.

Riis, Jacob A. **The Children of the Poor.** 1892.

Rural Poor in the Great Depression: Three Studies. 1938.

Sedgwick, Theodore.
Public and Private Economy: Part I. 1836.

Smith, Reginald Heber. **Justice and the Poor.** 1919.

Sutherland, Edwin H. and Harvey J. Locke.
Twenty Thousand Homeless Men: A Study of Unemployed Men in the Chicago Shelters. 1936.

Tuckerman, Joseph. **On the Elevation of the Poor: A Selection From His Reports as Minister at Large in Boston.** 1874.

Warner, Amos G. **American Charities.** 1894.

Watson, Frank Dekker. **The Charity Organization Movement in the United States: A Study in American Philanthropy.** 1922.

Woods, Robert A., et al. **The Poor in Great Cities.** 1895.